TO MY COUSIN
ERIC ALSCHULER
AND HIS LOVELY WIFE
AND CHILDREN,
WITH LOVE AND HOPES
FOR A SPEEDY RECOVERY
St. LOUIS, DEC. 2021
D.A.G.

THE HISTORICAL APOTHECARY COMPENDIUM

THE HISTORICAL
APOTHECARY
COMPENDIUM

A GUIDE TO TERMS AND SYMBOLS
~DANIEL A. GOLDSTEIN~

Schiffer
Publishing Ltd®

4880 Lower Valley Road • Atglen, PA 19310

Designed by Justin Watkinson
Type set in EngravrsRoman Bd BT/Zurich BT/Times New Roman

ISBN: 978-0-7643-4926-3
Printed in China

Published by Schiffer Publishing, Ltd.
4880 Lower Valley Road
Atglen, PA 19310
Phone: (610) 593-1777; Fax: (610) 593-2002
E-mail: Info@schifferbooks.com

For our complete selection of fine books on this and related subjects, please visit
our website at www.schifferbooks.com. You may also write for a free catalog.

This book may be purchased from the publisher. Please try your bookstore first.

We are always looking for people to write books on new and related subjects. If
you have an idea for a book, please contact us at proposals@schifferbooks.com.

Schiffer Publishing's titles are available at special discounts for bulk purchases
for sales promotions or premiums. Special editions, including personalized
covers, corporate imprints, and excerpts can be created in large quantities for
special needs. For more information, contact the publisher.

"There is no treatise on Pharmacy in the English language which can approach it in completeness or usefulness."—AMERICAN DRUGGIST.

PRACTICE OF PHARMACY.

A Treatise on the Modes of Making and Dispensing Officinal, Unofficinal, and Extemporaneous Preparations, with Descriptions of their Properties, Uses, and Doses. Intended as a Hand-Book for Pharmacists and Physicians, and a Text-Book for Students.

By Prof. JOSEPH P. REMINGTON, Ph.G.

1080 Pages, with nearly 500 Illustrations. 8vo. Cloth, $5. Sheep, $6.

FOR SALE BY ALL BOOKSELLERS AND WHOLESALE DRUGGISTS.

"We make no mistake when we assert that it is the best work on pharmacy that has ever been prepared. The subject of pharmacy in its treatment, description, language, and illustration is more complete, full, precise, and satisfactory than any other, and will hold the attention of the student as a guide into the mysteries he has not heretofore comprehended, while to the experienced pharmacist it will prove a help and constant reference of reliable value."

Pharmaceutical Record, New York.

"The arrangement of the book is excellent. It is remarkable, apart from its intrinsic value, from the fact that the author, as a practical pharmacist, runs a drug-store, and at the same time professes and demonstrates the theory and practice of pharmacy in a college. The fitness of such a man to write a book is unquestionable. The wonder is where the author found time in his busy life to write such a book."

Chemist and Druggist, London, Eng.

FOR SALE BY

P. BLAKISTON, SON & CO.,

1012 Walnut Street, Philadelphia.

Advertisement for Remington's Practice of Pharmacy from: Stewart FE. Quiz-Compends No.11, Pharmacy. P. Blakiston Son & Co., Philadelphia, PA, 1886.

T. W. DYOTT,

Wholesale and Retail Druggist, &c.

Nos. 137 & 139, NORTH-EAST CORNER OF SECOND AND RACE STREETS,

PHILADELPHIA,

Offers for Sale or Barter, at very reduced prices, a large and general assortment of choice and well selected *Drugs and Medicines, Patent Medicines, Chemicals, Dye Stuffs, Colours, Window Glass, Vials, Bottles, &c.* with a variety of other articles usually called for.

His extensive Stock, consisting chiefly of his own manufacture, or of goods purchased at the very lowest prices, for *Cash*, enables him to sell to Country Merchants, Druggists, Physicians, and Manufacturers, on the most advantageous terms, or take in *Barter* any of the following articles, *for which he will always give the highest market prices :* viz. Bright Rosin, Turpentine, Lampblack, Pink Root, Rice, Cotton, Tobacco, Sugar, Molasses, Coffee, Rum, Gin, Brandy, Bees-wax, Wheat Flour, Rye and Buckwheat Meal, Hams, Pork, Bacon, Butter, Lard, Cheese, Rye and Apple Whiskey, Peach Brandy, Mackerel, Shad, Pearl and Pot Ashes, Flaxseed, Flaxseed Oil, Logwood, Firewood, Castor Oil, Castor Oil Beans, Soap, Candles, Glass, Lead, Nails, Glue, Furs, Feathers, Rags, Paper, Bristles, Brushes, Shoes, Hats, Saddlery, Domestic Goods generally, Real Estate, in or near the city of Philadelphia, U. S. Bank Stock, &c. &c. &c.

From the extensive and general assortment of articles offered for sale by T. W. DYOTT, and the favourable terms on which he conducts business at his establishment for the accommodation of purchasers, he presumes that country merchants, manufacturers, and dealers in general (whom he solicits to give him a call,) will find it their interest to supply themselves as above.

N. B. Each article is warranted to be of the most pure and genuine quality of its kind.
☞ JAMES BEDFORD, New-Orleans, General Agent for T. W. DYOTT.

T. W. Dyott Glass Works, Philadelphia (electronically restored). Advertisement in *Whitley's Philadelphia Advertiser Directory* for 1820, from: Young, HJ, *The Toadstool Millionaire*, Princeton University Press, Princeton, N.J., 1961.

DEDICATION

To my wife, with her infinite tolerance for my collections,
and within whose loving home and arms all efforts seem possible.

To my mother and father, who with a few apothecary bottles,
of boundless curiosity to the youthful eye,
launched a lifelong fascination.

&

To my fellow collectors, whose enjoyment will, I hope,
be equally increased as my own by these efforts.

CONTENTS

Foreword 9
Acknowledgments 10

Chapter 1: Notes on the Structure and Use of This Book 11
    Introduction 11
    Sources and References 12
    Entries: Format & Use 12
    Illustrations 15

Chapter 2: Background Matter 17
    A Brief History of Apothecary Containers, Labels, and Labeling Practices 17
    Dating of North American Bottles 22
    Linguistics and Orthographics 24
    Weights and Measures 24
    Dosage Forms 25
    Therapeutic Actions 28
    Disease States 32
    Apothecary Processes 33
    Table of Elements 34
    Notes on Chemical Terminology 34

Color Plates 37

Chapter 3: The Compendium 53
    Abbreviations & Numbers 53
    Alphabetical list of terms 54

Appendices 295
    Notes on Latin 295
    Latin Abbreviations Commonly Used in Prescriptions 298
    Magistral Pharmacy 299
    Alchemical and Astrological Symbols 308
    Manufactures of American Apothecary Glass 321
    Manufacturers' Markings—American Apothecary Glass 324
    Botanical Parts and Terms 327

Guide to Sources 330
Credits 332

FOREWORD

Writing is putting one's obsessions in order
—Jean Grenier

Books are ships which pass through the vast sea of time
—Francis Bacon

Writing a book is an act of love, hope, and vanity. Certainly, the time and effort required for success require love for the subject at hand, if not outright obsession, and it would seem that I am a victim of the latter as pertains to antique apothecary bottles, patent medicines, and the often peculiar historical practices associated with them. As this is a compendium, there can be little doubt that I am attempting to put my obsession in order (alphabetical). One must also have a love of books themselves— as objects, art forms, and repositories of information—in order to muster the energy necessary for creation. This is particularly true today, as books are no longer the principal repositories of knowledge— but that is precisely where the hope comes in.

One hopes, above all else, that one's book will be read. Books such as this one attempt to span time, looking backwards to acquire information and packaging it in a form and context that will be of use and of interest to others—hopefully many others—in both the present and the future. Implicit is a belief that the book can survive the vagaries and vicissitudes of time, storage, and continual culling by librarians to reach the future reader. While electronic storage is tempting indeed, there are several reasons to think that the book may ultimately be the better vessel in which to cross the sea of time. First, electronic formats change rapidly and electronic media, especially electromagnetic media, have a very finite life. A book, on the other hand, requires nothing, save eye and mind, to read in the future. Second, if a book is an object of beauty and interest, as well as an information source, people will wish to collect it, hold it, enjoy it, and pass it onwards to the next generation. Third, if a book is perceived to have value, electronic versions will likely follow, often in the form of image files. The latter allow the object to be recreated as desired and, as image formats are fewer and more standardized, appear less subject to loss of readability as hardware and software evolve.

The true bibliophile cannot but be thrilled by holding their own book in their hand, and cannot but hope that others will admire, enjoy, covet, and acquire this offspring of their own creativity—and this is where, alas, vanity enters the picture. One must believe that one can, indeed, write a book and can do so sufficiently well that someone will want to publish it. Further, one must believe (and their publisher agree!) that one's own obsession is of great enough general interest to prompt others to buy, read, keep, and ultimately pass on the fruits of one's efforts far into the future. The goal (dare I say it?) is ultimately to matter to someone—anyone—at a time far distant from this one and likely far beyond the span of one's own years. Writing a book is little more than a feeble bid for some small measure of immortality—if that is not vanity, what is?

And so it is that I place my small, lovingly crafted ship upon the seas of time. I hope it finds you well, brings you joy, and that, in some small way, you also find me.

Daniel A. Goldstein, MD

ACKNOWLEDGMENTS

Creating this book has been a long, sometime arduous, journey. Thanks are therefore due to many who helped along the way and who immeasurably improved the vision, nature, and content of the compendium.

Much appreciation is due for the staff of the O. J. Cloughly Alumni Library of the St. Louis College of Pharmacy. Both Jill Nissen, MLIS, director of the library, and Teri-Ann Wallace, MA, ISLT, reference librarian and archivist, had a look at an early version of the compendium and encouraged me to proceed with expansion and publication. They also arranged for "hand's on" access to the library's collection of apothecary containers as well as access to, and guidance in, the archival reading room.

Thanks are also due to Callie Stapp, curator, and the staff of the Stabler Leadbeater Apothecary Museum in Alexandria, Virginia, who provided me unrestricted access to their collection of containers, labels, and other materials. This museum is a rare gem—a colonial apothecary shop still in its original location—and is a must-see destination for anyone with an interest in apothecary history, American history, or just beautiful buildings and objects. Access to stored collections was kindly provided by the St. Louis Science Museum. My thanks as well to Elizabeth Sherman and the staff of the New Orleans Pharmacy Museum. Special access to the display cases was provided during a visit to this essential destination, which is unique among US collections for the decidedly French influence on apothecary goods, labels, and styles.

Special thanks are due to Dr. Doug Holland, Director, and to Lucy Fisher and the staff of the Peter H. Raven Library, Missouri Botanical Garden. They jumped enthusiastically into this project when it was largely complete but lacking botanical illustrations. This deficiency was primarily due to the difficulties of plant identification across time and place. They were able to rapidly identify an illustrated textbook of *Medical Botany* (Woodville, 1700) which, vagaries of botany aside, allows one to know that an eminent medical botanist at that time (midway between American colonial times and 1930—the midpoint of the compendium) and in that place (England), thought that *this* was indeed the correct plant! The botanical illustrations add tremendously, I believe, to the value and enjoyability of the book. The library staff's enthusiasm, as well as the generosity of the Missouri Botanical Garden in allowing re-publication of the illustrations, are immensely appreciated.

My appreciation is extended, as well, to all of the individuals and organizations who assisted with permission for various images. Particular thanks goes to Cecil Munsey, whose book, *The Illustrated Guide to Collecting Bottles* (Hawthorn Books, 1970), has been a treasured gem in my personal library for many years. It was a thrill and a privilege to communicate with him in person, and permission to use his material is immensely appreciated. A debt of gratitude is owed as well to Adam McLean, creator and webmaster of the Alchemy Website (www.alchemywebsite.com), for use of the alchemical symbols from *Medicinish Chymisch und Alchemistisches* (1775). The availability of these electronic images, as well as a marvelous collection of materials related to alchemy (some available for purchase) reflects his thoughtful efforts. Thanks as well to Jane Surrey Pyne and James Rivington Pyne for assistance in seeking the copyright for the Whitall, Tatum & Co. Catalog of 1880, published by Pyne Press. I must also acknowledge the kind staff of the Copyright Office, United States Library of Congress, for guiding me through the card-file collection of filings and transfers for early (pre-1970) materials.

My sincere thanks are due to Pete Schiffer, and to Schiffer Publishing. Publishers for genre technical books can be difficult to find in today's market, but Pete responded to a very crude draft with enthusiasm and encouragement. I was afraid that I would need to shorten the text dramatically—but instead was encouraged to expand the compendium further. When I proposed the addition of hundreds of botanical illustrations late in the game, followed by color plates, Schiffer Books responded with "bring it on." Without their vision, the book may well have never gotten off my personal computer. As an inexperienced author, the guidebook provided by Schiffer Publishing was helpful, but paled in comparison to the assistance of my early-stage editor, Jesse J. Marth and check-in editor, Catherine Mallette, both of whom put up with a myriad of questions and anxieties and who patiently guided my way. Sincere thanks are also due to my copy editor, Douglas Congdon-Martin, for knocking the book firmly into final form, to Andrea Kiliany Thatcher for her assistance in marketing, and the Justin Wilkinson at Schiffer Publishing for the overall design and for the cover—far simpler and refined than my own vision, and clearly far superior.

Thanks are due both to my father, Bernard Goldstein, who purchased four bottles (color plate B) as a gift for my mother, and to my mother, Rosalie Goldstein, who cherished them. Together they initiated my own obsession with their own small collection of apothecary glass. My mother's skill as a professional editor is reflected heavily in my own writing, and indeed she was kind enough to take on the first editorial reading of this book.

Thanks to my children, Jennifer, Thomas, Wendy, and Caroline, for their enthusiasm and encouragement.

Lastly, but very far from least, I owe a boundless debt of gratitude to my loving wife, Sheila, for her faith, her patience, and her support. If I have succeeded in this or any other endeavor, it is only because she is always at my side.

Success is shared. Any failures, errors, and shortcomings—virtually inevitable in a compendium of this nature despite extensive effort—remain mine alone.

CHAPTER 1

NOTES ON THE STRUCTURE AND USE OF THIS BOOK

INTRODUCTION

The purpose of this text is to satisfy curiosity and to mollify the craving, so common among collectors of antiques and oddities, for knowledge about the object at hand. Such knowledge is often arcane and of little current practical utility, however vital it may once have been. With time, historical libraries will undoubtedly make historical materials available electronically, and electronic searching will facilitate finding even the most obscure information. The latter notwithstanding, the goal of this text is to put this information in one place—the palm of the collector's hand—in a form that is useful, concise, and interesting, and in a format which will hopefully be pleasing to the eye.

The terminology addressed in this compendium, and particularly the material in the background matter and appendices, is designed to assist the reader in interpreting not only apothecary jars, but a variety of related materials including other container types (tins, etc.), labels, catalogues, prescriptions, pharmacopoeias, advertisements, trade cards, pharmaceutical texts, medical texts, and other paraphernalia. Thus, I have included information on pharmaceutical processes, terms used to refer to disease states if no longer in use or if their meaning has substantially altered with time, dosage forms, weights and measures, and even commonly occurring decorative signs or symbols, such as those used in astrology and alchemy, the latter of which may occasionally appear in lieu of chemical names but are more often a decorative motif, frequently related to the contents.

My efforts have been directed at the apothecary and medical artifacts most likely to come into the hands of the North American collector, i.e., those objects and items actually made in the US and Canada or more popularly imported. Of necessity, I have limited the material primarily to terms in the English language or in the common languages of the medical arts since antiquity: true Latin, modern "Latinized" terms, and Greek, the latter as transcribed to Latin and thus presented using the common alphabet of the Romance languages.

The questions surrounding a particular container, label, or term may be multiple. What does it mean? What is the modern equivalent term (if any)? How was it made? What was it used for? Thus, I have tried to link each term, when applicable, back to a specific chemical or botanical name. The entry for the specific chemical name may contain additional information including synonyms and abbreviations, historical notes, and an indication of the therapeutic use of the material. Information on therapeutic use is generally restricted to American colonial times and later as a matter of practical utility, because the use and identity of *materia medica* has shifted considerably over time and because a comprehensive study of older uses across multiple cultures, locations, and centuries is impractical.

The ultimate value of any compendium is, by nature, determined by its degree of completeness. One can legitimately argue for performing entirely "original" research in older texts and sources, avoiding more contemporary works to avoid any concerns which may arise from the "taking" of other's accomplishments. This compendium is hardly complete—none ever

is—but after deep consideration, I determined that failure to build upon the work of others would be a disservice to the reader and would fail to push the compilation of knowledge beyond its current state. Even when working from alphabetized glossaries or dictionaries in this area, work is agonizingly slow, as one must coordinate each term with other terms in the compendium, identify similar or identical underlying chemical identities to link materials to one another, and reconcile numerous points of disagreement among sources by further research. This being said, and with due recognition to all of the authors of all sources relied upon, several sources require special mention.

The glossary of Drey's beautiful book, *Apothecary Jars,* was, in fact, my inspiration for undertaking this entire compendium. The use of European terms may extend back to ancient times, with only a subset of such terms making their way into North American apothecary usage. While I considered dispensing with these terms, antiquities and terminology have a way of migrating great distances. Further, the North American collector or those with a broader interest in apothecary terminology may well have need of such information and, lacking a copy of Drey's text, may have difficulty finding it.

Among historical documents, the seventh edition of the pharmaceutical classic, *Remington's Practice of Pharmacy* (1926, Cook and LaWall, editors), along with Mansfield's *Materia Medica, Toxicology and Pharmacognosy* (1937), and White's *Materia Medica and Therapeutics* (1896, Wilcox) formed the core of the reference material used in the compilation of terms. These references were chosen largely by chance, as they happened to be a part of my own modest collection.

The pocket handbook compiled by Igor Hughes, entitled *Dictionary of Synonyms and Trade Names in Common Use*, was produced in 1913 and contains an extensive listing of terms in use at that time and earlier. Each of these terms required considerable additional research to integrate into the compendium itself, but the reference deserves great credit for any approximation to completeness which might be achieved.

Among contemporary authors, the lovely volume from the American Institute of the History of Pharmacy, entitled *History of Drug Containers and Their Labels* (Griffinhagen and Bogard, 1999), contributed greatly on precisely the subject named. I also worked extensively from J. Worth Estes's *Dictionary of Protopharmacology*. Somehow I failed to discover this important document until this compendium was well underway, but I nevertheless added numerous entries and improved others using this carefully crafted source. In deference to the scholarly efforts of Dr. Estes, I have referenced his work where relied upon and have provided either quotation marks or explicit acknowledgment of his work when I have drawn material of significance directly from this source.

In many instances, Estes and other authors provide lists of pharmacological actions (diuretic, emmenagogue, etc.) for which no other term may be legitimately substituted; usually provided in their logical order (i.e., alphabetical). After much thought, I have concluded that mere rearrangement of the order of such words to avoid an appearance of plagiarism is a meaningless ruse. These lists therefore appear largely verbatim from various sources, which are of course referenced within the text.

A Warning!!

The reader is warned that the therapeutic recommendations in this book are historical in nature. **IN MANY CASES, THE USE OF THERAPEUTIC MATERIALS AS DESCRIBED HEREIN MAY BE AT BEST INEFFECTUAL AND VERY POSSIBLY DANGEROUS!!** Even for those materials which are therapeutically effective, this text does not provide sufficient information to properly prepare or administer the remedies described.

While one could consult an old pharmacopoeia for further details and attempt to use these agents "correctly" in the historical sense, even this is a decidedly poor idea. Please consult a current source of health information—book, website, doctor, nurse, pharmacist, etc. before instituting any medical treatment, lest you end up the victim of a therapeutic misadventure.

SOURCES & REFERENCES

Sources and references for this book are listed numerically in the back of the text. No effort has been made to place them in the order of occurrence in the text, the order primarily reflecting the order in which sources were identified and used. Throughout the book, reference numbers have been used in lieu of the more typical academic practice of using author's names. While the latter has much to commend it, I have opted instead to conserve space, as many references occur hundreds of times. Much information can be found in multiple sources, and I have not attempted to identify all cited references in which an item of information appears.

Selected additional references on related subjects, not relied upon in this book, are provided at the end of the reference list with the recognition that collectors rarely restrict themselves to a single line of goods and will likely be interested in any "gems" I may happen to find along the way. Criteria for inclusion are an informal mixture of interest, beauty, oddity, and practical utility, any one of which may alone suffice.

ENTRIES: FORMAT & USE

Entries in the compendium have a defined structure, but may be accompanied by a wide variety of information. The following general rules are applied, but exceptions occur, and these rules should not stop you from searching under each individual word on a particular label or artifact:

• Primary entries for **ingredients** are generally listed by Latin name. Common names are listed independently if the relationship to the Latin term is not obvious, but usually refer the reader to the Latin term. This has multiple advantages despite the fact that the reader is not likely fluent in Latin. Firstly, this is what is commonly on labels. Secondly, common names of plants are often multiple and may refer to more than one plant; hence the Latin is more specific. Finally, the common names of many things are already well known to the reader, and thus one is unlikely to look up "Extract of Cloves," but may well need assistance with "Fluidextractum Caryophyli."

• Most **formulated items** are listed under the primary botanical or chemical ingredient for which they are named, not under the type of preparation, i.e., mixture (mistura), tincture (tinctura), etc. For example, clove oil, Oleum Caryophyli, will be found under Caryophyli, oleum. This has the advantage of keeping formulations in close proximity to key ingredients and associated information, as little is gained by collecting all tinctures or mixtures in one location.

• The above being noted, difficulties arise with preparations not named after their primary chemical or botanical ingredient, i.e., Unguentum Aureum (golden ointment) or Aqua Cologniensis (Cologne water). English language glossaries would, of course, list by the primary noun (Unguentum or Aqua), but a reader unfamiliar with the fact that Cologniensis is not a botanical term will probably look for Cologniensis, Aqua. Space being limited, I have avoided widely using entries such as Aqua Cologniensis—see Cologniensis, aqua. Rather, I have exercised judgment in placing such terms where I think they will likely be looked for first. **If you do not find an item listed in the manner you expect, be sure to look under any other words in the inscription**.

• Exceptions to this rule are made for certain infrequent types of specialized formulations for which individual entries are difficult to justify. These include balneae (baths); cerioli (waxes); malti (malts); wools; injectiones hypodermicae, nebulae, parogens, pastilles, pessaries; pigmenta (paints); sera, solvellae; stupae; tabellae (chocolate tablets British Pharmaceutical Codex [BPC], not regular tablets, which are tablettae), troches specified in the BPC (numerous and based upon one of five specific formulae), and unguenta pro oculi (eye ointments) of the BPC.

• **Primary botanical or chemical names are generally listed first, followed by the formulations, even though the genitive form of the name may precede the nominative form alphabetically**, i.e., Eucalyptus (nominative, the plant name) comes immediately *before* associated preparations, which are listed under Eucalypti (genitive, meaning "of eucalyptus"). Explanatory notes are added to guide the reader when primary ingredients are alphabetically separated widely from their formulation, as in the case of pitch (*pix*), for which the genitive form ("of pitch") is *picis*.

• Eponymous preparations (Dewee's Mixture, Godfrey's Cordial, etc.) are usually listed under the inventor's or purveyor's surname, with given names following if commonly used on labels.

• Commercial, patent, and proprietary names are not generally listed unless they are so common as to appear on apothecary labels other than those of the manufacturer. For example, "Lysol" was such a common trade name for carbolic-acid-based disinfectants that it sprouted its own Latinized form, "Lysolum." Patent medicine trade names are generally listed only if they are indicated as being a synonym for a recognized official formulation, have a known composition, or are recognized in authoritative sources. Paradoxically, "Patent" medicines were rarely patented, as the latter act would require disclosure of the "secret formula," prompting copycat products. No attempt has been made to list the endless array of patent medicines, as little information can be found regarding their composition. Mercifully, the trade names of patent medicines, while tending toward the bombastic, generally indicate what conditions they are intended to treat.

If You Do Not Find What You Are Looking for...

• Be sure to scan the immediate area where a particular entry occurs (or should occur) for related terms or for variants of spelling. Alphabetizing is only approximate, as related terms may be clustered if not separated widely in the alphabet, and as primary ingredient terms for related entries are listed first for the sake of clarity, even if not strictly alphabetical.

• Be sure to check the compendium for each of the individual words from a label or other source, as word order in the original usage was variable to such a degree that listing of all historically extant word orders is neither feasible nor a worthwhile use of space.

• Beware of orthographic variants, especially at the beginning of a word. Particularly note "ae" for "e", "f" for "ph" (or vice-versa), "I" in place of "J" (*Iuniperi* for *Juniperi*) and "V" in place of "U" (vva for uva) in Latin terms.

• Be sure you are reading the spelling of the label correctly. Fused or closely adjacent letters are a particular problem if one is not familiar with apothecary terms. In my experience, the letter c is especially problematic and is easily mistaken for the letter o. Thus, coccus, when condensed, may easily look like "cooous" or even "cooois". Similarly the letters "vu" (as in *vulpus*, wolf), written as "vv" may be readily confused with "w." Also be alert to word fusions. I spent weeks trying to discover the origin of the French-sounding, and presumably eponymously named "Craborchard Salts," only to later discover, to my chagrin, a bottle neatly labeled Crab Orchard Salts.

• Be aware that irregular Latin possessive forms may move terms away from the immediate vicinity of the related noun. Thus, while formulations of almond, *amygdala*, appear nearby under *amygdalae*, formulations of pitch, *pix*, will appear under the genitive ("of pitch"), *picis*. Incorrect genitive forms (i.e., not native to correct Latin usage) also appear commonly. Thus, *picis* appears on labels as *pice* (the ablative) or *piciae* (not proper Latin at all).

• When looking for information about a particular compound, be sure to look for naming variants, especially for compounds of sodium or potassium. The former compounds mainly appear under *Sodii*, but *sodae*, *soda*, and *sodiae* are frequent variants. Potassium compounds appear mainly under *potassii*, but the variants *potassi* and *potassiae* are seen. The term *potassa*, technically referring to potash rather than potassium, is often seen, and the older name, kali (possessive of kalium, from which the chemical symbol for potassium, K, derives) is common. Magnesium salts have similar variants (*magnesii* vs. *magnesiae*), and barium salts, properly designated *barii*, are often designated *barytae* after the mineral source, baryta. In the interest of authenticity, I have reflected what I have found on actual labels rather than changing all of the terms to their "proper" Latin forms.

• Finally, note that **detailed information regarding botanical preparations will be clustered in accordance with the Latin name**. Thus, if one is looking for "Milk of Almonds," one should look up "Almond," which in turn will be cross referenced to "*Amygdala*," in the vicinity of which one will find numerous preparations, including "*Amygdalae, emulsum*," for which Milk of Almonds is listed as the English equivalent. Should one choose instead to begin by looking up "Milk," you would be referred to "_____, emulsum," prompting you to begin with "Almond" instead.

Failing all this, consider whether the container at hand is an apothecary container at all. The apothecary or "chemyst" was often the local purveyor of a wide variety of goods. Tobacco and tea containers are commonly found among pharmacy jar collections, as these goods were commonly carried in pharmacies. Tobacco jars are generally quite large, with openings sufficient to introduce a scoop or hand, and are often decorated with thematic representations of smoking, related paraphernalia (pipes, etc.), tobacco cultivation, or of Native Americans, often ridiculously attired (i.e., not in traditional clothing but with such items as top hats and Polynesian dress), engaged in smoking tobacco. Tea jars tended to be smaller in size, often presented in elaborately decorated, matched sets. Both tobacco and tea jars often carried a label as to type (ex.—*Jasmine*) or origin (ex.—*Ceylon*), often limited to a single word.

Far more confusing are the other chemical specialties carried in many pharmacies—dyestuffs, paints, household chemicals, and photographic supplies. Dyestuffs for home coloring of fabrics were commonly carried, as were artist's oil paints, watercolors, and paints for general household use. These containers are not difficult to comprehend if the label is in English. Dye containers and some paints may be labeled by color alone, but names such as Vermillion, Cadmium Red, or Paris Green can be far more confusing to the inexperienced, and some materials in fact had both medicinal and non-medicinal uses. Other common container goods included a variety of "sundries"—fly paper, insecticidal powders, hair combs, corks, sand paper, chalk, paint brushes, glaziers points, twine, etc. Manufactured, labeled containers and drawer pulls were available for these and many other items.

Structure of Glossary Entries

The basic forms are as follows (Items in brackets are optional and may not appear)

Definitional entries for simple terms (not ingredients):

> **Term** {*language*}(*descriptors*): definition (references)

> For example: **Pil.** (abr); **Pilulae**{*Latin*}: Pill or tablet. (2)

Brief entries for formulations. This will be used for most abbreviations, improper or trivial names, etc., other than a major entry for an ingredient or product. These entries will provide only a non-abbreviated form and the term associated with the major entry for a particular product.

> **Term** {*language*}(*descriptors*): {unabbreviated form if applicable} brief definition, including reference to an associated major entry if applicable. (reference)

> For example: **Spir. menth.vir.:** Spiritus menthae viridis: Spirit of peppermint, see mentha piperita. (2)

In general, the reader should refer to the major entry or entries associated with the ingredients (chemical or plant) noted. Exceptions will be made for information that is peculiar to the specific entry but which is not relevant to the underlying general term. Most commonly, this will be an explanation regarding the origin of a specific trivial name or slang term not relevant to the general entry.

Major entries. These are more comprehensive entries associated with particular ingredients (simples), mixtures (composites), or products in non-abbreviated form. While a particular chemical, plant, or other ingredient may appear in many locations throughout the compendium as a result of multiple names (trivial, botanical, chemical), abbreviations, and forms (root, leaf, powder, etc.), each plant, chemical, or other major ingredient will generally have only a single major entry in the compendium.

The term chosen for the location of a major entry will never be an abbreviated form, but is otherwise subject to the discretion of the author. For chemicals, the proper Latin chemical name will be used if one exists unless the trivial name is preferred in modern general use. For botanicals, the traditional Latin names will also be used almost exclusively, with cross references available from the common name(s) of the plant.

The detailed form of such entries will be highly variable as the nature and quantity of information regarding a particular ingredient varies widely.

> **Term** {*language*}(*descriptors*) {synonyms}: Definition with references to other indexed terms as appropriate. {Additional information} (references)

Synonyms will include abbreviations, alternate names including common or Latin if not used as the primary term, and chemical formulae. Additional information will vary widely, but for a botanical ingredient might include parts of the plant used, common dosage forms and dosage, the active principal if known (i.e., *Digitalis purpurea* produces digoxin), the therapeutic activity attributed to the plant, and other historical or technical information of interest.

Clustering of Entries

When in sequential alphabetical order, multiple related entries such as multiple abbreviations for a term will be clustered to conserve space, i.e.-

Pul.; **Pulv**.; **Pulver**.; **Pulverum**: Powdered, pulverized.

Entries of closely related items are also grouped by convenience, not necessarily in precise alphabetical order. This is especially seen with the botanicals, where the plant name in Latin or English, depending upon common usage, will come first, followed by various preparations. In general, these are listed in the order in which they would be obtained and used, i.e., oil or extracts would come directly from the plant, and then used to make pills or troches, etc. Thus the plant name would be listed, followed by the oil and/or extract, followed by the preparations.

Use of Parentheses and Brackets

Ornate brackets {text} indicate additional information, such as language or origin, related to a term.

Parentheses (text) in the *context of complete words* indicate information which may or may not appear, i.e., Aloes (Barbadensis) (Socotrinae) indicates that one may see Aloes alone or with one of the additional terms (which specify origin). When multiple parenthetical terms appear, it is generally obvious when they are mutually exclusive, so this has been indicated only when confusion may arise. I.e., it is evident that aloes cannot be from two places, and that formulations cannot be both strong (forte) and weak (mitis) or both concentrated (concentratum) and dilute (dilutum). However, *it is not necessary that any of the parenthetical terms appear at all.*

Parentheses (text) *within words* indicate optional letters. In some instances the letters may appear or not while in other instances the choices are mutually exclusive. For example, potassium chlorate is entered as *Potassae Chlor(in)ate*, indicating that *Potassae Chlorate* or *Potassae Chlorinate* may be seen.

Square brackets [text][text] in the context of *whole words* indicate mutually exclusive terms, *one (and only one) of which is expected appear*. For example, formulations of coffee in the US National Formulary were specified as being prepared from either green or toasted (roasted) beans, and are listed as *Coffeae* [*viridis*][*tostae*]..., indicating that you should expect to see one or the other term, but not both.

Square brackets [text][text] *within words* indicate mutually exclusive letters, one and only one of which is expected to appear. For example, a number compound formulations are found to be designated as *Composit*[*a*][*um*], indicating that one may see *Composita* or *Compositum*. In this case it is apparent that one will not see both endings together. It is somewhat less apparent, until one becomes used to Latin terminology, that at least one ending must appear, but this does not create a practical problem as one will not be looking up a term that one never finds (*Composit*).

Conventions for Terms, Use of Italics, Designations for Omitted or Unspecified Terms, etc.

Terms are followed by descriptors intended to clarify the nature of the term as, for example, a chemical name, abbreviated chemical name, proper botanical name, etc., and to identify linguistic origin. Common descriptors are abbreviated in the interest of space and are listed immediately preceding the compendium pages. Abbreviations will be designated as such (*abr*) only if the abbreviated nature is not readily apparent on the basis of punctuation or orthographic characteristics.

Omission of repeated words is signified by an em dash, —, applied to conserve space within the entries, for example:

Asafoetidae, emulsum; —, mistura; —, pilulae; —, tinctura refers to:

Asafoetidae, emulsum; Asafoetidae, mistura; Asafoetidae, pilulae; Asafoetidae, tinctura.

Unspecified terms will be designated by an underline, _____, i.e., "**Oleum** _____" could refer to any oil, and the entry will refer you onwards to "_____, oleum," indicating that you should look under the appropriate term for the source or type of oil. For example, if one wished to look up *Oleum Hedeoma* (oil of Pennyroyal), the entry under *Oleum* would indicate that one should instead look up "*Hedeoma, oleum.*" (Least you worry, the entry for Pennyroyal would refer you to *Hedeoma* as well.)

Terms from Multiple Languages

Terms from multiple languages will be clustered together as alphabetization permits. In these cases, the term may include multiple variants. Latin or English terms will lead, even if not alphabetically first, and will not be accompanied by a language designator unless necessary for the sake of clarity. Each variant will have a language designation, which refers only to the term immediately preceding it:

Sirupus; sirop {*French*}; **siropo** {*Italian*}; **siroppo** {*Italian*}: Syrup. (1)

In this example, **Sirupus** is clearly Latin (it is not designated and clearly not English), and remaining terms are specified by language.

Italics will be reserved for the titles of publications and for the proper Latin designations of a particular genus and species, as in *Papaver somniferum* (by convention: genus capitalized, species and variety designators not). However, there are numerous instances in which a Latin term is also the correct botanical name for the plant or animal to which it refers. In this circumstance, the glossary entry itself will *not* be placed in italics in order to keep the appearance of term listings consistent and to facilitate easy visual searching.

Use of Botanical Names and Illustrations

Botanical names were generally obtained from historical sources and proper Latin names (genus and species) will be provided when available. These will appear in italics within the definition (but not if listed as an entry term), with genus capitalized and the species not so, as is conventional in botany, notwithstanding reference to a proper name of a person or place, i.e., *Cannabis indica* refers to a plant native in India. Such names may not correspond to modern botanical designations. When a modern botanical term has been identified, it will be noted using the term "now" if certain, or "probably" if the correspondence is uncertain, i.e.:

Poison ivy (*Rhus toxicodendron,* now *Toxicodendron radicans*)

Unfortunately, disagreement remains frequent as to whether related plants, especially of widely scattered geographical origin, are the same species, a variant, a related species, or are, in fact, unrelated despite whatever similarities may be apparent. While my original intent was to identify current botanical nomenclature for each botanical entry, this was unachievable in practice; or in any event, clearly beyond the botanical skills of the author.

As a partial solution to difficulties in botanical identification, I have chosen the majority of illustrations from William Woodville's *Medical Botany*. Published between 1790 and 1795 in England, one can at least be certain that the illustrations represent an expert's opinion as to the correct identification at that time and place. While the Latin botanical names indicated on the original illustration may not match the preferred terminology in this compendium, Woodville provides a list of common names and Latin synonyms in the text which allow for reasonably certain identification. Additional illustrations of American species were obtained from F. Schuyler Mathews's *Fieldbook of American Wildflowers*, published in 1935, and then only if reliable association with the medicinal species could be established.

Lastly, the reader should not be surprised to discover that common plant names are often used to describe multiple different species and varieties of plants. While this may undermine the collector's desire to precisely identify a particular term, this is simply the nature of common language and cannot be avoided. It is also quite likely that a large number of local and trivial names for plants are missing from the *Compendium* altogether.

Descriptions of Usage

Uses, unless otherwise indicated, are based upon recognized uses in Europe and among European emigrant communities of North America. Indigenous knowledge of botanical remedies was extensive. While such knowledge is not to be denigrated and was often the origin of American medical use of materials not originally known to Europe, the simple reality is that the apothecary containers and other paraphernalia addressed in this compendium do not arise from these indigenous cultures. Thus, Native American or other historical uses will be identified only when of sufficient interest to warrant inclusion.

The reader should keep in mind that usage varied across time and place for any particular remedy, and probably varied significantly even at the level of the individual health practitioner. Today's medications tend to be highly specific to a particular condition or defined set of conditions, and have generally been selected to avoid side effects on other systems. In contrast, historical medications were taken as they occurred in nature, and were utilized for all of their various properties. While the occurrence of undesirable effects was noted, the sharp distinction between the desired effect and side effects did not exist then as it does now.

It should also be noted that little evidence of effectiveness was required, and many uses are anecdotally derived. Consequently, most materials will have a long list of uses, often seemingly unrelated, and

sometimes appearing utterly nonsensical to the modern reader. For example, "astringent" medications were believed to have a drying effect upon secretions and also cause vascular constriction, making them useful for control of bleeding. Further, while topical application occurred in a logical manner (gargling for the throat, a plaster or ointment for the skin, etc.), astringents were also used systemically (generally by mouth) to achieve either local effects on the gastrointestinal tract or to achieve effects on other organ systems. An oral astringent might be used for runny nose, eye discharges, phlegm in the throat, cough, asthma, respiratory congestion, mouth sores, bleeding ulcers, diarrhea, menstrual disorders, urinary bleeding, various skin disorders, etc. Similarly, the Compound Tincture of Lobelia and Capsicum was used for cramps (intestinal and muscular) as well as tetanus and convulsions—all of which involve some type of muscular spasm, but are now understood to be unrelated conditions.

Historical uses were also clustered around particular symptoms or organ systems. Thus, "fever" was thought of as a general condition, rather than a symptom of a more specific underlying disease, and any medication useful for fever could be used to treat virtually any febrile condition. Similarly, one will see medications that are generally used for conditions of the eye, and might be used for everything from cataracts to blindness to poor visual acuity. In some cases these associations were based upon the so-called "doctrine of signatures," a belief that a particular medicinal would carry some sign or symbol indicating its proper use. This was often a superficial resemblance to an organ such as a heart-shaped leaf or, in the case of mandrake, a bifurcated root with a human-like appearance; but could also include, for example, the use of a yellow-colored material to treat jaundice. In any event, the various conditions treated by a particular remedy often make little sense against the backdrop of modern medical diagnosis and treatment.

A very few remedies were considered to be "specifics" for a very particular condition. For example, digitalis for heart failure (dropsy) and colchicum (Autumn Crocus, the source of colchicine) for gout, both of which (in refined forms) continue to be used today.

ILLUSTRATIONS

Illustrations are obtained from original sources when feasible, but this has not always been practical, in which case I have tried to acknowledge both the primary and secondary source. Many of the illustrations taken from old texts are discolored, worn, faded, or damaged. These illustrations have been restored using digital techniques in order to improve image quality, but with the utmost respect for the original image. Text contrast has been increased, background lightened, and background soil digitally removed. Imprinted areas, where badly worn or abraded, have been retouched.

Several composite figures used to illustrate multiple variations of glassware are composed of various portions of images from one (or occasionally more than one) source. The reference for these figures will state that the image is compiled from a particular source or sources.

The image of Dr. Dyott's manufactory was particularly worn and was extensively retouched, including re-creation of the horse's forequarters and head (digitally obtained from the horse in the middle right) and restoration of other details in the lower left hand corner of the image.

Most botanical illustrations were obtained from William Woodville's *Medical Botany*. This collection was published between 1790 and 1793 as a three-volume set, with a supplemental volume published in 1794. Woodville (1752–1805) was an English physician, medical botanist, and

Fellow of the Linnaean Society, but was not himself an illustrator. Black-and-white illustrations for all four volumes were produced by James Sowerby (1757–1822), an English illustrator and naturalist whose works cover subjects from mineralogy to paleontology and whose own 36-volume set of color botanical plates is considered a major work of general botany. Unedited images were provided from the electronic collection of the Missouri Botanical Garden, as the volumes, which I had the privilege to briefly examine, are too fragile to allow repeated handling.

Additional botanical illustrations were taken from the lovely, 1905 *Fieldbook of American Wildflowers*, by F. Schuyler Mathews (1854–1938), which is part of the author's collection. Mathews was, like Sowerby, a naturalist and illustrator, and is perhaps best known for his *Field Book of Wild Birds and Their Music*, which provided not only illustrations but a transcription of birdsong in standard musical notation!

An 1891 view of the "Flint-Glass Factories" of Whitall, Tatum in South Millville.— *Illustration courtesy of Armstrong Cork Company*

From Whitall, Tatum and Co. Catalog, 1880, American Historical Catalog Collection, Pyne Press, Princeton NJ, 1971. Courtesy, Armstrong Company.

CHAPTER 2

BACKGROUND MATTER

A BRIEF HISTORY OF APOTHECARY CONTAINERS, LABELS, AND LABELING PRACTICES

General History

The taking of medications to alter, restore, or improve physical wellbeing is as old as humankind. Early therapeutic agents were restricted to botanical and mineral materials, often only to be had at particular locations or at particular times of year. Given the mobile existence of early human civilizations, it seems inevitable that the use of containers to store, preserve, and transport medicinal materials did not post-date by much, if at all, the first therapeutic interventions. Labeling, in at least some crude form, undoubtedly came soon thereafter. The earliest "labeling," given a lack of containers transparent enough to reveal contents, was probably the use of a distinctive container. Decorative markings probably soon followed, leading eventually to the symbolic and alphabetic labeling we know today— but all of this is lost in the depths of history.

Early containers were surely of natural origin —gourds, bark containers, leather, etc.—but few such containers survived to be studied in modern times, and this undoubtedly has biased our view of early apothecary practice. Thus, we are most familiar with the ceramic, stone, and later glass containers that have survived the ages. The history of these more durable apothecary containers is discussed at length by Griffenhagen and Bogard (5) and is augmented by more general histories of glass and ceramic objects (6). A brief history is presented here simply to set the stage for the information which follows.

By 2250 BCE, it is known that a trade in drugs and spices was in place between Egypt and Babylonia using clay and stone vessels. The earliest use of glass appears to have been the use of blue faience glazes on Egyptian ceramics, with glass beads and small objects following in the time frame of 1600 to 1500 BCE. The basic recipe for glass has changed little since that time—sand, soda (sodium carbonate), and lime. The Egyptians later developed a production method for glass bottles, performed using a sand core dipped in molten glass and/or wrapped with softened glass rod or fine threads to produce a decorative and functional container. These objects were difficult to manufacture, presumably expensive, and reserved for uses of greater priority than simple commercial transport of goods.

This situation pertained until roughly the third century BCE, when the development of glassblowing allowed much greater diversity in glass goods with a much reduced level of effort. Later Roman-era blown glassware is strikingly sophisticated and ranges from elaborately decorated objects of great expense to simple, mass-produced housewares and even window panes. The prevalence of glass manufacture followed the usual trends of technology in European history—tapering off with the fall of Byzantium, remaining sporadic, but not lost, through the Middle Ages, and expanding rapidly with the Renaissance. Leaded glass ("crystal") was introduced in England in 1676 by George Ravenscroft (6), the first major improvement in glass formulation since ancient times. Routine commercial wares, however, continued to be made with ordinary glass due to its low cost.

Non-glass containers have a long evolution as well. Considerable attention was paid to the proper storage of drugs by the Greeks and Romans, using stone (alabaster), clay, bone, lead, and silver containers in addition to glass. Ceramic items for apothecary use developed during the Middle Ages in the Middle East, and the use of such containers was spread by trade and conquest throughout Europe. One particular form, the *albarello*, is quite distinctive and widespread. This is a wide-mouth, ceramic container, most often of relatively tall aspect, somewhat like a vase, with a diameter such that the container could be easily held in the hand. The distinctive characteristic of such containers was the closure. The upper lip of the albarello was molded outwards in such a way that a groove or channel surrounded the top of the container, allowing a piece of fabric, hide, or other material to be tied atop the vessel. The number and variety of such containers, including squat containers used for ointments, is almost limitless. Whole sets were produced commercially, often including permanent labeling, for use as apothecary shop furnishings. Early materials were most often ceramic, but by the eighteenth century porcelain came into use for fine decorative containers and apothecary furnishings, and similar containers were later produced in glass as well.

Porcelain became commonplace in apothecary furnishings in the nineteenth century, and the albarello design was gradually replaced by the use of fitted lids. A variety of container forms became more commonplace, including syrup pots with pouring spouts. The commercial introduction, by Josiah Wedgwood, of cream colored, lead-glazed ceramic wares in 1762 resulted in the replacement of much porcelain ware with "*Queensware*" in England and the English colonies.

North American Wares

The history of apothecary wares in North America is, of course, comparatively brief. Early practices reflect the habits and available goods from the British Isles and from other colonial powers, as well as local production. North American wares are thus largely porcelain, earthenware, or glass, with the addition of metal tins and various wooden or paper containers, particularly for dispensing of tablets or for the sales of proprietary patent medicines.

There is evidence of the manufacture and export of glass wares, including drug "phials" (vials), from the American colony in Jamestown as early as about 1609, based upon the arrival of Dutch glassblowers in 1608. The early 1700s saw the development of several major glassworks in the colonies, the two best known being the Wistar and Steigel works.

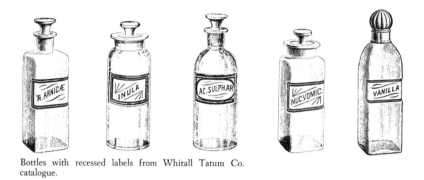

Bottles with recessed labels from Whitall Tatum Co. catalogue.

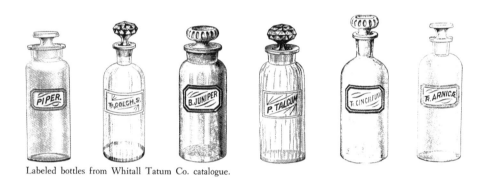

Labeled bottles from Whitall Tatum Co. catalogue.

Miscellaneous apothecary jars and globes from Whitall Tatum Co. catalogue.

Fig. 2-1 Apothecary Wares, from Munsey (6).

Show-window bottles from Whitall Tatum Co. catalogue.

Tablet jars from Whitall Tatum Co. catalogue.

Bottles with ground lettering from
Whitall Tatum Co. catalogue.

Fig. 2-2 Apothecary Wares, from Munsey (6).

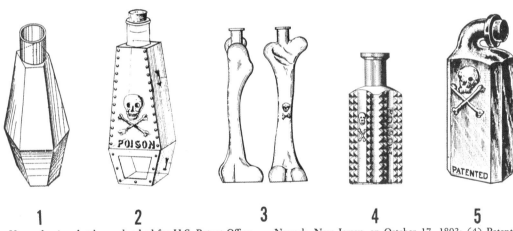

1   **2**   **3**   **4**   **5**

Unusual poison bottles as sketched for U.S. Patent Office (left to right): (1) Patent No. 183,117 granted to James W. Bowles, of Louisville, Kentucky, on October 10, 1876; (2) Patent No. 20,135 granted to Charles P. Booth, of Atlantic City, New Jersey, on September 9, 1890; (3) Patent No. 22,835 granted to Edward M. Cone, of Newark, New Jersey, on October 17, 1893; (4) Patent No. 541,133 granted to James H. Valentine, of Chatham, New Jersey, on June 18, 1895; (5) Patent No. 26,482 granted to Henry Lemmermann, of Hasbrouck Heights, New Jersey, on January 8, 1897. (George B. Griffenhagen, *Journal of the American Pharmaceutical Association*)

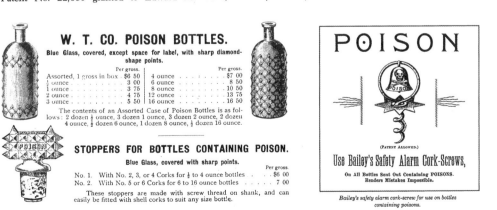

Fig. 2-3 Caveat emptor!! - Assorted poison bottles, stoppers, and corkscrew with bell. Compiled from Griffenhagen and Bogard (5) and Munsey (6).

Tincture-
mouthed shelf
bottle (round)

Salt-mouthed
shelf bottle
(round)

Tincture-
mouthed shelf
bottle (square)

Salt-mouthed
shelf bottle
(square)

Syrup bottle

Oil bottle

Syrup in an
ordinary
bottle

Fig. 2-4 Bottles for specific purposes, from Remington's (3). Tinctures have a narrow pouring lip, solids (salts) a wide mouth for easy access with a spoon or other instrument, syrups with an extended pouring lip to avoid dripping (the undesirable effects of which are seen in the last item, above), and for volatile oils, a small pouring outlet (removable with a ground-glass joint and an over-cap to minimize evaporation of the contents).

However, it is likely that many nondescript bottles and containers, such as pill vials, were made by numerous other small works in the northern colonies. By 1780, about one dozen glass manufactories are known to have been operating in the then United States, and the number of such businesses expanded rapidly thereafter. Of particular interest is the Philadelphia Glass Works, which began operation in 1771 and underwent several economic failures, later operating as the Philadelphia and Kensington Glass Works before being gradually acquired by Thomas Dyott, who bought into the firm in the 1820s. Dyott was a self-proclaimed "Doctor" and produced a wide variety of patent medications. His purchase of the firm was expressly to obtain the many bottles needed for his products; for many years he operated the company (less than modestly, as befits his trade) under the name of Dyottville Glass Works.

Several particular types of glass containers are of note in the Americas. The first of these are patent medicine bottles, imported first from Europe by the early colonists, but gradually supplanted by local production. The products are almost infinite in variety. Even the earliest bottles were sometimes embossed with labels or other details in order to reduce the ease of producing copy-cat products, but many early remedies and even later ones remained in plain bottles with paper labels.

The latter approach was commonly employed by pharmacies as well, using bottles produced inexpensively with custom plates inserted into standard bottle molds. These containers would be embossed with the name of the pharmacy or pharmacy chain (the best known examples being Owl Drug, later merging into the Rexall chain), as well as, frequently, volumetric markings.

An interesting side light is the poison bottle, an intentionally distinctive bottle intended to contain particularly poisonous remedies, materials not for internal use, or other toxic substances. Legislation requiring such bottles was considered in Britain in the 1850–1860s and a recommendation for such was made by the American Medical Association in 1872. The idea of poison bottles seems to have lasted from 1870 to the early 1930s, after which they fade from production. Such bottles were often oddly shaped (triangular, for example), colored (cobalt blue, brown), covered with irregularities, and, in some cases, even figural, i.e., molded to the shape of a skull-and-crossbones, a coffin, or in the form of a human femur.

Finally, of greatest interest here are the containers specifically produced for use by the apothecary. By far the most recognizable are the various recessed-label glass containers produced under a patent issued first to William N. Walton in 1862. Early versions utilized printed labels on paper or foil, over which a thin, conforming glass cover slip was applied using an adhesive, usually based on balsam. Later versions employed labels printed and fused directly to the glass slip and subsequently adhered or fused to the underlying glass container, which might have a recessed area intended for this purpose.

By far the best recognized manufacturer of such bottles was Whitall, Tatum and Company, which offered an entire line of apothecary furnishings from show globes (large multi-level containers usually filled with colored liquids and displayed in the window as a mark of the trade) to shelf bottles, as well as dispensing bottles, poison bottles, perfume bottles, etc. The company operating under this name was founded from several predecessor companies in 1857; by 1880 it offered an extensive assortment of apothecary goods (29). The bottle designs from this time period were specialized for particular uses and included wide-mouth jars for powdered and crystalline materials, like mineral salts (salt-mouth jars), stoppered containers for liquids (often with elaborate ground glass stoppers as well), lipped containers for syrups and oils, etc. Formally incorporated in 1901, production of apothecary goods at Whitall Tatum and Company appears to have peaked between 1900 and roughly 1910 (29). It has been suggested (29) that the introduction of automatic glassblowing equipment in 1903 foreshadowed the end of hand-manufactured goods as machine manufacture undercut price and eliminated the element of individual craftsmanship. By the early 1920s, the grand era of apothecary glass was in serious decline, and the era was arguably brought to a close with the purchase of Whitall, Tatum and Company by the Armstrong Cork Company in 1938 (29).

Labeling

There is, of course, a history of labeling independent of the history of containers, i.e., so long as the label was not physically embossed or otherwise permanently affixed to the container at manufacture, the label may be afforded a history of its own. This is discussed at length by Griffenhagen and Bogard (5), who first identify a concern for systematic labeling of storage and dispensing bottles in Europe in the sixteenth century. Lacking adhesive labels, one generally tied a paper tag or wooden chip label to the container with string, but few such containers have survived intact. By the eighteenth century in England, and presumably throughout much of Europe, labeling requirements were being strictly enforced.

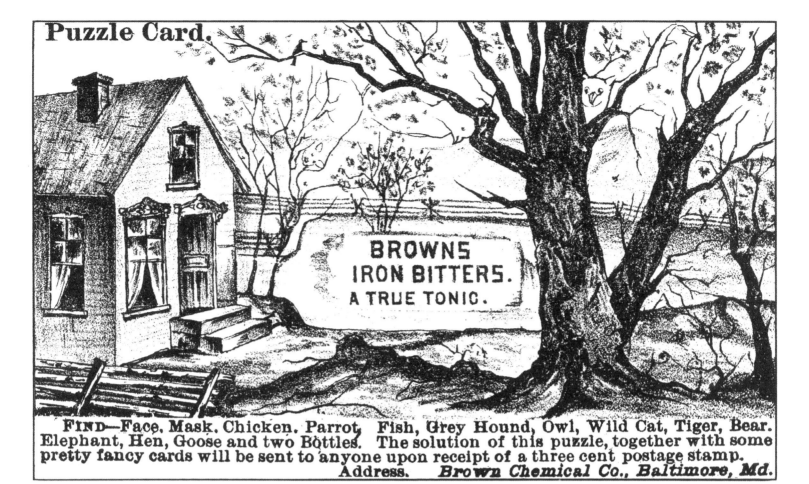

Fig. 2-5 A puzzle card advertising Brown's Bitters from Watson (27).

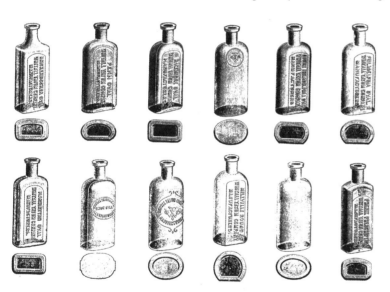

Fig. 2-6 Embossed dispensing wares from Munsey (6).

Fig. 2-7 Sample embossing plate images from Whitall, Tatum and Co. Catalog, 1880, American Historical Catalog Collection, Pyne Press, Princeton NJ, 1971.

The affixing of paper labels to containers is known to have been practiced in the latter part of the sixteenth century, and Griffenhagen and Bogard note that a book of pre-printed pharmacy labels, designed to be cut out and applied to containers, was printed in Nuremburg in 1603. From this time onwards, technology gradually moved from the use of woodcuts to copper engraving and movable type, allowing for increasing levels of detail and increasing quantities of information. Substantial competition arose among commercial label manufacturers in the early portions of the nineteenth century and since that time pre-printed labels have been the norm for use on all but fine apothecary furnishings.

The use of printing for labels and associated paraphernalia reached its zenith in the Americas during the nineteenth century, the heyday of so-called "patent" medications—perhaps better referred to as "proprietary," as few were actually patented. Competition was fierce, and the resulting need for brand-name recognition drove the development of distinctive labeling, advertisements in newspapers and magazines, trade cards, and various promotional items including pamphlets, songbooks, calendars, daybooks, medical handbooks, etc. This, arguably, represents the birth of modern advertising practice. While advertising content is generally better regulated today, we are in fact seeing a massive resurgence of "direct to consumer" advertisement of prescription drugs in the dawn of the twenty-first century, and little else has changed save for the addition of electronic media to the mix.

Fig. 2-8 Fused Glass Labels, Des Moines Drug Co. Catalog, 1906-07 (see also color plate of same)

Just as the introduction of the fused-glass label in 1862 moved much information off affixed labels and onto the container itself, the ready availability of mold-plates for the mass production of dispensing bottles created a plethora of customized bottles. This phenomenon began with the advent of glass blowing and was certainly popular for specific patent medicine products from early colonial times. One of the earliest known products imported to the American colonies was Turlington's Balsam of Life, sold in distinctively shaped and embossed bottles which would have been difficult to copy within the colonies. In later times, plate-molded bottles most often carried the name of the dispensing pharmacy or physician, with a paper label specifying the contents and instructions for use affixed at the time of dispensing.

DATING OF NORTH AMERICAN BOTTLES

The dating of bottles is difficult at best, and the problem has only been aggravated by the existence of copies of some types of decorative apothecary items and some of the more interesting patent medicine bottles. Establishing a date is difficult even for patent medicines with identifiable trade names, as many were produced for many decades. Indeed, Turlington's Balsam, believed to be among the first patent medications imported into the New World, was produced in England beginning in 1744 and was sold continuously in North America until almost 1900 (6). Appearance is notoriously unreliable as an index of age, as different glasses age differently under various conditions of environment and illumination, and methods of artificial "aging" for glass are sometimes employed by the unscrupulous.

A number of clues may prove useful to the collector in establishing a date, or at least an earliest date, of production. Much of this advice is drawn from Munsey's *Collecting Bottles* (6), which also contains illustrations of various molds and techniques, pictures of various empontilment markings, and diagrams of mold markings.

If one is fortunate enough to collect a bottle from an old pharmacy, waste heap, or other collection of contemporaneous materials, be sure to pay attention to associated items that may lead to an approximate dating. This is, unfortunately, a rare opportunity, especially with recent trafficking of antiques via the Internet. While the latter has certainly made items vastly more accessible to the collector, context is inevitably lost unless the seller has taken the trouble to provide it.

Containers or other objects making reference to plant materials native to the New World must clearly originate after the "discovery" of the American continents by Europeans in 1492. While earlier explorations are known, the voyages of Columbus clearly delineate the beginning of larger scale commerce between the Old World and the New.

Patent dates or, occasionally, copyright dates may be found on bottles or associated packaging. In most instances, patents reflect the method of manufacturing of the container or a unique closure, and the patent number is often on the bottom or even around the lip of the container. Collectors should keep in mind that "patent" medicines, despite the name, were rarely patented, as this would necessitate disclosure of the formula in a market rife with copy-cat products. When such medications do carry a "patent" date, it establishes a likely earliest date of manufacture, but may not be associated with an actual filing. One can also imagine that purveyors of patent medicines were not above exaggerating the age of their products.

Manufacturers names or symbols may also be helpful. The products of unsuccessful, and thus short-lived, manufacturers can be dated fairly accurately, but are likely to be a rarity. The products of a highly successful, and thus long-lasting, business venture will be found often, but are harder to accurately date unless a variation of marking or trade name allows greater precision.

US patent and commercial medications were taxed during the Civil War using tax stamps in various denominations (6). The Stamp Act was repealed in 1883 and re-instituted during the Spanish-American war of 1898 to 1900. These "stamps" could be government issued, but proprietary stamps were permitted. While some were typical, rectangular stamps very much like postage stamps, larger stamps and labels could be utilized as part of the packaging design, and paper bands designed to circle the container, as well as for use over the cork or seal of the bottle were common. Some, but by no means all, such stamps carried a denomination, typically of one to six cents, and usually designated by a digit somewhere on the stamp or seal. Proprietary stamps might also carry a trade name, trade mark, or portrait of the purveyor, and many were quite ornate. Unfortunately, at least for purposes of deducing a date, the required stamps quickly became part of the recognized packaging of well-known consumer products. Thus, the ornate stamps, bands, and seals persisted long after discontinuation of the Stamp Act, and one can only conclude that bottles with such stamps probably originated after the inception of the Civil War.

Closures can be helpful to some degree, especially for patent medicine and pharmacy dispensing bottles. The lower portion of bottles could be quite sophisticated in appearance even in colonial times, as this portion was blown into a mold. Following the molding process, the bottle was cut off the blow pipe and the neck either fire polished later or, following transfer to a pontil, subjected to further work. Most simple bottles prior to 1840 had a simple neck, fire polished to a smooth finish and designed for a cork closure (28). Following 1840, the addition of a glass ring to the top of the bottle to produce a more pronounced and sturdy lip became commonplace. After this time, the lips become more sophisticated; internal threading to accept a threaded cork became available in about 1855. External threading also increased, but did not become commonplace until after 1900. The turn of the century also marked the invention, by Michael J. Owens, of the bottle-blowing machine. The latter made mass production possible on an immense scale. Injection occurred from the bottom of the bottle, with the bottle neck and lip entirely molded and finished by a plunger mechanism, making outside threading easy to produce, and inside threading an impossibility. Because most apothecary ware was of superior quality, ground glass seals were standard from early times, and thus closures provide little insight into date of production.

The first patent on a recessed glass label was obtained in 1862. Such wares rapidly gained in popularity, presumably as a result of their neat appearance, durability, and effective protection of the label from damage, but virtually all date from the time of Civil War or thereafter.

Pontil markings are difficult to interpret, and provide little information as to date. A pontil, a blowpipe or solid rod, was affixed to the bottom of a blown bottle in order to allow working of the lip. This was then broken free of the bottle when complete, leaving a pontil-mark. The latter could, however, be ground off or fire polished. In the mid-nineteenth century, various boots or "snaps" were developed to hold the incomplete bottle without the need for a pontil (6). While machine blowing did away with the pontil altogether, this is worthy of mention, as a blowing machine leaves a valve-mark or cut-off mark of round or oval character which may be on- or off-center and is easily confused with a pontil-mark, especially if efforts had been employed to minimize or obliterate the latter. A clearly recognized pontil mark provides little insight into dating, but on a simple bottle suggests it was likely before the machine-blowing era. Likewise, a clearly recognizable machine marking places a bottle firmly after 1900.

Finally, mold marking may be of some utility in dating bottles. Practices varied widely, and such dates are, at best, approximations. Mold markings were easily concealed by fire polishing if desired, and this was typically done for bottles designed for sipping or drinking in order to provide a smooth surface free of sharp edges or irregularities. Early molds were dip-molds into which a bottle was blown. Such molds were of necessity simple, as they must be slightly tapered and must be free of any features or details other than vertical striations or markings to allow the bottle to be withdrawn. Such molds may leave a marking at the top of the mold, which may be accompanied by "blow over," a bulging of the bottle above the mold. However, both features depend on whether the mold was fully filled, whether the bottle was over-blown, and what further work the bottle received following molding.

Hinged molds coming to the shoulder of the bottle date back to the first century CE and continued to be used extensively until 1800 and even beyond for simple bottles. As these were hinged, they allowed for various features to be molded on the container. Full-height molds, coming to the lip of the bottle, entered common use after 1800. Bottom-hinged molds were common from 1810-1880 and have a seam across the bottom as well as on the sides of the bottle, the former sometimes interrupted by a pontil mark. A three-part mold, consisting of a bottom portion, much like a dip-mold, and two upper portions to form the shoulder and lip, was used mostly from 1870 to 1910. This did not allow details below the shoulder; while details on the upper portion of the bottle were possible, this was apparently infrequent. Full-height molds consisting of two, three, or (rarely) more parts were extensively used throughout the nineteenth century. The bottom portion of the mold was formed either by a post (typically round, but not necessarily so) or, alternatively, by a cup or depression. In either case, a circumferential mold mark appears on the bottom of the bottle. This may occur very close to the edge of the bottle, especially with a cup-bottom mold, in which case the mark could even be slightly up the side of the bottle if

Fig. 2-9 From Whitall, Tatum and Co. Catalog, 1880 (as reproduced with additional information, American Historical Catalog Collection).

the cup was a deep one. With post molds, the bottom seam could be farther from the edge, depending upon the diameter of the post relative to the bottle. As a rule, post-bottom molds were more popular, as two or more vertical mold sections could be hinged together and would self-center about the post when the mold was closed.

Notes on Glass Coloration

Simple soda glass is not water-white, but rather has a greenish-blue or aqua hue as a result of residual contamination with iron. Uncolored glass required the use of highly purified ingredients or other chemical treatment. Coloration of glass results not from dyes or pigments, but rather (despite the term "stained" glass) from the presence of specific metallic ions within the structure of the glass itself. Depending upon the oxidation state and the presence of other chemical materials, a given metal may produce a range of colors. Available colors span the range of hues from red (copper, selenium, gold), purple (nickel, manganese), green (chromium, copper), brown (carbon, nickel), green to yellow (iron), yellow to pink (selenium), and black (iron slag). Milk glass is produced in a variety of colors via the addition of tin or zinc salts, which in isolation produce a milky white color. While most apothecary wares tend to be clear glass, dark bottles do provide additional protection against the ravages of sunlight and thus were used for some purposes.

LINGUISTICS AND ORTHOGRAPHICS

Latin has long been the common language of medicine, fading into obscurity only in relatively modern times. Transcription from Greek to Latin, construction of pseudo-Latin terminology, and changes in spelling and usage over time, enhanced by individual peculiarities, have created many orthographic variants. This tendency is only encouraged by the fact that, while chemical and botanical names are often long, space on the surface of a container is limited, particularly if one wishes to apply an inscription which is distinctive, decorative, and readily visible (even before the advent of corrective lenses!) from a distance.

Orthographic variants will be included in entries when appropriate, as in Æther (ether) for example, but will generally be eliminated in the definitional portions of entries, which are based upon modern English usage. Thus, one will find entries related to the orthographic variant (not entirely disused) "sulphur," which is transcribed as sulfur for definitional purposes.

In addition to simple abbreviation, common variants in use (2) include *s* for *z*, *i* for *j* or *y*, f for ph, *e* for *ae* or *oe*, *v* for u (or ph, as in vial), and, of course, the reverse exchanges as well. One may also see, particularly in European applications of greater age:

- Overt omissions. (*Example* becomes *Expl*)
- The replacement of one or more letters with a dot, circle or other symbol. (*Ex•ple*)
- Minute letters, often elevated but sometimes interspersed (Ex^ample), often with the minute text underlined (Ex^ample).
- Use of a line above text to indicate one or more missing letters (Ex‾).
- Omission of spaces between words or word fragments.
- Limited examples of word completion on the bottom of the container (2).
- Inclusion of letters within other letters (usually within the letters C or O).
- Various fusions, such as HL, VL, HA, HP, etc., in which vertical or sometimes horizontal elements are shared.

Examples of orthographic variants derived from Drey (1) are shown in Figure 2.10:

CŒLQVINTIDA
Coloquintida

D'CLAMENTA
Dia Calamenta

ZVC̃ VꞶATO
Zuccharo Violato

A PLꞱTAGIŃS
A(qua) Plantaginis

UNG^TM E GIPTIAC̃
Unguentum Aegyptiacum

TIRICA·M·G
Theriaca Magna

Colloq̃tida
Colloquintida

SY̆ Đ CICRIA CMPOSTO
Syropo Di Cicoria Composto

Fig. 2-10 Orthographic variants (figure by author, based on images in Drey).

On American bottles, omissions are commonly denoted by a colon, as in "Glyc. Ac: Boric:", where "Glyc." is a standardized abbreviation (within a particular set of containers) for glycerate, and "AC:BORIC:" is boric acid, or Acidi Borici. The distinction between an abbreviation and a terminal omission is, in this case, arbitrary, although with other standard abbreviations such as "Spt." for spirit, the omissions may be in the middle of the word. In my experience, this combination of a standardized abbreviation, usually for the dosage form (tincture, spirit, powder, etc.) with a period, followed by non-standardized omissions represented by colons is extremely common in commercially produced sets. Another common American variant is the apostrophe for deleted text. Thus, for dilute nitrohydrochloric acid (*nitrohydrochloricum acidum dilutum*), one will find nit'hyd'chl. dil.

American manufactured commercial labels sometimes use minute letters in mid-word, but this was more common in European containers as noted above. Far more common is the use of one or more minute letters at the end of a word, with or without omitted letters, i.e., alumen ustum (burnt alum) as alumen ust^m.

American bottles commonly contain the usual letter fusions, Æ, æ, Œ (OE), and œ, but also often contain the peculiar combination of capital T and H (or h) into a single letter in which the first vertical line is crossed.

WEIGHTS AND MEASURES

Metric units of measure have, for reasons that will be readily apparent after review of the traditional units below, almost completely displaced more traditional English weights and measures during the latter half of the twentieth century. Today the apothecary system is preserved mainly in the dosage form of certain older medications such as the 325 milligram aspirin tablet, equivalent to 5 grains, and in the tendency to produce tablet sizes of 15 and 30 milligrams, roughly ¼ and ½ grain respectively.

Troy or Apothecary's Weight

The original unit of weight, the grain (gr.) reflect the definition of the English silver penny, or sterling, defined as weighing "*thirty-two grains of wheat, well dried and taken from the middle of the ear,*" as declared by Henry III of England, in 1266 (2).

One grain, approximately 64 milligrams (mg), forms the basis of the Apothecary System of weights, as follows.

Unit		Symbol/Abbrev.
grain		gr.
scruple	= 20 grains	Ɔ
drachm	= 3 scruples (60 gr.)	ʒ
ounce	= 8 drachms (24 Ɔ, 480 gr.)	℥
pound	= 12 ounces (5760 gr.)	—

Avoirdupois Weight

This corresponds to the standard US units of measure in modern times with units of ounce (oz.) and pound (lb.), the pound consisting of 16 ounces. While the Troy ounce weighs more than the Avoirdupois ounce (480 vs. 437½ grains respectively), the Avoirdupois pound weighs 7000 grains vs. 5760 grains for the Troy pound.

Apothecary's Measure (volume):

While this system is not much used today, one continues to see the apothecary fluid ounce symbol (fl ℥, or often just ℥) embossed on graduated dispensing bottles in current use.

The smallest unit of volumetric measure, the Minim, is often taken to be 1 drop (1/20 of a milliliter, or 0.050 cc, although it is correctly 0.06161 ml).

Unit		Symbol/Abbrev.
minim		♍
fluidrachm	= 60 ♍	fl ʒ
fluidounce	= 8 fl ʒ, or 480 ♍	fl ℥
pint	= 16 fl ℥	O. (octavo, i.e., 1/8ᵗʰ gal.)
gallon	= 8 O.	Cong. (congius, a Roman gallon)

Familiar intermediate measures include the cup (1/2 pint) and quart (quarto, a fourth part of a gallon).

Imperial Measure (volume):

In use primarily in the United Kingdom historically, but largely disused today, one occasionally still sees goods sold by the imperial gallon.

Unit		Symbol/Abbrev.
minim		min.
fluidrachm	= 60 ♍	fl dr.
fluidounce	= 8 fl dr.	fl oz.
pint	= 20 fl oz.	O.
gallon	= 8 O.	C.

The imperial pint is 20/16, or 5/4 of the apothecary (US) pint, and thus the imperial quart is 5/4 of the apothecary (US) quart, the Imperial Gallon (4 Imperial quarts) is equal to 5 US quarts, as is commonly known in the US.

Approximate Measures (volume):

Approximate measures of volume such as the household teaspoon (which may vary significantly from the official volume) remain in common use today, although the use of metric measures and the practice of providing properly graduated dosing devices (syringes, medicine cups—which may have both types of markings) are gradually supplanting this practice. Today, a teaspoon is assumed to be 5 ml (cc), but in fact this is quite variable and the 1926 edition of Remington's (3) notes the following:

Measure	Apothecary Equivalent	Metric
tumbler	fl ℥ viii (i.e., 8 fl. Oz)	240 cc
teacup	fl ℥ iv	120 cc
wineglass	fl ℥ ii	60 cc
tablespoon (Tbl.)	fl ℥ iv (i.e., 4 fluidrachms)	15 cc
dessertspoon	fl ℥ ii	8 cc
teaspoon (tsp)	fl ℥ i	4 cc

DOSAGE FORMS

Dosage forms are the ultimate product of the apothecary's art. Pills, liquids, and suppositories are obvious, but the scope extends much more broadly to include various ointments and creams, gargles, eye washes, and a variety of other forms, some of which (powders, troches) have largely passed from common use. For precisely this reason, a list of dosage forms is provided.

Liquid preparations are classified, in part, by use and, in part, by the primary solvent or carrier used to prepare the solution, most often water, alcohol, or some combination thereof. A distinction is made between *solutions*, in which all of the matter is fully dissolved in the solvent, and *liquids*, in which varying degrees of solid matter may be suspended.

Specific preparations in more modern times (*fluid extracts, abstracts,* and *triturations*) are defined in official pharmacopoeias on the basis of the quantitative relationship between the mass of extracted material and the original mass of starting material, or on occasion to some other point of reference.

One last modern addition, the capsule, has been added here with the other solid dosing forms. Dating to 1883 (3), the pre-manufactured capsule has become a common dosage form as a result of the simplicity of manufacture (the contents need few specific properties), great variety of sizes and colors, ease of marking, and relative ease of ingestion.

The materials are organized as per Stewart (2) or Cook (3), both of which reflect the original classification in *Remington's Practice of Pharmacy*. Processes referred to in this section (percolation, etc.) are discussed in the section regarding Apothecary Processes.

Liquids

Made without percolation or maceration:

Aqueous solutions
Waters (aquae)—Aqueous solutions prepared by dissolving material in cold or hot water, by filtration through an impregnated medium (powder, cotton), by distillation, or by passing a soluble gas through water.
Solutions or Liquor (liquors)—Particular water-based preparations described in official formularies.

Aqueous solutions containing sweet or viscid substances:
Syrups (syrupi)—Solutions based on a concentrated solution of sugar in water, the latter referred to as *Simple Syrup*, abbreviated S.S.
Honeys (mellita)—As with syrup, but using honey in place of sugar-based syrup.
Mucilages (mucilagenes)—Similar to syrup, but thickened using a gum or mucilaginous material such as gum tragacanth, gum arabic, etc.
Mixtures (misturae)—Solutions for internal use which also contain suspended solids.
Glycerites (glyceritae)—Based upon glycerin, often with egg yolk (*glyceritum vitelli*) or in conjunction with starch to form a clear jelly (*glyceritum amyli*).

Alcoholic solutions:

Spirits (spiritus)—Alcoholic solutions of volatile substances. May be made with or without maceration (the latter usually if derived from plants, i.e., spirits of peppermint), by passage of gas through alcohol, by distillation, or by direct chemical reaction in alcoholic solution.

Elixirs (elixira)—Aromatic, sweetened alcohol based substances with a small quantity of active medicinal substance.

Ethereal / Æthereal solutions:

Collodions (collodia)—Topical ether/alcohol based solutions of pyroxylin (gun cotton, nitrocellulose) that leave a flexible film behind on evaporation. May be used as such (flexible collodion dressing) or medicated to apply treatment to a skin lesion such as a wart.

Oleagenous solutions

Liniments (Linimenta)—Thickened rubs applied to skin, often with a volatile component such as camphor, with or without additional medication.

Oleates (oleata)—Produced by dissolving metal salts or plant alkaloids in oleic acid (a derivative of animal fat).

Made with percolation or maceration:

Aqueous liquids:

Elixir—See above. Elixirs may be made with or without maceration.

Infusions (infusa)—Liquid preparations made by soaking vegetable matter in hot or cold liquid. These tend to be variable and may be hazardous as concentration of active principals is unpredictable.

Decoctions (decocta)—Similar to infusions, but prepared by boiling.

Alcoholic liquids:

Tinctures (tincturae)—An alcoholic solution, generally of non-volatile medicinal ingredients (may be made without maceration or percolation in some cases). Spirits are very similar, but usually based on volatile active ingredients. Terminology is, however, used very inconsistently.

Wines(vina)—Solution made with wine. May be made with or without maceration or percolation, but most commonly contain vegetable matter.

Fluid Extracts (extracta fluida)— These are specialized alcoholic solutions or tinctures which have been produced or concentrated (by evaporation) so that one milliliter of the extract is derived from one gram of the starting medicinal material. Similarly, one minim of the extract will contain the material extracted from one grain of starting material. They may be designated by *extractum fluidum* or *fluidextractum*.

Liquid Extracts (extractum liquidum)—In the British nomenclature liquid extract is used in place of fluid extract.

Ethereal / Æthereal liquids:

Oleoresins (oleoresinae)—Very strong liquid extracts of essential oils or resins produced by extraction with ether and subsequent evaporation of the solvent.

Acetous liquids:

Vinegars (aceta)—Medication solutions prepared in vinegar which acts both as solvent and as a mild antiseptic.

Solids

Made by percolation or maceration (followed by drying or other solidification process)

Extracts (extracta)—Solid or semi-solid preparations prepared by extracting the starting material (often vegetable matter) with water, alcohol, a mixture thereof, or other solvent of choice, followed by evaporation of the solvent.

Abstracts (abstracta)—Extracts which are standardized by combination with sugar, dried milk, or other dry ingredients to achieve a standard concentration. Most typically the extract is made to weigh one-half the weight of starting material, i.e., has twice the potency of the starting matter.

Resins (resinae)—Prepared from a tincture by addition of water, in which the desired active principal is insoluble, resulting in precipitation.

Made without percolation or maceration:

These forms may incorporate any of the various liquid or, more commonly, solid preparations above in addition to various active ingredients in their native state and a variety of non-active ingredients to achieve the desired concentration and physical form. The latter are referred to as *excipients*.

Powders (pulveres)—These are simple powders, taken as such or dissolved or suspended in liquid. Some are effervescent.

Triturations (triturationes)—A class of powders introduced to the US Pharmacopoeia in 1880. Generally using 6 grains of active substance with 54 grains of powdered milk, the final powder consisted of ten percent active material.

Masses (massae)—Masses are prepared formulations used, after addition of active substances, to produce pills.

Confections, Electuaries or *Conserves*—These candy-like preparations (Latin—*confectiones, electuaria*) are an ancient dosage form which is now rarely used. Certain therapeutics in the form of chewing gum (nicotine, aspirin) are perhaps our closest modern equivalent.

Pills (pilulae) or *Tablets (tablettae)*—Pills (tablets) are rounded or ovoid bodies designed to be swallowed, and may be adhesive (sticky), firm to hard, or plastic in nature. The excipients used in pill production are numerous and complex. They were often coated with metal leaf (gold, silver), powders, gelatin, or other hard materials to retard sticking. This has largely been replaced with various commercial hard sugar coatings in various colors or by polymer films. In the late nineteenth and early twentieth centuries, small "pills" or tablets, typically 1/8 inch (3 mm) in size were provided for intravenous injection. They were diluted in the syringe prior to use. It should be noted that *Tabellae* (as opposed to tablettae, although usage is sometimes inconsistent) were chocolate-based tablets specific to the British Pharmaceutical Compendium, discussed in detail in the entry for tabellae.

Troches (trochisi)—Troches or lozenges are discoid or cylindrical items usually made from medicinal powders, sugar, and mucilage as a binder. Traditionally made from material rolled into sheets and cut with a lozenge cutting device (figure 2-11), they have been almost exclusively a commercially mass-produced product since the mid-nineteenth century.

Cerates (cerata)—Waxes designed to be soft enough to spread but not so soft as to liquefy on application to the skin. They are similar to ointments.

Ointments (unguenta)—Fatty preparations softer than waxes, designed to be applied by inunction, i.e., rubbing.

Plasters (emplastra, plasmae)—Plasters are designed to adhere to the skin and generally required heat to soften them and aid in application. Active ingredients were typically bound together with lead plaster, gum, resin, or pitch and then applied to fabric, paper, or other backings.

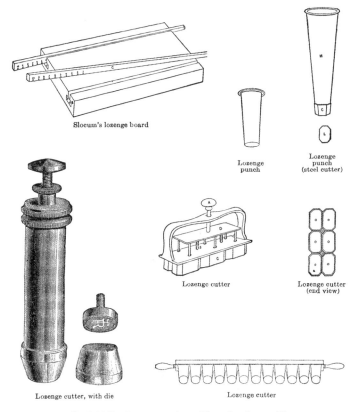

Fig. 2-11 Troche cutter, adapted from Remington (3).

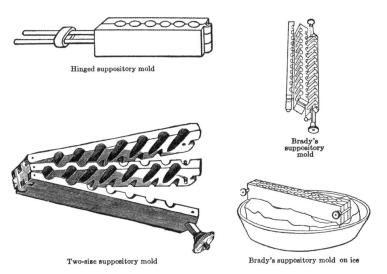

Fig. 2-12 Suppository manufacturing equipment, adapted from Remington (3).

Suppositories (suppositoria)—A dosage form designed for rectal insertion, vaginal insertion, or in historical time, urethral insertion. Generally based on gelatin, cocoa butter, or various waxes and fats, they were either rolled or, more commonly as time progressed, poured hot into suppository molds (figure 2-12) and allowed to harden.

Papers (charta)—Papers impregnated and/or coated with medications for topical use. A few forms, such as nitre paper, were burnt at the time of use to allow the smoke to be inhaled.

Capsules (capsulae)—This is a relatively modern dosage form, developed in 1833 by the French apothecary, A. Mothes. They are generally hard two-part gelatin capsules filled by hand or machine. Soft capsules and "pearles," which can be filled with liquid, are also in use today.

Cachet—A cachet consisted of a powder or mass contained within a small tissue envelope. The device shown (Fig. 2-13) was used to prepare and seal them.

Fig. 2-13 Cachet cutting equipment, adapted from Remington (3).

Additional Forms and Uses

A number of additional uses or forms exist, most based upon the general preparations described above.

NOTE: There is some degree of overlap between dosage forms and therapeutic actions, i.e., some dosage forms were used only for specific purposes, and in some cases you may be mistaken as to whether a term indicates a dosage form or intended activity. If you fail to find a term here, refer to Therapeutic Actions in the following section.

Apothem; Apozema—A strong infusion or decoction of a vegetable drug.

Aqua mulsa—See hydromel.

Bougie—A tapered device for dilating various strictures of the urethra, esophagus, etc., formed of cloth or thread dipped into a waxy or greasy material, and often medicated. (33)

Cataplasma—A watery (non-oily) poultice. (39)

Catapotia—Another term for pills. (39)

Ceratomalagmata—Cerates. (39)

Cerevisiae—A medicinal beer. (39)

Cerioli—Bougies or suppositories, but of a small size, rod-shaped, and for use in the nares or urethral opening. (42)

Clysma; Clyster—Enema. (40)

Collunarium—Nasal wash (pl.—collunaria)

Collution—Mouthwash. (39)

Collutor—Medication with honey consistency, applied to gums. (39)

Collutorium—Mouthwash (pl.—collutoria), occasionally also the Latin, Lavatio Ori.

Collyrium—Eye wash (pl.—collyria). (39)

Cyphi—Aromatic troches. (39)

Disc—See lamellae, below.

Draught—A liquid medication intended to be taken in several doses, haustus or potion are similarly used.

Eclegma—Sweet, sticky, semi-liquid formulation designed to be licked off a spoon. (1)

Ecusson—A plaster made with theriac. (39)

Emulsion; Emulsum; Emulsio—A stable admixture of immiscible materials, i.e., oil and water or a suspension of an insoluble solid in oil, etc. (This term was not used in the strict sense of a stable suspension of finely divided oily material in water.) Early Latin terms use *emulsum*, but later editions of the US National Formulary used *emulsio* to distinguish differences in preparation.

Enchiloma—Elixir. (39)

Enchristum—An unguent. (39)

Enchyta—Eyedrop. (3)

Enema—Enema (pl.—enemata).

Epicarpia—Plaster or cataplasm made with "sharp penetrating ingredients" to reduce local inflammation. (39)

Epiplasma—Same as cataplasm. (39)

Epithema—A topical preparation, usually liquid or cream, but may be any form.

Epulotica—Caustic plasters. (39)

Fluidglycerates—Fluidglycerates developed ca. 1900 as standard (National Formulary) preparations in a fifty percent mixture of glycerin and water, much like a fluidextract but with more body and some sweetness imparted by the glycerin, and alcohol free.

Fomentation—Epithem, a medication to be applied as a hot soak, in reference to the medication or to the plaster itself. (24)

Gargar; Gararisma—A gargle.

Gelatoglycerin—Gelatoglycerata developed ca. 1900 and consisted of a mixture of glycerin, gelatin, and the medication to be applied. They were formulated to melt at body temperature and were used to treat skin conditions.

Gilva—A plaster with a color similar to honey. (39)

Glyster—Clyster (orthographic variant). (39)

Haustus—Draught.

Hedychroum—A yellow (saffron) colored troche intended as an alexipharmic (panacea). (39)

Hedysmata—Aromatic unguents. (39)

Hydromel—Medication made with honey and water. (39)

Hydrosaccharum—Remedy made with sugar and water, i.e., simple syrup, or refers to sugar itself. (39)

Hypoglotis—Remedy made to place below the tongue. (39)

Incider—Remedy formulated with sharp particles to cut humors and reduce obstructions of the viscera. (39)

Julap; Julep—Julapium, a sweetened mixture containing an essential oil or medicated water. (34)

Lac—Milk, i.e., a milky formulation, often an emulsion or fine suspension. (39)

Lambative; Lambitive—Same as linctus. (39)

Lamellae—Lamellae (singular, lamellum), or disks, were standard in the BP and were small gelatin discs for insertion below the eyelid.

Lavement—Enema (French). (39)

Lexipyretus—A febrifugal plaster applied to the wrist. (39)

Linctus—A sweet, syrupy mixture or preparation. (34)

Lipara; Litus—Liniment. (39)

Lohoch—See eclegma above, generally made with honey. (1)

Looch—A lohoch, a lozenge, often sucked off the tip of a licorice stick. (39)

Magma—A soft remedy, which could be for oral or topical use. (39)

Mel, Mellita—Medicated honey (or honey-like remedy), hydromel, oxymel, etc. (39)

Melicratium—Same as hydromel. (39)

Migma—Mixture of several drugs. (39)

Mistura; Mixture—Used as a general term for complex formulations which do not fall readily into a more specific term such as a tincture, emulsion, etc. The use is at best irregular, and many materials traditionally called mixtures could as readily be placed in another category. (34)

Metrenchytum—Not actually a dosage form, but a syringe utilized for intra-uterine injection. (39)

Oleosacchara—A form consisting of a drop of any chosen essential oil triturated (mixed) with 2 grams of sugar.

Oxycoos—Remedy for earache. (39)

Oxycratum—Mixture including vinegar and water. (39)

Oxymel; Oxymil—A potion prepared by evaporating a mixture of honey and vinegar to a syrup. Oxymil is a common orthographic variant. (1)

Oxysaccharum; Oxysacchara; Oxyzacchara—Made by evaporating a mixture of sugar and vinegar, sometimes with pomegranate juice, to a syrup. (1)

Panis parvus—A "small bread," i.e., a troche. (39)

Pargyron—Can be a liquid medicine or a plaster. (39)

Pasta; Paste—A dry material admixed with water or other liquid to form a paste. This was sometimes for topical use, but in many cases was used as a pastille or troche. For example, a typical cough drop (now reincarnated as a candy) was the Jujuba troche, Pasta Jujube.

Pedilavum; Pediluvium—Footbath. (39)

Pessary—Most often a rubber appliance for intra-vaginal use, but may refer to a remedy designed for vaginal use, often for hysteria, which was attributed to uterine dysfunction. (39)

Picatio—Depilatory plaster. (39)

Placentula—A flat round troche, resembling a small "placenta," Latin for pancake. (39)

Posca—Same as oxycratum. (39)

Posset; Poscetum—A posset consisted of milk curdled by addition of alcohol, most often beer, and could also be medicated. (39)

Poterium; Potus—Any drink or potion. (39)

Potion—See draught.

Rob; Robub—A fruit juice boiled to concentrate. (39)

Saturation—An effervescent preparation in which a carbonate solution is, in the final moments of preparation, reacted with a vegetable acid (citric, tannic, etc.) and the bottle corked to retain the resulting carbon dioxide, i.e., a carbonated medication. (39)

Seplasaria—An aromatic unguent. (39)

Sparadrapum—A suppurative medication or plaster in which linen is soaked and then applied. (39)

Styli; Stylus—Medication in the form of a stick for application, usually to a local area of the skin or mucous membranes, as in a styptic pencil. Singular is stylus, but on containers the plural is usually seen, i.e., styptic pencils.

Stymmata—Preparation of dry aromatic materials in an oil or mixture of oils. (39)

Umbel (plaster)—A plaster surrounding a limb, circumferential plaster. (39)

Vectiaria—Violent cathartics. (39)

Xerocollyrium—Dry collyrium, i.e., an eye powder. (39)

THERAPEUTIC ACTIONS

There are a wide variety of therapeutic actions ascribed to drugs or other preparations (plasters, etc.). Many of these actions are described by now archaic terms which the reader will need to comprehend in order to fully understand older texts and prescriptions. A list of these terms is compiled below as derived from multiple references (4,7).

The use of terminology in patent or proprietary medicines has evolved in the marketing context to be quite different from recognized medical or apothecary usage. Terms used in patent medicine are specifically designated as such when indicated.

The late nineteenth and early twentieth centuries saw a fad for patent medications having alleged natural physical properties, demarcated with terms such as "*electric,*" "*magnetic,*" or "*volcanic,*" which generally have no basis in fact or origin and which have no specific therapeutic value or meaning.

NOTE: There is some degree of overlap between dosage forms and therapeutic actions, i.e., some dosage forms were used only for specific purposes, and in some cases you may be mistaken as to whether a term indicates a dosage form or intended activity. If you fail to find a term here, refer to Dosage Forms in the preceding section.

Absorbent—Absorbs liquids or other secretions, generally an alkaline material. According to Estes, by 1790 most were reclassified as antacids. (8,39)

Abstergent—A detergent or cleansing agent. (39)

Alexipharmic(a)—A universal antidote for poisonings; theriac.

Alexiteric—Same as alexipharmic.

Alleviator (patent medicine)—Relieves specified condition or symptoms. (4)

Alterative—Alters the processes of the body to re-establish normal function. A vague term used to describe many different actions. (8)

An(a)esthetic—Reduces the perception of pain. May be local (acts on the part to which it is applied) or general (induces a loss of consciousness). (8)

Anacollemata—Medication applied over and around the eyes. Evidently to prevent ill humors from entering the eye. (39)

Analeptic—A general restorative. (41) In modern use, a medication used to reverse stupor or coma and to stimulate or restore respiration, now a largely discredited concept.

Analgesic—Relieves pain. (8)

Anaphrodisiac—Reduces sexual desire. (8)

Anhidrotic—Reduces amount of perspiration. (8)

Annihilator (patent medicine)—Relieves specified condition or symptoms. (4)

Anodyne—A local medication which reduces pain by suppressing the function of nerve endings, roughly equivalent to a local anesthetic (8). Often appears in patent medicine context to describe an oral pain reliever.

Antacid—Neutralizes acid in the stomach. (41)

Antalgic (patent medicine)—Analgesic. (4)

Anthelmintic—Destroys intestinal worms or parasites. (8)

Antiarthritic—For "arthritis," usually gout. (41)

Anticephalic—See cephalic. (39)

Anticholegogue—Decreases the amount of bile secreted. (8)

Antiepileptic—For treatment of seizures and epilepsy. (39)

Antihectic—Relieves hectic fevers, i.e., in malaria. (39)

Antihydropic—Relieves dropsy (edema). (41)

Antihypochondriacal—For disorders of the hypochondria ("below the (chest) cartilage," i.e., abdomen), later associated with hypochondria, i.e., fixation or unjustified belief that one is ill. (39)

Antihysteric—Relieves nervous dysfunction or hysteria (a condition historically ascribed to a dysfunction of the uterus). (8)

Anti-icteric—For the treatment of icteris, i.e., jaundice. (39)

Antilienteric—For diarrhea. (39)

Antilithic—For prevention of stones (generally kidney or bladder). (39)

Antiperiodic—Treats periodic fever, i.e., malaria and other recurrent febrile illness. (8)

Antiphlogistic—A general anti-inflammatory. Phlogistin or phlogeston is the component of air responsible for combustion (i.e., oxygen) and was thus thought to be associated with the production of heat, i.e., inflammation. See Estes for a thorough discussion. (39)

Antipodagrica—For the treatment of gout. (39)

Antipyretic—Relieves fever. (8)

Antiscorbutic—For treatment of scurvy. (39)

Antiseptic—Prevents the growth of microorganisms (often used interchangeably with disinfectant). (8)

Antisialogogue—Decreases production of saliva. (8)

Antispasmodic—Relieves cramps and spasms, which may include neurological spasms (seizures) and cardiovascular spasms (rapid heart rate). (39)

Antisyphilitic—Used for the treatment of syphilis. (8)

Antitussive—For cough. (39)

Antizymotic—Terminates fermentation; may be either antiseptic or disinfectant. (8)

Aperient—Laxative, usually applied to patent medicines. (4)

Aphrodisiac—Increases sexual desire. (8)

Apodagritica—Reduces or eliminates tear production. (39)

Apophlegmatismus—Induces salivation when chewed. (39)

Araeotica—Remedy that thins humors and opens pores, i.e., a diaphoretic. (39)

Arcanum—A term for any compound remedy, after Paracelsus. (39) From the Latin, meaning "secret."

Arnica (patent medicine)—A stimulant, diuretic, diaphoretic, and emmenagogue, used in reference to therapeutic activity in patent medicines as opposed to the plant species. (4)

Aromatic—Having a spicy odor, used as a general stimulant. (8)

Arthitica—Treats arthritis or joint disorders. (39)

Ascaricide—Used to expel roundworms (i.e., ascaris and other species). (8)

Astringent—Contracts or dehydrates tissues and decreases the size of blood vessels. Thus typically used to limit excess secretions (respiratory, gastro-intestinal, genito-urinary, or even from wounds) and bleeding from nearly any site, either applied topically or taken systemically. (8)

Attenuantia—Divides up or disperses humors (causes of disease in the Galenic system of illness). (39)

Balm—In patent medicine, any soothing medication. Not necessarily used in reference to a topical application (4), i.e., Colbert's Balm of Gilead, which is taken orally. (4)

Balsam—Properly a class of natural resinous products containing benzoic or cinnamic acid in resin and volatile oil, with adhesive properties. In patent medicines, any soothing medication, not necessarily used in reference to a topical application, i.e., Fenton's Balsam of Horehound and Cherry, taken orally. (4)

Bitter—A bitter flavored medicine. A vague term used for various purposes. (8)

Blister—Vesicant, causes blisters. (41)

Califacient—Produces a sense of warmth. (41)

Cardiac depressant—Decreases action of the heart (i.e., heart rate or force of contraction). (8)

Cardiac stimulant—Increases action of the heart (rate, contractility). (8)

Carminative—Expels gas from the stomach and intestines. (8)

Catagmatica—An external remedy for bone fractures. (39)

Cathaeritica—Wound ointment. (39)

Cathartic—A purgative, causes evacuation of the bowels via irritation and/or stimulation. (8)

Catholicon—A universal remedy or cure, panacea. (4)

Catoterica—Empties the bladder, kidneys, and liver (gall bladder), a form of cathartic. (39)

Caustic—An escharotic or corrosive. Typically cathartic and anthelmintic if diluted and also dissolved stones if instilled in the bladder. (39)

Cephalic—A remedy for headache or other disorder of the head, i.e., epilepsy. (1)

Cerebral depressant—Decreases brain function, a sedative or hypnotic. (8)

Cerebral stimulant—Increases brain function. (8)

Chalastica—Emollients. (39)

Chalybeate—An iron supplement. (31)

Cholagogue—Increases the amount of bile either as a direct (increases secretion) or indirect (decreases resorption) activity. To cure bilious humors. (8,39)

Chronotrope—Increases the rate of the heart. (8)

Composing pill—Sleeping pill. (39)

Condiment—Used to make food more appetizing. (8)

Constringent—See astringent. (41)

Convulsant—Induces seizures. (41)

Cordial—A stimulating remedy, generally containing alcohol. (4)

Corrective—Used to correct or reduce unpleasant side effects of other medications, ex. an antispasmodic with a purgative to reduce cramping. (41)

Corrigent—Same as corrective. (41)

Corrector (patent medicine)—Corrects, alleviates, or cures stated condition or, if used alone, a general cure or panacea. (4)

Corroborant—Tonic. (39)

Counterirritant—Applied to irritate the skin in order to suppress the nervous function of underlying organs or viscera. (8)

Cynanchica—A sore throat treatment.

Demulcent—Protects the surface to which it is applied, an emollient to skin, a soothing and lubricating substance (usually mucilaginous) for the GI tract. (8)

Dentilavium—A medicated mouth wash, literally a "tooth wash" (Latin). (39)

Deobstruant; Deobstructant—A medicament for removing obstructions, i.e., from the GI tract, generally strong cathartic or purgative.

Deodorant—Absorbs, masks, or destroys undesirable odors. (8)

Depilatory—Removes hair. (41)

Depressant—Sedative. (41)

Depresso-motor—Reduces motor activity. (41)

Depurant—Agent to help cleanse or purify the body of, for example, toxins. (41)

Detergent; Detersive—A soap or detergent used as a cleansing agent. (8)

Diacatholicon—Catholicon, a universal antidote in reference to poisons, or a universal treatment, i.e., panacea.

Diaphoretic—Increases sweating. (8)

Digestant; Digestive—Generally a medication to improve digestion. In continental European usage, a topical wound treatment which encourages suppuration. (39)

Diluent—Increased blood volume or dilutes the blood, synergistic with diuretics. (39)

Disinfectant—Destroys microorganisms, often used interchangeably with antiseptic, which impedes the growth of microorganisms. (8)

Diuretic—Increases amount of urine produced. (8)

Drastic—Generally short for a drastic purgative (emetic and cathartic).

Dropax—Depilatory plaster. (39)

Dysenteric—To treat dysentery. (39)

Ecbolic—See oxytocic, stimulates uterine contraction. (8,39)

Eccoprotic—A laxative also causing mild emesis. (39)

Ecphractic—The opposite of a diaphoretic, closes pores, decreases sweating. (39)

Ectylotica—Removes calluses. (39)

Embrocation—In patent medicine, any liniment or rub. (4). More generally, an ointment for painful body parts. (39)

Emetic—Induces vomiting. (8)

Emmenagogue—Enhances or aids in menstruation. (8)

Emolient—A soothing and/or lubricating mixture, usually fatty or oily, which also prevents drying. Used topically on irritations, tumors, etc. (39)

Emotta—That which prevents motes, i.e., marks. Applied to pox or pustules to prevent scarring. (39)

Empasmata—Astringent powder to treat halitosis and excessive sweating. (39)

Emphrastica; Emplattomena—Same as ecphractica. (39)

Emulsifier—Allows formation of an emulsion (or water and oil). (8)

Enaemon—A styptic or agglutinating material that controls hemorrhage and encourages wound healing. (39)

Epispastic—A topical vesicant (severe blistering irritant) of the skin. (33)

Eradicator (patent medicine)—An agent that destroys a particular disease entity or symptom. A "specific."

Errhine—Causes nasal mucous discharge and sneezing, usually for headache, earache, or eye inflammation. (39)

Escharotic—A caustic or corrosive, destroys tissue. (8)

Evacuant—Purgative. (41)

Exipotica—Aids digestion. (39)

Excitant—Stimulant. (41)

Excito-motor—Increases motor activity. (41)

Expectorant—Retards the production and/or enhances expectoration of mucus in the chest. (8)

Extergentia—Detergent for topical use, to clean and dry wounds or exudative skin conditions. (39)

Extractor (patent medicine)—Removes or eliminates symptom or disorder, not necessarily via physical force (i.e., "pain extractor"). (4)

Febrifuge—Eliminates fever. (4)

Flavor—Used to impart taste to food or medication. (8)

Friction—Poultice to abrade skin and cause redness or counter-irritation. (39)

Frontal—Headache remedy for application to the forehead. (39)

Galactagogue—Enhances the secretion of milk, an aid to lactation. (8)

Galactopoetica—Same as galactogogue. (39)

Glutinoria—Same as enaemon. (39)

Glycea—Mild cathartic (i.e., glycerrhiza is licorice, a mild cathartic root). (39)

H(a)emagogue—Same as emmenagogue. (39)

Haematinic—Promotes the health of the blood, often containing iron. (8)

Haemostatic—Slows or stops bleeding. (8)

Hetica—Same as epispastic. (39)

Horetica—A digestive aid or aperient. (39)

Humectant—Moistening agent. (39)

Hydragogue—A form of cathartic, acting by drawing water into the gut, producing watery evacuation. (8)

Hypnotic—Induces sleep. (8)

Hypolata—Same as catoterica. (39)

Incitant—Stimulant, excitant. (39)

Incrassant—Coagulates or thickens bodily fluids. (39)

Inotrope—Increases the strength of contraction of the heart. (8)

Insiccant—Dries the body, i.e., a diuretic (not a topical desiccant as one might expect). (39)

Irritant—Causes irritation where applied. (8)

Keratoplastic—Dissolving or removing skin, i.e., a wart or corn remover. (31)

Lactogogue—Improves let-down or production of breast milk. (39)

Laxative—Increases evacuation of the bowels. (8)

Lenitive—A soothing, softening medication used orally as a laxative. (39)

Litho(n)triptic—Promotes dissolution of urinary stones. (8,39)

Malactica—Emollient internal or external remedy. (39)

Malagmata—Same as cataplasm. (39)

Meclita—Astringent remedy which is used to treat bleeding or hemorrhoids. (39)

Melanogogue—Encourages excretion of black bile or humors, to treat melancholia. (39)

Mesenterica—Treats disorders attributed to the mesentery (membrane to which intestines are attached), i.e., a digestive aid or appetite stimulant. (39)

Mochlia—A violent purgative which induces vomiting as well as bowel evacuation. (39)

Monohemera—A remedy that cures in a single day. (39)

Mydriatic—Dilates the pupil of the eye. (8)

Myotic; Miotic—Constricts the pupil of the eye. (8)

Narcotic—Induces sleep and relieves pain (an opiate). (8)

Nasalia—Same as errhines. (39)

Nephritic—Treats disorders of the kidneys. (39)

Nervine—After 1700, a substance having beneficial effects upon the nervous system, most often a sedative. Earlier usage was as a soothing unguent for ligaments and muscles. (39)

Neurotic—Acts on central nervous system. (41)

Nutriant; Nutrient—A nourishing substance. (8,41)

Odontalgia; Odontites—Toothache cures. (39)

Odontotrimma—Remedies to clean or strengthen the teeth. (39)

Opodeldoc (patent medicine)—A liniment or rub (4). Sometimes seen in use other than patent medicine to specify a liniment made of soap, saponis linimentum.

Oxycoos—Earache treatment. (39)

Oxytocic; Oxytotic—Accelerates childbirth, enhances uterine contraction. (8)

Oxyuricide—Destroys pinworm (*Oxyuris vermicularis*). (8)

Palliativa remedia A remedy that removes symptoms without relieving the cause of the disorder, i.e., use of opium for pain.

Panacea; Pancrestum (patent medicine)—Universal cure, from the same in Latin. (4)

Panchymogogue—Releases all humors, a universal purgative. (39)

Parasiticide—Destroys parasites. (8)

Peristaltic—Increase intestinal motility. (41)

Phlegmagogue—Releases pituitary secretions (believed to be the source of phlegm, hormonal function was of course not known until recent times). (39)

Phthartica; Phthoropoeum—A fatal poison. (39)

Phthoria—Hastens childbirth. (39)

Physic—In patent medicine, any medication, generally for oral use. (4) May also be used to describe non-surgical medicine, i.e., "Dr. of Physic."

Physogonum—A carminative. (39)

Pleonectica—Prevents accumulation of fluid, diuretic, diaphoretic, or cathartic. (39)

Pneumonica—Improves breathing. (39)

Polyanodyne—Rapidly acting pain reliever (usually opiate). (39)

Polychrestum—Panacea. (39)

Prolifica—Aphrodisiac. (39)

Prophylactic—Preventive, specifically an antidote or preventive for poisoning. (39)

Protective—Protects the surface to which it is applied. (8)

Psilothrum—Depilatory. (39)

Psorica—Remedy for itching, psoriasis, etc., often topical. (39)

Psyctica—Refrigerant. (39)

Ptyalagogue—Increases salivation. (41)

Purgative—Causes a purging or evacuation of the bowels. White's *Materia Medica* conveniently classifies the vegetable purgatives into laxative (ex.—prune), simple purgative (ex.—castor oil), and "drastic" (scammony, etc.). (8)

Purifier (patent medicine)—Purifies the body or tissue specified, usually blood.

Pustulant—Produces pustules when applied topically. (8)

Pyrotica—Same as escharotic. (39)

Ramich—A troche with tonic and astringent activity. (39)

Refective; Refectiva—Restorative, tonic. (39)

Refrigerant—Cools the skin (8), or in patent medicine use, reduces temperature/fever. (4)

Relaxant; Relaxania—An emollient and mild cathartic which releases humors for removal via the feces. (39)

Rennovator (patent medicine)—To make new, improve, or relieve a condition.

Repellentia—A remedy which immobilizes or prevents secretion of humors. (39)

Resolvent; Resolutiva—A medication causing resolution of some condition, or which causes dispersion of humors so that they may be transported in blood and exhaled or eliminated. Sometimes implying a panacea, but most often refers to a medication that resolves pain and inflammation. (34)

Respiratory depressant—Slows respiration, reduces respiratory drive. (8)

Respiratory stimulant—Increases respiration or respiratory drive. (8)

Restorative; Resumptive; Resumptiva (Patent medicine)—Restores health or vigor; a remedy that restores a patient, especially from pulmonary or alimentary internal disorders. (39)

Revulsant—Medication which causes irritation, drawing blood flow from a distant diseased part. Usually a vesicant. (41)

Restringent—Astringent. (39)

Rhyptica—Detergent. (39)

Roborant(ia)—A tonic. (39)

Rubifacient—Produces reddening of the skin. (8)

Saline Cathartic—A salt which causes bowel evacuation by drawing water into the bowels, one form of hydragogue. (8)

Sarcotica—A vulnerary, for treatment of wounds. (39)

Scelotyrbica—An anti-scorbutic. (39)

Sclerotic; Sclerontica—A remedy which hardens the flesh, generally topical. (39)

Scutum—A plaster applied over the heart or stomach to improve or restore function of the underlying organ. Alternatively, an ecusson (see miscellaneous preparations). (39)

Sedative—Relieves nervous excitement, may induce sleep. (8)

Septa—A corrosive. (39)

Sialogogue—Increases salivation. (8)

Smecticum; Smegma—Cleanses the skin. (39)

Solutive; Solutiva—Cathartic. (39)

Somnifacient; Somnifera; Soporific—Sedative. (39)

Sorbifacient—Causes or enhances absorption of another medication or in general. (41)

Specific—In traditional use, a remedy for a particular condition or symptom which does not act via an effect on the "humors" believed to be responsible for disease since ancient times. In patent medicine, it may be used in the same manner (4), but is often used with little specificity to disease, i.e., a "Female Specific," or in reference to organ systems, i.e., "Liver Specific."

Splanchnica; Splenetic(a); Splenica—For disorders of the spleen. (39)

Staltic(a)—Depress raised flesh surrounding a wound. (39)

Stegnotic(a)—Same as incrassant. (39)

Stephaniaea—Applied over cranial sutures (joints of the skull) to strengthen the neck and increase transpiration (removal of humors). (39)

Sternutatory—Causes sneezing. (8)

Stimulant—Increases mental and general activity. (41)

Stomachic—Increases gastric juice, relieves gastric distress. (8)

Stomatic—Pleasant detergent used orally, as a stomachic. (39)

Stupefacient(ia)—Sedative. (39)

Styptic; Stiptica—Checks bleeding or control hemorrhage. In modern usage usually a topical remedy (styptic pencil), but historically this could also be a systemic astringent. (8,39)

Sudorific—Increases sweating, a powerful diaphoretic. (24,39)

Suffitus; Suffimenta; Suffumigia—A fumigant, i.e., dry material which was burned in the sickroom. (39)

Synanchica—For treatment of sore throat. (39)

Syncoptica—Remedy for syncope (fainting). (39)

Syncritica—Relaxant. (39)

Teniacide—Destroys tapeworms (genus *Taenia*).

Tentipellium—Treats wrinkles of the skin. (39)

Theriac—A universal antidote to poisons.

Thermantica—Warming remedy, a diaphoretic. (39)

Tonic—See alterative—A vague term implying beneficial effect (8). In patent medicine, an agent which gradually restores strength and vigor. (4)

Toxica—Poison. (39)

Trachea—Various sharp, irritating, or ulcerating materials. (39)

Trigona—Narcotic remedies. (39)

Uncinaricide—Destroys hookworm (*Uncinaria americana*). (8)

Uricosuric—Eliminates uric acid, for gout.

Uterine sedative—Decreases uterine activity. (8)

Uterine stimulant—Increases uterine activity. (8)

Vapor; Vapores—Vapor. Not official in the USP, but a few materials were used specifically as vapor inhalants in the British Pharmacopoeia.

Vermicide—Eliminates worms by killing them. (8)

Vermifuge—Eliminates worms, usually by causing them to release from the gut. (8)

Vesicant; Vesecatory; Vesicatorium—Produces blisters on the skin. (8)

Vitilizer—To make alive (4), frequently used in patent medicines to describe a tonic or general agent intended to improve vigor or health (often a thinly veiled reference to sexual function) as opposed to restoring life.

Vulnerary—A healing agent for wounds. Generally but not invariably a topical. (8) In some cases a "sympathetic" unguent, i.e., applied to the weapon which inflicted the wound, not to the wound itself.

Xerophthalmica—Treatment for dry eyes. (39)

DISEASE STATES

Our understanding of disease states has evolved considerably across time and place, and thus a number of now peculiar terms appear in apothecary and patent medical literature which merit definition here. I make no claim that this list is complete, as there is no single source from which to derive such a glossary of terms. Rather, it is an accumulation of those terms I have encountered in my research. Terms commonly understood today and unchanged in general usage (epilepsy, diarrhea) are not listed.

One should recognize, especially in patent medicine usage, that the concepts of disease are often intermixed with symptoms (i.e., experiences reported by the patient such as pain or blurry vision), signs (physical findings by the physician such as swelling), or even with entire affected organ systems (as in "liver cures") or genders ("female cures").

Ague—An intermittent fever.

Apoplexy—Sudden loss of motor or sensory function, or loss of consciousness, usually the result of what would now be called a stroke (i.e., brain injury due to a failure of circulation to the brain, either due to hemorrhage or infarct). However, the term may be used for almost any sudden disabling illness of general collapse, including fainting.

Biliousness—Disordered digestion.

Bright's disease—Now a specific kidney disorder, previously used as a general term for disturbances due to kidney dysfunction, especially in patent medicines.

Canker—A mouth sore or sore throat.

Catarrh—Inflammation of mucous membranes, usually of the upper respiratory tract.

Chilblain—Inflammatory condition of the fingers and/or toes, usually due to cold. Frostbite, also probably other vascular disorders of the extremities, particularly what is now referred to as Reynaud's phenomenon.

Chill—Sensation of coldness, rigor, often accompanying fever.

Cholera—Infectious, epidemic diarrhea with copious stools and dehydration. Not limited to what is now known as cholera, i.e., infection with *vibrio cholerae*.

Cholera infantum—Epidemic diarrhea in infants, especially in cities during summer months, most probably of viral origin.

Cholera morbus—Sporadic (as opposed to widely epidemic) cholera (see cholera above).

Colic—Sporadic, spasmodic abdominal pain.

Constitutional—As an adjective, refers to an illness or condition affecting the whole body as opposed to being localized. In patent medicine use, often implies some intrinsic defect of physical or moral character resulting in disease. As a noun, a medication intended to treat a constitutional illness.

Consumption—A progressive wasting disease, generally tuberculosis.

Corpulence—Great obesity.

Croup—Inflammatory condition of the upper airways with laryngeal edema, resulting in inspiratory stridor (wheeze).

Debility—General weakness, diminution of strength or vigor.

Dropsy—Abnormal accumulation of fluid in an organ (locally, i.e., gallbladder obstruction might be described as "dropsy" of the gallbladder) or systemically (i.e., edema), the latter generally the result of congestive heart failure.

Dysentery—Inflammatory condition of the large intestine with fever and purulent, mucoid, and bloody diarrhea. Generally bacterial or amoebic in origin.

Dyspepsia—Difficult digestion.

Eczema—Inflammatory condition of the skin.

Flux—Abundant diarrhea.

Gangrene—Death (from loss of circulation) of a portion of the body, but can also be used to refer in general to the onset of death.

Gleet—Chronic gonorrhea.

Gonorrhea—Contagious genital inflammation, not necessarily restricted as in current use to describe specific infection with *Neiseria gonorrheae*.

Gravel—Small concretions or stones in the urinary tract.

Grippe—Influenza or epidemic catarrh (see catarrh above).

Heaves—Flatulence, as opposed to more modern slang term for vomiting.

Hectic fever—Erratic fever accompanying wasting diseases such as consumption (tuberculosis).

Humor—Any bodily fluid.

Hydrops—See dropsy.

Hypochondria—A state of malaise, depression, and dysfunction attributed to disorders in the midline upper abdomen (below the cartilaginous ribs and lower sternum called the hypochondrium, location of the liver, biliary tract and pancreas. Probably most akin to severe depression in modern terminology. This did not refer to psychosomatic illness or excessive concern with illness until well after the turn of the twentieth century.

Jag—State of drunkenness, a drinking binge.

King's evil—Scrofula (a form of tuberculosis affecting the lymphatic glands).

La grippe—See grippe.

Lumbago—Lumbar (low back) pain of usually sudden onset.

Morbilii—Measles.

Neurasthenia—General weakness, chronic fatigue, or malaise.

Neuralgia—Pain in the distribution of a particular nerve.

Prostration—Great loss of strength or energy, usually of relatively rapid onset (in contradistinction to a more chronic wasting disease such as consumption).

Pyrosis—Full of fire, i.e., heartburn, gastric indigestion.

Rheumatism—Inflammatory condition of the bones, joints, or connective tissues.

Salt rheum—Inflammatory skin disorder, chronic eczema.

Scrofula—A form of lymphatic tuberculosis, or refers to a constitutional predisposition towards tuberculosis.

Sprue—See thrush.

Summer Complaint—Diarrhea.

Tetter—A vesicular (blistering) eruption, eczema or perhaps shingles.

Thrush—Oral lesions or apthae (cold sores), or an oral or other mucous membrane infection with "yeast," i.e., *Candida albicans*.

Whooping cough—Acute infectious disease of childhood with characteristic cough, pertussis.

APOTHECARY PROCESSES

Understanding of apothecary instructions necessitates an understanding of the terminology used to describe apothecary processes. While some terms are in common use (boiling) or have remained in technical use (distillation), many other terms are archaic or specialized and will be unfamiliar to all but the pharmacist. As is traditional (see references 2 and 3), these will be grouped by functional category. The terms also appear in the alphabetical compendium for convenience of the reader.

Operations Requiring Heat

Vaporization— the process of heating a material to produce a gaseous or vapor phase.

Evaporation—Vaporization for the purpose of recovering the solid residue, or fixed part, i.e., a means of separating a desired solid from the solvent, the solvent being of no interest.

Distillation—A process in which a liquid is vaporized and the resulting vapor condensed and recovered. This process allows separation of a mixture of materials by boiling point, as the more volatile components vaporize at lower temperatures, allowing selective collection (fractionation) of the various components. This process is carried out historically in a device referred to as an alembic, an alchemical term, or more recently using a retort, condenser, and receiver.

Sublimation—Similar to distillation, but refers specifically to vapor formation above a solid phase. Specifically, this process allows the vaporized solid to be condensed and recovered.

Desiccation, Exsiccation, and *Granulation*—refer to heating of solids to drive off residual liquids and/or volatile components to end up with a solid or granular material. *Desiccation* is simple drying, *granulation* involves stirring while drying to end up with a coarse granular material, and *exsiccation* involves a more complete drying to drive off water trapped in a crystallized structure.

Alembic

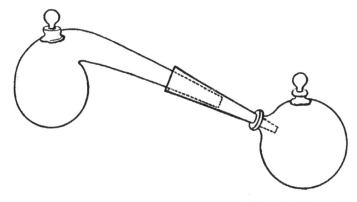

Fig 2-14 Alembic and distillation apparatus, adapted from Remington (3).

Boiling or Ebullition—The process of boiling can be used to facilitate distillation, but can also be used as a means of facilitating dissolution of a solid, of agitating a liquid, or of accomplishing clarification (see below).

Operations Not Requiring Heat

Comminution—The process of physically reducing a drug or material to a powder via cutting, rasping, grating, chopping, contusing, rolling, stamping, grinding, powdering, trituration, levigation, elutriation, granulation, etc.

Trituration—The reduction of a material to powder by means of a mortar and pestle.

Levigation—The application of trituration to a material in paste form using water or some other liquid.

Elutriation—The process by which a material of mixed granular size is suspended in water or another carrier in which it is insoluble. The coarser material will fall out first, allowing the finely divided material to be decanted with the liquid, with one or both parts being recovered as desired.

Pulverization by Intervention—A means of pulverizing material by dissolving in a solvent and then allowing the solvent to evaporate, i.e., camphor is readily powdered via intervention using alcohol.

Solution—the process of dissolving a solid in a liquid or, on occasion, dissolving a gas in a liquid by bubbling it through the solvent phase.

Operations Separating Liquids and Solids

Lotion or *Displacement*—The process of separating soluble matter from an insoluble portion by repeatedly pouring liquid over it.

Decantation—Pouring off a liquid portion from a solid, sometimes accomplished instead with a siphon apparatus.

Colation or *Straining*—Separation of a liquid from a coarse solid using a strainer or colander. This is a variation on filtration, generally involving coarser materials.

Filtration—Separation of a liquid from a solid using a filter which prevents passage of the solid material, made from paper, sand, asbestos, ground glass, charcoal, porous stone, etc.

Clarification and *Decoloration*—A variety of processes used to remove particulate matter and eliminate cloudy appearance or discoloration. The intent is generally to improve the quality of the resulting liquid fraction. This can be done with the application of heat, addition of water to decrease viscosity and allow settling, addition of albumin, gelatin, or other proteins (milk) to coagulate impurities, addition of paper pulp, via fermentation, or simply by prolonged standing. Decoloration may be facilitated by activated charcoal or other sorbents which adsorb colored materials, or by bleaching (chemical or sunlight).

Precipitation—The formation of an insoluble compound in solution via a chemical process. Several of the processes noted below can be used to isolate a precipitate once formed.

Crystallization—The process of inducing a material to crystallize in solution so that it may then be separated by various means. This is often done by producing a concentrated solution by evaporation of excess solvent, followed by cooling to reduce solubility and force crystal formation, but other chemical or physical manipulations may be used.

Dialysis—Material is placed in a semi-permeable membrane and placed in or exposed to water. The soluble material will transfer to the water by osmotic force.

Maceration—Soaking of a material, typically a plant material in a liquid until soluble materials are dissolved. Often the material is cut, shredded, or otherwise disrupted to facilitate the process.

Expression—Forcibly pressing a liquid from a solid via various presses or devices.

Percolation or *Displacement*—The process of extraction of desired material by flowing a liquid through a solid, as commonly done in the making of coffee. The solvent is referred to as a *menstruum*, the liquid recovered as a *percolate*.

TABLE OF THE ELEMENTS

Knowledge of the following chemical elements is sufficiently old that they are likely to appear in older texts. Rare or recently described elements have been omitted. The table provides the atomic number (number of protons), name of element, elemental symbol as used in chemical formulas, and date of discovery.

1	Hydrogen	H	1776
2	Helium	He	1895
3	Lithium	Li	1817
4	Beryllium	Be	1797
5	Boron	B	1808
6	Carbon	C	ancient
7	Nitrogen	N	1772
8	Oxygen	O	1774
9	Fluorine	F	1886
10	Neon	Ne	1898
11	Sodium	Na	1807
12	Magnesium	Mg	1755
13	Aluminum	Al	1825
14	Silicon	Si	1824
15	Phosphorus	P	1669
16	Sulfur	S	ancient
17	Chlorine	Cl	1774
18	Argon	Ar	1894
19	Potassium	K	1807
20	Calcium	Ca	1808
22	Titanium	Ti	1791
23	Vanadium	V	1830
24	Chromium	Cr	1797
25	Manganese	Mn	1774
26	Iron	Fe	ancient
27	Cobalt	Co	1735
28	Nickel	Ni	1751
29	Copper	Cu	ancient
30	Zinc	Zn	ancient
31	Gallium	Ga	1875
33	Arsenic	As	ancient
34	Selenium	Se	1817
35	Bromine	Br	1826
36	Krypton	Kr	1898
37	Rubidium	Rb	1861
38	Strontium	Sr	1790
40	Zirconium	Zr	1789

41	Niobium	Nb	1801
42	Molybdenum	Mo	1781
44	Ruthenium	Ru	1844
45	Rhodium	Rh	1803
46	Palladium	Pd	1803
47	Silver	Ag	ancient
48	Cadmium	Cd	1817
50	Tin	Sn	ancient
51	Antimony	Sb	ancient
52	Tellurium	Te	1783
53	Iodine	I	1811
54	Xenon	Xe	1898
55	Cesium	Cs	1860
56	Barium	Ba	1808
57	Lanthanum	La	1839
58	Cerium	Ce	1803
74	Tungsten	W	1783
76	Osmium	Os	1803
77	Iridium	Ir	1803
78	Platinum	Pt	1735
79	Gold	Au	ancient
80	Mercury	Hg	ancient
81	Thallium	Tl	1861
82	Lead	Pb	ancient
83	Bismuth	Bi	ancient
86	Radon	Rn	1900
88	Radium	Ra	1898
90	Thorium	Th	1829
92	Uranium	U	1789

NOTES ON CHEMICAL TERMINOLOGY

Important Ions

The tables below identify the common named acids and ions and allow them to be associated with their chemical formulas as well as, in the case of ions, their usual electrical charge (valence).

When combining to form a salt, the positive and negative ions must add to a net electrical charge of zero. This is sometimes important in deducing the chemical formula associated with a name. For example sodium chloride and calcium chloride both contain the chloride ion (1⁻), but since Sodium carries a 1^+ charge and calcium carries a 2^+ charge, the formulae must be NaCl and $CaCl_2$, respectively. This can be specified (i.e., calcium bichloride) but is often omitted. Conversely, iron bichloride and iron trichloride can be deduced to involve iron in the ferrous (2^+) and ferric (3^+) state respectively, and could be alternatively referred to as ferrous chloride ($FeCl_2$) and ferric chloride ($FeCl_3$).

When naming salts according to modern usage, the cation (positively charged ion) is named first, i.e., salt is sodium chloride, not chloride sodium. Older nomenclature often reverses this convention to give "Chloride of Sodium."

The Common Acids

Name	Formula
Acetic acid	CH_3COOH
Boric acid	H_3BO_3
Carbonic acid	H_2CO_3
Chloric acid	$HClO_3$
Chlorous acid	$HClO_3$
Formic acid	$HCOOH$
Hydrobromic acid	HBr
Hydrochloric acid	HCl
Hydrocyanic acid	HCN
Hydrofluoric acid	HF
Hydroiodic acid	HI
Nitric acid	HNO_3
Nitrous acid	HNO_2
Perchloric acid	$HClO_4$
Phosphoric acid	H_3PO_4
Phosphorous acid	H_3PO_3
Sulfuric acid	H_2SO_4
Sulfurous acid	H_2SO_3

Common Cations (Positively Charged Ions)

Trivial Name	Formula	Name
Aluminum	Al^{+3}	
Ammonium	NH_4^{+}	
Barium	Ba^{+2}	
Calcium	Ca^{+2}	
Chromium(II)	Cr^{+2}	Chromous
Chromium(III)	Cr^{+3}	Chromic
Copper(I)	Cu^{+}	Cuprous
Copper(II)	Cu^{+2}	Cupric
Hydrogen	H^{+}	
Iron(II)	Fe^{+2}	Ferrous
Iron(III)	Fe^{+3}	Ferric
Lead(II)	Pb^{+2}	
Lithium	Li^{+}	
Magnesium	Mg^{+2}	
Manganese(II)	Mn^{+2}	Manganous
Manganese(III)	Mn^{+3}	Manganic
Mercury(I)	Hg^{+1}	Mercurous
Mercury(II)	Hg^{+2}	Mercuric
Potassium	K^{+}	
Silver	Ag^{+}	
Sodium	Na^{+}	
Strontium	Sr^{+2}	
Tin(II)	Sn^{+2}	Stannous
Tin(IV)	Sn^{+4}	Stannic
Zinc	Zn^{+2}	

Common Anions (Negatively Charged Ions)

Name	Formula
Arsenate	AsO_4^{3-}
Arsenite	AsO_3^{3-}
Bicarbonate	HCO_3^{-}
Bromate	BrO_3^{-}
Bromide	Br^{-}
Carbonate	CO_3^{2-}
Chlorate	ClO_3^{-}
Chloride	Cl^{-}
Chlorite	ClO_2^{-}
Chromate	CrO_4^{2-}
Cyanate	OCN^{-}
Cyanide	CN^{-}
Dichromate	$Cr_2O_7^{2-}$
Dihydrogen phosphate	$H_2PO_4^{-}$
Fluoride	F^{-}
Hydride	H^{-}
Hydrogen sulfate	HSO_4^{-}
Hydroxide	OH^{-}
Hypobromite	OBr^{-}
Hypochlorite	OCl^{-}
Hydrogen phosphate	HPO_4^{2-}
Iodate	IO_3^{-}
Iodide	I^{-}
Nitrate	NO_3^{-}
Nitrite	NO_2^{-}
Oxide	O^{2-}
Perchlorate	ClO_4^{-}
Phosphate	PO_4^{3-}
Permanganate	MnO_4^{-}
Sulfate	SO_4^{2-}
Sulfide	S^{2-}
Sulfite	SO_3^{2-}
Thiocyanate	SCN^{-}
Thiosulfate	$S_2O_3^{2-}$

Chemical Identity and Terminology

While modern chemicals are generally reasonably pure and chemically consistent (save for natural mixtures, such as mineral oil or kerosene), older chemicals were often impure, inhomogeneous in composition, and confused with substances that had similar appearance, reactivity, function, or origin. Alchemy is discussed at length in the appendices, but it must be recognized that ancient chemical names were based upon appearance, physical properties, and the manner in which, or place from which, the material was created or obtained. If you could make something that looked like gold (heavy, shiny, and the correct color) then, for all practical purposes, it *was* gold. There was simply no understanding of elemental identity or chemical formula by which to conclude otherwise in the ancient world.

The reader will likely be frustrated, as was I, by ambiguities of chemical identity. While it is true that some materials we now accept as elements were known in ancient times, and while modern chemistry began to develop in the seventeenth century, the terminology used in apothecary practice is often ancient in origin. In many instances, it is not possible to be certain what, "exactly" (to the modern standard), was meant by an early chemical term. This is particularly true of sulphurettes and other complex mixtures of metals and counter-ions produced by heat, but can be true for the most mundane substances. Thus, a compound as common as potash (*potassa*), historically derived from heating the ashes of plant material ("pot-ash", from whence comes both potash and "pot-ash-ium," the modern potassium),was probably a mixture of potassium hydroxide and potassium carbonate. Historically, potash can refer to either compound and both, and that...is that!

No amount of research can resolve these "discrepancies," which arise from our natural and instinctive attempt to force historical reality into the model of modern chemistry. The author has done his best to explain these ambiguities when they could not be resolved, and the reader will simply have to tolerate them.

Mercury—Chemistry and Terminology

The element mercury plays a large role in apothecary medicine despite now being relegated primarily to the measurement of temperature or pressure in various medical instruments. Many compounds exist in different oxidation states, some of which were described and named long before their chemistry was clearly defined. In reviewing the compendium, I asked myself whether other elements might rise to a level requiring special attention, and no other such instances arose.

Naming

The Latin for Mercury is *Hydrargyrum*, literally "water-silver," for self-evident reasons. The proper genitive form "of mercury" is thus *Hydrargyri*. The peculiar form *Mercurius* is much less frequent, but is found. For purposes of this section, I will utilize the proper nomenclature, but do not be confused if you find listings in other forms. The naming does *not* reflect different oxidation states in any consistent manner, i.e., *Hydrargyri* or *Hydrargyrum* may reflect the mercuric or mercurous form, further explained below.

Oxidation States

In addition to the metallic state (Hg^0), mercury can take on a mercurous (Hg^{1+}) and a mercuric (Hg^{2+}) form. Thus, "mercury chloride" could be either mercurous chloride ($HgCl$) or mercuric chloride ($HgCl_2$). Similarly there are two oxides, mercurous oxide (Hg_2O, the "suboxide") or mercuric oxide (HgO).

"Non-compounds" and Color Variations

Some compounds, such as turpeth mineral, or hydragyri oxysulphatis, have a poorly defined or inhomogeneous chemistry. Turpeth mineral is created by boiling mercury and sulphuric acid to dryness and rapidly cooling the resulting mass in cold water to form a black "mineral" of poorly defined chemical composition. Further, one will see descriptions of various colors of oxide. Red (rubrum) or yellow (flavum), or indeed green (viridum), is generally mercurous oxide (Hg_2O) and black (nigrum) or grey is the mercuric form (HgO). Note that the same chemical "compound" (historically often quite impure) may take on a variety of colors related to the process of production, purity, or variations in composition.

Synonyms

The list provided below is derived from several reference sources (40,42) and from the general collection of terms in the compendium, but is undoubtedly incomplete. Many other mercury compounds appear in the compendium on one or a few occasions and are not included here.

Mercuric Ammonium Chloride—Ammoniated mercury, ammonio-chloride of mercury, calx hydrargyri alba, chloride of mercuric ammonium, infusible white precipitate, mercuric ammonium chloride, mercurius precipitatus albus, mercuroammonium chloride, white precipitate. This is $HgNH_2Cl$.

Mercurous Ammonium Chloride—Black mercury, black precipitate, Hahneman's mercury, nigri precipitatus. This is presumably Hg_2NH_2Cl, although chemical descriptions are ambiguous.

Mercuric Chloride—Hydrargyri corrosivum sublimatas, hydrargyri chloridum corrosivum, hydrargyri muriaticum corrosivum, hydrargyri perchloridum, hydrargyri permurias, hydrargyri supermurias, bichloride of mercury, corrosive chloride of mercury, corrosive sublimate, perchloride of mercury. This is $HgCl_2$.

Mercurous Chloride—Hydrargyri chloridum, hydrargyri chloridum mite (a weak solution), hydrargyri murias, hydrargyri submurias, colomelas, calomel, mercury chloride, mild mercurous chloride, mercurius dulcis sublimatis, muriate of mercury, protochloride of mercury, panacea of mercury, subchloride of mercury. This is $HgCl$.

Mercuric iodide—Hydrargyri iodidum flavum, hydrargyri pro-iodiret, hydrargyri iodidum viridi, brilliant scarlet, protoiodide of mercury, yellow iodide of mercury, subiodide of mercury. This is HgI_2.

Mercurous iodide—Hydrargyri iodidum rubrum, hydrargyri biniodide, deutero-ioduretum hydrargyri, biniodide of mercury, red iodide of mercury, red mercury iodide. This is HgI.

Mercuric sulfide—Hydrargyri sulfidum, Chinese red, cinnabar (the native form), Ethiop's mineral, Aetheops mineral, Aethiops mineralis, factitious cinnabar (when made in the laboratory), hydrargyrum cum sulphure, and hydrargyrum praecipitatum. This is HgS.

Mercuric Oxide—Hydrargyri oxidum flavum, hydrargyri oxidum rubrum, mercurius corrosivus rubrum, calcined mercury, monoxide of mercury, red oxide of mercury, red precipitate, yellow mercuric oxide, and yellow oxide of mercury, and hydrargyri nitrico-oxidum. This is Hg_2O.

Mercurous Oxide—Hydrargyri suboxidum, black oxide of mercury, dioxide of mercury, grey oxide of mercury, proto-oxide of mercury, and suboxide of mercury. This is Hg_2O.

Mercury (mercurous) Persulfate— Hydrargyri sulphas albus. This is $HgSO_4$.

Plate A Show globes. Show globes were the traditional sign of the apothecary, serving as advertisement even to the illiterate. There are many theories of origin, none with convincing documentation, but the evolution from practical container to trade symbol seems a small leap. Glass, height of center item, 25". No maker's mark, but the two right-hand items are identifiable in the catalogs of the Whitall-Tatum Co. (Photo by author, items from author's private collection.)

Plate B The originals. These four containers, belonging to the author's mother, decorated a living room bookcase in her Milwaukee home. Curiosity about these containers triggered the author's lifelong interest in apothecary containers and terminology. The items on either side are cylindrical show globes. Glass, with fused glass labels and powder-top closure, height of bottle set 12". No maker's marks, but almost certainly of American origin. (Photo by author, items from author's private collection.)

Plate C Bottles. Six bottles from a matched set of apothecary furnishings, surrounding a single bottle, unmatched. Glass with fused-glass labels. No maker's mark but almost certainly of American origin. (Photo by author, items from author's private collection.)

Plate D Bottles. Six bottles from a matched set carrying a maker's mark "Y-G-Co" of the York Glass Company, York, UK, surrounding an un-matched center bottle without maker's mark. Glass with fused glass labels and liquid closure other than the Pulv: Gallae bottle (2nd from left) with powder type closure. (Photo by author, items from author's private collection.)

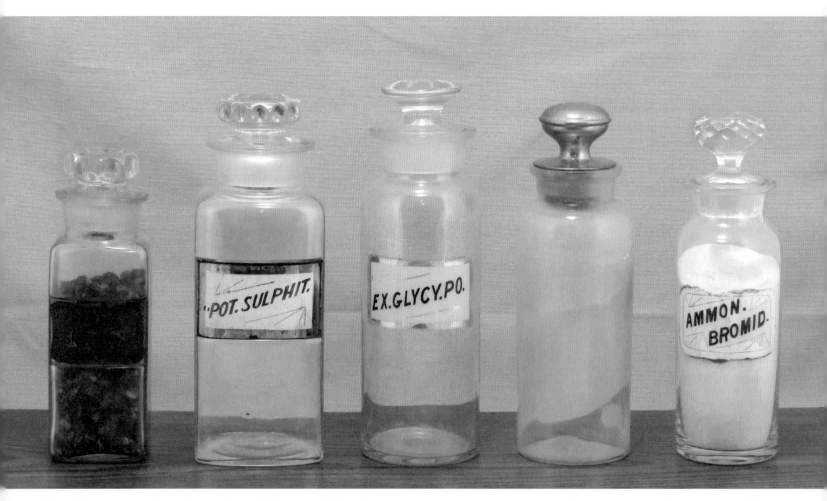

Plate E Bottles. Various with powder-type closure, height approx. 12". Ground glass closures were more typical than the metallic variety. Recessed labels (two items at left) were better protected than surface-mounted. Far left item likely had a fused glass label, but now carries a paper label Pulvis Scammon:, re-labeled Pulvis Manna and probably contains the latter. Ammonium bromide (far right) is normally white to yellow in color, actual contents unknown. (Photo by author, items from author's private collection.)

Plate F Large containers. Glass and ceramic (center) containers approximately 18" in height. No maker's marks. The glass containers have fused glass labels and are likely American in origin; the ceramic is French in origin, glazed with a hand-painted label in gold for powdered potassium nitrate. (Photo by author, items from author's private collection.)

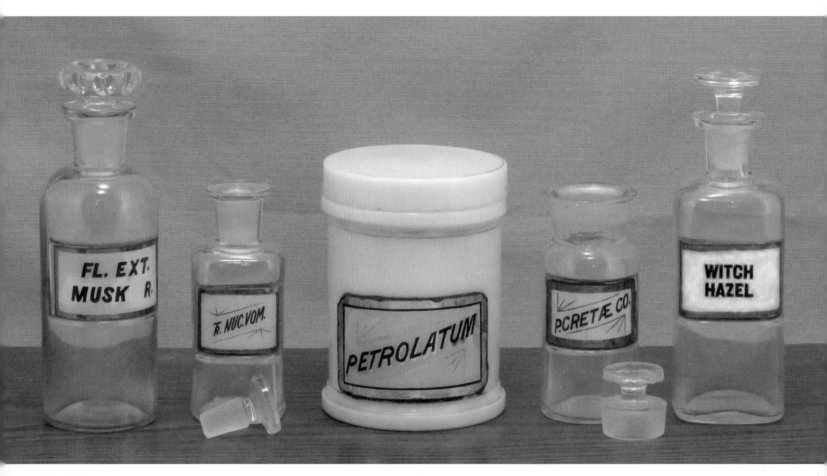

Plate G Small containers. An assortment of small (height approx. 6") clear or white (center) glass containers demonstrating appropriate closure type for content, whether liquid (stopper removed, tincture of nux vomicus), powder (stopper removed, compound powder of chalk), or an ointment (petrolatum), often found with a closure large enough to allow a large utensil or hand to enter. (Photo by author, items from author's private collection.)

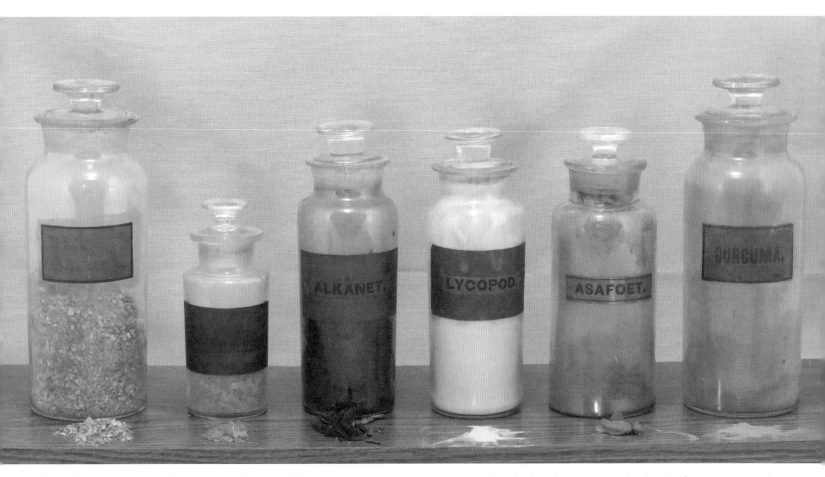

Plate H Bottles with contents. Rarely found, collectors should exercise caution as contents may not be as labeled and may have undergone deterioration. Contents may be toxic, may have become explosive, or may be illegal controlled substances. These bottles, however, do appear to contain the labeled contents (left to right): white shellac granules, sandarac resin, alkanet bark, lycopodium powder (spores), asafoetida powder, and curcumin powder. (Photo by author, items from author's private collection.)

Plate I Apothecary bottles, Uruguay, with closure types. Bottles purchased out of a large collection belonging to pharmacist's family in Montevideo, Uruguay, glass, height 6–14" with fused glass labels in either Latin or Spanish (the latter not covered in this text). Examples here include closures for ordinary liquids (Tr. Opii, Es. Eucalip.); powders or solids (Ipecac. P. and yodoform, or iodoform gauze); syrups or frequently poured non-volatile liquids (Ac. Alcanfor.) for which the inner pour is spout removable with a ground-glass joint, kept clean but not tightly sealed by glass cover shown; and volatiles like ether (Eter. Alcanf.) for which both an inner (stopper, missing) and outer ground-glass seal are provided. (Photo by author, items from author's private collection.)

Plate J Ceramic containers, Uruguay, purchased out of a large collection belonging to pharmacist's family in Montevideo, Uruguay, 10", with hand painted labels. The provenance is well documented and some labels here and on accompanying bottles (see previous plate) are in Spanish. An unexplained curiosity, the lion with unicorn accompanied by *Dieu et Mon Droit* (by the right of God) is the coat of arms of the British Monarchy (The lion being England, the unicorn, Scotland, and French spoken at court from the time of the Norman invasion). (Photo by author, items from author's private collection.)

Plate K Glass containers, modern. This set, including nine additional smaller (9") containers is glass with painted labels and gold banding. Labels refer to materials in ancient use (Theriac) through the early twentieth century (Pom Devine, a popular British hair dressing, not shown). This is clearly a modern reproduction, presumably decorative or promotional items, but nonetheless retains both beauty and historical interest. (Photo by author, items from author's private collection.)

Plate L Containers, French. A set of ceramic containers, 10″, with blue and gold painted labels and banding, late nineteenth or early twentieth century based on comparison with many similar containers available in the antiques market. They contained pills (Eponymously named compound valarian pills, presumably after Baron Guillaume Dupuytren, French anatomist famous for Dupuytren's contracture) or conserves (jellies) of rose hips (cynorrhodon, French) or angelica, so the container type is appropriate to labeled content. (Photo by author, items from author's private collection.)

Plate M Ceramic Jars. A pair of ceramic drug containers, glazed, height 9", according to seller salvaged by a family member from the building of the Philadelphia Dispensary, which operated from 1786 until the early twentieth century. They contained potato (Solanum tuberosum) starch and lead acetate. (Photo by author, items from author's private collection.)

Plate N Poison bottles. Glass, 2–8", characterized by odd shapes, colored glass, prominently textured surfaces, the words "poison" or "not to be taken," and often a skull-and-crossbones. Most common in North America from about 1855 when required by law in the US and UK (see Griffenhagen) through the early twentieth century when pre-packaged pharmaceuticals, elimination of highly toxic medications (mercurials, arsenicals) and better lighting made them obsolete. (Photo by author, items from author's private collection.)

Plate O Medical vaporizer. Vapo-Cresolene was a popular predecessor of modern sickroom medications and could be administered by adding to boiling water or by heating with a Vapo-Cresolene lamp. The latter is a diminutive Victorian oil lamp (device shown is 10" high), the heat from which rose under a shallow metal bowl containing the medication. See entries for creosote and for creosoti vaporis, balneum. (Photo by author, items from author's private collection.)

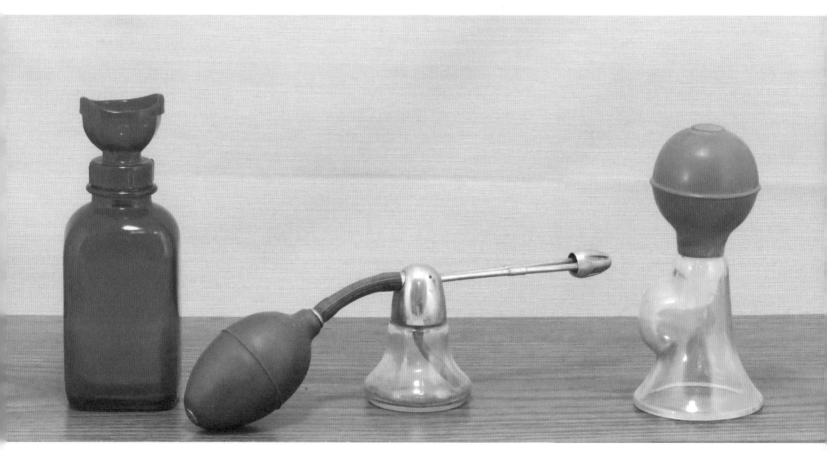

Plate P Sundries. Numerous odds and ends could be obtained from the apothecary, sometimes for administration of medication as with the eye wash bottle and eye cup combination (left) and nebulizer (center) and sometimes for other health-related purposes. The item on the right is a vacuum breast pump, in glass, not much different than available today in plastic.

Plate Q Apothecary labeling cabinet. Oak with brass interior hardware and drawer pulls, 27" x 20" x 8" and weighing nearly fifty pounds. The cabinet accommodated about seventy different paper labels purchased on rolls. Various widths were accommodated by various brass guides through which the labels were pulled and which provided a sharp edge to tear not-always-perforated labels. Manufactured by the McCourt Label Cabinet Company of Bradford, PA, in the late nineteenth and early twentieth centuries, in one to five row variants, the company remains a leading supplier of labels and related equipment. Purchased near Kansas City, it appears to have been used by Edward I. Dembrowski, a Polish pharmacist in Buffalo, NY, with labels in English, Latin, and Polish. (Photo by author, items from author's private collection.)

63 MANNA

64 SODII SULPH.

84 OL. LIMONIS

0 LIQ. CALCIS

92 PV. CINNAM.

114 VINUM ANTIMONII

21 LINI FARINA

42 BALS. COPAIBÆ

113 SP.ÆTHER. NITR.

52 SYR. SCILLÆ CO.

11 AQ. CAMPHOR.

1 TR. ACONITIR.

51 SYR. RHEI AR.

41 FL. EXT. CIMICIFUGÆ

4 G. ACACIÆ

2 PV. IPECAC.

7 AC. OXALIC.

5 OL. RICINI

9 MARANTA

13 PV. RHEI

201 VIN. IPECAC

ANY OTHER STYLE GLASS LABELS FURNISHED ON APPLICATION.

Latin titles will be used where customary, if not otherwise specified.   Prices furnished on Application,

Plate R Fused glass label styles. A variety of fused glass label styles were offered by the Des Moines Drug Company, a major Midwest supplier of drugs and equipment (long defunct) in their catalog for 1906–7. Bottles and other furnishings were also available along with bulk *materia medica* and prepared commercial medications. (Photo by author.)

CHAPTER 3

THE COMPENDIUM

ABBREVIATIONS & NUMBERS

The following abbreviations are used in the alphabetical compendium.

abr   Abbreviation. Distinguishes an abbreviation or abbreviated form of a term (used only when the abbreviated nature is not readily apparent).

adj   Adjective

bot   Botanical name, proper or trivial

BP   British Pharmacopoeia

BPC   British Pharmaceutical Codex

cc   Cubic centimeter, equivalent to a milliliter (ml, below).

eur   European (in origin)

gm   Gram. There are 1000 grams per kilogram (kg), about 28 gm per gravimetric ounce. One ml or cc of water weighs one gram.

lat   Latinate in origin. Note that much apothecary Latin is improper or is pseudo-Latin, i.e., a later term composed to look like classical Latin as with botanical names.

ml   Milliliter, one-one-thousandth of a liter, or 1 cubic centimeter (cc)

NF   National Formulary (US)

USP   United States Pharmacopoeia, i.e., item is found listed in one or more editions.

2, II, etc. "Of two," duabus(*f*) or duobus(*m*), i.e., *syrupus de duobus radicibus*, syrup of two roots, might be inscribed as *Sy. 2 Rad.* The Latin numbers beyond three are indeclinable, i.e., do not take a possessive form, but may be accompanied by "de" (of) in some uses. Digits are at times used for Greek prefixes (given parenthetically below), usually specifying a number of ingredients as in *unguentum dodecapharmacum* (ointment of twelve drugs).

2, II	duabus (*f*)/duobus(*m*)
3, III	tribus (tri)
4, IV	quattuor (tetra)
5, V	quinque (penta)
6, VI	sexies (hepta)
7, VII	septem (septa)
8, VIII	octo (octa)
9, IX	novem (nona)
10, X	decem (deca)
11, XI	undecem (undeca)
12, XII	duodecim (dodeca)

A

A.: At beginning of inscription: aqua (water); adeps (fat, grease, lard); axungia (unguent, ointment). At end of inscription: agaricus (of the field); alba (white); amara (bitter); Andromachus (of Andromachus); apium (of bees); aurea (yellow). (1)

A.B.C. liniment: See aconiti compositum, linimentum. (40)

A.B.C. powder: "Acid boric" (boric acid), Bismuth subnitrate, and Calomel in equal parts. (40)

A.C.E.: Anesthetic mixture of 1 volume absolute Alcohol, 2 of Chloroform and 3 of Ether. (3,40)

A. Mitrid. Dam.: Aqua or, more usually, axungia mithridatum damocratis.

A.R.: Analytical Reagent, designates a highly refined grade of purity. This would indicate a relatively recent label, probably twentieth century.

Abasier: Animal bone charcoal. (3)

Abatia: Leaves of *Abatia rugosa*, a black dye. (40)

Abele: White Poplar, see populus. (40)

Abelmoschus: Seeds of the aromatic plant, *Hibiscus esculentus*. See also moschus. (39)

Abercrombie's cough mixture: See scillae et opii, mistura. (40)

Abercrombie's lotion: An infusion of tobacco in water. (3,24)

Abernethy's mixture: Similar to sennae composita, mistura. (40)

Abernethy's pills: See colocynthidis et hydrargyri, pilulae. (40)

Abete {*Italian*}**; abezzo** {*Italian*}**; abies:** Of the genus *Abies*, fir tree. Twigs and resin used. (1)

Abies (canadensis): Hemlock spruce, *Abies* or *Pinus canadensis*. A source of pitch and turpentine, see terabenthine. (Not the poison hemlock, conium.) (32)

Abietis (canadensis), oleum; Abiet. can. ol.: Oil of *Abies canadensis*, the hemlock spruce, i.e., turpentine. See terebinthina.

Abietis, acidum: Aqueous extract of hemlock or pine resins, a diaphoretic, diuretic, and antiscorbutic, similar to turpentine. (39)

Abrastol: Calcium naphthol-sulphonate, analgesic, antipyretic and preservative. (40)

Abrus; Abri semina: Seeds of wild liquorice, Indian liquorice, jequirity bean, rosary pea, rosary bean or crab's eye, *Abrus precatorius*. A powerful cathartic. The alkaloid there in (abrin) is highly toxic, although the bean, if ingested whole, is usually inert. (33)

Abri, infusum: An infusion (BPC) of jequirity bean in water, as an eye medication. (42)

Abric: Sulfur. (3)

Abrotanum: Southernwood, *Artemesia abrotanum*. Anthelmintic, diuretic, and tonic, also externally used for hair loss and as an antiseptic. Figure 3-1. (1,39)

Absinth maritimum: Leaves of sea-absinth, *Absynthum maritima*, a diuretic. (39)

Absinth: An alcoholic beverage consisting of alcohol, water, and the oils of wormwood (absinthium) and anise. Hallucinogenic and subject to abuse. (1)

Absinthii, sal: Potassium carbonate. See sal absinthii. Unrelated to absinth proper. (1,3,39)

Absinthium; Absinthe; Absintio {*Italian*}**:** Wormwood, *Artimesia absinthum*, from which a volatile oil can be extracted. Leaves and flowering tops used. In combination with anise oil and alcohol, one can create absinth. An infusion of wormwood was said to be helpful for atony (loss of motility) of the stomach or intestines. The oil was not otherwise much used, but is said to be a stimulant, perhaps useful in neurasthenia, and has addictive properties. Figure 3-2. (1,8,42)

Absinthii, oleum; Absinth., ol.: Absinth oil as per above.

Absinthum (Romanum), conserva: Conserve of Roman absinth. Roman absinth appears to be a different species, *Artemesia pontica* (the Pope's absinth), said to be less bitter than common absinth and used as a stomachic and astringent for gastrointestinal disorders. (35)

Absolute alcohol: See alcohol, absolutum. (8)

Artemisia Abrotanum
Published by Dr. Woodville Dec.r 1. 1791

Fig. 3-1 Abrotanum.

Acacia; Acacia germanica; Acacia nostras: Inspissated juice of unripe Sloe, or Blackthorn berry. (1)

Acacia; Acaciae, gummi; Acaciae, g.: Gum arabic, the exudate of *Acacia senegal* of Africa or of related species such as *Acacia* (*Mimosa*) *nilotica*. The collected exudate resembles tears, and gradually dissolves in water to form a gum. Figure 3-3. (1, 8)

Acacia cortex: Babul bark, from *Acacia abrica* or *A. decurrens*, an astringent used for tannin content in the form of a gargle, lotion, or by injection. Botanically related to, but not the same as, source of gum acacia. (42)

Acacia cortex, decoctum: Decoction of bruised acacia bark in boiling water, an astringent similar to decoction of oak bark. (42)

Acaciae (Arabicae), mucilago; —, pulv.; —, syrupus: The mucilage of acacia was formed by dissolving acacia exudate (the powder, pulv.) in water to achieve the desired consistency. The syrup was approximately twenty-five percent mucilage of acacia with the remainder of simple syrup. Used as a binder or thickening agent or used alone as a demulcent. (8,40)

Acaciae composita, mucilago: Pill coating solution, of gums of acacia and tragacanth in chloroform and water, used as a solution to moisten pills prior to coating with powdered sugar, etc. (42)

Acaciae compositus, pulvis: Equal parts of gum acacia and tragacanth, a pill excipient. (42) In the NF of acacia, glycyrrhiza, and sugar, for same purpose. (46)

Acaciae, mistura: A mixture of powder of acacia and sugar in water. Similar to, if not synonymous with, the syrup. (34)

Acaciae, mistura: Acacia, sugar, and water; a demulcent, to be made freshly. (46)

Acalypha; Acalyphae liquidum, extractum: Entire plant of *Acalypha indica*. Usually used as the liquid extract in alcohol. Expectorant, laxative, and emetic. (40, 42)

Acalyphae, succus: Acalypha juice, used directly as an emetic and expectorant in India and eastern British colonies. (42)

Accroides: Gum from *Xanthorrhoea arborea*. (40)

Acerrimum, acetum: Concentrated (glacial) acetic acid. (3)

Acetanilid; Acetanilidum Acetanilid, phenylacetamide, antifebrin, formed by the reaction of glacial acetic acid (aceticum, acidum) and aniline (C_6H_5-NH_2) to form C_6H_5-NH_2-O-CO-CH_3. It is a close structural analog of phenacetin (acetaminophen) and was used as an antipyretic and general analgesic. (8)

Acetanilidi compositae (cum codeina), tablettae: Compressed tablets of acetanilide, caffeine citrate, sodium bicarbonate, glucose, and theobroma emulsion (theobromatis, emulsio) as an excipient. Codeine could be included if desired. Analgesic and antipyretic. (42)

Acetanilidi compositus, pulvis: Effervescent powder of acetanilid, of same with tartaric acid and sodium bicarbonate. An analgesic and antipyretic. (34,46) In the BPC this also contains caffeine, similar to many of today's headache remedies. (42)

Acetanilidum effervescens: Effervescent preparation of acetanilid from BPC, of same with sodium bicarbonate, tartaric acid, citric acid and sugar. (42)

Acetannin: Tannin reacted with acetic acid, diacetyl-tannin. A mild astringent for diarrhea. (40)

Acetate of ethyl: Ethyl acetate, a solvent. (40)

Acetatus, syrupus: Syrup of vinegar. (1)

Aceti, syrupus; Aceti, s.: See acetosus, syrupus. (35)

Acetic acid; Aceticum (dilutum) (glaciale), acidum: Acetic acid, CH_3-COOH, from distillation of sodium acetate plus sulfuric acid. Vinegar is three to five percent acetic acid. The concentrate is thirty-six percent strength, the dilute with water is approximately six percent. Glacial acetic acid is a dehydrated form, produced from dry sodium acetate and pure sulfuric acid, and is highly corrosive. (8)

Acetic (a)ether: See (a)ether, aceticus. (8)

Acetis _____: A "vinegar," see _____, acetata/acetatae, etc. (39) Vinegar itself being acetic acid, the "vinegar" of a metal would be the acetate salt. Vinegars of other substances would simply be a solution of that substance in vinegar.

Acetomorphine: Diamorphine, diacetylmorphine, i.e., heroin. (40)

Acetomorphinae, glycerinum: Glycerin of acetomorphine in glycerin, chloroform, alcohol, syrup of roses, and distilled water. For bronchitis, asthma, and laryngitis. (42)

Artemisia Absinthium

Published by D.º Woodville Dec.º 1.1791

Fig. 3-2 Absinthium.

Mimosa nilotica

Published by W.ª Woodville B&T J. 1793.

Fig. 3-3 Acacia, or gum arabic, tree.

Acetomorphinae et terpini, elixir: Elixir of acetomorphine (heroin) and terpin hydrate in alcohol, glycerin, and syrup of wild cherry. For chronic bronchitis and catarrh. (42)

Acetomorphinae, linctus: A preparation of acetomorphine, tincture of hyoscyamus, chloroform, and syrups of wild cherry and balsam of tolu with glycerin. Cough suppressant (acetomorphone) and drying (hyoscyamine) lozenge for cough. (42)

Acetone; Acetonum: Acetone is a volatile solvent occasionally used as an inhalant or internal antispasmodic in asthma. CH_3-CO-CH_3. (42)

Acetophenone: Phenyl-methyl-ketone. A hypnotic and anticonvulsant. (40)

Acetopyrin: Antipyrine acetylsalicylate, a febrifuge of both antipyrene and aspirin. (40)

Acetosa: Sorrel, *Rumex acetosa*. This is Common Sorrel as opposed to Yellow Dock, but is similar to (arguably same as in some sources) rumex. Figure 3-4. (1)

Acetosalic acid; Acetosalicum, acidum; Acetosalin: Acetylsalicylic acid, i.e., aspirin. (40)

Acetosella(e), sal: Potassium oxalate. (3,39)

Acetosella: See Luiula. (1)

Acetosus, syrupus (simplex): Syrup (simple syrup) of vinegar. (1, 35)

Acetous emetic tincture: See sanguinariae acetata composita, tinctura. (34)

Acetphenetidine: See phenacetin.

Acetum: Vinegar. (1)

Acetum aromaticum: Aromatic vinegar, with volatile oils of lavender, rosemary, juniper, peppermint, cinnamon, lemon and clove, dissolved in a mixture of alcohol, acetic acid and water. Used as a stimulating inhalant in a manner similar to smelling salts. (31)

Acetum destillatum: Distilled vinegar, in the USP, eight pints was used, from which seven were distilled, leaving various impurities behind. (44)

Acetum epispasticum: See cantharidis, acetum. (40)

Acetum fuscum: Brown, i.e., malt vinegar. (40)

Acetum gallicum: French wine vinegar. (40)

Acetum odoratum: Toilet or aromatic vinegar, of four percent acetic acid in water and alcohol, with oils of bergamot, cassia, clove, lavender, and lemon. Sprinkled in the room for control of odors, or inhaled via handkerchief as a restorative and for headache. (42)

Acetum plumbi: See plumbi subacetatis forte, liquor. (40)

Acetum prophylacticum: Toilet or prophylactic vinegar, i.e., an aromatic vinegar used as a disinfectant or to prevent contagious disease. This is the standard aromatic vinegar, acetum odoratum, above. (39)

Acetum saturni: See plumbi subacetatis forte, liquor. (40)

Acetyl-bromo-salol; Acetyl-iodo-salol: Analgesic, derivative of salol. (40)

Acetylsalicylic acid: Aspirin, from the reaction of acetic acid with salicylic acid. This is better tolerated than salicylate itself and is well absorbed. Unlike salicylate or other related compounds, aspirin also inactivates platelets when the acetate is cleaved to release salicylic acid.

Acetyltannic acid: Acetannin, an antipyretic material. (40)

Acetysal: Acetylsalicylic acid, aspirin. (40)

Ache {*French*}**:** See apium. (1)

Achicorea: Chicory. See chicorea.

Achillea: See millefolium. (32)

Acid, muriatic; Ac. muriatic: A crude hydrochloric acid.

Acid, spirit of: Glacial acetic acid, see acetic acid. (40)

Acid bath: Diluted nitro-hydrochloric acid. (40)

Acid carbonate: Bicarbonate of soda, i.e., sodium bicarbonate. (40)

Acid drops: Probably the same as elixir vitriol, i.e., sulfuric acid. (39)

Acid of sugar: Oxalic acid, non-therapeutic. (40)

Acid potassium tartrate: See potassii bitartras. (8)

Acid sulphate, ____: Bisulphate, a bisulfate salt. (40)

Acid tartrate, ____: Bitartrate, a bitartrate salt. (40)

Acidol: A trade name, betaine hydrochloride. (40)

Acidus, syrupus: Acid syrup, of dilute vitriol (sulfuric acid) and syrup of lemon, an astringent. (39)

Acipenser sturio: See ichthyocolla. (39)

Aconita: See aconitine. (42)

Aconite; Aconitum; Aconiti folium; —radix: Aconite is the tuber (radix) of *Aconitum napellus*, or monkshood, source of the highly toxic alkaloid, aconitine. Leaf (folium) also used. Aconitum is an effective topical anesthetic and will slow the rate of, and reduce the contractility of, the heart. It was used topically as well as systemically for a variety of febrile illnesses, although the benefits of this do not seem to have been clearly established. Figure 3-5. (1,8,44)

Aconiti, chloroformum: Chloroform of aconite, of powdered root soaked in ammonia to extract alkaloidal content, percolated with alcohol and chloroform. This was used as a paint on unbroken skin to relieve neuralgia. (42)

Aconiti, dentilinimentum compositum: Compound dental liniment of aconite. A 36 percent preparation of menthol and 13.5 percent chloroform in tincture of aconite (see aconiti, tinctura). A "powerful counterirritant and local anesthetic used in neuralgic conditions of the gums and in toothache. It should not be confounded with the compound liniment of aconite which is used externally." (31)

Aconiti, dentilinimentum et iodi compositum; Aconit., dentilin. et iod. co.: Compound dental liniment of aconite and iodine, with 2.2 percent each of menthol and iodine and 16.5 percent chloroform dissolved in tincture of aconite. "It is used for similar properties to the above but is less actively counterirritant but more antiseptic." (31)

Aconiti, extractum; —fluidum, extractum; —, tinctura: The dried extract, fluid extract, and alcoholic tincture of aconitum root, respectively. (8,34)

Fig. 3-4 Acetosa.

Aconiti (radix), linimentum (compositum); —, lin.: Aconitine liniment, of aconite root (radix), glycerin, and alcohol (US) or in the BPC, of aconite root and camphor in alcohol. Used as per aconite for systemic disorders such as gout, neuralgia, and rheumatism. The compound liniment of the BP also contained belladonna. (33)

Aconiti (radicis)(rad.)(folii)(fol.)(fortis), tinctura: Tincture of the root (radix) or leaves (folii) of aconite. The strong (fortis) tincture, Fle(e)ming's tincture, consisted of 70 parts (as opposed to 5 parts) of the root per 100 parts alcohol and was a topical anodyne for dental pain.

Aconiti alcoholicum, extractum: Alcoholic extract of aconite leaf, USP. (44)

Aconiti compositae, pilulae: Pills of aconite, stramonium, and valerianate of quinine. For febrile and inflammatory conditions and nervous irritability. (34)

Aconiti et chloroformi, linimentum: Liniment of aconite and chloroform, of fluid extract of aconite and chloroform in a mixture of alcohol and soap liniment. "It must not be confused with the dental liniment of aconite." (31)

Aconitine; Aconiti, unguentum; aconitinae, unguentum: The specific toxic alkaloid derived from monkshood by extraction with ammonia and precipitation. An ointment was prepared by dissolving aconitine in alcohol and suspending in lard. Used as per aconite, this had local anesthetic action. (8,42)

Aconitinae hydrobromas; —hydrochloras; —nitras: Various acid salts of—and used as per—aconitine. (42)

Aconitinae, ole(in)atum: Aconitine in oleic acid for topical treatment of rheumatism. Toxic if applied to abraded skin. (42)

Aconitir: This is Aconiti r(adix). When compacted on a label, fully capitalized, this can be confusing.

Aconitum fischeri: American aconite, said to be interchangeable with Japanese Aconite. (33)

Acor aceticus: Glacial (i.e., pure, water-free) acetic acid. (40)

Acorus; Acori calami, rhizoma; Acoro {*Italian*}**:** Root of the sweet flag, *Acorus calamus* or galingale. It is a typical bitter and is employed as such to improve appetite, and as a digestive and carminative. Figure 3-6. (1,8,40,42)

Acqua {*Italian*} Water. (1)

Acriflavine (, neutral): A powdered orange dyestuff used as a topical disinfectant.

Actaea alba: White cohosh. Use similar to black cohosh, see cimicifuga. (33)

Actea spicata: Root of red baneberry (Christopher), *Actea rubra*, used as a tonic and astringent. Figure 3-7. (39)

Actea; Actaeae compositus, syrupus; Actaeae, tinctura: Blue cohosh, see respectively cimicifuga; cimicifugae compositus, syrupus; or cimicifugae, tinctura. (34,40)

Actol: Silver lactate. (3)

Acusto: Potassium nitrate. (3)

Adalin: Uradal, a sedative bromine compound, urea derivative. (40)

Adamantanamine: See hexaminium.

Adansonia: Bark of the baobab tree, *Adansonia digitata*. (33)

Adder(s), oil of: See viperae, oleum. (40)

Adder's tongue: See erythronium. (39)

Adep(i)s ____: Fat, a fat-based preparation, see ____, adeps. (8)

Adep(i)s suillae: Mixture of lard and mutton fat. (39)

Adeps anserinus; —anseris: Goose grease. (3,40)

Adeps gadi: Cod liver oil. (3)

Adeps hominis: Human fat.

Adeps lana; Adeps lanae hydrosus: Fat of wool, i.e., (see) lanolin. (1,8)

Adeps myristicas: Expressed oil of nutmeg. See myristica. (40)

Adeps ovillus: Mutton (sheep) suet. (3)

Adeps praeparata: Prepared animal fat, generally lard. (40)

Adeps suis; —, sus: Pig fat, i.e—lard. (39)

Adeps; Adepis: From the Latin, fat or grease. When not otherwise specified, lard. Used in the preparation of benzoinated lard (see benzoin), cerates (waxes, typically three parts white wax to one part lard), and ointments (typically two parts wax to eight of lard, and thus softer than a cerate). (1, 8)

Adexolin: A proprietary concentrate containing vitamins A and D. (40)

Adhaesivum elasticum, emplastrum: Rubber adhesive plaster, similar to (see) emplastrum adhaesans. (42)

Adhatoda; Adhatodae liquidum, extractum: Fresh or dried leaved of *Adhatoda vasica*, of India, or the liquid extract in alcohol. In large doses, emetic; smaller dosages an expectorant in bronchitis, asthma, or tuberculosis. May be smoked for same effect. Noted in BPC to be used primarily in India and Eastern Colonies. (42)

Fig. 3-5 Aconite.

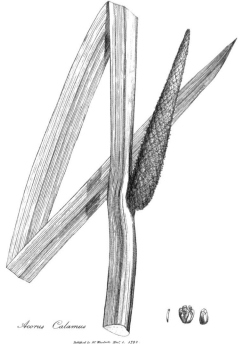

Fig. 3-6 Acorus.

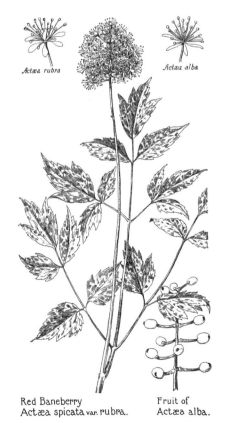

Fig. 3-7 Actea spicata.

A

Adhatodae, succus: Adhatoda juice, used directly as an emetic and expectorant in India and eastern British colonies. (42)

Adhatodae, tinctura: The alcoholic tincture of adhatoda. (42)

Adhesive plaster: See emplastrum adhaesans.

Adianthum; Adiantum: Term used for certain ferns, e.g. true maidenhair, *Adiantum capillus veneris*. (8)

Adipis lanae, unguentum: Ointment of lanolin and olive oil, emollient. (42)

Adipis, ceratum: Cerate of lard, of two parts lard (or other fat or oil as desired) and one of white wax. (44)

Adipsos: Licorice, see glycyrrhiza. (3)

Adjuvans, elixir: Elixir of glycyrrhiza, USP. (3)

Adonis; Adonidin: Adonidin is an alkaloid isolated from the false hellebore, or pheasant's eye *Adonis vernalis*. It is said to raise the blood pressure while lowering the heart rate, and to act as a diuretic primarily by increasing cardiac function. Use as per digitalis. (8,32)

Adonidis, fluidextractum; —, fluidum extractum: Fluid extract of adonis. (31,46)

Adragante; Adragante, gomme {*French*}**:** Tragacanth, i.e., gum tragacanth. (1,3)

Adrenalin; Adnephrin; Adrenal; Adrenamine; Adrenin; Adrin; Adrenina; Adrenine: Adrenaline, or epinephrine, originally isolated from the adrenal gland, a vasoconstrictor and stimulant, now used mainly for anaphylaxis and cardiac arrest. (40, 42)

Adreninae, suppositoria: Suppository of adrenine and boric acid in wool fat and cocoa butter, vasoconstrictor for hemorrhoids, especially if bleeding. (42)

Adreninae, unguentum: Adrenine ointment, of same with boric acid, water, lanolin, and soft paraffin, for application to hemorrhoids or to constrict mucous membranes of the nose. (42)

Adreninae album, unguentum: White adrenine (adrenaline) ointment, of same in castor oil, alcohol, hydrochloric acid, and soft paraffin. (42)

Adreninae boricus, liquor; —hydrochloricus, liquor: A solution of adrenaline with chloroform and either boric acid or hydrochloric acid plus sodium chloride in water, use as per adrenine inhalant. The hydrochloric solution could be used topically to control bleeding and via injection as a cardiac stimulant. (42)

Adreninae et cocainae, unguentum: Same as adreninae, unguentum with addition of cocaine as anesthetic and vasoconstrictor, for piles. (42)

Adreninae mitis, unguentum: Adrenine in oil of rose and paraffin, a weaker (mitis), scented form of adreninae, unguentum more appropriate for nasal use. (42)

Adrenine inhalant; Adreninae aromaticus, liquor: A solution of dilute adrenalin with alcohol, boric acid, eucalyptol, and oil of gaultheria in a base of castor oil. Nebulized or topical for relief of nasal congestion. (42)

Adstricta, aqua: Ice. (3)

Adstringens: Astringent (Latin, adjective).

Adstringens et escharotica, mistura: Astringent and escarotic mixture, of lead acetate, copper and zinc sulphate, and dilute acetic acid. (46)

Adstringens, lotio: An astringent lotion of sulphuric acid, oil of turpentine, and alcohol. (34)

Advita: A proprietary concentrate containing vitamins A and D. (40)

Aegle (marmelos): Fruit of the bilva, *Aegle marmelos*, of India. Highly effective laxative and carminative. (40) See bael fruit.

Aegyptiacum, unguentum: Egyptian ointment, made from basic copper acetate, vinegar, and honey. For topical treatment of ulcers. Escharotic, and not a true unguent, as it contains no fat or oil. (1,3,39)

Aer fixus: Carbonic acid gas, i.e., carbon dioxide. (3)

Aerata, aqua: Carbonated water. (3)

Aeratus, sal: Potassium bicarbonate, "usually applied at present (1926) to sodium bicarbonate." Source of carbon dioxide in effervescent formulations. (3) Sodium tartrate was also used for this purpose.

Aeris fixi, aqua: Water of "fixed air," i.e., carbonated water. (3)

Aerophorus laxantis, pulvis; Aerophorus (Seydlitzensis), pulvis: Effervescent laxative powder, see Seidlitz's powder. (1,3,34)

Aerosus lapis: Calamine, see calamina. (3)

Aeruginis ammoniata(e), aqua: Water of ammoniated copper, a green solution also called sapphire water. Verdigris (copper acetate) in ammonia water. A topical for skin ulcers and diluted for use as an eye wash. (39)

Aeruginis, linimentum; —, unguentum; —, oxymel: Ointment of verdigris (copper acetate) in honey and vinegar, used topically as a disinfectant for skin and eyes. (39,42)

Aerugo crystallisata: Crystalline copper subacetate. (40)

Aerugo; Aërugo: Crude copper acetate, verdigris, basic copper acetate, sometimes copper oxide. (1,3)

Aes aeratum: Copperas, crude ferrous sulfate (see ferri sulphas). A chemical misnomer from ancient times, probably based on the greenish color, but not actually a copper salt.(3)

Aes viride: Copper subacetate. (40)

Aes: Copper. (1,3)

Aesculus: The buckeye, *Aesculus glabra*, a nervous system stimulant and toxin much like strychnine (see strychnine). (32)

Aethacrinidini lactas: See ethacrinidine.

NOTE: Aether— if not listed here, or for structure and chemistry, see ether (8)

Aether, chloric: See chloroformi, spiritus. (40)

Aether, hydrochloric: This is chloroethane, a topical refrigerant anesthetic, now mainly a dry cleaning solution. See ethyl chloride. (40)

Aether, hyponitrous: See aetheris nitrosi, spiritus. (40)

Aether, methylatus; Ether, methylated: A crude mixture of dimethyl, diethyl, and methyl-ethyl ether with variable composition. A local refrigerant and inhalational anesthetic. (42)

Aether, nitrous: See aetheris nitrosi, spiritus and nitri dulcis, spiritus. (40)

Aether, ozonic(us): Solution of hydrogen peroxide in ether. By inhalation or by mouth for various conditions including diabetes, or nebulized, like carbolic acid, to disinfect an area. (40)

Aether, petroleum: See benzin(e). (8)

Aether, purificatus; ether, purified: Diethyl ether, purified by washing (extracting with water) and drying, for general anesthesia. (42)

Aether, spiritus: Spirit of ether, consisting of roughly one part ether and two parts alcohol. Hoffmann's drops. (8,31)

Aether, sulphuric; —, sulphuricum; —, sulphuricus: Sulfuric ether, made by distillation of wine and sulfuric acid. Sulfuric acid is a powerful dehydrating agent, resulting in the condensation of two alcohol molecules to form diethyl ether, the ether used for anesthesia. (39)

Aether, vitriolic; —vitriolicus: See aether, sulphuric. (39)

Aether aceticus: Acetic ether, or ethyl acetate, distilled from a mixture of sodium acetate (sodii acetas), alcohol, and sulphuric acid. Used as a stimulant, carminative, and antispasmodic. (Technically, this would now be called an ester, not an ether, $CH_3\text{-}COO\text{-}CH_2\text{-}CH_3$.) (8)

Aether bromatus: See ethyl bromide. (8)

Aether muriatic(us): Hydrochloric ether, not structurally a true ether, this is (see) ethyl chloride, i.e., chloroethane, used as a refrigerant topical anaesthetic spray. (40)

Aether soap: See saponis aetherea, solutio. (42)

Aether sulphuricus cum alcohole: A solution of ether in alcohol, for the same uses as ether itself. (39)

Aether vegetabilis: Acetic ether (see etheris acetatis). (3)

Aetherial extract; Aethereum extractum: An ether extract, generally evaporated down to an oleoresin. In general ____, aethereaum extractum is synonymous with ____, oleoresina. (34)

Aetherial oil of wine: See aetherium, oleum. (44)

Aetheris, syrupus: Syrup of ether, of sugar, alcohol, and ether. (34)

Aetheris chlorici, spiritus: See chloroformi spiritus. (40)

Aetheris composita, lotio: Compound lotion of ether, of same with, alcohol, ammonium acetate, and rosewater. A topical refrigerant. (34)

Aetheris compositus, spiritus: Compound spirits of ether, Hoffman's anodyne, consisting of ether (325 parts), alcohol (650 parts), and (a)ethereal oil (25 parts). (8,31)

Aetheris compositus, syrupus: Compound syrup of ether, from purified (diethyl) ether and alcohol in water and syrup, an antispasmodic and stimulant. (42)

Aetheris cum ammonia, mistura: A mixture of spirit of ether, aromatic spirits of ammonia, and water, orally as a stimulant, carminative, and antispasmodic. (42)

Aetheris muriaticus: See ethyl chloride. (40)

Aetheris nitrosi, spiritus: Spirit of nitrous ether, sweet spirits of nitre, distilled from a solution of sodium nitrite (sodii nitris), alcohol, and sulphuric acid to form ethyl nitrite, $C_2H_5NO_2$. (8)

Aetheris vitriolici aromaticus, spiritus: Aromatic spirits of vitriolic ether, of same with cinnamon, cardamom, piper longum, and angelica. A mild tonic. (39)

Aetherium, oleum; (A)etherial oil: Ethereal oil, a volatile liquid distilled from oil of wine, ether, alcohol, sulphuric acid, and distilled water, used to make compound spirits of ether (see aether, compositus, spiritus). (8) A poorly characterized product from distillation of a mixture of sulphuric acid, ether (diethyl) and alcohol, thought to be a mixture of ethylene in mono- and di-ethylsulfuric acid. (44)

Aethiops: A black substance. (39)

Aethiops absorbens: See hydrargyrum cum creta. (40)

Aethiops antimonial(is): A diaphoretic material made from mercury, aethiops mineralis, and antimony. (3,39).

Aethiops ferri: Black iron oxide. (39)

Aethiops martialis; Aethiops, martial: A black iron oxide formed by iron filings covered with water. (1,3)

Aethiops mineralis: 1. Mixture of mercuric sulfide and sulfur (3). 2. Black oxide of mercury (1).

Aethiops narcoticus: Mercury dissolved in nitric acid and precipitated with potassium sulphate. Narcotic effect said to be due to sulphur. Due to the mercury content, it was not constipating, like opium. (39)

Aethiops per se: Mercury oxide. (3)

Aethiops vegetabilis: Charcoal of seaweed. (3)

Aethyl; Aethylene _____: See ethyl or ethylene, respectively. This archaic nomenclature specifies the number of substitutions on the two-carbon ethylene (C_2H_6) molecule, i.e., ethyl chloride has one chlorine, ethylene chloride has two chlorines. (8)

Affium: Extract of poppy-heads (opium). (3)

African pepper: See capsicum. (8)

African saffron: See carthamus. (3)

Agallochum: See aloes, lignum. (1)

Agar; Agar-agar; Agarase: A dried mucilagenous material from *Gelidium corneum* or other algae, used as a demulcent, emollient, and laxative. An imporant culture medium for bacteriology. (7,40,42)

Agaric (, white)(, larch); Agaricus (albus): Agaric, white agaric, larch agaric, *Polyporus officinalis* a mushroom much like the common table mushroom, rind removed and dried. Sometimes said to be *Boletus laricis*, not related to the agarics. Used to control the night sweats of phthisis (tuberculosis). (1,3)

Agaric, fly: See muscarine. (32)

Agaricin; Agaricum, acidum: Agaricin, an organic acid derived from Larch Agaric. Said to paralyze nerve terminals of sweat glands and useful for night sweats in tuberculosis and other conditions. Emetic in larger doses. (42)

Ageratum: Maudlin, an herb, *Achillea ageratum*. (1)

Aggregativae, pilulae: Purgative pills made from aloes, scammony, larch agaric, colocynth, turpeth root, rhubarb, myrobalans, etc. For relief of headache or gastric discomfort. (1)

Agnus castus; Agnocasto {*Italian*}**:** Chaste tree, *Vitex agnus castus*. Fruit used, supposedly an anti-aphrodesiac or sexual sedative. Figure 3-8. (1)

Agomensin: A corpus luteum (ovarian) extract (progestin). (40)

Agotan: See chincophen. (40)

Agresta: Unripe grape. (1)

Agrimonia: Agrimony, cockle burr, stickwort, *Agrimonia eupatoria*. Herb used, especially for kidney disorders. Figure 3-9. (1,32)

Agrippae (Regis), unguentum: Ointment allegedly prescribed to King Herod Agrippa I of Judea. From squill, iris rhizome, bryony root, dwarf elder root, male fern rhizome, wax, etc. (1)

Agro {*Italian*}**:** Sour tasting or unripe, juice of a bitter fruit. (1)

Agro di limone {*Italian*}**:** Lemon juice. (1)

Fig. 3-8 Agnus castus or chaste tree.

Fig. 3-9 Agrimonia.

Agropyrum; Agropyrus; Agropyri; Agropyri liquidum, extractum: Couch grass, *Agropyrus repens* is confusingly referred to as triticum (a term now used for wheat), a closely related grass species. See tritici, fluidum extractum. A demulcent and diuretic used for catarrhal diseases of the genital and urinary tracts. (40,42)

Agropyri, decoctum: Decoction of couch grass or "triticum" (see immediately above). Demulcent and as a "suitable vehicle for bladder sedatives and antiseptics." See tritici fluidum, extractum. (40,42)

Ague bitters: See quininae composita, tinctura. (34)

Agurin: Theobromine-sodium-sodio-acetate. (40) Theobromine is similar to caffeine.

Ailanthus: Chinese sumach, tree of heaven, *Ailanthus glandulosa*. A stimulant. (32)

Airoform; Airogen: Bismuth oxyiodogallate. (40)

Airol: Bismuth iodogallate. (40)

Aitkin's (tonic) pills: See quininae sulphatis compositae, pilulae. (42)

Aitkin's syrup: See ferri, quininae et strychninae phosphatum, syrupus. (34)

Ajowan (, oil of): Seeds from *Ptychotis ajawon*, a spice, or the oil therefrom. (40)

Ajuga: See chamaepitys. (39)

Alabastic: A variety of gypsum, i.e., calcium sulfate. (3)

Alabastrinum, unguentum; alabastro, unguentum de {*Italian*}: Ointment of ground alabaster, chamomile flowers, rose petals, rose oil, white wax, etc. (1)

Alabastrum: Alabaster, generally ground to a powder. (1)

Alanin-mercury: Mercury amidopropionate. (3)

Alba; Albus; Album: White (Latin).

Alba, mixtura: Compound chalk mixture, see cretae, mistura. (3)

Alba veterinaria, lotio: Veterinary white lotion, resulting from reaction of zinc sulfate and lead acetate in water. Used topically. (31)

Albargin: Silver gelatin or glutin. See argein. (40)

Albi Rhasis, trochisci: Lozenges of white lead; see album Rhazes. (1)

Albocarbon: Naphthalene, literally "white carbon," in blocks or chunks, i.e., mothballs. (3)

Albright's solution: A solution of potassium and sodium citrate used to treat a specific renal dysfunction (renal tubular acidosis). (24)

Album: Ammoniated mercury, see hydrargyri ammonii chloridum. (40)

Album, linimentum: White liniment, egg liniment, of acetic acid, oil of lemon, turpentine, and yolk and white of egg with water, a stimulant and rubifacient ointment for sprains and rheumatism. (42)

Album, unguentum: White ointment, made of white lead, white wax, egg white, oil of roses, and rose water. For burns. (1,42)

Album Graecum; —, nigrum: Excrement of dogs or of rodents (mice or rats) respectively. (3)

Album refrigerans, ceratum: See refrigerans Galeni, ceratum. (1)

Album Rhazes: "White of Rhazes," or white lead acetate. (39)

Albumen (egg): Egg albumen, used as a nutritive and antidote. (8) Serum protein in blood is also referred to as albumen, but premodern uses or unspecified usually means egg albumen.

Albumen tannate: An antidiarrheal complex of albumen (the blood protein, not egg) and tannic acid. (40)

Albuminate of iron, albuminized iron, solution of: See ferri albuminati, liquor. (31)

Albus romanus, pulvis: White powder of Rome, magnesium carbonate. (3)

Alcermes, confectio: See alkermes, confectio. (1)

Alces: Elk. (8)

Alchechengi {*Italian*}: See alkekengi. (1)

Alchemilla: Lady's mantle, *Alchemilla vulgaris*. Used topically and internally for a variety of unrelated disorders, but particularly for female disorders. (1)

Alchermes, confectio: See alkermes, confectio. (1)

Alcohol (dilutum)(fortius): 1. A trivial term derived from the Arabic, al-kahūl, the essence. In alchemical terms, the essence or spirit of a material could be separated from the whole by physical processes such as distillation, and was considered to carry with it the essential properties or characteristics of the material from which it was derived. 2. In more modern terms, an alcohol is an organic (carbon based) compound bearing an –OH group on one or more carbons. 3. When not further specified the term refers to ethyl alcohol, the two carbon alcohol, CH_3-CH_2OH. Weaker (dilutum) or stronger (fortius) concentrations were specified in various sources. (44)

Alcohol, ammoniated; —, ammoniatum: See ammoniae, spiritus. (34,39)

Alcohol, ethyl: A ninety-one percent solution consisting of ethyl alcohol (C_2H_6O). This is generally obtained by distillation from a fermented spirit, treated with anhydrous potassium carbonate and calcium chloride to reduce water content. Alcohol and water, when distilled, form an azeotrope, i.e., a fixed mixture which cannot be further separated by distillation, and hence no concentration greater than approximately ninety-one percent can be achieved by distillation. (8) See alcohol absolutum.

Alcohol, methyl(ic); —, methylicum: Methanol, wood alcohol, CH_3OH. It has narcotic and sedative effects but is little used due to high toxicity. (40,42) A single ounce may cause permanent blindness.

Alcohol absolutum: Ethyl alcohol containing less than one percent water. As noted (see alcohol, ethyl), this cannot be formed by distillation, but is rather formed by percolating ethyl alcohol through freshly formed lime, which reacts with and removes water. The mixture is then re-distilled under a vacuum to purify the absolute alcohol. (8)

Alcohol deodoratum: Alcohol purified by distillation over fused sodium acetate, which removes residual (non-alcohol) odors. (8)

Alcohol dilutum: Approximately forty-one percent alcohol (ethyl) in water. (8)

Alcohol sulphuris: Carbon disulfide, a solvent. (3)

Alcoholic eye wash: See opthalmicus, spiritus. (46)

Alcoolat {*French*}: A distilled spirit. (3)

Alcoolature {*French*}: An alcoholic tincture of a fresh plant (green tincture). (3)

Alcoolé {*French*}: An alcoholic solution of a substance entirely soluble in alcohol. (3)

Alcornoque (, devine): Wood of the various cork-oak species, used as an astringent and for phthisis and liver disorders. (39)

Aldehyde; Aldehydum (dilutum): If not further specified, usually acetaldehyde, CH_3-CHO. Used in diluted (fifteen percent) form in medicinal applications. A topical antiseptic, especially for nasal membranes. (40,42)

Aldehydum ammoniatum; Aldehyde, ammoniated: A crystalline substance formed by reacting acetaldehyde and ammonia, which readily decomposes into the parent compounds. Mainly useful for preparing quantitative reference solutions of acetaldehyde, which, in turn, are used in quality analysis of fermented spirits. (42)

Alder buckthorn: See rhamnus frangula. (40)

Aldrich's mixture: A one percent solution of gentian violet, for treatment of burns. (24)

Ale(o)phanginae, pilulae: Scented pills of aloes, aloe-wood, cinnamon, nutmeg, cloves, myrrh, rose petals, etc. For treatment of epilepsy, vertigo, migraine, and melancholy. (1,39)

Alegar: Ale vinegar, by fermenting ale on raisins or vine (presumably grape) cuttings. (3)

Alembroth, sal: Mixture of mercuric and ammonium chlorides, i.e., sal ammoniac with calomel. (3,39)

Alessandrino, electuario {*Italian*}: Purgative electuary, after Alessandro Petronio, physician to Pope Gregory XIII, originator. (1)

Aletodin: Acetylsalicylic acid, aspirin. (40)

Aletris: Unicorn Root, Star Grass, Starwort, *Aletris farinosa*, rhizome and root used. A diuretic for dropsy, uterine tonic, and for rheumatism. The genitive is aletridis. (7,42)

Aletridis compositum, elixir: Compound elixir of aletris, of the fluid extracts of aletris, mitchella, helonias and caulophyllum with viburnum opulus. Intended for dysmenorrhea. "As none of these drugs are of much value and as the quantities present are ridiculously minute it is evident that the elixir is of no great use." (31)

Aletridis, elixir: Elixir of liquid extracts of aletris and licorice in simple elixir and water. A "uterine tonic." (42)

Aletridis, fluidextractum; —, fluidum extractum; —liquidum, extractum: Fluid extract of aletris. (31,42,46)

Alexandrina, aurea: See aurea Alexandrina. (1)

Alexandrinum, julapium: See regius, syrupus. (1)

Alexipharmacum: A general antidote for poisons. (1) In later use, a cure-all or panacea.

Alexiterius, pulvis: See ipecacuanae compositus, pulvis. (40)

Alfalfa: See medicago. (32)

Algaroth, powder of: Antimony oxychloride. Also referred to as "vital mercury," mercurius vitalis, this was a recrystallized antimony "murate" (chloride), later found to be the oxychloride. (3)

Alhandal; Alhandali, trochisci: Alhandal, equivalent to colocyntha, or lozenges thereof. (1,39)

Alia creish: Black sugar, i.e., succus glycyrrhizae, licorice juice. (40)

Alisma: Water Plantain, *Alisma plantago*, leaves used for urinary conditions. (33)

Alkali fixum vegitabile: Potassium hydroxide. "Fixed" by heating of vegetable alkali, the carbonate, releasing carbon dioxide. (39)

Alkali, vegetable; —, vegitabile: Potassium carbonate. (3)

Alkali, volatile: Ammonium carbonate. (3) Ancient term for ammonia. (44)

Alkalina aerata, aqua: Aerated alkaline water, of potassium carbonate and water, saturated with carbon dioxide; carbonated water. (39)

Alkalina composita, pulvis: Compound alkaline powder, of sodium bicarbonate, sodium chloride, and borax, to be dissolved in water as a nasal douche for catarrh. (42)

Alkaline aromatic solution: See aromaticus alkalinus, liquor.

Alkaline bath: Balneum alkalinum, an alkaline bath salt official in the BPC, but there were many variants. (40)

Alkaline elixir: See hydrastis compositum, elixir. (31)

Alkaline lixivia: Caustic soda, potassium hydroxide. (39)

Alkaline nasal wash: See liquor alkalinus, (40)

Alkaline salt: Potassium carbonate. (39)

Alkalinus (antisepticus), liquor: A variant of aromaticus alkalinus, liquor. A solution of potassium (or sodium) bicarbonate and carbolic acid (phenol) or other antiseptic (eugenol, eucalyptol, etc). Used as a nasal or eyewash or for other topical irrigation.

Alkalinus, lapis: Alkaline stone, i.e., caustic potash, see potash. (3)

Alkalinus, syrupus: Alkaline syrup, of sodium tartrate and simple syrup, for use as antacid. (39)

Alkalinus comp., pulvis: See bismuthi compositus, pulvis. (40)

Alkalinus fixus fossilis, sal: Barilla or natron, a natural mixture of sodium carbonate and bicarbonate. (39)

Alkalinus fixus vegetabilis, sal: Fixed vegetable alkalai, variably potassium hydroxide or carbonate, see potash. (39)

Alkanna; Alkanet: Dyer's bugloss, *Alkana tinctoria*, a colorant (purple or red). See buglossum and see illustrations and discussion under anchusa. (33)

Alkekengi: Winter cherry, *Physalis alkekengi*. Berries used. Diuretic and aperient. Figure 3-10. (1,39)

Alkermes, confectio: A preparation named after the kermes insect, source of red dye, one of the ingredients. (1) Various sources describe multiple and varying ingredients including silk, apple juice, gold, rose water, or crushed pearl, flavored with cinnamon and sweetened with sugar or honey—inevitably colored red. Purported to be a strong general and cardiac tonic.

All-fours: A "domestic" (UK, probably meaning "unofficial") cough remedy of oil of peppermint, oil of anise, tincture of opium, and compound tincture of camphor. (40)

Alliaria: Jack-by-the-hedge, *Sisymbrium alliaria*; or leaves of sauce alone, *Erysimum alliaria*. Diaphoretic and deobstructant, external antiseptic. Figure 3-11. (1,39)

Allium: Garlic, bulb of *Allium sativum*, of Asia and Southern Europe, but widely cultivated. It is used as a general stimulant, digestive aid, and in the postinflammatory recovery from catarrhal and pectoral conditions. Figure 3-12. (1,8)

Allii, syrupus; Allio, syrupus ex {*Italian*}**:** Syrup of garlic, 200 parts garlic, 800 sugar, and diluted acetic acid to a total of 1000 parts. For cough and infantile catarrh. (8,34)

Allspice: See pimenta. (8)

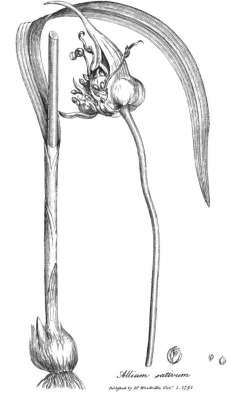

Fig. 3-10 Alkekengi or winter cherry.

Fig. 3-11 Alliaria.

Fig. 3-12 Allium or garlic.

Allume {*Italian*}**:** See alumen. (1)

Allyl-thiourea; Allyl-thiocarbamide: See thiosinamina. (42) A photographic chemical. (40)

Almond, bitter; Almond, Jordan; Almond, sweet: Bitter almond, see amygdala amara. Sweet or Jordan almond, see amygdala dulcis. (8)

Alnus: Tag alder, *Alnus rubra*, a stomachic. (32)

Alnus glutinosa: Common European alder, bark used as per oak bark. Unofficial. (44)

Alocol: Colloidal aluminium hydroxide, antacid. (40)

Aloe: Barbadoes aloes, Curacoa aloes, the inspissated juice of the leaves of *Aloe vera,* or of the socotrine aloe, *Aloe Perryi* or *Aloes socotrina*. This is a hard orange-brown mass. Aloe is used as a stimulant and laxative, as well as an emmenogogue. Like senna, it tends to see use in many formulations involving multiple laxative agents. Figure 3-13. (1,8)

Aloe, lignum: See aloes, lignum.

Aloe, natal: Not always distinct from aloe above, but said to be from *Aloe bainsii*. (40)

Aloe capensis: Cape aloe, *Aloe spicata*, of North America. (44)

Aloe pills, mild: See aloes dilutae, pilulae. (42)

Aloe purificata: Purified aloe, by solution in alcohol, straining to remove foreign material, and evaporation to dryness. (8)

Aloe socotrina; Aloe doc. pulv.: Aloes obtained from the island of Socotra, *Aloes (perfoliata) socotrina*, or a powder therefrom. Figure 3-13. (1, 29)

Aloephanginae, pilulae: See alephanginae, pilulae. (1)

Aloes, enema: Enema of aloes, potassium carbonate, glycerin, and mucilage of starch, for bowel evacuation. (42)

Aloes (barbadense)(socotrinae), extractum (aquosum); Aloes Aq., E.: Aqueous extract of aloes, for which Socotrine or Barbadense may be specified. Aloe is disintegrated in water, which is separated, filtered, and evaporated to dryness. (8,42)

Aloes, glyceritum: Glycerite of aloes, topical emollient for various skin conditions. (34)

Aloes, hepatic: Liver-coloured aloes. (40)

Aloes, lignum: Aloe wood, eagle wood, agalloch, the resinous wood of the East Indian tree, *Aquilaria agallocha*. (1)

Aloes, oil of: Oil obtained from Socotrine aloes, see aloe. (40)

Aloe perfoliata Socotrina

Fig. 3-13 Socatrine aloe.

Aloes (barbadense)(socotrinae), pilulae: Pills of purified aloe and soap, in the BPC also with oleum carui and confection of roses. Laxative. (8,42)

Aloes, tinctura: Tincture of aloes made with aloe, licorice root (glycyrrhiza), and dilute alcohol. Cathartic. (8,42)

Aloes, vinum: Wine of aloes, of purified aloes, cardamom, and stronger white wine (vinum album fortius). For constipation. (34)

Aloes cape pulv.: Powdered cape aloes, a type of aloe, *Aloe capensis*. See aloes. (29)

Aloes composit(a)(um), tinctura: Alcoholic extract of aloes with myrrh and crocus, for a wide variety of internal conditions. In the BPC, of aloes, gentian, rhubarb, zedoary, and saffron in alcohol. Purgative. (39,42)

Aloes compositae, pilulae: Compound pills of aloe, anti-dyspeptic pills. Extracts of boneset, mandrake, and ginseng, powdered aloe, capsicum and lobelia seed powder, soap, and oil of cloves. For dyspepsia, constipation, jaundice, and amenorrhea, and a general cathartic. (34) In the BPC, of powdered aloes, ipecac root, and scammony with green extract of hyoscyamus and syrup, also cathartic, with hyoscyamus to reduce cramping. (42)

Aloes compositum, decoctum: Compound decoction of aloes, with aloes, myrrh, potassium bicarbonate, and licorice. (3) In the BPC, extract of aloes, powdered myrrh, saffron, potassium carbonate, extract of licorice, compound tincture of cardamom, and water. This is a purgative. (42)

Aloes cum colocynthide, pillule: Pill of aloes, scammony, vitriol, antimony, colocynth, caryophyllus and gum arabic. For headache or used as a cathartic. (39)

Aloes cum guaiacum, pillule; —, pulvis: Pills or powder of aloes and guaiac. Diuretic and cathartic. (39)

Aloes dilutae, pilulae: Mild aloe pills, of aloe, extract of licorice, soap, treacle, and water as needed, laxative. (42)

Aloes et asafoetedae, pilulae: Pills of aloe and asafetida with soap. For gastric upset, flatulence, and constipation. (8,34,42)

Aloes et canellae: A formulation of aloe and canella, probably in reference to the powder, below. (29)

Aloes et canellae, pulvis: A powder of socotrine aloes and canella bark, a purgative and emmenagogue, one of several items referred to as hiera picra. (42)

Aloes et colocynthidis, pillulae; Aloes et Coloc., pilula: See colocynthidis compositae, pilulae. (40)

Aloes et ferri, pilulae: Pills of aloe and iron, of purified aloe, ferrous sulphate, aromatic powder, and confection of rose. For amenorrhea and constipation in anemic or otherwise debilitated women. (8,34) In the BPC also with compound cinnamon powder and syrup. (42)

Aloes et mastiches, pilulae: Pills of aloe and mastic with red rose. For constipation and poor bowel function, the mastic is said to keep the pill intact, allowing for effects in the lower intestinal tract. Minor variants include this and other "dinner pills," i.e., Chapmans', Cole's, Hall's, or Lady Webster's dinner pills, with various additional ingredients such as glycyrrhiza or jalap to enhance cathartic effects. (8,34)

Aloes et myrrhae, pilulae: Pills of purified aloe and myrrh with aromatic powder and simple syrup. For uterine disorders with constipation and debility. A similar tablet in the BPC was compounded with refined sugar and theobromatis, emulsio. (8,31,34,42)

Aloes et myrrhae, tinctura: Tincture of aloe and myrrh, Elixir Proprietatis Paracelsi, of purified aloe, myrrh, licorice root, alcohol, and water, or in the BPC, of aloes, saffron, and myrrh. Purgative. (8,42)

Aloes et nucis vomicae et belladonnae, tablettae: Tablet of powdered aloes, extract of nux vomica, alcoholic extract of belladonna, sugar, etherial solution of theobroma, and alcohol. For chronic constipation. (42)

Aloes et nucis vomicae, pilulae: Aloes, extract of nux vomica, and extract of belladonna formed to pills using alcohol. Laxative. (42)

Aloes et podophylli compositae, pilulae: Compound pills of aloes and podophyllum, of same with extract of belladonna leaf and extract of nux vomica. Cathartic. (34)

Aloes petrolatum, unguentum; Aloes petrol., ung.: Ointment of aloes made with petrolatum in place of the usual base material, lard.

Aloes pulvis; Aloes pv.: Powdered aloe.

Aloes Socotrinae, pilulae: Socotrine aloe pills with hard soap, oil of nutmeg, and confection of roses. Cathartic. (42)

Aloeticus, pulvis: See hiera picra. (40)

Aloin; Aloinum: In the USP, a standard pill of aloes, strychnine, and belladonna. In the BPC, the active principal of aloes, usually Curacao aloes, used as per aloe. (33,42)

Aloini, strychninae et belladonnae (compositae), pilulae: Pills of aloin (aloe), strychnine, and belladonna, for habitual constipation. The compound pills contained rhamnus pershiana as well. (34)

Aloini compositae, pilulae: Compound pills of aloin, with podophyllum and extract of belladonna. (34) In the BPC of aloin, extract of nux vomica, ferrous sulfate, myrrh, and hard soap or later of aloin, powdered ipecac, extract of nux vomica, sugar, and theobromatis, emulsio. For chronic constipation. (42)

Aloini et podophylli compositae, pilulae: Aloin and oleoresin of capsicum, jalap resin, podophyllum resin, extract of nux vomica, and green extract of hyoscyamus. Purgative. (42)

Aloini et strychninae compositae, pilulae: Aloin, strychnine, powdered ipecac, milk sugar, and green extract of belladonna. Purgative. (42)

Alphacaine: Alpha-eucaine, local anesthetic. (40)

Alphol: Alphanaphthol salicylate, antiseptic and anodyne taken internally. (40)

Alquermes, confectio: See alkermes, confectio. (1)

Alsol: Fifty percent solution of (see) aluminii aceto-tartrate. (42)

Alstonia: Australian fever bark, bitter bark, Alstonia bark, *Alstonia constricta.* An antimalarial. (32)

Alstonia scholaris: Dita bark, from *Alstonia scholaris*, of India. Antimalarial, said not to be as effective as *A. constricta*, above. (33)

Alstoniae, infusum: An infusion (BPC) of alstonia, a bitter tonic and for malaria and chronic diarrhea. (42)

Alstoniae, tinctura: Tincture of alstonia and alcohol, a bitter. (42)

Alterantiae composita, mistura; Alterative mixture, compound: Compound alterative mixture, or tonic mixture, of sodium phosphate, quinine sulphate, strychnine, ammonia water, sugar, and dilute sulphuric and phosphoric acid. A general tonic in chronic and wasting diseases. (34)

Althaea; Althea; Altheae flor: Marsh-mallow, *Altheaea officinalis*, or the flower thereof. Root generally used. Note that this is the marsh mallow, not the mallow (see malvae folium). Figure 3-14. (1,5,7)

Althaeae (vs Altheae): British (and proper Latin) spelling of the genitive form of althaea. In the US, altheae is often seen, although althaeae is official. Figure 3-14.

Althaeae, decoctum: Decoction of marshmallow root, sliced and boiled. Commonly used for cough, bronchitis, and as a general demulcent. (42)

Althaeae, trochisci: Marshmallow lozenge, of althaea powder, sugar, gum acacia, orange flower water, and egg white. Demulcent for irritant cough. (42)

Alth(a)eae, Fernel's syrup of: A deobstruent based on the marsh mallow created by Dr. Fernel of Paris in 1593. (39)

Alth(a)eae, syrupus: Syrup of althea, from althea and containing ten percent glycerin and three percent alcohol. Used as per syrup of acacia. (31,34) In the BPC, of macerated althea root extract, sugar, and water. A demulcent for cough. (42)

Alth(a)eae, unguentum compositum; Althaeae ung. c.: Compound unguent of marshmallow, of the root with fenugreek, linseed, olive oil, wax, resin, and turpentine. (35)

Althein: Asparagin, aminosuccinamic acid, a diuretic. (40)

Alum; Alumen: Alum, or potassium alum is aluminum potassium sulfate, $Al_2K_2(SO_4)_2$. This is a mild astringent used orally or nasally, including for treatment of oral ulcers, a topical haemostatic and wound treatment (coagulates proteins when applied to wounds), and may be used as an emetic or laxative if given in large doses. (8) For compounds and formulations, see aluminis or aluminus (not to be confused with other aluminum compounds, under alumini or aluminii).

Alum, burnt: Burned, burnt, or dried (exsiccatus) alum is the crystalline material heated to drive off the water normally incorporated at crystallization. The resulting powder was a very effective desiccant used topically to dry and clean wounds or open skin lesions.

Alum, cake: Aluminum sufate. (3)

Alum, chrome; Alumen, Chromicum: Chrome alum, from potassium and chromium sulfate. Used as a mordant in dyeing, not pharmaceutical. (42)

Alum, concentrated: Aluminum sufate. (3)

Alum, cube: Potassium alum. (3)

Alum, exsiccatus; Alum exs.: Dried alum. See alum, burnt.

Alum, ferri; —, ferric: See ammonii ferri alum.

Alum, patent: Aluminum sufate. (3)

Alum, porous: Sodium aluminum sufate. (3)

Alum, rock; —, Roche; —, Roman; Alumen Rupeum: Lump alum, as naturally occurs. (3)

Alum root: See heuchera. (39) A British source indicates this may also be geranium. (40)

Alumen plumosum: Asbestos. (3)

Alumen pulv.; Alumen Pv.; Aluminii Pulv.: Powdered alum.

Alumen Romanum: See roche alum. (40)

Alumen rubrum: Rock salt. (3)

Alumen ustum; Alumen Ustm: See alum, burnt.

Aluminae, super-sulphas et potassae (exsiccatus): Alum (dried). (39)

Aluminum: While aluminum is the metallic component of compounds listed here (some, like alum, being ancient), metallic aluminum does not appear in older medical references as the base metal was not refined and identifed until 1881 and the material remained extraordinarily valuable until the electrolytic refining process was introduced after the turn of the twentieth century.

Fig. 3-14 Althea or althaea.

A

Alumini(i) acetatis, liquor: Solution of aluminum acetate, Liquor Burowii, Burow's solution, an aqueous solution of neutral aluminum acetate (i.e., aluminum triacetate), made by the reaction between lead acetate (see plumbi acetatis) and aluminum sulphate, from which lead sulphate precipitates, leaving the aluminum compound in solution. An astringent and antiseptic. Note also, alumini subacetatis, below. (31) In the NF, directly prepared from aluminum sulfate by conversion with acetic acid and calcium carbonate in water. (46)

Alumini(i) et potassii sulphas; Aluminii et pot. sul.; etc.: This is aluminum potassium sufate, i.e., alum.

Alumini(i) hydras: Aluminum hydrate, i.e., aluminum hydroxide, $Al_2(OH)_6$. (8)

Alumini(i) subacetatis, liquor: Solution of aluminum subacetate, aqueous solution of basic aluminum acetate (i.e., aluminum monoacetate dihydrate), made from aluminum sulphate, acetic acid, precipitated calcium carbonate and water. An active germicide, as well as astringent used as a gargle and surgical dressing, generally diluted with 4 to 8 parts water. (31)

Alumini(i) sulphas: Aluminum sulfate $Al_2(SO_4)_3$. Used as per alum as a topical astringent and mild caustic for enlarged tonsils, nasal polyps, mucous membrane ulcerations, and discharges from mucous membranes. (8,42)

Aluminii acetatis, carbasus: Antiseptic gauze treated with dilute ammonium acetate and dried. (42)

Aluminii acetici, solutum: See aluminii acetatis, liquor. (40)

Aluminii aceto-tartrate; Aluminum aceto-tartrate: By action of aluminum hydroxide on a mixture of acetic and tartaric acids, this is a modest astringent and non-toxic germicidal agent, used as a topical solution in wounds, and as a gargle, mouthwash, douche, and eyewash. (42) In the NF, directly prepared from alum, sodium carbonate, glacial acetic acid, tartaric acid, and water. (46)

Aluminii chloridum: Aluminum chloride, an antiseptic and astringent for topical use, occasionally given systemically. (42)

Aluminii naphthol-sulphonas; Aluminium naphthol-sulphonate: Cutol, a proprietary powder used for skin conditions. (42)

Aluminis, gargarisma: Alum gargle made up in infusion of roses, for pharyngitis. (42)

Aluminis, glycerinum: Powdered alum in glycerin and water, an astringent for the oropharynx. (42)

Aluminis, glyceritum: Glycerite of alum, used for same astringent purposes as alum itself. (34)

Aluminosae, aquae: Aluminated waters, a mineral water. (39)

Aluminus composita, aqua: Compound alum water, of alum and zinc sulphate, as a topical astringent and disinfectant for skin, eyes, and mucous membranes of the genital tract, i.e., for venereal disease. (39)

Aluminus composita, pulvis: Compound alum powder, a styptic, of alum with gum kino. (39)

Amadou: Punk or tinder. (3)

Amande {*French*}**; Amandola** {*Italian*}**:** Almond. See amygdala. (1)

Amanita (muscaria): See muscarine. (32)

Amapola (flora); Amapol, Flor: Amapola is Spanish for poppy. This is the flower of poppy, presumably opium poppy.

Amara, tinctura: Bitter tincture, stomachic tincture, bitter stomachic drops, stomach drops, made from gentian, centaury, bitter orange peel (aurantii amari, cortex) and zedoary, it is a bitter tonic. (31)

Amara; Amarum; Amarus: Bitter tasting (adj., Latin). (1)

Amaranthus hypochondriacus: Prince's feather, *Amaranthus hypochondriacus*, topical astringent. Unofficial. (44)

Amarum, sal: "Bitter salt" or magnesium sufate, i.e., Epsom salts. (3)

Amber, Crato's: A mixture of amber with socotrine aloes, agaricus, and aristolochia made into a pill with honey. A cathartic and antispasmodic. (39)

Amber, oil of, factitious: Oil distilled from copal or dammar. (40)

Amber, oil of, liniment: See succini compositum, linimentum. (34)

Amber seed: Seed of the musk mallow, see malva. (40)

Ambergis; Ambergrisia; Ambra grisea: Whale oil, spermaceti. (1) Ambergris is a solid material said to be formed in the intestine of the whale and found in the sea. (39)

Ambra, citrina: Amber (resin). (1)

Ambrettas, tinctura: Tincture of musk seed, see abelmoschus. (40)

Ambrosia trifida: Tall ambrosia, ragweed, *Ambrosia trifida*, an astringent, stimulant, hemostatic, and antiseptic. (33)

Ambusta, unguentum ad: Burn ointment. (1)

Amec(h), confectio: See Hamech, confectio. (1)

American ashes: Crude potassium carbonate, potash. (40)

American copal: Resin of *Hymenasa courbaril*. (40)

American elder: See sambucus (canadensis). (40)

American oil: Scandinavian term for castor oil. (3)

American senna: See cassia (marilandica). (40)

Amianthus (, lapis): Asbestos. (3)

Amidala {*Italian*}**:** Almond. See amygdala. (1)

Amidol: See diamidophenol. (42)

Amidon: Starch. (3)

Amidosuccinic acid (amide): See asparagin. (42)

Aminic acid: Trivial name for formic acid. (40)

Amino-acetparaphenetidin hydrochloride: Phenocoll hydrochloride, analgesic. (40)

Amino-mercuric chloride: Ammoniated mercury. See hydrargyri ammonii chloridum. (3)

Aminoform: Hexamine, see hexaminium. (40)

Aminophylline: The diphenhydramine salt of theophylline, a bronchodilator for asthma.

Aminosuccinamic acid: See asparagin. (40)

Ammi: Plants of the genus *Ammi*, i.e., bishop's weed. Seeds used. (1)

Ammonaldehyde: Hexamine, see hexaminium. (40)

Ammonia: Ammonia, NH_3, or the solution thereof. (44)

Ammonia, hepatised: Ammonium sulfide. (40)

Ammonia, spirit of: A solution of ammonia; see ammoniae liquor. (40)

Ammonia praeparatus: Usually ammonium carbonate, sometimes calcium carbonate, for numerous conditions including snake envenomations and as an antacid. (39)

Ammoniac; Ammoniacum: When otherwise unspecified, this is generally gum ammoniac, a gum resin obtained from *Dorema ammoniacum*, of the Middle East. Not to be confused with sal ammoniac (ammonium chloride). Employed in a manner similar to other volatile oils such as clove (see caryophyllus). (8,39)

Ammoniacalis camphorata, lotio: Ammoniated camphor wash, aqua sedativa, sedative water, eau sedative de Raspail. An aqueous solution containing sodium chloride and ammonia water, with ten percent spirit of camphor. Used as a nervous sedative. (31)

Ammoniaci, emplastrum: Plaster of sal ammoniac and dilute acetic acid (vinegar). (46)

Ammoniaci, emulsum: A milk-like emulsion formed by grinding ammoniac with water. (8)

Ammoniaci, lac; Ammoniaci, mistura; Ammoniacum mixture: A mixture of ammonia, syrup of balsam of tolu, and water, a milky mixture used in the treatment of bronchitis. (42)

Ammoniaci caustici dzondii, spiritus: Liquor of the stronger spirit of ammonia, see ammoniae, spiritus. After Carolus Henricus Dzondi (i.e., Carl Heinrich, German, 1770-1835). (34)

Ammoniaci cum hydrargyr[um][o], emplastrum: Ammoniac plaster of mercury, of oleate of mercury (hydrargyri, oleatum), ammoniac (the gum resin), diluted acetic acid, and lead plaster (plumbi, emplastrum). (8) In the BPC, of ammoniac, mercury, olive oil, and sublimed sulphur. For glandular enlargements and synovial swelling of joints. (42)

Ammoniacum, gummi: Ammoniacum or gum ammoniac, a gummy resin exuded from the stem of *Dorema ammoniacum*. (1)

Ammoniacum, sal; Ammoniac sal: Sal ammoniac, i.e., ammonium chloride. Not to be confused with Ammoniac(um), the resin of *Dorema ammoniacum*, see ammoniac. (1,3)

Ammoniacum martiale, sal: Iron ammonio-chloride. (3)

Ammoniacum secretum glauberi, sal: Ferrous sufate (which is not Glauber's salt). (3)

NOTE—Ammoniae vs Ammonii: Both variants occur regularly, depending on source. USP and BP seem to prefer the former. See both sets of entries for compounds and formulations of ammonia.

Ammoniae, aqua (fortior): Ammonia (NH_3) water, a ten percent solution of ammonia gas in water. Ammonia was used topically as a counterirritant, by inhalation as a stimulant, or as a gastric stimulant. A similar solution was prepared using sal ammoniac in water. USP specified a standard and stronger (fortior) solution of 26% and 32.5% respectively. (8,39,44)

Ammoniae, hydro(-)sulphuretum: A sedative which also produces dizziness, vomiting, and reduced heart rate. Probably ammonium sulfide or hydrosulfide. (39)

Ammoniae, linimentum; Ammonia liniment: Liniment of ammonia, volatile liniment; composed of ammonia water, alcohol, and cottonseed oil. (8)

Ammoniae (fortis), liquor: A solution of ammonia in water, a rubifacient and applied to insect stings. The stronger form is equivalent to aqua ammoniae fortior. (42)

Ammoniae, murias: Sal ammoniac, i.e., the product of muriatic acid (HCl) and ammonia, ammonium chloride. (39)

Ammoniae, spiritus salus: Healthful spirits of ammonia, see ammoniae, aqua. (39)

Ammoniae, spiritus: Spirits of ammonia, ten percent ammonia (NH_3) in alcohol. (8)

Ammoniae acetatae (, liquor); Ammoniae acetatis: Ammonium acetate solution in water, used as an aperient, diaphoretic, and febrifuge. (39,40)

Ammoniae anisatus, liquor; —, spiritus: Anisated spirit or solution of ammonia, of anethol in ammonia water and alcohol. (31)

Ammoniae aromaticus, spiritus; Ammon Ar. Sp.: Aromatic spirits of ammonia, or smelling salts, of ammonium carbonate, ammonia water, oil of nutmeg, oil of lemon, alcohol, oil of lavender flowers, and water. Used as an inhaled stimulant and in production of various ammoniated tinctures (i.e., guaiaci, valerianae). (8)

Ammoniae composita, tinctura: Strong solution of ammonia with a small amount of mastic, alcohol, and oil of lavender. Stimulant and antispasmodic. (42)

Ammoniae compositum, spiritus; Spt. ammon. co.: Compound spirits of ammonia. This is the same as the aromatic spirits of ammonia, or smelling salts. See ammoniae aromaticus, spiritus.

Ammoniae cum senega, mistura: A mixture of ammonium carbonate, wine of ipecac, and infusion of senega in distilled water, a powerful expectorant. (42)

Ammoniae detergens, liquor: A solution of ammonia with oleic acid and alcohol in water, for general skin cleansing. It is noted that the milky appearance of typical household ammonia solutions can be achieved using tap water instead of distilled water as the haze is caused by precipitation of hard water minerals. (42)

Ammoniae fetidis, spiritus; ammoniae foetidis, spiritus: Fetid spirits of ammonia, of asafoetida in strong solution of ammonia, distilled. For hysteria, flatulence, colic, gastric acidity, and gastric upset. (34)

Ammoniae fortior, aqua; —, liquor: Stronger solution of ammonia (NH_3) in water (twenty-eight percent). (8,39)

Ammoniae hydriodas: See ammonii iodidum. (40)

Ammoniae hydrochloras: Ammonium chloride, see ammonii chloridi. (40)

Ammoniae succinatus, spiritus: Amberized spirits of ammonia, of ammonia water and oil of amber, as a smelling salt and for snakebite. (39)

Ammoniae sulphas: Ammonium sulfate. (44)

Ammoniareti cupri, pilluli: Pill of the ammonium salt of copper, with bread crumbs. (39)

Ammoniatum, oleum: Ammoniated oil, i.e., ammoniae, linimentum. (39)

Ammonic: Irregular chemical name for the ammonium ion, NH_4^+. For compounds see ammonii. (29)

NOTE: Ammonii vs Ammoniae: Both variants occur regularly, depending on source. USP and BP seem to prefer the latter. See both sets of entries for compounds and formulations of ammonia.

Ammonii acetas; Ammonium acetate: Ammonium acetate is a mild diaphoretic and expectorant used especially in childhood, usually as the liquor. (42)

Ammonii acetatis (fortior), liquor: Ammonium acetate, approximately seven percent with small amounts of acetic and carbonic acids, by addition of ammonium carbonate to acetic acid. A mild diaphoretic and diuretic. The BPC also specified a four-fold stronger (fortior) version. (8,42)

Ammonii acetatis concentratus, liquor: Similar to fortius preparation, but in NF from neutralization of acetic acid with ammonium carbonate, followed by dilution water. (46)

Ammonii benzoas: Ammonium benzoate, the ammonium salt of benzoic acid. See benzoicum, acidum. Used similarly, it is primarily an expectorant. (8,42)

Ammonii bicarbonas: Ammonium bicarbonate, primarily a stimulant used in place of ammonium carbonate as it is less unpleasant. (42)

Ammonii bromidi, elixir: Elixir of ammonium bromide, made with ammonium bromide and diluted, sweetened aromatic elixir. See amonii bromidum and also bromide. (31)

Ammonii bromidum effervescens: An effervescent preparation, with sodium bicarbonate, tartaric acid, citric acid, and sugar. Sedative. (42)

Ammonii bromidum: Ammonium bromide, from neutralization of hydrobromic acid (see hydrobromicum dilutum, acidum) with ammonia or ammonium carbonate. Primarily used as a sedative and for control of epilepsy, see bromide. (8)

Ammonii carbonas [aqua]: Ammonium carbonate, $(NH_4)_2CO_3$, or the solution thereof. A general stimulant, emetic, gastric stimulant, and carminative. (8,39)

Ammonii caustici spiritosus, liquor: Liquor of the stronger spirit of ammonia, see ammoniae, spiritus. (34)

Ammonii chloridi, lotion: A simple solution of ammonium chloride, used as a resolvent and sedative. (34)

Ammonii chloridi, mistura: Mixture of ammonium chloride and purified extract of glycyrrhiza in water. An expectorant. (34,46)

Ammonii chloridi, tabellae; Ammon. Chlor., tabellae: Ammonium chloride tablets. Such tablets are still available for acidification of urinary pH in humans and veterinary use and as a supplement for chloride or following net loss of hydrochloric acid, i.e., following vomiting. (The ammonium ion is excreted, leaving behind a proton and chloride ion, thus this is a replacement for HCl, which is too acidic to be taken by mouth.)

Ammonii chloridi, troschisci: Troches of ammonium chloride, licorice extract, tragacanth, sugar, and syrup of tolu. (8)

Ammonii chloridi, vapor: Ammonia inhaled via a solution of hydrochloric acid so that ammonium chloride salt was inhaled. (42)

Ammonii chloridum: Ammonium chloride, NH_4Cl. Used to increase secretions of the mucous membranes, mild cholegogue, diaphoretic, and diuretic. (8)

Ammonii citras: Ammonium citrate, a mild expectorant and diuretic. (42)

Ammonii citratis (fortior), liquor; Ammonii citri, liquor; Ammon. citr., liq.: A solution of ammonium citrate 12.5%. The pharmaceutical use of this material is unclear. It is, however, used as a clearing agent in black and white photographic processing, and such chemicals were carried by pharmacists with some regularity. The BPC also specifies a four-fold stronger (fortior) version. (8,42)

Ammonii ferri alum; Ammon. Ferri Alum: Ammonium ferric alum, or ferric alum, i.e., ferric ammonium sulfate, $FeNH_4(SO_4)$, made by combining ferric sulfate and ammonia solutions. Pharmaceutical use is poorly documented, but may be a source of iron. This is primarily a photographic chemical.

Ammonii fluoridum: Ammonium fluoride, toxic, used in "very dilute solution" orally for enlarged spleen or goiter. (42)

Ammonii hydrochloras: Ammonium hydrochloride, NH_4Cl. (44)

Ammonii hypophosphitis, syrupus: Syrup of ammonium hypophosphite, of ammonium hypophosphite flavored with compound spirit of vanillin (vanillini compositus, spiritus). (31)

Ammonii ichthosulphonas: See ichthymol. (42)

Ammonii iodidi, linimentum: A non-staining topical iodine preparation with oils of rosemary and lavender, and camphor. (34,46)

Ammonii iodidum: Ammonium iodide, NH_4I, is used as an iodine supplement and is the primary ingredient in "colorless tincture of iodine," used as an antiseptic. (42) From potassium iodide and ammonium sulphate. For syphilis. (8)

Ammonii muriae (pulv.); —murias; —mur.; —muriat.: This is the salt of ammonia with muriatic (hydrochloric) acid, i.e., ammonium chloride (powdered). See ammonii chloridum and related entries.

Ammonii nitras: Ammonium nitrate, NH_4NO_3, by action of nitric acid on ammonium carbonate. A diuretic, but rarely used therapeutically. Primarily used in the preparation of nitrous oxide, i.e., laughing gas. (8,42)

Ammonii persulphas: Ammonium persulfate, used in the preparation of other persulfate compounds. (42)

Ammonii phosphas: Ammonium phosphate, a mild expectorant, diuretic, and diaphoretic and for "spasmodic labor pains." (42)

Ammonii sesquicarbonas: Ammonium carbonate, see ammonii carbonas. (40)

Ammonii valeratis, elixir: Elixir of ammonium valerate, made with ammonium valerate and chloroform dissolved in aromatic elixir, colored and flavored with vanilla, see valariana.

Ammonii valerianas: See valeriana. (8)

Ammonii valerianatis (et quininae), elixir: Elixir of ammonium valerianate with or without quinine, as specified by NF, see valariana. (45)

Ammonio-chloride of mercury; Ammonio-mercuric chloride: Ammonium chloride and corrosive mercuric chloride were dissolved in water and allowed to co-crystallize. Highly antiseptic, but less corrosive than mercuric chloride. Used as a treatment for gauze or lint to create a wound dressing, which was colored with aniline blue and which turned white as the dressing was soaked through, making it easy to identify when dressings required changing. It was also given by injection as a convenient and non-irritating form of mercury for the treatment of syphilis. (8)

Ammonio-ferric alum: See roche alum. (40)

Ammonio-formaldehyde: Hexamine, see hexaminium. (40)

Ammonium carbonicum pyro-oleosum: A mixture of ammonium carbonate with animal oil. (3)

Ammonium hydrosulphide: Ammonium sulphide. (40)

Ammonium ichthosulphonate: See icthamol. (40)

Ammonium iso-valerianate: Ammonium valerianate, see valariana. (40)

Ammonium muriaticum; Ammon. mur.: See sal ammoniac. (29)

Ammonium sulpho-ichthyolate: Ichthyol. (3)

Ammonium sulphydrate: Ammonium sulphide. (40)

Ammonium valerate: See ammonii valerianas. (40)

Amomi, semen: See pimento. (40)

Amomi repentis, tinctura: See cardamomi, tinctura. (40)

Amomum repens; —zingiber: See cardamom and zingiber (ginger), respectively. (39)

Amomum; Amomum granum paradisum: Term used for zingiberaceous plants, including cardamom, grains of paradise. (1)

Ampelopsis: American ivy, Virginian creeper, five leaves, woodbine, false grape, wild wood vine, *Ampelopsis quinquefolia*, an alterative, tonic, astringent, and expectorant. (33)

Amphion: Opium. (3)

Amphotropin: Hexamine camphorate. (40)

Amplosia: Unfermented grape juice. (3)

Amygdala amara: Bitter almond, seed of *Prunus amygdalus* var. *amara*. Figure 3-15. (1, 8)

Amygdala dulcis: Sweet almond, or Jordan almond, the seed of *Prunus amygdala* var. *dulcis*. Figure 3-15. (1, 8)

Amygdala: Almond, *Amygdala communis*, which has sweet and bitter variant below. Figure 3-15. (8)

Amygdalae (expressum), oleum; —, emulsum: Oil of sweet almond, which is expressed by crushing, not by distillation. The emulsion, or milk, of sweet almond was formed using sweet almond, sugar, and acacia in water. (8)

Amygdalae amarae, essentia: Essence of bitter almond, i.e., the essential oil distilled from the almond, often diluted with some alcohol.

Amygdalae amarae, mistura: A mixture of bitter almonds and water, triturated together and filtered. A base for skin lotions (BPC). (42)

Amygdalus communis
Published by IC Woodville May 1. 1791.

Fig. 3-15 Amygdala or almond, bitter or sweet variants.

Amygdalae amarae, oleum; —, aqua; —, spiritus: The oil of bitter almond, obtained by crushing and distillation; water of bitter almond, of the oil plus water; or spirit of bitter almond, from the oil with alcohol. Per the US dispensatory (1912), "the spirit is intended for medicinal use; it must not be used for flavoring foods." (8)

Amygdalae composita, essentia: Compound essence of almond, of the essential oil, tincture of vanilla, and simple tincture of benzoin. A flavoring agent. (42)

Amygdalae compositum, elixir: Compound elixir of almond, a flavoring elixir of very low alcoholic strength, containing oil of bitter almond (amygdalae amarae, oleum), vanillin, and orange flower water (aurantii florum, aqua). (31)

Amygdalae compositus, pulvis; Amygd. co., pulv.: Powdered almonds in sugar and gum of acacia.

Amygdalae persicae, oleum: Oil derived by crushing peach kernels. (40)

Amygdalae, lac: Milk of almonds, of sweet almond kernels in sugar water. (39)

Amygdalae, mistura: See amygdalae (expressum), oleum. In the BPC, compound powder of almonds mixed in water, a demulcent mixture used as a pleasant tasting vehicle. (42)

Amygdalae, syrupus: Syrup of almond, containing both sweet and bitter almond, sugar, orange flower water, water, and simple syrup. (8)

Amygdalarum, conserva: See amygdalae compositum, pulvis. 40)

Amygdalinum; Amygdalin: Alkaloid from bitter almond or seeds of other plants, which liberates hydrocyanic acid on hydrolysis in the stomach, used as per almond, i.e., expectorant. (42)

Amygdalus persica: Peach tree, *Amygdalus persica*, a stomachic. Figure 3-16. (32)

Amyl alcohol; Alcohol amylicum: Fusel oil, n-penatanol, a five-carbon linear alcohol, used to make amyl nitrite and as a solvent in some reactions. (8)

Amyl colloid: A preparation of amyl hydrate, aconitine, and veratrine in collodion. The anesthetic effect of the alkaloids was enhanced by the evaporative cooling of the amyl hydride (amyl alcohol). Very effective for topical treatment of neuralgia. (8)

Amyl hydrate; Amylenum hydratum; Amylene hydrate: Amylic alcohol, a five carbon alcohol (technically, tert-amyl alcohol, $(C_2H_5\text{-})(CH_3\text{-})_2C\text{-OH}$). A sedative hypnotic. (8,40)

Amyl hydride: A trivial name for the five-carbon hydrocarbon, pentane.

Amyl nitras; Amyl nitrite: Amyl nitrite, the nitrite of the 5-carbon amyl (pentyl) alcohol, from the reaction of sodium nitrite (sodii nitris) and amyl alcohol. This was provided in a glass capsule which could be crushed in a handkerchief and the volatile liquid inhaled, causing a rushing sensation due to dilation of blood vessels, rapid heart rate, and a "high" sensation of short duration. In 1867, Brunton noted that peripheral vessels were constricted in cases of angina pectoris, and suggested using amyl nitrite therapeutically, which was highly effective. We now recognize angina pectoris as due to coronary artery constriction, and continue to use nitrites and nitrates for this condition, including nitroglycerin (glonoini, spiritus). Amyl nitrite remains an inhalational drug of abuse. (8)

Amyl nitritis, mistura: A mixture of amyl nitrite in alcohol, simple syrup, and distilled water with gum tragacanth, an oral vasodilator. (42)

Amylase: Diastase, an enzyme that breaks down starch. Taken as digestive aid or added to starchy food to assist in digestion. (40,42)

Amylene chloral: Sedative mixture of amylene and chloral hydrates. (3,40)

Amylhydride: A trivial name for the five-carbon hydrocarbon, pentane. (3)

Amyli et acidi borici, cataplasma: Poultice of starch with boric acid. Used as antiseptic for ulcerated wounds. (42)

Amyli, cataplasma: Poultice of starch and water. Used for superficial ulcerations. (42)

Amyli, decoctum; Amyli, mucilago: Decoction or mucilage of starch, of starch in water, briefly boiled. A demulcent and ingredient in other preparations. (34,40)

Amyli, glycerinum; —, glyceritum: Glycerite of starch, ten percent starch in glycerin, a thick, clear substance used in preparing other materials. (8) A topical emollient for skin. (42)

Amyli pulvis: Powdered starch.

Amylodextrin: Soluble starch. (3)

Amyloform: An iodinated amyl alcohol, used as a disinfectant. (40)

Amylum: Starch, generally corn starch. Used as a carrier for dusting powders or material to be insufflated. The glycerite (see glyceritum amyli) is used as a base for suppositories. (1,8)

Amylum iodatum: Iodized starch, used internally for syphilis or cachexia, and topically as a wound dressing. (42)

Amylum tritici; Amyl. tritic.: "Wheat starch," i.e., flour.

Amytal: Amyl-ethyl-barbituric acid, amobarbital, a sedative. (40)

Anacahuite wood: Wood from Mexico, said to be effective in phthisis. Unofficial. (44)

Anacardium: Cashew tree, *Anacardium occidentale*. "Nuts" (anacards, cashew nuts) used are not a true nut, but portion of cashew fruit (cashew apple). (1)

Anacyclus: See pyrethrum. (39)

Anaesthyl: Mixture of methyl and ethyl chlorides. Topical refrigerant anaesthetic. (40)

Anagallis: Common pimpernel, *Anagallis arvensis*, and possibly other plants such as water speedwell, *Veronica anagallis-aquatica*. (1)

Amygdalus Persica

Published by W. Woodville June 1 1790.

Fig. 3-16 Amygdalus Persica, the peach.

A

Anagallis arvensis: Red chickweed, red pimpernel, scarletpPimpernel, poor man's weather glass, *Anagallis Arvensis*. Said to be stimulant. (33)

Analgen: See quinalgen. (40)

Analgene; Analgesine: Antipyrin, antipyrene, an antipyretic. (3,40)

Analgesic balsam; Analgesicum, compositum, unguentum: See methylis salicylatis compositum, unguentum. (42)

Anamirta cocculus: See cocculus. (39)

Anaphromeli: Clarified honey, see mel despumatum. (3)

Anarcotine: See narcotine. (40,42)

Anas; Anatra {*Italian*}**:** Duck. (1)

Anchusa(e); Anchusa officinalis: Common alkanet, *Anchusa officinalis* (sometimes *tinctoria*), and related plants. A red coloring agent. Root and herb used. See buglossum. Figures 3-17 and 3-18. (1,42) There is considerable confusion between *Alkana* and *Alkanet*, with later creation of the genus *Anchusa* and with variable use of *officinalis* or *tinctoria* for the official Common Alkanet or Dyer's Bugloss, the current official name being *Anchusa officinalis*.

Anda, oil of: Oil of *Anda brasiliensis* seed, purgative. Unofficial. (44)

Andeer's lotion: Resorcinol solution in water, disinfectant. See resorcini, lotio. (40,42)

Anderson's Scot(t)s pills: Aloes with colocynth and gamboge, a cathartic. Variant of aloes et mastiches, pilulae. See grana angelica. (34,39)

Andira: Cabbage tree bark, *Andira inermis*, a purgative and anthelmintic. (33)

Andrographidis, infusum; —, liquor: An infusion or solution (BPC) of andrographis, bitter and stomachic. (42)

Andrographis; Andrographidis, tinctura: *Andrographis paniculata* is a plant native to India, used primarily as a bitter in tincture form with alcohol, official in India and eastern British colonies. (40,42)

Andromachi, theriaca; Andromachus: Theriac per the formulation of Andromachus, Roman physician, first century CE, who originated varieties of mithridatum (a universal antidote) and theriac. (1)

Andromeda arborea: Sorrel-wood tree. Unofficial. (44)

Andropogon citratus: See lemon grass, oil of. (40)

Androsaemifolium: See apocynum. (39)

Anemone nemorosa: Wind Flower, *Anemone nemorosa*, very toxic, used for a variety of unrelated conditions, if used at all. (33)

Anemone Patens; —, Praetensis; —, Meadow: American pPulsatilla, Pasque flower, *Anemone patens* or *A. pulsatilla*, used for a wide variety of illnesses, but particularly for eye conditions, including transient blindness. Figure 3-19. (33,39,44)

Anemopsis: Yerba Del Manza, *Anemopsis californica*. For many conditions, including tuberculosis. (32)

Anestile: Mixture of methyl and ethyl chlorides. Topical refrigerant anesthetic. (40)

Anethol: An aromatic substance obtained from oil of (see) anise. Carminative and expectorant. (42)

Anethum; Anethi fructus; Aneto {*Italian*}**; Anethi, aqua; Anethi, oleum:** Dill, dried fruit (fructus) of *Peucidanum graveolens* (*Anethum graveolens* or *Anethi fructus*). Herb and seed used, from which a water is prepared by soaking and from which an oil may be distilled. Use is as per caraway or anise. Antiflatulent, said to be particularly useful for children, and the water is said to be a good vehicle for children's medications (i.e., tastes good!). Figure 3-20. (1,8,42) Note that *Anethum foeniculum* (or *dulce*) is sweet fennel, see foeniculum dulce.

Anetra {*Italian*}**:** Duck. (1)

Angelica seed: Seed of *Angelica atropurpurea*. (40)

Angelica; Angelicae radix: Angelica plant, *Angelica archangelica*, now *Archangelica officinalis*. Root used. Figure 3-21. (1)

Angelicae radicis, fluidextractum; ——, fluidum extractum: Fluid extract of angelica root. A stimulant and expectorant. (31,42,46)

Angelicae, pillulae: Angelic or Frankfurt pill, of aloes and rhubarb, unrelated to Angelica plant. (39)

Angelicae, vin(um): Angelica wine, a sweet wine fortified with brandy to increase alcohol content. This is said to have originated in California and is perhaps named for the city of Los Angeles. One might assume that this is a wine with angelica root, but no documentation suggests that this was the case.

Angineurosin: Nitroglycerin. (3)

Anglicum, sal: "English salt," i.e., that from Epsom, magnesium sufate. (3)

Angustura bark; Angustura, cortex; Angusturae, ___: Alternate name for Cusparia. (8) Infusum angusturae is specified in the USP. (44)

Fig. 3-17 Anchusa tinctoria or alkanet.

Fig. 3-18 Anchusa officinalis.

Fig. 3-19 Anemone.

Anhalonium: Peyote, *Lophophora williamsii* or *Anhalonium lewini*, hallucinogen, used to treat cardiac disturbances. (32)

Anhydro-glucochloral: See glucochloral. (40)

Aniline (oil); Anilinum: Aniline, amido-benzene, starting material for aniline dyes, generally quite toxic. Occasionally used by inhalation with eucalyptus, anise, peppermint, or wintergreen (gaultherium) oil for phthisis, or orally in glycerin for epilepsy. (42)

Aniline red; Anilina rubra; Anil. Rub.: A synthetic dyestuff. There are many analine dyes, red being the most commonly used as a colorant in medicines. Apothecary shops dealt routinely in dyes for clothing and other purposes. Other colors of aniline dyes may well be found.

Anima articulorum: "Life of the joints," a name given to colchicum for its ability to cure gout. (3)

Anima hepatis: Ferrum vitriolatum, or ferrous sulfate. (39)

Anima rhei: Aqueous tincture of rhubarb. (3)

Animal oil; Animale Dippelii, oleum: Dippel's animal oil, bone oil. Oily preparation derived from hartshorn per J. C. Dippel, German physician (1673-1734), originator. (1,3)

Animale foetidum, oleum: Crude oil of hartshorn or Dippel's animal oil, immediately above. (3)

Animé; Gum animé: Gum of *Hymenaea courbaril*, of South America. Unofficial. (44)

Anise; Anisum; Anisi, fructus; Anisi oleum: Anise, the fruit of *Pimpinella anisum*, of Asia. Used interchangeably with star anise, illicium. A volatile oil is distilled directly. Usage was as per other volatile oils such as clove (see caryophyllus). Stimulant, carminative, antiseptic, and the oil is used for flavoring many other formulations. Figure 3-22. (1,8,42)

Anise [fruit], star: See anisum estrellatum. (42)

Aniseed cordial: See anisi, elixir. (40)

Anisi, aqua; —, spiritus; —, elixir: Water of anise, from the oil and water, spirit of anise, from the oil in alcohol, or the "elixir" (cordial). The latter misnamed (not a true elixir) per the 1926 US Dispensory. Of anethol, oil of fennel, spirit of bitter almond, syrup, water, and a small quantity of alcohol. A flavoring and carminative favored for children. (3,8,31,42)

Anisi, essentia: Essence of anise, i.e., the distilled essential oil, often diluted with some alcohol.

Anisi, semen; Anisi sem.: Anise seed.

Anisi stellati fructus; Anisum estrellatum; —stellatum: Star anise, *Illicium verum*. (1)

Anisic Acid; Anisicum, acidum: Para-methoxy-benzoic acid, an organic acid from oxidation of anethol, derived from anise. Intestinal anti-inflammatory similar to salacetic acid, liberates salicylate in the intestine. (42)

Anitra {*Italian*}: Duck. (1)

Annatta; Annatto: Fruit pulp of *Bixa orellana*. Seed is used as a source of red colorant. (40,44)

Annidalin: Aristol, trade name antiseptic, thymol di-iodide. (3)

Anodyne balsam: See opiatum, linimentum. (39)

Anodyne drops: See Hoffmann's anodyne. (40)

Anodyne electuary: Confection of opium, BP, similar to opiata, confectio. (40)

Anodyne liniment: See opii, linimentum. (34)

Anodyne necklace: A necklace of peony wood, said to relieve pain and cure epilepsy. (39)

Anodyne; Anodynum: Anodyne, i.e., a remedy for pain. Containers sometimes carry this label alone, the contents presumably known to the apothecary. (1)

Anodynin: Antipyrine, analgesic and antipyretic. (40)

Anodynus (Hoffmanni), liquor: Hoffmann's anodyne, see etheris compositus, spiritus. (3)

Anodynus mineralis, liquor: See etheris compositus, spiritus. (40)

Anonis: Plant of genus *Ononis*, the rest-harrow. Herb and root used. (1)

Anser: Goose. (1)

Ansyncriticum, medicamentum: A remedy beyond criticism or unparalleled, a panacea. (39)

Ant oil, artificial: Furfural, an organic solvent. (3)

Ant. et Pot. Tart.: See antimonii et potassii tartras. (29)

Antacrida, tinctura; Antacrid tincture: A tincture of the corrosive chloride of mercury (corrosive sublimate), guaiac, Canada turpentine, oil of sassafras, and alcohol. It is anti-acrid, i.e., disinfectant and deodorant. (46)

Antennaria margaritiacea: Life everlasting plant, astringent and expectorant. Unofficial. (33,44)

Anethum graveolens

Fig. 3-20 <u>Anethum</u> or dill.

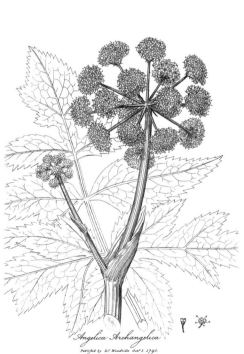

Angelica Archangelica

Fig. 3-21 Angelica.

Pimpinella Anisum

Fig. 3-22 Anisum or anise.

Anthemidis et papavaris, decoctum: Decoction of chamomile with bruised poppy capsule (as a source of opium), said to be used hot as an anodyne for abscesses. (42)

Anthemis; Anthemidis, aqua; —, oleum; —, infusum (concentratum); liquidum, extractum: Chamomile, the flower heads of *Anthemis nobilis*. It is a typical bitter and is employed as such (see columba for detail of use), in the form of a water, tea (infusum), or liquid extract. Chamomile is of course also a popular tea used in convalescence from various illnesses even today. The oil of chamomile was standard in the BP and used as a stomachic and carminative. A concentrated infusion with a small amount of oil of chamomile was also specified in the BPC. Figure 3-23. (8,34,42)

Anthemis cotula: See cotula (fetidis). (39)

Antherosperma moschata: Australian sassafras, the bark of which yields an oil said to be diaphoretic and diuretic as well as a cardiac sedative. Unofficial. (44)

Anthion: Potassium persufate. (3)

Anthora: Unidentified mountain plant similar to wolfsbane. (1)

Anthos, conserva; —, c.; —, oleum: Conserve or oil of rosemary. (3)

Anthos; Anthos flores; —herba: Rosemary, or the flowers or herb. See rosmarinus. (1,3)

Anthrakokali (sulphuretted): A coal-derived material, plain or sulphuretted, for scrofula, rheumatism, and other maladies. (3,44)

Anthrapurpurin diacetate: A synthetic purgative, which stains the stool bright red. (40)

Anthraquinone; Anthraquinonum: Anthraquinone is used in preparation of anthrapurpurin and other derivatives. (42)

Anthrarobine: Dioxyanthranol, leucoalizarin, a dermal antiseptic obtained by reduction of alizarin red dye. (3,42)

Anthriscus cerefolium: Chervil. See cerefolium. (39,44)

Anti-infective vitamin: Vitamin A. (40)

Anti-neuritic vitamin: Vitamin B-1, thiamin. (40)

Antiasthmatic elixir: See euphorbiae compositum, elixir.

Antibilious physic: See jalapae compositus, pulvis. (34)

Antibilious pills, Dixon's: A proprietary formulation of the nineteenth century, primarily a cathartic, being made of aloes, scammony, rhubarb, and antimony tartrate. (39)

Fig. 3-23 Anthemis or chamomile.

Anticatarrhal powder; Anticatarrhalis, pulvis: Catarrh snuff or powder, of morphine hydrochloride, acacia, and bismuth subnitrate. (46)

Anticatarrhal salts: See eucalyptus compositus, vapor. (40)

Antidiarrheal mixture: See camphorae acida, mistura. (34)

Antidotum fuchsi: Hydrated ferric oxide, supposed arsenic antidote. (3)

Antidotum h(a)emagogum: Emmenagogue from root of long birthwort, root of elecampane, pellitory of Spain, seeds of rue, lupin, myrrh, etc. (1)

Antidysenterica, mistura: See camphorae acida, mistura. (34)

Antidyspeptic pills: See pilulae antidyspepticae. (34)

Antifebrin; Antifebrinum: See acetanilid.

Antifungin: Magnesium borate. (3)

Antihypo: Potassium percarbonate, a photographic chemical. (3)

Antihysteric plaster: See emplastrum antihystericum. (39)

Antihystericum, sal: Potassium acetate. (3)

Antiia gastrica: Stomach pump. (3)

Antilusin; Antilytic serum: Normal horse serum. (40)

Antimonial ointment: See antimonii tartarati, unguentum. (34)

Antimonialis (co.)(compositis), pulvis: Antimonial powder, James' powder, of antimony oxide and calcium phosphate. (8)

Antimoniated hydrogen: Antimony hydride, highly toxic but rapid means to deliver antimony. Unofficial. (44)

Antimonii, butyrum: See butter of antimony. (39)

Antimonii, cerussa: "Wax of antimony," antimony nitrate, used as a cathartic. (39)

Antimonii, crocus: Antimony oxide, now known to be partially the oxysulfite. (39)

Antimonii, emplastrum: Plaster of antimony tartrate and potassa in burgundy pitch. (44)

Antimonii, essentia: See antimonium vitrificatum. (39)

Antimonii, flores: Antimony flowers, the antimony sesquioxide (trioxide). (3)

Antimonii, tinctura: Tincture of antimony, containing antimony potassium tartrate (antimonii et potassii tartras) in water and alcohol, colored with caramel and flavored with acetic ether (ether, aceticum). "Tincture of antimony may be dispensed when vinum antimonii (wine of antimony) is ordered." (31)

Antimonii, vinum: Antimonial wine, from antimony potassium tartrate, or tartar emetic. This is a powerful drug, and the wine is said to provide a convenient way to administer small quantities (see antimonii et potassii tartras). (8,31)

Antimonii, vitrum: Glass of antimony, by heating of the sulphurette until fused. Antimonial medication, but said to be quite variable as it is an unpredictable mixture of oxides and sulfides, (and probably irregularly absorbed) and thus little used. Unofficial. (44)

Antimonii, butyrum: See butter of antimony. (39)

Antimonii, cerussa: "Wax of antimony," antimony nitrate, used as a cathartic. (39)

Antimonii, crocus: Antimony oxide, now known to be partially the oxysulfite. (39)

Antimonii, emplastrum: Plaster of antimony tartrate and potassa in burgundy pitch. (44)

Antimonii, essentia: See antimonium vitrificatum. (39)

Antimonii, flores: Antimony flowers, the antimony sesquioxide (trioxide). (3)

Antimonii (tartarati), unguentum: Tartar emetic ointment, unguentum stibiatum. Of antimony tartrate in a simple ointment base. Produces a pustular eruption as a means of counter-irritation, but could cause serious skin injury and scarring. (34)

Antimonii chloridi (liquor): Antimony chloride liquor, a solution of antimony in hydrochloric acid. Corrosive. Occasional escharotic for infected wounds or cancerous growths. (8,42)

Antimonii compositi, pillulae: Compound pills of antimony, Plummer's pills, of mild mercurous chloride (hydrargyri chloridum mite), sulphurated antimony (antimonii sulphuratum), guaiac, and castor oil. A cathartic. (8)

Antimonii et potassii tartras: Antimony and potassium tartrate, tartrated antimony, tartar emetic, by action of potassium tartrate (potassii tartras) on antimony trioxide (antimonii oxidum). A popular and effective emetic agent. (8)

Antimonii oxidum: Antimony oxide, antimony trioxide, Sb_2O_3, by reaction of the chloride with water and subsequent treatment with sodium carbonate. Expectorant and diaphoretic in small doses, but a violent emetic followed by collapse and toxicity in larger doses. (8,42)

Antimonii oxysulphuret: See antimonii sulphuretum. (40)

Antimonii potassio-tartrate: Tartarated antimony, see antimonii et potassii tartras. (40)

Antimonii sulph(ureticum) aureum: Golden sulphurated antimony. (40)

Antimonii sulphidum (purificatum): Antimony sulfide, Sb_2S_3, naturally occurring or purified. (8)

Antimonii sulphuret(ic)um praecipitatum; Antimonii Sulph. Praecip.: A mixture of antimony and its vitriol (crude sulfate), said to be red antimony sulfide, Sb_2S_5. (39,40)

Antimonii terchloridi, liquor: See antimonii chloridi, liquor. (44)

Antimonii vitrum ceratum: A mixture of vitrified antimony (antimonium vitrim or vitrificatum) and yellow wax. Cathartic, emetic, and relatively toxic. (39)

Antimonine: Antimony lactate. (3)

Antimonium, vitriol: Sulfurated antimony, or kermes mineralis, see antimonium sulfuratum below. (39)

Antimonium album: An archaic term, "white antimony" is properly bismuth. (3)

Antimonium calcareo phosphoratum: See antimonialis, pulvis. (39)

Antimonium calcinatum: Calcined antimony nitrite, a weak diaphoretic and emetic. (39)

Antimonium diagrediatum: A mixture of antimony and scammony. (39)

Antimonium diaphoreticum (lotum)(nigrum): Diaphoretic antimony, produced by heating antimony and nitre. Same as antimonium calcinatum. (8,39)

Antimonium muriatum: Thought to be antimony chloride, now understood to be the oxychloride. Corrosive reagent not used in therapeutics, but rather in the preparation of antimony tartrate. (39)

Antimonium nigrum (purificatum); Antim. nig.: Black antimony, i.e., the naturally occuring sulphide ore of antimony, Sb_2S_3, or a purified form. For preparation of the sulphuratum, below. (29,40,42)

Antimonium sulphas (nigrum): See stibum sulphur nigra. Ancient chemistry being inexact, this is actually a tin compound.

Antimonium sulphuratum: Sulphurated antimony, mainly the sulfide (see antimonii sulphidum), with some residual antimony oxide (see antimonium oxidum). Also called kermes mineral, as the red color is reminiscent of kermes insect, from which a red dye is obtained. See antimonii sulphuret(ic)um praecipitatum. A cholegogue in gout and rheumatism and ingredient in other materials. (8,40)

Antimonium tartaratum; Antimonium tartrate: Tartar emetic, antimony tartrate or tartarated antimony, a popular emetic. (42)

Antimonium ustum cum nitro: See antimonium calcinatum. (39)

Antimonium vitrificatum: See antimonii, vitrum. (39)

Antimony: See antimonium (metallic), antimonii (compounds). (8)

Antimony, black: See antimonium nigrum. (40)

Antimony, calcario-phosphorated: Same as antimonialis, pulvis. (39)

Antimony, diaphoretic: Potassium antimonate. (3)

Antimony, liver of: See antimonii, crocus. (40)

Antimony, muriate of: See antimonii, chloridi. (40)

Antimony, prepared sulphuret of: See antimonii sulphuret(ic)um praecipitatum. (40)

Antimony, protoxide of: See antimonii oxidum. (40)

Antimony, regulus of: Metallic antimony. (40)

Antimony, saffron of: See antimonii sulphureticum. (40)

Antimony, sesquicarbonate of: See antimonii oxidum. (40)

Antimony, sulphide of: See antimonium nigrum purificatum. (40)

Antimony needles: Antimony sulphide. (3)

Antimony sulphas nigra; Antimony sulphurette: See stibum sulfur nigra and also antimonii sulphuret(ic)um praecipitatum. (40)

Antineuralgicae, pilulae; Antineuralgic pills: Gross' antineuralgic pills were of quinine sulphate, morphine sulphate, strychnine alkaloid, arsenous acid, and extract of aconite. (34) See also Brown-Séquard's pills. (46)

Antipepsin: Monobromocetanilid, paramonobromo-phenylacetamide. Antipyretic analgesic. (3)

Antiperiodic pills: See pilulae antiperiodicae. (46)

Antiperiodica (sine aloe) (Warburg or Warb.), tinctura; Antiperiodic Tincture: Antiperiodic tincture, Warburg's Tincture with or without (sine) aloe. A complex tincture made from rhubarb, angelica fruit, elecampane, saffron, fennel, gentian, zedoary, cubeb, myrrh, camphor, white agaric, black pepper, cinnamon, ginger, quinine bisulphate, and extract of aloes. "The dose of Warburg's tincture depends on the kind used-whether with aloes or without, and the intended purpose....The larger quantity is given when Doctor Warburg's original directions are followed for administering the remedy in remittent fevers, which were as follows: One-half ounce to be given alone without dilution, after the bowels have been evacuated by any convenient purgative, all drink being withheld. After three hours, another half ounce is to be given." It is an antiperiodic. (31)

Antipestulentiales, pilulae: See pestilentiales, pilulae. (8)

Antiphthisica, tinctura: A tincture of cerussa acetata (lead acetate), used to inhibit sweats in tuberculosis and other lung disorders. (39)

Antipyrin(e); Antipyrina; Antipyrinum: Antipyrin, phenyl-dimethyl-pyrazolone, an antipyretic analgesic employed for relief of fever, pain, and inflammatory conditions. (8)

Antipyrina effervescens (cum caffeina); Antipyrine (with caffeine), effervescent: An effervescent powder of antipyrine, which may also include caffeine for activity against migraine. (42)

Antipyrinae salicylas; Antipyrine salicylate: A compound of antipyrine and salicylic acid which decomposes and delivers both medications. Antipyretic and anti-inflammatory. (42)

Antipyrinae, tablettae: Tablets of antipyrine and starch. (42)

Antirachitic vitamin: Vitamin D. (40)

Antirrhinum linarea: Common toadflax. Unofficial. (44)

Antirrhinum: Plant of genus *Antirrhinum*. (1)

Antiscorbutic vitamin: Vitamin C. (40)

Antiseptic(us): Capable of killing microbes, a disinfectant. Sterile goods are described by "aseptica." (42)

Antiseptic perchloride tablets: See hydrargyrum perchloras. (40)

Antiseptica, tinctura: Alcoholic solution of boric and benzoic acids, thymol, eucalyptol, and oils of peppermint, wintergreen, and thyme. A few drops were dissolved in a glass of water to form an antiseptic mouthwash or gargle. (42)

Antisepticus, liquor: Antiseptic solution, a water and alcohol solution containing 2.5% boric acid with traces of thymol, eucalyptol, menthol and methyl salicylate. "While it possesses feeble antiseptic properties, it is chiefly useful to flavor mouth-washes." (31)

Antiseptol: Cinchonine iodosulphate. Antiseptic. (3)

Antispasmodic tincture: See lobeliae et capsici composita, tinctura. (34)

Antithyroidin, Moebius': Antithyroid serum, outdated treatment for hyperthyroidism. (40)

Ants, oil of: See formicarium, oleum. (40)

Antuitrin: A preparation of dried anterior pituitary. (40)

Aper: Wild boar. (1)

Aperient effervescing powders: See effervescens compositus, pulvis. (34)

Aperientes, quinque radices: Aperient of five roots, i.e., fennel, smallage, parsley, asparagus, butcher's broom. (1)

Aperientis: Laxative, aperient. (1)

Aperione: Phenolphthalein, a mild laxative cathartic. (40)

Aperitivum, elixir: Compound tincture of aloes, probably same as aloes, tinctura or a closely related formula, but not offical. (3)

Aphrodine: Yohimbine derived alkaloids, see yohimbe. (40)

Apii (graeolens), semen; Apii (grav.) s.: Celery seed.

Apii compositus, infusium: Compound infusion of apium (celery) with horseradish, squill, white mustard, mandrake, and queen of the meadow, infused in cider. Particularly used for dropsy, as squill is an active cardiotonic and queen of the meadow a diuretic. (34)

Apii fructus, fluidextractum: Fluid extract of celery fruit. Filtered through an alcohol-wetted filter to remove any separated oil. (31)

Apii graveolentis compositum, elixir; Apii grav. co., elix.: Compound elixir of celery (*Apium graveolens*). Elixirs of celery date to ancient times and varied widely. The NF specifies a nerve stimulant and tonic of celery seed, coca (cocaine), kola, and viburnum prunifolium.

Apii mundificativum: See mundificativum (de apio), unguentum. (1)

Apiol (, liquid); Apiolum: A material obtained from the fruit of *Petroselinum sativum* by extraction with benzine. Emmenogogue used to treat amennorrhea, dysmenorrea, or scanty menstruation when believed due to ovarian failure. (8)

Apiol, white: Crystallized apiol. (40)

Apis (extractum): Bee (i.e., the insect), from which an extract is produced by shaking bees in alcohol. (8,32)

Apium; Apium graveolens; Apium grav. (variant, gray.); Apii graveolentis, fluidum extractum: Smallage, wild celery, *Apium graveolens* or the fluid extract. Root and seed used. (1,46)

Apium dulce: Celery. (1)

Apocodeinae hydrochloridum; Apocodeine hydrochloride: From the action of zinc chloride and hydrochloric acid on codeine. An emetic and expectorant, but less potent than apomorphine. (42)

Apocyni, tinctura: Tincture of Canadian hemp, of same in alcohol, tonic and diuretic for dropsy. (42)

Apocynum (cannabinum); Apocyni fluidum, extractum: The root of Canadian hemp, *Apocynum cannabinum*, or the fluid extract. A diuretic said to be helpful in dropsy, and perhaps having some of the beneficial cardiac effects of strophanthus. (8,42,44)

Apocynum androsaemifolium: Dog's bane, of North America, emetic. (44)

Apomorphinae, syrupus: Syrup of apomorphine hydrochloride with dilute hydrochloric acid in alcohol, water, and syrup. (42)

Apomorphinae hydrochloras; —hypochloridum: Apomorphine hydrochloride, from dehydration (extraction of a water molecule) of morphine in a closed ampoule using hydrochloric acid. Apomorphine is a powerful emetic, and is largely lacking in other actions of the narcotics. Still in use today as an emetic for treatment of overdoses, although syrup of ipecac is generally preferred, in part due to the prolonged vomiting sometimes induced by apomorphine. (8,40)

Apostolicum, unguentum; Apostolorum, unguentum: Ointment of the Apostles, also known as unguentum dodecapharmacum, or ointment of twelve ingredients: myrrh, frankincense, bdellium, galbanum, opopanax, rosin, turpentine, gum ammoniac, root of long birthwort, verdigris, litharge, and white wax. Used to treat wounds and ulcers. (8)

Apothem; Apozema: A strong decoction or infusion of any vegetable drug. (1,39)

Appio {*Italian*}: Smallage. (1)

Apple acid: Malic acid. (3)

Apple of Peru: See stramonium. (39)

Apple oil: Amyl valerate. (3)

Apyonin {*French*}: Designation for yellow pyoktanin, an antiseptic. (3)

Apyrothium: Sulfur. (3)

Aqua: Water, either refers to water itself (distilled is assumed) or to a specific medicated water, usually derived by distillation from water containing a particular plant. Later uses can refer to water for a particular purpose, i.e., a tonic water or eye water. (1,4)

Aqua ____: Water, a water solution, see ____, aqua if not listed below. (8)

Aqua; Aqua destillata; —distillata: Water, distilled water, H_2O. Distilled water was generally used in the formulation of remedies. Water in its various forms (steam, ice) and at various temperatures was also used extensively as an external therapeutic in the form of baths or soaks of the body or various body parts. The latter becoming an entire specialty, balneology. (8)

Aqua aerata; Aqua aeris fixi: Aerated water or water of "fixed air" (carbon dioxide), i.e., carbonated water. (39)

Aqua aluminus, composita; Aqua aluminosa, Bateana: Compound aluminum water or Bate's aluminum water. (39) Variously described, but usually a solution of alum and zinc sulfate (vitriolated zinc), used as a topical astringent.

Aqua anthos: See rosmarinae, aqua. (40)

Aqua benedicta co.: This is aqua calcis compositus, the compound water of lime, also known as Benedict's solution. (40)

Aqua binelli: "Italian nostrum," styptic, thought to contain creosote. Unofficial. (44)

Aqua cardiaca: Cardiac (heart) water, a solution with cardamom, cinnamon, ginger, and orange peel, similar to the cardiac electuary. (39)

Aqua concentrata(e) ____: Concentrates of the standard waters of the BPC, used for later formulation. They were about 40-fold concentrates and are described as aqua concentrata anethi, camphorae, carui, chloroformi, cinnamomi, foeniculi, menthae (piperitae and viridis), and pimentae. See corresponding water under ____, aqua. (42)

Aqua dulcis: "Sweet water," chloroform water, see chloroformi, aqua. Used as a flavoring or preservative. (40)

Aqua epidemica: See aqua odorifera.

Aqua fluvialis: River water. (44)

Aqua fontana: Spring water.

Aqua fortis: "Strong water," an alchemical term for a crude nitric acid solution made from saltpeter. In later use, this simply referred to nitric acid.

Aqua(e) medicata(e): Standard medicated waters of the BPC, of a volatile oil triturated with calcium phosphate and subsequently dissolved in water at about 0.2 percent. They are described for anethi, anisi, carui, cinnamomi, foeniculi, menthae (piperitae and viridis), and pimentae. In the USP, they are produced instead using powdered talc or pulp from filter paper to disperse the oil. (42)

Aqua nigra: See lotio, nigra. (3,31)

Aqua odorifica; Aq. odorif.: Scented water, aqua epidemica, or plague water. A perfumed water used to treat homes or clothing as a defense against plague.

Aqua phaeged[ae][re]nica flava; —nigra: See lotio flava for the former and for the latter, also called lotio nigra, see hydrargyri flava, lotio. (34)

Aqua phaged[ae][re]nica mitis; —nigra: See nigra, aqua. (40)

Aqua regia: "Water of Kings" or "Royal Water," this is a mixture of hydrochloric and nitric acids, which will dissolve gold. See nitrohydrochloric acid.

Aqua sedativa: See ammoniacalis camphorata, lotio. (31)

Aqua vitae: Water of life, i.e., alcohol or brandy. Note that this is not a reference to the necessity of alcohol, but rather the archaic recognition of distilled spirits or essences (quintessence) conveying the life force. See appendix regarding alchemy. (1)

Aquifolium: Holly plant, *Ilex aquifolium*. (1)

Aquila alba: Calomel. (3)

Aquilegia vulgaris: Columbine, diuretic, diaphoretic, and antiscorbutic. Unofficial. (44)

Ar.; Aromatic(a)(um)(us): Aromatic (adj.) Latin feminine, neuter, masculine respectively.

Arabica, emulsio: See amygdalae, lac. (39)

Arabicae, pillulae: Arabian pills, of aloe, bryonia, myrobilan, citrus and multiple additional ingredients. (39)

Arabicum, gummi: Gum arabic. (1)

Arabicus, costus: See costus. (1)

Arachis; —, oleum: Peanut, *Arachis hypogea*; peanut oil. (40)

Aragon, unguentum: See arogon, unguentum. (1)

Aralia; Araliae, fluidextractum; —, fluidum extractum: American spikenard, spignet, *Aralia racemosa*, rhizome and roots used, or the fluid extract therefrom. An alterative, for rheumatism. (7,31,46)

Aralia (hispida): The Dwarf-elder, *Aralia hispida*, for dropsy. Aralia, not otherwise identified, is more likely to be *A. racemosa*, the Spikenard. (see below). (32)

Aralia nudicaulis: American, wild, or false sarsaparilla, small spikenard, wild licorice, shot bush, *Aralia nudis*, used as per sarsaparilla. (33)

Aralia spinosa; Araliae (spinosa), tinctura: prickly elder, angelica tree, Hercules' club, toothache bush or tree, southern prickly ash, or the tincture thereof, a purgative and for syphilis and rheumatic conditions. (33,34)

Araliae, syrupus: Syrup of aralia or spikenard, of spikenard, yellow-doc and burdock root, guaiac wood, bark of sassafras root and southern prickly ash, elder flowers, and blue flag root, extracted in alcohol and water, filtered and with added sugar. A general alterative for many chronic conditions from ulcers to syphilis. Said to be equivalent to compound syrup of sarsaparilla. (34)

Aranea diadema: Web of the diadem, papal cross, garden or cross Spider, *Aranea diadema*. See tela araneae. (33)

Arantium: See aurantium (1)

Araroba; Araroba powder: A crude powder of chrysarobinum. (1,42)

Arbor vitae: Tree of life, genus *Thuja*. (1)

Arbutus uva ursi: See uva ursi. (39)

Arcaei, balsamum; —, linimentum; —, unguentum: An ointment (balsam, liniment) made from gum elemi, lard, and turpentine per Francesco Arcaeus, physician, Spain (1493–1567). (1,3)

Arcanum: Any compound remedy, i.e., having multiple therapeutic ingredients. From the Latin, meaning "secret." (39)

Arcanum corallinum: 1. Crude form of red mercuric oxide, literally a "red secret." (1) 2. Coral secret, red nitrate of mercury as prepared and named by Paracelsus. (39)

Arcanum duplicatum: "Double secret," residue from evaporation of saltpeter and vitriol, crude potassium sulfate. (1,3)

Arcei balsamum; —linimentum: See Arcaei. (1)

Archangelica atropurpurea: Purple angelica, masterwort, high sngelica, great angelica, *Archangelica atropurpurea*. A close relative of *Archangelica officinalis* or *Angelica archangelica*. See angelica. (33)

Archil: A purple liquid prepared from lichens. See lakmus. (40)

Arctium lappa: Burdock, see lappa. (40)

Arctostaphylus uva ursi: See uva ursi. (39)

Ardea: Heron (bird). (1)

Areca (nut); Areca po.: Betel nut or powder of same. See betel nut.

Aregon, unguentum: See arogon, unguentum.

Argein: Silver proteinate, a complex of proteinaceous material and metallic silver. A topical disinfectant, for gonorrhea among other uses. (40)

Argemone (mexicana): Prickly Poppy, *Argemone mexicana*, an emetic, purgative, anodyne, and narcotic; juice used topically for eye conditions. (33,44)

Argentamin: Ethylene-diamine-silver phosphate, an astringent and disinfectant. (40)

Argenti, sal: Silver nitrate. (3)

Argenti, tectum: "Cover silver" which is bismuth, condensed out in the cover of a retort or other equipment used in refining of other metals. (40)

Argenti citras: Silver citrate, used as a topical powder to dry and clean wounds and ulcers and as an injection for gonorrhea and cystitis. (42)

Argenti cyanidum: Silver cyanide, from potassium cyanide and silver nitrate, AgCN. Used to prepare solutions of hydrogen cyanide. Toxic, and will evolve cyanide gas on contact with moisture or acid. (8)

Argenti iodidum: Silver iodide, AgI. (8)

Argenti nitras fusas; —induratus: Toughened, or fused silver nitrate, a stick or styptic pencil formed from molten silver nitrate and a small amount of hydrochloric acid. Lunar caustic. Used topically to cauterize or control bleeding. (8)

Argenti nitras mitagatus: This is similar to the fusas or induratus preparation, but less potent (mitigatus) due to the use of about two parts potassium nitrate for each one part of silver nitrate. (42)

Argenti nitras: Silver nitrate, $AgNO_3$, by action of nitric acid on silver. Used in various dilutions as a caustic to obliterate growths or lesions, to cauterize wounds, to control bleeding, or as a topical for skin, oral, and even gastro-intestinal disturbances. Still in use as a topical cauterizing agent and topical antimicrobial. (8)

Argenti oxidum: Silver oxide, Ag_2O. Used orally for gastric pain, internal bleeding, and menorrhagia, usually as a pill with kaolin. It is poorly absorbed and has primarily local activity in the GI tract. (8,42)

Argentic quinaseptol: Silver oxychinolin-sulphonate, a disinfectant powder. (40)

Argentic: Irregular chemical name for the silver ion, Ag^{2+}. For compounds see argenti. (29)

Argentina: Silver Weed, Wild Tansy, Goose Tansey, Goose Grass (*Potentilla anserina*). (1)

Argentol: Silver oxychinolin-sulphonate, a disinfectant powder. (40)

Argentum: Silver (i.e., the metal). (1)

Argentum ____: A variant of argenti, i.e., for silver nitrate one sees argentum nitratum in place of the proper argenti nitratum. (39)

Argentum créde; —colloidum: Colloidal silver, a finely divided form of metallic silver, antimicrobial. (40)

Argentum fugitivum: "Fugitive" (fleeing) or "quick" (alive) silver, i.e., mercury. (3)

Argentum musivum: "Mosaic silver" a pigment used in mosiac tile, of tin and bismuth amalgamated with quicksilver. (3)

Argentum vivum: Quick (i.e., live) silver, i.e., mercury metal. (1,3)

Argil; Argilla: Clay, or in pharmacy, alum. (3,39)

Argilla sulphurica alcalisata: Alum. (3)

Argol(s) (red)(white): See tartar. (3) This is a crude potassium hydrogen tartrate (often containing significant calcium tartrate) derived from wine (hence red or white). (42)

Argonin: Silver caseinate, a complex of metallic silver and milk protein. Antiseptic. See also: silver albuminate. (40)

Argyrol: See silver albuminate. (40)

Aristol: Diiodo-thymol. Disinfectant. (40)

Aristolochia: See serpent(in)aria. (8) Aristolochia is an official equivalent in India for serpentaria. (42) Aristolochia, or "royal birth" was used to assist with difficult labor.

Aristolochia longa: Long birthwort. Root used, to assist in childbirth. Figure 3-24. (1)

Aristolochia rotunda: Round birthwort. Root used, to assist in childbirth. (1)

Aristolochiae concentratus, liquor: A solution of powdered aristolochia in water, a bitter used in India and British colonies. (42)

Aristolochiae, tinctura: See serpentinariae, tinctura. (42)

Armel {*Italian*}**:** Wild rue (see harmula). (1)

Armeniaciae, gummi: Apricot gum, dried gum from branches of apricot tree. (1)

Armeniacum: Gum ammoniac (see ammoniacum, gummi). (1)

Armeniacum, sal: Ammonium chloride, sal ammoniac. (3)

Armoracia (radix); Armoraciae compositus, spiritus: Root of horseradish, *Cochlearia armoracia*, or the compound spirit containing horseradish, oil of bitter orange, nutmeg, alcohol, and water. Chiefly a condiment, but could be used much like mustard oils as a stimulant and mild diuretic. Figure 3-25. (8,42)

Arnica (montana); Arnica (montana) (flores((radix); Arnicae, rhizoma: The flowers or roots of arnica, mountain tobacco, or leopard's bane, *Arnica montana*. Used topically for bruises and the oil used as per other volatile oils (see caryophyllus). Figure 3-26 (1,8,32)

Arnica opodeldoc: See arnicae, linimentum. (40)

Arnicae, emplastrum; —linimentum: Plaster of arnica root, from the extract with resin plaster, or a liniment of same. (8)

Arnicae (radicis), extractum; —fluidum, extractum; —, tinctura: Dried extract, fluid extract, and alcoholic tincture of arnica root. (8)

Arnicae alcoholicum, extractum: Alcoholic extract of powdered arnica, USP. (44)

Arnicae flor(ae)(um) fluidum, extractum: Fluid extract of arnica flowers. (46)

Arnicae flor(ae)(um), tinctura: Alcoholic tincture of flowers of arnica, official in the North American British colonies. (8,42)

Arnotta: Annatto. (40)

Arogon, unguentum: From the Greek "arogo"—to help, an ointment of rosemary, marjoram, sage, bay-laurel, bryony, frankincense, oil of bay-laurel berries, bear's grease, etc. Used to treat nervous disorders. (1)

Aromatic cascara: See cascarae, elixir. (40)

Aromatic mixture of iron: See ferri aromatica, mistura. (34)

Aromatic powder; Aromatic fluid extract: See pulvis aromaticus. (8)

Aromatic spirits of ammonia: See ammoniae aromaticus, spiritus. (8)

Aromatica, tinctura: Aromatic tincture, made from cinnamon, ginger (zingiber), galangal, clove (caryophyllum), and cardamom. A carminative and aromatic. (31)

Aromaticum, vinum: Aromatic wine, see hippocraticum, vinum. (1)

Aromaticum (rubrum), elixir: See elixir aromaticum. (8)

Aromaticus alkalinus, liquor: Alkaline aromatic solution, liquor antisepticus alkalinus, containing two percent each of sodium borate and potassium bicarbonate with small amounts of thymol, eucalyptol and methyl salicylate, sweetened with glycerin and colored with cudbear. (31)

Arquebuscade (water): 1. A distillate of multiple antiseptic and aromatic plants used to treat wounds from an arquebus (sixteenth century gun). (39) 2. Agreeably smelling vulnerary water, "compound sage water" (see salvia). (3)

Arrack: A fermented beverage of various fruits, grain, and sugar cane juice or palm sap. (40)

Arrhenal: Sodium metharsonite, antimicrobial. (40) See sodii metharsenis. (42)

Arrow root, Portland: Starch from arum (specifically, *A. maculatum*). (40)

Arrow root (Brazilian): For arrow root (of the West Indies) see maranta. For Brazilian arrow root (i.e., tapioca) see manihot. (33)

Ars.: Generally in reference to arsenic, arsenii, etc. In Latin, ars (not abbreviated) means "art" and can apply to any specific skill or to a work of art.

Arsacetin: Sodium acetyl para-aminophenyl, antipyretic. (40)

Arsenatis et bromidi, liquor; Arseni et bromidi, liquor: See potassii arsenatis et bromidi, liquor. (40)

Arseni: Variant of (see) arsenici. (44)

Arsenic: See arsenum for metallic, arseni(i) for compounds. (8)

Arsenic, sesquioxide of: See arsenous acid. (40)

Arsenic, white: See arsenum album. (39)

Arsenic acid: H_3AsO_4, or $AsO(OH)_3$, the pentavalent acid of arsenic. Not commonly used in medicine as the pentavalent form is the more toxic. See arsenous acid.

Arsenic antidote; Arsenici, antidotum: See ferri oxidum hydratum cum magnesia. (8)

Arsenic trioxide: See arsenous acid.

Arsenicalis, liquor: See potassii arsenitis, liquor. (40)

Arsenici, solutio mineralis: See potassii arsenatis, liquor. (39)

Fig. 3-24 Aristolochia longa.

Fig. 3- 25 Armoracia or horseradish.

Fig. 3-26 Arnica montana.

Arsenici et hydrargyri iodidi, liquor; Ars. e. hyd. i. (, l.); Ars. et hydr. iod., liq.: A solution of arsenic acid and mercuric iodide, Donovan's solution. "Iiod," presumably typographical error, has been observed on commercial labels. (8,44)

Arsenici hydrochloricus, liquor: A solution of arsenious acid in water with dilute hydrochloric acid, essentially the same as liquor acidi arseniosi. (42)

Arsenicum: Arsenic. (1)

Arsenii bromidum: Arsenic bromide, $AsBr_3$. Used as per arsenious acid via pills of milk sugar and tragacanth, as it decomposes in solution. (42)

Arsenii chloridum: Arsenic chloride, $AsCl_3$. See discussion under the bromide. (42)

Arsenii iodidum: Arsenic iodide, AsI_3. See discussion under the bromide. (8,42)

Arseniosum, acidi; Arsenosi, acidi liquor: Arsenous acid or solution of arsenous acid in hydrochloric acid. (8,42)

Arsenious anhydride: See arsenous acid. (40)

Arsenious wool: A dental fiber (floss) treated with arsenic. (40)

Arsen(i)um: Arsenic. Common arsenic salts are in the trivalent (3+, arsenous) or pentavalent (5+, arsenic) form, as in arsenates (AsO_4^{3+} salts). Arsenic has value as a corrosive agent, as a gastrointestinal stimulant, and for systemic treatment of various skin disorders such as psoriasis. (8)

Arsenium album; Arsenicum album; Arsenious acid; —anhydride: White arsenic, generally the trioxide above. (40)

Arsenobenzene; Arsenobillon: Arsenobenzene, Arsenobillon, Arsphenamine, Kharsivan, Salvarsan, or compound 606, was the first "Magic Bullet" antimicrobial compound with reduced human toxicity developed by Erlich, and introduced the era of synthetic antimicrobials. (40)

Arsenobenzol: An organoarsenic compound, antisyphilitic. There were a number of compounds (see immediately above) referred to by this term over time and in various locations.

Arsenosi acidi, liquor; Arsen., ac., lic.: A solution of arsenous acid, i.e., of arsenic trioxide. (8)

Arsenous acid; Arsenosum, acidum: Arsenous acid, As_2O_3, white arsenic, arsenic trioxide. (8)

Arsinyl; Arsonate; Arsamin: Sodium aminarsonate, antimicrobial. (40) See sodii metharsenis. (42)

Arsphenamin(e): See arsenobenzol. (40)

Artanita: See arthanita. Astringent and aperient. (1,39)

Artemesia: Mugwort, *Artemesia vulgaris*. Herb used, primarily for flavoring. Figure 3-27. (1)

Arthanita: Sowbread (*Cyclamen europaeum*). Tuber used. (1)

Arthemesia: See artemesia.

Artis, sal: "Salt of the (healing) art," a mixture of mercuric and ammonium chlorides. (3)

Arum ([maculatum][triphilum]); Arum trip.: 1. Dried corm (bulb) of the Indian turnip, Jack-in-the-pulpit, dragon root, or wake robin, *Arisaema triphyllum*, or *Arum triphyllum*. (33); 2. Lords-and-ladies, *Arum maculatum*. Rhizome used. Figure 3-28. (1,39)

Arundo: Reed. (1)

Asa dulcis: Benzoin. (3)

Asafetida; Asafoetida: A gum-resin obtained from the root of *Ferula foetida (F. assafoetida)*, of the Middle East. It contained a volatile oil usually extracted in formulation rather than isolated. Use was as per valerian, with particular use as a purgative and with limited success for mental disturbances. It was not used externally. Figure 3-29. (1, 8)

Asafoetida compound tablets; Asafoetidae compositae, tabellae: See galbani compositae, tablettae. (42)

Asafoetidae, emplastrum: Plaster composed of lead plaster (see plumbi, emplastrum) with asafoetida, galbanum, yellow wax, and alcohol. (46)

Asafoetidae, emulsum; —, mistura; —, pilulae; —, tinctura: The emulsion or mixture, also known as milk of asafoetida, was made by rubbing asafoetida in a warm mortar with water, followed by straining. Pills were formed with asafoetida and soap, and the tincture by maceration with alcohol followed by filtration. (8)

Asaf(o)etidae, enema: Enema of tincture of assafoetida and mucilage of starch, for flatulent distention. (42)

Asafoetidae, lac: Milk of asafoetida, an emulsion of same in water, an antihysteric orally or via enema. (39)

Asafoetidae, syrupus: Syrup of asafoetida, with sugar and water, often combined with antispasmodics, such as black cohosh for intestinal disorders. (34)

Asaf(o)etidae composita, mistura: A mixture of fresh asafetida, liquid extract of cascara sagrada, and ammonium carbonate in infusion of valerian, described (somewhat disturbingly) as "a laxative mixture with a nauseous smell and taste, for use specially in hysterical and nervous conditions, with the object of producing a profound psychical effect." (42)

Fig. 3-27 Artemesia.

Fig. 3-28 Arum maculatum.

Fig. 3- 29 Asafetida or asafoetida.

Asafoetidae compositae, pilulae: Compound pills of asafetida, of same with opium and ammonium carbonate, for nervous and hysterical disorders. See galbani compositae, pilulae. (34,40)

Asaprol; Asaprolum: Calcium beta-naphthol-alpha-sulfate, a surfactant and antiseptic said to be useful in epidemic influenza, relieving fever and pain; also for dyspepsia and rheumatism. (3,8)

Asarabacca; Asarum: In American usage, wild ginger (*Asarum canadensis)*, figure 3-30. In Europe, asarabacca or hazelwort (*Asarum europaeum*), figure 3-31. Rhizome and root used. Emmenagogue, tonic, diaphoretic, and as an errhine. (1,7,32,39,40)

Asarabacca, oil of: Oil from root of asarabaca. (40)

Asari compositus, pulvis: Compound powder of asarabacca (asarum), of same with marjoram, marum syriacum, and lavender, a strong errhine used as a snuff for headache and ophthalmia. (39)

Asari compositus, syrupus: Compound syrup of asarum, from asarum root, alcohol, cochineal, potassium carbonate (potassii carbonas), fluid extract of ipecac (ipecachuanae fluidum, extractum), sugar, and water. An expectorant. (31,34)

Asbolin: An alcoholic distillate of soot. (3)

Asclepiadis compositus, pulvis: Compound powder of pleurisy root, of same with spearmint, sumach berries, bayberry bark, skunk cabbage, and pulverized ginger. For cough, colds, and febrile illness. (34)

Asclepias; Aesclepiadis fluidum, extractum: Pleurisy root, root of *Asclepias tuberosa*, of the eastern United States, or fluid extract thereof. It is a diaphoretic, carminative, and expectorant used primarily in the treatment of pleuritic chest pain and pectoral conditions. (8)

Asclepias (incarnata) (decumbens)(syriaca)(tuberosa): 1. Swamp milkweed, flesh-colored asclepias, *Asclepias incarnata*. Per Ellingwood: "Emetic, diuretic, anthelmintic, stomachic. Swamp milkweed affects the heart and arteries, like digitalis, and is a speedy and certain diuretic…" 2. Root of butterfly weed or pleurisy root, *A. decumbens* or *tuberosa*, a diaphoretic, expectorant, febrifuge, cathartic, and carminative. 3. Root of common milkweed, *A. syriaca*, an anodyne, expectorant, antispasmodic, and antitussive. (32,39)

Asclepias curassavica: Bastard Ipecacuanha, anthelmintic. Unofficial. (44)

Asenzio: See assenzio. (1)

Aseptica (vs Antisepticus): Aseptica indicates sterility, referring to items like carbasus aseptica, sterile gauze. Antisepticus refers to antiseptic activity. (42)

Aseptol: Sozolic acid, orthophenylsulphonic acid. See sulphocarbolic acid. (3)

Asfalto {*Italian*}: Bitumin of Judea, see asphaltus. (1)

Ash, manna: See fraxinus. (40)

Asiatic pill; Asiaticae, piluli: Arsenious acid pills, of same with (in BPC) black pepper and extract of gentian. (40,42)

Asimina: See carica (papaya). (33)

Aspalathi, lignum; Aspalathum; Aspalato {*Italian*}: Rosewood. (1)

Aspalto {*Italian*}: Bitumen of Judea, see asphaltus. (1)

Asparagin; Asparaginum: Amidosuccinic acid amide, found in asparagus and other plants, a powerful diuretic used in dropsy and kidney disease. (42)

Asparagus (officinalis): Asparagus plant, *Asparagas officinalis*, a diaphoretic, aperient, and deobstruant. Seeds and root used. (8,39)

Asperula: Woodruff (*Asperula odorata*). (1)

Asphaltum: Pix mineralis, mineral pitch tar, see asphaltus. (40)

Asphaltum, oil of: Oil obtained from asphaltum, bituminous oil or tar. (40)

Asphaltus: Bitumen of Judea, or asphalt. Bituminous material found on the surface of the Dead Sea. Used as an emollient. (1)

Aspidium; Aspidii, oleoresina; —, fluidextractum; —, liquid extract: Male fern, the rhizome of *Dryopteris filix-mas* (see filix mas and figure 3-103) or *D. marginalis*, from which an oleoresin ("solid extract") can be derived by percolation with ether and subsequent evaporation. This is an effective anthelmintic, especially for tapeworm. It is noted that it may be flavored with peppermint or ginger, and that castor oil should be given before and after treatment with aspidium. The "liquid extract" or "fluidextract" are not technically correct, it is a resin. (8,34)

Aspidosperma; Aspiodospermatis fluidum, extractum: Quebracho, the bark of *Aspidospermia quebracho-blanco*, or the fluid extract. Many alkaloidal components were identified, but the root was used in its natural form for therapeutic purposes, primarily as an appetite aid and for the treatment of asthma and other bronchial conditions. (8)

Aspidospermine: A commercial extract of Aspidosperma, containing a mixture of active alkaloids and used in place of the whole root. (8)

Aspirin: A Bayer trade name for acetylsalicylic acid in most countries, but not legally trademarked in US, and hence used as a generic name. See acetylsalicylic acid. (8)

Asplenium: Ceterach, see polytrichum. (1)

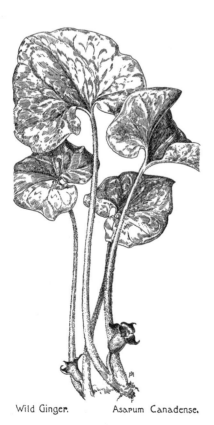
Fig. 3-30 American asarabacca.

Fig. 3-31 European asarabacca.

Assafoetida: See asafoetida. (1)

Assaieret, pilule: Cleansing pills, a cathartic of hiera picra, mastiche, citrus, myrobilans, aloe, and stechas. (39)

Assentio; Assenzio {*Italian*}: Wormwood, see absinthium. (1)

Astacus: See cancrorum lapilli. (39)

Aster puniceus: Red-stalked aster, cocash, meadow scabish, or squaw weed, *Aster puniceus*, root used as a stimulant and diaphoretic. (33)

Asthma paper: See potassii nitratis, charta. (40)

Asthma powder: See lobelia compositus, pulvis as specified in the BPC. (42)

Asthmaticus, elixir: Antiasthmatic elixir, see opii camphorata, tinctura. Sometimes refers to laudanum. (39)

Astragalus tragacantha: Gum tragacanth. (39)

Astral oil: Kerosene. (3)

Astringent and escharotic mixture: See adstringens et escharotica, mistura. (34)

Astringent lotion: See adstringens, lotio. (34)

Ater; Atra: Black (the color), less commonly used equivalent to niger. (3)

Athanasia magna: From Greek for immortality, (a, not + thanatos, death) elixir of opium, poppy seed, costus root, spikenard, saffron, myrrh, etc. Analgesic and hypnotic. (1,39)

Athens, spiritus: See vitrioli dulcis, spiritus. (40)

Atophan: See chincophen. (40)

Atoxyl: Sodium aminarsonate. Antimicrobial. (40)

Atrahens, emplasturm: Attracting plaster, see cerae compositum, emplastrum. (39)

Atramentum heberdenii: See ferri aromatica, mistura. (40)

Atramentum: 1. Alchemical term, copper and/or ferrous sulfate. 2. Atrament, any pigment used in black ink. 3. Ink in general. (1)

Atramentum; —indicum (sinense); —nigrum: Black ink or India ink, respectively. (3)

Atriplex: Plants of genus *Atriplex*, esp. *A. hortensis* (garden orach, mountain spinach). Leaves used. (1)

Atriplex foetida: Stinking atriplex, leaves of stinking orach, *Chenopodium vulvaria*, an antihysteric. Figure 3-32. (39)

Atropa belladonna; —mandragora: See belladonna. *A. mandragora* is a related species, said to be of lower potency. (39)

Atropia; Atropiae, liquor: Atropia is a variant of atropinae, the liquor was a simple solution of atropine in water. (44)

Atropinae, chloroformum: Chloroform of atopine, of same dissolved in chloroform extract of alkanet root. This was used as a paint on unbroken skin to relieve neuralgia. (42)

Chenopodium Vulvaria

Published by D. Woodville May 1.1792.

Fig. 3-32 Atriplex foetida.

Atropinae, collodium: Collodion with atropine, as a topical counterirritant on skin. (42)

Atropinae, glycerinum: Atropine sulfate in glycerin and water with compound tincture of lavender. (42)

Atropinae, guttae: Eyedrops (BPC) consisting of atropine 0.25-1%, mydriatic. (42)

Atropinae, linimentum: Liniment of atropine sulfate, compound tincture of lavender and alcohol. A non-staining liniment. (42)

Atropinae, ole(in)atum: Atropine in oleic acid with alcohol and olive oil, as a topical for pain. (42)

Atropinae, unguentum: Atropine in oleic acid, used for local neuralgias. (34)

Atropinae cum chloroformo, linimentum: Liniment of chloroform with linimentum atropinae, a non-staining liniment. (42)

Atropinae et cocainae, guttae: Eyedrops (BPC) consisting of atropine and cocaine, mydriatic and anesthetic. (42)

Atropinae et morphinae, pilulae: Pills of atropine sulfate, morphine hydrochloride, lactose, and binder of simple syrup. (42)

Atropinae salicylas: Atropine salicylate was used as a topical mydriatic in ophthalmology. (42)

Atropinae sulphas; Atropinae sulphatis: Atropine sulfate, a soluble salt of atropine. See belladonna. The BPC specifies a liquor with salicylic acid, used as per atropine or belladonna. (8,42)

Atropine; Atropina: Atropine, an alkaloid derived from belladonna. Atropine was (and is) used to dry secretions and decrease gut or urinary tract motility, to reduce night sweats, to increase heart rate, and for asthma. Topically, used to dilate the pupils. (8,42)

Attar: See Otto. (40)

Attar of rose: See rosae, oleum. (8)

Auramin: Yellow pyoktanin, an antiseptic. (3)

Aurantii, aqua: See aurantii florum, aqua.

Aurantii, elixir: Elixir of oil of bitter orange in simple syrup, alcohol, and cinnamon water, a flavoring. (42)

Aurantii (amari), elixir: Elixir of (bitter) orange, of oil of (bitter) orange, tincture of (bitter) orange peel, and orange flower water as the flavoring constituents. (31)

Aurantii, infusum: An infusion (BPC) of bitter orange peel in water, as a vehicle. (42)

Aurantii, spiritus; Aurantii compositus, spiritus: The spirit of orange oil (see aurantii corticus, oleum) is fifty percent orange oil in alcohol. The compound spirit contains oil of orange, lemon, coriander, and anise in deodorized alcohol. Both primarily flavoring agents. (8)

Aurantii (dulcis), syrupus; Aurantii dulcis, tinctura: The syrup or alcoholic tincture of sweet orange. Primarily a flavoring agent. (8)

Auranti(i), tinctura: Tincture of orange. A flavoring, of bitter orange peel extracted in alcohol. (42)

Aurantii, vinum: Orange wine, made by the fermentation of a sugar solution to which fresh bitter-orange peel (aurantii amari, cortex) has been added, used as a vehicle. (31)

Aurantii amari fluidum, extractum; —, tinctura: The tincture or fluid extract of bitter orange. The two preparations differ mainly in the higher alcohol content of the tincture. Primarily a flavoring agent. (8)

Aurantii compositum (concentratum), infusum: Infusion of orange and lemon peel and cloves, used as a carminative. The BPC specified a concentrate with alcohol and chloroform water that could be stored and reconstituted. (34,42)

Aurantii compositum, elixir: Elixir of the tinctures of orange and lemon in orange-flower water, alcohol, syrup, and distilled water. (42)

Aurantii compositum, vinum; Aurantiorum compositum, elixir: Compound wine of orange, consisting of sherry with bitter orange peel, absinth, menyanthes leaves, cascarilla, cinnamon, and potassium carbonate. (34)

Aurantii compositus, spiritus: Compound spirit of orange; oils of orange, lemon, coriander, and anise in alcohol. Flavoring. (42)

Aurantii cortex; —amari cortex; —, C.: Bitter orange peel from *Citrus vulgaris*, of northern India. It is classified as a bitter (see columba for details of use), but is primarily used as a flavoring agent. (8)

Auranti[um][orum] cortex, conserva; Cort. Aur. C.: Conserve of orange peel, i.e., candied orange peel. (35)

Aurantii cortex indicus: Indian orange peel, locally used from orange varieties grown in India or Asia. (42)

Aurantii corticus, oleum: Oil of orange peel, a volatile oil expressed from the orange and used primarily as a flavoring. (8)

Aurantii dulcis, cortex (, tinctura): Sweet orange peel from *Citrus aurantium*, or the alcoholic tincture from same. It is classified as a bitter (see columba for details of use), but is primarily used as a flavoring agent. (8)

Aurantii flor[um][is], aqua; —fortior, aqua; —syrupus.: Largely used as flavoring agents, water of orange flowers consists of bitter orange-flower oil in water. The precise strength of the water versus the "stronger" water (fortior, or "triple") is not clearly defined. The syrup is made from the water combined with simple syrup. (8)

Aurantii (amari) florum, oleum: Oil of orange flowers, distilled from the flowers of the bitter orange, *citrus vulgaris*, of India. (8)

Aurantii recentis, tinctura: Tincture of fresh bitter orange peel. A flavoring. (34)

Aurantiorum compositum, elixir: Compound elixir of orange peel and gentian. Various sources suggest this is similar to vinum aurantii. (3)

Aurantium (hispanalense): Orange (i.e., the fruit). Hispanalense means Spanish. (39)

Aurantium: Orange (fruit). Figure 3-33. (1)

Aurea Alexandrina: 1. Mixture made from gold leaf, silver leaf, pears, powdered ivory, red coral, mandrake root, opium, myrrh, etc. (1) 2. Gold of Alexander, a complex drug made with gold and opium, attributed eponymously. (39)

Aureas, pulvis: Face powder of gold leaf, iron oxide, galingale, cinnamon, and aniseed. (1)

Aureoline: Hair bleach, diluted hydrogen peroxide. (3)

Aureum, unguentum: Any golden colored ointment. (39) "Gold ointment," made of saffron, olive oil, yellow wax, frankincense, colophony, and other resins, used as a vulnerary. (1)

Auri bromidum: Gold tribromide, use as per gold itself. (42)

Auric acid: Gold peroxide. Antirheumatic. (40)

Auri chloridum: Gold chloride as the aurochloric acid salt, $HAuCl_4$. Use as per gold. (42)

Auri et arseni(i) bromidi, liquor: Solution of gold and arsenic bromide, a reddish brown solution resulting from the interaction of arsenic trioxide, bromauric acid and bromine. "It was at one time lauded as a remedy for diabetes." (31,46)

Auri et sodii chloridum: Gold and sodium chloride, $AuCl_3$ and NaCl. Used in the treatment of dyspepsia and other gastric and internal disorders, and in the treatment of syphilis. (8)

Auri philosophicum, sal: Potassium bisulphate. (40)

Auripigmentum: Orpiment, arsenic trisulfide, which is golden yellow in color. (1)

Aurochloric acid: See auri, chloridum. (42)

Aurum: Gold, metallic. Although toxic, gold remains in use as a treatment for refractory rheumatoid arthritis. Used for a wide range of other conditions including epilepsy in the past. (39)

Aurum musivum: Mosaic gold, tin bisulphide, a gold pigment used in mosaic tiles. (3)

Aurum potabile: Potable gold, applied to certain metallic preparations having gold to yellow color, term probably of alchemical origin. (1)

Australian copal: Fossil resin obtained from *Agathis australis*. (40)

Australian fever bark: See alstonia. (32)

Avantine: Isopropyl alcohol. (40)

Avellana; Aveline {*French*}**:** Hazelnut. (1)

Avena decorticata: Decorticated wheat, i.e., groats. (40)

Avena(e) farina: Oat bran or flour, oatmeal. (40,44)

Avenae sernina: Oats. (40)

Avena sativa; Avenae sativae, fluidextractum: Cultivated white oats, *Avena sativa*, grain used. A nutrient and demulcent used to treat hoarseness and, of course, for food, or the fluid extract therefrom. (7,31)

Avens: See caryophyllum. (39)

Avertin: Tribromethylalcohol. Antiseptic. (40)

Avicenna: A corruption of Ibn Sina, renowned Arabic physician (980-1037 CE), to whom a variety of pharmaceutical materials are ascribed, often without firm basis. (1)

Avoleum: Vitamin A concentrate. (40)

Avorio {*Italian*}**:** Ivory. (1)

Axungia: Grease, fat, or lard, synonym for adeps, or an ointment, usually in a fatty base. (1,3)

Axungia oxygenata: Fatty material obtained by treating pork fat with nitric acid. (1)

Axungia pedum tauri: See bubulum. (34)

Axungia porci(num); Axungia porc.: Porcine fat, i.e., lard.

Azadiractae indicae, infusum: An infusion (BPC) of Indian azadirach, a bitter. (42)

Azedarach (, Indian); Azadiracha indica; Azadiractae indicae, tinctura: Neem or Margosa bark, or the alcoholic tincture of same. Bark of the root of pride of India, pride of China, bead-tree, Indian lilac, African lilac, or Persian lilac, *Melia azedarach*. Mainly a bitter but also anthelmintic, diuretic, emetic and narcotic. (33,42)

Azotic acid: Nitric acid. (3)

Azure: See smalt. (44)

Azurite: Native copper carbonate. (3)

Citrus Aurantium

Fig. 3-33 Aurantium or orange tree.

B

B.: At beginning of inscription: bacca (berry); balsamum (balm); baume {*French*} (balm). At end of inscription: bianco {*Italian*} (white); blanca {*French*} (white). (1)

B.I.P.P.: See bismuth iodoform paraffin paste. (40)

Babul bark: Acacia bark. See acacia cortex. (40)

Bacca; Baccae; Baie {*French*}**:** Berry (Bacca) or berries (baccae). (1)

Badiani, semen: Fruit of star anise, see anise. (40)

Bael fruit (, Indian); Belae fructus; Belae liquidum, extractum: Dried, partially ripe fruit of the Bèl, Bael fruit, Indian quince, Indian Bael, or Bengal quince, *Aegle marmelos*, of Malabar, or the fluid extract. Used to treat diarrhea in India, the dried, imported fruit is stated to be useless, but Kings' states it has refrigerant properties and is used in hypochondria, melancholia, palpitations, asthma, and habitual constipation. (8,33)

Bagot's mixture: A local anesthetic consisting of cocaine and spartein in water. (24)

Bailie's pills: See digitalis compositae, pilulae. Closely related formula with additional digitalis leaf. (42)

Baird's aperient powder: See rhei cum hydrargyro et soda, pulvis. (42)

Baird's pills: An aloe pill. See aloes, pillulae. (40) See aloes compositae, pilulae (BPC). (42)

Baker's ammonia: Ammonium subcarbonate. (3)

Baking soda: See sodii bicarbonas. (8)

Balata: A caoutchouc-like product resembling chicle. (3)

Balaustium: Wild pomegranate tree, see granata. Flowers used. (1)

Baldmoney: See meum. (39)

Baldwin's phosphorus: Calcium nitrate, which, when heated and exposed to light, becomes luminous, i.e., phosphorescent. (3)

Ballston (mineral) water: Water from the famous spa in New York State. A cathartic, diuretic, and tonic. (39)

Balm drops: Friar's balsam, or compound tincture of benzoin, see benzoini composita, tinctura. (8,40)

Balm of Gilead: See gileadense, balsamum. (3)

Balm water: See carmelitana, aqua. (39)

Balm, oil of: Volatile oil from (see) melissa. (40)

Balm; Balm mint: Balm, i.e., the plant. See melissa. (8,39)

Balmony: See chelone. (33)

Balneum ____; Balnea (plural)**:** A bath from the British Pharmaceutical Codex, or other variant. The BPC notes the following official forms, made up in 30 gallon quantities:

- **Acidi borici**—with boric acid, antiseptic, for skin disorders.
- **Acidum**—with nitrohydrochloric acid, for congestion of the liver.
- **Alkalinum**—with sodium carbonate, for skin disorders, gout, and rheumatism.
- **Calidum**—hot water at 37–43° C.
- **Effervescens**—with sodium bicarbonate and sodium acid sulphate, with or without sodium and calcium chloride, for heart disease.
- **Frigidum**—of cold water at 15° C.
- **Sinapis**—with mustard, for chills and febrile conditions.
- **Sodii chloridi**—with salt, for gout and rheumatism.
- **Sulphuratum**—with sulphurated potash, a parasiticidal bath for scabies and other infestations.
- **Tepidum**—of warm water at 30–35° C.
- **Vaporis creosoti**—is not really a bath, see creosoti vaporis, balneum. (42)

Balsam; Bals.: Generally a sap or resin from a tree or shrub.

Balsam, Canada; Balsamum canadensis; Balsam drops: See terebenthina canadensis. (8)

Balsam, Carpathian: See balsam, Riga (first definition). (40)

Balsam, Hungarian: Exudation from *Pinus pumilo*. (3)

Balsam, Persian: See benzoini composita, tinctura. (40)

Balsam, Riga: 1. Balsam from distillation of leaves of *Pinus cembra*, thin fluid with odor resembling juniper and character similar to turpentine. (3) 2. Oils of lavender, cloves, cinnamon, thyme, mace, and lemon, with balsam of Peru; oil of sage, and tincture of saffron; in alcohol. (40) There are many variants involving different herbal components, and the term also applies to a traditional Latvian preparation of herbs in an alcoholic base, now usually vodka but variable in the past.

Balsam, sulphur: Sulphurated linseed oil. (3) See also, sulphuratum, oleum. (39)

Balsam fir: See abies (balsamea). (40)

Balsam flavus: Yellow balsam, turpeth mineral. See hydrargyri subsulphas flavus. (39)

Balsam of copaiba: See copaiba. (8)

B

Balsam of fern: Liquid extract of male fern, see aspidium. (40)

Balsam of life: Compound decoction of aloes, see aloes compositum, decoctum. (40)

Balsam of Peru; Balsam peruvianum: A balsam obtained from *Toluifera pereirae*, of Central America. Similar in use to volatile oils, like clove (see caryophyllus), but especially as a disinfectant and treatment for skin disorders or injury or for sore nipples and cracked lips, for which one part of balsam of Peru and seven parts lard are recommended. An effective scabicide and treatment for skin parasites, for which a mixture with olive oil and petrolatum may be prepared. (8)

Balsam of soap: Soap liniment, see saponis, linimentum. (40)

Balsam of storax: Prepared storax, see storax. (40)

Balsam of sulphur: Sulfur and olive oil, heated together until combined. (40) See Oleum sulphuratum. (44)

Balsam of tolu; Balsam tolutanum: A balsam obtained from *Toluifera balsamum*, of Latin America. Similar to balsam of Peru, but usually used only as an expectorant. Figure 3-34. (8)

Balsam tranquilans: Proprietary formulation of olive oil and various aromatic and narcotic plants, topical. Unofficial. (44)

Balsami tolutani, tinctura: See tolutana solubilis, tinctura. (40)

Balsamica, tinctura: See benzoini composita, tinctura. (40)

Balsamicae Mortonii, pilulae: Morton's anti-tussive pills from balsam of Peru, sublimate of benzoin, gum ammoniac, saffron, etc. (1)

Balsamicum, unguentum: See elemi, unguentum. (40)

Balsamicus, syrupus: Syrup of tolu, see tolutana, syrupus. (1,3)

Balsamina: Balsam apple, fruit of *Mormordica balsamina*. (1)

Balsamita: Leaves of costumary, *Chrysanthemum* (or *Tanacetum*) *balsamita*, said to be an ineffective antihysteric and an antidote to opium. (39)

Balsamum: Balsam, balm, aromatic resinous substance. (1)

Balsamum commendatoris: Compound tincture of benzoin, see benzoini composita tinctura. (40)

Balsamum dipterocarpi: See gurjun oil. (40)

Balsamum filicis: Liquid extract of male fern, see aspidium. (40)

Balsamum peruvianum: See balsam Peruvianum. (42)

Balsamum styracis: Prepared storax, see storax. (40)

Balsamum sulphuris: Balsam of sulphur, made by heating flowers of sulfur in olive oil. (1)

Balsamum terebinthinae: See Dutch drops. (40)

Balsamum tranquillans: See hyoscyami oleum (compositum). (40)

Fig. 3-34 Balsam of Tolu, Balsamum tolutanum.

Balsamum traumaticum: See benzoini composita, tinctura.

Balsamum universale: Compound tincture of benzoin, see benzoini composita tinctura. (40)

Bamberger's fluid: An (egg) albumen containing solution of mercury, used to treat syphilis. (24)

Banana oil: Amyl acetate. (3)

Bane: Old English "bana," murderer. A material or individual that opposes, kills, or is otherwise bad for a person, animal, or illness. Henbane, dogsbane, wolfsbane, etc. drive off or kill the respective creature. (39)

Banilloes: Vanilla pods. (40)

Banks oil: Cod liver oil. (3)

Bannal: See scoparius. (3)

Baptisia (tinctoria); Baptisiae, fluidextractum: Wild indigo, *Baptisia tinctoria*, or the fluid extract therefrom, used to produce a yellow coloration and also as a cathartic and hepatic stimulant. Also called *Sophora tinctoria*. (3,31,39)

Baptisiae, unguentum: Ointment of wild indigo, of the root in butter, beeswax, tallow, and alcohol, for various skin diseases and for piles. (34)

Baptisiae compositae, pilulae: Compound pills of baptesia with leptandra, podophyllum, and sanguinarine (isolate of sanguinaria). Cholegogue, laxative, and for typhoid fevers. (34)

Baptista, lapis: Ancient name for talcum. (3)

Barbados nuts: Seeds of *Curcas purgans*, purgative. Unofficial. (44)

Barbados tar: Bitumen or mineral tar, see asphaltus. (40)

Barbaloin: Aloin from Barbados aloes. (40)

Barbitone: Malourea, a barbiturate sedative. (40)

Barbotine: Herb of the genus *Artemesia*, same as or related to santonica. (3)

Barbul; Barbura bark: Acacia bark. See acacia. (40)

Bardana: Burdock, see lappa. (1,3)

Baric: Irregular chemical name for the barium ion. For compounds see barii. (29)

Baricis: Barium sulfate. (39)

NOTE: Barii vs Barytae: Barium compounds can be specified either way, Barytae was official in the USP. (44)

Barii chloridi, liquor: Solution of barium chloride in water, deobstruant and anthelmintic and for cancer and scrofula. (44)

Barii chloridum: Barium chloride. Soluble barium salts were used to slow the heart and improve cardiac function, and are said to act like digitalis. Also used for atonic bladder or intestine or to treat hemorrhage. Soluble salts are highly toxic, causing nausea, vomiting, and paralysis. Barium has fallen out of therapeutic use entirely except that the insoluble salts (sulfate) are used as contrast agents in radiographic studies, i.e., "barium enema." (8)

Barii dioxidum: Barium dioxide, BaO_2, used to produce aqua hydrogenii dioxidi, i.e., hydrogen peroxide. (8)

Barii hypophosphis: Barium hypophosphite. (42)

Barii sulfidum: Barium sulfide, BaS. Depilatory, applied in a paste of starch or of starch and zinc oxide and scraped off in 5-10 minutes. Little used internally, but pills can be prepared. (42)

Barilla: See natrium, barilla is identical to natron. (39)

Barium: The element, see baryta. (44)

Bark, Carthagina; —, Pitaya; —, Bogata; —, Maracaybo; —, Santa Martha: Unofficial barks similar to cinchona, largely named by geographical point of origin. There are many associated descriptors for color (yellow, red, pale / flava, rubra, pallida), or consistency (hard, spongy, fibrous/dura, spongeosa, fibrosa). (44)

Bark, Honduras: See cascara amarga. (7)

Bark, Panama: See quillaia bark. (40)

Bark, tincture of: See cinchonae composita, tinctura. (40)

Barker's (post partum) pills: See laxativae post partum, pilulae. (46)

Barley: See hordeum. (8)

Barm: Yeast. (3)

Barosma(e): Synonym for buchu. (34,39)

Baryta, muriate of: Barium chloride, for the solution, see barii chloridi, liquor. (44)

Baryta; Barytes: Soil or mineral from which barium can be derived, usually in the form of the oxide. (19) Barium sulfate. (39) Barium Oxide. (40) Barium compounds may be named as barytae as opposed to barii. (44)

Baryta mixture: A mixture of barium salts derived from baryta. (19, 29)

NOTE: Barytae vs Barii: Barium compounds can be specified either way, Barytae was official in the USP. (44)

Barytae carbonas: Barium carbonate, used to prepare the chloride. (44)

Bartyae sulph. Orthographic variant or typographical error for Barytae, below.

Barytae sulphas: Barium sulfate, virtually insoluble, it was sometimes used as a white pigment (permanent white), much like white lead. It is commonly used today as a radiological contrast agent for "barium enemas." (44)

Basham's mixture: See ferri et ammonii acetatis, liquor. (8)

Basil, wild: See pycnanthemum. (33)

Basilicon, unguentum; —[ointment][, axunguinum]; Basilicum (nigrum), unguentum: A black ointment, from Greek "basilicon" for "royal," made from wax, pitch, olive oil, myrrh, frankincense, and other resins and used to treat wounds. (1,39)

Basilicon, yellow: Ointment of yellow wax, resina alba, olibanum, and pig's fat, closely related or same as basilicon, unguentum. (39)

Basofor: Trade name for barium sulfate. (3)

Bassora gum: See hog gum. (40) Plant gum named for region in the Mediterranean, botanical source unknown. (44)

Bassorin paste: See tragacanth, gum. (40)

Bastard saffron: Safflower. (40)

Bastard saffron thistle: See carthamus. (39)

Bataviae compositus, pulvis: See os sepiae. (30)

Bateman's (pectoral) drops: See Opii et gambir composita, tinctura. (31)

Bate's (Dr.) Pacifick pill: Formula after Dr. William Bates, London, mid-seventeenth century, containing opium along with crocus, tartaric acid, anethum, and soap as a binding material. (39)

Batiste: A fine cambric cloth of cotton and linen, for plasters. (40)

Battery acid: Sulfuric acid and potassium dichromate. Non-therapeutic item carried by some "chemysts." (3)

Battley's solution; Battley's sedative solution of opium: A solution of boiled opium, saffron, nutmeg, and other ingredients. See opii sedativus, liquor. (8,40)

Baume {French}: Balsam, balm. (1)

Baume de vie: Balm of life, see aloes compositum, decoctum. (3,39)

Bay; Bay leaf, Bay oil; Bay spirit; Bay rum: See myricae, oleum. (8,40)

Bay, English: See laurus. (40)

Bay, Sweet: American usage may refer to either of *Magnolia virginiana* or *Pimenta acris*. British usage, see laurus. (40)

Bay berries, oil of: Oil from (see) lauri, baccae. (40)

Bay berries: Fruit of the laurel, *Laurus nobilis*. See laurus. (40)

Bay laurel: See myrcia acris. (40)

Bayliss(') solution: Gum acacia, six or seven percent in saline. (40)

Bay salt: Sea salt. (3)

Bdelium; Bdellium, gummi: Bdellium resin, resin from certain trees of the genus *Balsamodendron* and *Commiphora*. (1,39)

Bearberry: See uva ursi, Latin for "berry of the bears." (8)

Bear's foot: See helleboraster. (39)

Beaume de Mecca: See balm of Gilead. (40)

Beberiae sulphas: Crude reaction product of beeberu bark with sulfuric acid, probably same as or similar to beeberine sulfate. (44)

Bebe(e)rine sulphate, Bebe(e)rine sulphas; Bebe(e)rinae sulphas: Purified alkaloids of bebeeru, dissolved and neutralized with dilute sulfuric acid, use as per bebeeru, mainly a bitter, can be used for quinine. (42)

Beberine sulphate; Beeberine sulphate: Beberine sulfate, extracted from beeberu bark, for headache. (40) Not the same as berberine.

Beccabunga: Brook-lime or speedwell, *Veronica beccabunga* (or *officinalis*) and related species. Herb used. Antiscorbutic, detergent, and mild stimulant bitter. Figure 3-35. (1,39)

Beccheri, pilulae; Becheri, pilulae; Becher, pilules de {French}: Alterative pills per Johann Becher, German chemist (1635-82), composed of aloes, rhubarb, myrrh, etc. (1)

Becchiche, pilulae; Bechicae, pilulae; Bechicae, trochisci; Bechiche, pillole {Italian}: From Greek for "cough," anti-tussive pills from iris rhizome, etc. (1)

Becher's tonic: Cathartic, diuretic, and tonic preparation after Johann Becher (see Becheri, pillulae), of black hellebore, myrrh, and carduus benedictus. Particularly for dropsy. (39)

Bechici, troschisci (albi)(nigri)(cum opio): Similar to troches of tussilago, but per Estes, the latter had disappeared as an ingredient and was replaced with gum arabic (white pectoral troches, albi), with optional addition of licorice (black pectoral troches, nigri), or with licorice and opium (cum opio). For respiratory disorders. (39)

Béchiques, pilules {French}: See bechicae, pilulae. (1)

Bechium; Bechio {Italian}: Coltsfoot, see tussilago. (1)

Beck's paste: Injectable form of bismuth subnitrate. (40)

Bedeguar: Excrescences of various plants of the rose family, produced by insect damage and containing insect larvae, used as anthelmintic and for toothache. Unofficial. (44)

Beeberu bark; Bebe(e)ru bark: The bark of the bebeeru tree, *Nectandra rodioei*, of British Guiana, from which beberine is isolated. Bitter stomachics similar to calumba, they are believed to be mildly antipyretic and antiseptic, but generally considered inferior to alternatives. (8) Placements of the letter "e" are highly variable, but current, correct botanical name seems to bebeeru.

Been album; Behen album: White behen, uncertain plant, possibly *Centaurea behen*, *Silene inflata*, or *Silene armeria*. (1)

Begbie's mixture: An English remedy for cough and respiratory irritation, of dilute hydrocyanic and nitric acids, glycerin, and quassiae, infusum.

Veronica Beccabunga.
Publish'd by D. Woodville, Feb. 1. 1790.

Fig. 3-35 Beccabunga.

Bela; Belae fructus: See bael fruit. (33,44) The genitive of bael is invariably seen as belae, not baelae.

Belac liquidum, extractum: Extract of bael fruit in water and alcohol, for dysentery and diarrhea, especially in children. (42)

Belgimi; belgioni {*Italian*}**:** See benzoinum. (1)

Bellad.; Belladonna; Belladonnae folia (or folium); Belladonnae radix: Belladonna, or deadly nightshade, *Atropa belladonna* or the leaves (folia) or root (radix) thereof. Belladonna is the source of atropine, hyoscyamine, and other similar alkaloids. Eyedrops derived from belladonna were used historically to dilate the pupil and thereby make women more attractive, hence the derivation from the Italian, *bella donna*, or beautiful woman. Atropine and related compounds inhibit the parasympathetic nervous system, responsible for bladder and bowel function, and will dry all secretions, increase heart rate, dilate the pupil, and cause nervous stimulation progressing to agitated delirium and seizures. Often employed in laxative or purgative preparations to reduce "grippe," or cramping. It is useful in drying secretions and dilating the airways in asthma. Figure 3-36. (8)

Belladonna, liquid plaster: See belladonnae, collodium. (42)

Belladonna plaster, green: See belladonnae viride, emplastrum. (42)

Belladonnae, chloroformum: Chloroform of belladonna, of powdered root, soaked in ammonia to extract alkaloidal content, percolated with alcohol and chloroform. This was used as a paint on unbroken skin to relieve neuralgia. (42)

Belladonnae, collodium: Collodion with belladonna, as a topical counterirritant on skin. Prepared from liquid extract of belladonna, Canada turpentine, castor oil, camphor, and pyroxylin, not by addition to collodion. (42)

Belladonnae, collyrium: Extract of belladonna in distilled water, soothing eyewash and mildly dilates the pupil. (42)

Belladonnae (mitius), emplastrum: A plaster from extract of belladonna with resin and soap plaster bases, the mitius form being half-strength. Applied to relieve pain and diminish secretions, used locally for pleurisy or cardiac pain. (8,42)

Belladonnae, extractum (foliorum alcoholicum) (radicis fluidum): Extract of belladonna (unspecified part), an alcoholic extract of leaves, or a fluid extract of roots, respectively. By percolation with alcohol and water, followed by evaporation to dryness, concentration adjusted via addition of milk sugar in the BPC. (8,42)

Atropa Belladonna.
Publish'd as the Act directs by D: Woodville Jan 1.1790.

Fig. 3-36 Belladonna or dadly nightshade.

Belladonnae, glycerinum: Green extract of belladonna (belladonna liquidum viridis, extractum) in water and glycerin, a topical for pain relief and to suppress lactation. (42)

Belladonnae, linimentum: Belladonna liniment, of fluid extract of belladonna root with approximately five percent camphor. (8)

Belladonnae, succus: Fresh juice of belladonna leaves (three parts), to which is added alcohol (one part) as a preservative. (34)

Belladonnae, suppositoria: Suppository of alcoholic extract of belladonna in cocoa butter, for local pain. (42)

Belladonnae, tinctura: Tincture of liquid extract of belladonna in alcohol or, in earlier BP, from direct extraction of leaves. (42)

Belladonnae, unguentum: Belladonna ointment, of the alcoholic extract of belladonna in benzoinated lard. Applied for local neuralgia and painful joints, to dilate the pupil and the uterine os, for local pain relief or muscle spasm, and in violent tetanus, delirium tremens, and puerperal convulsions (toxemia). (8,34)

Belladonnae alcoholicum, extractum; Belladonna alch. ext.: Dry alcoholic extract of belladonna leaf, USP. (44) See belladonna siccum, extractum. (40)

Belladonnae cum chloroformo, linimentum: Liniment of chloroform mixed with linimentum belladonnae. (42)

Belladonnae exsiccatum, extractum: Dry extract of belladonna leaf as per the BPC. (42)

Belladonnae fluidum, emplastrum: See belladonnae, collodium. (42)

Belladonnae foliorum, tinctura: Tincture of belladonna leaves, by maceration in alcohol. (8)

Belladonnae liquidum, extractum: Liquid extract of the root, BPC. (42)

Belladonnae viride, emplastrum: Green plaster of belladonna, of the green extract in alcohol and water, thickened with resin. Approximately equivalent to belladonnae mitius, emplastrum. (42)

Belladonnae viride, extractum: Green extract of belladonna, BPC. Of leaves and young branches in alcohol, with chlorophyll added back to give the green (viride) coloration. Said to be used in pill form for diarrhea or with purgatives to reduce cramping, as a topical (skin or eye) and even as a suppository. (42)

Belladonnas siccum, extractum; Bellad. sic., ext.: A standardized alcoholic extract of dried, powdered belladonna used in place of the fresh material in compounding. (40, 33)

Bellericus, myrobalanus: See myrobalanus bellericus. (1)

Bellostii, pilulae; Belloste, pilules de {*French*}**:** Pills used in the treatment of skin disorders after Augustin Belloste, French surgeon (c. 1650–1730), composed of mercury, aloes, scammony, rhubarb, black pepper, and honey. (1)

Bemax: Commercial wheat germ rich in vitamin B, i.e., "B-max." (40)

Benedicta, herba; **Benedetta, herba** {*Italian*}**:** Common avens, herb bennet, *Geum urbanum*. Herb and root used. A topical astringent, aromatic, tonic, febrifuge, etc. Figure 3-37. (1)

Benedicta laxitiva: "Blessed laxative," a pleasant laxative electuary made of turpeth root, hermodactylus, gromwell, etc. (1) or per Estes (39) of senna, tamarind, cassia, prunus galica, corriander, and licorice.

Benedictum, unguentum: Ointment of mercury, litharge, white lead, frankincense, and lard. (1)

Benedict's solution: A solution of sodium citrate, sodium carbonate, and copper sulfate which changes color from blue to yellow in the presence of sugar. Used in urinalysis, i.e., to detect diabetes. (24)

Bengal isinglass: Agar. (3)

Benguin's sulphuretted spirit: Ammonium sulphide. (40)

Benjamin(, sal): Benzoin or benzoic acid. (3)

Benjamin, oil of: Oil obtained from benzoin, after sublimation to remove benzoic acid. (40)

Benne; Benne oil: Sesami; sesame oil. See sesami, oleum. (8)

Benzaldehydum: Benzaldehyde, the chief component of oil of bitter almonds, prepared synthetically and used as a flavoring or replacement of the oil, see amygdalae amaris, oleum. (42)

Benzanalgene: See quinalgen. (40)

Benzin; Benzine; Benzinum (purificatum): Petroleum ether. This is a petroleum distillate of mixed composition, defined by boiling point. It is used as a solvent for extraction. Benzene, the aromatic hydrocarbon C_6H_6, is often confused with benzin(e) and, in fact, could be used interchangeably in many instances. "Purified" is rinsed with an aqueous solution of potassium permanganate mixed with sulfuric acid and then separately with sodium hydroxide. The acid and alkaline washes extract impurities oxidized by the permanganate. (8,42)

Benzoas, ammoniae; Benzoas, lithii; Benzoas, sodii: The ammonium, lithium, or sodium salt of benzoic acid, obtained by treatment of benzoic acid with ammonia, lithium carbonate, or sodium carbonate. For therapeutic uses, see benzoin. (8)

Benzocaine: Para-amino-benzoic ethyl-ester, an injectable topical anaesthetic. (40)

Benzoes, flores: Benzoic acid. (3)

Benzoic acid; Benzoicum, acidum; Benzoini, flores: Benzoic acid, by sublimation of benzoin, producing fine crystals known as flowers (flores) of benzoin. Primarily utilized as various salts (see benzoas, ____). Therapeutic use is identical to that of benzoin. (8,45)

Benzoic ether: Ethyl benzoate. (3)

Benzoin; Benzoinum; Benzoes, resin.; Bengioino {*Italian*}; Bengivo {*Italian*}: Benzoin, gum benzoin, gum benjamin. A balsamic resin obtained from *Styrax benzoin*, of Asia, in the form of milky white tears, from which benzoic acid is obtained by sublimation. Benzoin and benzoic acid are considered powerful antiseptics and were applied topically as irritants, counterirritants, and antimicrobials. Lint soaked in the compound tincture was particularly favored. It was used internally as a disinfectant for the urine as well as an expectorant, and was said to have antipyretic value similar to or greater than salicylic acid. Placed in heated water, benzoin could be inhaled as an expectorant and disinfectant for bronchitis, laryngitis, tuberculosis, or other chest conditions. Figure 3-38. (1,8)

Benzoin, sal: Benzoic acid. (3)

Benzoin odoriferum: Spicewood, vermifuge and substitute for allspice as a flavoring component, mainly from bark and berries of various American shrubs in the laurel family, such as *Lindera benzoin*. Unofficial. (44)

Benzoinatus, adeps: Benzoinated lard, consisting of 20 parts benzoin for every 1000 parts of lard. The benzoin served to add a pleasant odor and presumably kept the material well preserved due to the antimicrobial properties, as one would expect plain lard to become rancid. Benzoinated lard was one of the most common bases for the preparation of ointments, either alone or in combination with waxes, vaseline, etc. to achieve a desired texture. (8)

Benzoini, lotio: Lait virginal, or virgin's milk, of the simple tincture of benzoin in rose water and optionally with glycerin, as a cosmetic preparation. (42)

Benzoini (composita), tinctura: Tincture of benzoin, of benzoin macerated in alcohol. Compound tincture consisted of benzoin, storax, balsam of tolu, and aloes, digested in alcohol and filtered. A similar compound tincture is still used topically on skin prior to the application of tape dressings to protect the skin and improve adhesion. (8)

Benzoini, unguentum: See benzoinatus, adeps. (34)

Benzol: See benzene (not same as benzine). (42)

Benzoline: Petroleum spirit, see benzin(e). (40)

Benzonaphthol: Betanaphthylbenzoate, an intestinal antiseptic. (3)

Benzophenone; Benzophenonum: Diphenylketone, a C=O group with a phenyl (6-carbon ring) structure on each side, a sedative-hypnotic. (42)

Benzophenoneid: Yellow pyoktanin; an antiseptic. (3)

Benzosol: Benzoyl-guaiacol, guaiacol benzoate, an antitubercular. (3)

Benzosulphinidum (, sodii): Saccharin or the sodium salt, which is more readily dissolved. Sweetener. (40)

Benzoyl hydrate: Benzoic acid. (40)

Benzoyl-glycocoll: Hippuric acid. (40)

Benzoylamino-ethoxy-quinoline: See quinalgen. (40)

Benzyl benzoate; Benzyl succinate: Both benzoic acid derivatives used as "antispasmotics," i.e.-bronchodilators for cough or asthma. (40)

Benzylmorphinae hydrochloridum: Benzylmorphine, product of benzoic acid (chloride) and morphine, a narcotic similar to acetomorphine. (42)

Beprochin: See plasmochin. (40)

Berber(id)is, conserva; Berberor, conserva: Conserve of barberry. (35)

Berberidis, fluidextractum; —, liquor; —, tinctura: Fluid extract, liquor or tincture of berberis. (31,42)

Fig. 3-37 Benedicta or Common Avens.　　　Fig. 3-38 Benzoin.　　　Fig. 3-39 Berberis or common barberry.

Berberina; Berberine (sulphate): Alkaloid extracted from barberry, *Berberis vulgaris*, with antimicrobial and anthelmintic activity.

Berberinae (carbonas)(hydrochloridum)(phosphas)(sulphas): Carbonate, hydrochloride, phosphate and sulfate salts of berberine, used in the same manner. (42)

Berberis; Berberidis, cortex: Common barberry, *Berberis vulgaris*. Bark, seeds, berries used. Primarily a simple bitter or mild laxative. Figure 3-39. (1,7)

Berberis (vulgaris); Berberis vulgaris fluidum, extractum: In US or European use, usually barberry, but also Oregon grape, mountain grape, *Berberis aquifolium* or *Mahonia aquifolia*. A stimulant emetic. (32) Dried stem of *Berberis aristata*, of India and Celon and official in those areas according to the BPC. (42; 46)

Bergamii, essentia: Essence of bergamot, i.e., the distilled essential oil, often diluted with some alcohol.

Bergamot oil; Bergamottae, oleum; Bergamii, oleum: Oil of bergamot, a volatile oil expressed from the fresh fruit of the bergamot orange, *Citrus bergamia*, of Sicily. Although having therapeutic properties similar to other volatile oils (see caryophyllus), it was used almost exclusively in perfumery. (8)

Berlin blue: Prussian blue. (3)

Berthollet's neutral carbonate of ammonia: Ammonium bicarbonate. (40)

Bertoni's ether: Amyl nitrite. (40)

Bestuscheff's tincture: 1. See ferri chloridi aetherea, tinctura. (31)**:** 2. See golden drops. (39)

Betacaine (hydrochloride)(lactate); Beta-eucaine; Betacainum (hydrochloridum)(lactas): Betacaine or its hydrochloride or lactate salt, local anesthetic. (40,42)

Betanaphthol benzoate: Naphthol benzoate. (40)

Betanaphtholum: See naphthol.

Betel (leaf): Leaves of *Piper betle*. This relative of the pepper plant has leaves with mild stimulant activity. It is chewed together with lime (the chemical) by indigenous peoples of Latin America. (40) Not the same as betel nut.

Betel nut: Areca nut or betel nut, from *Areca catechu*. Chewed as a stimulant in Asian native cultures along with lime (the chemical). This is similar to the leaf in use, despite geographical and botanical differences. Medicinal use primarily as a veterinary vermifuge. (3,42)

Beth root: See trillium. (7)

Betol: Betanaphthyl salicylate, an intestinal antiseptic. (3)

Betonica (officinalis); Bettonica {*Italian*}: Wood betony, *Stachys bentonica*. Herb used. Root is emetic and purgative, herb used for many conditions historically. Figure 3-40. (1,44)

Betton's British oil: See brick oil. (39)

Betula: Birch tree. Bark and leaves used. (1)

Betula alba: Common European birch, used as per other betula species. Unofficial. (44)

Betulae (albae) (pyroligneum), oleum; Betulas, oleum; Betulinum (pyroligneum), oleum: Empyreumatic oil of birch, oil of Russia leather, see betula. (3,40)

Betulae compositum, linimentum: Liniment of menthol and oil of eucalyptus with oil of camphor, dissolved in methyl salicylate (oil of wintergreen), for joint and muscular pain. Similar rubs are common today. (42)

Betulae compositum, unguentum: See methylis salicylatis compositum, unguentum. (42)

Betulae volatile, oleum; Betulas lentas, oleum: Volatile oil of Betula, volatile oil distilled from bark of sweet birch, *Betula lenta*. This is nearly identical to oil of gaultherium and is chemically identical to methyl salicylate. (8)

Beyer's pill: See Frankfurt pill. (39)

Bezoar: 1. Concretion or stone found in the stomach or intestines of certain animals. (1) 2. Powder of the liver and heart of a snake (seventeenth century). (39)

Bezoardicum, acetum: Aromatic vinegar, see acetum aromaticum. (3)

Bezoardicum minerale: "Mineral bezoar," obtained by action of nitric acid on antimony trichloride. An alchemical term. (1,19)

Bhang: Cannabis, i.e., cannabis indica. (3)

Biacca {*Italian*}: Ceruse, white lead oxide. (1)

Bianco {*Italian*}: White. (1)

Bibiru bark: Bebeeru bark. (40)

Biborate of soda: Borax. (40)

Bibron's antidote: A treatment for snakebite consisting of potassium iodide, mercury bichloride (corrosive sublimate), and bromine. (24)

Bicalcic phosphate: Calcium phosphate, dibasic. (3)

Bice, green: Native copper carbonate. (40)

Bichiche, pillole: See bechiche, pillole.

Bicreol: Injectable form of finely divided metallic bismuth, anti-infective, especially for syphilis. (40)

Biden bipinnata; Bidens: Spanish Needles, *Bidens bipinnata*, root and seeds used primarily for menstrual disorders. (33)

Bikh; Bish: Root of *Aconitum ferox (A. virorum)*, a relative of monkshood. Homeopathic. (40)

Bile salts: Sodium taurocholate and glycocholate, from animal sources, as a digestive aid. (40)

Bilis bovinum: Ox gall. (3)

Billroth's cambric: A cotton fabric commonly used for plasters. (40)

Bilva: See aegle (marmelos). (40)

Binelli, aqua: Creosote water, see creosote. (3)

Biniodide, soluble tablets (strong) (weak): See solvellae, specifically hydrargyri et potassii iodidi (fortes). (42)

Biogen: Manganese peroxide. (40)

Bipalatinoid: "Gelatin capsule divided by a partition, to keep two powders separate until swallowed." (3)

Birch tar (oil): Oil or tar from wood of the birch, *Betula alba*. (40) See betulae, oleum. (42)

Bird lime: See calx avis. (40)

Bird pepper: See piper indicum. (39)

Bisantiis, syrupus de; Bisantino, siropo {*Italian*}: See byzantiis, syrupus. (1)

Bisenna: See mesenna. (44)

Bish: See bikh.

Bismalva: See althaea. (40)

Fig. 3-40 Betonica or betony.

Bismostab: Injectable form of bismuth metal, for syphilis. (40)

Bismuth; Bismuthum: Bismuth was introduced into medicinal use in approximately 1800, per Estes, by Dr. Louis Odier, as an antispasmodic. It remains in use as bismuth subsalicylate (as in Pepto Bismol ™) for the same purposes. (39)

Bismuth, cosmetic: See bismuth subchloride. (40)

Bismuth, trisnitrate of: Bismuth nitrate. (40)

Bismuth, white (oxide of): See bismuthi subnitras. (39)

Bismuth beta-naptholate: Bismuth naphtholate, anthelmintic. (40)

Bismuth carbolate: See bismuth phenate. (40)

Bismuth cream: Glycerin of bismuth carbonate. (40)

Bismuth dithiosalicylate (, basic): A topical disinfectant used as per iodoform. (40)

Bismuth iodoform paraffin paste; Bism. et iodof. pasta; B.i.p.p.: An official paste (BPC) of bismuth oxide and iodoform in paraffin, a disinfectant. (40)

Bismuth oxycarbonate: See bismuthi subcarbonas. (40)

Bismuth oxychloride: See bismuth subchloride. (40)

Bismuth oxygallate: See bismuthi subgallas. (40)

Bismuth oxyhydrate: See bismuthi hydroxidum. (40)

Bismuth oxynitrate: Bismuth subnitrate. (40)

Bismuth subiodide: Bismuth oxyiodide. (40)

Bismuthi, carbonatis, glyceritum: Glycerite of bismuth carbonate, BPC (1923), similar to bismuthi, glyceritum. (40)

Bismuthi, cremor: Glycerite of bismuth carbonate, BPC (1923), similar to bismuthi, glyceritum. (40) In the NF, see bismuthi oxidum hydratum.

Bismuthi, elixir: Elixir of bismuth, made from glycerite of bismuth, glycerin, distilled water, and aromatic elixir; used as an intestinal astringent. (31) In the BPC, of bismuth and ammonium citrate, distilled water, solution of ammonia, and aromatic elixir.

Bismuthi, flores: Bismuth oxide. (3)

Bismuthi, glyceritum: Glycerite of bismuth, made from bismuth subnitrate, nitric acid, tartaric acid, sodium bicarbonate, glycerin, and distilled water. It is used in making other preparations containing bismuth. "As the bismuth in this compound is in a soluble form it does not represent the virtues of bismuth subnitrate which are largely due to the insolubility of that salt." (31)

Bismuthi, liquor: Solution of bismuth, made from glycerite of bismuth, alcohol, and distilled water, used as an intestinal astringent, "but does not possess the therapeutic virtues of the insoluble bismuth salts." (31,46)

Bismuthi, mistura: A mixture of glycerin of bismuth and water. (42)

Bismuthi, trochisci: Troche of bismuth subnitrate, magnesium carbonate, carbonate of lime, sugar, and gum arabic. For local inflammation or systemic administration of bismuth. (44)

Bismuthi, unguentum: Unguent of bismuth subnitrate in lard, for pruritis and skin inflammation including chilblains. (42)

Bismuthi carbonas: See bismuth subcarbonate. (42)

Bismuthi carbonatis, glycerinum: Glycerin of bismuth carbonate, of the nitrate with ammonium carbonate, glycerin, and distilled water. An alternate means to administer bismuth. (42)

Bismuthi citras: Bismuth citrate. Use as per the subcarbonate. (8,42)

Bismuthi composita (cum morphino)(cum pepsino)(cum soda), mistura: A mixture of bismuth citrate, solution of ammonia, chloroform, tincture of nux vomica, dilute hydrocyanic acid, solution of carmine (colorant), and water. A "gastric sedative" used in pyrosis and gastric catarrh. One could also add morphine to reduce motility and suppress vomiting, pepsin to assist digestion, or "soda" (sodium bicarbonate) as an antacid. (42)

Bismuthi compositum, pulvis: Compound powder of bismuth, of magnesium carbonate, bismuth oxynitrate, and cretae aromaticus, pulvis. (40)

Bismuthi concentratus, liquor: A solution (BPC) of bismuth oxynitrate, nitric and citric acids, sodium bicarbonate, solution of ammonia, and solution of ammonium citrate in water; twice the strength of bismuthi, liquor, but for same uses. (42)

Bismuthi et ammonii citra(ti)s (effervescens): Bismuth and ammonium citrate. This is readily soluble and used as an astringent orally. Also specified in an effervescent solution. (8,42)

Bismuthi et morphinae, insufflatio: Bismuth subnitrate and morphine hydrochloride in powdered gum acacia, for insufflation into the nose for catarrh. (42)

Bismuthi et sodii bicarbonatis, tablettae: Tablet of sodium bicarbonate, bismuth oxycarbonate, gum acacia, talc, and water to bind, for gastric catarrh. (42)

Bismuthi et zinci, pasta; Past. Bism. et Zinc: Paste of bismuth and zinc, BPC (1923). (40)

Bismuthi hydroxidum: The hydrate, or oxyhydrate, of bismuth, use as per the subcarbonate. (42)

Bismuthi naphtholas: Bismuth naphtholate, combining astringent effects of bismuth salts with disinfectant and antiparasitic properties of naphthol, for intestinal disorders. (42)

Bismuthi nitras: Bismuth nitrate, converts to subnitrate in dilute solutions, soluble in glycerin and used to treat skin diseases. (42)

Bismuthi oleas: Bismuth oleate, used as a dusting powder or ointment for skin conditions. (42)

Bismuthi oleatus, unguentum: Ointment of bismuth oleate in paraffin, topical astringent for skin conditions. (42)

Bismuthi oxidum (hydratum): Bismuth oxide, use as per the subcarbonate. (42) In the NF (46) the hydratum (hydrated form) is prepared from bismuth subnitrate treated with nitric acid, ammonia water, and washed with sodium bicarbonate.

Bismuthi oxyiodidum: See the subiodide. For ulcers internally (as with the subcarbonate) or topical astringent disinfectant in place of iodoform, or injection for gonorrhea. (42)

Bismuthi oxyiodo(sub)gallate: Bismuth oxyiodogallate. Mainly a topical for skin diseases. (40,42)

Bismuthi phenate; —phenolate: Bismuth phenate, oral anti-infective and anthelmintic. (40)

Bismuthi salicylas: Bismuth sub-salicylate, a non-irritating intestinal antiseptic for the treatment of intestinal catarrh, diarrhea, and general gastric upset. It is the active ingredient in Pepto-Bismol™. (8)

Bismuthi subcarbonas; Bism. dubcarb.: Bismuth subcarbonate, probably mainly $(BiO)_2CO_3$. An insoluble salt. At one time thought to have emetic effects, this was due to arsenic impurities in early bismuth preparations. The material is mildly astringent and used as a topical protective and astringent for the skin and gastrointestinal tract. While this salt has fallen from use, the subsalicylate salt is still in use for gastro-intestinal treatment in the form of Pepto-Bismol™ and related medications. (8)

Bismuthi subchloridum: The subchloride, BiOCl, a fine lustrous powder that is still used to provide "shimmer" in cosmetics, also a topical disinfectant for open skin conditions or wounds. Can be applied to mucous membranes by insufflation or used in suppositories. (42)

Bismuthi subgallas: Bismuth subgallate, a non-toxic, non-irritant topical disinfectant, also used internally for fermentative dyspepsias and diarrhea due to tuberculosis or typhoid. (8)

Bismuthi subnitras: Bismuth subnitrate, probably mainly $BiONO_3$. Used as per the subcarbonate. (8)

Bismuthi tannas: Bismuth tannate combines two astringents and was used for diarrhea and dysentery. (42)

Bismuthose: Bismuth albuminate. Antacid. (40)

Bismuthum album: See bismuthi subnitras. (40)

Bismuthum carbonicum, etc.: Probably bismuth carbonate. The "bismuthum" in place of bismuthi is common in homeopathic formularies. See additional bismuth salts above.

Bismuthyl iodide: Bismuth oxyiodide. (40)

Bisodol: Proprietary brand antacid, of sodium bicarbonate with calcium and magnesium carbonate.

Bissy nuts: See kola nut (40)

Bistort(a): Bistort, snakeweed, adderwort, *Polygonum bistorta*. Rhizome used. Astringent and styptic. Figure 3-41. (1)

Bisulfite: See discussion of metabisulfite.

Bisulphate of potash: Acid potassium sulfate, see potasii sulphas. (40)

Bitartrate of potash: Acid potassium tartrate, see potassii tartras. (40)

Bitter almond: See amygdala amara. (8)

Bitter apple: See colocynth. (8)

Bitter bark: See alstonia. (32)

Bitter drops: See Stoughton's bitters. (39)

Bitter purging salts (, Moult's): Magnesium sulfate, i.e., Epsom salts. (39)

Bitter tincture: See amara, tinctura. (31)

Bitter wine of iron: See ferri amarum, vinum. (8)

Bitter wood: See quassia. (40)

Bittera febrifuga: Bitter ash, febrifuge. Unofficial. (44)

Bittersweet: See dulcamara. (8)

Bittersweet, false: For American usage see celastrus. British usage is *Solarium dulcamara*, see dulcamara. (40)

Bitumen, sulfonated: Bitumen processed with sulfuric acid to produce a variety of sulfur derivatives of the aromatic carbon compounds contained therein. Used topically as per icthyol, which is similarly produced.

Bitumen Judaicum: Asphalt, see asphaltus. (1,3)

Bitumen petroleum: See petroleum barbadense. (39)

Bituminis sulphonati, collodium: Collodion of sulphonated bitumen (ichthyol), ichthyol collodion, ten percent sulphonated bitumen in flexible collodion. See ichthyol. (31)

Bituminis sulphonati, unguentum: Ointment of sulphonated bitumen, ichthyol ointment, ten percent sulphonated bitumen in petrolatum. (31)

Bituro; Biturro {*Italian*}: Butter. (1) In ancient chemistry, a chloride salt of a metal, see butter.

Bizantiis, syrupus de: See byzantiis, syrupus. (1)

Black balsam: Peru balsam. (3)

Fig. 3-41 Bistorta or bistort.

Black basilicon ointment: Black ointment made with pitch. (3)

Black bryony: The herb, *Tamus communis*, not the same as bryony (bryonia). Use appears to be homeopathic. (40)

Black cohosh: See cimicifuga. (8)

Black draught: A compound infusion of senna (see sennae compositum, infusum), "must not be confounded with Black Drop." (3,8)

Black drop: Vinegar of opium. See opii crocatum, acetum. (3,8)

Black elder: Hemp agrimony, see eupatorium. (40)

Black flux: Mixture of charcoal and potassium carbonate. If referring to a diagnosis, this is diarrhea containing blood, which turns black if of upper gastrointestinal origin. (3)

Black haw: See viburnum prunifolium. (31)

Black jam: See sennae, confectio. (40)

Black lead: Graphite. A sundry use as a lubricant, non-therapeutic. (40)

Black lotion; Black wash: See nigra, lotio. (31)

Black oxide of iron: Magnetic oxide of iron, magnetite. (40)

Black oxide of mercury: Mercurous oxide. See hydrargyri suboxidum. (40)

Black powder: See pulvis nigrum. (34)

Black Samson: See echinacea. (32)

Black sassafras: See cinamomum oliveri. (40)

Black snakeroot: Black cohosh, see cimicifuga. (8)

Black sugar: Licorice extract in sticks, or succus glycyrrhizae, licorice juice. (40)

Blackberry: See rubus. (8)

Bladder wrack: See fucus. (40)

Blanc [de fard][de perle][d'Espagne]: Pearl white, white of Spain, a precipitated bismuth subchloride or mixture of zinc oxide with bismuth. Primarily to add "shimmer" to cosmetics. (40)

Blanc de baleine: Spermaceti. (40)

Blanc de Troyes: Prepared chalk. (3)

Blanc fixe: Artificial barium carbonate or sulfate. (3)

Blanc {*French*}: White. (1)

Blancard's pills: Pills of ferrous iodide. (3)

Blankit: A proprietary bleaching compound of sodium formaldehyde sulphoxylate. (3)

Blatta: Dried, pulverized bodies of the common cockroach, *Blatta orientalis*, a diuretic. One presumes it was rarely, if ever, identified to the patient by anything other than the Latin term. (32)

Blatta bysantia: Shell of *Murex inflatus* and certain other molluscs. (1)

Blaud's pills: See ferri carbonatis, pilulae. (8) The BPC indicates (see) ferri, pilluli instead. (42)

Blaud's tablets: See ferri, tablettae. (42)

Blazing Star: See helonias. (7)

Bleaching liquid: Solution of chlorinated lime, see calx chlorata. (40)

Bleaching powder: See calx chlorata. (8)

Bleaching solution: See calcis chlorinatae, liquor. (42)

Blister beetle, Chinese: *Mylabris Phalerata* and related species. See cantharis. (40)

Blister(ing) flies or beetles: See cantharis. (8)

Blistering liquid: Liquor epispasticus, same as cantharidis, linimentum. (40)

Blistering paper: See epispastica, charta.

Blistering plaster: See cantharidis, emplastrum. (40)

Block juice: A commercial extract of licorice. (40)

Blois, bole of: See bolus blesensis. (39)

Bloodroot: See sanguinaria. (8)

Blue, Berlin: Prussian blue. (3)

Blue, Chinese: Prussian blue. (3)

Blue acid: Prussic or hydrocyanic acid. (3)

Blue black: A name for ivory-black (charcoal of ivory). (3)

Blue butter: See blue ointment; hydrargyum, unguentum. (40)

Blue cohosh: See caulophyllum. (40)

Blue copperas: Copper sulfate, see cupri sulphas. (3)

Blue flag: See iris. (8)

Blue gauze: See carbasus salis alembroth. (40)

Blue gum tree: See eucalyptus. (40)

Blue lint: See linteum salis alembroth. (40)

Blue mass; Blue pills: Mercury mass (for pill manufacture) or pills. See hydrargyri, massa or piluli, accordingly. (8)

Blue ointment; —unction: Unguentum mercuriale, see hydrargyrum, unguentum. (40)

Blue paint: Brilliant green and crystal violet dyes, one percent each, in rectified spirits and water, a topical antimicrobial. (40)

Blue pill: Mercury pill, see hydrargyri, pilluli (40)

Blue plaster: See hydrargyri, emplastrum. (39)

Blue wool: See gossypium salis alembroth. (40)

Bluestone; Blue vitriol: Copper sulfate (see cupri sulphas). (3)

Boldo (folia); Boldus; Boldi, fluidextractum; —fluidum, extractum; —, tinctura: Boldo, a tree or shrub native to Chile, *Peumus boldus*, or the fluid extract or alcoholic tincture therefrom, used as an alterative and tonic. (3,31,32,42,46)

Bole: See bolus.

Bole, Armenian; —, red: See bolus Armenia. (40)

Bole, white: Kaolin, China clay, see bolus alba. (40)

Boletus: See agaric. (32)

Bolus: 1. Bole, a fine clay or earth (terra) of various sources, i.e., Armenia (*bolus Armenius*), Lemnos (*terra Lemnia*), Bohemia (Bohemian bole), etc. Formed into cylinders or pressed into tablets and stamped to assure authenticity, it was referred to as *terra sigillata* (signed or stamped earth). They disintegrate slowly in the mouth, and were used as astringents, diaphoretics, and general alexipharmics (panaceas). (1,39) 2. A large soft pill, weighing from 10 to 20 grains. (40)

Bolus alba: Kaolin clay. (3)

Bolus Armenia (rubra): Armenian bole, a soil from Armenia. (3)

Bolus blesensis: Bole of Blois, a fine yellow bole (clay) which effervesces strongly in the presence of acid. (39)

Bombax: Cotton plant. (1) Cotton is more commonly referred to by the current genus name, *gossypium*.

Bombyx: Silkworm, species *Bombyx*. (1)

Bonain's solution: A topical anesthetic for the ear drum, of menthol, eucalyptiol, and cocaine. (24)

Bonduc: Bonduc plant, *Caesalpinia bonducella,* an alternative antimalarial agent, native to India. (32)

Bone ash; —earth: Crude calcium phosphate. (3,40)

Bone black; —char(coal): Animal charcoal. (3)

Bone marrow, red: Marrow of young calf bones. (40)

Bone oil: See Dippel's oil. (3)

Bones, spirit of: A solution of ammonia, see ammoniae liquor. (40)

Boneset: See eupatorium. (8)

Bonney's blue: See blue paint. (40)

Bontius, water pill of: Latinized form in reference to Jacob de Bondt, Dutch physician in the East Indies (1598-1631). The water pill was a diuretic and cathartic of aloe and scammony. (1,39)

Boracic acid; Boric acid; Boricum, acidum: Boric acid, H_3BO_3, from the action of hydrochloric acid on borax (see sodii boras). Primarily a disinfectant. Room temperature saturated solutions of boric acid are conveniently isotonic (same overall ionic concentration) with body fluids and not corrosive, and hence are useful as irrigants for the eye, mouth, or in wounds. (8)

Boracis, acidum, glyceritum; Boric., ac., Glyc.: See glyceritum boroglycerini. Colons in latter entry appear in original.

Boracis, gargarisma: Four percent borax in water, as a gargle for throat ulcers. (42)

Boracis, glycerinum: Borax in glycerin, for topical application in the oropharynx. (42)

Boracis, lotio (cum morphinae): Borax lotion, a solution of sodium borate, usually with rosewater, for use as a general irrigant, particularly an eye wash. Saturated sodium borate has a concentration conveniently near the concentration of ions in body fluids (i.e., is isotonic) and thus is well tolerated. Could include morphine for additional analgesia. (34)

Boracis, mel; Boratis, mel: Borated honey, with sodium borate. (34)

Boracis, unguentum; Boric: ung: Borax ointment, of powdered borax and lard. (36) Ointment of borax in spermaceti ointment base. (42) Colons in latter entry appear in original.

Boracis compositus, liquor: Compound solution of borax, a dilute solution of borax (boric acid) containing sodium bicarbonate and carbolic acid. Nasal disinfectant and irrigant. (42)

Borago; Borrago; Boragine {*Italian*}**:** Common borage, *Borrago officinalis*. Herb or flower used for many purposes, inconsistent in various sources. Figure 3-42. (1)

Boral: Aluminium borotartrate. (40)

Borate of soda: Borax. (40)

Borax, red: Red oxide of mercury. (3)

Borax; Boracis, sal acidum; Borace {*Italian*}**:** Sodium borate, used for many purposes—astringent, diuretic, emmenagogue, sedative, etc. See sodii boras. (8,39)

Borici, acidi, [et zinci], collyrium: Boric acid eye wash, with or without a small quantity of zinc sulfate to enhance astringency, for conjunctivitis or other inflammations of the eye. (42)

Borici, acidi, carbasus: Antiseptic gauze soaked in a solution of saturated boiling boric acid and a small amount of aniline red dye, pressed and dried. (42)

Borici, acidi, et amylis, pulvis: Powder of equal parts boric acid and starch, a dusting powder for skin. (42)

Borici, acidi, glycerinum: Boric acid in glycerin, as a topical antiseptic paint in the throat, or diluted with water to make an antiseptic solution or gargle. (42)

Borici, acidi, gossypium: Absorbent cotton soaked in boric acid and dried. (42)

Borici, acidi, lotio: Three percent boric acid in water, antiseptic surgical irrigant. (42)

Borici, acidi, unguentum: Ointment of boric acid, of same, in paraffin. (34)

Boricum, acidum (, [p.][pv.][pulv.]): Boric acid (powdered).

Borneal; Borneol; Borneo camphor; Bornyl alcohol: Borneo camphor, originally a crude mixture derived from various plants, later a specific camphor-like terpene compound synthetically produced. A topical refrigerant and disinfectant.

Boroboracic acid; Boroboric acid: Mixture of equal parts of borax and boric acid. (3)

Borago officinalis

Published by B:Woodville Feb:ʸ 1. 1794.

Fig. 3-42 Borago or borage.

Borocaine: Ethocaine borate, a topical local anesthetic. (40)

Boroglyceride: Proprietary form of boroglycerinum. (42)

Boroglycerini, suppositoria: Suppositories of boroglycerin, of glycerinated gelatin, glycerin, and glyceratum boroglycerini. (31)

Boroglycerin(um): Boroglycerin, a forty-seven percent borax in glycerin, a mild topical disinfectant. (42)

Borrusic acid; Borussicum, acidum: Hydrocyanic acid. (3,40)

Bos: Ox (Latin). (1)

Botany Bay kino: See kino eucalypti. (42)

Botrys: Leaves and seed of Jerusalem oak, *Chenopodium botrys*. (39)

Bougie: A device for the dilation of strictures (esophageal, etc.) made by dipping strips of cloth or bundles of thread into greasy, waxy, or other plastic materials and forming a tapered shape by rolling on a slab. They could contain additional medications. The stated material was repeatedly applied in coats and baked, resulting in a hard device which was ground with pumice and polished to a smooth finish. See also: cerioli. King's American Dispensatory notes the following bougies (42):
- **Bell's**—lead plaster, yellow wax, and olive oil.
- **Elastic**—boiled linseed oil, amber, oil of turpentine, caoutchouc.
- **Goulard's**—yellow wax with Goulard's extract of lead.
- **Hunters**—olive oil, yellow wax, red lead.
- **Piperdet's**—yellow wax, olive oil.
- **Swediaur's**—white wax, spermaceti, lead acetate.

Bouin's fluid: A fixative for microscopy, of formaldehyde, picric acid, and acetic acid. (24)

Boulton's solution: See iodi phenolatus, liquor. (31)

Bourrache {*French*}**:** Borrage, see borrago. (1)

Bovinus, succus: Beef "juice"—squeezed from fresh beef and used to make beef tea or as a nutritive and gastric stimulant. (42)

Bowman's root: See gillenia. (33)

Box berry: See gaultheria. (40)

Boxwood: See cornus (florida). (39)

Boyle's fuming liquor: Ammonium sulphide, see ammoniae, hydro-sulphuretum. (40)

Bran oil: Furfural, an organic solvent. (3)

Branalcane: A commercial boric acid preservative. (40)

Brandish's solution: Impure solution of potash. (40)

Brandy mixture: See vini gallici, spiritus, mistura. (34)

Brandy, Indian: See tincture, Indian. (40)

Brasium: Malt. (3)

Brassica: Cabbage and related species. This large family contains cabbage, brussels sprouts, rapeseed, broccoli, cauliflower, etc. Possibly antiscorbutic. (1,39)

Brassica marina: Leaves of sea colewort, Scot's scurvygrass, or soldanella, *Convolvulus soldanella*. A powerful cathartic. (39)

Brassil: Pyrite, iron sulfide mineral commonly called fool's gold, use unclear. (3)

Brayera: See cusso. (8)

Brayerae, infusum: Infusion of brayera (see cusso) which must be freshly prepared. (31)

Brazil nut: Brazil nut as currently consumed, the oil of which could be used for ointments. Unofficial. (44)

Brazil wax: Carnauba wax. (3)

Brazil wood: The species *Caesalpina echinata*, one alternative source of sanguis draconis. (39)

Brazilian cacao: Guarana. (3)

Breakstone: *Alchemilla arvensis*, parsley piert. Mainly a topical demulcent and refrigerant, but also diuretic and supposedly effective for urinary stones. (40)

Breast tea: See species pectorales. (31)

Bresille wood: Red sanders wood, see santalum. (40)

Brick oil: Brick oil, from distillation of bricks soaked in oil and powdered. Originally of rosemary oil, later petroleum oil, this is related to philosopher's oil (see philosophorum, oleum) obtained from the bricks of alchemical furnaces. Michael and Thomas Betton marketed this as an antiscorbutic and antirhumatic product called Betton's British Oil ca. 1740. (39)

Brimstone: See sulphur, roll.

Brionia: See bryonia. (1)

Britannica, herba: See lapathum. (39)

British gum: Dextrin. (40)

British oil: See brick oil. (39)

Brodie's (Sir Benjamin) gout pills: Colchici et hydrargyri compositae, pilulae. (42)

Bromalin: Bromethylformin, a disinfectant. (40)

Bromatum, oleum: See bromopin. (40)

Bromcamphora: Camphor bromide. Used for sedative effects of bromide and also in the homeopathic formulary.

Bromi, aqua: Same as (see) bromi, liquor. (42)

Bromi (fortis), liquor: Solution of bromine and potassium bromide, a stronger (fortis) version being specified in the BPC. (34,42,46)

Bromidorum, syrupus: Syrup of the bromides, made from potassium, sodium, ammonium, calcium, and lithium bromides (five bromides—see immediately above), with tincture of vanilla, compound tincture of cudbear (see persio), compound syrup of sarsaparilla and simple syrup. Used as a nerve sedative. (31)

Bromidorum quinque, elixir: Elixir of five bromides. "What the advantage is of having five different salts of hydrobromic acid in combination, is not very obvious; they are sodium, potassium, calcium, lithium and ammonium bromides." (31)

Bromidorum trium, elixir: Elixir of three bromides, ammonium, potassium and sodium bromides. As with bromidorum quinque, elixir, the therapeutic advantage of this combination is not clear. (31)

Bromine; Brominum; Bromum: Bromine, a volatile liquid at ambient temperatures, Br_2. Obtained from seaweed. All of the bromide salts are used primarily for their sedative effect, and are also known to be cardio-depressant and to mildly suppress respirations. The latter effects are probably secondary to nervous system suppression. The sedative effects are undoubtedly responsible for the slang term, bromide (as in "that old bromide") in reference to a soothing or sedating song or saying. (8,44)

Brominol; Bromipin: Sesame oil with bromine. Disinfectant. (40)

Bromochloral compositus, liquor: A solution (BPC) of chloral hydrate, juice of hyoscyamus and potassium bromide in syrup and water, with liquid extract of licorice, and tinctures of orange and Indian hemp. A sedative. (42)

Bromoform; Bromoformum: Bromoform, tribromomethane, $CHBr_3$. Primarily an anesthetic, useful for whooping cough. (8)

Bromol: Tribromophenol, an antiseptic. (3)

Bromolyptol: Formolyptol, a disinfectant. (40)

Bromphenobis: Xeroform, bismuth tribromophenate, a disinfectant still in use. (40)

Brompton('s) (Hospital) Mixture; Brompton('s) Cocktail: There is considerable confusion among these related materials. Brompton's Cocktail refers to a variety of narcotic pain relieving and cough suppressant medications, with some variant formulations even including cocaine. These were directed primarily at the treatment of cough due to tuberculosis at the Royal Brompton Hospital in London. Brompton's Hospital Mixture properly refers to mistura acidi hydrocyanici composita (BPC, see hydrocyanici, mistura acidi, composita), a mixture of dilute hydrocyanic (Prussic) acid and morphine, with both components directed at managing cough. This being said, the terms "mixture" and "cocktail" seem to be used haphazardly, with or without "hospital," usually in reference to a pain relieving narcotic. (40)

Bromural: Uvaleral, a brominated urea compound with sedative-hypnotic activity. (40)

Brooklime: See beccabunga. (39)

Broom: See scoparius. (8)

Brown Holland: A plain linen or cotton fabric, for plasters. (40)

Brown mixture: See glycyrrhizae composita, pulvis. (8)

Brown ointment: Eye ointment similar to (see) zinci oxidi compositum, unguentum. See also fuscum, unguentum. (31,34)

Brown plaster, camphorated: See fuscum camphoratum, emplastrum. (31)

Brown soap plaster: Soap plaster, see saponis, emplastrum. (40)

Brown-Sequard's fluid: Spermin, an extract of testes. This was claimed to restore "vigor" to older men and is part of a long history of both legitimate and (far more often) fraudulent treatment based upon organ extracts or transplants. (40)

Brown-Séquard's (antineuralgic) pills: A complex pain remedy after the eminent neurologist Charles-Edouard Brown Séquard, of extracts of hyoscyamus, conium, ignatia, opium, aconite leaf, cannabis indica, and stramonium with alcoholic extract of belladonna leaf. (46)

Browning: Burnt sugar, i.e., caramel. (40)

Bruciato; Brugiato {*Italian*}**:** Burnt. (1)

Brucine: See nux vomica. Related to strychnine and used in a similar manner. (8)

Brucite: Magnesium hydroxide. (3)

Brugnatelli's vermafuge powder: Tin sulfide. (39)

Bruisewort: See saponaria. (39)

Brunella: See prunella. (1)

Bruscus: See ruscus. (1)

Bryonia; Brioniae radix; Brioniae, tinctura; Bryony: This is the root of common bryony, *Bryonia alba* or *B. dioica*. The root or tincture was used as a powerful cathartic as per scammony. Figure 3-43. (1, 8,7)

Bubon (galbanum): See galbanum. (39)

Bubulum, oleum: Neat's-foot oil. This is a form of bone oil expressed from the feet and shin bones of the pig. (3,39)

Bucco: See buchu. (8)

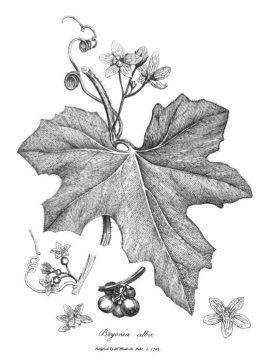

Fig. 3-43 Bryonia or common bryony.

Buchu; —fluidum, extractum; —liquidum, extractum; —, elixir; —, infusum (concentratum); —, tincture: The leaves of *Barosma betulina*, of southern Africa, from which the oil is obtained as a fluid extract, further used to produce an elixir, or leaves may be extracted in alcohol to prepare a tincture. Buchu has most of the actions attributed to volatile oils in general (see caryophyllus), but was especially used as a diuretic and urinary disinfectant as well as for irritable bladder, gonorrhea, pyelonephritis, etc. The elixir consists of the fluidextract, alcohol, and aromatic elixir (aromaticum, elixir). (8,31,42) An infusion is also noted, as well as a concentrate with alcohol and chloroform water for storage and reconstitution. (40,42) The infusion is said to be one of the best ways to administer this material. (34)

Buchu, juniperi et potassii acetatis, elixir: Elixir of buchu, juniper, and potassium acetate. "The proportion of active ingredients is so small that one is forced to the conclusion that the most potent substance, in this elixir, is the alcohol." (31)

Buchu composita, mistura: A mixture of potassium citrate and tincture of hyoscyamus in infusion of buchu. Diuretic and urinary sedative, for cystitis, bladder catarrh, nervous urinary retention, or incontinence. (42)

Buchu compositum, elixir: Compound fluid extract (below) of buchu is used instead of the simple fluid extract (see above) to produce this elixir. See buchu. (31)

Buchu compositum, fluidextractum; —fluidum, extractum: Compound fluid extract of buchu, with cubeb, juniper and uva ursi. (31,46)

Buchu et potassii acetatis, elixir: Elixir of buchu and potassium acetate, used in cystitis with acid urine. (31)

Buchu, foliae; Buchu fol.: Buchu foliage, i.e., leaves.

Buckbean: See trifolium. (39)

Buckeye: See aesculus. (32)

Buckthorn: See frangula. (8)

Buckthorn berries, syrup of: See rhamni catharticae, syrupus. (31)

Bufo: Toad (Latin). (1)

Bugleweed: See lycopus. (32)

Bugloss (, dyer's); Buglossum; Buglossa {*Italian*}**:** Bugloss, the common alkanet, *Anchusa* (formerly *Alkanna*) *officinalis* and related members of the borage family, *Boraginaceae*. See alkanna and especially discussion under anchusa. (1,33)

Bullientis, aqua(e): Boiling water. (3)

Bur(r)ow's solution; Burowii, liquor: See alumini acetatis, liquor. (31)

Burdock: See Lappa. (8)

Burgundica, pix; Burgundy pitch: See pix burgundia. (8)

Burnet saxifrage: See pimpinella. (39)

Burnett's fluid; Burnett's solution: Twenty percent solution of zinc chloride, used as an antiseptic and disinfectant on equipment and surfaces. (8)

Bursa pastoris: Shepherd's purse, *Capsella bursa pastoris*. Herb used. (1)

Butcher's broom: See ruscus. (39)

Butea gum: Gum (kino) from *Butea frondosa*, bastard teak, of India. Astringent, like kino. (40,42)

Buteae semina: Seeds of butea, aperient and anthelmintic, used as a topical rubifacient in lemon juice. (42)

Buteae seminum, pulvis: Powder of butea seed, anthelmintic and laxative, official in India and eastern British colonies. (42)

Butipyrine; Butyl-amidopyrine: An analgesic, see trigemin(e). (40)

Butter (of antimony, tin, lead, zinc): The chloride salt of the respective metal. (3,39) Etymology unclear.

Butter color: Annatto. (3)

Buttercup: See ranunculus. (39)

Butternut: See juglans. (8)

Butyl chloral hydrate: Butyl chloral, a sedative, much like chloral or chloral hydrate, useful for trigeminal neuralgia. (8)

Butyl hypnal: Butylchloral-antipyrin, hypnotic and antipyretic anti-inflammatory as a result of antipyrin content. (3)

Butyl nitris; Butyl nitrite: A vasodilating nitrite compound that gives a "rush" sensation and euphoria. See amyl nitrite, as butyl nitrite can be used similarly. (40)

Butyl-chloral hydras, mistura: A mixture of butyl-chloral hydrate, glycerin, chloroform, and water, for facial neuralgia. (42)

Butyl-chloral hydratis, syrupus: Butyl chloral hydrate in simple syrup. (42)

Butyl-cresyl iodide: A powerful antiseptic. (40)

Butyrum majoranae: Ointment of sweet marjoram (see majorana). (3)

Butyrum nucistae: Expressed oil of nutmeg (see myristica). (3)

Butyrum: 1. Butter (dairy product). (1): 2. A chloride salt of a metal, see butter (of). (39)

Buxus (sempervirens): Box, boxwood, *Buxus sempervirens*, leaves used as cathartic, sudorific, alterative, and anthelmintic. (33)

Byne(s); Bynin: "Apparently a favorite name in England for malt and malted preparations." (3) See malt. (8)

Bysantia, blatta: See blatta bysantia. (1)

Byzantiis, syrupus de: Syrup made from bugloss, endive, smallage, hops, and sugar, used in the treatment of liver disorders. (1)

C

C.: In the beginning or middle of inscription: most commonly an abbreviation for the Latin *cum* (i.e., with), often as the letter c or C with a bar above, frequently in reduced font size. Corteccia {*Italian*} or cortex (bark, peel) is also common, but may also be compositum (composite); conditum (sweetmeat); confectio or confeczione {*Italian*} (confection); conserva (conserve); or costus (the plant species). At the end of the inscription: compositum or composto {*Italian*} (composite). (1)

C. aurant.: See aurantii, cortex. (29)

C.A.: Cum agarico, with larch agaric, see agarica. (1)

C.C. (succinatus), liquor: See cornu cervi, liquor or cornu cervi succinatus, liquor. (3)

C.C.: Cornu cervi, i.e., antler or harts horn. (1) See also sal c:c.

C. fl. ros. pall.: See rosae pallidae, confectio flores.

C.O. salts: See Crab Orchard salts.

C.P.: Commercially purified, a chemical grade, quality just below that of analytical reagent, suitable for commercial use. This would indicate a relatively recent label, probably twentieth century.

C.R.: Cum rubarbaro (with rhubarb) or cum rheo (with poppy). (1)

Cabardine musk: Inferior grade of musk from Tibet; see moschus. (40)

Cabbage oil: Oil derived from cabbage, genus *Brassica*, said to be an approximation to (presumably a replacement for) oil of elder; see sambucinum, oleum. (40)

Cabbage tree: See geoffroea. (39)

Cabotz: See cusso. (40)

Cacao, syrupus: Syrup of cocoa, syrup of chocolate, chocolate syrup, a pleasant flavoring agent of chocolate, tincture of vanilla, and sugar. (31)

Cacao: Chocolate, from the seed of the cacao plant, *Theobroma cacao*. (39)

Caccharatum: Orthographic variant or error for saccharatum.

Cachectic powder; Cachecticus, pulvis: Cachectic powder, a restorative with sugar, iron, and cinnamon. (39)

Cachecticus, syrupus: Syrup of senna, larch agaric, polypody rhizome, agrimony and maidenhair leaves, safflower seeds, cinnamon, etc., to treat chachexia. (1)

Cacodylic acid; Cacodylicum, acidum: Dimethylarsinic acid, an organoarsenical used mainly as an herbicide, but also for antimicrobial properties, especially for tuberculosis, and for a wide range of other conditions from asthma or diabetes to neurasthenia. (3,40)

Cactus (grandiflorus); Cacti grandiflori, tinctura: Cactus grandiflorus, or night-blooming cereus, *Cactus grandiflorus* or *Selenicereus grandiflorus*, or the tincture therefrom. The latter by maceration and expression, then further percolation in alcohol. "It is supposed by some to act as a regulator of cardiac arrhythmias." See cerius (grandiflorus). (7,8,31)

Cacumina; Cacuminae: Tops or shoots of a plant, Latin.

Caddis: Cotton wool, lint; see gossypium. (40)

Cade, oil of; Cadinum, oleum: See juniper, oil of. (8)

Cadmia: An impure zinc oxide. Cadmia was the deposit in the chimney of zinc smelting operations and contained mixed oxides of zinc, cadmium (named for this source), and other metals. (1)

Cadmii iodi; —iodidum: Cadmium iodide, applied externally to enlarged glands and joints and as a topical for chilblains and other skin conditions. (42,44)

Cadmii iodidi, unguentum: Ointment of cadmium iodide in simple ointment base, applied to enlarged glands. (42)

Cadmii sulphas: Cadmium sulfate, astringent and emetic. (44)

Cadmium: Introduced in USP in 1868, for purpose of preparing the sulfate or iodide. (44)

Caerulea, pilula: Mercury pills or blue pills, see hydrargyri, massa. (8,40)

Caerulea; Caeruleus; Caeruleum: Blue (Latin), but cerulea, etc. is a common variant.

Caeruleum (mite), unguentum: Blue ointment (mild), from mercury, hog's lard, and turpentine, as a treatment for venereal disorders. (1)

Caffa: Camphor. (3)

Caffea: Coffee, bean (techically, seed of the fruit) of the coffee tree, *Caffea arabica* or *C. robusta*. See also—coffea for additional entries with that spelling variant. Figure 3-44

Caffeae; syrupus: Coffee syrup, a flavoring.

Caffeina; Caffeine: Caffeine, also referred to as guaranine or theine. Generally from hot water extraction of tea leaves (*Thea sinensis*) or coffee bean (*Cafea arabica* or *C. robusta*). Used, as today, as a nervous stimulant, as well as to stimulate the heart and as a diuretic. (8)

Fig. 3-44 Caffea, coffea, or coffee tree.

Caffeina citrata (effervescens); Caffeinae citras: Caffeine citrate, from isolated caffeine and citric acid, or in effervescent powder form when prepared with sugar, tartaric acid, and sodium bicarbonate. (8)

Caffeinae, elixir: Elixir of caffeine specified in NF, of same with diluted hydrobromic acid in a mixture of aromatic elixir and syrup of coffee. (45,46)

Caffeinae hydrobromidum (effervescens): Combines the vasoactive effects of caffeine and sedative effects of bromide, used primarily for migraine or "nervous headache" as a solution or effervescent powder. (42)

Caffeinae iodidum: Caffeine iodide, readily soluble and dissociating (iodine releasing) compound used for rapid relief of pain, said to be effective in gout or rheumatism. (42)

Caffeinae salicylas: See caffeinae sodio-salicylate. (42)

Caffeinae sodio-benzoa[s][te]: Caffeine sodio-benzoate is highly soluble and is used as an injectable form of caffeine. (42,46)

Caffeinae sodio-salicylas; Caff. sod.-sal.: Caffeine sodio-salicylate powder containing equal parts caffeine and sodium salicylate. A stimulant analgesic, similar to modern formulations of caffeine and aspirin used for headache. (31)

Caffeinae valerianas: Caffeine valerianate, used as per caffeine for headache or hysterical conditions. (42)

Caffeine, citrated: See caffeina citrata. (42)

Cahina: Black wood of Brazil, diuretic, purgative, emetic. Unofficial. (44)

Cahinca: The bark of the root of cahinca, snowberry, cluster-flowered snowberry, cainca, David's root, *Chiococca racemosa*. (33) Homeopathic, various sources also suggest allopathic use as a purgative and diuretic.

Cajaput oil; Cajaputi, linimentum; —, oleum: Volatile oil distilled from the leaves of *Melaleuca leucadendron*, of the East Indian Islands, or a liniment made from same. Use as per clove oil (see caryophyllus). Figure 3-45. (8)

Cajaputi composita, mistura: Compound mixture of cajaput, of oils of cajaput, peppermint, clove, and anise in alcohol. Said to be a very useful stimulant and antispasmodic which "should be kept by every physician and druggist." (34)

Cajaputi, spiritus: Oil of cajaput in alcohol, stimulant and antispasmodic. (42)

Melaleuca Leucadendron

Fig. 3-45 Cajaput (source of).

Cajuputol: See eucalyptol. Clove (cajuput) and eucalyptus oil contain similar aromatic compounds. In current use, this is generally referred to as eucalyptol. (40)

Calabar bean: See physostigma. (8)

Calamentum: See calamintha. (1)

Calami, cortex radicis; Calam. rad. c.: Bark (cortex) or the root (radix) of calamus, see acorus.

Calamina; Calaminaris lapis; Calamine (pv.): Calamine, i.e., basic zinc carbonate, generally a powder (pv.). (1) Estes (39) states this is a zinc silicate.

Calamina factita: Artificial calamine, of zinc sulfate and sodium carbonate with a small amount of ferric chloride, the precipitate of which is heated in a crucible. Resulting ferric oxide imparts a slight pink color. (42)

Calamina praeparata: Prepared calamine, a calcined preparation of native zinc carbonate. Naturally pink due to residual iron oxides, but may be tinted with various red substances such as tumeric, jeweler's rouge, carmine, or bolus Armenia. (42)

Calaminae (compositum), lotio: Calamine lotion, of prepared calamine and zinc oxide (see zinci oxidi) in lime water with a little glycerin. Used topically for itching as per modern use. The compound (compositum) formula is a ten percent solution of liquid phenol in calamine lotion. (31)

Calaminae, ceratum: See calaminae, unguentum. (44)

Calaminae, linimentum: Calamine liniment, eight percent each prepared calamine and zinc oxide (zinci oxidi) suspended in lime liniment (calcis, linimentum). (31)

Calaminae, unguentum; Calaminare, unguentum: Calamine ointment, Turner's cerate, contains seventeen percent calamine in ointment base. "This sedative protective ointment has properties similar to those of the ointment of zinc oxide, over which it has the advantage of being a pinkish color and hence not so conspicuous when applied to the skin." (31)

Calaminaris, lapis: Impure zinc carbonate. (3)

Calamintha: Common calamint (*Calamintha officinalis*) and related species. Flowering herb used. (1)

Calamus; Calami, fluidum, extractum: See Acorus, the sweet Flag, or the fluid extract therefrom. It is a typical bitter and is employed as such (see columba for detail of use). (8)

Calamus; Calamus aromaticus; Calamo {*Italian*}: Calamus, uncertain plant of Eastern origin, from biblical times. (1)

Calcatrepola; Calcitrapa: Caltrop, star thistle, *Centaurea calcitrapa*. Herb used. (1)

Calcic _____: Irregular chemical name for the calcium ion, Ca^{2+}. For compounds see calcii. (29)

Calcidin: Calcium iodide, see calcii iodidi. (40)

Calciferol: Vitamin D. (40)

Calcii bromidi, elixir: Simple elixir of calcium bromide, NF, sedative. (45)

Calcii bromidum: Calcium bromide, CaBr$_2$. From reaction of calcium carbonate (calx carbonatus) and hydrobromic acid. Primarily used as a sedative and for control of epilepsy. See bromine. (8)

Calcii carbonas praecipitatus: Precipitated calcium carbonate, CaCO$_3$. Precipitated from sodium carbonate and calcium chloride. Used in preparation of other materials including pulvis morphinae compositus and syrupus calcii lactophosphatus. See cretae, praecipitatum. (8)

Calcii chloridi, elixir; Calcium chloride elixir: See calcii chloridi, syrupus. (42)

Calcii chloridi, liquor: A solution of sixteen percent calcium chloride. The principal use was for dispensing or preparation of other materials as this is a deliquescent salt and thus difficult to store in solid form. Deobstruant. (42,44)

Calcii chloridi, syrupus: Syrup of calcium chloride and citric acid with water and simple syrup. Calcium source. (42)

Calcii chloridum (anhydrosum): Calcium chloride, $CaCl_2$. Formed from calcium carbonate and hydrochloric acid, followed by drying. Used for reducing enlarged lymph glands and as a general source of soluble calcium. The anhydrous form is made by fusing the salt with heat, and is prepared mainly to avoid the variability in composition of the hydrated form. (8,42)

Calcii chlorohydrophosphatis, syrupus: Syrup with water, hydrochloric acid, spirit of lemon, and precipitated calcium phosphate. (46)

Calcii et sodii glycerophosphatum, elixir: Elixir of calcium and sodium glycerophosphates. (31)

Calcii et sodii hypophosphitum, syrupus: Syrup of calcium and sodium hypophosphites, made of same along with hypophosphorous acid, sugar and water. (31)

Calcii formas: Calcium formate, used for the formate content as a "tonic." (42)

Calcii glycerophosphas (effervescens): Glycero-phosphate of calcium, by reaction with glycerophosphoric acid, used as a tonic in neurasthenia and a component of many other formulations. Also formulated as an effervescent powder. (42)

Calcii hippuras: Calcium hippurate is used for gout and urinary stones, "but without benefit." (42)

Calcii hydras: Calcium hydroxide, slaked lime. Astringent and antacid. (42)

Calcii hypophosphis: Calcium hypophosphite, $Ca(PH_2O_2)_2$. Given in general debility as in tuberculosis. often in mixtures with other hypophosphites. (8,42)

Calcii hypophosphitis, elixir: Alterative and reconstructive elixir of calcium hypophosphite, NF. (45)

Calcii hypophosphitis, syrupus: Syrup of calcium hypophosphite, of hypophosphorous acid, sugar, and water. (31)

Calcii iodas: Calcium iodate, as a topical dust or ointment for disinfection or in dilute solutions as an intestinal antiseptic, gargle, or mouthwash. (42)

Calcii iodidi, syrupus: Syrup of calcium iodide, from iodine, iron wire, precipitated calcium carbonate, sugar, distilled water, and syrup. "This may be used for the same purpose as the other iodides, but is by some believed to be especially valuable in asthma." (31)

Calcii iodidum: Calcium iodide, as a general source of iodine in formulations and as a topical solution for chronic ulcers. (42)

Calcii lactas; Calc. lact.: Calcium lactate, the calcium salt of lactic acid. A common inert ingredient in pills and other formulations. Abbreviated form could also mean calcium lactophosphate, but the official USP abbreviation for calcium lactate is Calc. Lact., whereas the lactophosphate is officially abbreviated Calc. Lactophos.

Calcii lactophosphatis cum ferro, syrupus; Calcii lactophosphatis et ferri, syrupus: Syrup of calcium lactophosphate and iron. It is made from ferrous lactate, potassium citrate, water, and syrup of calcium lactophosphate. (31)

Calcii lactophosphatis, syrupus: Syrup of calcium carbonate, lactic acid, concentrated phosphoric acid, sugar, water, and orange flower water, pleasant calcium source, especially for children. (42)

Calcii lactophosphatis, syrupus; —, elixir; Calc. Lactophos. El.: Syrup, also called elixir, of calcium lactophosphate. Composed of calcium carbonate, phosphoric acid, lactic acid, orange flower water, sugar, water. (8,31) In the NF this was of calcium lactate and phosphoric acid in water, syrup, and aromatic elixir. (46)

Calcii lactophosphatis; Calc. lactophos.: Mixture of calcium lactate and calcium phosphate produced from calcium carbonate, lactic acid, and phosphoric acid, evaporated to dryness. A calcium source in various nutritive formulations and products. (3,42)

Calcii naphthol-sulphonas: Calcium naphthol-sulphonate, both a topical antiseptic and an analgesic antipyretic said to be similar to aspirin. (40,42)

Calcii peroxidum: Calcium peroxide, CaO_2. Like hydrogen peroxide, an antiseptic. Said to be particularly good for digestive disturbances in children, and in acid dyspepsia, and can be given in milk. (42)

Calcii phosphas (praecipitatis): Precipitated calcium phosphate from bone ash digested with hydrochloric acid. Used in other remedies, i.e., pulvis antimonialis. (8)

Calcii sulphas (exsiccatus): Dried, finely ground calcium sulfate, i.e., gypsum, used to make calx sulphurata. This is "plaster of Paris," and when mixed with water, forms a smooth paste which rapidly hardens. Used to form "hard bandages" (orthopedic casts) as well as to form "casts" (molds for anatomical models) of injuries and abnormalities. (8)

Calcinaphthol: See calcii naphthol-sulphonas. (40)

Calcined plaster: Plaster of Paris. (3)

Calcinol: Calcium iodate, $Ca(IO_3)_2$. (40)

Calcis, aqua; Calcis, liquor; Calcis, syrupus: Solution (water based liquor) or syrup of lime (i.e., calcium oxide or hydrate, not the fruit). See calx. (8)

Calcis (aquae), linimentum: Lime (calcium oxide) liniment, or Carron oil, of lime and linseed oil. Used in the topic treatment of burns. See calx. (8, 39)

Calcis, muriatis: Calcium chloride. See calcii chloridum. (39)

Calcis carbonas praeparata: See calcii. (44)

Calcis chlor(in)atae, liquor: A solution of chlorinated lime. (42,44)

Calcis chlorinatae et acidi borici, pulvis: A powdered preparation of chlorinated calcium (probably the hypochlorite) and boric acid. No official preparation was located. Presumably a topical antiseptic. (40)

Calcis composita, aqua; Calc. co., aq.: The compound water of lime, see Benedict's solution. (40)

Calcis hydras: Slaked lime, hydrated calcium oxide. (44)

Calcis phosphas praeparata: See calcii. (44)

Calcis saccharatus, liquor: A solution of calcium hydroxide and sugar in water, antacid, especially for children. (42)

Calcis sulphurata(e), liquor: Solution of sulphurated lime, solution of oxysulphuret of calcium, Vlemincks' solution, Vleminck's lotion. Made by boiling lime, sublimed sulfur and water, used topically for skin diseases. (31)

Calcitea; Calcitria: Sulfuric acid. (3)

Calcithos: Copper subacetate. (3)

Calcium dioxide: See calcii peroxidum. (42)

Calcium oxide: See quicklime. (39)

Calcium phosphate, neutral: Calcium phosphate, see calcii phosphas. (40)

Calcium Sandoz: A proprietary formulation of calcium gluconate. (40)

Calcium superoxide: See calcii peroxidum. (42)

Calendula; Calendulae, conserva; Calendulae, tinctura; —fluidextractum; —fluidum, extractum: Florets of the garden marigold, *Calendula officinalis*, or the conserve, alcoholic tincture or fluid extract thereof. White's (1894) notes that it was "formerly supposed to be antispasmodic, sudorific, and an emmenagogue, but is now believed to have no therapeutic value." (1,8,35,46)

Calib.; Calyb.: Abbreviations for chalybeatae or chalybis, meaning iron containing. (39)

Calisaya; Calysaya: See chinchona.

Calisaya (, ferrated)(ferri et bismuthi)(, ferri, bismuthi et strychninae) elixir (, alkaloidal); —, essence: Calisya is an alternate name for chinchona, or Peruvian bark, source of quinine. See Peruviana, cortex and Cinchonae alkaloidorum (et ferri), elixir, etc. (7,8)

Callitriche: Water-starwort, water chickweed, *Callitriche verna*, a useful diuretic. (33)

Calloxylin: See pyroxylin. (8)

Calomel: See hydrargyri chloridum mite. (8)

Calomel lozenges: This appears to be an extemporaneous formulation (i.e., not standardized), and consisted of lozenges or tablets containing calomel, mixed with a variety of other purgative, laxative, or anthelmintic materials (castor oil, jalap, etc.) to act as a purgative or to expel worms.

Calomel ointment; Calomelanoe, unguentum; Calomelanos, unguentum: See hydrargyri subchloridi, unguentum and hydrargyri chloridi mitis, unguentum. (31,34,40)

Calomel tablets: See hydrargyri chloridi mitis, tabellae. (31) See hydrargyri subchloridi, tablettae. (42)

Calomelanos: Calomel. (3)

Calomelanos composita, pilula: See antimonii compositi, pillulae. (40)

Calomelanos et colocynthidis (et hyoscyami), pilulae: Pills of mercurous chloride and compound extract of colocynth. Purgative, with optional addition of hyoscyamus to reduce cramping. (42)

Calomelos et [acidi borici][amyli][zinci oxidi], pulvis: Dusting powders of one part calomel and three parts of boric acid, starch, or zinc oxide, respectively. (42)

Calorific wool: Capsicum tissue or wool, of wool soaked in oleoresin of capsicum, used as a topical counterirritant for the pain of rheumatic disorders, much like heating plasters available today. (40)

Calotropus; Calotropis, tinctura: Members of the milk-weed family. Toxic, primarily homeopathic or herbal use. Diaphoretic in small doses, emetic in large. The BPC specifies a tincture official in India and the eastern British colonies. (42)

Calotropis gigantea: Madar or Mudar plant, bitter bark, mainly for rope manufacture but some purported medicinal use. (44)

Calox: Proprietary tooth powder with calcii peroxidum. (42)

Caltha officinalis: See calendula. (40)

Calumba; Calumbae radix: Calumba or columbo is the root of *Jateorhiza palmata*, of Africa. Used as a typical bitter to improve appetite, with mild carminative effect, and in the treatment of dyspepsia. Bitters were used to treat general depletion or exhaustion from physical effort or disease, such as tuberculosis. Bitters, in general, are antiseptic and disinfectant and can be administered rectally to treat threadworm. Bitters are generally to be avoided in the presence of acute or chronic gastric disease such as ulcer or gastritis, and should not be administered for too long a time or in too high a concentration to avoid irritation of the stomach and GI tract. (8)

Calumbae (fluidum), extractum; —concentratus, liquor; —, infusum (concentratum); —, pulv.; tinctura: The fluid extract, solution, infusion, powder or alcoholic tincture of calumba root. (8) The BPC also specified a concentrated infusion with tincture of calumbae, alcohol, and chloroform water for storage and reconstitution. Primarily a bitter. (42)

Calx: Lime, quicklime, calcium oxide, CaO. Lime has been produced since ancient times by heating of calcium carbonate in its naturally occurring forms, such as marble or oyster shell, with the liberation of carbon dioxide. Lime was used as an astringent, an antacid, and an antidote to poisoning with acids. (1,8)

Calx avis: Bird lime, a sticky pitch-like material applied to branches or surfaces to catch birds. Non-pharmacologic, but it is not beyond imagination that an apothecary would carry this material, as pest control products were among materials commonly provided. (40)

Calx bismuthi: Bismuth subnitrate. (3)

Calx chlor(ata); Calx chlorinata: Calcium chlorate, more properly, calcium hypochlorite, or bleaching powder. From the action of chlorine on lime. A general disinfectant. (8,39)

Calx hydrargyri alba: White calx of mercury, a precipitate of calomel with sal ammoniac and lye, used to prepare ointments. (39) Ammoniated mercury, see sydrargyri ammoniatum. (40)

Calx sulphurata: Sulphurated lime, a crude calcium sulfide, CaS, with some residual sulfate. From heating a mixture of calcium sulphate, charcoal, and starch. A scabicide (see sulphur). Also for prevention of infection in boils, carbuncles, or acne, and used as a topical dipilatory as per barium sulphide. (8)

Calx viva: Quicklime, see calx. (3)

Calybeatae, pilulae: See chalybeatae, pilulae. (1)

Cam wood: See camwood. (44)

Camaemelum; camomilla {*Italian*}**:** See chamomilla. (1)

Cambogia: See gambogia. (7)

Cambogiae compositae, pilulae: Powdered gamboge, aloes, and cinnamon in hard soap. A laxative. (42)

Camellia; Camelliae fluidum, extractum: *Camellia thea* is an alternate name for tea, *Thea pecco*. The NF specifies a fluid extract. See thea. (46)

Camel's hay: The aromatic grass, *Andropagon schoenanthus*, of India, from which an aromatic oil, called geranium oil, is obtained. (39)

Cammock: See restharrow. (39)

Campeche; Campechense, lignum; Campeachy wood: Logwood, see haematoxylon. (1,40)

Camphine: Oil of turpentine. (40)

Camphire: Orthographic variant of camphor. (39)

Campho-Phenique: A proprietary mixture of camphor and phenol, for topical use on sore throat, cold sores, skin lesions, etc. (40)

Camphor; Camphora: Camphor is a stearoptin, an oxidation product of the ten-carbon terpene products found in turpentine (see terebenthina). It is obtained from the laurel, *Cinnamomum* (or *Laurus*) *camphora* (Figure 3-46) by exposing the branches and wood to the vapor of boiling water, driving off the camphor. Borneo Camphor (sometimes referred to as Sumatra or Barus Camphor) is obtained instead from *Dryobalanops camphora*, and is often substituted. It is sometimes referred to as Oil of Camphor, although it is not a true oil, and can be confused with Camphorated oil, i.e., cottonseed oil to which camphor has been added (see camphorae, linimentum). Camphor has a pleasant aromatic odor and is used topically as an antiseptic and cutaneous stimulant, irritant, and counterirritant, causing a sensation of warmth. It is a GI stimulant, mild diaphoretic, and purported aphrodisiac, with variable effects on the nervous system. In overdose, it generally causes over-stimulation and convulsions and may be lethal. Topical preparations with thymol and chloroform are particularly good anodynes for toothache. (8)

Camphor, bromated: Monobromated camphor, see camphora monobromata. (40)

Camphor, carbolated: A mixture 1:1 of phenol (carbolic acid) and camphor. Topical. (40)

Camphor(ae), liniment(um): See camphoratum, unguentum album. (40)

Camphor(ae), Tinct.: Tincture of camphor. A ten percent solution of camphor in alcohol in the US Dispensatory of 1850, seemingly equivalent to spirits of camphor.

Laurus Camphora

Published by DC Woodville July 1.1793.

Fig. 3-46 Camphor.

Camphor, tonka bean: Coumarin, an aromatic compound deriverd from the tonka bean, *Diptyrix odorata*, of Latin America. (3) An anticoagulant, it was used primarily in perfumery. See tonka. (42)

Camphor ice: See camphorae compositum, ceratum. (3) A variety of proprietary products of the same name seem to have been sold at various times.

Camphor julep; —mixture: Camphor mixture, see camphorae composita, mistura. (3)

Camphor salicylate: A topical mixture of these two materials used as a counterirritant for local pain. (40)

Camphor wash, ammoniated: See ammoniacalis camphorata, lotio. (31)

Camphora cum creta: Camphorated chalk, by trituration of camphor in alcohol with addition of chalk, about ten percent camphor. Used as a refreshing powder and especially as a toothpaste. (42)

Camphora monobromata: Brominated camphor, from treatment of camphor with bromine in benzene, and crystallization. Use is as per camphor and as a sedative hypnotic said to be useful in delerium tremens, chorea, or hysteria. (8,42)

Camphorae, aqua; —, linimentum; —, spiritus; —, ceratum; —, unguentum: The water, liniment, spirit, and wax (cerate) of camphor, respectively. The water is made with camphor triturated in water with calcium phosphate and filtered; the liniment or unguent, also known as camphorated oil, consists of twenty percent camphor in cottonseed oil; the spirit is ten percent camphor in alcohol; and the cerate consists of the camphor liniment (camphorated oil) in a mixture of white wax and lard. (8)

Camphorae, essentia: Essence of camphor, of camphor in oil, used for catarrhal respiratory illness, presumably via inhalation of vapor. (42)

Camphorae (durum), unguentum: Ointment of camphor in mixture of hard and soft paraffin, camphor ice. (42) Paraffin mixture adjusted to acheive soft or hard (durum) consistency.

Camphorae acida, mistura: Acid mixture of camphor, antidiarrheal mixture, mistura antidysenterica, or Hope's mixture. Of nitric acid, tincture of opium, and camphor water. For diarrheal illness. (34)

Camphorae ammoniatum, linimentum: Liniment of camphor, oil of lavender, strong solution of ammonia, and alcohol, for rheumatism. (42)

Camphorae aromatica, mistura: Compound tincture of lavender, sugar, and camphor water, Parrish's camphor mixture. (46)

Camphorae composita, mistura: Paregoric, compound mixture of camphor, of oils of camphor, peppermint and spearmint waters in deodorized tincture of opium. This and related preparations were used to control diarrrhea. (34)

Camphorae composita, tinctura: Alcoholic tincture of benzoic acid, camphor, and oil of anise. Paregoric (in the BPC), a cough remedy. (42)

Camphorae compositae, pilulae: Compound pill of camphor, opium, kino, capsicum, and conserve of roses. For Asiatic cholera, general stimulant, anodyne, and antispasmodic. (34)

Camphorae compositum, ceratum; —, linimentum: Compound camphor cerate ("camphor ice"), of camphor, white wax, castor oil, spermaceti, carbolic acid, oil of bitter almond, and benzoic acid; or a liniment of camphor, oils of hemlock, oregano, sassafras, and turpentine, with capsicum, used as a topical anesthetic and for local joint pain or other inflammation. (3,34) The liniment in BPC refers to (see) camphorae ammoniatum, linimentum. (42)

Camphorae compositus Tully, pulvis: See morphinae compositus, pulvis. (34)

Camphorae compositus, pulvis: A powder of tannic acid, kino, camphor, and opium, especially useful for cholera. (34)

Camphorae compositus, spiritus: Compound spirit of camphor, of same with benzoic acid, oil of anise, and liquid extract of licorice, in alcohol. Mild expectorant and base for other cough syrups, especially for children. (42)

Camphorae compositus, syrupus: Compound syrup of camphor, of same with oil of anise, benzoic acid, glacial acetic acid, tincture of opium, vinegars of ipecacuanha and squill, refined sugar, burnt sugar (caramel flavor), and water. An expectorant and sedative cough syrup. (42)

Camphorae forte, spiritus: A concentrated spirit of camphor, see camphorae, spiritus. (40)

Camphorata: An herb with a camphor-like odor, i.e., *Camphorosma monspeliaca*. (1) See also camphoratum.

Camphorated oil: See camphorae, linimentum. (8)

Camphorated spirit of wine: Liniment of camphor in spirits of wine. (39)

Camphoratum: Camphorated, an irregular Latin usage, see also the proper term, camphorae, "of camphor." For various formulations. (34)

Camphoratum, chloroformum: Chloroform of camphor, of same dissolved in about half its weight of chloroform. A topical for toothache. (42)

Camphoratum, oleum: See camphoratum, unguentum album. (40)

Camphoratum, unguentum album; Camphor., u. alb.: White unguent of camphor, made with white lead oxide and camphor in ointment base. (36)

Camphoratum, unguentum alkalinum: See unguentum alkalinum, camphoratum. (34)

Camphoric acid; Camphoricum, acidum: Camphoric acid, from treatment of camphor with nitric acid. It is a mild stimulant and disinfectant astringent used especially for chronic inflammatory conditions of the mouth and nose. May be given systemically to suppress night sweats. (8,42)

Camphossil: See camphor salicylate. (40)

Campolon: Proprietary injectable liver extract, mainly for treatment of anemia. (40)

Camwood: Wood of *Baphia nitida*, African Sandalwood, from which a red dye is obtained. (40)

Canada balsam: See terebenthina canadensis. (8)

Canada liniment: See opii compositum, linimentum. (31)

Canada turpentine: See terebenthina canadensis. (8)

Canadense, balsamum; Canada, baume du {*French*}: Canada balsam or Canada turpentine, resin from the balsam fir, *Abies balsamica*. (1)

Canadian ash: Potassium carbonate; see potassii carbonas. (40)

Canadian fleabane: See erigeron canadense. (40)

Canadian hemp: Apocynum cannabinum. (40)

Canadian moonseed: See menispermum. (8)

Canadol: Trade name, petroleum ether. (3)

Canariensis, semen et flora; Canary seed: Appears to refer to canary seed and flowers, seed of *Phalaris canariensis*, noted to be used commonly as a bird food, but the seed was also crushed to produce a plaster, and could be crushed to flour and consumed.

Cancer: Crab. (1)

Cancer chelae; Cancrorum chelae: Crab's claws. (3,39)

Cancrorum lapilli: Crabs' stones (concretions found in stomach of European crawfish). (3)

Cancrorum oculi: Crab's eyes, properly cancrorum lapilli, above. (39)

Cancrum exulceratum, unguentum ad: Ointment for an ulcerated cancer, of castor oil, white lead, and hydrargyrus praecipitatus. (39)

Candelae fumales: Fumigating pastilles or candles. (3) While prepared by pharmacists, their purpose was perfumery and, to some degree, pest control (as with mothballs). Numerous eponymous formulas and suggestions can be found.

Candy Carrot: See daucus creticus. (39)

Canella (alba); Canella bark; Cannaelae cortex: Bark of *Canella alba*, white cinnamon, of Florida and the Bahamas, an aromatic bitter stomachic not commonly prescribed. Figure 3-47. (8,1)

Canfora {Italian}: Camphor. (1)

Canna (starch)(fecula): Starch (fecula) prepared from sugarcane, or an alternative term for arrowroot flour, see maranta. (39,40) In the USP said to be starch from rhizome of undetermined or unspecified varieties of canna. (44)

Cannabine; Cannabis resin; Cannabinonum; Cannabinone: Cannabinone and related active principals derived from marijuana, see cannabis. (40)

Cannabinum tannas: Cannabine tannate, a hypnotic and also used in dysmenorrhea and menorrhagia. It is free of intoxicating effects but noted to be "generally of little value." (42)

Cannabis (sativa): Marijuana, generally identified as "Indian cannabis" in historical sources. See cannabis indica. (1,8)

Cannabis indica: Marijuana, female plant of the species *Cannabis sativa*, of Indian origin. Various active components were known, but not generally isolated. Used then, as now, for its relaxant and intoxicating properties. The use in medicine was primarily by ingestion of prepared extracts, not by smoking. (8)

Cannabis indicae, extractum; —, fluidum extractum; —, tinctura: Dried extract, fluid extract, and alcoholic tincture of cannabis. (8)

Cannabis purificatum, extractum: Dried alcoholic extract of cannabis. (44)

Cannella: See canella. (1)

Cantharidatum, collodium: Similar to cantharidini, collodium, but prepared with cantharides rather than the purified cantharidin. Useful where blistering plasters cannot be readily applied—behind the ear, for example. (42)

Cantharidini, acetum: Vinegar solution of cantharidin. In the BPC from cantharides "bruised," i.e., whole insect with acetic and glacial acetic acid. Stimulant for hair growth. (40,42)

Cantharidini, collodium: Cantharidin collodion, of purified cantharidin in collodion. (42)

Cantharidini, emplastrum: In the BPC, plaster of cantharidin (purified from cantharides), yellow beeswax, suet, chloroform (to dissolve cantharidin), and resin. This is more potent than emplastrum cantharidis and thus more useful for blistering than as a rubifacient. (42)

Cantharidini, tinctura: Tincture of cantharidin dissolved in a small amount of chloroform and subsequently diluted with alcohol. (42)

Cantharidini, unguentum: Ointment of cantharidin in chloroform, beeswax, and olive oil, use as per ointment of cantharides. (42)

Cantharidinum; Cantharidin(s): An active component derived from cantharides. (42)

Cantharis ([P.][Pulv.]); Cantharides; Cantharides, tinctura; Cantharidis, acetum.: A powder of the dried insect *Cantharis vesicatoria* or a tincture or vinegar solution from same. Cantharides are highly toxic by mouth, producing severe and often bloody purging. They were used as powerful topical irritants and counterirritants as well as vesicants and to treat a variety of proliferative skin lesions such as skin cancer or warts. The tincture and vinegar were used topically to stimulate hair growth. Taken orally it is a urethral irritant said to be aphrodesiac, i.e., Spanish fly. (8,34)

Cantharidis, charta: Small cantharidin paper plasters, of cantharides, white wax, spermaceti, olive oil, turpentine, and water, applied to paper and dried. (46)

Cantharidis, emplastrum; —, unguentum: Cantharide ointment, ointment of Spanish fly, of cantharide in yellow wax and olive oil, sometimes with resin and turpentine as well. In the BPC, of bruised cantharides in benzoinated lard. A counterirritant and rubifacient. (34,42)

Cantharidis, linimentum: Liniment (NF) of about fifteen percent cantharides in oil of turpentine. (46)

Cantharidis extracti, ceratum: Cerate of cantharides in resin, yellow wax, lard, and alcohol to soften as needed, used like the emplastrum. (46)

Canthianus, pulvis: Powdered crab stones, powder of Kent. See cancrorum, lapilli. (39)

Canton's phosphorus: Calcium sulphide. After British physicist John Canton. A slightly phosphorescent material, poorly characterized, of calcined oyster shells combined with sulfur. (40)

Caoutchouc, liquor: A solution of India rubber in benzene and carbon disulfide, an adhesive or substitute for collodion. (42)

Caoutchouc: Rubber, see India rubber for details and illustration. (8)

Caper(s); Capparis; Capari, olio de {Italian}: Capers, flower buds of shrub, *Capparis spinosa*. Pickled buds are an appetite stimulant, today largely a garnish. Oil (olio) of capers (observed, probably Italian). Figure 3-48. (1,39)

Caphura: Camphor. (1)

Capillaire: See capillus veneris. (40)

Capillaire, syrupus: See aurantii florum, syrupus. (40)

Capillaris, spiritus; Capillorium, spiritus: See resorcini, spiritus. (42)

Capillorum veneris, syrupus; Capill. vener. s.: Syrup of maidenhair, for a variety of internal disorders of the chest and abdomen. (35)

Capillus veneris: True maidenhair, Venus maidenhair, *Adiantum capillus veneris*. Fronds used. (1)

Capita papaveris: Poppy-heads. Poppy being the source of opium. (3)

Capivi: See copaiba. (39)

Capparis spinosa: Caper-bush, diuretic and for conditions of liver and spleen. Unofficial. (44)

Capretto {*Italian*}: Kid (i.e., juvenile goat). (1)

Caprokol: Proprietary hexylresorcinol, a topical anodyne for the throat and mucous membranes. (40)

Capsella: See bursa pastoris. (32)

Capsici, gossypium: Absorbent cotton soaked in liquid extract of capsicum and dried, often dyed red with eosin. Rubifacient and counterirritant, applied to the chest for bronchitis, or to joints. (42)

Capsici, linimentum: Liniment (BPC) of stronger tincture of capsicum with oleic acid, oil of lavender, and alcohol. General use counterirritant for chest and musculoskeletal afflictions. (42)

Capsici, oleoresinae, unguentum: Ointment of oleoresin of capsicum in beeswax and benzoinated lard, counterirritant in chest and pulmonary complaints. (42)

Canella alba.

Published by D.ʳ Woodville Dec.ʳ 1791

Fig. 3-47 Canella alba.

Capsici (et lobeliae), trochisci: Capsicum troches, of capsicum powder, sugar, and gum tragacanth for irritations of the throat and for "relaxed uvula," with or without oil of lobelia, which added expectorant and stimulant properties. (34)

Capsici, unguentum: Ointment of bruised capsicum fruit in spermaceti and olive oil, a counter irritant for rheumatic joints. (42)

Capsici compositum, linimentum: Compound liniment of tinctures of capsicum, opium and camphor, oils of oregano and cinnamon, and ammonia water. For local inflammation or injury. (34)

Capsici compositum, linimentum: This is a liniment (BPC) of black pepper powder, capsicum powder, hard soap, camphor, and oils of rosemary, lavender, clove, and cinnamon with solution of ammonia and water. (42)

Capsici compositus, liquor: See capsici compositum, linimentum (BPC). (42)

Capsici et myrrhae, tinctura; Caps. e. myrrh., tr.: Tincture of capsicum and myrrh, Hot Drops, Thomsonian Number Six, made from capsicum and myrrh. "It is a powerful gastric stimulant and carminative." (31)

Capsici fluidum, extractum; —liquidum, extractum; —, oleoresina; —, tinctura; —, pulv.; —emplastrum; —unguentum: Fluid extract, oleoresin, alcoholic tincture, powder, plaster, and unguent of pepper. The oleoresin is extracted with ether and evaporated. The plaster typically consisted of gauze impregnated with resin plaster followed by painting on of the oleoresin. The unguent was of five percent oleoresin in a base of petrolatum and paraffin. Primarily a topical rubifacient and counterirritant for pain. The tincture was given as a carminative and for dyspepsia, and to treat craving in alcoholics. (8,31,42)

Capsici fortior, tinctura: Turnbull's tincture of capsicum, of thirty-three percent capsicum fruit (as opposed to five percent in the standard tincture) in alcohol, topical counterirritant and hair growth stimulant. (42)

Capsicum, compound solution of: See capsici compositum, linimentum (BPC). (42)

Capsicum (annuum)(fructus): Cayenne or African pepper, the fruit of *Capsicum fastigiatum* (*C. frutesiens*), of tropical Africa. An oleoresin derived from capsicum could be used much like other volatile oils (see caryophyllus). It is a condiment and used as a stomachic and carminative. *C. annuum* is the same as piper indicum. Figure 3-49. (8,39)

Capsicum tissue: See calorific wool. (40)

Capsula gelatini; Capsulae: Gelatin capsules. Of gelatin, syrup, glyceri, and distilled water, the hardness of which is controlled by using more or less glycerin in the mixture. (42)

Capsulae amylaceae: "Starch capsules," i.e., wafer cachets, thin starch wafers between which material was enclosed and the edges sealed to form a cachet or lozenge. (40)

Capsule(s), glutoid: Capsules treated with solution of keratin and dipped in formaldehyde, to bypass dissolution in the stomach, an early enteric coating. (42)

Capuchins, powder of; Capuchin monk's powder: A powder of *Staphisagria nicotiana*, and sabadilla. (39)

Caput mortuum vitrioli: Ferric oxide (jewellers' rouge), see ferri rubigo. (40)

Caput mortuum: "Dead head," residual potassium chloride precipitated in distillation of sal ammoniac, or equivalent to ferri rubigo. (39)

Carabe; Carabi: Amber. (1)

Carabi, trochisci de: Troches of amber, with red coral and multiple other ingredients, for pulmonary conditions, especially hemoptysis. (35)

Caramania gum: An inferior gum tragacanth. (40)

Caramel: Caramel, as in common usage, i.e., partially burnt sugar. A flavorant and colorant. (7)

Caranna, gummi: Gum of a South American tree. (1) Resin of *Amyris caranna* and other species, said to resemble tacamahac. Unofficial. (44)

Caraway: See carum.

Carbamide: Urea, used as a topical exfoliant, to make isotonic solutions for irrigation, and other purposes. See urea. (40,42)

Carbanilic ether: Phenyl-urethane, an antiseptic. (40)

Carbasus (absorbens) (aseptica): Linen, canvas, or fabric. In apothecary usage, gauze or other dressing. May be steam sterilized (aseptica). (42)

Carbasus antisepticus: Antiseptic gauze, generally treated with an iodine based ointment, carbolic acid ointment, or similar antimicrobial, and very much like, if not identical to, today's iodoform gauze.

Carbasus salis alembroth: A gauze treated with sal alembroth, i.e., sal ammoniac, an antiseptic packing or dressing. (40)

Carbasus styptica: Gauze treated with Stockholm tar and resin dissolved in benzol, then dried. (42)

Fig. 3-48 Caper or capparis.

Fig. 3-49 Capsicum.

Carbazoticum, acidum; Carbazotic acid: Picronitric acid, see picric acid. (3,40)

Carbo animalis (purificatus); Carb. anim.: Charcoal, animal charcoal, from bones charred without access to air. The purified form was treated with hydrochloric acid, washed extensively, and then heated to red hot in a closed crucible. (8)

Carbo; Carbon: Carbon, elemental. While there are many sources of carbon, the traditional sources in pharmacology are wood charcoal (carbo ligni) and bone charcoal (carbo animalis). Charcoal itself was used as an antiseptic and deodorant for foul wounds, although it probably has no significant antimicrobial activity. It was also used as a tooth powder and for the treatment of poisonings, particularly with vegetable poisons (strychnine, etc.). Activated charcoal (treated with steam to remove organic material and increase surface area) remains in use for the latter purpose. The sorbent ability of purified charcoal (see carbo animalis purificatus) made it an effective deodorizer and decolorizer in the preparation of a variety of materials. (8)

Carbo ligni: Charcoal, wood charcoal, i.e., wood charred without access to air. (8)

Carbol-fuchsin solution: A dark purple solution of fuchsin, resorcinol, and phenol, dissolved in acetone, alcohol, and water. Used as a topical treatment for fungal skin infections. (24)

Carbolate: A phenol (carbolic acid) salt. (40)

Carbolic acid water: See phenolata, aqua.

Carbolic acid, iodized: See phenol iodatum. (42)

Carbolic acid, ointment; Carbolic acid, glycerite; Carbolicum acidum, glycerit.: Ointment and glycerite of carbolic acid. See carbolicum, acidum. (8)

Carbolic camphor: Twenty-five percent phenol in camphor, used topically for toothache. (42)

Carbolici, acidi, carbasus: Gauze treated with five percent carbolic acid in a mixture of resin and wax. Usually used to form a bandage. (42)

Carbolici, acidi, et boracis, lotio: A mixture of the glycerin of carbolic and boric acids and water, diluted five-to-ten fold for use as a disinfectant gargle or mouthwash. (42)

Carbolici, acidi, gargarisma: Phenol gargle, five percent in distilled water. (42)

Carbolici, acidi, glycerinum; —, glyceritum: Phenol in glycerin, as an analgesic and antiseptic paint for the throat or diluted to produce gargle or disinfectant solution. (42)

Carbolici, acidi, lotio: Five percent solution of carbolic acid (phenol) in water as a surgical irrigant and disinfectant. (42)

Carbolici, acidi, plasma: Plasma (plaster) of carbolic acid, with glycerin and chalk. An antibacterial surgical and wound dressing. (34)

Carbolici, acidi, suppositoria: Suppository of carbolic acid (phenol) in beeswax and cocoa butter, antiseptic and antipruritic for hemorrhoids. (42)

Carbolici, acidi, unguentum: Ointment (five percent in ointment of choice) of carbolic acid, i.e., phenol. Used as a topical disinfectant, deodorant, and anesthetic. (8)

Carbolici compositum, acidi, unguentum: Compound phenol ointment, of mercuric nitrate ointment with sublimed sulfur, carbolic acid, olive oil, and beeswax, parasiticide and in diluted form a disinfectant for chronic skin conditions. (42)

Carbolicum, acidum; Carbolic acid: Carbolic acid, i.e., phenol, purified from crude carbolic acid, C_6H_5-OH. Carbolic acid is used as a disinfectant and deodorant. An aerosolized solution was used to disinfect operating rooms, gloves, and equipment as suggested by Lister. Remains in common use as a topical anesthetic in throat lozenges, as well as use in various disinfectant or cleaning products. (8) See acidi carbolici.

Carbolicum crudum, acidum; Carbolic acid, crude: Crude carbolic acid is a coal-tar derivative consisting of various aromatic alcohols, mainly cresol and phenol. (8)

Carbolicum iodatum, acidum: See phenol iodatum. (46)

Carbolicum liquifactum, acidum: Liquefied carbolic acid, of carbolic acid (which is nearly liquid at room temperature) with approximately ten percent water. (42)

Carbolisatum, gossypium: Absorbent cotton soaked in carbolic acid (phenol) in ether and dried. (42)

Carbolized oil: See oleum carbolatum. (34)

Carbon, disinfecting: Naphthalene in blocks, one form of mothball (the other being para-dichlorobenzene), but the vapor is also disinfectant. (40)

Carbon disulphide; Carbonei disulphidum; Carbonei bisulphidum: Carbon disulfide, CS_2, used as a solvent, especially for rubber. (8)

Carbonas: A carbonate, not to be confused with carbonis (carbon). Often seen as orthographic variants or errors, i.e., one sees Carbonas Ligni in place of Carbo(nis) Ligni for wood charcoal, etc. When in doubt, see both headings. Note also, carbonici, which means carbonated, i.e., effervescent. (39)

Carbonas barytes: Barium carbonate. (39)

Carbonas calcis praeparata: Same as creta praeparata, prepared chalk, i.e., calcium carbonate. (39)

Carbonas calcis, sal: Calcium carbonate, i.e., chalk. See creta. (39)

Carbonas ferri: Iron carbonate, but said by Estes to be likely the red oxide (rust). A tonic. (39)

Carbonas magnesiae: Magnesium carbonate, same as magnesia alba. (39)

Carbonas plumbi: White lead carbonate. (39)

Carbonas potassae (impurus): Potassium carbonate, lixivia. (39)

Carbonas potassae purissimus: "Most pure" potassium carbonate, equivalent to sal tartari, which is the carbonate obtained by calcination of potassium tartrate. (39)

Carbonas sodae: Sodium carbonate, purified barilla, an antacid, deobstruent, lithontriptic, diaphoretic, and tonic. (39)

Carbonas zinci impurus praeparatus: See calamine. (39)

Carbonas zinci: Zinc carbonate, mainly for use in eyewash. (39)

Carbonate of iron: Ferri oxidum praecipitatum rubrum, see ferri rubigo. (40)

Carbonate of potash: Potassium bicarbonate; see potassii bicarbonas. (40)

Carbonate of soda: Sodium bicarbonate; see sodii bicarbonas. (40)

Carbonatis ammoniae, aqua: Same as aqua ammoniae. (39)

Carbonatis calcis, potio: See cretae, mistura. (40)

Carbonici, acidi, aqua: Carbonated water, the dissolution of carbon dioxide results in formation of carbonic acid. (44)

Carbonicum, acidum; Carbonic acid; —anhydride; —snow: Carbonic acid, fixed air, i.e., the product of the dissolution of carbon dioxide in water, which forms carbonic acid. "Snow" would be the frozen material as ejected from a carbon dioxide fire extinguisher. (39)

Carbonis, cataplasma: Poultice of powdered wood charcoal, bread crumbs, and crushed linseed. Used for deodorizing and disinfecting foul wounds. (42)

Carbonis animalis, tabellae: Tablets of compressed animal charcoal, replacing trochisci carbonis ligni, each compressed tablet containing 0.3 grams. (31)

Carbonis bisulphidum: See carbon disulphide. (42)

Carbonis detergens, liquor: See picis carbonis, liquor. (31)

Carbonis ligni compositus, pulvis: Compound powder of charcoal, of same with rhubarb and sodium bicarbonate. For dyspepsia, acid indigestion, loss of appetite, and constipation. (34)

Carburet of iron: Graphite, or alternately a mixture of carbon and iron, used primarily as blacking, occasionally as a pill or as an ointment after grinding to powder. (40,44)

Cardamine: The flowers of l adies' smock, or cuckoo-flower, *Cardamine pratensis*, used as a diuretic, antispasmodic, and diaphoretic. Figure 3-50. (39)

Cardamom, lesser; Cardamomae, minus: Lesser cardamom, or *Eleteria cardamomum*. Aromatic, carminative, and diaphoretic. (39) Many sources indicate this is the official form.

Cardamom; Cardamomum; Cardamom[a][i] semina: Cardamom, the fruit (seeds) of *Elettaria (or Amoma) repens*, of Malabar. Use is as per clove oil (caryophyllus). It is especially useful to provide a pleasant flavor to various preparations. (8) Cardamomum in some sources consists of seed capsules of *Elettaria cardamomum,* the lesser cardamom, below. Figure 3-51. (1)

Cardamomae composita, pulvis: See pulvis aromaticus. (40)

Cardamomi, semen; Cardam., sem.; **Cardam., s.:** Seeds of cardamom. (7)

Cardamomi, tinctura: The alcoholic tincture of cardamom. (8)

Cardamomi composita, tinctura; Card. com. tr.; Card.com. tinct., etc.: The compound tincture of cardamom with caraway, cassia cinnamon, cochineal, and glycerin. (34) Similar formulation in the BPC consisted of cardamom seed, caraway fruit, raisins freed from seeds, cinnamon bark, and cochineal in alcohol. (42)

Cardamomi compositum, elixir; Card. co., elix.: Compound elixir of cardamom, of low alcoholic strength (nine percent), used as a vehicle and flavoring agent. (31)

Cardamomi compositus, spiritus: Compound spirit of cardamom, made from oils of cardamom, orange, cinnamon, clove (caryophylli, oleum), and caraway plus anethol, in alcohol. A flavoring. (31)

Cardiac drops: See aqua cardiaca. (39)

Cardialgia tabellae: Literally, heart-pain tablets, for digestive discomfort or heartburn. (39)

Carduus benedictus: Blessed thistle, holy thistle, *Cnicus benedictus* or *Centaurea benedicta*. Flowering tops used. A tonic, diaphoretic, and emetic. Figure 3-52. (1,39)

Carduus marianus: Our Lady'smMilk thistle, *Silybum marianum*. (1)

Carduus sanctus: See carduus benedictus. (1)

Carduus stellatus: See calcitrapa. (1)

Carica papaya: See papaya. (32)

Carica: Dried fig, see ficus. (1)

Caricae fructus: Figs, see ficus. (40)

Cariocostinum, electuarium: See caryocostinum, electuarium. (1)

Cariophylli: See caryophylli. (1)

Carlina: Carline thistle, *Carlina acaulis*. Root used as a diaphoretic, alexipharmic, and emetic. (1,39)

Carlsbad powder, effervescent: See carolinum factitium (effervescens), sal.

Carlsbad salt: A cathartic salt of sodium and potassium sulfate, sodium chloride, and sodium bicarbonate. (24)

Carmania gum: Gum of unclear origin said to resemble or to be used to adulterate tragacanth. Unofficial. (44)

Carmelitana, aqua: Water from the Carmelite monastery. A panacea, made with melissa, lemon peel, nutmeg, coriander, caryophyllus (clove) and cinnamon. (39)

Carminativa, mistura; Carminative mixture: Carminative or Dalby's mixture, of magnesium carbonate, potassium carbonate, tincture of opium, oil of caraway, oil of fennel, oil of peppermint, and syrup. (34) In the BPC, sodium bicarbonate with spirits of ammonia, tincture of cardamom, glycerin, and dill water. (42) Either these or other variants used for dyspepsia, acidity, and loss of appetite.

Carminativa, tinctura: Carminative tincture, BP, consisting of cardamom, tincture of ginger, oils of cinnamon, caraway, and clove, and rectified spirits. A stimulant and carminative, but mostly a flavoring for other formulations. (8,42)

Carminativa Dewees, mistura: See magnesiae et asafoetidae, mistura. (34)

Carmine; Carminum; Carmini, liquor: Solution of carmine in ammonia water, glycerin and water. Carmine is the red dye derived from the cochineal bug, used as a coloring agent. See also: cocci, liquor. (31)

Carmini, glycerinum: A solution of carmine in ammonia, water, and glycerin, a colorant. (42)

Carnauba wax: Wax from leaves of *Copernicia cerifera*. (40)

Carneolus(, lapis): Cornelian or carnelian, a semi-precious stone. (1)

Carnis et ferri, elixir: Elixir of beef and iron. Similar to *vinum carnis et ferri*, "there is little material difference …except in flavor. The old preparation was enormously abused; let us hope the change in flavor will lessen its popularity as a tipple." (31)

Fig. 3-50 Cardamine.

Fig. 3-51 Cardamom.

Fig. 3-52 Carduus benedictus or blessed thistle.

Carnum, extractum: Meat extract, useful as a nutrient and stimulant in starvation, prostration, and fatigue. Used in place of formula for infants not tolerating milk, and said to be useful in combination with capsicum in the management of alcoholism or delirium tremens. (8)

Carolina pink: See spigelia. (8)

Carolinum factitium (effervescens), sal: Artificial Carlsbad salt, of potassium sulphate, sodium chloride, sodium bicarbonate and sodium sulphate. Dissolved in water to prepare Carlsbad water. The effervescent form is made so in the usual manner, with sodium bicarbonate, tartaric acid, and citric acid. "It is rarely used except in the effervescent form." (31)

Carota; Carrot: Wild carrot, *Daucus carota*, a mild stimulant and diuretic. Figure 3-53. (33)

Carotene: The orange pigment in carrots and other plants, a vitamin A precursor. (40)

Carpobalsamum: Fruit of tree *Commiphora opobalsamum* and related trees (see opobalsamum, xylobalsamum). Used in theriac. (1,39)

Carrageen: Irish moss, see chondrus crispus. (40)

Carrel-Dakin fluid: See Dakin's solution. (24)

Carron oil: Carron oil is formed when linseed oil (lini, oleum) is mixed with a solution of lime (calcium oxide). See calcis, linimentum. (8)

Carrot (, wild): See carota.

Carthamin: Red coloring matter of safflower. (40)

Carthamus: Safflower, bastard saffron, saffron thistle, dyers' saffron, *Carthamus tinctorius*. Seeds used as diuretic and cathartic. (1,33,39)

Carthusianus, pulvis: Carthusian monk's powder, sulphurated antimony, a crude antimony sulfate. (39)

Carui; Carui, fructus; Carui, semen: This is caraway or caraway seed (semen). Figure 3-54. (34)

Carui, aqua: Of caraway fruit in water, a carminative and flavoring. (42)

Carui, spiritus; Carui (olei) tinctura: Spirit of caraway, essence of caraway, of the oil in alcohol. For flatulence and nausea. (34)

Carum; Cari, oleum; Cariol; Caruon: Caraway, the fruit of *Carum carvi or carui*, from which an oil is distilled. Use is as per anise or coriander and other typical volatile oils (see caryophyllus). Figure 3-54. (8)

Carvacrol: Isopropyl-orthocresol, from oil of oregano, a "powerful antiseptic." An iodide compound can be formed and used in place of iodoform. (42)

Carvol; Carvone; Carvonum: Active principal derived from oils of caraway (carum) and various other plants. Aromatic and carminative. (40)

Carvum; carvi (*eur, orth var*): Caraway, see carum. Carvum or carui are variants of caruum, a variant of carum. (1)

Caryocostinum, electuarium: Purgative electuary from cloves, costus root, scammony, etc. Used for gout or bilious attacks. (1)

Caryophyllata: See benedicta, herba. Root of water avens, *Geum urbanum*, a tonic and stomachic, stringent, and antiseptic. (1,39)

Caryophylli: Cloves, dried flower buds of tree, see caryophyllus and Figure 3-56. (1)

Caryophyllum rubrum: Dried flowers of *Dianthus caryophyllus*, a cardiac and alexipharmic, noted to be used chiefly for flavoring, i.e., a substitute for cloves. Figure 3-55. (39)

Caryophyllus (aromaticus); Caryophylli, infusum (concentratum); —, oleum: The dried, unexpanded flower of *Eugenia (or Caryophyllus) aromatica*, the clove, from which can be distilled a volatile oil. Source of eugenol. Clove oil was widely used among the volatile oils and serves as a prototypical example. Externally it was used as a stimulant, rubifacient, irritant, and counterirritant and gives rise to tingling followed by local anesthesia. It is effective against parasites and is antiseptic. Internally it causes a burning sensation in the mouth with vascular dilation and increased salivation. It is a gastric stimulant and appetite is increased, with increased motility of the stomach and intestines. It increases the rate and force of the heart, and is said to be helpful for a variety of spasmodic conditions such as intestinal or muscular cramping. It is excreted across mucous membranes of all types and will serve as an expectorant, although it was not often used in this manner. The infusion (tea) was used especially for nausea and for pains associated with flatulence. (8,34) The BPC also specified a concentrated infusion with alcohol for storage and reconstitution. Figure 3-56. (42)

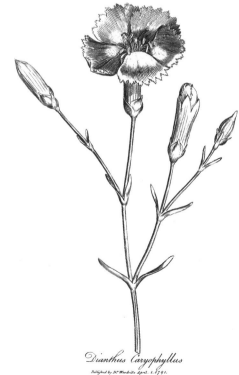

Fig. 3-53 Carota or wild carrot.

Fig. 3-54 Carum or caraway.

Fig. 3-55 Caryophyllum rubrum or dianthus.

Caryophyllus, conserva: Conserve of cariophyllus. (35)

Casca bark: Bark of the African casca, casca bark, sassy bark, or ordeal bark tree, *Erythrophloem guineense*. Tonic, astringrent, and according to some sources, having digitalis-like effects upon the heart.

Cascanea: Variant of castanea.

Cascara; Cascara sagrada: This is the bark of *Rhamnus purshiana*, i.e., sacred bark, or chittem bark, still used as a laxative today. A simple laxative and aperient, causing little "grip," or cramping. (8)

Cascara amarga: Bark of same, i.e., Honduras bark, not to be confused with the laxative cascara sagrada. An alterative and bitter. (7)

Cascara sagrada, compound elixir of: See rhamni purshianae compositum, elixir. (46)

Cascara sagradae, tablettae: Tablet of cascara sagrada with potato starch, etherial solution of theobroma, and alcohol, for constipation. (42)

Cascara, aromatic: See cascarae, elixir. (42)

Cascarae, elixir: Elixir of liquid extracts of cascara sagrada and licorice in glycerin and alcohol, flavored with oils of anise, peppermint, cloves, dill, and cinnamon. Cathartic. (42)

Cascarae aromaticus, syrupus: Syrup from liquid extract of cascara sagrada with tincture of orange, alcohol, cinnamon water, and simple syrup. Pleasant form of cascara for chronic constipation. (42)

Cascarae et belladonnae, pilulae: Pill of extracts of cascara sagrada and nux vomica with alcoholic extract of belladonna to reduce cramping. Cathartic. (42)

Cascarae et euonymini, elixir: Elixir of dry extract of euonymus, tincture of lemon, tasteless liquid extract of cascara sagrada (liquidum insipidum, below), and glycerin. Cathartic. (42)

Cascarae et euonymini, pilulae: Extract of cascara with euonymin and green extract of hyoscyamus. Cathartic. (42)

Cascarae sagradae (composita), mistura: A mixture of liquid extracts of cascara and licorice with aromatic spirits of ammonia and chloroform water, a purgative. The compound mixture also had tinctures of belladonna and nux vomica, which increase purgative action while reducing (due to atropine in belladonna) the griping (cramping) sensation. (42)

Cascarae sagradae (compositum), elixir: Elixir of cascara sagrada, a mixture of equal parts of aromatic fluid extract of cascara and elixir of glycyrrhiza. The compound elixir also contains small amounts of senna and juglans. A laxative. (31)

Cascarae sagradae aromaticum, fluidglyceratum: Aromatic fluidglycerate of cascara sagrada, from cascara sagrada by removing its bitter taste with calcium oxide and flavoring with fluidglycerate of licorice and oils of fennel, clove, and cinnamon. (31)

Cascarae sagradae liquidum insipidum, extractum: Tasteless liquid extract, of the liquid extract boiled with alkali (potash) until bitterness is eliminated. It is said to be appropriate in place of the liquid extract for essentially all uses of the latter, but especially in preparations for children. (42)

Cascarae sagradae liquidum, extractum: Liquid extract in water and alcohol, same as extractum rhamni purshianae. (42)

Cascarae sagradae miscibile, extractum: Liquid extract in water with glycerin and a small amount of strong solution of ammonia. (42)

Cascarae sagradae, extractum: Dry extract of cascara sagrada (BPC). (42)

Cascarae sagradae, fluidglyceratum: Fluidglycerate of cascara, a laxative. (31)

Cascarilla; Cascarillae, tinctura; Cascarillo: The bark of *Croton eluteria (Clutia elutheria spp. cascarilla)*, of the Bahamas, or tincture therefrom. It is a typical bitter and is employed as such (see columba for detail of use). Figure 3-57. (1,8,40)

Cascarillae composita, mistura: A mixture of compound tincture of camphor and vinegar of squill in the infusion of cascarilla, as an expectorant in chronic bronchitis or emphysema. (42)

Cascarillae, infusum (concentratum): An infusion of cascarilla. A bitter. The BPC also specified a concentrate with alcohol and chloroform water for storage and reconstitution. (42)

Casein; Caseinum: Milk casein, a protein derived from acidification of milk. Mainly nutritive, sometimes a component of ointment bases. (42)

Caseus: Cheese. (1)

Cashew nut: See anacardium. (40)

Cashoo: Extract of cutch; see catechu. (3)

Cashub: See lixivia. (39)

Cassia; —fistula; —fistularis; —stick tree: Cassia, pulp from pods of tree, *Cassia fistula,* whose pulp is administered as a mild laxative alone or with senna as confectio sennae. Figure 3-58. (1,8,40)

Cassia, electuarium e: Electuary of cassia pulp with tamarind, syrup of roses, and manna. Laxative. (35)

Cassia acutifolia: See senna. (32)

Fig. 3-56 Caryophyllus or clove.

Fig. 3-57 Cascarilla.

Cassia bark; Cassia(e) cortex: Cassia cinnamon bark, this is cassia lignea, below, a substitute for cinnamon, see cinnamoma.

Cassia buds; —flores: Buds of *Cassia fistula*, which closely resemble cloves.

Cassia lignea: Cassia cinnamon, cassia bark, i.e., bark of tree, *Cinnamomum cassia*. A substitute for cinnamon. (1,39) Much modern "cinnamon" is in fact cassia bark.

Cassia marilandica: American senna, same use as cassia fistula, above. (44)

Cassia senna: See senna. (39)

Cassiae pulpa; Cassia pulp: See cassia fistula above. (42)

Cassius' purple (powder of): A compound of tin with gold oxide. Antivenereal. (3,39)

Castanea; Castaneae fluidum, extractum: Leaves of the American chestnut, *Castanea dentata*, of North America, or the fluid extract. A mild sedative and antispasmodic said by White's *Materia Medica* to be used only for whooping cough due to the combined antispasmodic, expectorant, and sedative effects (8)

Castanea vesca; —vesica: Chestnut, *Castanea vesca,* botanical relationship to above unclear, but used for same purposes. Vesca is current proper botanical name, vesica is noted as an orthographic variant or error.

Castellani's mixture: A mixture of tartar emetic (antimonii et potassii tartras), sodium salicylate, potassium iodide, and sodium bicarbonate in water, used to treat yaws (a spirochetal venereal infection similar to syphilis.). (24)

Castellani's paint; —solution: See carbol-fuchsin solution. (24)

Castille soap: See sapo. (8)

Castor (fiber); Castoreum; Castorio *{Italian}***; Castoreo** *{Italian}***; Castoriae, (ammoniata) tinctura:** Castor, castoreum, substance with empyreumatic odor, obtained from the beaver. An alcoholic tincture or ammoniated tincture can be prepared. Note that the genus *Castor* refers not to the castor bean, but to the beaver, see immediately below. (1)

Castor (bean) oil: See ricini. (8)

Castor oil, emulsion: See both ricini, olei, emulsum (for US) and the similar rincini, olei, mistura (BPC). (42)

Castor oil lozenges: See calomel lozenges. (40)

Castor oil pills: Aperient, i.e., compound rhubarb pills (see rhei compositae, pilulae) containing castor oil. (40)

Castorei canadensis, tinctura; Castor. can., tinct.: This is an alcoholic tincture derived from the reproductive glands of the North American beaver, *Castor canadensis*, not to be confused with castor oil, derived from the castor bean (*Ricinus communis*). Used primarily for dysmenorrhea and "hysterical" illness, the latter believed to be of uterine origin at the time.

Casumunar: Said to be the tuberous root of an unknown plant frpm the East Indies. Antihysteric, stomachic, and carminative. (39)

Catalpa: Bark of the cigar tree, *Catalpa bignonioides*. (33) Botanical relationship to next entry is unclear as both receive little mention.

Catalpa cordifolia: Catalpa or catawba tree, unclear activity and possibly toxic. Unofficial. (44)

Cataplasma fermenti: See yeast poultice. (40)

Cataplasma: Cataplasma, or poultice, a plaster. (1)

Cataria: Catmint, Catnep, Catnip, the plant *Nepeta cataria*, European, naturalized in North America. It is a carminative and aromatic used for flatulence. (7)

Catariae et foeniculi, elixir: Elixir of catnep and fennel, of ten percent fluid extract of catnep with sodium bicarbonate and trace oil of fennel (foenicula) and spearmint (mentha viridis). It is intended as a carminative for infants. (31)

Catariae, fluidextractum: Fluid extract of catnep. (31)

Catarrh powder; —snuff: See pulvis anticatarrhalis. (34)

Catartico imperiale: See imperiale, catartico. (1)

Catawba: Found on a fused glass label pharmacy bottle with a ground glass stopper, this is presumably catawba red wine, see vinum.

Catechol: Pyrocatechin or catechol, a six-carbon ring compound with two adjacent alcohol (OH) groups, closely related to phenol (carbolic acid, one OH group) and having similar topical anesthetic and disinfectant properties. (40)

Catechu (, black); Catechu composita, tinctura; Catechu, extractum; —, infusum; —, trochisci: An extract from the wood of the Acacia, *Acacia (*or *Mimosa) catechu*, of India. It could be used to prepare a compound tincture consisting of catechu and cassia cinnamon or for troches of catechu, sugar, tragacanth, and stronger orange flower water (aurantii fortior, aqua). Used as a typical astringent (see tannicum, acidum). Infusion used particularly for diarrhea. Figure 3-59. (1,8,34)

Catechu compositum, infusum: Compound infusion of catechu with cinnamon powder. (44)

Fig. 3-58 Cassia fistula.

Fig. 3-59 Catechu.

Catechu compositus, pulvis: Compound powder of catechu, of same with kino, krameria, cinnamon, and nutmeg. For diarrheal illness. (34,46)

Catellus: Small dog, puppy. (1)

Cathartic dulcis: "Sweet cathartic," i.e., gentle cathartic, or calomel. (39)

Cathartic pills, compound; Catharticae compositae, pilulae: 1. In the USP compound cathartic pills of mild mercurous chloride (hydrargyri chloridum mite), extract of colocynth, extract of jalap, and gamboge. A cathartic. A very similar form is found in the BPC. 2. Eclectic or herbal pills of the same name, of leptandra, scammony, gamboge, podophyllum resin, and soap. (8)

Cathartica, pilula: See colocynthidis compositae, pilulae. (40)

Catharticae (compositae) vegetabiles, pilulae: Compound vegetable cathartic pills, of compound extract of colocynth with hyoscyamus, jalap, extract of leptandra, resin of podophyllum, oil of peppermint, and water. (8)

Catharticum compositum, elixir; Cathar. co. elix.: Compound cathartic elixir, consisting of frangula, senna and rhubarb (rheum), flavored with peppermint and aromatic elixir. (31)

Catharticus, sal: Cathartic salt (unspecified)—usually "vitriolated soda," or sodium sulfate, but usage is inconsistent per Estes. (39)

Catharticus amarus, sal: Bitter cathartic, magnesium sulphate. (3)

Catharticus Anglicanus, sal: "English salt," i.e., that from Epsom, magnesium sulfate. (3)

Catharticus Glauberi, sal: Glauber's salt, sodium sulfate. See sal catharticus, Glauberi. (1,3)

Catheter oil: See oleum lubricans. Also a synonym for oil of eucalyptus. (40,42)

Catheter paste: See pasta lubricans. (42)

Catholicon; Catholicum, electuarium: See diacatholicon, electuarium. (1)

Catholicon, acid: Sulfuric acid. (3)

Catholicon; Cathol.; Catholico.: This may refer to catholicon or may be an abbreviated form of diacatholicon, especially in reference to an electuary (electuarium diacatholicon). (35) Catholicon is not a religious reference, but a reference to universal applicability—i.e., an alexipharmic or panacea. Almost invariably a cathartic.

Catholicum, extractum: A compound extract of rhubarb. (3) Various sources indicate different formulations under this term, especially in Europe. All contain rhubarb, but other ingredients appear to vary widely.

Catmint; Catnep; Catnip: See cataria. (7)

Cauda equina: See equisetum. (1)

Caules: Twigs (Latin).

Caulibus, lohoch de: Lohoch made from red cabbage juice, sugar, and honey, used to treat chest ailments. (1)

Caulis: Red cabbage. (1)

Caulophylli, fluidextractum; —fluidum, extractum; —liquidum, extractum: Fluid extract of caulophyllum. (31, 42,46)

Caulophylli, resina: Dried resin from an alcoholic tincture of blue cohosh. Use as per the herb. (34)

Caulophylli composita, tinctura: Compound tincture of blue cohosh, with ergot, water-pepper, oil of savin and alcohol. For uterine and menstrual disorders. (34)

Caulophylli et pulsatillae, liquor: A solution made by extraction of caulophyllum root and pulsatilla powder with dilute sulphuric acid, alcohol, and water. For dysmenorrhea and uterine disorders. (42)

Caulophyllum: Blue cohosh, squaw root, papoose root, the rhizome and roots of *Caulophyllum thalictroides*, of eastern North America. Blue Cohosh was well known to the indigenous population of the Americas as an aid to facilitate labor. It was given as an ecbolic and in the treatment of various menstrual disorders, and has been used as an abortifacient. Figure 3-60. (8)

Caustic alcohol: Sodium ethylate, see sodii ethylas. (40)

Caustic alkaline lixivia; Caustic ley: Lye (potassium hydroxide), ley is a variant. (39)

Caustic soda: See soda. (8)

Causticus, lapis: Potassa (in sticks). (3)

Caustique perpetuel {*French*}**:** Perpetual or permanent caustic, i.e., silver nitrate. (39)

Cauterium potentiale: Caustic potash, i.e., potassium hydroxide. (40)

Cavallo {*Italian*}**:** Horse. (1)

Cavretto {*Italian*}**:** Kid (juvenile goat). (1)

Cayenne pepper: See capsicum. (8)

Ceanothi compositus, syrupus: Compound syrup of red root with lactuca, cimicifuga, asclepias root, asarum, lobelia, and sanguinaria root, for cough and hepatic disorders. (34)

Ceanothus: Red root, New Jersey tea, *Ceanothus americanus*, an astringent and expectorant. Also *C. thrysiflorus*, the California lilac or deer bush, for similar uses. (32)

Cedar (red), oleum; Cedar ol.: Cedar oil, i.e., turpentine-like substance derived from distillation of (red) cedar wood.

Cedrae (de Cedro), oleum: Oil of lemon. (3)

Cedrat, oil of: Oil of citron (lemon) peel. (40)

Cedri, oleum: Cedar oil, see cedar, oleum. (42)

Cedro {*Italian*}**:** Citron fruit, sometimes lemon. (1)

Cedron: Seed of *Simaba cedron*, said to be used in Central America for serpent bite. Unofficial. (44)

Celandine: See chelidonium. (8)

Celandine, lesser: See cheladonium minus. (42)

Celandine, wild: In American usage, *Impatiens aurea*; in British usage, *Ranunculus ficaria*. (40)

Celanese: Trade name, cellulose acetate, used to make collars and collar stays, but also various appliances such as pessaries, catheters, etc. (3)

Celastrus: False bittersweet, staff tree, climbing staff tree, staff vine, climbing bittersweet, waxwork, or fever twig, *Celastrus scandens*. (33)

Celidonia {*Italian*}**:** See *Chelidonium majus*. (1)

Celloidin: Concentrated collodion. (40)

Centaurea benedicta: See *Carduus benedicta*. (39)

Centaurium major: Major centaury, *Centaureum umbellatum* or *Chlora perfoliata*, a tonic, astringent, and vulnerary. (39)

The fleshy covered cadet blue seeds showing groups in pairs after bursting of the ovary.

Blue Cohosh.   Caulophyllum thalictroides.

Fig. 3-60 Caulophyllum or blue cohosh.

Centaurium minus: Common or lesser centaury, *Erythraea centaurium, Centaurium ramocissimum,* or *Chironia centaurium.* At times centaurium major (above). Dried flowering tops used, primarily as an aperient. Figure 3-61. (1,39)

Centaury, American: 1. Tops of American centaury, *Centaurea americanus,* as a substitute for centaurium major. 2. Same as sabbatia. (39)

Centinodium: See polygonum. (1)

Cepa: Onion. (1)

Ceph(a)eline; Cephalina: An active alkaloid derived from ipecacuanha root, a potent emetic. (42)

Cephalanthus: Bark of buttonbush, buttonwood, pond dogwood, crane willow, or globe flower, *Cephalanthus occidentalis,* used as a tonic, febrifuge, aperient, and diuretic. (33)

Cephalic powder: See myricae compositus, pulvis. (34)

Cephalic(um): Drug for relief of headache. (1)

Cera (alba): Wax, typically bees wax if not otherwise specified. White (alba) wax was prepared from yellow wax by bleaching by exposure to air, sun, and moisture. Used in the preparation of cerates and ointments. (8)

Cera alba placent(a): White beeswax, in cakes (*placenta,* Latin, flat cake or pancake). Yellow beeswax is bleached in the sun, or later chemically, to obtain white beeswax. (40,42)

Cera aseptica: Beeswax with almond oil and salicylic acid, heated and stored in sterile (aseptica) bottles. This is used as a bone wax to control bleeding, especially for cranial surgery. Much the same material is used as "bone wax" today. (42)

Cera flava: Yellow beeswax. (42)

Cera sigillata: Sealing wax. (3)

Cerae aetherea, solutio: Solution of white beeswax in methylated ether, a pill coating. (42)

Cerae compositum, emplastrum: 1. Composite wax plaster, of yellow wax, suet, and oil of turpentine. Often used as a dressing following blistering. (39) 2. Same as atrahens, emplastrum, the attracting plaster, a compound plaster evidently based upon wax. (39)

Cerasi, aqua: Cherry water, of the bruised fruits and seeds in water. Mild cathartic. (39)

Cerasi, syrupus: Sour cherry syrup, a flavoring, made from the cherry, *Prunus cerasus.* (7)

Cerasorum, aqua: Diluted bitter almond water. (3) This is likely the same as or similar to aqua cerasi, made from cherry pits, which, like almonds, produce hydrocyanic acid.

Cerasum: Cherry. (1)

Cérat de Galien {*French*}**:** See refrigerans Galeni, ceratum. (1)

Cerate; Ceratum: Cerate, a waxy ointment generally compounded with a wax and an oil with other therapeutic ingredients as desired. (1) Also spermaceti, or whale oil. (8) In the US formulary, 30 parts white wax, 20 petrolatum, and 50 benzoinated lard. (45)

Cerate liniment: Liniment of calamine in wax and oils, an astringent. (39)

Cerate, white: See ceratum album. (40)

Cerati saponis, emplastrum: See saponis fuscum, emplastrum. (40)

Ceratum album: White cerate, spermaceti ointment, a simple wax ointment of wax and whale oil. (40)

Ceratum calaminae: See epuloticum, ceratum. (40)

Ceratum cantharidis: See cantharidis, unguentum. (40)

Ceratum cetacei: Same as ceratum album (cetacei being a reference to whales).

Ceratum epuloticum: See epuloticum, ceratum. (1)

Ceratum (refrigerans) galeni: See refrigerans Galeni, ceratum. (1)

Ceratum labialis: Lip cerate, or lip balm, see ceratum rosatum.

Ceratum lithargyri acetati: Cerate of lead acetate, similar to plumbi acetatis, unguentum. (40)

Ceratum paraffini: Paraffin cerate, of six percent white beeswax in paraffin. Used as an ointment base. (42)

Ceratum plumbum compositum; Ceratum plumb. co.: Compound cerate of lead, similar to plumbi acetatis, unguentum.

Ceratum resinae compositum; Cerat. Resin. Co.: Compound rosin cerate, Deshler's salve, a popular cerate of rosin, yellow wax, suet, turpentine, and linseed oil, used as a stimulating dressing. (31)

Ceratum resinae: Simple cerate with rosin. (45)

Ceratum rosatum: Rose lip salve. This preparation consisted of wax, oil of almond (flavoring), alkanet or carmine (red colorant), and oil of roses, with abundant variants noted. (40)

Ceratum sabina: See sabinae, unguentum. (40)

Ceratum stomachale; ceratum stomachicum: See stomachale, ceratum. (1)

Cerecloth salve: See ferri, emplastrum (in lump form). (40)

Cerefolium: Chervil, *Anthriscus cerefolium.* Herb used as aperient and diuretic. (1,39)

Cereoli: Medicated bougies, see bougies. (40)

Cereoli (BPC): A rod- or pencil-shaped bougie or suppository for use in the nares or urethra, specified in the BPC. Nasal bougies were of cocoa butter or gelatin, urethral bougies of cocoa butter. These typically offer one or more of: the pain relief of a narcotic, the anticholinergic activity of atropine or belladonna (to dry the membranes), an antiseptic (iodoform) and an astringent such as tannic acid or zinc sulfate. The BPC (42) specifies the following Cereoli:

- **Acidi tannici et opii,** with tannic acid and opium in cocoa butter.
- **Atropinae,** with atropine in cocoa butter.
- **Belladonnae,** with extract of belladonna in cocoa butter.
- **Bismuthi et plumbi,** of bismuth oxynitrate and lead acetate in cocoa butter.
- **Cocainae,** of cocaine hydrochloride in cocoa butter.
- **Iodoformi,** of iodoform in cocoa butter.
- **Iodoformi et belladonnae,** with both iodoform and belladonna in cocoa butter.
- **Iodoformi et eucalypti,** with iodoform and eucalyptus oil (to clear nasal secretions) in cocoa butter.
- **Iodoformi et morphinae,** of iodoform and morphine in cocoa butter.
- **Zinci sulphatis** of desiccated zinc sulfate in cocoa butter.

Ceresin: Earth-wax, impure paraffin. (3)

Chironia Centaurium

Fig. 3-61 Centaurium minus or lesser centaury.

Cereum, unguentum: Wax ointment, see unguentum simplex. (40)

Cereus grandiflorus: The night-blooming cereas, a cactus, *Cactus grandiflora*, of the tropical Americas. A fluid extract could be prepared. This material appears to have affected autonomic function, strengthening the heart, slowing the rate, but increasing contractile force. It could be used much like digitalis for treatment of heart failure or dropsy, but was also useful in certain conditions where digitalis was contraindicated. Also used for enlarged heart of diverse causes, in recovery from typhoid, to treat sexual exhaustion, etc. (8)

Cerevasia fermenti; Cerevisiae fermentum: See yeast. *Cerevasia fermenti* is the former Latin name of brewer's yeast, *Saccharomyces cerevisiae*. (8)

Ceridin; Cerolin: Extracted fatty acids of yeast. (40)

Cerii nitras [effervescens]; Cerii oxalas [effervescens]: Cerium nitrate or oxalate. Cerium salts resemble bismuth in activity and were given for dyspepsia and vomiting, especially during pregnancy. These are not absorbed. Formulated in solutions or tablets, and also specified in BPC as effervescent formulations. (8,42) Cerium oxalate was said to be a sedative and useful to "arrest vomiting in gastralgia following a debauch." (45)

Ceroneum, emplastrum: Poultice of litharge, fenugreek, myrrh, yellow wax, etc. Used as emollient and for muscular pain. (1)

Ceroto; Cerotto {*Italian*}: Poultice, plaster. (1)

Cerous _____: Compound of cerium, see Cerii. (42)

Cerralina: See galla. (39)

Cerratum, unguentum; Cerat. u.: Wax ointment, of white wax, spermaceti, and olive oil. (35)

Cerule[a][us][um] (orth. var): Blue, see listings for correct Latin term, caeruleum.

Ceruse; Cerussa: 1. Ceruse, white lead, basic lead carbonate. 2. Identical with cerussa acetata. (1,3,39)

Cerussa acetata: Lead acetate. (3)

Cerussa antimonii: See antimonii, cerussa. (39)

Cerussae acetata, unguentum: Cerate of lead acetate, a cooling and desiccating ointment. (3,39)

Cerussae, unguentum: See plumbi carbonatis, unguentum. (40)

Cervus; Cervus elaphus: Stag, or horn of stag, hartshorn. (1,39)

Cetacei, unguentum; —, Ung.: Ointment of spermaceti, of same with white beeswax, almond oil, and benzoin. An emollient for excoriations, vesications, and wounds. (34)

Cetaceum; Ceti, oleum; Cetaceae, ceratum: Spermaceti, the oil obtained from the head cavity of the sperm whale, *Phyester macrocephalus*. The wax (cerate) consisted of 100 parts spermaceti, 350 white wax, and 550 olive oil. Spermacetti was an emollient and the cerate served as a base for various ointments. (8,40)

Ceterach: Common Spleenwort, *Asplenium ceterach*, possibly other ferns. See polytrichum. (1)

Ceti, unguentum: See cetacei, unguentum. (40)

Cetraria (islandica); Cetrariae, decoctum: Icelandic moss, *Cetraria islandica*. This is actually a lichen, not a moss, and was used to form a demulcent preparation, decoctum cetrariae, by boiling in water. Primarily used for sore throat and as a demulcent. (8)

Cetylacetic acid: Stearic acid. (3)

Cevadilla: Variant of sabadilla. Cevadilla is official in the BPC. (39,42)

Cevadilline; Cevine; Cevedine: See sabadilline. (40)

Cfy: Irregular abbeviation for cyanoferrate or ferrocyanide ion, see prussate. (29)

Chabaud's mixture: A tissue specimen fixative of alcohol, phenol, formalin, and acetic acid. (24)

Chaberti, oleum: Rectified animal oil. (3)

Chaerefolium: See cerefolium. (1)

Chalabeata, mistura: See ferri amara, mistura. (42)

Chalabeate plaster; Chalybeate plaster: See ferri, emplastrum.

Chalcanthum: 1. Copperas, zinc sulfate. (3) 2. Ferrous sulfate. (40)

Chalibeatae, pilulae; Chalyb(e)ate pills: Iron pills, purgative pills of iron oxide, aloes, saffron, etc. See ferri carbonatis, pilulae. (1,8)

Chalibeatus, syrupus; Chalybeatus, syrupus: Syrup of iron oxide and other ingredients. Used to treat anemia. (1)

Chalk, French: See creta Gallae. (40)

Chalk, precipitated: See calcii carbonas praecipitatus. (40)

Chalybeate: An iron containing medicinal used as a tonic and astringent. The specific chemical referred to is often unclear or ultimately proved to be incorrect in any event, i.e., iron tartrate usually oxidized and was in fact the oxide; sal chalybis is the sulfate, etc.

Chalybeated tartar: Tartarated iron, see ferrum tartarisatum. (40)

Chalybeatum, vinum: See ferri citratis, vinum. (31)

Chalybis rubigo praeparatus: Iron rust, see ferri rubigo. (40)

Chalybis, sal: Ferrum vitrolatum, i.e., iron sulfate. (3,39)

Chamaedrys: Common germander, wall germander, *Teucrium chamaedrys*. Herb used as diaphoretic, diuretic, stomachic, and emmenogogue. Figure 3-62. (1)

Chamaelirium; Chamoelirium: See helonias. (33)

Chamaemelum; Chamaemilla: See chamomilla. (1)

Chamaepithys; Chamaepitys: Ground pine, gout ivy, *Ajuga chamaepitys*. Leaves used as aperient, vulnerary, and antirheumatic. (1,39)

Chamomile, Dog; —, Wild: See cotula. (33)

Chamomilla; Chamomile; Chamomile (, German/ Roman(ae))(, Hungarian/Vulgaris): Roman chamomile (*Anthemis nobilis*); German (Hungarian) chamomile (*Matricaria chamomilla*), and possibly other related plants of family *Compositae*. The uses of this remedy were multiple, from antihysteric to vermifuge. (1,7,39)

Chamomillae citratum, oleum: Oil of lemon distilled over German chamomile. (3)

Chamselaea: Daphne mezereum, see mezereum. (40)

Chapman's dinner pills: See aloes et mastiches, pilulae. (34)

Chapman's mixture: A variant of copaibae composita, mistura. Copaiba, spirit of nitrous ether, compound tincture of lavender, potassa, simple syrup, and mucilage of dextrin. A diuretic, for gonorrhea, and for various urinary conditions. (34)

Charas: Resin from Indian hemp. See apocynum (cannabinum). (40)

Chardon bénit {*French*}: See carduus benedictus. (1)

Teucrium Chamædrys

Fig. 3-62 Chamaedrys or germander.

Charlton white: See lithopone. (3)

Charpie: Lint. (3)

Charta _____: Paper (as a dosage form or means of application), see _____, charta. (8)

Chartreux, poudre de {*French*}**:** Powder of Chartreux, see kermes mineralis. (39)

Charyophylli: See caryophilli. (1)

Chaubert's oil: A three to one mixture of turpentine and hartshorn oil. (40)

Chaulmogra; Chalmugra; Chalmoogra oil; Chaulmoogree, oleum: Chaulmoogra oil. See gynocardia. (7,33)

Chaulmoograe, unguentum: Chaulmoogra oil and paraffin, for chronic skin conditions, including leprosy. (40)

Cheatle's green: A solution of malachite green and mercuric chloride. No specific medicinal use identified. (40)

Chebulus, myrobalanus: See myrobalanus chebulus. (1)

Cheiri: Wallflower, *Cheiranthus cheiri*. Flowers used. (1)

Chelae cancrorum: Crab claws, given as per prepared chalk, as antacid or absorbent. Unofficial. (44)

Chelarum cancri compositus, pulvis: Compound powder of crab's claws, of crabs claws and red coral. (39)

Chelen: Kelene, i.e., ethyl chloride, a topical refrigerant anesthetic. (3)

Chelidonium majus: Greater celandine, *Chelidonium majus*, of European origin, but cultivated in North America. Leaves and root used as a powerful cholegogue, aperient, diuretic, and diaphoretic, and especially for jaundice as the root is yellow, suggesting under the doctrine of signatures that it should be effective for "yellow conditions." Figure 3-63. (1,8,39)

Chelidonium minus: Lesser celandine, *Ranunculus ficaria*. Leaves and root used. Also called pilewort, and was used in folk medicine under the doctrine of signatures, i.e., the root resembles hemorrhoids and was used to treat same. (1,39)

Chelone (glabra): Herb, especially leaves, of balmony, snakehead, turtlehead, turtlebloom, shellflower, or salt-rheum weed, *Chelone glabra*. A tonic, cathartic, and anthelmintic, valuable in jaundice and hepatic diseases. (33,44)

Chelsea pensioner: An antirhumatic electuary named for the Chelsea Hospital (eighteenth century), of variable formulation, but usually including guaiac, rhubarb, and sulfur. (39) See guiaci composita, confectio. (42)

Cheltenham salt: An artificial mineral salt of sodium sulphate, magnesium sulphate, and sodium chloride. (40)

Chemical food: See ferri phosphatis compositus, syrupus. (42)

Chemick: A cold dilute solution of chlorinated lime (calx chlorata), usually a bleaching agent in textile industry, but also used in the synthesis of chloroform. (3)

Chenopodii composita, mistura: Compound mixture of chenopodium, or worm mixture, of wormseed oil, anise oil, and tincture of myrrh, all in castor oil. A vermifuge. (See also atriplex foetida.) (34)

Chenopodium; Chenopodium, oleum: American wormseed, fruit of *Chinopodium ambrosoides*, of India and Central America, but naturalized in the United States, and source of a volatile oil distilled from the dried seed. An effective anthelmintic. May also be *Atriplex Foetida*. (8)

Chenopodium botrys; —anthelminticum: Jerusalem oak, *Chenopodium botrys*, leaves and seeds used as anthelminthic, emmenagogue, carminative, and pectoral. (39)

Chenopodium vulvaria: See atriplex foetida. (39)

Chequer berry: Wintergreen berry or associated plant, see gaultherium. (40)

Cherefolium: See cerefolium. (1)

Chermes: See kermes. (1)

Cherry laurel: See laurocerasus. (8)

Chervil: See cerefolium. (39)

Chestnut (, horse) (, water): For chestnut, see castanea. For horse chestnut or water chestnut, see respectively hippocastanum or water caltrop. (8,39)

Chian turpentine: Oleoresin from *Pistacia terebinthus*, the Turpentine Tree, of the Mediterranean. Related to, but not the same as the pistachio tree. (40)

Chicorea intybus, extractum; Cich. Int., Ext.: Extract of chicory, *Cichorum intybus*. (1)

Chicory; Chicorium; Cicorea {*Italian*}**; Cicoria** {*Italian*}**; Chicorée** {*French*}**:** Chicory, succory, or wild succory, *Cichorium intybus*. Root, leaves, flowers, seeds used. Aperient and mild laxative. Figure 3-64. (1,33)

Fig. 3-63 Chelidonium majus or greater celandine.

Fig. 3-64 Chicory or chicorium.

Chimaphila; Chimaphilae fluidum, extractum; —, decoctum: The leaves of *Chimaphila umbellata*, the pipsessewa or prince's pine, or the fluid extract or simple decoction. Used as a diuretic, tonic, and astringent. Figure 3-65. (8,44)

China, pride of: See azederach. (39)

China (root): "China" may refer to cinchona or to the China root, rhizome of *Similax china*, a diaphoretic and diuretic used for venereal and skin disorders. Figure 3-66. (1,39)

China berry: See azederach. (39)

China blue; Chinese blue: Prussian blue. (3)

China chinae; Chinae cortex: See peruvianus cortex. (1)

China clay: Kaolin, a clay, for diarrhea. (40)

China oil: Balsam of Peru. (3)

China red; Chinese red: Vermillion. See cinnabar. (33,40)

China white; Chinese white: Zinc oxide. (3)

Chinae, extractum spissum; —, Extr. Spiss.: Dried extract of quinine, see peruvianus, cortex.

Chinalgen: Quinalgen, a quinine related antimalarial. (40)

Chinchona (, yellow)(, red); Chin.: Chinchona is an orthographic variant on cinchona, or quinine, see peruvianus, cortex. (1)

Chinese ____: See also: China ____.

Chinese sumach: See ailanthus. (32)

Chinic acid: Quinic acid, from quinine. (40)

Chininium; Chinium: Quinine. (3,40)

Chinoidin; Chinolin: Quinoidine and quinoline, respectively, from quinine. (40)

Chinotropine: Hexamine quinate, antimalarial related to quinine. (40)

Chinquapin: See castanea. (39)

Chinse cortex: Cinchona bark. (40)

Chinsol: See oxyquinoline sulphate. (40)

Chionanthus; Chionanthi, fluidextractum: Fringe tree, *Chionanthus virginica*, bark of root used, or the fluid extract therefrom. (7,31)

Chips, bitter: Quassia. (3)

Chirata; Chiratae fluidum, extractum; —concentratus, liquor; —infusum (concentratum); —, tinctura: The entire plant, *Swertia chirata*, of India, or the fluid extract, liquor (concentrate only specified), infusion, or alcoholic tincture therefrom. It is a typical bitter and is employed as such (see columba for detail of use). The BPC also specified a concentrated infusion with alcohol and chloroform water for storage and reconstitution. (8,42)

Chirayta(e): Variant of chirata, above.

Chiretta: Said to be the stem and roots of *Ophila* or *Agathotes chirayta*, this appears to be identical with chirata (*Swertia chirata*). (39)

Chironia centaurium: Probably equivalent to centaurium minus. (39)

Chittem bark: See cascara sagrada. (8)

Chloral; Chloral hydrate; Chloralum hydratum: Chloral hydrate, CCl_3-CH=O, from reaction of dry chlorine with absolute alcohol (alcohol, absolutum). Chloral hydrate is an effective antiseptic topically, but is an irritant and will cause blister formation. It is a very powerful hypnotic used to induce sleep, and accordingly depresses respiration and cardiac function. Dependence on this drug was recognized. Chloral hydrate is readily disguised in alcoholic beverages, and the combination is commonly referred to a "Mickey Finn." Chloral hydrate is still in use as a sedative, primarily for medical procedures. (8)

Chloral (, sol.) (, solut.); Chloral Hydrate (solution); Chloralum hydratum (, sol.) (, solut.): Solution of chloral hydrate.

Chloral and phenol: See chloral carbolate. (42)

Chloral camphorata cum cocaina: Camphorated chloral with cocaine, equal parts camphor and chloral hydrate triturated with cocaine, ten percent. Topical for toothache. (42)

Chloral camphoratum: Camphorated chloral, eutectic mixture (i.e., having a lower melting point than either component alone) of equal parts of hydrated chloral and camphor, used as a local anodyne and counter-irritant. (31)

Chloral carbolate: Carbolic acid (phenol) in equal amount of chloral hydrate. Topical for carious teeth and treating dental discomfort. (42)

Chloral carmine: Staining fluid (for microscopy) of carmine, dehydrated alcohol and chloral hydrate. (3)

Chloral formamide; Chloralum formamidatum: Chloral-formamide degrades to chloral, and is used as a sedative-hypnotic. (8)

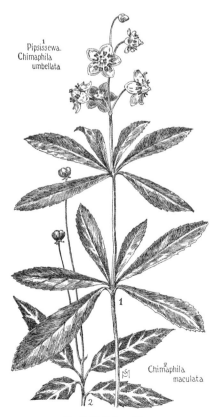

Fig. 3-65 Chimaphila.

Fig. 3-66 China root or similax china.

Chloral, syrupus: Syrup of chloral hydrate in simple syrup. A sedative. (34,42)

Chlorali et potassii bromidi composita, mistura: Compound mixture of chloral (hydrate) and potassium bromide, containing tincture of cannabis indica and extract of hyoscyamus, used as a sedative. (34) The NF specified a similar mixture of chloral, potassium bromide, extracts of cannabis indica, hyoscyamus, tincture of quillaja, and water. (46)

Chloralose: A chlorinated aliphatic hydrocarbon related to chloral, used as a sedative-hypnotic. See gluco-chloral. (40)

Chloramide composita, mistura: A mixture of chloramide, potassium bromide, alcohol, and water, a sedative-hypnotic and for sea sickness. (42)

Chloramide of mercury: See hydrargyri ammonii chloridum. (40)

Chloramide: See chloral formamide, a proprietary name for this sedative. (40)

Chloramine—T; Chlorazene: Sodium N-chloro-tosylamide, a chloramine compound which releases free chlorine. A disinfectant. (40)

Chlorazotic acid: Aqua regia, hydrochloric and nitric acid. (3)

Chlorbutol; Chlor-butyl alcohol: Chlorobutanol, disinfectant still in use in pharmaceutical preparations, also with some sedative and muscle relaxant properties.

Chlorcosane: See paraffin chlorinatum. (40)

Chloretone: See chlorbutol. (40)

Chlorhydric acid: Hydrochloric acid. (40)

Chlori, aqua; —, liquor: Chlorine water, from passage of chlorine gas through water. (8)

Chlori, gargarisma: Gargle of dilute potassium chlorate in water, a disinfectant for diphtheria, scarlatina, and "septic" throat. (42)

Chlori compositus, liquor: Compound solution of chlorine, made by reacting potassium chlorate with hydrochloric acid and dissolving the products in water. Used as an intestinal antiseptic. (31)

Chloric ether: See chloroformi, spiritus. (8)

Chloride of lime: See chlorinated lime. (40)

Chloride of mercury and quinina: See hydrargyri et quiniae chloridum. (44)

Chloride of mercury, corrosive; Chloride of mercury, mild: Mercuric ($HgCl_2$) and mercurous (HgCl) chloride, respectively. See, respectively, hydrargyri chloridum corrosivum and hydrargyri chloridum mite. (8)

Chloridorum, elixir: Elixir of four chlorides. This complex elixir contains bichloride of mercury, arsenic trioxide, ferric chloride, and diluted hydrochloric acid. (31)

Chlorinated lime: Lime (calcium carbonate) treated with chlorine, used in the manufacture of chloroform.

Chlorine; Chlorum: Elemental chlorine gas, Cl_2. This is generated by heating hydrochloric acid and manganese dioxide. Chlorine salts (other than common salt, NaCl) are generally not used internally except as a mouthwash, but are useful as sanitizers and disinfectants. See chlorum, chlori, chlorata, and chloridum for salts as chloride. (8)

Chlorine poultice: See sodae chlorinatae, cataplasma. (42)

Chlorine water: See chlori compositus, liquor. (31)

Chlorinii, aqua: See chlori compositus, liquor. (44)

Chlorodyne; Chlorodynum: A popular mixture of laudanum, tincture of cannabis, and chloroform, for cholera, diarrhea, neuralgia, migraine, etc. Tinctura chloroformi et morphinæ composita was intended as an official generic substitute for this proprietary remedy. The BPC gives the ingredients as chloroform, morphine hydrochloride, tincture of Indian hemp, tincture of capsicum, liquid extract of licorice, gum acacia, treacle (molasses), glycerin, and oil of peppermint, in about fifty percent alcohol. (42)

Chlorodyni, trochisci: Troche with morphine hydrochloride, tragacanth, chloroform, ether, oil of peppermint, tincture of capsicum, sugar, and mucilage of acacia, for cough, gastric pain, or flatulence. (42)

Chloroform; Chloroformum (purificatum): Chloroform, $CHCl_3$. Distilled from a mixture of water and alcohol over chlorinated lime. (This was ethyl alcohol; the 2-carbon alcohol is converted to chloral and then decomposes to release chloroform.) Used to cool the skin, sometimes to the point of local anesthesia, and of course for general anesthesia as well. (8)

Chloroform anodyne: See chloroformi et opii, mistura. (34)

Chloroform of ____; Chloroformum ____: A chloroform solution, see ____, chloroformum. (42)

Chloroformi (diluta), aqua: Chloroform water, by agitation of chloroform and water, with the excess chloroform settling to the bottom. Flavoring and mild carminative. The standard water was approximately 0.25 percent, the dilute 0.1 percent chloroform. (8,42)

Chloroformi, emulsio: Emulsion of chloroform, tincture of quillaia, and water in the BPC, or in the USP of chloroform, water, and dried tragacanth. Primarily a flavoring and preservative. (42)

Chloroformi, linimentum: Chloroform liniment, a mixture of chloroform in soap liniment. A topical anesthetic. (8,34)

Chloroformi, mistura: Mixture of chloroform, camphor, egg yolk, and water. (44)

Chloroformi, oleum: Mixture of chloroform and olive oil. (40)

Chloroformi, spiritus: Chloric ether, spirit of chloroform. Six percent chloroform in alcohol. (8)

Chloroformi (et morphinae), tinctura: Tincture of chloroform, with or without morphine. The former of chloroform, rectified spirits, and compound tincture of cardamom, the latter of chloroform, rectified spirits, morphine hydrochloride, dilute hydrocyanic acid, oil of peppermint, fluid extract of licorice, treacle, and simple syrup. An anodyne and, with morphine, for cough and colic. (34) In the BPC, of chloroform, morphine hydrochloride, dilute hydrocyanic acid, tinctures of capsicum and cannabis Indica, oil of peppermint, glycerin, and alcohol, and noted to be used as a gastrointestinal sedative and for general relief of pain in addition to above. (42)

Chloroformi composita, mistura: A mixture of morphine hydrochloride, dilute hydrobromic acid, chloroform, tincture of cudbear, syrup of wild cherry, and simple syrup; a sedative mixture for cough, especially chronic cough in phthisis. (42)

Chloroformi composita, tinctura: Compound tincture of chloroform, consisting of compound tincture of cardamom, fifty percent, with ten percent chloroform and forty percent alcohol. Carminative, but mainly a flavoring. (42)

Chloroformi compositum, elixir: Compound elixir of chloroform NF, with spirit of camphor, opium, aromatic spirits of ammonia, and cinnamon oil. (45)

Chloroformi compositum, vapor; Chlorof. co., vap.: See A.C.E. mixture. (40)

Chloroformi et cannabis indicae composita, mistura: Compound mixture of chloroform and cannabis indica, with ether, tincture of capsicum, morphine sulphate, glycerin, and peppermint oil, dissolved in alcohol. For painful conditions. (34,46)

Chloroformi et morphinae composita, tinctura: Compound tincture of chloroform, with morphine hydrochloride, dilute hydrocyanic acid, tinctures of capsaicin and Indian hemp, oil of peppermint, glycerin, and alcohol. For cough. (34)

Chloroformi et opii, mistura: Mixture of chloroform and opium, also called chloroform anodyne, for pain. (34)

Chloroformum camphorae: Chloroform in which camphor is dissolved. Used topically as per camphor itself. (8)

Chloroformum venale: Commercial grade, i.e., ninety-eight percent or better, chloroform.

Chloro-hydrargyricum, acidum: Mercuric chloride, i.e., calomel. (40)

Chlorohydrophosphate of lime, syrup of: See calcii chlorohydro-phosphatis, syrupus. (46)

Chloro-methyl: Methyl chloride, primarily a fumigant. (40)

Chloromorphine (, tinctura); Chlor-morph, tr.: This appears to be a non-standard tincture of chlorinated morphine (6-chloromorphine), used as a sedative and analgesic.

Chloronitrosum, acidum: Nitrohydrochloric acid. (3)

Chlorophyll [liquidum] [spissum]; Chlorophyllum: Chlorophyll from plants, the nature of which was not understood, at least as of 1907. It was available as a liquid or dry (spissum) green product, used for coloring alcoholic beverages, soaps, and oils. No medicinal value. (42)

Chloryl anaesthetic: Ethyl chloride, a topical refrigerant anesthetic. (40)

Chlor-zinc iodine: See Schulze's solution. (40)

Chocolate: See cocoa (source of) or pasta theobromatis (the confection). (42)

Chocolate nut: See theobroma. (40)

Chocolate tablets (BPC): See tabellae. Note, distinct from compressed tablets, tablettae. (42)

Cholagogum, electuarium: Purgative electuary for bilious disorders. (1)

Cholera mixture, board of health: See cretae compositus, pulvis or, according to BPC, a similar liquid formulation, cretae compositus, mistura. (40,42)

Cholera mixture: See diarrhea mixture. (34)

Cholera pills: See camphorae compositae, pilulae. (34)

Choline di-stearo-glycero-phosphate: Lecithin. Emulsifier. (40)

Chondrae, decoctum: Decoction of Irish moss, a demulcent and nutritive, for cough, bronchitis, and "catarrh of the bladder." (42)

Chondri, mucilago: Mucilage of Irish moss. (34)

Chondri compositus, syrupus: Compound syrup of Irish moss, with squill, senega, camphorated tincture of opium, and talcum. A demulcent and expectorant. (34)

Chondrodendron (tomentosum): See pareira (brava). (39)

Chondrus (crispus): Irish moss, *Chondrus crispus* or *Gigartina mamillosa*, of the Atlantic Ocean. This is a seaweed, not a moss, despite the name, and is also called carragheen, the source of the thickening agent, carrageenan. It is boiled in water to form a mucilage or gelatinous mass. It is used directly as a demulcent to treat gastric upset, but more commonly as a binder for various preparations or in foods. (8)

Choralamide: See chloral formamide. (40)

Chrisma: Soft paraffin. (40)

Chrismol: A liquid paraffin. (40)

Christmas rose: See helleborus niger. (39)

Chrome orange: Lead oxychromate. (40)

Chrome red: Lead dichromate. (40)

Chrome yellow: Lead chromate. (3)

Chromic trioxide; Chromicum, acid[i][um] (, liquor): Chromic acid, H_2CrO_4 or the anhydrous form, chromic trioxide, CrO_3. A disinfectant and sanitizer sometimes applied in dilute solutions to ulcers and sores. The liquor is a one:three dilution in water specified in the British *Pharmacopoeia* and is used to destroy skin lesions. A solution of approximately twenty-five percent chromic acid in water, a topical corrosive for warts, etc. applied "by means of a pointed glass rod," or diluted as a gargle, paint, or lotion. Chromium has no internal use. (8,42)

Chromii trioxidum: See chromicum, acidum. (45)

Chromule: See chlorophyll. (40,42)

Chrysarobin; Chrysarobinum; Chrysarobini, unguentum: Chrysarobin was a neutral substance obtained from goa (araroba) powder, a substance found deposited on the wood of *Andira araroba*, of Brazil. An unguent was prepared as five percent chrysarobin in benzoinated lard. It was a powerful skin irritant and antiparasitic used for ringworm. It is a powerful cathartic, causing vomiting and purging if given orally. It would stain skin, linens, and the urine brown. (8)

Chrysophanic acid; Chrysophanicum, acidum: Chrysophanic acid is derived from araroba, and was used primarily for topical treatment of a wide variety of skin conditions, usually as an ointment. (33)

Chrysophyllum: Bark of monesia, *Chrysophyllum glyciphloeum*, from which an extract (also called monesia), is prepared. A mild stimulant and astringent. (33)

Churchill's iodine caustic: See iodi causticus, liquor. (46)

Churchill's tincture (of iodine): See iodi, tinctura. (46) See iodi fortior, tinctura and iodi composita, tinctura. (31,34)

Chylista: Antimonium vitrificatum with mastiche dissolved in spirits of wine. This is a variant of vinum antimonii, and was used as a cathartic. (39)

Chymosin: Pepsin. (3)

Cibus deorum: Asafetida. (3)

Cicer; Cicera: Chick-pea, *Cicer arietinum*. Seeds used. (1) However, cicera (Latin plural) usually refers to small balls, i.e., pills as immediately below.

Cicera tartari (Mynscht's): "Peas of tartar," a pill made of terebintha (turpentine) and cream of tartar, iris florentina, niter, and water of violets; a deobstruent after Adrian Mynscht, 1600s. (39)

Cicerbita: See sonchus. (1)

Cichorium: See chicorium. (33)

Cicuta (maculat(a)(um)): Water hemlock or spotted cowbane, *Cicuta maculata (*formerly *C. virosa)*. A potent narcotic and sedative, as well as topical discutient. This is deadly toxin, causing seizures and death by paralysis. Not to be confused with poison hemlock, the supposed poison of Socrates (see conium). Figure 3-67. (1,39)

Cicuta virosa: In current use, northern water hemlock or cowbane, highly toxic and largely replaced by cicuta maculata, above. Unofficial. (44) Many older sources use this term for *C. maculata*.

Cicutas, tinctura: See conii, tinctura. (40)

Cicutine: Coniine, active principal (toxin) of conium (poison hemlock). (40)

Cidonia: See cydonia. (1)

Cidro {*Italian*}**:** See cedro. (1)

Ciguë {*French*}**:** See cicuta. (1)

Cilidonia: See celidonia. (1)

Cimicifuga; Cimicifugae rhizoma; Cimicifugin: The black s nakeroot, rhizome and roots of *Cimicifuga racemosa*, of North America. In addition to typical uses for a bitter (see columba for details of use), it was used for menstrual disorders and to enhance uterine contraction, i.e., to assist in labor or as an abortifacient. Cimicifugin is the supposed active component or concentrate. (8,40,42)

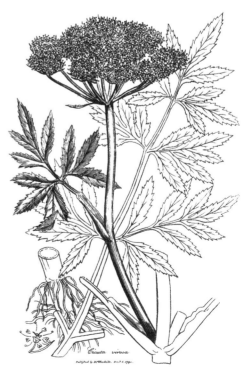

Fig. 3-67 Cicuta maculatum or water hemlock.

Cimicifugae, extractum; —fluidum, extractum; —liquidum, extractum; —, tinctura: The extract, fluid extract, and alcoholic tincture of cimicifuga, the black snakeroot or black cohosh. (8,42)

Cimicifugae, resina: Dried resin from an alcoholic tincture of black cohosh. Use as per the herb. (34)

Cimicifugae composita, tinctura: Compound tincture of black cohosh, of tinctures of black cohosh, blood-root and poke-root, admixed. Particularly good for pulmonary illness, hepatic diseases, and dyspepsia. (34)

Cimicifugae compositae, pilulae: Compound pills of black cohosh, with scutillaria and valerianate of quinine, for restlessness, insomnia, and some uterine conditions. (34)

Cimicifugae compositus, syrupus: Compound syrup of black cohosh, with fluid extracts of cimicifuga, glycyrrhiza, and senega, wild cherry, and fluid extract of ipecac, in water. For lung disorders. This formulation was, according to *King's Formulary*, misnamed as Syrup of Actaeae in the original USP. (34)

Cimolite: Purified fuller's earth, see terra fullonica. (40)

Cina flores: Santonica. (3)

Cina {*Italian*}**:** See China. (1)

Cinae, semen: See santonica. (1)

Cinara: See cynara.

Cinchona (calisaya): Bark of *Cinchona officinalis*, originally of South America. Calisaya is a synonym for cinchona, so that bottles labeled "Cinchona Calisaya," although sold commercially, are redundant (see also calisaya). This is the source of quinine, the essential anti-malarial and general febrifuge (antipyretic) of the New World, and one of the most sought-after agents for the treatment of human disease. Additional alkaloids, many of which were isolated and used independently, include quinidine, cinchonine, and cinchonidine. This was used primarily to treat fevers in general, as well as being a specific for malaria due to the ability of quinine to kill the malarial parasite. It is no longer in use for the latter purpose due to the development of resistance, and has been replaced by more effective, and less toxic antipyretics (aspirin, phenacetin, etc.). Toxicity with quinine, cinchonism, was well described, with ringing in the ears, visual disturbances leading to blindness, and cardiac and respiratory failure. (8) There are many varieties of cinchona plant giving rise to powders of varying color (flava, rubra, pallida), not always with a clear association between species and resulting color. Figure 3-68. (44).

Cinchona, pale; —pallida: Pale cinchona, bark of *Cinchona officinalis*. (40) Other sources suggest other species of questionable differentiation, including *C. condaminea* and *C. micrantha*. (44)

Cinchona, red: Bark of *Cinchona succirubra* (probably *C. rubra*, below). (40)

Cinchona febrifuge: Mixed cinchona alkaloids. (40)

Cinchona flava (, tinct.) (, Pv.): Yellow cinchona, a closely related species or perhaps the same as *C. officinalis*, depending upon source of information. For the tincture, see cinchonae, tinctura.

Cinchona flava; Cinchona, yellow: Bark of *Cinchona calisaya*. (40)

Cinchona rubra (, tinct.) (, Pv.): Bark of a tree closely related to cinchona, the red conchona, or *Cinchona rubra*, of Ecuador and vicinity or the tincture or powder. Used for the same purposes as cinchona. For the tincture, see cinchonae, tinctura. Figure 3-69. (8)

Cinchonae (detannata), tinctura: Tincture of Peruvian bark, of same with glycerin, alcohol and water. The detannated form is treated with iron tersulphate, ammonia, and ferric hydrate to remove (precipitate) tannins and clarify the material. (34)

Cinchonae (et ferri), elixir: Tonic elixir of cinchona with or without iron as a hematinic, NF. (42,45)

Cinchonae (ferratum), vinum: Cinchona wine, used as a bitter, optionally with iron and ammonium citrates to create a tonic bitter. (42)

Cinchonae (flavae)(rubrae), decoctum; Cinchona, infusum; —, extractum; —fluidum, extractum; —liquidum, extractum; —, tinctura: Infusion, fluid extract, and tincture of cinchona. Astringent, the decoction or infusion was used as a base for bitters. (8,42)

Cinchonae, ferri et [bismuthi] [bismuthi et strychninae] [calcii lactophosphis] [pepsini] [strychninae], elixir: Various tonic elixirs specified in the NF, with iron as hematinic as well as combinations of bismuth (stomachic), strychnine (stimulant), lactophosphite (nutritive), or pepsin (digestive). The first comma, following cinchonae, is in the original. (45)

Cinchonae, glycerinum: Preparation of the liquid extract of cinchona with water, glycerin, and gum tragacanth, equivalent in strength to the tincture of cinchona. (42)

Cinchonae, liquor: See cinchonae, extractum. (40)

Cinchonae, pepsini et strychninae, elixir: Tonic, digestive, and stimulant elixir of cinchona with pepsin to aid digestion and strychnine, NF. (45)

Fig. 3-68 Cinchona, source of quinine.

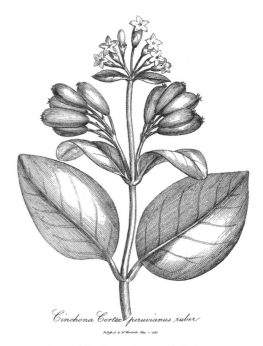

Fig. 3-69 Cinchona rubra or red cinchona.

Cinchona(e) acida, mistura: A mixture of liquid extract of cinchona with dilute nitric acid, aromatic syrup, and distilled water, as a simple bitter and tonic. (42)

Cinchonae acidum, infusum: An infusion (BPC) of cinchona with sulfuric acid, a bitter tonic. (42)

Cinchonae alkaloidorum (et ferri), elixir: Elixir of cinchona alkaloids; elixir calisaya, alkaloidal. An elixir made from the isolated alkaloids (instead of the bark) in aromatic elixir colored with cudbear (see persio). Used as a bitter. The ferrated form contains soluble ferric phosphate and was used as a tonic. (31)

Cinchonae alkaloidorum, ferri et bismuthi, elixir: Elixir of cinchona alkaloids, iron, and bismuth. Described as "polypharmaceutical," and probably no less "irrational" than the version containing strychnine, below. (31)

Cinchonae alkaloidorum, ferri et strychninae, elixir: Elixir of cinchona alkaloids, iron and strychnine, used as a bitter tonic. (31)

Cinchonae alkaloidorum, ferri, bismuthi et strychninae, elixir: Elixir of cinchona alkaloids, iron, bismuth and strychnine, described as an "irrational elixir." (31)

Cinchonae aromaticum, vinum: Peruvian bark, coriander, and cinnamon bark, macerated in alcohol and evaporated to resin, then suspended in Madeira wine, sugar, and tartaric acid. A general tonic. (34)

Cinchonae composita, tinctura; Cinch. Co., Tr.: A preparation of red cinchona, bitter orange peel, serpentinaria, glycerin, and water. (8,34)

Cinchonae detannata, tinctura: Tincture of cinchonae detannated by addition of the solution of tersulphate of iron, with alcohol, ammonia water, and water. (46)

Cinchonae detannatum, elixir: Elixir of detannated tincture of cinchona with syrup, glycerin, and aromatic elixir. (46)

Cinchonae et hypophosphitum, elixir: Tonic and reconstructive elixir, NF, of calcium and sodium hypophosphites, citric acid, water, and elixir of cinchona. (45)

Cinchonae ferrata, tinctura: Ferrated tincture of Peruvian bark, similar to the detannated form. The compound tincture is treated with hydroxide of iron and ammonio-citrate of iron to remove tannins. (34)

Cinchonae flavae, tinctura: Simple tincture of yellow cinchona bark. (42)

Cinchonae rubrae cortex: Red cinchona bark, said in the BPC to be from *Cinchona succiruba*, of India. Use as per cinchona. (42)

Cinchonine; Cinchonineae sulphas; Cinchonidine; Chinchonidinae sulphas: Cinchonine and cinchonidine are minor alkaloids derived from cinchona, and were isolated as their respective sulfate salts. (8,42)

Cinchophen; Chincophan: Phenylcinchoninic acid, anti-inflammatory introduced ca. 1910, used particularly in gout. Chincophen is correct, chincophan a variant. The latter undoubtedly arose due to several trade names (atophan, quinophan) suggesting the use of "phan." (40)

Cineol: Eucalyptol. (40)

Cineres clavellati: Crude potassium carbonate, lixivia. (3,39)

Cinn(amon)aldehyde: Aldehyde related to cinnamic acid, from oil of cinnamon or synthetic. (45)

Cinnabar; Cinnabaris (nativa): Vermillion, red mercuric sulphide, the ore of mercury. (1,3,39)

Cinnamic acid; Cinnamicum, acidum: Cinnamic acid is an organic acid obtained from storax, balsam of Peru, or tolu by oxidation of cinnamon oil, or made from benzaldehyde. Similar to benzoic acid, used for tuberculosis. (42)

Cinnamomi, aqua; —, spiritus; —, tinctura. —, syrupus: Cinnamon water is produced with cinnamon oil and water, used as a flavoring and carminative for children. Spirit, or essence, of cinnamon is approximately ten percent cinnamon oil in alcohol. The tincture is derived by percolation of cinnamon in a mixture of glycerin, water, and alcohol. The syrup (NF) consists of cinnamon, alcohol, sugar, and cinnamon water. (8,31,42)

Cinnamomi, essentia: Essence of cinnamon, i.e., the essential oil distilled from the bark, often diluted with some alcohol.

Cinnamomi, oleum: Cinnamon oil, a volatile oil distilled from cinnamon. Use is as per other volatile oils such as clove (see caryophyllus). (8)

Cinnamomi, pulvis; Cinnam. pv.: Powdered cinnamon bark.

Cinnamomi composita, pulvis: See pulvis aromaticus. (40)

Cinnamomi composita, tinctura: Compound tincture of cinnamon, with cardamom, prickly ash berry, and ginger. In the BPC, of cinnamon bark, cardamom seed, piper longam, and ginger, all bruised and extracted with alcohol. For flatulence or gastric disturbances. (34)

Cinnamomi, syrupus: Syrup of cinnamon water, sugar, alcohol, and coarse cinnamon powder, filtered to remove residual solids during preparation. (46)

Cinnamomum oliveri: Oliver's bark, of the Australian tree, *Cinnamomum oliveri*, a substitute for cinnamon. (40)

Cinnamon; Cinnamomum; Cinnimomum cassia; —saigonicum; —ze(y)lanicum: Cinnamon is the bark of the cinnamon tree. Celon (Zelanicum or Zeylanicum) cinnamon is derived from *Cinnamomum ze(y)lanicum*. The specific source of Saigon (Saigonicum) and Chinese (Cassia) cinnamon is unclear and perhaps is the same species. It consists of a rolled inner bark, commonly available in grocery stores as "cinnamon sticks." It is used to prepare an oil as well as numerous other preparations. Figure 3-70. (1,8)

Cinnamon, Chinese: Cassia, see cinnamon. (40)

Cinnamon bark, wild: Canella bark, see canella. (40)

Cinnamylic acid: Cinnamic acid, from cinnamon. (40)

Cinoglossa {*Italian*}**:** See cynoglossum. (1)

Cinorrhodon, cinosbatos: See cynorrhodon, cinosbatos. (1)

Cinque radici, sciroppo di {*Italian*}**:** See quinque radicibus, syrupus de. (1)

Cinquefoil; Cinquefoglio {*Italian*}**:** See pentaphyllum. (1,39)

Cinse semen: Santonica seed. (40)

Cipero {*Italian*}**:** See cyperus. (1)

Fig. 3-70 Cinnamon.

Cipheos, trochisci: See cyphi, trochisci. (1)

Cirsium (arvense): Root of the Canada, or cursed thistle, *Cirsium arvense*. A tonic and astringent, usually boiled with milk. (33)

Cissampeli, decoctum: Decoction of cissampelos, official in India as a substitute for pareira. (42)

Cissampeli liquidum, extractum: Liquid extract of cissampelos in water and alcohol. (42)

Cissampelos: Dried root of *Cissampelos pareira*, of West Indies, India, and Ceylon, a source of berberine. BPC notes it was used locally in place of pariera. Figure 3-71. (42)

Citarin: Sodium anhydro-methylene-citrate, supposedly liberated formaldehyde in the blood to help solubilize uric acid, i.e., for gout. (40)

Citonium: See cydonium. (1)

Citrago; Citrace {*Italian*}**; Citraggine** {*Italian*}**:** Balm, lemon-balm, see melissa. (1)

Citral: See geranaldehyde. (42)

Citramin; Citraminoxyphen: See formamol. (40)

Citreum, unguentum: Ointment of lemons, white coral, frankincense, etc. Used for removal of skin blemishes. (1)

Citri aurantii, syrupus: See aurantii, syrupus. (40)

Citri, oleum: Citrus, i.e., lemon oil.

Citric acid; Citricum, acidum: Citric acid, obtained from citrus fruit, usually lime. (8)

Citrici, acidi syrupi: A dilute solution of citric acid in simple syrup, with a small amount of spirit of lemon. (8) This is an easily reconstituted sweet lemon juice not dependent on fresh fruit, essentially lemonade. It was used alone or with carbonated water to produce a cooling beverage for febrile illness and for rehydration. (34)

Citrici, syrupi cortici; Citri., s. cort.: Syrup of citrus (i.e., lemon or lime) peel. See limonis, syrupus. (40)

Citricum saccharatum, acidum: Saccharated citric acid, of same with finely powdered sugar. (46)

Citrin {*French*}**:** Lemon-colored, yellow. (1)

Citrine ointment (, yellow): See hydrargyri nitratis, unguentum. (31)

Citrini, ceratum: Resin cerate, see ceratum resinae. (3)

Citrinum, unguentum: Ointment of mercuric nitrate. Used as an escharotic. (1)

Citrinus, myrobalanus: See myroblanus citrinus. (1)

Citron {*French*}**:** Citron, lemon. (1)

Citron ointment: See citrine ointment. (40)

Citronellae, oleum: Oil of citronella, obtained from citronella grass, *Cymbopogon nardus*. Used mainly in perfumes and, in higher concentrations, as an insect repellent, particularly in the form of citronella candles.

Citronum, syrupus e corticum; Citr., s. e. cort.: Syrup of citrus peel, i.e., lemon peel. (35)

Citrophen: Phenacetin citrate, analgesic. (40)

Citrosalic acid; Citrosalicum, acidum: Novaspirin, a condensate of citric acid and aspirin, analgesic. Reported in New and Non Official Drugs (AMA) in 1921. (40)

Citrullus: Watermelon, *Citrullus vulgaris*. Seeds used, see pepo, semen. (1,39)

Citrum; citrus (medica): Lemon or citron (*Citrus medica*). (1)

Citrus aurantium: Orange (i.e., the fruit), see aurantium. (39) Citrus, not otherwise specified, is invariably lemon or lime (not differentiated historically); while preparations of various orange species are generally entitled aurantium or the genitive, aurantii.

Civet; Civit: Excretions of anal glands of certain cat species, antispasmodic, related to castor, and used mainly in perfumery. (44)

Clark's liver pills (, Sir Andrew): See aloini compositae, pilulae. (40)

Clary: See horminium sativum. (39)

Clavos pedum, emplastrum: A plaster for nails (clavos, Latin) or corns, of pitch, galbanum, diachylon, verdigris, and sal ammoniac. (39)

Clematis: Fresh stems, leaves, and blossoms of virgin's bower, ladies' bower, love vine, or traveler's ivy, *Clematis virginiana*. Corrosive and irritant, used for a variety of skin (topically) and systemic conditions. See flamula. Figure 3-72. (33)

Clemens' solution: See potassii arsenatis et bromidi, liquor. (40)

Clove: See caryophyllus. (8)

Cnicus benedictus: Leaves and flowers of *Cnicus benedictus*, the blessed or holy thistle. Primarily a tonic, diaphoretic, and emmenagogue. (33)

Fig. 3-71 Cissampelos.

Virgin's Bower. / Purple Virgin's Bower.
Clematis Virginiana. / Clematis verticillaris.

Fig. 3-72 Clematis.

Co. (*lat.*): Compositum, i.e., composite, not a simple remedy.

Coal tar: See pix liquida. Although pine tar was the official USP form, coal tar was used similarly. (8)

Coal-tar naphtha: Benzol. (3)

Cobalt(um); Cobaltum nitricum; —chloridum: Metallic cobalt or the nitrate salt. This was used homeopathically in the form of soluble salts, most commonly the nitrate, but also possibly the chloride. Cobaltum is indeclinable, i.e., the genitive form is not used.

Cobweb: Spider web, a styptic, but various webs were accorded an assortment of medicinal properties, all unlikely. Unofficial. (44)

Coca; Cocae folia; Cocaina; Cocaine: Leaves from the coca plant, *Erythroxylon coca*, source of the alkaloid cocaine (not the cocoa tree, source of cocoa powder, *theobroma cocoa*). The leaf was chewed by indigenous peoples of middle Americas with little evidence of significant abuse. The alkaloid was isolated in 1855, and the purified form rapidly saw both medicinal use and abuse. Soluble cocaine salts are highly effective topical anesthetics (and the first injectable local anesthetics), powerful vasoconstrictors used in surgical procedures and dilate the pupil. Systemically, cocaine is a powerful stimulant, which is highly addictive and widely abused. (8)

Cocae, elixir: Elixir of cocaine, from the liquid extract of coca and simple elixir, a "cerebral stimulant and gastric sedative." (42)

Cocae, tinctura: Simple tincture of extracted coca leaves, a cerebral stimulant and gastric sedative. (42)

Cocae, vinum: Cocaine wine, elixir of coca (cocaine) in wine with sugar. This became a popular agent of abuse in the form of Vin Mariani before the active substance was controlled in the early 1900s. (42)

Cocae et guaranae, elixir: Stimulant elixir of cocaine and guarana (caffeine), NF. (45)

Cocae fluidum, extractum; —liquidum (miscible), extractum: Liquid extract of coca leaf in alcohol. The miscible form was further purified to remove waxes and improve water solubility, but with resulting lower potency. (42)

Cocainae, guttae: Eyedrops (BPC) consisting of cocaine sulphate and hydrochloride, mydriatic and anesthetic. (42)

Cocainae, ole(in)atum: Cocaine in oleic acid with alcohol and olive oil, as a topical for pain, neuralgia, or pruritis. (42)

Cocainae, oleum: Two percent cocaine in almond oil. Topical anesthetic. (40)

Cocainae, unguentum: Cocaine in oleic acid and lard, topical anesthetic for piles, shingles, urticaria, and pruritis. (42)

Cocainae hydrochloras; —hydrochloridum: Cocaine hydrochloride was produced by extraction with acidified alcohol and water, followed by alkalinization, extraction from the aqueous phase with ether, and evaporation to dryness. Being water soluble, salts—mainly the hydrochloride—were generally used in formulation. (8,42)

Cocainae nitras: Cocaine nitrate, used as per other cocaine salts such as hydrochloride. (42)

Cocainae salicylas: Cocaine salicylate, recommended as injectable treatment for spasmodic asthma, although said to be no better than the hydrochloride. (42)

Cocci, glycerinum: Glycerin of cochineal in water and glycerin with potassium carbonate and citrate, a useful non-alcoholic red colorant. (42)

Cocci, liquor; Coccineus, liquor; Cocci (cacti), tinctura: Cochineal color, made from cochineal bug. The liquor with potassium carbonate, alum, potassium bitartrate, alcohol, glycerin, and water; the tincture with alcohol. Like the solution of carmine, a coloring agent. (31)

Cocciae (major(es)), pilulae: Purgative pills of aloes, scammony, colocynth, etc. In USP usage, colocynthidis compositae, pilulae. (1,34,39)

Cocciae minor(es), pilulae: Same as cocciae, pilulae, above, but with rhamnus catharticus as additional ingredient. A strong purgative. (39)

Coccinilla: See cochinilla. (1)

Cocculi, unguentum: Ointment of cocculus indicus, kernels beaten into lard. Used for skin conditions and as a pediculocide. (34)

Cocculin: See picrotoxin. (40)

Cocculus; Cocculi fructus: Fish berry, Indian berry, *Cocculus indicus* or *Anamirta cocculus*. Berry used primarily for destruction of pediculi (lice, etc.). (7)

Coccus: See cochineal. May also refer to lacca. (8)

Cochia pills; Cochiae (majores)(minores), pillulae: See cocciae, pillulae. This is the strong (majores) and weak (minores) purgative formulation. (1,34,35)

Cochia pilula(e); Cocci, —: Approximately same as colocynthidis compositae, pilulae. (40)

Cochineal; Cochinilla: Cochineal is the red coloring material derived from the cochineal bug, *Coccus cacti*, of Central America and Mexico. It was valuable as a red dye generally, but was used, and remains in use, as a colorant for medications and foods. The Latin form is coccus, or coccus cacti, the latter in reference the cactus plant inhabited by the beatle. (8,34)

Cochlearea: See cochlearia, spelling appears to have been preferred in some early sources.

Cochlearia (officinalis): Scurvy grass, *Cholearia officinali*s. Herb used. An effective anti-scorbutic (i.e., source of vitamin C). Used orally and in mouthwashes for scorbutic gum degeneration. Figure 3-73. (1,39) Note that cochleare (cochl.) is a teaspoon. See measures. Also note that horseradish is *Cochlearia armoracia*, and some terms (see below: chochleariae, spiritus) refer back to horseradish instead of *C. officinalis*.

Cochlearia compositus, succus: Compound juice of cochlearia, of same with nasturtium, Spanish orange, and nutmeg. For scurvy. (39)

Cochleariae, spiritus: Spirits of cochlearia, obtained by distillation of the bruised herb in alcohol. Note that Hughes relates this instead to horseradish, *Cochlearia armoracia*. See armoraciae compositus, spiritus. (40)

Cochlearia officinalis.

Publifhed by D.ᵗ Woodville June. 1. 1790.

Fig. 3- 73 Cochlearia or scurvy grass.

C

Cochlearia marina: Sea Scurvygrass, *Cochleraria Anglica*, an antiscorbutic. (39)

Cochleariae compositus, syrupus: Compound syrup of horseradish, of same with boneset, snakeroot, acetic acid, water, and sugar. For chronic or persistent upper respiratory conditions. (34)

Cocillaña; Cocillana; Cocillanae, fluidextractum: 1. The bark of *Physocarpus rusbyi*, of Brazil, from which an unofficial fluid extract, syrup, and tincture could be made. A stimulant of mucus glands, it was used as an expectorant and as a mild laxative. (8) Possibly same as or similar to: 2. Grape bark, dried bark of *Guarea rusby*, or the fluid extract. Used as an expectorant, and described as similar to ipecachana. (3,31)

Cocoa: See cacao. (39)

Cocoa butter: Cocoa butter, oil of theobroma, or oleum theobromatus is the butter-like fat derived from the cocoa bean, *Theobroma cacao*. It is a solid at room temperature, but melts readily and is most commonly used to form suppositories. (8)

Cocois (nucitera), oleum; Cocos, oleum: Oil of coconut. (3,40)

Cocos butyracea: Cocoa butter, sometimes used interchangeably for palm oil. (39)

Coctum, oleum: Fixed oil (olive oil) infused with one or more herbs. (3)

Coctus, sal: Same as sal muriaticus, i.e., hydrochloric acid. (39)

Cod liver oil: Cod liver oil, or oleum morrhuae, see morrhuae, oleum for related entries. The expressed oil from the liver of the codfish, *Gadis morrhua*. The liver was placed in boiling water, and the fat skimmed from the surface, sometimes deprived of hard fats by partial freezing. The oil is well absorbed across skin and following ingestion, and will lead to nausea, indigestion, and diarrhea. External application was used rarely, due to the odor. Internally it was said to be of great value for tuberculosis, rickets, and a variety of wasting diseases, rheumatism, and many other maladies such as "general feebleness." Due to the unpleasant nature, a variety of deodorized (with ether) oils, flavored oils (generally with peppermint oil), jellies, and other non-official preparations were created. (8)

Cod liver oil, pancreatized cream: See morrhuae pancreaticus, cremor. (42)

Codeina: Codeine, derived from opium following removal of morphine by precipitation with caustic soda and extraction and recrystallization from ether. (8)

Codeinae, gelatinum: Codeine jelly (BPC). Codeine with citric acid, gelatin, glycerin, terpeneless oil of lemon, balsam of tolu, and water. For chronic cough and laryngitis. (42)

Codeinae, linctus: Syrup of codeine with citric acid, emulsion of chloroform, glycerin, and mucilage of tragacanth, a lozenge for cough. (42)

Codeinae, syrupus: Simple syrup with one percent codeine sulfate. (46)

Codeinae (phosphas), syrupus: Syrup of codeine phosphate, cough suppressant and general narcotic. (40,42)

Codeinae hydrochloras: Codeine hydrochloride, a soluble salt of codeine, for formulation purposes. (42)

Codeinae phosphas: Codeine phosphate is readily water soluble and a useful form of codeine for formulations. (42)

Codeinae sulphas: A soluble codeine sulfate salt, used as per the phosphate or hydrochloride. (42)

Codium: Poppy head, i.e., source of codeine, derived from opium poppy. (1)

Codoil: Rosin oil. (3)

Coelocline polycarpa: A yellow dye-tree of Africa, topical as a powder or decoction for ulcers. Unofficial. (44)

Coeruleum, acidum: Blue acid, hydrocyanic acid. (3)

Coeruleum, unguentum: See caerulium, unguentum. (1)

Coeruleus, lapis: Copper sulfate (see cupri sulphas). (3)

Coffea; Coffeae [viridis][tostae] fluidum, extractum: Alternate for caffea. The NF specified a fluidextract of green (viridis) or toasted (tosteae) coffee. (46)

Coffeae (tostae), fluidextractum; —, syrupus: Fluidextractum of (toasted) coffee, prepared using glycerin, alcohol, and water as menstruum. The syrup could be used (per King's) to "make a good cup of coffee." (31,34)

Coffee, soudan: See kola. (3)

Coffein; Coffeinum: Orthographic variant of caffeine.

Cohosh, black; Cohosh, blue: For black cohosh, see cimicifuga; for blue cohosh, see caulophyllum. (8)

Cohosh, white: See actaea alba. (33)

Coing {*French*}: See cydonium. (1)

Cola: See kola. (1)

Colagogum, electuarium: See cholegogum, electuarium. (1)

Colchici, acetum; —aceticum, extractum: Vinegar of colchicum, of dried colchicum bulb (corm) in distilled vinegar. For gout.

Colchici, extractum: Simple extract of colchicum corm in water. (44)

Colchici [radicis][cormae][semen], extractum; —fluidum, extractum; —, vinum: The dry extract, fluid extract, or wine of colchicum root (radix or cormus) or seed (semen), respectively. The wine was particularly popular for gout. (8)

Colchici, mistura: A mixture of wine of colchicum with magnesium carbonate and sulphate in peppermint water, a saline purgative used in "gouty conditions." (42)

Colchici, semen; Colchic. sem.: Seed of colchicum. Use is same as the root, above. (8)

Colchici ammoniatus, spiritus: See colchicum composita, tinctura. (40)

Colchici composita, tinctura: Tincture consisting of colchicum seed in aromatic spirits of ammonia, for gout. (42)

Colchici cormi fortior, tinctura: Stronger tincture of colchicum, an alcoholic tincture of colchicine, for gout. (31)

Colchici et aloes, pilulae: Extracts of colchicum and aloes, and green extract of hyoscyamus with powder of acacia to bind. Cathartic and for gout. (42)

Colchici et hydrargyri (compositae), pilulae: Extract of colchicum with mercury pill mass (hydrargyri, massa) and compound extract of colocynth, purgative. The compound pill also had extract of rhubarb. (42)

Colchici flores: Flowers of colchicum, containing small amounts of colchicine. A non-official tincture can be prepared for gout but is low potency and would seem to be unpredictable. (42)

Colchici florum, tinctura: Alcoholic tincture of fresh colchicum flowers, for gout. (42)

Colchici semini(s), extractum; —fluidum, extractum; —, tinctura; —, vinum: The dry extract, fluid extract, tincture, or wine of colchicum seed, respectively. (8,34,42)

Colchicina: Colchicine is the active alkaloid of colchicum, useful for gout but is highly toxic in larger doses. (42)

Colchicinae salicylas: Colchicine salicylate, for gout. (42)

Colchicum composita, tinctura: Compound tincture of colchicum seed, black cohosh, and alcohol. (34)

Colchicum; Colchici cormus; Colchicum cormus; Colchici radix: Colchicum root, the corm (bulb-like structure) of the autumn crocus, *Colchicum autumnale*, originally of southern and central Europe. Colchicine, the active principal, is a potent anti-inflammatory still in use as a specific remedy for gout, and was used for virtually nothing else. It is a powerful emetic and purgative in larger doses, but is now recognized to impede cell division and is a potent toxin in overdose. Figure 3-74. (8)

Colcothar of vitriol: Same as ferrum vitrolatum exsiccatum, a crude dry iron sulfate. (39)

Colcothar: Colcothar, ferric(iron) oxide. (1,3)

Cold cream: See rosae aquae, unguentum. (8)

Cole's dinner pills: See aloes et mastiches, pilulae. (34) This variant contained aloes, mercury mass (hydrgyri, massa), jalap, and antimony and potassium tartrate. (46)

Colic root: See aletris. (40)

Coliniensis, aqua; Colin. aq.: A variant of Cologniensis, Cologne water.

Colla piscium: Isinglass. (3)

Collargol: Colloidal silver, see argentum créde. (24)

Collaurin: Colloidal gold, see aurum. (3)

Collinsonia; Collinsoniae, tinctura: Stone root, *Collinsonia canadensis*, a stomachic, or the tincture therefrom. Figure 3-75. (32)

Collip's extract: Parathyroid extract, source of parathormone, which reduces calcium levels. Judging by reports of hypocalcemia, this particular endocrine extract was clearly active. (40)

Collodii compositum, liquor: See salicylicum compositum, collodium. (40)

Collodion; Collodium: Pyroxylin, 30 parts, dissolved in 750 parts ether and 250 alcohol. Used as a vehicle for other topical materials and to seal wounds, although it tends to crack, so flexible collodion (below) is preferred. (8)

Collodion, blistering: See cantharidatum, colodium. (42)

Collodion, cantharidal; Collodium cantharidatum: Cantharides is percolated in chloroform, which is filtered and evaporated to dryness. The dry extract thus obtained is dissolved in flexible collodion. Topical cantharides are used to treat proliferative skin lesions such as warts, granulomas, or skin cancers. They remain in use today, especially for venereal warts. (8)

Collodion, flexible; —, elastic; Collodium, elasticum: A mixture of 920 parts collodion with 50 of Canada turpentine (terebinthina) and 30 of castor oil. This dries to a transparent, flexible material and was used as a self-adhesive liquid bandage to seal wounds. (8,40)

Collodium anodynum: Collodion with aconitine and veratrine, applied to intact skin for neuralgia, sciatica, muscular rheumatism, etc. (42)

Collodium callosum: Collodian for calluses. See salicylicum compositum, collodium. (40)

Collodium elasticum; —flexile: See collodion, flexible. (40,42)

Collodium salicylicum; Collod. Salicyl. Co.: See salicylicum compositum, collodium. (40)

Collodium stypticum: Styptic collodion, a self-adhesive mixture of collodium, ether, alcohol, and tannic acid (see tannicum, acidum). (8)

Collodium vesicans: See cantharidatum, colodium. (42)

Collunarium acidi carbolici compositum: See boracis compositus, liquor. (40)

Collunarium alkalinum: See liquor alkalinus. (40)

Collunarium: Nasal wash.

Collyrium: Eye wash, eye salve. (1)

Colocynth; Colocynthis; Colocynthedis, pulpa: The bitter apple, squirting cucumber, watermelon-like fruit of *Citrullis (*or *Cucumis) colocynthis*, a bitter and a powerful purgative. It causes severe gripping and was not generally used alone. Figure 3-76. (8)

Colocynthidis, extractum: Dry extract of colocynth. (8)

Colocynthidis, tinctura: Alcoholic tincture of colocynth pulp, a drastic purgative. (42)

Colocynth and henbane pill: See colocynthidis et hyoscyami, pilulae. (40)

Colocynthidis alcoholicum, extractum: Dry alcoholic extract of colocynth, USP. (44)

Colocynthidis compositae, pilulae: Compound pills of colocynth, with aloes, scammony resin, and oil of cloves. Referred to also as pilulae cocciae or cochia pills. Purgative. (34,42)

Colocynthidis compositum, extractum; Colocynth Co., Ext.: Compound extract of colocynth, of extract of colocynth with aloes, cardamom, resin of scammony, soap, and alcohol; melted, strained, and reduced to powder when cool. Purgative. (8)

Colocynthidis et hydrargyri (compositae), pilulae: Colocynth and mercuric chloride tablets, purgative. (40) The BPC compound pill (compositae) adds green extract of hyoscyamus to reduce cramping. (42)

Colocynthidis et hyoscyami, pilulae: Pills of colocynth, aloes, resin of scammony, oil of clove, and extract of hyoscyamus to prevent cramping. Purgative. (34)

Colocynthidis et podophylli, pilulae: Pills of colocynth, aloes and resin of podophyllum. Purgative. (34)

Cologne spirit; —, eau de: See colonensis, spiritus. (42)

Fig. 3-74 Colchicum, source of colchicine.

Note the long lower lip of the corolla and its slightly fringed edge.

Rich Weed. Collinsonia Canadensis.

Fig. 3-75 Collinsonia.

Cucumis Colocynthis

Fig. 3-76 Colocynth.

Cologne water; Cologniensis, aqua: See odoratus, spiritus. (31)

Colonensis, oleum aqua pro; Colon., aqua pro, ol.: Oil for Cologne water, i.e., a mixture of oils used to prepare cologne or used to create scented goods.

Coloniensis, aqua; Colon. aq.: Cologne water. See odoratus, spiritus. (3)

Coloniensis, spiritus: Cologne (spirits), of oils of bergamot, lemon, orange-flower, rosemary, and thyme as well as undiluted orange water in alcohol. (42)

Colophonia; Colophony: Colophony, rosin, i.e., residue from distillation of turpentine. (1)

Coloquint(id)a {*Italian*}**:** See colocynthis. (1)

Columbo: See calumba. (8)

Columbo, American: See frasera. (32)

Colutea arborescens: Bladder senna, a weak substitute for senna as a decoction or infusion. Unofficial. (44)

Colza oil: Oil of rapeseed. (3) The plant currently known as "canola" is a variety of oilseed rape.

Com. (*lat.*)**:** Compositum, i.e., composite.

Comino {*Italian*}**:** Cumin or caraway, see cyminum or carvum. (1)

Commander's balsam; Commandeur, baume de: Commander's balm, a liniment panacea containing iron, originated about 1680 by Gaspart, Lord of Pernes, who was commander of the Knights of Malta. According to Ellis, by the 1800, this was a simple liniment, much like tincture of benzoin. (39) See benzoini composita, tinctura. (40)

Com(m)itissae: Commitissa is the Latin for countess, commitisae the possessive. Not a botanical. (39)

Com(m)itissae palmae pulvis: Powder of the countess of Palma, magnesium carbonate. (3)

Com(m)itissae, pulvis: Powder of the countess (of Cinchona), i.e., cinchona. (39)

Com(m)itissae, unguentum: Ointment of medlars, bilberries, etc. after Contessa di Vadra, fifteenth century, to whom it was prescribed. (1)

Communis, aqua: Common water, not distilled, etc. (3)

Communis, emulsio: Common emulsion, see amygdalae, lac. (39)

Communis, pilula: Common pill, see aloes et myrrhae, pilulae. (40)

Communis, sal: Common or table salt, sodium chloride. (3)

Communis, syrupus: Common syrup, i.e., molasses. (3)

Composite; Compositum; Composto {*Italian*}**:** A compound remedy, i.e., having more than one ingredient (as opposed to *simplex*, i.e., simple). (1)

Composition powder: See myricae compositus, pulvis. (34)

Compound 606: See arsenobenzol. (40)

Compound [spirit][tincture] of lavender: See lavandulae composita, tinctura. (8)

Compound cathartic pills: See catharticae compositae, pilulae. (8)

Compound dental liniment (of aconite and iodine): See dentilinimentum aconiti compositum or dentilinimentum aconiti et iodi compositum. (31)

Compound digestive elixir: See pepsini compositum, elixir. (31)

Compound elixir of orange: See aurantii compositum, vinum. (34)

Compound pills of antimony: See antimonii compositi, pilulae. (8)

Compound spirit of aether: See (a)etheris compositus, spiritus.

Compound syrup of squill: See scillae compositus, syrupus. (8)

Comptonia; Comptonia asplenifolia; Comptoniae asp.; Comptae asp.: Sweet fern, meadow fern, or ferngale, *Comptonia asplenifolia*, a tonic, astringent, and alterative. Unofficial. A pillow of the leaves from this plant is said to be beneficial for rickets—a doubtful proposition. Tonic and astringent used for diarrhea. (33,44)

Comtissae, unguentum: See comitissae, unguentum. (1)

Con.; Conc.: Concentrated. (29)

Con^ d'enul^ campa^: Observed, most likely confectio of elecampane, i.e., (see) enula.

Conchinine: Quinidine, in German chemical usage. (3)

Conditum; Condito {*Italian*}**:** Sweetmeat, made by boiling sliced fruit and rinds with sugar and water, followed by evaporation, i.e., candied fruit. (1)

Condurango; —, cortex; —, fluidextractum; —liquidum, extractum: Condurango, *Marsdenia condurango*, native to Ecuador, bark used, or the fluid extract, an alterative and stomachic. (7, 31,42)

Condy's red (solution): A concentrated solution of potassium permanganate used to sanitize and deodorize bedpans and other items. See potassii permanganas. (8)

Confectio; Confezione {*Italian*}**:** Confection, syrupy preparation of drugs, usually with honey. Often, but by no means always, a solid. (1)

Confectio amygdalae: See amygdalae compositum, pulvis. (40)

Confectio aromatic(a)(um): See cretae aromaticus, pulvis. (34)

Confectio aromatica: Aromatic confection, see electuarium aromaticum. (39)

Confectio cardiaca: 1. Aromatic chalk powder. (3) 2. Composite preparation of rosemary, juniper berries, saffron, etc., used as a cordial. (1) 3. Similar to aromatic electuary. (39)

Confectio damocratis: Damocrates' confection, a complex aromatic and astringent confection of some sixty-four ingredients, including opium. (3)

Confectio thebaica: Confection of opium; see electuarium opiatum (40)

Confectio universalis: Universal confection, a panacea. Composition unknown. (39)

Confection, aromatic: Aromatic confection, see electuarium aromaticum. (40)

Conicine; Conine; Coniina; Coniine: Coniine, the active principal of *Conium maculatum*. (40,42)

Conii, cataplasma: Poultice of juice of conium with crushed linseed. Used topically to control pain from ulcerated or cancerous lesions, which would be effective as conium interferes with nerve conduction. (42)

Conii, extractum; —, fluidum extractum; —liquidum, extractum; —, tinctura; —, unguentum: Dried extract, fluid extract, tincture or unguent of conium, respectively. (8,34)

Conii, oleum: Oil of poison hemlock (*Conium*).

Fig. 3-77 Conium or poison hemlock.

Conii, succus: Fresh juice of conium leaves (three parts), to which is added alcohol (one part) as a preservative. It is used internally for sedative and anti-spasmodic actions but is quite toxic. Use of the leaves, as opposed to the fruit, seemingly assures somewhat lower dosage of the active principal. (34,42)

Conii alcoholicum, extractum: Dry alcoholic extract of dried poison hemlock, USP. (44)

Conii compositae, pilulae: Compound hemlock pills, of extract of conium, powdered ipecac root, and treacle to bind. (42)

Conii folia: Conium leaves, used in the preparation of conii, succus. (42)

Coniinae hydrobromidum; —hydrochloridum: Bromide and chloride salts of coniine, which are soluble and thus used in systemic (non-topical) formulations. (42)

Conium; Conii fructus: The fruit of *Conium maculatum*, the poison hemlock, classical poison of Socrates. The nicotine-like poison, conine, causes muscular paralysis. While used at one time for tetanus and other spasmodic conditions such as whooping cough and chorea, it was highly unpredictable due to variable concentrations of the active ingredient, and was little used as a therapeutic. Topically, the ointment was effective as an anesthetic for piles or other painful conditions, like shingles. Figure 3-77. (8)

Coniura: See cicuta and also conium. Coniura comes from the Latin to conjure or plot, and this is an alternative (and more ominous) name for poison hemlock. (40)

Connecticut lead: Barytes, the ore of barium. (3)

Conserve of ____; Conserva ____: See ____, conserva.

Conserve; Conserva: Conserve, a preparation made with finely cut herbs or flowers and sugar. (1)

Consolida; Consoude {*French*}**:** Comfrey, see symphytum; or same as solida. (1,39)

Constant white: Barium sulfate. (3)

Contessa, unguentum: See comittissae, unguentum. (1)

Contra, semen: Seeds of santonica. (40)

Contra diarrhoem, mistura: See diarrhea mixtures. (34)

Contra pestem, pilulae: Anti-pestilential pills, i.e., to prevent plague. Composition variable. (1)

Contrayerva: In Spanish a contraction of "against-herb," the Contrayerva plant, *Dorstenia contryerva*. Root used as a general alexipharmic, diaphoretic and astringent tonic. Figure 3-78. (1,39)

Contrayerva Germanorum: German contrayerva, see vincetoxicum. (39)

Contrayervae compositus, pulvis: Compound powder of contrayerva, of powdered contrayerva and compound powder of crab's claws (chelarum cancri compositus, pulvis). Alexipharmic and diaphoretic. (39)

Convallamarin: Active glucoside obtained from convallaria, with digitalis-like action on the heart. (42)

Convallaria polygonatum: European plant, Solomon's seal, decoction used for piles and skin rash due to certain plants. Unofficial. (44) See sigillum salomonis.

Convallaria; Convallariae radicis, fluidextractum; —liquidum, extractum: 1. Rhizome and root of *Convallaria majalis*, the lily of the valley, or the fluidextract therefrom. Acts upon the heart in a manner similar to digitalis. Figure 3-79. (8,42) 2. According to Estes, this is properly Solomon's seal (*Convallaria polygonatum*, above), and lily of the valley is properly Convallium. Authoratative sources appear to disagree on this point.

Convallariae flores; —flores fluidum, extractum: Flowers of Lily-of-the-Valley, or fluid extract thereof. Not usually used, but convallamarin and convallarin can be obtained from the flowers. (42,46)

Convallariae, tinctura: Convallaria flower tincture of same in alcohol, used for action on heart similar to digitalis. (42)

Convallarin: Active glucoside obtained from convallaria, with digitalis-like action on the heart. (42)

Convallium (lilliorum): Lily of the valley, see convallaria, above. (39)

Convolulus jalapa: See jalap. (39)

Convolvulin: See jalapin. (42)

Convolvulus (scammonia): When not otherwise specified, convolvulus is probably scammony. (32)

Convolvulus panduratus: See mechoacanna. (39)

Convolvulus soldanella: See brassica marina. (39)

Copahu(e), balsamum; Copaivae, balamum: Copaiba, oleoresin from bark of certain trees of genus *Copaifera*. (1)

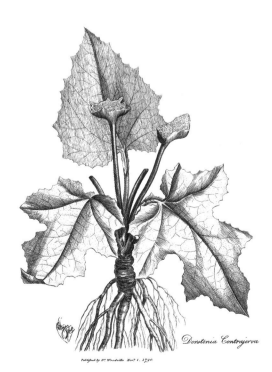

Fig. 3-78 Contayerva.

Lily of the Valley.
Convallaria majalis.

Fig. 3-79 Convallaria or lily of the valley.

Copaiba; Copaibae, oleum; —, resina: An oleoresin obtained from *Copaiba langsdorffii* (or *Copaifera officinalis*) of Latin America. From this a volatile oil can be distilled (oleum), leaving a resinous residue (resina). Copaiba shared all of the actions of other major volatile oils, of which clove oil is an example (see caryophyllus). It was particularly used for urinary disorders in a manner similar to buchu. Figure 3-80. (8)

Copaibae, liquor: A solution of copaiba extracted into alcohol, water, and solution of potash. Diuretic and urinary antiseptic. (42)

Copaibae, mistura: A mixture of copaiba and gum acacia in water, a diuretic and antiseptic for cystitis and gonorrhea. (42)

Copaibae, pilulae: Pills of copaiba in white wax, for gonorrhea. (34)

Copaibae, resina; Copaibicum, acidum; Copaivic acid: Dried resin from an alcoholic tincture of copaiba, copaivic acid, acidum copaibicum. Use as per the herb. (34)

Copaibae composita, mistura: Compound mixture of copaiba with nitrous ether, camphor, oil of almonds, copaiba, and oil of turpentine. A diuretic, for gonorrhea and for various urinary conditions. Other variants include Lafayette's and Chapman's mixtures (see accordingly). (34) In the NF, of copaiba, spirit of nitrous ether, compound tincture of lavender, solution of potassa, syrup, and mucilage of dextrin. (46)

Copaibae compositae, pilulae: Compound pills of copaiba, with solidified copaiba oil (adsorbed to magnesia), etherial extract of cubeb, resin of podophyllum, gum myrrh, and alcoholic extract of nux vomica. For gonorrhea, prostate inflammation, and other male urological conditions. (34)

Copaibae et buchu et cubebae (cum santalo), liquor; Copaibae et santali, liquor: The former was a solution of copaiba with extracts of buchu and cubebs, to which could be added oil of sandalwood and cassia (cum santalo); the later was simply of copaiba and the added oils. For urinary disorders and gonorrhea. (42)

Copaiva; Copaya; Copayba: Presumably variants of copaiba or the genitive copaibae as these are listed as variants of the botanical name and no other likely candidate is evident. (39)

Copal: Hard resin from certain tropical trees or, per Estes, from the shrub (see) *Rhus copallina*. (1)

Copal, West African: Copal (resin) derived from *Copaifera guibourtiana*. (40)

Copal, Zanzibar: Copal (resin) from Copal tree, *Trachylobium hornemannianum*. (40)

Copper: See cuprum (metallic), cupri (compounds). (8)

Copper, persulphate of: Copper sulfate, see cupri sulphas. (40)

Copper acetate: Usually cupric (sub)acetate, $Cu(CH_3\text{-}COO^-)_2$, if unspecified, but could be cuprous acetate, $Cu(CH_3\text{-}COO^-)$. Verdigris. (39)

Copper oxyacetate: See cupri subacetas. (40)

Copper pill: See ammoniareti cupri, pilule. (39)

Copperas, blue: Blue vitriol, or crude copper sulfate. (39)

Copperas (unspecified); Copperas, green: Similar to ferrum vitriolatum, iron sulfate. (39)

Copperas (white): Zinc sulfate. (3)

Copra oil; Coprah oil: Coconut oil. (3,40)

Copra: The dried meat of the coconut. (3)

Coptis (trifolia); —, fluidextractum; —fluidum, extractum: Coptis, goldenthread, dried plant of *Coptis trifolia*, or the fluid extract. Used primarily as an astringent mouthwash or gargle for cancerous sores or sore throat. Figure 3-81. (3,31,46) Estes states that coptis is equivalent to nigella. (39)

Copya; Copyba; Copyus: Probable variants of copaiba or the genitive copaibae, as these are listed as variants of the botanical name and no other likely candidate is evident.

Coral; Corallium (album; rubrum): Coral, white or red respectively. Corallium rubrum can also be red nitrate of mercury (hydrargyri nitratis ruber), see arcanum corallinum. (1,39)

Corallina: Corallina, sea moss, *Corallina officinalis*. (1)

Corallorhiza: Crawley, coral root, *Corallorhiza odontorhiza*, a diuretic. (32)

Cordia myxa: See sebestena. (39)

Cordial julep: Refers to any non-oily, sweet, clear liquid, often containing camphor. (39)

Cordiale aromaticum: Aromatic cordial (syrup), often used as a vehicle. If unspecified, usually blackberry or raspberry.

Cordialis, syrupus: Syrup with tonic properties, of saffron, cloves, ambergris, etc. (1)

Fig. 3-80 Copaiba.

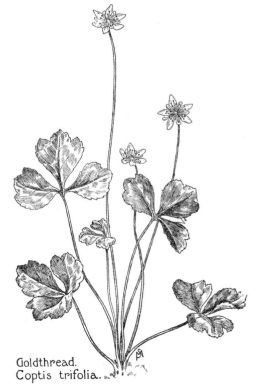

Fig. 3-81 Coptis.

Coriandrum; Coriander; Coriandri fructus; Coriandri, oleum: Coriander, fruit of *Coriandrum sativum*, from which a volatile oil is distilled. Usage was as per other volatile oils such as clove (see caryophyllus). Used extensively as a flavoring, especially to mask rhubarb or senna. Figure 3-82. (8)

Coriaria: Currier's sumach, leaves of *Coriaria myrtifolia*, also referred to as *Rhus Coriaria*, of the Mediterranean. Said to be extremely toxic, medicinal uses are unspecified. Figure 3-83. (33)

Corn collodion: See salicylicum compositum, collodium. (31)

Corn ergot: See ustilago. (32)

Corn paint: See salicylicum compositum, collodium. (40)

Corn plaster: See salicylicum compositum, emplastrum. (40)

Corn rose: Red poppy. See papaver rhoeas. (1,40)

Corn silk: See zea. (8)

Corn sugar: Dextrose. (3)

Cornachinus, pulvis: Purgative of scammony, cream of tartar, and antimonium diaphoreticum, after Marco Cornacchini, Prof. of Medicine, Pisa. (1)

Corne de cerf {*French*}**:** Stag's horn, hartshorn. (1)

Cornu cervi: Hartshorn, ammonium carbonate. (3)

Cornu cervi, liquor: Solution of ammonium carbonate, with empyreumatic oil. (3)

Cornu cervi, sal: Ammonium subcarbonate. (3)

Cornu cervi (foetidum), oleum: Crude animal oil. (3)

Cornu cervi succinatus, liquor: Solution of ammonium succinate. (3)

Cornu cervi ustum (nigrum): Bone-black, i.e., burnt antler. (3,33)

Cornu cervi volitilis, liquor; Cornu cervi liq. volat.: A solution of ammonia. (40)

Cornus (florida); Corni, fluidextractum; —fluidum, extractum; —, decoctum: Dogwood bark, of *Cornus florida*, or the fluid extract or simple decoction, believed to be a mild astringent and stomachic, and possibly antiperiodic. (31,44,46)

Cornus circinatae fluidum, extractum: Extract of *Cornus circinata*, Round-leaved dogwood or green osier. While the British term osier is usually taken as willow, the botanical name is assigned now to a variety of dogwood and is specified as such in the USP. (44, 46)

Cornus sericea: Fruit and bark of swamp dogwood, *Cornus sericea*; similar in all respects to cornus florida, above. (39)

Cornutine: Impure ergotoxine, active component of (see) ergot. (40)

Corpus luteum: Desiccated corpus luteum from the ovaries of cow, pig, or sheep, source of progesterone and various estrogens. (7)

Corrigens, elixir: Aromatic elixir of yerba santa (see eriodictyi aromaticum, elixir). (3)

Corrosive chloride of mercury; Corrosive mercuric chloride; Corrosive sublimate: See hydrargyri chloridum corrosivum.

Cortex; Corteccia {*Italian*}**:** Bark or peel. (1)

Cortex, Carthagina; —Pitaya; —Bogata; —Maracaybo; —Santa Martha: See bark.... (44)

Cortex aurantiorum: Orange peel. (1)

Cortex A~G, H~M, etc.: Drawer or cabinet pull for alphabetical filing of various barks.

Cortex citri: Lemon peel. (1)

Cortex magellanicus: See wintera. (33)

Cortex miscel.: Miscellaneous barks (drawer or cabinet pull).

Cortex peruviana; —peruvianus: See Peruvianus, cortex. (1)

Cortex querus: Oak bark. (1)

Cortex winteranus; —winteri: See wintera. (33)

Corticus peruvian(a) composita, tinctura: See cinchonae composita, tinctura. (40)

Cortin: Adrenal gland extract. (40)

Corydalis: Corydalis, turkey corn, squirrel corn, *Dicentra cucullaria* or *D. canadensis*, bulbs used. Source of various alkaloids (corydaline, bulbocapnine, etc.). A diuretic and alterative used in kidney disorders and cutaneous diseases. Figure 3-84. (7)

Corydalis, compositum, elixir: Compound elixir of corydalis. The compound elixir contained about three grains of potassium iodide in one fluidrachm and small quantities of the fluid extracts of corydalis, stillingia xanthoxylum, and blue flag (iris). (31)

Corydalis, fluidextractum; —fluidum, extractum; —, tinctura: Fluid extract or alcoholic tincture of corydalis. (31,46)

Corydalis composita, tinctura: Compound tincture of corydalis, with yellow-dock, bark of tag alder, and leaf and root of figwort, added to syrup of mandrake root. An alterative for multiple chronic conditions. Scudder's alterative. (34)

Corydalis compositus, syrupus: Syrup of turkey-corn, of corydalis, twin-leaf, blue-flag root, and sheep-laurel leaves, in sugar and water. An alterative for many chronic diseases. (34)

Fig. 3-82 Coriandrum or coriander.

Fig. 3-83 Coriaria.

Fig. 3-84 Corydalis.

Coryl: Proprietary mixture of methyl and ethyl chlorides, used as a topical refrigerant anesthetic. (40)

Corylus: Hazelnut. (1)

Corynanthe (yohimbe); Corymbenine; Corymbine; Corynanthine; Corynine: Corynanthine; Corymbenine; Corynine; Corymbine: The yohimbe plant and various active principals. See yohimbine. (32,40)

Coscinium; Coscinii concentratus, liquor; Coscinii, infusum; —, tinctura: Dried stem of *Coscinium fenestratum*, of India and Ceylon, or the liquor or tincture prepared therefrom. A bitter, much like (see) columba, used in India and British colonies. (42)

Cosimo, powder of father: Corrosive topical escharotic based on red mercuric oxide (cinnabar). (39)

Cosmetic mercury: Ammoniated mercury, see hydrargyri ammonii chloridum. (40)

Cosmoline: Soft paraffin. (40)

Coster's paste: A paste of iodine in light oil of wood tar, for skin disorders. See pigmentum picis cum iodo. (8,40)

Costinum, oleum; Costino, olio {*Italian*}**:** Liniment of *costus* root, sweet marjoram, cassia bark, white wine, and olive oil. (1)

Costumary: See balsamita. (39)

Costus; Costus arabicus; Costo {*Italian*}**:** Plant native to Asia, believed to be *Saussurea lappa* (*Compositae*), formerly called *Auklandia costus*. Root used. Expectorant. (1,39)

Cotarnine; Cotarnina; Cotarninae hydrochloridum; —, phthalas: An oxidation product obtained from opium alkaloids, usually used as a soluble hydrochloride or phthalate salt. This has no narcotic activity, but is considered a styptic and is used for uterine hemorrhage as well as topically as a wool or gauze preparation to control bleeding. (42)

Coto (bark); Coto, tinctura; —fluidum, extractum: Bark of *Drimys winteri*, of Venezuela or a tincture or fluid extract therefrom. Promotes intestinal absorption of fluid and used to treat diarrhea of various causes. Source of cotoin and paracotoin. (8,46)

Cotoin: A bitter alkaloid derived from bark of coto, and used for same purposes. (8,42)

Cotonea; Cotogno {*Italian*}**:** See cydonia. (1)

Cotton; Cotton root: See gossypium. (8)

Cotton; Cottonseed oil: See gossypium or for the oil, gossypii seminis, oleum. For gun cotton, see pyroxylin. (8)

Cotula (foetida): May-weed, wild chamomile, dog fennel, dog chamomile, *Maruta cotula*, a tonic, emetic, antispasmodic, emmenagogue, and epispastic. (33,39)

Cotyledon major: See umbilicus veneris. (1)

Cotyledon umbilicus: Navel or penny wort, tonic. Unofficial. (44)

Couch grass: See triticum. (8)

Couch syrup: See scillae compositus, syrupus. (34)

Cough drops: See sanguinariae composita, mistura. These are liquid drops, i.e., guttae, not solid candies as are modern "cough drops." (34)

Cough moss: See marrubii, syrupus or scillae, oxymel. (40)

Cough pill: See ipecacuana cum scillae, pillule. (40)

Coumarin(um): An alkaloid obtained from various plants, particularly tonka bean, used for treatment of lymphedema. It is a structural relative, and chemical precursor, of coumadin, the anticoagulant. Primarily a flavoring and odorant in older uses, but could be employed for anticoagulant properties.

Count(ess) Palma's powder: Magnesium carbonate. (40) Usually attributed to the countess as this was a fine powder for cosmetic purposes.

Countess(') powder: Cinchona bark powder, see cinchona. (40) Note the specific powder of the Countess of Palma, above.

Cow parsnip: See heracleum. (39)

Cowhage; Cowitch: See dolichos. (39)

Cowrie gum: See dammar gum. (40)

Coylus rostrata: Beaked hazel, nut of which is covered in tiny hairs, used as anthelmintic as per cowhage. Unofficial. (44)

Crab eye (seeds): If a seed, the rosary pea or jequerity bean, see abrus. See also crab's eyes, below.

Crab ointment: Blue ointment, i.e., mercurial ointment, see hydrargyri, unguentum. (40)

Crab orchard salts; Craborchard salts; C.o. salts: Properly Crab Orchard Salts, although in labels with all capitals it is often run together. A salt obtained from formations in Crab Orchard, Kentucky, and said to be particularly of use for diarrhea.

Crab's eyes: Prepared chalk, see creta praeparata. (40)

Cramp bark: See viburnum opulus. (8)

Cranberry: Equivalent uva ursi. (39)

Cranesbill: See geranium. (8)

Crataegus: See oxycantha. (32)

Cream of tartar, soluble: Potassium boro-tartrate. (40)

Cream of tartar: See potassii bitartras. (8)

Creasote; Creasotum, etc.: Variant of creosote. (44)

Credé's antiseptic: Silver citrate. (24)

Credé's ointment: Ointment of collargol (colloidal silver), water, white wax, and benzoinated lard, for septicemia and local skin infections, carbuncles, boils, etc. (24)

Creme imperatrice: See bismuthi et zinci, pasta. (40)

Cremor tartari: Cream of tartar, potassium hydrogen tartrate. (1,3)

Creolin; Creolinum: Creolin is a cheap but effective antiseptic used as per carbolic acid. It is a crude distillate of coal tar, containing various phenols, cresols, etc, somewhat like creosote. Used pure or in solution, in soaps, or occasionally internally to treat dysentery or typhoid fever. (8)

Creosotal; Creosote carbonate; Creosoti carbonas: Carbonate salts of creosote, by extraction of creosote with sodium carbonate. Use as per creosote, especially for pulmonary disorders. (40)

Creosote [Beechwood]; Creosotum; Creosoti, aqua; Creosoti, liquor: Creosote is a complex mixture of phenols, cresols, and other aromatic organic alcohols derived by distillation of wood tar, especially that of the beech tree. It is an effective disinfectant and topical anesthetic. Creosote water or liquor consists of one percent creosote in water. Before the use of carbolic acid (purified phenol), creosote was used for toothache and as an oral or inhaled (for treatment of tuberculosis) antiseptic. Oral administration was in the form of various non-standardized emulsions or tablets. (8,42)

Creosoti vaporis, balneum: A "bath" of creosote vapor in the BPC, actually not a bath at all, but a vapor treatment consisting of heated creosote in a porcelain or metal dish, much like modern vaporizer preparations for the sick room. Considered disinfectant and thus used to treat whooping cough and other chest infections, now used for symptomatic relief of congestion. (42)

Creosoti, mistura: 1. Glacial acetic acid and creosote dissolved in water, with syrup and spirit of juniper, an antiemetic. (34) 2. A BPC mixture of creosote, spirit of juniper, syrup, and distilled water, for flatulence or dyspepsia, and as a respiratory disinfectant for phthisis. (42)

Creosoti, pilulae: Pills of creosote and powdered licorice root in powdered curd soap. (42)

Creosoti, spiritus: Creosote in alcohol, for chronic bronchitis and phthisis, expectorant. (42)

Creosoti, unguentum: Ointment of creosote in simple ointment base. For skin infections, ulcers, and burns. (34)

Creosoti, vapor: Creosote in boiling water, inhaled for phthisis and bronchitis. (42)

Cresol; Cresolum crudum: A component of creosote, dihydroxytoluene, also refered to as orcin, orcine, or orcenol in various sources. (42)

Cresol saponatus, liquor: A mixture of cresol in soft soap, disinfectant. (40)

Cresolis compositus, liquor: A solution of cresol, linseed oil, potassium hydroxide, alcohol, and water, an external antiseptic. (42)

Cresolis glycerinatus, solutio; Cresolis saponatus, solutio: Cresol soap solution, a powerful disinfectant of cresylic acid (cresol), linseed oil, potassium hydroxide, alcohol, glycerin, and water. (42)

Crespigny's pills, Lady: See aloes et mastiche, pilule. (40)

Crespino {*Italian*}**:** See berberis. (1)

Cresyl hydrate: See cresol. (40)

Creta: Chalk, i.e., calcium carbonate. (1)

Creta fullonica: Purified fuller's earth, see terra fullonica. (40)

Creta gallae, pulvis; Cret: gall:, pulv; Creta gallica: French chalk, powdered. French chalk is actually fine talcum, a magnesium silicate hydroxide, not true chalk, which is calcium carbonate. This was used to mark cloth, for cosmetic purposes, and to coat pills following application of syrup or other material to promote adhesion. See talcum. (42)

Creta praecipitata; Creta praecip.: Precipitated chalk, i.e., calcium carbonate. Chalk is naturally occurring, but this form is made by precipitation from calcium chloride solution with sodium carbonate. See calcii carbonas praecipitatus. (8)

Creta praeparata; —preparata; —praep.: Prepared chalk, i.e., calcium carbonate, $CaCO_3$. An effective antacid, mild astringent, mild abrasive (i.e., for use as a dentifrice), and used topically to dry wet skin eruptions. (8)

Creta(s) composita mistura: See cretae compositus, pulvis. In the BPC, this was specified as aromatic powder, aromatic spirits of ammonia, tincture of catechu, compound tincture of cardamom, and tincture of opium in chalk mixture, and was known as Board of Health Cholera Mixture.

Cretacea: Orthographic variant of cretae. (40)

Cretaceus, pulvis; Cretae aromaticus (cum opio), pulvis: Aromatic powder of chalk, confectio aromatica, of chalk, cinnamon, saffron, nutmeg, cloves, and cardamom, or a variant with opium. For diarrheal illness. (40,34) BPC equivalent of (see) cretae compositus cum opio. (42)

Cretae (pulv[is][.].), mistura: Chalk mixture, compound chalk water (see cretae compositus, pulvis) in cinnamon water, and in the BPC also sugar and gum tragacanth. (8,29,42)

Cretae, troschisci: Troches of chalk, acacia, spirit of nutmeg, sugar, and water. For mild diarrhea or gastric acidity. (8,34)

Cretae, unguentum: Ointment of chalk in spermaceti, mild astringent for acne and burns. (42)

Cretae compositus (cum opio), pulvis; Cretaceus compositus, pulvis; Creta co., pv.: Compound chalk powder, of chalk, acacia, and sugar, often with other ingredients (cinnamon, gum arabic, nutmeg, tormentilla, and piper longam per Estes). Used for diarrhea, especially in children, and for acid gastric upset. With (cum) or without opium. (8,34,39)

Cretae compositus, pulvis (BPC): In the BPC, the USP formulation called cretae compositus was referred to as cretae aromaticus. Cretae compositus (BPC) consisted of chalk, gum acacia, and refined sugar. (42)

Cretae cum camphor, pulv.: Pulverized chalk with camphor, one of a number of aromatic chalks.

Creyat: See andrographis. (40)

Crinalis, lotio: A hair lotion of almond oil, strong solution of ammonia, oil of rosemary, alcohol, and honey water. (42)

Crisalbine: Gold and sodium thiosulfate, a proprietary gold preparation used as an antirheumatic. (40)

NOTE—Botanical uses of crocus appear first below, followed by the archaic metalurgical uses of the term.

Croci, glycerinum: Glycerin of saffron, with fifty percent alcohol, a flavoring and golden colorant. (42)

Croci (, p. or pulv.): Powdered crocus, saffron.

Croci, syrupus; —, tinctura: Syrup of saffron, of glycerin of saffron and syrup; or the simple tincture in alcohol. Coloring agents. (42)

Crocomagma: Saffron ointment, same as confectio democratis. (39)

Crocus (sativum)(sat); Croci, tinctura: The crocus, *Crocus sativum (or sativis)*, is the source of saffron, which are the stigmata (pollen bearing organs) of the crocus flower. (For autumn crocus, source of colchicine for the treatment of gout, see colchicum autumnalis.) The tincture is made by maceration of saffron in alcohol, followed by filtration. Used as a coloring agent only, the color being so intense that one or a few thread-like stigmata can color a large volume of material. It has no therapeutic value. Figure 3-85. (8) See also, crocus (non-plant) definition, below.

Crocus in Fasno: Saffron, in reference to a specific location in Italy. (40)

Crocus in placenta: Cake saffron (placenta being Latin for pancake), noted to be frequently adulterated (saffron being very costly). (40)

NOTE—Botanical uses of crocus appear above, archaic metalurgical uses below.

Crocus: In archaic chemical use, any yellow to red oxide of a metal. (39) See also botanical definition, above.

Crocus antimonii: See crocus metallorum. (39)

Crocus martis: Ferric oxide. (3)

Crocus martis astringens: Iron rust, see ferro rubigo. (40)

Crocus martis; Crocus martis aperiens; Crocus martis apertivus: Red oxide of iron, ferric oxide. Used as a deobstruant and emmenagogue. (1)

Crocus metalorum (antimonii): Brown antimony oxide. The original (seventeenth century) formula apparently also contained sal niter and wine. (3,39)

Crocus saturni: Red lead oxide. (1,3)

Crocus veneris: Copper oxide. (1)

Croll's styptic (plaster): After Oswald Croll, 1608, a complex styptic mixture of thirty-one ingredients including various lead oxides, calamine, hematite, mother of pearl, etc. (39)

Crosswort: American usage, see eupatorium; British usage, *Galium cruciata*. The latter being an herbal (non-official) remedy in Europe. Deobstruant. (40)

Crosta di pane, emplastro di {*Italian*}: See crusta panis, emplastrum de. (1)

Croton chloral hydrate: See butyl chloral hydrate. (This is a chemical misnomer). (8)

Croton eleutheria: See cascarilla. (39)

Crocus sativus

Fig. 3-85 Crocus or Saffron.

Croton oil: Oil expressed from the seeds of *Croton tiglium*. The oil was administered on a lump of sugar or in castor oil or vaseline, with only a few drops producing catharsis. Croton oil is severely irritant to the skin and rapidly causes pustules. It was used as a counterirritant and rubifacient, but may cause severe injury with scarring and was not widely used. It can be an irritant to the stomach and produce a severe enteritis (inflammation of the intestines) if used in excess. Skin application also causes catharsis, leading to the presumption that the oil contains some agent which directly causes increased motility. This was recommended in very limited doses, only for stubborn constipation. A dilute liniment of fifteen percent in oil of cajuput and alcohol was recommended in the BP for stimulation of the scalp in the event of hair loss. (8)

Crotonis eleuthereae, tinctura: See cascarillae, tinctura. (40)

Crotonis, aqua: Water from Croton Lake, New York. (3)

Crotonis, linimentum: Liniment of croton oil with oil of cajuput and alcohol. General use counterirritant for chest and musculoskeletal afflictions. (34,42)

Crow fig: Nux vomica. (3)

Crude oil: Petroleum. (3)

Crudum; Crudus: Crude, unrefined (adj., Latin). (1)

Crurin: See quinoline bismuth salicylate, probably an antidiarrheal. (40)

Crusta panis, emplastrum de: Poultice of bread crusts, red coral, mastic, oil of quinces, etc. (1)

Cryst alba: "White crystals," refined naphthalene, disinfectant (mothballs). (3)

Crystalli tartari: Cream of tartar (see potassii bitartras). (3)

Crystalli: Literally, "crystals," but unspecified this is said to be tartaric acid crystals. (40)

Crystallose: Soluble saccharin. (3)

Crystallus mineralis: See sal prunellae. (39)

Crystals of venus: Cupric acetate. (3)

Cubeb; Cubeba; Cubebae fructus; Cubebae, oleum; Cubebae, oleoresin: Unripe fruit of *Piper cubeba*, of Java, from which an oil was distilled or from which an oleoresin could be extracted with ether. While this shared all of the actions of other major volatile oils, of which clove oil is an example (see caryophyllus), it was particularly used for urinary disorders and as a diuretic. (1,8)

Cubeb paste: Powdered cubebs mixed with copaiba. While a specific use was not identified, both of these ingredients were diuretic and used for urinary disorders, so one would presume the same for the combination. (40)

Cubeba, extractum: This irregular use actually refers to the oleoresin of cubebs, as opposed to the official fluid extract. (40)

Cubebae, vapor: Oil of cubeb and magnesium carbonate in water, inhaled vapor for chronic bronchitis. (42)

Cubebae fluidum, extractum; —liquidum, extractum; —, tinctura; —, trochisci; —, oleoresina: Fluid extract and tincture of cubeb. The oleoresin was equivalent to the fluid extract. The troches were made of cubeb oleoresin, sassafras oil, licorice extract, acacia, and syrup of tolu. (8,40,42)

Cubebar: Variant of cubebae, above.

Cubic nitre: Sodium nitrate, see sodii nitras. (40)

Cuca: Cocaine, see coca. (3,8)

Cucumis: Cucumber (*Cucumus sativis*). Seeds used. (1)

Cucumis, unguentum: Ointment of cucumber, of pulped cucumber juice in lard and veal suet. These are heated together and cooled, the ointment coagulating above the liquid. An emollient for chapping, etc. Prone to spoilage, it was suggested that it be kept in a glass jar covered with rose-water. (34)

Cucumus agrestis: Juice from the fruit of the wild, or squirting, cucumber, *Ecballium elaterium* or *Mormordica elateria*. An irritant cathartic. Figure 3-86. (39)

Cucumus colocynthis: See colocynthis. (39)

Cucurbita; Cucurb. (pepo) (semen or S.): Gourd, especially pumpkin, *Cucurbita pepo*. Seeds (semen) used. See also next entry. (1)

Cucurbita (citrullis): Watermelon, *Cucurbita citrullus*, a diuretic. The family *cucurbitaceae* contains all of the squashes and melons as well as cucumbers, resulting in some inconsistencies of botanical use. (32)

Cucurbitae semina praeparata: Melon or pumpkin seed, outer husk removed, and used fresh, not roasted, as a taenicide (i.e., for flatworms). (42)

Cudbear: See persio. (31)

Culilawan (, cortex): Bark of *Cinnamomum culilawan*, closely related to cinnamon. Unofficial. (44)

Culinaris, sal: Cooking salt, common or table salt, sodium chloride. (3,40)

Culver's root: See leptandra. (8)

Cum: With (i.e., the preposition, Latin). (1)

Cumaric anhydride: See coumarin. (40)

Cumene; Cumenum: Isopropyl benzene, an aromatic solvent. (42)

Cuminum; Cumini fructus; Cumini, oleum: Cumin or cumin oil, from *Cuminum cyminum*. Figure 3-87. (1)

Cuniculus: Rabbit. (1)

Fig. 3-86 Cucumus agrestis.

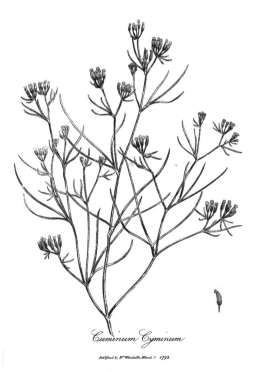

Fig. 3-87 Cuminum or cumin.

Cunila: Whole herb of American or mountain dittany, stonemint, *Cunila mariani*, a stimulant, carminative, antispasmodic, and diaphoretic. (33)

Cuppa emetica: Emetic cup, essentially vinum antimonium, of wine standing over (see) antimonium vitrificatum. (39)

Cuprea bark: Bark of *Remijia* species, a substutute for cinchona. (40)

Cupreinae sulphas: Cupreine sulfate is an alkaloid salt derived from cuprea bark, use similar to quinine. (42)

Cupressus: Cypress tree, *Cupressus sempervirens*. Wood and nuts used. (1)

Cupri, sulphatis composita, solutio: See cupri vitriolati compositum, aqua. (39)

Cupri acetas; Cupri acetum: Vinegar of copper, i.e—copper acetate.

Cupri alkalinus, liquor: See Fehling's solution.

Cupri nitras: Cupric nitrate, or copper nitrate, used as per copper sulfate as an astringent. (42)

Cupri oleas: Copper oleate, by dissolution of copper sulphate in hard soap, primarily used in unguentum cupri oleatus, as an astringent, antiseptic, and parasiticide, for ringworm, and topically for warts, corns, and bunions. (42)

Cupri oleatis, unguentum: Ointment of copper oleate in lard, for ringworm, corns and bunions. (42)

Cupri subacetas: Copper subacetate, i.e., copper acetate. (29)

Cupri sulphas (venalis): Copper sulfate, blue vitriol, bluestone, $CuSO_4$, from action of sulfuric acid on copper. The venalis (commercial) form is purified by recrystallization. A caustic, astringent, and emetic. Powder or concentrated solutions can be used to eliminate skin growths or granulomas, fungal infections, etc., including around the eye, as it is less irritating and corrosive than similar zinc salts. Small doses are said to be helpful for severe diarrhea via pill or enema. It is a rapid emetic, and hence suggested for poisonings. (8)

Cupri sulphatis, guttae: Eyedrops (BPC) consisting of 0.5% copper sulfate, astringent. (42)

Cupri sulphatis, plasma: Plasma, or thickened solution (not blood plasma) of copper sulfate with glycerin and starch. A topical used on the mucous membranes, especially the eyes. (34)

Cupri vitriolati composita, aqua: Compound water of copper vitriol, a solution of copper sulfate (vitriol) and alum used as a styptic. (39)

Cuprum: Copper. (1)

Cuprum aluminatum: See lapis divinus. (40)

Cuprum ammoniacum: Ammoniated copper, a pill formed of ammonia and blue vitriol (copper sulfate). A presumably ineffective remedy for epilepsy. (39)

Cuprum scoriatum: Crude copper acetate, verdigris. (3)

Curacao (oleum); Curaçao; Curassao, ol.: Oil of the Curaçao or Curasso orange tree, *Citrus aurantium currassuviensis*, of Latin America, derived from the peel of the fruit and possibly also from the leaves. The fruit is similar to bitter orange, and the oil is used as per the oil of bitter orange. See aurantia amara.

Curara; Curare; Curare hypodermica, injectio: Curare is derived from the poison-arrow frog and is used as a paralytic agent for surgery or as a treatment for tetanus to relieve muscle spasm. hypodermally or intravenously injected. (8)

Curassao, elixir: Flavoring specified in NF, of spirit of curassao, iris root, alcohol, citric acid, syrup, magnesium carbonate, and water. (45)

Curassao, spiritus: Oils of curassao, fennel, and bitter almond in deodorized alcohol. (46)

Curatio paraffini; Curat. paraf.: "Under this peculiar title is a paraffin softened by the addition of white petrolatum and olive oil, and containing one percent resorcinol and two percent eucalyptol." It was used to dress burns. (31)

Curcas purgans: Purging nut, physic nut, or barbadoes nut, seeds of *Curcas purgans*, whose pharmacological abilities are apparent from the name alone. (33)

Curcuma longa; Curcuma(e), tinctura: Tumeric, *Curcuma longa* or the alcoholic tincture thereof. Rhizome used. Tonic, aperient, emmenagogue, and anti-icteric. Figure 3-88. (1,39,42)

Curcuma zedoaria: See zedoaria. (39)

Curd soap: See sapo animalis. (8)

Curdling fluid: Rennet. (40)

Curshmann's solution: Camphor and anesthetic ether in olive oil, injected for the treatment of heart failure or "cardiac weakness." (40)

Cursuta: Said to likely be the same as gentian, root of plant formerly called *Gentiana purpurea*. (39)

Cuscuta; Cuscutha: Plant of genus *Cuscuta* (i.e., Dodder). Herb used. (1)

Cusparia bark; Cuspariae cortex; —concentratus, liquor; —, infusum (concentratum): Bark of *Galipea cusparia*, of tropical South America, or the aqueous concentrated liquor or infusion. Used as a bitter and stomachic. (8) The BPC also specified a concentrated infusion with alcohol and chloroform water for storage and reconstitution. (42)

Cusso; Cusso fluidum, extractum; —, infusum: Cusso, Brayera, Kooso, or Kousso, the female flower of *Hagenia abyssinia*, or the fluid extract or infusion. This or the active principal, koussin, was used for tapeworm. (8,34)

Cutch: Dark (black) gum catechu. A preparation from the heartwood of catechu, mainly a dye. (8,40)

Cutol: See aluminium naphthol-sulphonate. (40)

Cy: Irregular abbreviation for cyanide ion, i.e., the hexacyanoferrate ion may be designated by $FeCy_6$. (29)

Cyanegg; Cyanfran: Trade names, egg-shaped lumps or granules of sodium cyanide, respectively. (3)

Cyanide gauze: See hydrargyri et zinci cyanidi, carbasus. (42)

Cyanus: Cornflower, *Centaurea cyanus*. Flowers used. (1)

Cyclamen: Tuber of the cyclamen, sow bread, or hog's bread, *Cyclamen hederaefolium*, a "drastic cathartic." (33)

Cycloform: A local anesthetic. (40)

Fig. 3-88 Curcuma longa.

Cydonia; Cydonium: Quince tree, *Cydonium malum* or *Pyrus cydonia*. Fruit and seeds used. Figure 3-89. (1)

Cydonii, decoctum: Decoction of quince, used as a vehicle for eye lotions as it is mucilaginous and less readily removed by tears, also an adjunct in skin lotions and creams. (42)

Cydonii, mucilago: Mucilage of cydonia, mucilage of quince-seed. A soothing demulcent. (34)

Cyminum: See cuminum. (1)

Cynae, semen: See santonica. (1)

Cynanchum vincetoxicum: White swallow-wort, of Canada, *Cynanchum vincetoxicum*. Emetic and purported alexipharmic. Unofficial. (44)

Cynara: Juice of the artichoke, *Cinara (or Cynara) scolamus (or scolymus)*. Figure 3-90. (1)

Cynoglossum; Cygnoglossus: Hound's tongue, *Cynoglossum officinale*. Root used. Figure 3-91. (1,39)

Cynorrhodon; Cynosbatos: Dog-rose, *Rosa canina*, and other wild roses. Fruit (rose hip) used. (1)

Cynosbastae; Cynosbatae; Cynosbastus: Rose hips, primarily used as a binding agent in formulations, also cooling and astringent. (3,39) See rosae caninae.

Cynosbasti, conserva: Conserve of rose hips. Said to be "lithontriptic," i.e., capable of breaking up (kidney) stones. (35)

Cynosbati confectio: Confection of rose hips. See rosae caninae, confectio. (40)

Cyperus: Plant of genus *Cyperus*, e.g.—English galingale, *Cyperus longus*. Root used. Stomachic and carminative. (1,39)

Cyphi, trochisci: Aromatic lozenges from cinnamon, myrrh, bdellum resin, cassia bark, spikenard, galingale, etc. Used against rheumatism and pestilence. (1)

Cypress powder: See unguent, cosmetic. (39)

Cypressus: See cupressus. (1)

Cypripedii compositus, pulvis: Compound powder of yellow ladies' slipper, nerve powder, of same with pleurisy root, skunk cabbage, and scullcap, for excessive excitability. (34)

Cypripedium; Cypripedii fluidum, extractum; —, oleoresina: Lady's slipper, *Cypripedium parviflorum (or C. pubescens)*, containing a volatile oil prepared as a fluid extract by maceration and percolation in alcohol and water, which can be evaporated to obtain the oleoresin. Use, as per valerian, was variable, but especially for nervous disorders. Figure 3-92. (8,34)

Cys(s)ampelos: See cissampelos

CyS; Cy S: Irregular abbreviation for sulphocyanide, i.e., thiocyanate group (-S=C=N). (29)

Cystamin; Cystogen: Hexamine, see hexaminium. (40)

Cytisus: May refer to either genista or scoparius. (39) Unofficial in USP in reference to laburnum, *Cytisus laburnum*, with a variety of unrelated indications for use. (44)

Fig. 3-91 Cynoglossum or hound's tongue.

Fig. 3-89 Cydonium or quince tree.

Fig. 3-90 Cynara or artichoke.

Fig. 3-92 Cypripedium or lady's' slipper.

D

D.: At beginning or middle of inscription: de (of); decoctum (decoction); di {*Italian*} (of); sometimes dilutum (dilute). At the end of inscription: often dilutum (dilute); Damocratis (see Mithridatum D.); double (double); dulcis (sweet); duplicatum (double). (1)

D.T.O.: Deodorized tincture of opium, see opii deodorata, tinctura. (8)

Dactylus; Dactyli (plural): Date (i.e., the fruit). (1,3)

Daffy's elixir: Compound tincture of senna, after Rev. Thomas Daffy, ca: 1650. (3,39)

Dagget oil; —, oil of; Dagutt: Empyreumatic oil of birch (oil of Russia leather). (3)

Daisy: See leucanthemum. (33)

Dakin's antiseptic; —fluid; —solution (modified): A dilute solution of sodium hypochlorite (bleach), used as a disinfectant. (24)

Dalby's carminative; —mixture: See carminativa, mistura. After J. Dalby, apothecary, London, ca. 1780. (34)

Damiana: The leaves of several plants (*Bigelovia venata*; various species of *Turnera* including *T. aphrodisiaca* and *T. diffusa*), native to Mexico. It is poorly characterized and said to be a general tonic as well as possible specific for "sexual atony" (impotence). (8,32)

Damiana, phos. et. nuc. vom. (comma in original): Probably damiana with phosphorus (in the form of hypophosphites) and nux vomica, i.e., damiana, phosphorus et nucis vomicis. Various sources suggest that damiana was generally combined with phosphorus in some form and with strychnine (nux vomica). Damiana was also used as a proprietary trade name for this and similar preparations recommended as a general stimulant and to enhance sexual performance or desire. Probably same as, or very similar to damianae composita, mistura.

Damianae, elixir: Extract of damiana (turnera) in alcohol, glycerin, and aromatic elixir. (46)

Damianae, extractum; —, fluidextractum; —liquidum, extractum: Solid or fluid extract of damiana, or fluidextractum turnerae. "It is attributed, but probably erroneously so, with aphrodisiac powers." (31,42)

Damianae composita, mistura: A mixture of liquid extracts of damiana and nux vomica with calcium and sodium hypophosphites in chloroform water. (42)

Damianae compositae, pilulae: Extract of damiana and nux vomica with phosphorated suet, chloroform, compound powder of tragacanth, and mucilage of acacia. (42)

Dammar gum: Gum dammar is a resin obtained from various trees of the genus *Dipterocarpaceae*, native to India. Primarily in use as a varnish today. (40)

Damocrates: Servilius Damocrates, Roman physician, first century CE., purported originator of a variety of mithridatum and theriac preparations. (1)

Damocratis confectio; Damocratis, mithridatium: See mithridatum, see also Damocrates. (1)

Dandelion: See taraxacum. (8)

Danish ointment: A sulfur ointment for scabies. (40)

Daphne gnidium: Spurge flax, a laxative, mainly cited in the herbal literature. (40)

Daphne mezereum: See mezereum. (39)

Datura [folia][semina]: In the BPC, leaves and seeds of *Datura fastuosa*, of India, used as per the leaves of belladonna or stramonium, or the seeds of datura stramonium, respectively. (42)

Datura stramonium; Daturae, tinctura: Jimson or loco weed. See stramonium. A simple tincture was specified in the BPC for use in India and eastern colonies, a respiratory sedative and antispasmodic. (8)

Daturina; Daturine: Active alkaloid of datura, similar to hyoscyamine, used primarily in ophthalmology as a mydriatic ointment or as gelatin ophthalmic "disks." (42) Closely resembles atropine. (42)

Daturinae, guttae: Eyedrops (BPC) consisting of 0.5 percent daturine, a mydriatic. (42)

Daucus (carota): See carota. Carrot, *Daucus carota*, but may be referring as well to wild carrot, Queen Ann's lace, a closely related species (*Daucus sylvestris,* below). (1, 39)

Daucus creticus: The candy carrot, *Athamanta cretensis*, seeds used as a diuretic and carminative. (39)

Daucus sylvestris: "Forest carrot," Queen Ann's lace, or wild carrot, *Daucus sylvestris.* Used mainly in plasters but also as a carminative, diuretic, antiscorbutic, and anthelmintic. (39)

De citro, tabellae: Tablets of citrus rind. (39)

De duobus, sal: Potassium sulfate. (3)

De mel: "Of or from honey," see mel. (39)

De morbo: See Neapolitan unguent. (39)

Deba: Diethylbarbituric acid, or Veronal, i.e., barbital, a sedative barbiturate. (40)

Decoctum; Decoctio; Decoctum _____: Decoction. For preparations see _____, decoctum if not listed below. (1)

Decoctum ad icteros: Jaundice decoction, a cholegogic cathartic decoction consisting mainly of celandine, see chelidonium. (8)

Decoctum album: A kind of chalk mixture, see creta. (3)

Decoctum diaphoreticum: Compound decoction of guaiacum. (3)

Decoctum lignorum: Compound decoction of guaiacum wood. (3)

Defensivum, unguentum: Ointment of dragon's blood (i.e., the plant, *Sanguis draconis*), Armenian bole, rose oil, vinegar, and wax. Used to treat inflammation. (1)

Degras: Crude wool fat. (3)

Delphinii, tinctura: Tincture of larkspur, of the seed, by maceration and percolation. "This tincture is rarely used internally, but is commonly employed externally to destroy body vermin" (lice, etc.). (31)

Delphinium: Larkspur, *Delphinium ajacis*, dried ripe seed used, preparations primarily pediculocidal. (7)

Demo(s)cratis(,) confectio; Democratis, mithridatium: See Mithridatum, see also Damocrates. (1,40)

Dens: Tooth. (1)

Dens leonis: See taraxacum. (1)

Dental tablets, antiseptic: See solvellae antisepticae. (42)

Dentif.; Dentifricium: Dentifrice or tooth powder typically of soap, sugar, flavoring, prepared chalk, precipitated calcium carbonate and five percent sodium perborate. (31)

Dentifricus, pulvis: Tooth power made from, for example, powdered pumice, white coral, cuttle bone, iris rhizome, and mastic. (1)

Denver mud: Cataplasm of kaolin. (3)

Deodorized alcohol: See alcohol, deodoratum. (8)

Dermatol: See bismuthi subgallas. (8)

Derosne's salt: Narcotine, an alkaloid derived from opium or related species of *Papaverae*. (3)

Des(s)iccativum, unguentum: See rubrum des(s)icativum, unguentum. (1)

Deshler's salve: See ceratum resinae compositum (31)

Despumatum, mel: See mel despumatum. (1)

DeValangin's solution: An orally administered solution of arsenious acid in hydrochloric acid and distilled water, for systemic delivery of arsenic. (40)

Devie (, elizir): Orthographic variant of the French, elixir of life, elixir de vie.

Devil's dung: See asafetida. (40)

Dewee's carminative: See magnesiae et asafoetidae, mistura. (34)

Dewee's tincture (of guaiac): See guaiaci composita, tinctura. (31)

Dextrin: A partially hydrolyzed starch, or starch gum, dissolved in water to produce a mucilage. (29)

Dextrini, mucilago: Mucilage of dextrin in water. (34)

Dextrose: Glucose.

Di sodic hydric phosphate: Disodium hydrogen phosphate, see sodii phosphas. (29)

Di(-)acetyl-tannin: See acetannin. (40)

Di(-)acetylmorphine: Heroin, see same and also see opium.

Dia…: A prefix indicating "made from," ex: diacassia (made from cassia); diacodium (made from codium, i.e., poppy, head). Contracted in combination with substances beginning with the letter "a," i.e., "of anise" is dianisum, not diaanisum. If not listed below, refer to root term for additional information. (1) Note that some occurrences refer to di-substituted compounds, especially "diacetyl" or "diamino" or to diaphoresis (sweating, Greek, to carry from).

Diabetin: See levulose. (40)

Diabolus metallorum: Tin. (3)

Diaboracis: Antihysteric powder of borax. (39)

Diabotanum: "Of plants," generally referring to a plaster made from multiple plant species. (39)

Diabryonias, electuarium: Cephalic and mild cathartic preparation of bryony. (39)

Diabryonias, unguentum: Ointment of bryony with cucumber, scilla, arum maculatum, ebulus, and iris florentina as well as an unspecified type of fern. (39)

Diabuglossi: Cardiac powder made from bugloss (see buglossum). (39)

Diacalaminthes: A complex formulation based on calamine, used as a stomachic, carminative, and expectorant. (39)

Diacaron: "Of nuts," see dianucum. (39)

Diacarthami: Cathartic and expectorant electuary, made of carthamus. (39)

Diacassia; Diacasia cum manna: See cassia, electuarium e. (39,40)

Diacastoreum: Cephalic and antihysteric electuary based on castoreum. (39)

Diacatholicon, electuarium; Diacatholicum, electuarium: Purgative electuary "of everything" (catholicon) of senna leaf, tamarind pulp, cassia pulp, polypody rhizome, cucumber and fennel seed, rhubarb, licorice, etc. (1) Catholicon is not a religious reference, but a reference to wide inclusion of ingredients and universal applicability—i.e., an alexipharmic or panacea. Many variants, almost invariably cathartic.

Diachalciteos: See palma, emplastrum. (39)

Diachyli, unguentum; Diachylon, unguentum: Unguent of lead oxide containing lead plaster and oil of lavender. See plumbi, emplastrum. (8)

Diachylon, emplastrum; Diachylon, E.; Diacylon plaster: A plaster of lead and olive oil, also referred to as Theriac of Diachylon or by the variant Diatchylon (Diat.). See plumbi, emplastrum. (8,40)

Diacinnabaris: Antiepileptic powder made from the mercury ore, cinnabar. (39)

Diacinnamomi: Cordial and stomachic powder of cinnamon (see cinnamoma) or clove (see caryophyllus). (39)

Diacnicum, syrupus: Syrup of saffron thistle. (1)

Diacodii, syrupus: Syrup of poppy-heads. (3)

Diacodium: Poppy-heads, old name for syrup of poppies. May also be a weak solution of opium. (39)

Diacorum: A complex electuary made from calamus (acorus) aromaticus. (39)

Diacretae: An astringent powder made from chalk (creta). (39)

Diacridium; Diacrydium: See diagridium. (1,39)

Diacrocum: A powder made from crocus. Tonic, diaphoretic, and antihysteric. (39)

Diacrysalli: A lactogogue. The composition of this powder is unknown. (39)

Diacymini: A cephalic, antihysteric, and stomachic powder prepared from cumin. (39)

Diadamascenum cholegogum: Cholegogue of Damascus, see diaprunum solitivum. (39)

Diadictamnum ceratum: A vulnerary liniment of dictamnus. (39)

Diafarfarae: Pectoral pills of tussilago. (39)

Diafoenicum, electuarium: See diaphoenicum, electuarium. (1)

Diagalangae: A stomachic and antihysteric powder of galanga. (39)

Diagridium; Diagrydium: Scammony, or mucilage made by trituration of powdered scammony with fruit juice. (1,3)

Diahyssopi: Stomachic and antiasthmatic powder from hyssop. (39)

Diaireos: Pectoral and antiasthmatic powder of iris. (39)

Diajalapae: Powder of jalap, cathartic and hydrogogue. (39)

Dialaccae: Antihysteric tonic of lacca. (39)

Dialauri: Carminative and antihysteric powder of laurel. (39)

Dialthea, unguent: Ointment of marshmallow (althea). (39)

Dialthiae: See althiae a contraction of *Di* or *De althiae* (of marshmallow). (35)

Dialunae: "Of the moon," the moon being the symbol for silver, i.e., an antiepileptic powder made with silver. (39)

Dialyzed iron: See ferrum dialysatum. (8)

Diamanna(e): Mild cathartic electuary made of manna. (39)

Diamargaritum (simplex): Cordial tonic powder of margarita. The simplex form was a pill rolled in sugar. (39)

Diambrae, pillulae: Diambra pills, a variant of aromatic pills, made with a powder (species) or aromatic materials which seem to generally include cinnamon. (35)

Diamera: Powder made of spermaceti, a cordial, cephalic, and stomachic. (39)

Diamidophenol [hydrochloride]: Amidol, a photographic developer. (42)

Diamorium compositum: Juice (rob) of morus (mulberry) with honey, verdigris, myrrh, crocus, and sapa. (39)

Diamoron(is), syrupus: Syrup "of morus" (mulberry). See morus. (35)

Diamorphine: Heroin, see same and also see opium, contraction of diacetylmorphine.

Diamorum simplex: Simple syrup of mulberry. (39)

Diamorusia: Stomachic and antihysteric made with diamorum compositum and other ingredients. (39)

Diamoschi dulcis: Cordial and tonic powder made with moschus. (39)

Diampholyx, unguentum: An ointment of zinc oxide, white lead, juice of belladonna, and olibanum. (39)

Diamumiae: Tonic powder of powdered mummy. (39)

Diamurcurii: A mercurial powder, anthelmintic. (39)

Diana: Silver, i.e., Diana, goddess of the moon, associated with silver. (3)

Dianisi: Digestive, carminative, and anthihysteric powder made of anise. (39)

Dianitri: Powder made of nitre, a diuretic. (39)

Dianthos: Cephalic powder of rosemary. (39)

Dianthus: See caryophyllum rubrum. (39)

Dianucum: "Of nuts," a rob made of green walnuts (see juglans) and honey. (39)

Diaolibani: Antiepileptic powder of olibanum. (39)

Diapalma (, emplastrum): Plaster of palm and olive oil, water, and white lead. (39)

Diapenta; Diapente: Literally, "of five" (Latin), accoding to Beasley "[t]his should be made with equal parts of myrrh, gentian, ivory-dust, bay-berries, and birthwort." However, historical references vary widely as to exactly what five items might be used to prepare this formulation. (36,40) Any tonic powder or electuary of five ingredients. (3)

Diapeperios, ceratum: "Wax of peppers," a wound ointment containing piper nigrum. (39)

Diaphaenicum: Orthographic variant, see diaphoenicum. (39)

Diaphoenicum, electuarium: Purgative electuary dates, scammony, turpeth root, etc. Used to treat lethargy, dropsy, paralysis, and other conditions. (1)

Diaphoretic antimony: Equivalent to the antimony oxide, crocus antimonii. (39)

Diaphoretic mixture: See mistura diaphoretica. (39)

Diaphoretic powder: See ipecacuanae et opii compositus, pulvis. (34)

Diaphoretica, pilula(e): See antimonii composti, pillulae. (40)

Diaphoreticum, electuarium: Electuary with sudorific properties, of contrayerva root, nitre, and syrup of orange peel. (1)

Diaphoreticum Joviale: Diaphoretic of Jupiter, symbol of tin, although this is actually an antimonial diaphoretic, see antimonium calcinatum. (39)

Diaphoreticum minerale: See antimonium tartarisatum, i.e., antimony tartrate. See antimonium diaphoreticum. (1,39)

Diaphoreticum solare: Diaphoretic of the sun, symbol of gold, i.e., of gold salts combined with antimony, said to also be a stomachic. (39)

Diaplantaginis: Astringent powder of plantago. (39)

Diapompholigos, unguentum; Diapompholygos, unguentum: 1. Ointment of pompholyx with juice of belladonna berry and white and red lead. For treatment of ulcerous skin disorders. (39) 2. Ointment of impure zinc oxide. (3)

Diaprassi: A complex preparation based on marubium. (39)

Diaprunum simplex: Simple laxative based on prune. (39)

Diaprunum solitivum: Cathartic electuary of prune and scammony. (39)

Diapyrites: "Of pyrite," the iron sulfide ore known as fool's gold. A vulnerary liniment. (39)

Diarhodon: Medicinal tonic of red rose petals and other components. (1)

Diarhodon, pilule: Rose pills, cathartic and stomachic. (39)

Diarhodon abbatis: A cathartic and stomachic pill, based on rose, attributed to an unspecified abbot, medieval. (39)

Diarhodon trochisi: Rose troches, cordial, stomachic, and astringent. (39)

Diarrhea mixture; Diarrhoeae; mistura pro; Diarrhoeam, mistura contra: A group of related antidiarrheal mixtures based upon opium, including (34,46):
- **Diarrhea mixture; Cholera mixture; Sun mixture**—of tinctures of opium and rhubarb with spirits of camphor and peppermint.
- **Loomis'**—of tinctures of opium and rhubarb, compound tinctures of catechu and lavender, and oil of sassafras.
- **Squibb's**—of tinctures of opium and capsicum, spirit of camphor, chloroform, and alcohol.
- **Thielemann's**—of wine of opium, tincture of valerian, ether, oil of peppermint, and fluid extract of ipecac in alcohol.
- **Velpeau's**—of tincture of opium, compound tincture of catechu, and spirits of camphor.

Diasarum: Cathartic and emetic electuary preparation based on asarum. (39)

Diasaturni: "Of Saturn," symbol of lead. Antiasthmatic and antitubercular powder with salts of lead and antimony. (39)

Diasatyrion, electuarium: Electuary of satyrion, or orchid root. See satyrion and salep. (35)

Diascordium, electuarium: Electuary of scordium and other ingredients. Useful for the treatment of "fluxes" (diarrhea). Invented as a plague remedy in the early sixteenth century by Giralomo Fracastoro. (35,39)

Diasebesten: Cathartic electuary of sebesten. (39)

Diasenna; Diasennae: A catharic powder based on senna. Estes identifies the former as only cathartic, the latter as cathartic and a melanogogue. (39)

Diaspermatum: "Of seeds," an apparently variable mixture made of various seeds. (39)

Diastase: A digestive enzyme, see amylase. (42)

Diasuccini: Astringent and narcotic powder based on amber oil (succini, oleum). (39)

Diasulphuris: Antiasthmatic powder of sulfur. (39)

Diasulphuris, ceratum; —, emplastrum: "Wax of sulphur," a wound dressing with sulfur. (39)

Diasulphuris, tabella: Antiasthmatic tablets of sulfur. (39)

Diatameron: Stomachic powder, of dactylus. (39)

Diatartari (of Castelli): A cathartic and hydrogogue made of cream of tartar, senna, manna, ginger root, cinnamon, and red sugar, after Pietro Castelli, Messina, seventeenth century. (39)

Diatchelon; Diat.; Diatylon: Variant of diachylon.

Diatessaron, theriaca: A complex electuary made with gentian, laurel, juniper, and aristolochia. See theriaca diatessaron. (1,39)

Diatomaceous earth: See kieselguhr. (40)

Diatragacanthae, pulvis: An agglutinating and pectoral powder of starch, licorice root, gum arabic, and sugar. (3,39)

Diatragacanti (frigidi), species: Agglutinating and pectoral powder of gum tragacanth, gum arabic, marshmallow (althea), and licorice (glycerrhiza). (39)

Diatrium piperon, pulvis; Diatrionpipereon; Diatrium piperum: Powder of three kinds of pepper (dia + tri + piper), with ginger, thyme, and anise seed. Used as a digestive aid. (1,39)

Diatrium santalorum: Cordial powder of sandalwood (see santalum). (39)

Diaturbith: Cathartic, expectorant, and hydrogogue powder or electuary of turpethum. (39)

Diaturbith minerale: Emetic electuary of hydrargyrus vitriolicus, i.e., mercuric sulfate. (39)

Diazingiber: Stomachic, carminative, and digestive powder of ginger (zingiber). (39)

Diazingiber laxativum: Cathartic and expectorant laxative made with ginger (zingiber). (39)

Dictamnus albus: White dittany, *Dictamnus albus*. Root used. Figure 3-93. (1)

Dictamnus creticus: Dittany of Crete, dittany of candy, *Origanum dictamnus*. Leaves used. Many and variable uses, often for female disorders. Figure 3-94. (1)

Diervilla: Root, leaves, and twigs or the bush honeysuckle, or Gravelweed, *Diervilla trifida*, a diuretic, astringent, and alterative. (33)

Diet drink: See sarsaparilla, decoctum compositum. (39)

Diethyl-barbituric acid: Barbitone or barbital, a sedative barbiturate. (40)

Diethyl-malonyl-urea: Barbitone or barbital, a sedative barbiturate. (40)

Diethylenediamine: See piperazine. (32)

Diethylsulphone-diethylmethane: See ethylsulfonal. (42) Related to sulphonal. (40)

Difensivum, unguentum: See defensivum, unguentum. (1)

Digalen: Proprietary solution of digitoxin. (40)

Digallic acid: See tannicum, acidum. (8)

Digestivum sylvii, sal: Digestive salts of Sylvius, see caput mortuum. (39)

Digestivum, unguentum; Digestivo, unguento {*Italian*}**:** Ointment of white wax, turpentine, and rose or olive oil; used to treat suppurative inflammation. (1)

Digestivus, pulvis: Powdered pepsin, digestive enzyme, as a digestive aid. See pepsini compositus, pulvis. (40,46)

Digestivus, pulvis: Rhubarb, saltpeter, and cream of tartar. (3)

Digipuratum: A standardized extract of digitalis. (40)

Digitaline; Digitalin(um); Digitalin verum: See digitalis. Digitalin is a general term for glycosides (sugar derivatives of alkaloids) derived from foxglove. (40)

Digitalinum pulverisatum purum germanicum: See digitalin, this is said to be a standardized form in regards to strength. (40)

Digitalis [folia]: Leaves of the foxglove plant, *Digitalis pupurea* and source of digoxin and related compounds (digitoxin) still used extensively to treat congestive heart failure. Digitalis was effective in increasing the contractile force of the heart, diuresing accumulated fluid in heart failure (edema, or "dropsy"), increasing blood pressure in heart failure, and decreasing heart rate in pathological conditions causing increased rate (atrial fibrillation). While sometimes regarded as a diuretic, it has little if any affect on the kidney itself but instead dramatically increases the effectiveness of the failing cardiovascular system, allowing the mobilization of retained fluid and excretion via the kidney. Figure 3-95. (1,8)

Digitalis, extractum; —, fluidum extractum; —, tinctura; —, pulv.: Dried extract, fluid extract, alcoholic tincture, or powder of digitalis, respectively. (8)

Digitalis, infusum: Infusion of digitalis in cinnamon water, boiling water, and alcohol. (8) The BPC also specified a concentrated infusion with alcohol and chloroform water for storage and reconstitution. (42)

Digitalis, succus: Juice of fresh leaves of digitalis, combined with alcohol, use similar to tincture. (42)

Digitalis alcoholicum, extractum: Dry alcoholic extract of dried digitalis, USP. (44)

Digitalis compositae, pilulae: Pills of powdered digitalis leaf, powdered squill, mercury pill mass (hydrargyri, massa), and glucose syrup to bind. For dropsy. (42)

Digitalis et opii compositae, pilulae: Pills of powdered digitalis leaf, opium, ipecac root and quinine sulfate with syrup for binder. For dropsy. (42)

Digitalis et scillae, pilulae: See digitalis compositae, pilulae. (42)

Digitoxin: Alkaloid from digitalis, with similar activity. (42)

Dihydroxysuccinic acid: See tartaric acid. (42)

Di-iodo-isopropyl alcohol: A disinfectant. (40)

Dil.: Dilute(d). (29)

Dilapsus: Adjective applied to salts, meaning effloresced, or made into "flowers" (crystals) by evaporation of the solution. (3)

Fig. 3-93 Dictamnus albus or white dittany.

Fig. 3-94 Dictamnus creticus or dittany of crete.

Fig. 3-95 Digitalis purpurea or foxglove.

Dill; Dill oil: See anethum. (8)

Dimatos: See kieselguhr. (40)

Dimethyl(-)arsinic acid: See cacodylic acid. (40)

Dimethyl-ethyl-carbinol: See amylene. (40)

Dimethyl-piperazine tartrate: Compound evidently used for dissolving urate kidney stones. (40)

Dimethylketone: Acetone. (40)

Dimethylxanthine: Theobromine (2,3-dimethylxanthene), from tea or chocolate, similar in activity to caffeine. (40)

Dimol: Dimethyl-methoxyphenol. Pharmaceutical use unclear, not to be confused with modern commercial product of this name, which is a silicone anti-gas medication. (40)

Dinitrocellulose: See pyroxylin. (40)

Dinner pills (Champan's) (Lady Webster's): See aloes et mastiches, pilulae if not specified. (34) For eponymous preparations, see the associated sirname.

Dio...: See entry for prefix dia...

Dionin: Ethylmorphine, a narcotic. (40)

Dioscorea; Dioscoreae, fluidextractum: Wild yam root, *Dioscorea villosa*, rhizome and roots used. Fluid extract of dioscorea. A questionable diaphoretic, used in rheumatism. (7,31)

Dioscoreae, trochisci: Troches of dioscorea extract, ginger, peppermint oil, and gum tragacanth, for "colic, flatulency, borborygmi…and bilious colic." (34)

Dioscorides: Greek physician and botanist, ca. 50-100 CE. (1)

Diosma; Diosmae: Synonym for buchu. (34,39)

Diosmus, infusum: Infusion of buchu. (40)

Diospoliticon: Antihysteric and emmenagogue powder, after a location in Egypt. (39)

Diospyros: The bark and unripe fruit of persimmon or date plum, *Diospyros virginiana*, a tonic and astringent. (33)

Dioxygen: A patent or proprietary medicine, composition unknown. The manufacturer produced apothecary jars carrying the trade name for dispensing this product. Chemically, dioxygen is a term used for, and the normal state of, oxygen in the atmosphere (O_2) but this bears no apparent relationship to the trade name.

Dioxyphenyl-ethanol-methyl-amine: Adrenaline. (40)

Dioxysuccinic acid: Tartaric acid. (3,42)

Dioxytoluene: Orcin(e), orcinol, an isomer of cresol. (3)

Diphenylketone: See benzophenone. (42)

Dippel's acid elixir: See sulphuricium aromaticum, acidum. (40)

Dippel's oil; Dippelii, oleum animale: See animale, Dippelii, oleum. (1,39) "… an evil smelling distillate from bones or other animal matter." (3)

Dipping acid: Sulfuric acid. (3)

Dipsacus: Plant of genus *Dipsacus* (teasel), especially wild teasel, *Dipsacus sylvestris*. (1)

Diptamnus albus: See dictamnus albus. (1)

Dipterix: Tonka bean. (3)

Dirca: Leatherwood, moosewood, American mezereon, or wickopy, *Dirca palustris*. Fresh bark is a vesicant, preparations from the bark are emetic, cathartic, and sudorific. (33)

Discutient ointment: See stramonii compositum, unguentum. A "discutient" removes skin or tissue. (34)

Disodium methyl arsinate: See sodii metharsenis. (42)

Dispermin: See piperazidine. (40)

Distillat[a][us][um]: Distilled. (1)

Dita Bark: Bark of *Alstonia scholaris*, see alsotonia. (40)

Dithymol diiodide: See thymol iodide. (40)

Dittamo {*Italian*}**:** See *Dictamnus albus*. (1)

Dittany, American; —, mountain: See cunula. (33)

Dittany of Crete: See dictamnus albus. (39)

Diuretic drops: See copaibae composita, mistura. (34)

Diuretic salt; Diureticus, sal: Potassium acetate. (3,39)

Diuretin: See theobromine sodio-salicylate. (8)

Divinus, lapis: Copper aluminate. (3)

Dixon's pills: See antibilious pills. (39)

Dobel(l)'s solution: See sodii boratis compositus, liquor. (24,31)

Dock, bitter; —, curly-leaved; —, narrow-leaved: See rumex obtusifolis, rumex crispus and rumex acutus, respectively. (39)

Dodecapharmacum, unguentum: "Unguent of 10 ingredients." See apostolorum, unguentum. (1)

Dolce {*Italian*}**:** Sweet. (1)

Dolichos (pruriens); Dolichi pubes: Stiff down or hairs (literally translated, itchy or pubic hairs) from pods of cowhage, *Mucuna* or *Dolichos pruriens*. These small hairs are ingested by internal parasites and are anthelmintic. Figure 3-96. (39)

Donovan's solution: See arsenici et hydrargyri iodidi, liquor. (8)

Doom bark: Sassy bark, see erythrophloeum. (8,40)

Dormiol: Amylene-chloral, a sedative mixture of amylene and chloral hydrate. (3,40)

Doronicum: Leopard's bane, *Doronicum pardalianches*. Herb and root used. (1)

Doronium germanicum: "German gift," see arnica montana. (39)

Dorstenia contrayerva: See contrayerva. (39)

Dover's powder; Doveri pulv.; Dover's tincture: See ipecacuanae et opii, pulvis or tinctura. (8,29,42) Estes (39) provides a detailed history, indicating that this was originally of opium, ipecac, licorice, niter, and potassium sulphate, but later was primarily opium and ipecac. Introduced ca. 1730 by Dr. Thomas Dover, London.

Dr. Tinker's weed: See triosteum. (33)

Draco mitigatus: Calomel. (3)

Draconis, resina: Dried resin exuded from the seed pod of dragon's blood. Use as per the herb, sanguis draconis. (34)

Draconis, sanguis: See sanguis draconis. (1)

Dracontium: Roots and seeds of skunk cabbage, skunk weed, meadow cabbage, polecat weed, or foetid hellebore, *Dracontium foetidum*, a stimulant. Preparations are sometimes labeled symplocarpus. (33)

Dracunculus: Tarragon, *Artemesia dracunculus*. Herb used. (1)

Dragante {*Italian*}**:** See tragacantha. (1)

Drago mitigatus: Calomel, see hydrargyri chloridi mitis. (40)

Dragon's blood: See sanguis draconis. (39)

Dragon's root: See arum maculatum. (39)

Drawing ointment: See resinae, unguentum. (40)

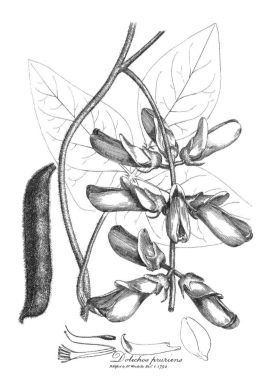

Fig. 3-96 Dolichos or cowhage.

Dreuw's salve: Salicylic acid, chrysarobin, birch tar and green soap in petrolatum. (24)

Drosera; Droserae, fluidextractum: Drosera, youthwort, lustwort, or sundew, *Drosera rotundifolia* or related species *D. anglica* or *D. longifolia*, or the fluid extract. Used in chronic bronchitis, whooping cough, and tuberculosis "but is apparently of little value." (31,32)

Drumstick: Cassia fistula. (3)

Duabus radicibus, syrupus de: See duobus radicibus, syrupus de. (1)

Duboisia; Duboisine sulphate; Duboisinae sulphas: The corkwood elm, *Duboisa myoporoides,* or an alkaloid obtained from same. This is believed to be identical with hyoscine (see hyoscyamus). Used to dilate the pupil in ophthalmology. (8,32)

Dugong oil: Oil derived from from the marine mammal of the same name, *Halicore australis* or *H. dugong.* This is claimed to have benefit in tuberculous consumption and other conditions. (40)

Dulcamara caules: Bittersweet (dulcamara) twigs. (40)

Dulcamara; Dulcamarae fluidum, extractum; —, infusum; —, decoctum: Bittersweet [dulca (sweet) + amara (bitter)] or bitter nightshade, *Solanum dulcamara* or the fluid extract or infusion (decoction). Source of active principals, solanine and dulcamarin. Young branches used. Said to possess feeble narcotic, analgesic, and mydriatic properties. Figure 3-97. (1,8)

Dulcified spirits of niter: Same as sweet spirits of niter. See niter dulcis, spiritus. (39)

Dulcified spirits of salt: Muriatic (hydrochloric) acid and wine in equal parts, heated. A diuretic, febrifuge, and panacea. (39)

Dulcin: A sweetening agent, paraphenetolcarbamide, or Sucrol. (3)

Dulcis: Sweet. (1,8)

Duobus radicibus, syrupus de: "Syrup of two roots," of fennel and parsley root. (1)

Duobus, pilulae de: Purgative "pills of two," i.e., colocynth and scammony. (1)

Duobus, sal de: See arcanum duplicatum. This is potassium sulfate. (39)

Duodenalis, liquor: A solution prepared from the duodenal intestinal membranes of ox, pig, or sheep, a digestive aid given orally or by injection. It was believed to contain the hormone secretin, which induces production of pancreatic juices in mammals. (42)

Duodenalis, pulvis: Duodenal powder, of cleaned and stripped duodenal lining from swine, source of secretin, a pancreatic stimulant peptide. (42)

Duodenin: See secretin. (40)

Duotal: Guaiacol carbonate, see guaiacol. (40)

Duplicatum: Double. (1)

Dutch drops: Dutch drops, or Haarlem oil, a patent remedy made up in turpentine. Not the same as Dutch oil or liquid. (3) A preparation made by heating linseed oil with sulfur and dissolving in turpentine. (40)

Dutch liquid; —, oil: "The chloride of olefiant gas," i.e., of ethylene, specifically 1,2—dichloroethylene. A solvent and dry cleaning fluid. Presumably a sundry item. (3,8,19)

Dutch metal: Imitation gold leaf, of copper and zinc. (3)

Dutch tea: A variety of St. Germain's tea. (3)

Dutch white: White lead. (3)

Dwale: *Atropa belladonna*, see belladonna. (40)

Dwarf elder: See ebulus. (40)

Dya: Orthographic variant, see dia. (1)

Dysmenorrhoea mixture: See antacrida, tinctura. (46)

Solanum Dulcamara

Fig. 3-97 Dulcamara or bittersweet.

E

E.: Within an inscription: usually an abbreviation for the Latin *et*, meaning "and," but sometimes for the Latin *e(x)*, meaning "of" or "from." In American commercial shopware it often appears as the letter e or E with a bar above, often in reduced font size. At the beginning or end of an inscription: eau {*French*} (water); electuarium, electuario {*Italian*} (electuary); elixir (elixir); empiastro {*Italian*}, emplastrum (plaster); erba (herb), essentia (essence); extractum (extract). (1)

Earl of Warwick, powder of: See cornachinus, pulvis. (39)

Earth, bitter: See magnesia. (3)

Earth nut (oil): Peanut, or peanut oil. (3,40)

Earth wax: Ceresine, crude paraffin. (3)

Easton's pills: See ferri phosphatis cum quinina et strychnina, pilulae. Sometimes with addition of arsenious acid. (42)

Easton's syrup: See ferri, quininae et strychninae phosphatum, syrupus. (34)

Eau d'Arquebus(c)ade {*French*}**:** Wound water, see arquebuscade. (40)

Eau de Broccherai {*French*}**:** Creosote. (3)

Eau de Javel(le) {*French*}**:** Chlorinated potash solution, by passing chlorine through aqueous sodium or potassium hydroxide, i.e., bleach, used medicinally as a disinfectant. Named after French town of Javelle. (40)

Eau (de) Luce {*French*}**:** Aromatic spirits of ammonia. (3) In the BPC, see a similar preparation, ammoniae composita, tinctura.

Eau de Laitue {*French*}**:** Lettice water, see lactucae, aqua. (40)

Eau de Naphe {*French*}**:** Orange-flower water, see aurantii floras, aqua. (40)

Eau (de) Rabel {*French*}**:** See Haller's elixir. (3)

Eau de Raspail {*French*}**:** Aqua sedativa. See ammoniacalis camphorata, lotio. (31,40)

Eau de vie {*French*}**:** "Water of life," i.e., brandy. (40)

Eau sedative {*French*}**:** Aqua sedativa. See ammoniacalis camphorata, lotio. (31,40)

Eau {*French*}**:** Water. (1)

Ebulus: Dwarf elder, danewort, *Sambucus ebulus*. Herb and root used as a powerful cathartic. (1,39)

Ebur ustum: Bone-black or ivory black. (3)

Ebur: Ivory. (1)

Ecballium: See cucumus agrestis. (39)

Ecboline: See ergotoxine. (40)

Echinacea; Echinaceae, fluidextractum: Echinacea, purple coneflower, black samson, *Echinacea augustafolia*, rhizome and roots used, or the fluid extract therefrom. (7, 31)

Echtroth: A brilliant red dye. In modern times, an aniline dye, but appears to have been used variably for intense red or orange dyes over time, as use of the term preceded aniline chemistry. (40)

Eclegma: Sweet, semi-fluid medication intended to be licked off spoon. (1)

Écorce {*French*}**:** Bark, peel, or rind. (1)

Edera {*Italian*}**:** See hedera. (1)

Effervescens; Effervescent preparations: See sodii citro-tartras, effervescens for the general formulation. (42) The powder immediately below is typical. These could be freshly prepared for immediate use or confined to a sealed bottle as with a carbonated beverage.

Effervescens compositus, pulvis: Compound effervescing powder, or Seidlitz powder, consisting of two components often dispensed in different colored papers. One component was potassium and sodium tartrate plus sodium bicarbonate. This was dissolved first and on addition of the second component, tartaric acid, would effervesce. Consumed while effervescing for gastric disorders. (8)

Effervescens laxans, pulvis; Effervescentes aperientes, pulveres: See Effervescens compositus, pulvis. (34,40)

Effervescing draught: See potassae citratis, liquor. (39)

Egg liniment: See album, linimentum. (42)

Egg yolk: See vitellus. (8)

Egyptiacum, unguentum; Egitiaco, unguento {*Italian*}**; Egiptiac. U.:** See Aegyptiacum, unguentum. (1)

Egyptian mimosa: Gum arabic. (39)

Egyptian privet: Henna. (3)

Egypticum, ____: See Aegypticum, ____.

Ehrlich-Hata: See arsenobenzol. Erlich and Hata were the joint discoverers of Salvarsan. (40)

El. f. q. et ars.: See ferri quinini et arsenii, elixir.

El.; Elix.: Elixir.

Elapi: See hartshorn. (39)

Elastica; Elastica, resina: India rubber. (1,3)

Elaterin; Elaterium; Elaterinum; Elaterini, trituratio; Elaterii, extractum: This is a material deposited by the juice from the fruit of an African or Southern European plant, *Ecballim elaterium*. It could be prepared as a trituration with milk sugar. It is said to be "violently purgative, producing profuse watery evacuations, attended with gripping and much prostration." It increases salivation, and will purge following injection. It is stated to be the most powerful purgative in the USP. It could be useful for removal of large amounts of fluid in cases of ascites or renal failure, but needed to be used with care, especially in those with heart disease. Unlike true extracts, the US Dispensatory notes that this "extract" deposits spontaneously from the juice on standing. See also cucumus agrestis. Elaterine, or Elaterinum in pseudo-Latin, is an active alkaloid derived from elaterium. (1,8,41,42)

Elaterini compositus, pulvis: Powder of elaterine in milk sugar, a drastic purgative. (42)

Elaterium elder: See sambucus nigra. (40)

Elatteria: See cardmom minus. (39)

Elder: See sambucus. (8)

Elder, dwarf: In American use, *Aralia hispida*; in English use, *Sambucus ebulus* (see ebulus). (40)

Elecampane: See inula. (8)

Electrolyte acid: Sulfuric acid, a sundry item. (3)

Electropoeicus, liquor: Battery acid consisting of sulfuric acid and potassium dichromate. The later NF specified variants for several battery types including an ammonium chloride solution for the Leclanche zinc-carbon cell. (3)

Electrum: Amber. Also may refer to an alloy of gold with approximately forty percent silver. (3)

Electuarium: Electuary. (1)

Electuarium aromaticum: Aromatic electuary or confection. Estes reports several formulae: cinnamon, cardamom, ginger, and orange peel; zedoaria, crocus, cancer lapilli, cinnamon, nutmeg, and caryophyllus (known as confectio aromaticum); or pulvis aromaticus and syrup of orange peel. (39)

Electuarium gingivale: Gingival electuary, of myrrh, cream of tartar, and cloves, in honey, colored with cochineal. Specific for the treatment of gingivitis. (39)

Electuarium piperis: See piperis, confectio. (40)

Elemi gummi, unguentum e: See arcaei, unguentum. (35)

Elemi; Elemi, unguentum: A resinous exudate primarily, but not exclusively, from *Canarium commune*, of Manilla, used as a topical stimulant and disinfectant. (8)

Elemi, Brazilian; —, Manila; —, Mauritius; —, Mexican: Elemi (see above) derived from *Idea icariba*, *Canarium commune*, *Canarium mauritianum* or *Amyris elemifera*, respectively. (40)

Elephant louse: Cashew nut. (3)

Elescoph, electuarium: See episcopi, electuarium. (1)

Elettuario {*Italian*}: Electuary. (1)

Eleutheria: See cascarilla. (39)

Elixir; El^x: Elixir. A liquid formulation for oral consumption. (1)

Elixir _____: See _____, elixir.

Elixir adjuvans: Elixir of glycyrrhiza, USP, see glycerrhizae, elixir. (3)

Elixir aromaticum: Aromatic elixir contains compound spirit of orange (see aurantii compositus, spiritus), syrup, and deodorized alcohol. A flavoring agent. May be colored red with cudbear (*Lecanora tartarea*), a lichen from which a red dye is derived. (8)

Elixir de vie {French}; **Elixir Devie** (orth var.): "Elixir of life." Occasionally seen as Elixir Devie, an elixir of aloes, of which varieties abound. The term is still in use for various anti-aging products. (40)

Elixir digestivum compositum: Compound digestive elixir (NF), containing pepsin, pancreatin, diastase, lactic and hydrochloric acids, and aromatic elixir. Digestive aid. (45)

Elixir laxitivum; Elixir, laxative: See rhamni purshianae compositum, elixir. (46)

Elixir magnum: See Stoughton's bitters. (39)

Elixir of long life: Modification of well-known Swedish bitters. (3)

Elixir of longevity: See elixir de vie. (40)

Elixir of vitriol, acid: See sulphuricum aromaticum, acidum. (40)

Elixir of vitriol: See vitrioli aromaticum, acidum. (40)

Elixir proprietatis paracelsi: A proprietary "elixir" attributed to Paracelsus. Said to be aloes et myrrhae, tinctura. (8)

Elixir sacrum: Compound tincture of rhubarb, see rhei composita, tinctura. (39)

Elixir salutis: See sennae composita, tinctura. (34)

Elixir simplex; Elix. simpl.: See elixir aromaticum. (8)

Elixir stomachicum: See gentianae composita, tinctura. (40)

Elixir traumaticum: See benzoini composita, tinctura. (40)

Elkonogen: Sodium amidobetanaphthol-betamonosulphonic acid, a photographic developer. (3)

Elleboro {*Italian*}: See helleborus. (1)

Elm: See ulmus. (8)

Emagogum, antidotum: See antidotum haemagogum. (1)

Embelia: Dried fruit of *Embelia ribes*, of India, source of embelic acid, anthelmintic used India and eastern British colonies. (42)

Embilicus, myrobalanus: See myrobalanus embilicus. (1)

Emerald green: Copper acetoarsenite or copper arsenite. (3)

Emerald lemonade; Emeralds: See limonata smaragdina. (39)

Emetic powder: 1. See lobeliae compositum, pulvis. (34) 2. See Algaroth, powder of. (39)

Emetic tincture: See sanguinariae acetata composita, tinctura. (34)

Emetic weed: See lobelia (inflata). (39)

Emetic wine: See vinum antimonii. (39)

Emetine: Active alkaloid derived from ipecacuanha. (42)

Emmaenagogicae, pilulae; emmenagogae, pilulae: Emmenagogic pills of birthwort, saffron, myrrh, etc. (1)

Emmenagogue pills: See ferri compositae, pilulae. (34)

Emmenagogue powder: See pulvis nigrum. (34)

Emol keleet: Purified fuller's earth, see terra fullonica. (40)

Emolliens, unguentum: Cold cream, see rosae, aqua, unguentum. (40)

Empirin: A proprietary name for aspirin, also available as Empirin with Codeine. The manufacturer produced various apothecary wares bearing this brand name. This line of products remains available today.

Emplastrum _____: Plaster, see _____, emplastrum. (8)

Emplastrum, devinus: Devine plaster, a plaster with tonic and vulnerary effects. (39)

Emplastrum; Empiastro {*Italian*}: Plaster, poultice, cataplasm. (1)

Emplastrum adhaesens; Emp. adhaes.; Emplastrum adhaesivum elasticum: Adhesive plaster. There is little mention of this term in apothecary texts. Nonetheless, the adhesive plaster has a long history, beginning in ancient times with various gums, resins, or pastes applied to cloth to produce a self-adhesive dressing. Early adhesive plasters often had medicinal materials incorporated into the adhesive matter. Later versions sometimes incorporated a separate area or dressing pad to protect the wound and carry any desired medication, which could be either pre-applied or added later. The BPC (42) provides a formulation of diced India rubber, resin, Japan wax, benzoated beef tallow, wool fat, sesame oil, methyl salicylate (wintergreen oil, for odor), thymol (antimicrobial), and lead oleate, dissolved in the necessary quantity of benzol to achieve the desired consistency. It appears from advertisements that around 1850 commercially produced products replaced most do-it-yourself efforts. The current iteration in this eternal saga was developed in 1874 by R. W. Johnson and G. J. Seabury of East Orange, New Jersey, the former being the founder of the Johnson & Johnson Company, from whence comes the omnipresent Band-Aid. The precise content of older containers bearing this label is unknowable. If produced after about 1900, it is probably just a fancy band-aid jar.

Emplastrum album: White plaster, a murcurial plaster of calomel. (40)

Emplastrum antihystericum: A plaster applied to the umbilical area, consisting of litharge (white lead), assafoetida, galbanum, and yellow wax. An antispasmodic, emmenagogue, expectorant, and anthelminthic. (39)

Emplastrum aromaticum: Plaster composed of lead plaster (see plumbi, emplastrum) with cinnamon, ginger, capsicum, camphor, and cotton seed oil. (46)

Emplastrum calefaciens [mylabridis]: "Heat-making" plaster. Generally a plaster of cantharides (Spanish fly) designed as a rubifacient and blistering agent. For example, see cantharidis, emplastrum. (40) The BPC indicates about four percent powdered cantharides in a mixture of yellow beeswax, resin, resin plaster, and soap plaster. The mylabridus form uses powder of another insect, (see) mylabris, in place of cantharides. (42)

Emplastrum cephalicum: See picis burgundicae, emplastrum, compositium. For headache or other head disorders. (39,40)

Emplastrum commune: Common plaster, lead plaster, see plumbi, emplastrum. (40)

Emplastrum gummosum: See galbani, emplastrum. (40)

Emplastrum lyttae: A cantharides plaster used for blistering. (40)

Emplastrum magneticum: Magnetic plaster, a suppurative plaster of "arsenical magnet," see magnes arsenicalis. For topical treatment, presumably of syphilitic lesions as per magnes arsenicalis. (39)

Emplastrum pauperis: Pauper's plaster, poor man's plaster, see picis burgundicae, emplastrum. (40)

Emplastrum roborans: Tonic plaster, similar to emplastrum thuris compositum, one variant example contained white lead, pine resin (turpentine), yellow wax, olive oil, and colcothar. (39) See also the British use of this term under ferri, emplastrum. (40)

Emplastrum thuris compositum: Compound plaster of frankincense, a tonic and astringent, of frankincense (thus, genitive thuris), sanguis draconis, and white lead, and said to be suitable for children. (39)

Empyreumatic: As a process, distillation at a high temperature, generally in reference to an oil. It may also refer to any strongly scented material, also usually an oil, which may or may not be derived via this process, and to various resins or pitches.

Empyreumatica liquida, resina: Tar, see pix. (3)

Empyreumatica solida, resina: Pitch, see pix. (3)

Empyreumaticus, syrupus: Molasses, generally blackstrap molasses, which has a high sulfur content. (3,39)

Emulsio (vs. emulsum): Emulsio was a preferred term for emulsions in later versions of the NF. (45)

Emulsio...(of volatile oil not specifically noted): The NF indicates that emulsions can be prepared for any volatile oil as per terebinthinae, olei, emulsio. (46)

Emulsio communis: See amygdalae (expressum), oleum. (3)

Emulsio purgans cum scammonia: See scammonii, lac. (34)

Emulsum _____: An emulsion, or "milk," a suspension of an oily material in water. See _____, emulsum. (8)

Endiva; Endivia: Endive, *Chicorium endiva*. Root and leaves used as an aperient. (1,39)

Enema, domestic: Common enema, usually of salt water and olive oil or with aloe and chamomile, sometimes with opium added to reduce diarrhea. (39)

Enema nutriens; —, nutrient: Nutrient enema of beef tea, egg yolk and white, and milk, as a retention enema. (42)

English powder: A preparation of quinine (cinchona) with rose flowers and lemon juice or with succus petroselinus and anise water. (39)

English salts: Magnesia vitriolata, magnesium sulfate, or Epsom salts, from Epsom, England. (39)

English white: Calcium carbonate. (3)

Enixum, sal: Potassium bisulfate. (3)

Ens: A Paracelsian term for essence or essential spirit. (39)

Ens martis: Essence of Mars (symbol of iron), ammoniated iron. (3)

Ens veneris: Essence of Venus, a mixture of sal ammoniac and vitriol (ammonium chloride and sulfuric acid). (39)

Enula (campana): Elecampane, *Inula helenium*. Rhizome used. See inula. (1)

Enulatum, unguentum: Unguent of enula, a topical for itching and as an expectorant, diaphoretic, cathartic, stomachic, and emmenagogue. (35)

Enulatum cum mercurio, unguentum: Same as above, with mercury. (1)

Eosot: Guaiacol valerianate, a proprietary creosote derivative used for tuberculosis. (40)

Epatica: See hepatica. (1)

Ephedrini hydrochloridi: Ephedrine hydrochloride, derived from the ephedra plant *Ephedra sinica*, or Ma Huang. A stimulant and decongestant. See adrenaline. (40)

Epigaea; Epigaeae, infusum: Trailing arbutus, *Epigaea repens*, for urinary symptoms, especially with uric acid crystals in the urine, often as an infusion. (32)

Epilobium: Wickup, willow herb, *Epilobium angustifolium*. Astringent, tonic, emollient, and demulcent. (32)

Epinephrine: See adrenaline. (40)

Epiphegus: Beech drops or cancer root, *Epiphegus virginiana*, an astringent and hemostatic. (33)

Episcopi, electuarium: "The Bishop's Electuary," purgative of scammony, turpeth root, polypody rhizome, etc. (1)

Epispastica, charta: Blistering paper, paper strips impregnated with a heated mixture of wax, resin, spermacetti, and cantharides. (40)

Epispasticum, emplastrum: Vesicatory poultice from cantharides and other ingredients. (1)

Epispasticus (concentratus), liquor: Same as cantharides, linimentum, a vesicant. The BPC also had a double-strength (concentratus) version. (34,42)

Epithema: Epithem, fomentation. Any topical dosage form, generally for use on skin. Most typically a liquid, cream, or plaster. (1)

Epithymi, syrupus; Epithimo, syrupus de {*Italian*}: Syrup of thyme dodder, with a myriad of other ingredients. For melancholy and other disorders of the stomach and liver (recall that melancholy was believed to be a biliary disorder). (35)

Epithymus; Epitimo {*Italian*}: Thyme dodder, epithyme, *Cuscuta epithymum*. Herb used. (1)

Epsom Salts: Magnesium sulfate, from the English town of Epsom, where the mineral occurs in natural form. See magnesii sulphas (8)

Epuloticum, ceratum: Ceratum calaminaris, Turner's cerate. (3) A wound ointment of calamine, olive oil, and wax. (1)

Equisetum: Common horsetail, scouring rush, *Equisetum arvense*. Dried green stems and leaves used. Primarily a diuretic and for urinary disorders. (1,32)

Equus: Horse. (1)

Erba {*Italian*}: Herb. (1)

Erechtites; Erechtitis, oleum: Plant or oil of fireweed, *Erechtites hieracifolia*. (33)

Ergosterol, irradiated: Vitamin D, formed by action of ultraviolet light on ergosterol in milk, still in use for the supplementation of vitamin D levels in milk. (40)

Ergot; Ergota: Ergot, or secale cornutum, a fungus, *Claviceps purpurea*, affecting the grain of rye. Ergot is highly active and remains in use today in various forms for migraine headache and in obstetrics and gynecology. It is a powerful vasoconstrictor and intestinal stimulant, haemostatic, and oxytocic (ecbolic) used to stimulate uterine contractions to facilitate labor and as an abortifacient. Neurological side effects, especially numbness or abnormal sensations, were common. Excessive vasoconstriction could lead to gangrene of the extremities and other complications. (8)

Ergotae, extractum; —fluidum, extractum; —, liquidum, extractum; —aquosum, extractum; —, infusum; —, tinctura; —, vinum: The dry extract, fluid/liquid (NF and BPC) extract, aqueous extract (NF), infusion, alcoholic tincture, or wine of ergot, respectively. The extract was prepared with acetic acid and alcohol, and evaporated to dryness. Wine of ergot was prepared using white wine and alcohol. (8,34,42)

Ergotae, mistura: A mixture of liquid extract of ergot and dilute sulfuric acid in chloroform water, use as per ergot in uterine conditions. (42)

Ergotae, tinctura: Simple tincture of powdered ergot. (42)

Ergotae ammoniata, tinctura; Ergotae ammoniatum liquidum, extractum: Ammoniated tincture of ergot. (34)

Ergotas, liquor; Ergotinae, liquor: Solution of ergot. (34)

Ergotoxine; Ergotinine: Pharmacologically active components of ergot. Now a specific compound among others, ergonovine, etc., but historically purity was probably variable. (40,42)

Erigeron (canadense); Erigeron, oil of; Erigerontis, oleum: Oil of fleabane, *Erigeron heterophyllum* or *E. Philadelphicum*; or Canadian fleabane, *E. Canadense*. Used as per turpentine (terebinthina), although said to be less potent. Figure 3-98. (8,44)

Eringium: See eryngium. (1)

Eriodictyi aromaticum, elixir; Eryiodict. arom., el.: Aromatic elixir of eriodictyon, aromatic elixir of yerba santa, or elixir corrigens. Made from fluid extract of eriodictyon, syrup, and compound elixir of taraxacum; used chiefly as a vehicle for disguising the taste of quinine sulphate and other bitter substances. (31)

Eriodictyi aromaticus, syrupus: Aromatic syrup of eriodyction, aromatic syrup of yerba santa, comprised of the extract of eriodyction, potassa, tincture of cardamom and oils of sassafras, lemon, and clove in a mixture of alcohol, sugar, and water. Primarily a flavored vehicle. (34)

Eriodictyon; Eriodictyi fluidum, extractum; —, syrupus aromaticus: Yerba santa or mountain balm, leaves of *Eriodictylon glutinosum*, of western United States, or the fluid extract. Used as a bitter tonic and stimulating expectorant, useful for chronic bronchitis, and as a masking vehicle for the bitterness of quinine. The aromatic syrup (NF) is of fluid extract flavored with compound tincture of cardamom, oils of sassafras, lemon, and clove, alcohol, sugar, and water. (8,31)

Ermodattilo {*Italian*}**:** See hermodactylus. (1)

Eruca: Garden rocket, *Eruca sativa*. Seeds used. Said to be aphrodesiac. (1,39)

Eruginis, linimentum: See aegypticum, unguentum. (40)

Erygeron heterophyllum; —philadelphicum: The daisy fleabane, *Erigeron annuus*, and the common daisy, *E. philidelphicus*, diuretics. (39)

Eryngium: 1. Water eryngo, sea holly, *Eryngium maritimum*. Root used as diaphoretic, aperient, expectorant, and other purposes. Figure 3-99. (1,39) 2. Button snakeroot, *Eryngium aquaticum*, for various conditions, especially urogenital. (32)

Eryngo: Common eryngo, *Eryngium campestre*, an aperient, diuretic, and aphrodesiac. (39)

Eryotictylon (*orth var*)**:** See eriodictyon.

Erysimum; Erysimi o: Hedge mustard, *Erysimum officinale*. Herb used. Figure 3-100. (1) Last letter possibly c or e. Erysimi o observed elsewhere, but no information located. Most likely the oil (oleum) as an oil is described in modern literature (could be extract or confection, but not cortex as this small plant has no bark).

Erythritol tetranitrate; Erythrol tetranitrate; Erytrolis tetranitras: A vasodilator for hypertension and angina, still in use. (42)

Erythrol nitratis: Erythritol tetranitrate. (42)

Erythrol nitratis, tablettae: Erythritol tetranitrate, cocoa powder, gum acacia, refined sugar, and ethereal solution of theobroma. Like nitroglycerin, chewed for angina. (42)

Erythronium: Leaves and root of adder's tongue, dog's-tooth violet, fellow snowdrop, rattlesnake violet, or yellow erythronium, *Erythronium americanum* (or *E. lanceolatum*). Said to be "Emetic, emollient, and antiscrofulous when fresh; nutritive when dried." (33)

Erythrophloeine; Erythophloeinae hydrochloridum: Hydrochloride salt of active alkaloid from erythrophloem, used for same purpose and also with eugenol in dentistry to relieve pain. (42)

Erythropleum; Erythrophloeum; Erythrophloei, cortex; —, tinctura: Sassy, saucy, mancona, or ordeal bark, the bark of *Erythophleum guineense*, of Africa, or the tincture thereof. It is said to be therapeutically identical to digitalis. (8,33)

Erythroxyli (aromaticum), vinum: Coca wine, fluidextract of erythroxylon and sugar in claret wine. The aromatic form contained fluidextract of erythroxylon, compound elixir of taraxacum and syrup of coffee in sherry. A tonic and stimulant. A popular preparation available to the public in late 1800s and early 1900s was Vin Mariani. (34)

Erythroxyli (et guaranae), elixir: Elixir of fluid extract of erythroxylon with alcohol, syrup, tincture of vanilla, and aromatic elixir; guarana can be added. See elixir cocae (et guaranae). (46)

Erythroxylon (coca); Erythroxylum: *Erythroxylon coca*, source of cocaine. See coca and related entries. (8, 46)

Eserine; Eserinae; Eserinae (et cocainae), guttae: See physostigminae. (8,42)

Esipo {*Italian*}**:** Wool fat, i.e., lanolin. (1)

Essence; Essentia: Volatile oil or essence in most uses. Proper use refers to a volatile oil condensed after distillation from a liquid or solid state, i.e., anise oil, which may be distilled directly from leaves. In many cases, these were then diluted with absolute alcohol to a desired strength. Occasionally, this refers to a concentrated form of a material as in essence of vinegar, i.e., acetic acid. (1,3)

Essence of ginger: See zingiberis fortior, tinctura. (34)

Fig. 3-98 Erigeron or rleabane species.

Fig. 3-99 Eryngium maratimum or water eryngo.

Fig. 3-100 Erysium or hedge mustard.

Essence of muirbane: Nitrobenzol, artificial oil of bitter almonds. (3)

Essence of peppermint: In addition to peppermint oil proper, a patent medicine, by John Juniper, London, ca. 1760. (39)

Essence of pepsin: See pepsini et rennini compositum, elixir. (31)

Essence of venus: See ens veneris. (39)

Essence of vinegar: Concentrated acetic acid. (3)

Essentia _____: Essence, see _____, essentia.

Essentia bina: Caramel. (3)

Essentia pepsini: See pepsini et rennini compositum, elixir. (31)

Essentiale tartari, sal: Tartaric acid. (3)

Esula: Leafy spurge, *Euphorbia esula*, possibly other related *Euphorbia* species. Root used. (1)

Ethacrinidine (lactate); (A)ethacrinidini lactas: Ethacrinidine is a dye used as a topical antiseptic, usually as the lactate salt.

Ethanol: See alcohol, ethyl. (8)

Ethene chloride: See ethylene bichloride. (8)

NOTE: Ether and related formulations, if not listed here, see aether

Ether, pyroacetic: Acetone. (3)

Ether: A general class of organic compounds containing a C-O-C linkage, when otherwise unspecified referring to diethyl ether, CH_3-CH_2-O-CH_2-CH_3. Used for inhalational anesthesia, topical anesthesia (by evaporative cooling of the skin) and as a cardiac stimulant. Also referred to as sulphuric ether as it is formed from a mixture of sulfuric acid and alcohol. The former dehydrates the alcohol to form di-ethyl ether, which is distilled away from the solution and condensed for use. The true structure was not published until ca. 1845. (8,39)

Ethiops martialis; —mineral; —mineralis: See aethiops. (1,40)

Ethocaine (borate): Novocaine or borocaine, topical anesthetics. (40)

Ethyl acetate: See (a)ether, aceticus. (8)

Ethyl alcohol: See alcohol, ethyl. (8)

Ethyl bromide; (A)ethyl(is) bromidum: Ethyl bromide, C_2H_5Br, from alcohol and potassium bromide in the presence of concentrated sulfuric acid. A general anesthetic by inhalation, used as with ether. (Note, ethylene bromide, C_2H_3Br, is a topical refrigerant introduced in more modern times and used to freeze skin lesions.) (8,42)

Ethyl chloride; Ethyl(is) chloridum: Monochloroethane, a rapidly evaporating chlorinated hydrocarbon (not an ether, although referred to as hydrochloric or muriatic ether). Still used as a topical refrigerant and local anesthetic. (42)

Ethyl hydroxide: Ethyl alcohol. (40)

Ethyl nitratis, liquor: An unstable solution of ethyl nitrite in alcohol with sodium nitrite and dilute sulphuric acid, on ice. Diaphoretic, diuretic, and antihypertensive, must be diluted at time of use. While seemingly suboptimal, it is actually more stable than ethyl nitrite itself. (42)

(A)ethyl nitrite, spirits; (A)ethylis nitritis, spiritus; (A)ethylis nitratis spiritus: See (A)etheris nitrosi, spiritus. (3)

Ethyl urethane: Urethane. Sedative. (40)

Ethylene bichloride; Ethyleni bichloridum: Ethylene chloride, or 1,2-dichloroethane, $C_2H_4Cl_2$. An inhalational anesthetic used in a manner similar to ether, safer (less flammable) but more expensive. (8)

Ethylene dibromide; Ethyleni dibromidum: Ethylene dibromide (1,2 dibromoethylene), a sedative and anesthetic. (42)

Ethylenimine: Piperazidine. (40)

Ethylic alcohol: Absolute (anhydrous) ethyl alcohol. (40)

Ethylmorphine hydrochloride; Ethylmorphina hydrochloridum: Ethylmorphine hydrochloride, by action of ethyl iodide on morphine. Much like codeine, a cough suppressant. (42)

Ethylsulphonal: Diethylmethane-diethylsulphone, a sedative related to sulphonal, but more readily soluble in alcohol solutions. (40,42)

Eucaine: Benzamine, a topical anesthetic. (40)

Eucalypt(i)(us) compositus, vapor (BPC); Eucalyp., vap.: A preparation of eucalyptus for addition to boiling water, administered via inhalation. Various formulations typically contained oil of eucalyptus, pine oil, camphor, and other volatiles. In the BPC, carbolic acid, oil of eucalyptus and of pine, strong solution of iodine, camphor, and ammoniated alcohol. Sawdust or other material could also be saturated with this mixture and the vapors inhaled for coryza, hay fever, influenza, etc. (42)

Eucalypti, elixir: Elixir of eucalyptus with syrup of coffee and compound elixir of taraxacum, antiperiodic and tonic. (45)

Eucalypti, tinctura: Simple tincture of powdered eucalyptus leaf in alcohol, for asthma, cough, and chronic bronchitis. (42)

Eucalypti, unguentum: Ointment of eucalyptus, oil of same in paraffin, as an antiseptic and topical stimulant to promote healing of old ulcers. A good dressing for odorous wounds or ulcers. (34)

Eucalypti, vapor: Oil of eucalyptus triturated with magnesium carbonate in water, the vapor being inhaled for nasal catarrh, phthisis, bronchitis. (42)

Eucalyptae rostratae, syrupus; Eucalypti compositus, syrupus: Eucalyptus gum and oil with refined sugar and mucilage of acacia and water, astringent for diarrhea and dysentery. (42)

Eucalypti compositum, elixir: Elixir of the fluid extract of eucalyptus with alcohol, magnesium carbonate, syrup of coffee, and compound elixir of taraxacum. (46)

Eucalypti gummi (rubri) liquidum, extractum: Liquid extract of eucalyptus gum in alcohol, applied as a styptic on cloth or lint or as a nasal wash for epistaxis. (42)

Eucalypti gummi, syrupus: Liquid extract of eucalyptus gum and refined sugar, as an astringent for the throat. (42)

Eucalypti gummi, tinctura: Tincture of eucalyptus gum in alcohol, astringent for diarrhea and as a component of gargles for pharyngitis. (42)

Eucalypti gummi, trochisci: Troches of eucalyptus gum, or red gum; red gum lozenges, for pharyngitis. (31)

Eucalypti gummi; —, kino: See eucalyptus gum. (40)

Eucalyptol: Eucalyptol is the semivolatile oil obtained from eucalyptus, with a camphor-like odor. (33)

Eucalyptus; Eucalypti, folia; —, oleum; Eucalyptol: Leaves of the eucalyptus, *Eucalyptus globulus*, or the volatile oil therefrom. Eucalyptol is purified from the crude oil by fractional distillation and purification. Oil of eucalyptus is less irritating topically than other volatile oils, but can produce vesication and pustulation if confined against the skin. It is an antiseptic and disinfectant, stomachic, and stimulant expectorant, and is otherwise employed much like oil of cloves (see caryophyllum). Eucalyptus gauze can be used to dress and deodorize wounds, or an ointment can be made from eucalyptus, iodoform, paraffin, and vaseline. (8,42)

Eucalyptus gum; Eucalypti gummi: A ruby red exudate from the Eucalyptus, *Eucalyptus rostrata*, of Australia. A powerful tannin-containing astringent used for diarrhea and dysentery. Suppositories could be prepared for hemorrhoids, and it could be used topically as a mouthwash, vaginal douche, or enema. (8)

Eucasin: A preparation of casein treated with ammonia. Nutritive typically added to beverage for use. (3)

Euchinin: Quinine ethyl carbonate. (40)

Eucortone: Adrenal cortex extract. (40)

Eucupin: Isoamylhydrocupreine. A topical anesthetic. (40)

Euflavine: See acriflavine. (40)

Euforbium: See euphorbium. (1)

Eufragia {*Italian*}; Eufrasia {*Italian*}: See euphrasia. (1)

Eugallol: Pyrogallol monoacetate, see pyrogallol. (40)

Eugastrol: Hog's stomach extract, a digestive aid. (40)

Eugenia caryophyllata: See caryophyllum. This is an alternate name for cloves, from which is named the primary component of clove oil, eugenol. (39)

Eugenia (jambolana): See jambul. (32)

Eugenol; Eugenic acid: See caryophyllum, or clove. Eugenol is the primary component in clove oil and was used as a flavoring agent, to mask sickroom odors, and as a topical disinfectant astringent in dentistry. (40)

Eunulatum, unguentum: Ointment of elecampane rhizome, oil of wormwood, turpentine, and lard. Used to treat skin disorders. (1)

Euonymi compositum, elixir: Compound elixir of tincture of euonymus, iridin (from iris), stronger glycerin of pepsin, bismuth and ammonium citrate, and simple elixir, colored with solution of cochineal. A digestive and cholegogue. (42)

Euonymi et [cascarae][iridini], liquor: A solution of euonymus extract in alcohol with liquid extract of cascara sagrada or of euonymus extract and iridin in water and alcohol. Aperient and either laxative (cascarae) or outright purgative (iridin). (42)

Euonymi et pepsini, elixir: Elixir of euonymus and pepsin, of tincture of euonymus, crystalline pepsin, dilute hydrochloric acid, glycerin, and water. A digestive aid. (42)

Euonymi(n), tinctura: Simple tincture of bark in alcohol, purgative and to slow the heart, like digitalis. (42)

Euonymi, elixir: Elixir of the fluid extract of euonymus with syrup of coffee, and compound elixir of taraxacum. (46)

Euonymi, extractum (siccum); —, fluidextractum; —liquidum, extractum; —, liquor: Extract of euonymus (powdered), prepared by exhausting the powdered drug with diluted alcohol, evaporating to dryness and diluting with starch, or the fluid extract or liquor made therefrom. "It has been stated that the absorption of euonymus in the gastrointestinal tract is uncertain and irregular. To avoid possible toxic or cumulative action, the physician should carefully guard the dosage and determine in each case the tolerance of the patient and regulate the dosage accordingly." (31,42)

Euonymin, brown: Same as euonymi, extractum. (42)

Euonymus; Euonymi cortex: Bark of the wahoo or spindle tree, *Euonymus atropurpureus*, of the eastern United States. It was a useful cholegogue and cathartic, with some diuretic and expectorant effects, and was used specifically for cases in which constipation was accompanied by liver disorders. (7,8)

Eupad: See calcis chlorinatae et acidi borici, pulvis. (40)

Euparatone: A parathyroid extract. (40)

Eupatoriae compositae, oleoresinae, pilulae: Compound pills of the resin of *Eupatorium perfoliatum,* with oleoresins of xanthoxylum and strychnine. A stimulant diuretic for multiple conditions. (34)

Fig. 3-101 Euphragia or eyebright.

Eupatorium; Eupatorio {*Italian*}**:** Hemp agrimony, *Eupatorium cannabinum*. Herb used as tonic, aperient, antiscorbutic, cathartic, and narcotic. (1,39)

Eupatorium (perfoliatum); Eupatorii fluidum, extractum: Flowers and tops of the thoroughwort, queen-o-the-meadow, or boneset plant, *Eupatorium perfoliatum*, or the fluid extract thereof. Used as a tonic, diaphoretic, and aperient as well as in the early stages of catarrhal illness, influenza, or muscular rheumatism, and for urological disorders. (8,33)

Eupatorium pilosum: Leaves of hairy thoroughwort or purple boneset, *Eupatorium pilosum*, tonic diaphoretic, and mild cathartic. (39)

Euphakin: See paraphakin. (40)

Euphorbia; Euphorbium: Euphorbium, dried latex from stem of *Euphorbia resinifera* and related *Euphorbia* species. Potent emetic, cathartic, and vesicant, used mainly as an errhine (topical nasal medication) to increase mucus discharge. (1,39) For *Euphorbium ipecacuanha*, see ipecacuanha. (39)

Euphorbia corollata: Root of flowering spurge, *Euphorbia corollata*. Diaphoretic and expectorant, cathartic and emetic with large doses, and topical vesicant. (39)

Euphorbia ipecacuanha(e): American ipecac, *Euphorbia ipecacuanhae*. See ipecacuanhae. (39)

Euphorbiae, fluidextractum: Fluid extract of euphorbia. Prepared by using diluted alcohol as the menstruum. "The change of name (formerly it was fluidextractum euphorbiae piluliferre) is, in our opinion, unfortunate as other species of Euphorbia with very different medicinal properties are used in medicine." (31)

Euphorbiae, tinctura: Simple tincture of euphorbia in alcohol, for asthma, coryza, and hay fever. (42)

Euphorbiae compositum, elixir: Compound elixir of euphorbia, antiasthmatic elixir, contains fluid extracts of euphorbia and lobelia, sodium bromide, sodium iodide and spirit of nitroglycerine. For treatment of asthma. (31)

Euphorbiae herba: Dried above-ground portion of *Euphorbia pilulifera*, of India, used locally as a decoction, infusion, or tincture for asthma. (Not same as source of euphorbium.) (42)

Euphorbiae piluliferre, fluidextractum: See euphorbiae, fluidextractum.

Euphorin: See phenylurethane. (40,42)

Euphragia; Euphrasia: Eyebright, *Euphrasia officinalis*. Leaves used for eye, ear, and respiratory disorders, measles, etc. Figure 3-101. (1,32)

Euquinine: Quinine ethyl carbonate, see cinchona. (40)

Euresol: Resorcin monoacetate, see resorcin. (40)

Europhen: Diisobutyl-ortho-cresol iodide, a disinfectant used in place of thymol. (8)

Eusol: See calcis chlorinatae et acidi borici, pulvis. (40)

Evaporating lotion: See (a)etheris composita, lotio. (34)

Everitt's salt: Potassium ferrous ferrocyanide, $K_2Fe(Fe(CN)_6)$. (24) Reducing agent, medicinal use, if any, unclear.

Exalgin; Exalginum: Methylacetanilid, methylphenyl-acetamid, a powerful analgesic and antipyretic, although used almost exclusively for pain. More toxic than acetaminophen, it has been displaced. 3,(8)

Excestrense, oleum; Exeter oil: 1. Exeter oil, liniment from various herbs, olive oil, and wine. (1) 2. Oil of elder, mixed with euphorbium, mustard, etc. (40)

Expectorant mixture; Expectorans, mistura (Stokes): A mixture of solution of ammonium acetate, vinegars of squill and ipecac, and glycerin in chloroform water, a diaphoretic and expectorant. (42) In the NF, of ammonium carbonate, fluid extracts of squill and senega, and camphorated tincture of opium. (46)

Exsiccat[a][us][um]; Exs.: Dry or dried.

Extract of apples, ferrated: See ferri pomatum, extractum and ferri pomata, tinctura. (31)

F

F.: At beginning or middle of inscription: farina (flour); fel {*Italian*} (bile); feuilles {*French*} (leaves); fiori {*Italian*}, fleurs {*French*}, flores (flowers); foglie {*Italian*}, folia (leaves). At end of inscription: fernelium (see same); fina (fine); flava, flavus, flavum (yellow); Fracastoro (see same). (1)

Faba: Bean. (1)

Faba porcina; —, suilla: Fruit of hyoscyamus. (3)

Faba purgatrix: Castor bean. (3)

Faba sancti ignatii: See St. Ignatius' bean. (40)

Fabiana: See pichi. (8)

Face seeds: See hyoscyamus. (40)

Factiti[a][us][um]: Artificial, i.e., mimicking a natural product as in artificial Carlsbad salt, see Carolinum factitium, sal.

Faecula: Starch, see amylum. (3)

Faetidae, pilulae: See foetidae, pilulae. (1)

Faex: Dregs or residue, Latin.

Faex medic(in)alis: See yeast, residue of fermentation. (40,42)

Faex sacchari: Same as treacle, i.e., molasses, residue of sugar. (40)

Faex vini: Dregs of wine, see tartar, cream of. (39)

Faexin extract: Fatty acids extracted from yeast. (40)

Faexin: Dried yeast. See yeast. Faex is Latin for dregs of wine, i.e., residual yeast from fermentation. (40)

Fagi pyroligneum, oleum: Fagi is Latin for sticks (English-faggots). This is "oil of burnt sticks", i.e., tar of beechwood sticks, see betulinum, oleum. (40)

Fahnestock's vermifuge: Mixture of castor oil, wormseed oil, anise oil, tincture of myrrh, oil of turpentine, and croton oil, for intestinal worms. (34)

Faivre's cachets: See oxyquinotheine cachets. (40)

False unicorn: See helonias. (7)

Family pills: Aperient pills, a digestive aid. (40)

Fantus' antidote: Supposed antidote for mercury poisoning, intravenous calcium sulfide. (24)

Farfara {*Italian*}; Farfaro {*Italian*}; Farfarae folia: Coltsfoot leaves, see tussilago. (1,40)

Farin[a][i]____: See ____, farina or farini if not listed below.

Farina; Farini: Flour, pulverized grain, from the Latin. Farina is the proper feminine noun, farini is often observed, but in the genitive, should be farinae.

Farina hordei praeparatus: Barley flour, steamed for about thirty hours. (3)

Farini tritici: Wheat flour, see flour, wheat. (1,8)

Farrant's solution: A microscopy slide-mounting solution of glycerin, water, arsenous acid, and gum arabic. (24)

Febrifuge salt: Potassium chloride. (This has no known action against fever.) (40)

Febrifugum, sal: Potassium acetate. (3)

Febrifugus: Febrifuge, i.e., antipyretic, to treat fever. (1)

Febris: Fever. (1)

Fecula: A fine starch, see canna. (44)

Fehling's solution: Consists of two components, a solution of copper sulfate and a solution of potassium sodium tartrate (alum), mixed at the time of use. For detection of sugar in urine, i.e., diabetes. See potassio-cupri tartratis, solutio. (24,34,42)

Fel {*Italian*};—tauri; —taurinum; Fele {*Italian*}: Ox bile. (1)

Fel bovinum; —bovis; —bovi purificatum: Fresh bile of the ox. Purified oxgall is concentrated by evaporation to one third of the original volume, dissolved in alcohol, filtered, and then evaporated to remove residual alcohol. It was used as a cholegogic purgative for constipation in which the pale color of the stool suggested inadequate bile flow. It could also be dissolved in water and given an as enema for impacted feces. (8,42)

Fel tauri inspissatum: Purified ox bile. (40)

Felis; Feles: Cat. (1)

Felix: See filix. (39)

Fellandrium: See phellandrium. (1)

Feniculum; Fenocchio {*Italian*}; Fenouil {*French*}: See foeniculum. (1)

Fenner's guaiac mixture: See antacrida, tinctura. (46)

Fenner's mixture: See mixture, dysmenorrhoea. (3)

Fenugraecum: See foenugraecum. (1)

Fer ascoli: Nuclein combined with iron. (40)

Fermentationis, oleum: Fusal or fusel oil, an oil derived from fermented matter, often grapes, primarily amyl (five carbon) alcohols. (3)

Fermenti, cataplasma: Fermenting plaster, of flour and yeast. This would naturally ferment in place, like rising bread. (39)

Fermentum: Yeast, brewer's yeast, formerly *Cerevisiae fermentum*, now *Saccharomyces cerevisiae*. (44)

Fern, ethereal extract; Fern, oleoresin of: See aspidii, oleoresina. (34)

Ferneli[anis][us], syrupus: A syrup after Fernelius, i.e., Jean Fernel, 1497–1558, physician and professor at University of Paris, author of *Universa Medica*. (1)

Ferrated extract of apples: See ferri pomatum, extractum and ferri pomata, tinctura. (31)

Ferri, emplastrum: Iron or chalybeat plaster; of ferric oxide (ferri oxidum hydratum), Burgundy pitch, lead plaster (plumbi, emplastrum), and olive oil. (8)

Ferri, pilulae: Exsiccated ferrous sulfate and sodium carbonate with gum acacia, tragacanth, syrup, and glycerin. (42)

Ferri, quininae et strychninae (phosphatum), elixir: General tonic elixir, NF, with quinine and strychnine and either ferric chloride or ferric phosphate. (45)

Ferri, quininae et strychninae (phosphatum), syrupus: A syrup of iron phosphates (see ferri phosphas solubilis), strychnine, and quinine. For treatment of iron deficiency anemia and as a tonic. (8)

Ferri, quininae et strychninae, elixir: Elixir consisting of tincture of citro-chloride of iron, quinine hydrochloride, strychnine sulfate, alcohol, and aromatic elixir. (46)

Ferri, super-carbonatis aqua: A solution of ferrous carbonate, but see discussion under ferri carbonas (praecipitatus). (39)

Ferri, tablettae: Hematinic tablet of exsiccated ferrous sulfate, sugar, and gum acacia mixed and combined in turn with a mixture of sodium bicarbonate and (see) emulsio theobromata to make a pill mass. Each pill ended up with one grain of ferrous carbonate. (42)

Ferri, trochisci: Iron troches, of ferric oxide (ferri oxidum hydratum), vanilla, sugar, and gum tragacanth. For treatment of iron deficiency anemia. (8)

Ferri, vinum: See ferri citratis, vinum. (31)

Ferri acetatis (fortior), liquor: Solution of ferric acetate, from ferric sulfate precipitated with ammonia and extracted with glacial acetic acid. The standard solution was 12.5 percent, the fortior four-fold stronger. (8)

Ferri acetatis, tinctura: Tincture of acetate of iron, of sulphate of iron in sulphuric and nitric acid, potassium acetate, and rectified spirits. Astringent and chalybeate. In the BPC, of ferric acetate and acetic acid in alcohol and water. (34,42)

Ferri albumin[as][atum]: A preparation of iron in egg albumen, supposedly better tolerated than non-protein containing iron supplements. A similar material was made from peptone or a variety of other proteins at various times. (31,42)

Ferri albuminati(s), liquor: Solution of ferric albuminate, solution of albuminized iron, albuminate of iron. Made by dissolving albuminized iron (ferri albuminatum) in an aromatic vehicle. An iron supplement. (31,42)

Ferri amara, mistura: A bitter mixture of the solution of ferric chloride and syrup in infusion of quassia, an astringent iron tonic "apt to derange digestion." (42)

Ferri amarum, vinum: Bitter wine of iron, from soluble iron and quinine citrate (see ferri et quininae citras, solubilis), tincture of sweet orange peel, syrup, and white wine. For treatment of iron deficiency anemia. (8)

Ferri ammoniata, mistura: Ammoniated iron mixture, of solution of ferric chloride and aromatic spirit of ammonia in syrup and water, more pleasant than ferri amara, mistura as it is less bitter. (42)

Ferri ammonio-citras: See ferri et ammonii citras. (40)

Ferri aromatica, mistura: Heberden's mixture, aromatic mixture of iron, of cinchona bark, calumba root, bruised cloves, and iron wire, macerated in peppermint water, to which is added tincture of orange peel and compound tincture of cardamom. A tonic and antianaemic. (34,42)

Ferri arsenas: A mixture of ferrous and ferric arsenates and some oxides. It could be used when the actions of both iron and arsenic were desirable. (8)

Ferri arsenatis, syrupus: Syrup of sodium arsenate and citrate of iron. A tonic. (34)

Ferri arsenicalis, mistura: A mixture of arsenical solution (BPC) with iron and ammonium citrate, tincture of calumba, and water, for patients needing both iron and arsenic in the form of a bitter. (42)

Ferri arsenicalis, pilulae: See ferri et arsenici, pilulae. (42)

Ferri bromidi (cum quinina(et strychnina)), syrupus: Syrup of ferric bromide, a tonic. In the BPC, of bromine, iron wire, sugar, and water. The cum quinina form, with or without powdered strychnine, also contained quinine acid hydrobromide and dilute hydrobromic acid, and was used as a hematinic and bitter. (34,42)

Ferri cacodylas: Ferric cacodylate, for anemia (iron source) and skin disorders (arsenical component). See cacodylic acid. (42)

Ferri carbonas (praecipitatis) (solubilis): See ferri rubigo. (40) Ferri rubigo, being the red oxide, makes little sense and various sources describe this as either the precipitated carbonate or the oxide. It is described as white, red, or brown, and modern literature indicates that attempts to isolate iron carbonate result in a mix of ferric and ferrous carbonates which rapidly oxidize to form iron oxides or hydroxides with release of carbon dioxide. In short, the precise chemical species represented by this term is unclear and probably variable.

Ferri carbonas effervescens: Ferrous carbonate in effervescent formulation consisting of ferrous sulfate, sodium bicarbonate, tartaric and citric acids, and refined sugar. (42)

Ferri carbonas saccharat(a)(us) (variant, caccaratus, noted): Saccharated ferrous carbonate, a powder of ferrous carbonate, ferrous sulfate, sodium bicarbonate, and sugar. For treatment of iron deficiency anemia. (8,44)

Ferri carbonatis composita, mistura: Compound mixture of ferrous or iron carbonate, of same with glucose, syrup, gum acacia, tincture of myrrh, spirit of nutmeg, and rose water, said to be more stable than mistura ferri composita. (42)

Ferri carbonatis, massa: Mass of ferrous carbonate, i.e., a pill mass, Vallet's mass, consisting of ferrous sulfate, sodium carbonate, clarified honey, and sugar, for treatment of iron deficiency anemia. (8)

Ferri carbonatis, pilulae: Ferrous carbonate pills, of ferrous sulphate, potassium carbonate, sugar, tragacanth, althaea, glycerin, and water. Ferruginous, Chalybate, Griffith's or Blaud's pills. In the BPC, of iron carbonate with licorice root powder and syrup. For treatment of iron deficiency anemia. (8,42)

Ferri carbonatis, tablettae: Tablet of iron carbonate, glucose, starch, liquid glucose, water, and ethereal solution of theobroma. For anemia. (42)

Ferri chloridi aetherea, tinctura: Ethereal tincture of ferric chloride, Bestuscheff's tincture, Lamotte's drops, from solution of ferric chloride (ferri chloridum), ether, and alcohol. Used as chalybeate, i.e., iron supplement. (31)

Ferri chloridi, liquor; —, tinctura: The liquor was a ferric chloride solution of approximately 37.8 percent made directly as per ferri chloridum, not from dissolution of the solid. The tincture was an alcoholic solution of approximately 25% concentration, from dissolution of the salt in alcohol. (8)

Ferri chloridum: Ferric chloride, $FeCl_3$, by action of hydrochloric acid on iron, addition of nitric acid (to oxidize iron from ferrous to ferric state), and precipitation. Generally used as a topical astringent, including for gastro-intestinal bleeding. Too irritating for use in treatment of anemia. (8)

Ferri citras: Ferric citrate (crystalline), from evaporation of the solution. For treatment of iron deficiency anemia. (8)

Ferri citrates, vinum: Wine of iron citrate, vinum ferri, wine of iron, vinum chalybeatum. Of iron and ammonium citrate in orange wine (vinum aurantii), shaken occasionally for three days and filtered. (31) Alternately of iron and ammonium citrate (ferri et ammonii citras), tincture of sweet orange peel, syrup, and white wine. (8)

Ferri citratis, liquor: Solution of ferric citrate, from ferric sulfate precipitated with ammonia and extracted with citric acid. (8)

Ferri citro-arsenias ammoniatus: Ammoniated citro-arsenate of iron, water soluble greenish crystals used as an iron source, an antiperiodic for malaria, and as a general source of iron or arsenic when desired by injection. (42)

Ferri citro-chloridi, tinctura: Tincture of ferric citro-chloride, tasteless tincture of ferric chloride, tasteless tincture of iron, made of the solution of ferric chloride with sodium citrate, alcohol and water. Used as a chalybeate. (31)

Ferri citro-iodidi, syrupus: Syrup of iron citro-iodide, tasteless syrup of iodide of iron. Of iodine, iron wire, potassium citrate, sugar, and distilled water. (34,46)

Ferri composita(e), pilula; Ferri co., pil.: 1. Compound pills of iron, of myrrh, sodium carbonate, iron sulphate, and syrup. This was specified in the USP of 1880. 2). Compound pills of iron, or emmenogogue pills, of Vallet's carbonate of iron, resin of podophylum, and white turpentine. An emmenogogue, per King's of 1905, "not to be confounded with" pills of the same name specified in the USP of 1880. (34) See ferri cum myrrha, piluli. (40) In the NF, of myrrh, sodium carbonate, sulfate of iron, and syrup. (46)

Ferri composita, mistura: Compound mixture of iron, ferrous sulphate, potassium carbonate, myrrh, sugar, spirit of lavender, and rose water. It is a dark green solution containing a mixture of iron sulfate and carbonate. Griffith's mixture. For treatment of iron deficiency anemia. (8)

Ferri cum myrrha, piluli: Iron and myrrh pill, of iron sulfate, myrrh, sodium carbonate, and sugar. (39)

Ferri dialysatis, liquor: A solution of ferric chloride and ammonia in water, as an iron source. For dialyzed iron, see ferrum dialysatum. (42)

Ferri et ammonii acetatis, liquor: Solution of iron and ammonium acetate, Basham's mixture. (8)

Ferri et ammonii citras (viridis): Iron and ammonium citrate scales formed from solution of ferric citrate and ammonia. For treatment of iron deficiency anemia. The green form (viridis) has more citrate and less ammonia, resulting in a greenish color. (8)

Ferri et ammonii citras effervescens: Effervescent formulation of iron and ammonium citrates in sodium bicarbonate, tartaric and citric acids, and refined sugar. (42)

Ferri et ammonii sulphas: Ferric ammonium sulfate, ammonio-ferric sulfate, ammonio-ferric alum, $Fe_2(NH_4)_2(SO4)_4$, from precipitation of ferric sulfate in ammonia. For treatment of iron deficiency anemia. (8)

Ferri et ammonii tartras: Iron and ammonium tartrate, scales formed from precipitate of ferric sulfate with ammonia dissolved with tartaric acid. For treatment of iron deficiency anemia. (8)

Ferri et arsenici, pilulae: Exsiccated ferrous sulfate and arsenous acid (arsenic trioxide), milk sugar and syrup. (42)

Ferri et magnesi sulphas, mistura: A mixture of solution of ferric chloride, magnesium sulfate, and glycerin in infusion of quassia, a "chalybeate aperient." (42)

Ferri et mangani iodidi, syrupus: Syrup of iron and manganese, of iron wire, manganese sulfate, potassium iodide, and sugar. A tonic. (34)

Ferri et potassii tartras: Iron and potassium tartrate, potassio-ferric tartrate, a solution of iron and potassium tartrate from ammonia, ferric sulphate, and potassium bitartrate. For treatment of iron deficiency anemia. (8)

Ferri et quininae (et strychninae) citra(ti)s (solubilis) (effervescens): Iron and quinine citrate, crystallized from solution of ferric citrate (ferri citras), quinine, and citric acid. Optionally formulated with strychnine. Soluble form is similar, but solution also contains ammonia. An effervescent version was specified in the BPC and NF. For treatment of iron deficiency anemia. (8)

Ferri et quininae compositae, piluli: Compound tablets of iron sulfate and quinine sulfate, quadruplex pills. In the NF, with purified aloes and extracts of nux vomica and gentian. (34)

Ferri et quininae et strychninae phosphatum, glycerinum: Glycerite of soluble iron phosphate, quinine, strychnine, and phosphoric acid with glycerin and water, a stimulant tonic. (42)

Ferri et strychninae citras: Iron and strychnine citrate, scales formed from solution of iron and ammonium citrate (ferri et ammonii citras), citric acid, strychnine, and water. (8)

Ferri ferrocyanidi compositae, pilulae: Compound pills of iron ferrocyanide (iron hexacyanoferrate, i.e., Prussian blue) with quinine sulphate, and extract of black cohosh. A tonic and alterative for "all diseases attended by periodicity" (intermittent fever), epilepsy, chorea, etc. (34)

Ferri ferrocyanidum; Ferri ferrocyanuretum: Iron ferrocyanide (iron hexacyanoferrate), i.e., Prussian blue. Tonic, febrifuge, and alterative. (39)

Ferri filum: Iron wire. (40)

Ferri formas: Iron (ferric) formate. An alternative salt for iron supplementation. (42)

Ferri glycerophosphas: Glycerophosphate of iron, a yellow powder, for neurasthenia and anemia. (42)

Ferri hydrogenio reductum; Ferr. hydrog. red.: See ferrum reductum.

Ferri hypophosphis: Iron hypophosphite, $Fe_2(PH_2O_2)_6$, from the reaction of ferric chloride with sodium hypophosphite. (8)

Ferri hypophosphitis (fortis), liquor: A solution of ferric sulfate, ammonia, citric acid, sodium hypophosphite, sodium citrate, and a small amount of chloroform. Used primarily to prepare syrups of hypophosphites. (42) In the NF, from iron and ammonium sulfate crystals, sodium hypophosphite, potassium citrate, glycerin, and water. (46)

Ferri hypophosphitis, elixir: NF elixir of iron hypophosphite, of the solution of same plus aromatic elixir. Alterative and hematinic. (45,46)

Ferri hypophosphitis, syrupus: Solution of ferric hypophosphite in simple syrup, with (NF) potassium citrate and orange flower water, iron supplement for children. (42)

Ferri iodidi (fortis), liquor: A solution of iron (from wire), iodine, diluted hypophosphorous acid, and water, used as stock solution to prepare syrupus ferri iodidi. (42,46)

Ferri iodidi, pilulae: Pills of ferrous iodide, from trituration of iron and iodine, followed by addition of glycyrrhiza, extract of glycyrrhiza, acacia, balsam of tolu, and ether, evaporated to a pill mass. Needed to be protected from light as they did not store well. For treatment of iron deficiency anemia. (8) In the BPC, iron wire, iodine, and licorice in refined sugar and distilled water. (42)

Ferri iodidi, syrupus: Syrup of ferrous iodide, from iron wire, iodine, sugar, and water. Primarily astringent or for iron deficiency. (8)

Ferri iodidum saccharatum: Saccharated ferrous iodide, from iron wire, reduced iron (ferrum reductum), distilled water, and milk sugar (lactose), triturated and reduced to a powder. For treatment of iron deficiency anemia. (8)

Ferri iodidum: Ferric iodide, FeI_2. (42)

Ferri lactas: Ferrous lactate, from action of lactic acid on metallic iron. For treatment of iron deficiency anemia. (8)

Ferri lactatis, elixir: NF elixir of iron lactate, potassium citrate, and aromatic elixir. Alterative and hematinic. (45)

Ferri lactophosphatis, syrupus: Syrup of iron lactate and phosphoric acid. A tonic. (34)

Ferri limatura praeparata: Prepared iron filings, same as ferri rubigo, i.e., rust or iron oxide. (39)

Ferri limatura purificata: Iron filings, "purified" by drawing through gauze using a magnet. (39)

Ferri malascrudus; Ferri malatis crudi, tinctura: See ferri pomatum, extractum and ferri pomata, tinctura, respectively. (31)

Ferri muriatis, tinctura; Fer.mur., tr.: See ferri chloridi, tinctura. (34)

Ferri nitra(ti)s, liquor: Solution of ferric nitrate, $Fe_2(NO_3)_6$, by precipitation of ferric sulfate with ammonia, followed by treatment with nitric acid. Generally used as a topical astringent, including for gastrointestinal bleeding. Too irritating for use in treatment of anemia. (8,44)

Ferri oxidati solubilis, syrupus; Ferri saccharati solubilis, syrupus: Syrup of saccharated iron, of iron chloride, soda, and sugar in water. (34)

Ferri oxidum (praecipitatum) rubrum: Red iron oxide (precipitated). See ferri rubigo. (40)

Ferri oxidum (precipitatum) fuscum: See ferric oxide. (40)

Ferri oxidum calcinatum: Red iron oxide, calcined (heated to drive off water). See ferri rubigo. (40)

Ferri oxidum hydratum cum magnesia: Ferric hydrate with magnesia, arsenic antidote. Ferric hydrate and magnesia were kept in separate bottles and mixed immediately before use. Said to be an effective antidote for arsenic poisoning, although there is no reason to believe it would be specifically effective for that condition. (8)

Ferri oxidum hydratum: Ferric hydrate, ferric oxide, hydrated ferric oxide, $Fe_2(OH)_6$, from precipitation of ferric sulfate with ammonia. (8)

Ferri oxidum magneticum: Magnetic iron oxide, the black oxide of iron, aethiops martialis. (42)

Ferri oxidum nigrum: Black iron oxide, purified filings powdered to a black material, probably a mixed metallic and oxide state. (39)

Ferri oxidum saccharatum: Saccharated ferric oxide, soluble ferric oxide, ferrum oxydatum saccharatum. Freshly precipitated ferric hydroxide is dissolved in a heavy sugar syrup by addition of sodium hydroxide, evaporated, and sugar added to obtain desired weight. (31)

Ferri oxychlorati, liquor; Ferri oxychloridi, liquor: Dialyzed iron, see ferrum dialysatum. (3)

Ferri oxydati solubilis, syrupus: See ferri saccharati solubilis, syrupus. (31)

Ferri oxysulphatis, liquor: Solution of iron sulfate, nitric acid, and water. (46)

Ferri peptonas; —peptonatum; Ferri peptonati(s) (et mangani) (cum mangano), liquor: Solution of peptonized iron, made from pepsin, fresh egg albumen, hydrochloric acid, solution of ferric oxychloride, alcohol, and sodium citrate in a pleasantly flavored preparation with oil of orange, acetic ether, and vanillin, using glycerin, syrup, and distilled water. May be made with or without addition of soluble manganese citrate. An iron supplement. (31,42)

Ferri perchlorate, liquor; Ferri perchloridi (fortis), liquor; Ferri perch. liq.; Ferri perchloridi, tinctura: Liquor (solution) of ferric perchlorate. A styptic. The BPC had a four-fold stronger (fortis) solution as well. (29,40,42)

Ferri perchloridi, gossypium: Absorbent and styptic cotton soaked in ferric chloride solution and dried. (42)

Ferri perchloridi, tinctura; Ferri perchlorate tinct.: Tincture of ferric perchlorate. (29)

Ferri perchloridum: Ferric perchloride, Fe_2Cl_6. (42)

Ferri pernitras; Ferri pernitratis, liquor: Ferric nitrate or the solution of same, as an iron source. (42)

Ferri peroxidum (humidum); Ferri peroxidum hydratum: Ferric oxide. The oxide and hydroxide can be readily interconverted by hydration. (40)

Ferri persulphatis; Ferri persulphat; Ferri persulph., liquor: Iron persulfate or the solution of same. In modern use, probably $FeSO_5$. Older preparations were characterized by sulfur in an apparently higher oxidation state than sulfate (SO_4), either $FeSO_5$ or FeS_2O_8, in which the oxidation state of sulfur is unchanged, but one or more oxygens is replaced with a peroxide (-O-O-) group. (29,42)

Ferri phosphas (solubilis)(saccharatus): Soluble ferric phosphate, scales formed by evaporation of a mixture of ferric citrate and sodium phosphate. (8)

Ferri phosphatis compositus, syrupus: Compound syrup of ferrous phosphate, Parrish's syrup, or chemical food. Of iron wire reacted with concentrated phosphoric acid, calcium carbonate, potassium bicarbonate, sodium phosphate, cochineal, sugar, and orange flower water in water. Iron supplement for debilitated children with anemia, rickets, or tuberculous bone disease. (42)

Ferri phosphatis cum quinina et strychnina, pilulae: Ferrous phosphate, quinine, and strychnine with milk sugar, formed using concentrated phosphoric acid for liquid to bind. (42)

Ferri phosphatis effervescens, pulvis: Effervescent powder of phosphate of iron, saccharated sodium bicarbonate, and saccharated tartaric acid. Iron supplement. (46)

Ferri phosphatis et quinina et strychnina, pilulae: See ferri phosphatis cum quinina et strychnina, pilulae. (42)

Ferri phosphatis, cinchonidinae et strychninae, elixir: Elixir of phosphate of iron, potassium citrate, cinchonidine sulphate, strychnine sulphate, alcohol, water, and aromatic elixir. (46)

Ferri phosphatis, elixir: NF elixir of ferric phosphate, water, and aromatic elixir. Nerve tonic and hematinic. (45)

Ferri phosphatus [et][cum] quininae (et strychninae), elixir; Ferri Phos et. Q(u). (et S.): See ferri, quininae et strychninae phosphatum, syrupus. (34)

Ferri phosphatus, liquor; —, syrupus: Syrup of iron phosphate, of iron sulphate, sodium bicarbonate, concentrated phosphoric acid, sugar, and water. A tonic. Prepared from the more concentrated liquor. The latter produced by reaction of iron wire with phosphoric acid. (34,42)

Ferri phosphorici cum chinino et strichnino {Italian}: See ferri, quininae et strychninae phosphatum, syrupus. (34)

Ferri pomata, tinctura: Tincture of ferrated extract of apples, tincture of crude malate of iron, tinctura ferri malatis crudis. This tincture is made from ferrated extract of apples (ferri pomatum, extractum), alcohol, and cinnamon water. Used as a chalybeate. (31)

Ferri pomatum (fluidum), extractum: Ferrated extract of apples, ferri malascrudus, crude malate of iron, made from iron wire, fresh apple juice and water, and is used as a chalybeate (iron supplement). The apple (*malus*) serves as a source of malic and other organic acids, solubilizing the iron. (31,46)

Ferri potassio-tartras: See ferrum tartaratum. (40)

Ferri protochloridi, syrupus; —, liquor: Syrup of the "protochloride" of iron, i.e., ferrous chloride, with glycerin and orange water. (34) The NF specified a solution made with iron wire reacted with hydrochloric acid, from which ferric chloride crystals were isolated, followed by addition of glycerin, water, and diluted hypophosphorous acid. (46)

Ferri protosulphureticum: See ferri sulphureticum. (44)

Ferri pulvis: Iron powder, i.e., reduced (metallic) iron. (40)

Ferri pyrophosphas (solubilis): Iron pyrophosphate, $Fe_4(P_2O_7)_3$. Soluble ferric pyrophosphate, scales formed from solution of ferric citrate, and sodium pyro-phosphate. For treatment of iron deficiency anemia. (8,42)

Ferri pyrophosphatis, elixir: NF elixir of ferric pyrophosphate and aromatic elixir. Nerve tonic and hematinic. (4,465)

Ferri pyrophosphatis, quininae (et strychninae), elixir; —, syrup; Ferri Pyrophos. et Q (et S): Elixir ferric pyrophosphate, quinine (and strychnine), differs from the formerly official elixir of iron, quinine, and strychnine phosphates in containing soluble ferric pyrophosphate instead of phosphate, while the quinine in the former elixir is replaced by quinine sulphate. Also prepared as a syrup. (31,34)

Ferri pyrophosphatis, syrupus: Soluble pyrophosphate of iron in syrup, a tonic. (34)

Ferri quinini et arnesii, elixir; F. q. et ars., el.: The full inscription has not been located, only the abbreviated form. This appears to be a modified elixir of iron and quinine tonic, to which arsenic has been added.

Ferri ramenta: Iron filings, same as ferri limatura purificata. (39)

Ferri rubigo: Red iron oxide, i.e., rust. (39)

Ferri saccharati solubilis, syrupus: Syrup of soluble saccharated iron, syrupus ferri oxydati solubilie, syrup of saccharated oxide of iron, or syrup of soluble oxide of iron. It is made from saccharated iron (ferri carbonas saccharatus), distilled water and syrup. In the NF, of the solution of iron chloride, soda, solution of soda, sugar, water, and syrup. (31,46)

Ferri salicylatis, liquor: Solution of ferric salicylate, of sodium salicylate, tincture of ferric citro-chloride, ammonium carbonate, citric acid, methyl salicylate, glycerin, and distilled water. For cases of chronic rheumatism, especially if complicated with anemia. (31)

Ferri scobs: Iron filings. *Scobis* is Latin for sawdust or filings, but the literature consistently uses the apparent corruption, scobs. (3)

Ferri sesquichloridi, tinctura: See ferri chloridi, tinctura. (34) See ferri perchloridi, tinctura. (40)

Ferri sesquioxidum (solubile): See ferri oxidum rubrum. (40)

Ferri subcarb.; —subcarbonate; —subcarbonas: Irregular name for ferric hydroxide, not related to carbonate ion. See ferric hydroxide. See discussion under ferri carbonas (praecipitatus). (29) Red iron oxide (see ferri oxidum rubrum). (40)

Ferri subcarbonatis, trochisci: Lozenge of iron carbonate, sugar, and vanilla with gum tragacanth. (44)

Ferri subchloridi, syrupus: Syrup of ferrous chloride, of iron wire reacted with hydrochloric acid, citric acid, water, and simple syrup. Iron supplement. (42)

Ferri subsulphatis, liquor: A poorly characterized solution of ferrous sulfate partially oxidized with nitric acid to the ferric state, Monsel's solution. The formulation was variable in composition. Generally used as a topical astringent, including for gastrointestinal bleeding. Too irritating for use in treatment of anemia. (8)

Ferri sulph c.p.: Probably ferric sulfate, commercially purified, see C.P.

Ferri sulphas, (exsiccat[a][us]) (granulat[a][us]): Ferrous sulfate, $FeSO_4$, or green vitriol, from action of sulfuric acid on iron. Used as an iron supplement, but also in preparation of numerous other iron compounds. May be dried (exsiccatus) or granulated (granulatus). For treatment of iron deficiency anemia or as an astringent. (8)

Ferri sulphureticum: Sulphuret or protosulphuret of iron, from reaction of iron and sublimed sulfur. For production of "sulphuret of hydrogen," or hydrogen sulfide. (44)

Ferri tersulphatas, liquor: Solution of ferric sulfate, $FeSO_4$, by boiling of ferrous sulfate in sulfuric and nitric acid. (8)

Ferri valerianas: See valeriana. (8)

Ferri valerianatis compositae, pilulae: Pills of iron, quinine, and zinc valerianates formed with milk sugar and syrup. (42)

Ferric alum: See ammonii ferri, alum.

Ferric chloride, basic solution of: See ferri oxychloridi, liquor. (40)

Ferric hydroxide: $Fe(OH)_2$, also called (incorrectly) ferric subcarbonate in some sources.

Ferric oxide, saccharated; Ferric oxide, soluble: See ferri oxidum saccharatum. (31)

Ferric oxyhydrate: See ferric oxide. (40)

Ferrier's snuff: See bismuthi et morphinae, insufflatio. (42)

Ferro-alumen: See ferri et ammonii sulphas. (40)

Ferro pagliari: Solution of ferrous chloride. (3)

Ferrochloride of ammonia: Ferric ammonium chloride. (40)

Ferrocitrate of ammonia: See ferri et ammonii citras. (40)

Ferrocyanide: See Prussate.

Ferropyrin: Antipyrine (analgesic) with ferric chloride. (40)

Ferroso-ferric oxide: See ferric oxide. (40)

Ferruginous pills: See ferri carbonatis, pilulae. (8)

Ferrugo: Iron rust. (3)

Ferrum: Iron. Iron has long been associated with the treatment of anemia, which is often the result of iron deficiency. These solutions are also astringent, particularly the chloride and nitrate. Iron commonly occurs in two different oxidation states, the 2+ (ferrous) and 3+ (ferric) form.

Ferrum (rubrum) praecipitatum, tinctura: Tincture of (red) iron rust, a tonic. (39)

Ferrum alcoholisatum: Finely powdered iron (not same as reduced iron). (3)

Ferrum ammoniatum; —ammoniacale: Ammoniated iron, actually the product of ammonium chloride and iron, i.e., ferric chloride, an aperient, antihysteric, and tonic. (39) Ferric ammonium chloride. (40)

Ferrum dialysatum: A precipitated ferric hydrate, further purified by dialysis in pure water. It is used as a treatment for arsenic poisoning, not for iron supplementation. (8)

Ferrum limatum: Iron filings. (3)

Ferrum oxydatum saccharatum: See ferri oxidum saccharatum. (31)

Ferrum pomatum: Iron malate. (3)

Ferrum pulveratum: Powdered iron (metal).

Ferrum reductum; —redactum: A preparation of iron oxide treated with hydrogen gas and heat, it consists of variable amounts of the oxide and the metallic (reduced) form. Used to make pilulae ferri iodidi and ferri iodidum saccharatum. (8,29)

Ferrum tartaratum; —tartarisatum; —tartarizatum: Iron tartrate, a tonic. See ferri et potassii tartras. (39,40)

Ferrum vitriolatum (exsiccatum): Vitriolated iron (dried), i.e., iron reacted with sulfuric acid, iron sulfate, which may be dried using heat. (39)

Ferula asafoetida; —persica; —tingitana: See asafoetida, sagapenum, and silphium, respectively. (39)

Fetid tincture; —powder; —pill: A formulation whose primary ingredient was asafoetida. (39)

Fetidae, pilulae: See foetidae, pilulae. (1)

Fetron salve: three to five percent anilide of stearic acid in petrolatum. (24)

Feuille {*French*}: Leaf. (1)

Fever drops: See cinchonae composita, tinctura. (40)

Fever root: See triosteum. (39)

Fibrolysin: Thiosinamine-sodium salicylate, a febrifuge. (40)

Ficorum, syrupus: Syrup of cut figs and sugar in water, strained. A laxative for children. (42)

Ficorum compositus, syrupus; Ficorum, elixir: Compound syrup of figs. "This unfortunately named syrup is prepared from figs, fluid extract of senna, aromatic fluidglycerate of cascara sagrada, oil of fennel (foeniculi, oleum), spirit of peppermint, sugar, and water." A laxative. (31) In the BPC, of compound tincture of rhubarb, liquid extract of senna pod, spirits of cinnamon and nutmeg, and tasteless extract of cascara sagrada in syrup. (42)

Ficus (carica): Fig, the fruit of *Ficus carica*, used whole as a mild laxative. Figure 3-102. (1,8,39)

Fiddle gum: Same as tragacanth. (40)

Fiel {*French*}; **Fiele** {*Italian*}: Gall, bile. (1)

Fieno greco {*Italian*}: See foenugraecum. (1)

Fife; Fife's snuff: White snuff, a menthol and cocaine snuff. (40).

Fig: See ficus. (8)

Figwort: See scrophularia. (32)

Filicis liquidum extractum: See filicis maris, oleum.

Filicis maris, oleum; —, oleoresinae: Liquid extract of filix mas. (40,44)

Filicis; Filicis maris: See aspidium and associated listings (aspidii), a partial botanical name for *Aspidium filicis maris*. (34)

Fig. 3-102 Ficus or fig.

Filix (mas): Male fern, *Dryopteris (or polypodium) filix-mas*, figure 3-103. See aspidium and also see polypodium and associated figure 3-199. (1) Note the genitive form, filicis maris.

Filix foemina, asplenium: Female fern. Various fern species, substituted for male fern. Unofficial. (44)

Filonium; Filonio {*Italian*}: See philonium. (1)

Filosofi, olio de {*Italian*}: See philosophorum, oleum. (1)

Fin[a][um][us]; Fino {*Italian*}: Fine or choice. (1)

Finnocchio {*Italian*}: See foeniculum. (1)

Fiore {*Italian*}: Flower. (1)

Fiovarenti, baume de: Balm after Leonardo Fiovarenti, Bologna, ca. 1650; a tincture of canella, cloves, nutmeg, ginger, and multiple other ingredients, as a cure for arsenic poisoning. (39)

Fir tree (oil): See pini sylvestris and pini sylvestris, oleum. (8)

Fir wool oil: See pini sylvestris, oleum. (40)

Fish berry: See cocculus. (7)

Fistula armata: Enema apparatus, a clyster syringe. (40)

Fixed air: Carbon dioxide. (3)

Fixed nitre: Potassium carbonate, see potasii carbonas. (40)

Fixed vegetable alkali: Lixivia, potassium carbonate. (39)

Fl. ext.: Fluid extract. See primary substance, i.e., _____ extractum, fluidum.

Flake lead; —white: Lead carbonate. (3)

Flamula jovis: Leaves of the virgin's bower, *Clematis vatalba*. A vesicant and, internally, a highly dangerous tonic. (39) See also clematis.

Flav[a][us][um]: Yellow (Latin). (1)

Flava, aqua; Flava, lotio: Yellow lotion, yellow wash, aqua phagedrenica flava, of corrosive mercuric chloride in lime (calcium oxide) water, the mercury being present as a yellow hydroxide. It is used externally in skin diseases. (3,31)

Flava, resina: Rosin (colophony). (3)

Flavine: See acriflavine. (40)

Flavum praecipitatum: Yellow precipitate, specifically mercury sulfate (hydrargyrus vitriolatus). (39)

Flax, purging: See linum catharticum. (39)

Flax, toad: See linaria. (39)

Flax seed: See linum. (8)

Fldext.: See fluidextract

Fldglyc.: A fluidglycerite, generally see _____, fluidglyceritum.

Flea seeds: Seeds of Nigella. (3)

Flea wort: Psyllium seeds, used in chronic constipation. See psyllium. (3,39)

Fleeming's tincture; Fleming's tincture (of aconite): See aconiti, tinctura. (42) A formulation of aconitum with nearly twice the strength of the official USP formulation. (8)

Flesh liquor: Lard. (40)

Flor.: Usually an abbreviation flora / florae, i.e., flowers. Note that in relation to the iris, it is an abbreviation for Florentina, i.e., the Florentine iris. See Iris.

Florae; Flores; Fleurs {*French*}: Flowers, either botanical or chemical, the latter being a substance obtained by sublimation or crystallization, as in flowers of sulfur. (1)

Florence oil: Olive oil imported from Leghorn, Italy. (3,40)

Flores martiales: Flowers of iron, ammonio-chloride of iron, i.e., ferric ammonium chloride. (40)

Flores salis ammoniaci martiales: Ammonio-chloride of iron, i.e., ferric ammonium chloride. (40)

Flores sulphuris: See flowers of sulphur. (39)

Florum omnium, aqua: Water of all flowers, efficiently produced by grazing cows, this was cow urine. One must suspect that the true nature of this material was rarely, if ever, disclosed to the patient. Used orally for intestinal disorders and topically for skin disorders. (39)

Flos: Flower (Latin singular), plural flores. (1)

Flos aeruginis: Copper acetate. (3)

Flos cordialum: Flower of cordials, a superior cordial whose composition was probably variable, but now unknown. (39)

Flos salis: Sodium subcarbonate. (3)

Flour (, wheat): Wheat flour, used to produce bread for bread crumbs (mica panis) to make pills and cataplasmata. (8) If unspecified, flour is generally wheat flour.

Flower de Luce: See iris pseudacorus. (39)

Flowers of antimony: Oxide of antimony. (3)

Flowers of arsenic: Arsenous anhydride, white oxide of arsenic, see arsenium album. (40)

Flowers of benjamin; Flowers of benzoin: See benzoic acid. (3,40)

Flowers of brimstone; Flowers of sulphur: Sublimed sulfur, see sulphur sublimatum. (8,40)

Flowers of zinc: Oxide of zinc. (3)

Fluidextract; Fluidextractum: Fluidextract, i.e., fluid extract (pl.— fluidextracta). Generally listed as _____, fluidum, extractum. The fused term, fluidextract, tended to be used later, especially in the US National Formulary. (31)

Fluoric acid: Hydrofluoric acid. (40) For etching glass, not therapeutic.

Fluorol: Sodium fluoride. (3)

Fluorspar; Fluor spar: Calcium fluoride. (3)

Fluvialis, aqua: River water. (3)

Fly agaric: See muscarine. (32)

Fly blister: See cantharidis, emplastrum. (40)

Fly stone: Mercuric chloride in lump form, see hydrargyri chloridum corrosivum. (40)

Fly trap (, Venus): See melilotus. (32)

Flystone: A mixture of cobalt and arsenic. (3)

Foeniculi pv. s.; Foeniculi semen pulv.: Powdered fennel seed.

Foeniculum (fructis); Fennel; Foeniculi, oleum; Foeniculi, aqua: Fennel, the fruit of *Foeniculum capillaceum*, from which an oil is distilled. Water of fennel consists of the oil triturated into water. Use is as per anise or coriander and other typical volatile oils (see caryophyllus). (1,8)

Foeniculum dulce: Seed and root from sweet fennel, *Anethum foeniculum*, or *Foeniculum vulgare*, aromatic, carminative, expectorant, resolvent and lactogogue. Figure 3-104. (39)

Polypodium Filix mas   *Published by Dr Woodville Oct. 1. 1790.*

Fig. 3-103 Filix mas or male fern.

Foenum graecum (semina); Foenugraecum: Fenugreek, *Trigonella foenum graecum.* Seeds used. Figure 3-105. (1,33)

Foetida antihysterica, aqua: A distillate from asafetida, galbanum, myrrh, valerian, etc. (3)

Foetidae, pilulae: "Stinking pill," a pill of gum asafoetida and eighteen or so other ingredients. (1,39)

Fold sheet: See gutta percha tissue. (40)

Folium; Foliae; Foglia {*Italian*}**; FOL.; Fol.:** Leaf or leaves. (1)

Fontana, aqua: Spring water. (3)

Fonticulos, emplastrum ad: "Plaster for the small fountain," an apt pseudonym for the aphrodesiac, Spanish fly. See cantharides, unguentum. Applied topically as a sparadrapum, i.e., on a cloth backing. (39)

Food of the gods: Asafetida. (40)

Food, chemical: See phosphatum compositus, syrupus. (31)

Fool's gold: Pyrites, iron pyrite. (3)

Forbes' emulsion (of oil of turpentine): See terebinthinae, olei fortior, emulsio. (46)

Ford's laudanum: See opii, vinum. (40)

Formal: Formaldehyde. (40)

Formaldehydi, liquor: A solution of formaldehyde (BPC), about thirty-seven percent, to be diluted and used as a disinfectant. (42)

Formaldehydi, nebula: A nebulized solution of dilute formaldehyde. This appears to have been an attempt to use formaldehyde as a disinfectant to treat tuberculosis. (40)

Formaldehydum cresolatum: Cresolated formaldehyde, a mixture of orthocresol (see cresol) with formaldehyde, used as a disinfectant. (31)

Formaldehydum polymerisatum: See paraformaldehyde. (40)

Formalith: A commercial formaldehyde solution. (40)

Formamina; Formamine: See hexaminium. (40,42)

Formamol: Hexamine-methylene citrate, supposedly liberated formaldehyde in the blood to help solubilize uric acid, i.e., for gout. (40)

Formamylum: An iodinated amyl alcohol, used as a disinfectant. (40)

Formatum, elixir: Elixir of formates, of sodium and potassium formate in simple elixir. Said to be a pleasant means to give formates, although the purpose of doing so is not clearly described. (42)

Formatum et strychnina, elixir: Elixir of formates with strychnine, of calcium and potassium formate with strychnine in simple elixir. A muscular tonic and stimulant. (42)

Formic acid; Formicum, acidi: Formic acid. (33) Formic acid (the one carbon organic acid, H-COOH) was first discovered in the venom of stinging ants, genus *Formicae*, hence both the name of the acid and odd name, spirit of ants.

Formic aldehyde: Formaldehyde, CH_2O. (40)

Formicae cum acervo: A distillate of ants (see historical note, formic acid) in water, i.e., a solution of formic acid, used as an aphrodesiac. (39)

Formicarium, oleum: This is a formulation of ants in oil used to treat skin conditions. See formic acid for explanation.

Formicarium, spiritus; Formicar., spir.: Spirit of formicarium, literally, spirit of ants. See formic acid. (31)

Formici, acidi, spiritus: Spirit of formic acid, spiritus formicarum; spirit of ants (see formic acid), containing four percent formic acid in alcohol and distilled water. A powerful disinfectant. (31)

Formin: See hexaminium. (40)

Formochlorol: A commercial saturated formaldehyde solution. (40)

Formol: Formaldehyde. (3)

Formyl tribromide: See bromoform. (40)

Formylum chloratum: Chloroform. (3)

Forte; Fortior: Strong, fortified.

Fosselline: Similar to petrolatum, i.e.-vaseline. (3)

Fossil alkali: Sodium carbonate. (3)

Fossil flour: See kieselguhr. (3)

Fossil salt: Rock salt, i.e., sodium chloride. (40)

Fossil wax: Crude paraffin. (3)

Fossilis, sal: Rock salt, i.e., sodium chloride. (3,39)

Fothergill's cough mixture: See scillae, mistura. (42)

Fothergill's pills: A pill of calomel, digitalis, and squill, for heart disorders and dropsy. (24)

Fousel: See fusal oil. (40)

Fowler's solution: See potassii arsenitis, liquor. (8)

Foxglove: See digitalis. (8)

Frac.: (*abr Lat.*)**:** 1. Fractura, i.e., fractured or broken. 2. See Fracastoro. (1)

Fracastoro; Fracastorius: Girolamo Fracastoro, 1484-1553, Italian physician, biologist, physicist, and astronomer, investigator of syphilis and other contagious diseases, and originator of diascordium, an electuary believed to be a panacea. (1)

Fragaria: Wild strawberry, *Fragaria vesca.* Roots, leaves, fruit used. (1)

Fig. 3-104 *Foeniculum dulce* or sweet fennel.

Fig. 3-105 *Foenum graecum* or fenugreek.

Francis' (triplex) pills: A variant of triplex pills, of aloe, scammony, mercury pill mass (hydrargyri, massa), croton oil, oil of caraway, and tincture of aloes with myrrh. (46)

Frangula (cortex); Frangulae fluidum, extractum; Frangula bark: Bark of the buckthorn, *Rhamnus frangula*, collected at least one year before use, or the fluid extract thereof. The fresh bark is said to be a "violent gastro-intestinal irritant," but the aged bark produces a laxative effect which is mild and is recommended in children. (8,40)

Frangulae, elixir: Elixir of buckthorn, of the fluid extract with alcohol, compound elixir of taraxacum, and aromatic elixir. Laxative. (45)

Frangulae liquidum, extractum: See rhamni frangulae liquidum, extractum. (42)

Frankenia: Yerba reuma, *Frankenia grandifolia*, an astringent, for intestinal and genitourinary disorders. (33)

Frankfurt pill: A cathartic of rhubarb and aloe, after the German, J.H. Beyer, 1600s. See angelicae, pillulae. (39)

Frankincense: American usage, a concrete, turpentine-scented material scraped off the frankincense pine, *Pinus toeda* or *P. australis*. For European or ancient frankincense, see olibanum. Used as other resins (see resina). (8)

Frankincense plaster: See ferri emplastrum. (40)

Frankincense, common: Resinous oil from *Thus americanum*, not a substitute for true frankincense, which is a solid resinous material. (40) Formulations may be listed as "thus" or use the irregular genitive form, "thuris."

Frasera: American Columbo, *Frasera canadensis* or *F. walterii*, a stomachic. (32)

Fraude reagent: Perchloric acid, analytical reagent used to test for alkaloids, producing a red color. (3)

Fraxini (Americanae), vinum: Wine of white ash, of white ash bark in stronger white wine (vinum album fortior). (34)

Fraxinus; Frassino {*Italian*}: Ash tree. Bark, leaves, seeds used. Figure 3-106. (1)

Freezing salt: Calcium chloride or crude sodium chloride, rock salt, i.e., as used for making ice cream. A sundry item. (3,40).

French brandy: See vini gallici. (34)

French chalk: See talcum. (42)

French mixture: See iodi phenolatus, liquor. (31)

French polish: An alcoholic solution of shellac. (3)

French white: Pulverized talc. (3)

Friar's balsam: 1. Compound tincture of benzoin, see benzoini composita, tinctura. (8) 2. See balsamum traumaticum and benzoini composita, tinctura. (45)

Fringe tree: See chionanthus. (7)

Fructose: Levulose, fruit sugar. (3)

Fructus: Fruit. (1)

Fruit salt: A variety of Seidlitz's or Seltzer aperient. (3)

Frumenti opt[.][imus], spiritus: Fermented spirits, i.e., whisky, forty-four to fifty percent alcohol, sometimes designated as "best" or "finest" (optimus). (8)

Ft.: Forte, i.e., strong(er).

Fuchsine: Magenta or aniline red dye. (40)

Fucus; Fuci, extractum; —, fluidextractum; —fluidum, extractum; —liquidum, extractum: Fucus, or bladderwrack, *Fucus vesiculosus, F. serratus,* or *F. silignosus*, or the solid extract or the fluid or liquid extract therefrom. Employed for weight control, but "probably of little value." (3,31,42,46)

Fucus digitatus: A seaweed used as per laminaria. (33)

Fuga daemonum: "Flight of the demons," see hypericum, St. John's wort. The herb, hung in the window on the feast of St. John (December 27), would drive away demons and spirits. (39)

Fuliginis, pulv.: Powdered soot, powdered ashes.

Fuliginis, sal: Ammonium carbonate. (3)

Fuliginis, unguentum: Ointment of soot, powdered wood soot in lard, for burns, open skin infections, tinea, and other skin conditions. (34)

Fuligo (ligni): Soot, typically wood (ligni), see soot. (1,39)

Fuligokali: An alkaline solution of soot, evaporated to dryness. (3)

Fuller's earth: Purified fuller's earth, see terra fullonica. (40) See note regarding etymology under fuller's herb.

Fuller's earth, white: See talcum. (42) See note regarding etymology under fuller's herb.

Fig. 3-106 Fraxinus or ash tree.

Fig. 3-107 Fumaria or fumatory.

Fuller's herb: See saponaria. Note that this does not refer to an individual named Fuller, but to a fuller, one who beats wool fabric. Fuller's herb, or soapwort, was added as a lubicant and to remove excess fats from wool fabric. Fuller's earth was added as a mild abrasive and to take up residual fats. Fuller's herb is not to be confused with fuller's teasel, a thistle plant used to brush wool fabric to raise the nap, and not a medicinal. (33)

Fulv[a][um][us]: Brown or yellow in color (Latin).

Fumans boylii, liquor: Ammonium hydrosulphide. (3)

Fumaria; Fumeterre {*French*}**; Fumosterno** {*Italian*}**:** Common fumitory, *Fumaria officinalis*. Herb used. Figure 3-107. (1)

Fumifera, charta: Fuming (literally fume-making) paper. See potassii nitratis, charta. (40)

Fumigatio balsamica: See pulvis fumalis.

Fumitory: See fumaria. (39)

Furfur: Bran. (3)

Furol; Furfural(dehyde): Furfuraldehyde (furfural), a solvent, derived historically from oat hulls (bran). (3)

Furunculine: Dried yeast, see yeast. (40)

Fusal oil; Fusel oil: See amyl alcohol and also fermentationis, oleum. (3)

Fuscum camphoratum, emplastrum: Camphorated brown plaster, camphorated mother plaster, of red oxide of lead (see lead, red), olive oil, yellow wax, and camphor. Used as a skin protective. (31)

Fuscum, unguentum: Brown ointment, unguentum matris, mother's salve, of fifty percent camphorated brown plaster (fuscum camphoratum, emplastrum) with remainder equal parts olive oil and suet. (31) "Dark ointment," salve of pine tar, frankincense, mastic, wax, etc. Used in treatment of ulcers. (1)

Fuscus, syrupus: Brown syrup, i.e., molasses. (3)

Fustic, old; —, young; Fustic wood; Fustet: The wood of (old) fustic, *Morus tinctoria* (now *Maclura tinctoria*), or (young) *Rhus cotinus* respectively. Sometimes seen as "fustet." Alternatively, Fustic wood in British use is said to be *Chlorophora tinctoria*. In any event, a yellow to orange colored wood used primarily as a colorant. (3,40)

G

G.: At beginning of inscription: gummi, gomme {*French*} (gum); grasso {*Italian*} (grease). At end of inscription Galeni, Galeno {*Italian*}, Galien {*French*} (of Galen, see Galenus). (1)

Gabriel's injection: Phenol five percent in almond oil. (40)

Gadberry's mixture: See spleen mixture. (46)

Gadus morrhuae, oleum: See morrhuae, oleum. (40)

Galactic: Lactic. (3)

Galam, beurre de {*French*}: Galam butter, shea butter, fatty material from seeds of *Butyrospermum parkii* and other *Sapotaceae*. (1)

Galanga(l) (, lesser); Galangae, rhizoma: Galingale, rhizome of certain East Asian plants, esp. *Alpinia officinarum (*now *A. galanga*, greater galengal or blue ginger*)* and *Kaempferia galanga* (lesser galangal or sand ginger). A stomachic bitter, aromatic and carminative. (1,39,42)

Galbani, emplastrum; Galbanum plaster: A plaster of galbanum, sal ammoniac, and lead plaster (plumbi, emplastrum). In BPC, also contained beeswax. Mild irritant for use on painful joints. (33,40,42)

Galbani compositae, pilulae: Compound pills of galbanum, with myrrh, assafetida, and syrup, employed in hysteria and "mucous profluvia." (34,42)

Galbani compositae, tablettae: Tablet of asafoetida, galbanum, myrrh, refined sugar, alcohol, and ethereal solution of theobroma. (42)

Galbani compositum, emplastrum: Plaster of galbanum, turpentine, burgundy pitch, and lead plaster (plumbi, emplastrum). (44)

Galbanum: Green resin tears of *Ferula galbaniflua, F. rubricaulis*, and probably related species. Figure 3-108. (1,8)

Galega; Galegae, fluidextractum: European goat's rue or ruta capraria; *Galega officinalis*, or the fluid extract. Used as a diaphoretic and galactagogue. (1,3,31)

Galen(us); Galeno {*Italian*}**; Galien** {*French*}**:** Galen of Pergamon, 130–201 CE. One of the most influential physicians of ancient history, promoted the humoral theory of disease which would predominate in Western medicine for the some seventeen centuries to follow. (1)

Galena: Lead sulfide, a naturally occuring crystalline ore. (3)

Galene: A variant of mithridatum. (39)

Galeni, ceratum; Galen's cerate; Galien, cérat de {*French*}**; Galeni, unguentum:** Cold cream, see rosae, aqua, unguentum and refrigerans Galeni, ceratum as well as Galenus, above. (1,3,40)

Galingale: See galanga, specifically *Galanga minor*. (39)

Galium: Cleavers, *Galium aparine*, for urinary inflammatory conditions. (32) Decoction used topically for scrofula. Figure 3-109. (44)

Galium verum: Yellow ladies' bedstraw, cheese rennet. roots and flowers used for red or yellow dye, respectively, and bruised plant used to impart yellow color to cheese as well as assist coagulation. (Not same as animal derived rennet now used to coagulate cheese.) Unofficial. (44)

Fig. 3-108 Galbanum (source of).

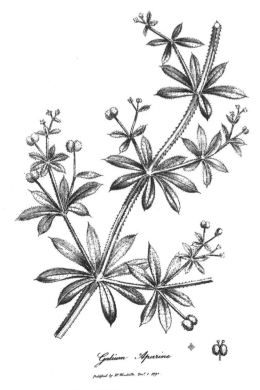

Fig. 3-109 Galium or cleavers.

Galla: Nutgall, an excrescence on oak of the species *Quercus lusitanica*, resulting from insect damage (other oaks have similar galls). Principal components are tannic and gallic acid. An astringent, used in a manner similar to tannic acid (tannicum, acidum). (8)

Gallacetophenone: Methylketo-trioxybenzene, alizarin-yellow dye "C." Colorant. (3)

Gallae, decoctum: Decoction of galls, a topical astringent for bleeding and to lessen discharges from inflamed mucous membranes. (42)

Gallae (cum opio), unguentum: Ointment of nut-gall, of same in benzoinated lard, for hemorrhoids, rectal prolapse, and foul smelling ulcers. Powdered opium could be added to produce an ointment said to be of particular value as a topical in rectal prolapse, piles, and for vaginal relaxation. (34)

Gallae pulv.; Gallae, tinctura: Powdered nutgall or tincture of nutgall, made from nutgall and glycerin in alcohol. Used as an astringent. (29, 31)

Gallas compositum, unguentum: See gallae cum opio, unguentum. (40)

Gallein: Coal-tar derived color, used as a pH indicator. (3)

Gallia moschata: French musk, a cordial and stimulant troche of musk, aloes, and amber. Perhaps identical to galliae moschatae, trochisci. (39)

Galliae moschatae, trochisci: Lozenges of aloe wood, musk, ambergris, gum tragacanth, and rose water. Used as a restorative. (1)

Gallici, acidi unguentum: Ointment of gallic acid in benzoinated lard, for rectal disorders and foul skin infections or ulcers. (34)

Gallicum, acidum; Gallic acid; Gallicum, acidum, glyceritum: This is a mild astringent obtained from tannic acid (tannicum, acidum). It does not coagulate protein effectively and is thus of lesser topical use, but could be given orally to achieve some of the remote effects of oral tannic acid on the bladder or gastrointestinal tract, for example, with a lesser degree of local astringency in the mouth and stomach. The glycerite was used for inflammatory conditions of the mucous membranes. (8,34)

Gallicus bolus: French earth or clay, French bolus. (39)

Gallipoli (oil): An impure olive oil. (3)

Gallobromol: Dibromogallic acid, astringent similar to gallic acid. (3)

Gallotannic acid: See tannicum, acidum. (8)

Gambi(e)r: A gummy dried extract prepared from the leaves and shoots of pale catechu or gambier, *Terra japonica*. It is medicinally astringent, used for diarrhea and hemorrhoids and also as a reddish-brown dye and in tanning of hides. (7,40)

Gambi(e)r, trochisci: Troches of gambir with tragacanth and sugar, flavored with oil of cinnamon. (38)

Gambi(e)r composita, tinctura. Gambir Co., Tr.: Compound tincture of gambir, of same and cinnamon, in alcohol. (38)

Gambi(e)r compositus, pulvis: Compound powder of gambir with kino, krameria, cinnamon and nutmeg. (38)

Gamboge; Gambogia; Gambogium: The gum resin of *Garcinia Hanburii*, of Southeast Asia. It is a "drastic purgative" not unlike elaterin. (1,8)

Gambogia India: Indian camboge or gamboge, similar to the Asian variety above. (42)

Gambosiae compositae, pilulae: Compound pills of gambosia (cambosia), with scammony, elaterium, croton oil, and extract of hyoscyamus. For obstinate constipation and dropsy. (34)

Gamene: Madder, a dyestuff. (3)

Ganja: Indian hemp, see apocyum. (40)

Gannal's solution: Solution of aluminum acetate. (3)

Garance {*French*}: See rubia tinctorum. (1)

Garantose: Saccharin. (3)

Garcinia: See gamboge. (39)

Gardenia grandiflora: Tree from China, used primarily as source of yellow dye, although fruit of related *G. campanula* used as cathartic and anthelmintic. Unofficial. (44)

Gargarisma acidi tannici: See glyceritum acidi tannici.

Garget: See phytolacca decandra. (39)

Garlic: See allium. (8)

Garofano {*Italian*}: Clove (see caryophylli) or Clove-gillyflower (see tunicae, flores). (1)

Garou {*French*}: See thymelaea. (1)

Gas black: Lampblack. (3)

Gascoign(e)'s powder; Gasgoyn's powder: Seventeenth-century formulation of bezoar, amber, hartshorn, coral, crab's claw, and margarite. (39) Approximates cretae aromaticus, pulvis. (40)

Gaseosa, aqua: Carbonated water. (3)

Gaster siccata: Desiccated hog's stomach, as a digestive aid. (40)

Gastown black: Lampblack. (3)

Gaultheria: Wintergreen plant, *Gaultheria procumbens*.

Gaultherii, spiritus; Gaultherium, oleum: Oil of wintergreen, distilled from the leaves of the wintergreen plant, *Gaultherium procumbens*, or the "spirit" in alcohol. Chemically, this is methyl salicylate. Used for flavor or scent (to mask odors) or as per other aromatic oils, see caryophyllum. (8)

Gautier, emplastrum: A sparadrapum (plaster applied on cloth backing) of unknown formula. (39)

Gauvain's formula: A mixture of guiacol, iodoform, ether, and sterile olive oil used as a lavage solution in empyema (infection of the space surrounding the lung). (24)

Gauze, _____: See carbasus _____ or _____, carbasus. (42)

Gauze, sublimate: See hydrargyri perchloridi, carbasus. (42)

Gauze, tarred: See carbasus styptica. (42)

Gavelle's extract: Extract of common mallow, see malva. (40)

Gayac {*French*}: Orthographc variant of gaïac. See guaiaci, lignum. (1)

Gaïac {*French*}: See guaiaci, lignum. (1)

Gelanthum: An aqueous mixture of gelatin and gum tragacanth, used as a pill varnish and as a carrier for topical medications. (40)

Gelatin; Gelatina; Gelatinum: Gelatin, useful for formation of suppositories, pessaries, bougies, capsules, lozenges, and as a pill coating. Still in extensive use today for production of capsules. (8)

Gelatina vituli: Calf's foot jelly, a veal aspic, as a nutritive. (40)

Gelatinum chondrae: Irish moss gelatin, see chondrus. (34)

Gelatinum glycerinatum; Gelato-glycerinum: A base material for gelatin suppositories and nasal bougies, of 33 parts gelatin, 40 glycerin, and 40 water, or adjusted as needed for greater strength (more gelatin). (42)

Gelatum petrolei: Petroleum jelly, see petrolatum. (40)

Gelsemin; Gelseminae hydrochloridum: Active component of gelsemium or the hydrochloride salt, a stimulant. (42)

Gelsemium; Gelsemii radix; Gelsemii, fluidextractum; —liquidum, extractum; —, tinctura: Root of *Gelsemium sempervirens*, yellow jasmine or jessamine, or the fluid extract or tincture therefrom. Contains a nicotine-like alkaloid used as a cardiodepressant and as a muscular relaxant in tetanus or other spasmodic illnesses, like whooping cough. Due to severe side effects, primarily muscular paralysis, it was evidently little used. (8, 31,42)

Gemmae, sal: Sodium chloride. (3)

Gemmae populi: Poplar buds, used to prepare demulcent material, see Gilead, balm of and also populus. (1)

Geneva: Gin, see juniperi, spiritus. (40)

Gengero {*Italian*}; **Gengiovo** {*Italian*}: Ginger, see zingiber. (1)

Geniévre {*French*}: See juniperus. (1)

Genista: Common broom, *Cytisus scoparius* or *Spartium scoparium*. Leaves, flowers, seeds used. See scoparius. A cathartic and emetic. Figure 3-110. (1,39)

Genista tinctoria: Dyer's broom, dyer's weed, or green weed, a dye source and diuretic for dropsy, said to be used in Eastern Europe to prevent hydrophobia (rabies). Unofficial. (44)

Genoa (oil): Fine olive oil. (40)

Gentian; Gentiana (lutea); Gentianae radix: The root of *Gentiana lutea*, of central Europe, or the fluid extract therefrom. It is a typical bitter and is employed as such (see columba for details of use). Figure 3-111. (8,32,42) In American use, root of *Gentiana saponaria*.

Gentian, white: "A German rural domestic medicine, which is dried white dog-dung." (3) See also gentiana (lutea) above.

Gentian ft., inf.: Probably a strong (forte) infusion of gentian. No specific reference to this formulation was identified.

Gentiana catesbaei: Blue gentian, it is "little inferior to the European..." (44)

Gentiana purpurea: Purple gentian, the root is said by Woodville to be indistinguishable from white gentian, above.

Gentianae, elixir: Elixir of Gentian, made from fluid extract of gentian flavored with compound spirit of cardamom. It contains too small an amount of gentian to be therapeutic, used as a vehicle. (31) In the NF, of fluid extract of gentian with compound spirits of cardamom, solution of tersulphate of iron, water of ammonia, alcohol, water, and aromatic elixir. (46)

Gentianae (et ferri phosphatis), elixir: Elixir of gentian or of gentian and ferric phosphate, chalybeate and tonic. (31,45)

Gentianae, extractum; —fluidum, extractum; —composita, tinctura; —, infusum: The extract, fluid extract, or infusion (in water) of gentian. The compound tincture consisted of gentian, bitter orange peel, and cardamom macerated and percolated in alcohol, then filtered. (8,31)

Gentianae (et sodae), mistura: A mixture of macerated gentian root, bitter orange peel, and coriander fruit extracted into alcohol and water, for dyspepsia and as an appetite stimulant. (42)

Gentianae acida, mistura: A mixture of diluted nitro-hydrochloric acid and spirit of chloroform in compound infusion of gentian, a bitter. (42)

Gentianae composita, tinctura: Compound tincture of gentian, with bitter orange peel, cardamom, and alcohol. (34)

Gentianae compositum (fortior), infusum (concentratum); Gent. Co. Conc., Inf.: Compound infusion of gentian with coriander and orange peel, in standard or stronger (fortior or concentratum) form, a tonic and stomachic. See also: infusum amarum. (34,39) The BPC also specified a concentrated infusion with alcohol and chloroform water for storage and reconstitution. (42)

Gentianae cum tinctura ferri chloridi, elixir; Gentianae et ferri, elixir; Gent. Ferratum, Elix.: Elixir of gentian and iron, elixir of gentian with tincture of ferric citro-chloride. Tincture of citro-chloride of iron with elixir of gentian. Used as a bitter tonic. (31)

Gentianae et sodae, mistura: A mixture of sodium bicarbonate in compound infusion of gentian, antacid, and aperient. (42)

Gentianae glycerinatum, elixir: Glycerinated elixir of gentian, containing small amounts of gentian and taraxacum in sweetened, flavored sherry wine. "The last is its most active ingredient." (31) Bitter tonic and stomachic of gentian, taraxacum, and phosphoric acid in glycerin and white wine and flavoring of sweet orange peel, compound tincture of cardamom, and acetic ether. (45)

Gentina: See cursuta. (39)

Geoffroea: Cabbage tree, *Geoffroea* (or *Geoffroya) inermis*, bark used as an anthelmintic. Figure 3-112. (39)

Geosot: Guaiacol valerianate, a proprietary creosote derivative used for tuberculosis. (40)

Geranii compositum, infusum: Compound infusion of geranium, witchhazel, black cohosh, and goldenseal, with or without alum. An astringent for mouth ulcers and other oral conditions as well as for female complaints. (34)

Geraniol: Primary component of oil of geranium, primarily used in perfumery. (42)

Geranium oil: See camel's hay as well as geranium. (39)

Spartium scoparium

Published by Dr Woodville June 1 1791.

Fig. 3-110 Genista scoparius or common broom.

Gentiana lutea

Published by Dr Woodville, Augst 1, 1792.

Fig. 3-111 Gentian, white or European.

Geoffroya inermis.

Published by Dr Woodville Nov. 1 1791.

Fig. 3-112 Geoffroea.

Geranium robertanium: Herb Robert, a type of geranium rare in US, common in Britain, internal for fever, consumption, hemorrhage, and kidney and liver disorders. Unofficial. Figure 3-113. (44)

Geranium; Geranii fluidum, extractum: The rhizome of the geranium or cranesbill, *Geranium maculatum*, of North America. Used as per tannic acid (tannicum, acidum). The fluid extract was obtained by percolation with water, alcohol, and glycerin. Geranium was commonly used in diarrhea, dysentery, and for various hemorrhages, as it was widely available in North America. (8)

Gerardia: Bushy gerardia, lousewort, fever weed, American fox-glove, *Gerardia pedicularia*, astringent, antiseptic, and sedative, for various infectious and inflammatory conditions. (33)

Germander; Germander, water: See chamaedrys or scordium, respectively. (39)

Geronaldehyde: A ten-carbon aldehyde derived from oil of geranium and other plants such as lemon grass, citrus, etc. Primarily a flavoring, said to be the primary flavor component of lemon oil and about fifteen times as potent. (42)

Geum (rivale)(urbanum): See benedicta, herba. (1,39) A powerful astringent and cathartic. (44)

Ghatti gum: Gum from India, often gum acacia, but could be other tree gums. (40)

Giacinto {*Italian*}: Jacinth (a gem). (1)

Gialappa {*Italian*}: See jalapium. (1)

Giallo {*Italian*}: Yellow. (1)

Giancintina, confezione {*Italian*}: See hyacintho, confectio de. (1)

Giglio {*Italian*}: See lilium. (1)

Gilead, balm of; Gileadense, balsamum: Balm of Gilead. 1. In North America, balm of poplar buds, of various species, *Populus niger* (black poplar), *P. candicans*, or *P. balsamifera*. 2. In Europe, sap of *Commiphora opobalsamum* or *Amyris gileadensis*, but difficult to obtain and often replaced with Canada balsam or balsam of copaiba. Figure 3-114. (3,39)

Gilla theophrasti; —vitrioli: Zinc sulfate, an emetic. (39)

Gillenia: Bark of the rhizome of Indian physic, American ipecac, Indian hippo, and sometimes Bowman's root, *Gillenia trifoliata* and *Gillenia stipulacea*. Emetic action, much like ipecac. (33)

Gilmour's pills: See digitalis compositae, pilulae. Closely related formula with additional digitalis leaf. (42)

Gilson's solution: A tissue fixative containing mercuric chloride, nitric acid, and glacial acetic acid. (24)

Ginepro {*Italian*}: See juniperus. (1)

Ginestra {*Italian*}: See genista. (1)

Gingembre {*French*}; **Ginger:** See zingiber. (1,8)

Ginger, wild: See asarum for American usage, in British usage, see zingiber (officinale). (7,40)

Ginger mint tablets: See zingiberis compositae, tablettae. (42)

Gingilli; Gingelly oil: See sesami, oleum. (40)

Ginseng: Ginseng, *Panax ginseng (schinseng)* or in N. America, *see Panax quinquefolium*. Root used. Figure 3-115. (1,39)

Giulebbe {*Italian*}; **Giuleppo** {Italian}: Julep. (1)

Giusquiamo {*Italian*}: See hyoscyamus. (1)

Glacial acetic acid: See aceticum, acidum. (8)

Glacies mariae: Isinglass stone, muscovy glass, a form of calcium sulfate. (3)

Glacies: Ice. (3)

Glandes quercus (tostae): Acorns (toasted). (3)

Glandular rottleras: See Kamala. (40)

Glaseri, sal: See potassae sulphas cum sulphure. (3)

Glass, soluble: Water-glass, sodium silicate. See silicate of soda. (40,44)

Glass of antimony: Vitrified antimony oxide. (3) See antimonii, vitrum. (44)

Glass wool: Fiberglass, long fibers of clear glass used as a filtering material.

Glauber's salt; Glauberi, sal catharticus: See sal catharticus Glauberi. See also: sodii sulphas. (1,8)

Glauber's secret (sal ammoniac): Ammonium sulfate. (39)

Glauber's spirit (of niter): See niter, sweet spirit of. (39)

Glauber's spirit of salt: Hydrochloric acid. (39)

Glechoma(tis) hederacea: See hedera terrestris. (1,44)

Glechoma: Ground ivy, cat foot, or gill-go-over-the-ground, *Glechoma hederacea*, a stimulant, tonic, and pectoral. (33)

Globularia alypum: European wild senna, cathartic, taken as a decoction. Unofficial. (44)

Globuli martiales: Crude iron tartrate balls or marbles. (3)

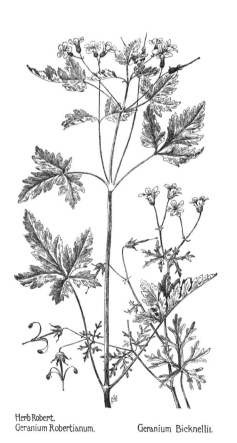

Herb Robert.
Geranium Robertianum.   Geranium Bicknellii.

Fig. 3-113 Geranium robertanum.

Amyris gileadensis.

Published by D[r] Woodville March 1, 1793.

Fig. 3-114 Balm of Gilead (European).

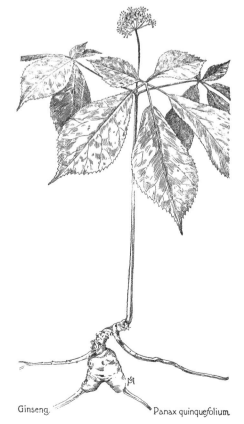

Ginseng.   *Panax quinquefolium.*

Fig. 3-115 Ginseng (American).

Glonoin; Glonoini, spiritus; Glonoinum, spirit of: Spirit of glonoin, glyceryl trinitrate, Trinitrin, i.e., nitroglycerin. From nitration of glycerin with nitric and sulfuric acids. Nitroglycerin separates as an oily layer from the reaction mixture and can be further refined. See amyl nitrite for discussion of nitrites and nitrates in cardiac disease. This is noted to be "largely taken by persons liable to cardiac pains." It may be used topically, orally, or sublingually (as tablets) and remains in common use today. (8)

Glonoini, liquor: One percent solution of nitroglycerin, a vasodilator for angina and hypertension. (40)

Glonoini, pilulae: Nitroglycerin pills, of spirit of glonoin in althea powder, with rose water. For sublingual use in angina pectoralis. (34)

Glucochloral: A chloral hydrate derivative used as a sedative. (40) Prepared by reaction of chloral with dry glucose in a sealed container over heat. Also used for sea sickness. (42)

Glucosi, syrupus: Liquid glucose and simple syrup, used as a pill excipient. (42)

Glucosum: Glucose. (7)

Glucosum liquidum: A liquid sweetener made by hydrolysis of starch, similar to today's corn syrup. Used as a base syrup or pill excipient (binder). (42)

Glucusimide; Gluside; Glusidum (solubile): Saccharin. The soluble form is produced by neutralizing a solution with sodium carbonate or bicarbonate and recrystallizing the resulting material. (40,42)

Glue: A term applied to crude gelatin, used to prepare capsules, not an adhesive. (44)

Glusidi, elixir: Elixir of saccharin, sweetener. (42)

Glusidi, tablettae: Tablet of sodium bicarbonate and gluside (saccharin) with excipient etherial solution of theobroma. This is equivalent to a modern saccharin tablet, used for sweetening tea, etc. (42)

Glutol: Formaldehyde gelatin, a commercial gelatin-formaldehyde mixture used as a thickener. (Currently a trade name for oral glucose used in glucose tolerance tests.) (3,40)

Glutton's febrifuge spirit: See ethyl chloride. (40)

Glyceratum boroglycerini: A solution of boric acid and glycerin. Used as a topical disinfectant, including as a mouthwash and wound irrigant. (8)

Glycerin; Glycerina; Glycerine; Glycerinum: Glycerin, archaic use often with a terminal "e," is obtained from the decomposition of vegetable or animal fats or from fixed oils. Glycerin is a three-carbon tri-alcohol, i.e., $CH_2OH\text{-}COH\text{-}CH_2OH$. Fats consist of glycerin to which three fatty acids are attached. Cleavage of fats by alkali, as in the making of soap, forms salts of the fatty acids (i.e., soap) and liberates glycerin, which can be freed from soap via the kneading process. As soap is a major commodity item, glycerin was always in ample supply. Also used as a general emollient, ingredient in various formulations, and as a starting material for (tri) nitroglycerin. It is a clear, syrupy substance used to make a variety of preparations, including various "glycerites," in which the active ingredient is dissolved in glycerin or a mixture containing glycerin. As it is actually a short chain sugar, it adds a sweet flavor to any preparation. It is a soothing additive to topical preparations for the skin, and produces purging with large oral doses. (8,44)

Glycerin of borax: A solution of borax with glycerin and water, applied to mouth ulcers and as topical disinfectant. (8)

Glycerin suppository: See suppositoria, glycerini. (8)

Glycerin tonic: See gentianae glycerinatum, elixir. (45)

Glycerini, lotio: Glycerine lotion, one-half ounce in a half pint of distilled water, as a general soothing irrigant and irrigant of the ear canal for deafness. (34)

Glycerini, suppositoria: Suppository of glycerin and gelatin, lubricating, to assist in evacuation of bowels. (42) A typical formula would include glycerin 60 parts, sodium carbonate 3 parts, stearic acid (from olive oil) 5 parts. This would be melted and poured in a mold. These can be used to treat constipation or rectal difficulties, or any desired active substances can be added to the mixture when warm to create a variety of suppositories. An alternative formulation is based on cocoa-butter. (8)

Glycerini compositum, lotio; Glycerin, compound lotion of: Lotion of hard beeswax, lard, hard soap, salicylic acid, glycerin, almond and rose oils, chloroform, and water. (42)

Glycerinum et acidum tannicum; Glyc. E. Ac. Tannic.: See tannici, acidi, glyceritum.

Glycerinum glycerophosphatum compositum: A compound glycerophosphate in the BPC. Calcium, potassium, sodium, magnesium, and iron glycerophosphate in glycerin and water, with citric acid, cudbear, chloroform, alcohol, orange-flower water and cherry-laurel water. Noted to be used in place of the compound syrup when sugar was undesirable (diabetes). (42)

Glycerinum glycerophosphatum cum medulla rubra: See the compositum above, with the addition of red bone marrow extract as an iron source. (42)

Glycerite of egg yolk: See vitelli, glyceritum. (31)

Glycerite of glyceryl borate; Glycerite of boroglycerin: See glyceratum boroglycerini. (8)

Glyceritum _____: Glycerite, see _____, glyceritum.

Glycerol: See glycerin. (40)

Glycerolé {_French_}: Liquid glycerin preparations. (3)

Glycerophosphat[um][is] compositum, elixir; —, syrupus: Compound elixir of glycerophosphates, of the glycerophosphates of sodium, calcium, iron, and manganese with quinine and strychnine. (31) In the BPC, also contained caffeine, cudbear (colorant), refined sugar, alcohol, and water. (42) A general tonic for debility, neurasthenia, and wasting conditions.

Glycerophosphat[um][is] cum formatibus, syrupus; —, elixir: Compound syrup of glycerophosphates with formates, essentially the compound syrup of glycerophosphates (BPC) with addition of potassium and sodium formates, and used for same purposes. (42)

Glycerophosphoric acid: Glycerol phosphate, i.e., the phosphate ester of glycerol. Supposedly a nerve tonic. (40,42)

Glyceryl trinitrate: See glonoini, spiritus. (8)

Glycocaine: A local anesthetic. (40)

Glycocol; Glycocolum: The amino acid, glycine. Pharmaceutical use unclear.

Glycocoll-paraphenetidin hydrochloride: Phenocoll hydrochloride, see phenocol. (40)

Glycogelatinum: In the BPC, a mixture of gelatin, glycerin, distilled water, orange-flower water, sugar, citric acid, oil of lemon and carmine colorant, used as a basis for pastilles (lozenges). (42)

Glyconin: See vitelli, glyceritum. (31)

Glycyrrhiza: Licorice (liquorice) root, the root of _Glycyrrhiza glabra_. Licorice root was used as a demulcent, but also added flavor and served as a modest thickening agent in various formulations, and is of course well known for its laxative effects and for use in food confections. Figure 3-116. (1,8)

Glycyrrhizae, elixir: Simple elixir, NF, of fluid extract and aromatic elixir. (45)

Glycyrrhizae, extracti, liquor: Solution of the purified extract of licorice, alcohol, water, and glycerin. (46)

Glycyrrhizae, fluidglyceratum: Fluidglycerate of glycyrrhiza, used as a flavoring agent. (31)

Glycyrrhizae, radix, (pulv.); Glycyrrh. r. (pulv.); etc.: Liquorice root (powdered). This term often used in place of glycyrrhizae alone in any liquorice preparation, as only the root was used.

Glycyrrhizae, succus: Licorice (root) juice, black sugar. Mainly for flavoring.

Glycyrrhizae (et opii), trochisci: Troches of licorice root (and opium), of licorice root, acacia, sugar, and oil of anise, with or without powdered opium. For cough and catarrh. (8,34)

Glycyrrhizae aquosum, elixir: Aqueous elixir of glycyrrhiza, aqueous elixir of licorice. A new (ca. 1926) non-alcoholic flavoring elixir of fluid extract of licorice (glycyrrhizae composita, mistura), compound spirit of cardamom (cardamomi composita, tinctura), and orange flower water (aurantii florum, aqua). (31)

Glycyrrhizae aromaticum, elixir: Aromatic elixir of licorice, of the fluid extract and aromatic elixir with oils of clove, cinnamon, nutmeg, and fennel. A flavoring. (45)

Glycyrrhizae composita, mistura: Compound mixture of licorice, or brown mixture, of extract of glycyrrhiza, sugar, mucilage of acacia, camphorated tincture of opium, wine of antimony, and spirit of nitrous ether in water. (8)

Glycyrrhizae composita, trochisci: Compound troches of licorice, of licorice root, ammonium chloride, hydrochlorate of morphine, gum arabic, oil of sassafras, oil of stillingia, and tincture of balsam of tolu. For cough, irritation of the throat, and bronchitis. (34)

Glycyrrhizae compositus, pulvis: Compound powder of licorice (glycyrrhiza), of senna, glycyrrhiza, oil of fennel, washed sulphur, and sugar. (8)

Glycyrrhizae depuratum, extractum: Solid extract of licorice, NF, from extraction of licorice sticks in water, boiled to concentrate. Not same as glycyrrhizae purum extractum. (46)

Glycyrrhizae extractum pulvis; Glycyrrh., pv. ex.; Glycyrrh. po., ext.: Powdered extract of licorice root.

Glycyrrhizae pulvis; Glycyrrh. pv.: Powdered licorice (root).

Glycyrrhizae purum, extractum; —fluidum, extractum; —, syrupus: Pure licorice extract was obtained by boiling licorice in ammonia water, followed by evaporation to dryness. The fluid extract was similarly produced, but not dried. The syrup (NF) is of the fluidglycerate and simple syrup. (8,31)

Glycyrrhizae spirituosum, extractum: Spirituous extract of licorice, i.e., with alcohol. This was official in India and British colonies where the alcohol content prevented fermentation in warm climates. (42)

Glycyrrhizinum ammoniatum: Ammoniated glycyrrhizin, produced by extraction of licorice root in ammonia water, followed by precipitation of the alkaloid by addition of sulfuric acid. Said to be used mainly as a masking agent for quinine and other bitter medications. (33)

Gnaphalium: See Life Everlasting. Multiple medicinal indications, unofficial. (33,44)

Goa; Goa powder: See chrysarobinum. (8)

Goddard's drops: Proprietary aromatic spirits of ammonia, after Wm. Goddard, London, ca. 1790. Originally Estes notes that this was an oil extracted from human bones, to which spirits of niter and wine were added at a later date. (39)

Godfrey's cordial: See sassafras et opii, mistura. After Ambrose Godfrey, London, cq. 1660. (34)

Gold chloride: See auri, chloridum. (42)

Gold tribromide: See auri, bromidum. (42)

Gold: See aurum (metallic), auri (compounds). (8)

Golden drops (of General LeMothe): Golden drops, or Bestucheff's Tincture, a tincture of perchloride of iron and ether. (39)

Golden hair dye: Hydrogen peroxide. (40)

Golden sulphur of antimony: See sulphur antimonii, praecipitatum. (39)

Golden sulphurette: Sufides of antimony in sulfur. See antimonii sulphuret(ic)um praecipitatum. (39)

Goldenrod: In North America, see solidago. In Europe, this was *Virga aurea*. (39)

Goldenseal: See hydrastis. (8)

Goldenthread: See coptis. (3)

Gomme {*French*}: Gum, gum resin. (1)

Gommeline: Crude dextrin. (3)

Gommeuse, potion {*French*}: See mistura acaciae. (42)

Gondret's pomade: See unguentum ammoniacale. (34)

Goodyera: Net-leaf plantain, scrofula weed, adder's viola, or rattlesnake leaf, *Goodyera pubescens*, for scrofula. Figure 3-117. (33)

Gooroo nuts: See kola. (40)

Gorit: Proprietary version of calcii peroxidum. (40,42)

Gossypii, tinctura: Tincture of cotton root bark in alcohol, a "doubtful" substitute for ergot. (42)

Fig. 3-116 Glycyrrhiza or licorice.

Fig. 3-117 Goodyera.

Gossypii liquidum, extractum; Gossypii radicis corticus liquidum, extractum: The fluid extract of gossypium root bark, as named in the BPC. (42)

Gossypii radicis corticis, decoctum: Decoction of cottonroot bark, a substitute for ergot, as emmenagogue and to control hemmorhage. (42)

Gossypii seminis, oleum: Cottonseed oil, expressed from the seed of cotton, *Gossypium herbaceum*. It is a bland, nutritious oil used in formulations, particularly liniments, and in food. (8)

Gossypium; —radicis cortex; —radicis fluidum, extractum; —corticus, fluidextractum: Cotton, *Gossypium herbaceum*, the root bark of cotton, or the fluid extract thereof. It was used in a manner similar to ergot for uterine disorders and to facilitate labor. It was an emmenogogue, abortifacient, and for menorrhagia or metrorrhagia of various causes, but especially for uterine fibroids. Cotton fiber was also utilized for absorbent purposes in dressings and as a raw material for the preparation of pyroxylin (gun cotton, see pyroxylinum) from whence is made collodion. (8)

Gossypium (purificatum): Cotton, "purified," usually as cotton balls. (7)

Gossypium fulminans: Gun cotton, see pyroxylin. (40)

Gossypium salis alembroth: Cotton treated with sal alembroth, i.e., sal ammoniac, an antiseptic packing or dressing. (40)

Gossypium stypticum: Styptic cotton, made by impregnating purified cotton with diluted solution of ferric chloride, glycerin and water. "It should be kept in well closed containers." (31)

Goto: See coto. (40)

Goudron: A Norwegian tar, presumably a pine tar. (40)

Goulard's cerate: See plumbi subacetatis, ceratum. (8,39)

Goulard's extract (of Saturn); —lotion; —water: See plumbi subacetatis, liquor. Saturn was the symbol for lead. (8,39) A dilute solution of lead acetate (plumbi acetatis). (24)

Goulard('s) powder: Lead acetate, see plumbum acetatis. (40)

Gower's solution: A solution of sodium sulfate, glacial acetic acid, and water used as a reagent in counting red blood cells. (24)

Grain oil: Amyl alcohol. (3)

Grains d'Ambrette: Musk seeds, see moschus (the botanical definition). (40)

Grains d'Avignon: French berries (*Rhamnus infectorius*). (3)

Grains of paradise: See grana paradisi.

Graisse {*French*}**:** Grease. (1)

Gramen; Gramigna {*Italian*}**:** Couch-grass, *Agropyrum repens* or quickgrass, *Triticum repens*. Rhizome used as aperient and blood purifier. (1,39)

Graminis citrati, oleum: Lemon grass oil. (42)

Gram's solution: A bacteriological stain. (24)

Gran.: Granulated, see granulata.

Grana actes: Elderberries, see sambuca. (40)

Grana angelica: Angelic grains or Anderson's Scots pills, after Patrick Anderson, ca. 1635, of aloes, jalap, gamboge, and anise. Sold by his daughter to Dr. Thomas Weir, Edinburgh, and patented as a panacea ca. 1690. According to Estes, by the 1800, the pills were made of aloe, jalap, and oil of anise. (39)

Grana paradisi: A spice from west Africa, *Aframomum or Amomum melegueta,* used as a condiment, carminative, and an ingredient in occasional non-standard remedies. (3,39)

Grana tiglia: Croton seeds, see croton. (40)

Granata; Granata malus: Pomegranate tree, *Punica granatum*. Rind of fruit, bark of stem, and bark of root used. (1)

Granata fructus cortex: Fruit rind of pomegranate. (44)

Granata radicis cortex: Bark of the root of pomegranate, astringent. (44)

Granati cortex: Refers to pomegranate bark, see granatum, below. (42)

Granati corticis, decoctum: Decoction of pomegranate bark, of powdered bark in water, astringent, and anthelmintic. (42)

Granati fructi cortex: Rind of the pomegranate fruit, a strong astringent. (42)

Granati radicis, decoctum: Simple infusion of pomegranate root in water. (44)

Granatum: 1. Pomegranate fruit. (1) 2. Bark and stem of the pomegranate tree, *Punica granatum*, of India and southwestern Asia. It can be used to prepare an astringent decoction and was believed to be anthelmintic, especially for the tapeworm. Figure 3-118. (8,39)

Granatus: Garnet (gem). (1)

Granula(e) dioscoridis: Arsenic granules or pills. (40)

Granulat[a][us][um]: Granulated, granular.

Granum: Grain, seed. (1)

Grape bark: See cocillana. (3)

Fig. 3-118 Granatum or pomegranate.

Fig. 3-119 Gratiola or hedge hyssop.

THE COMPENDIUM

Grape root (, Oregon): See berberis. (7)

Grape sugar: Glucose (despite the term, not fructose). (40)

Graphite: This may have the modern meaning of graphite (a form of carbon, as in pencil "lead"), but in older use was the black lead ore. See plumbago. (40)

Grarus, elixir: Syrup with alcohol, distillate of aloes, and spices. (3)

Grasso {*Italian*}: Grease, fat. (1)

Gratia dei: "Thanks be to God." 1. Herb-Robert (*Geranium robertianum*), meadow crane's bill (*Geranium paratense*) and other plants. Herb used. (1) 2. A vulnerary plaster similar to the plaster made from bentonica. (39) A pitch plaster similar to picis, emplastrum. (40)

Gratiola: Hedge hyssop, *Gratiola officinalis*. Herb used. A strong cathartic. Figure 3-119. (1,39)

Great Cordial Elixir: See Stoughton's bitters. (39)

Green oil: Oil of elder, see sambuca. (40)

Green soap: See sapo mollis. (8)

Green treat: A plaster of sweet clover, see melilotus. (40) Many formulations for such a plaster are found with widely varying ingredients.

Greenheart bark: Nectandra or bebeeru bark. (40)

Gregory's (Dr.) pills: See colocynthidis compositae, pilulae. (40,42)

Gregory's powder (, improved): See rhei compositus, pulvis, second item. After James Gregory, Edinburgh, late eighteenth century. (8,34,39)

Gretas: This is a variant, or more likely a transcription error, of cretas (chalk). It is found in a few secondary sources, but does not appear in any primary listings of preparations and lacks a proper translation in Latin.

Grey lotion: See nigra, aqua. (40)

Grey ointment: See hydrargyri, unguentum. (40)

Griffith's mixture: See ferri composita, mistura. (8)

Griffith's pills: See ferri carbonatis, pilulae. (34)

Griffith's white: See lithopone. (3)

Grindelia; Grindeliae fluidum extractum; —liquidum, extractum: Leaves of wild sunflower, *Grindelia robusta* or *G. squarrosa*, or fluid extract thereof. A mild stomachic and cardiac sedative, but primarily a bronchodilator used in the treatment of asthma. (8)

Grindeliae, elixir: NF elixir made of fluid extract of grindelia with compound spirit of orange, alcohol, and compound elixir of taraxacum. (45)

Grossularia: Gooseberry bush. Fruit used. (1)

Gross' antineuralgic pills: See antineuralgicae, pilulae. (34,46)

Ground nuts: "Nuts" of *Arachis hypogaea*, i.e., peanuts. (40)

Groundsel: The plant *Senecio vulgaris*, refrigerant and antiscorbutic. (39)

Grutellum: Groats (i.e—hulled grains of a cereal crop). (40)

Guacamphol: Guaiacol camphorate, see guaiacol. (40)

Guaco: Central and South American term for a variety of ill-defined plants believed to be alexipharmic. Unofficial. (44)

Guaiac; Guiacum; Guaiaci lignum; Guaiaci, resina; Guaiaci, tinctura; Guaiaci ammoniata, tinctura: Guaiacum wood, the dense heartwood of lignum vitae ("wood of life"), *Guaiacum officinale* and *Guiaicum sanctum*, of the West Indies and Americas. The wood is the source of guaiac resin, or gum guaiac. It was usually in the form of raspings or turnings. From the wood, which is denser than water, is made an alcoholic tincture and an ammoniated tincture by maceration in alcohol or ammoniated spirits, respectively. Guaiac resin is described in White's *Materia Medica* as "so disagreeable and its value so doubtful that it is rarely ordered." The powdered wood, or a lozenge of the powder in black currant paste, was said to be effective in chronic sore throat, especially in the case of syphilis, and produces a warm feeling in the stomach, resulting in use as a general gastric stimulant. It is a mild purgative, sometimes given as a pill for constipation, and was employed as well for chronic rheumatism. Figure 3-120. (1,8)

Guaiaci, glyceritum: Glycerite of guaiac, of the powder, solution of potassa, glycerin, and water. (46)

Guaiaci, lac; —, mistura: Mixture of guaiac, of powdered guaiac, sugar, and acacia, in cinnamon water. Said to be popular for syphilis, but undoubtedly inactive. (40)

Guaiaci, mistura: Guaiac mixture, of guaiac powder, sugar, acacia, and cinnamon water. Usage as per guaiac (34,42)

Guaiaci ammoniata, tinctura; Guaiaci composita, tinctura: Compound or ammoniated tincture of guaiac, Dewee's tincture of guaiac. The compound tincture (Dewee's) is made from guaiac, potassium carbonate and pimenta in diluted alcohol, used for rheumatism and as an emmenagogue. The term is also used for the ammoniated tincture, which is of guaiac extract in aromatic spirits of ammonia. (31,34)

Guaiaci composita, confectio: Compound confection of guaiac, "Chelsea Pensioner," of powdered guaiac resin, powdered rhubarb, acid potassium tartrate, powdered nutmeg, sublimed sulphur, and clarified honey. A "popular remedy for gout and rheumatism." (42)

Guaiaci compositum, gargarisma: Compound gargle of guaiac of ten percent each of ammoniated tincture of guaiac and compound tincture of cinchona, with twenty percent clarified honey, and four percent potassium chlorate, with oil of peppermint to desired flavor. "Used as a local stimulant for the throat." (31)

Guaiaci compositum, tinctura: See guaiaci ammoniata tinctura. (40)

Guaiacol; Guaiacoli(s) benzoas; —camphoras; —carbonas; —cinnamas; —phosphas; —salicylas; —valarianas: Guaiacol is a crude fraction of beachwood tar, purified by treatment with ammonia, and consists of sixty to ninety percent creosote. It is used directly or as various salts (benzoate, camphorate, carbonate, cinnamate, phosphate, salicylate, valarianate) in the same manner as creosote. (8) In the BPC (42), the benzoate is said to be good for diarrhea in phthisis and in diabetes mellitus, the camphorate for night sweats and diarrhea in phthisis, the carbonate as a disinfectant for phthisis and typhoid fever, the cinnamate for intestinal phthisis, bladder catarrh, typhoid, cystitis, and gonorrhea, the phosphate in phthisis and typhoid fever, and the valarianate for tuberculosis, bronchial disorders, chlorosis, and diarrhea.

Guano: The dried excrement of sea fowl, source of phosphate. (3) Said to be used in South America both internally and topically as a cataplasm with clay for leprosy and joint inflammation. Unofficial. (44)

Guaiacum officinale

Published by Dr. Woodville April. 1. 1790.

Fig. 3-120 Guaiac or heart of lignum vitae.

Guarana; Guaranae, fluidextractum: A paste formed from crushed seeds of the guarana plant, *Paullinia cupana*, of Brazil or of related species, or the fluid extract therefrom. The active principal, guaranine, is identical to caffeine, and the plant was used for the same purposes. (8, 31)

Guaranae, elixir: Elixir of guarana, of fluid extract of guarana, aromatic elixir and compound elixir of taraxicum. (31) In the BPC, of guarana powder, oil of cinnamon, syrup, and alcohol. (42) Effects similar to caffeine and used for headache.

Guaranae, tinctura: Simple alcoholic tincture of powdered guarana, for "sick-headache," noted to act chiefly by virtue of caffeine content. (42)

Guaranae et apii, elixir: Elixir of guarana and celery, from the fluid extracts of guarana and celery (apium). (31)

Guaranine: Structurally identical to caffeine, active principal of guarana. (8)

Guaza: Cannabis (i.e., cannabis indica). (3) Indian hemp. See apocynum (cannabinum). (40)

Guhr: See kieselguhr. (3)

Guiaci, gum(mi); Guiac gum: Gum guaiac, equivalent to the resin noted above (guiaci, resina).

Guide's balsam: Liniment of opium, for example, see opiatum, linimentum. (40)

Guiggiola {*Italian*}; **Giugiuba** {*Italian*}: Jujube, fruit of the jujube tree. See jujuba. (1)

Guilandina moringa: See nephriticum lignum. (39)

Guimauve: Marsh-Mallow. See altheae. (40)

Guinea grains: See grana paradisi. (3)

Guinea pepper: Capsicum fruit, pepper. See capsicum. (40)

Gulancha: See tinospora. (42)

Gum: A gummy substance used as a binder for pills or troches or a thickening agent. The most commonly used were gum tragacanth and gum arabic. (8)

Gum animi: See copal. (40)

Gum arabic: See acacia. (8)

Gum barbary, brown: See acacia. (3)

Gum benjamin: See benzoin. (3)

Gum camphor: See camphor. (40)

Gum catechu: Gum of catechu. (40)

Gum dragon: Tragacanth. (3)

Gum elemi: See elemi gummi. (40)

Gum guaiacum: See guiaci, gum(mi). (40)

Gum juniper: See sandaraca, presumably the botanical definition. (40)

Gum kino: Although there is a specific plant known as kino, gum kino appears to be a general term for gum derived from a variety of tropical plants.

Gum kordofan: See acacia. (40)

Gum pill: See asafoetidae compositae, pilule. (39)

Gum saline solution: Injectable solution of gum acacia in nomal (0.9%) saline. (40)

Gum sanguis draconis: Dragon's blood, see sanguis draconis. (40)

Gum scammony: See scammonii, resina. (40)

Gum senegal: See acacia. (40)

Gum thus: Frankincense, or sometimes turpentine, oleoresin. See frankincense, common. (3,40)

Gummae et resinae: Gums and resins (drawer or cabinet pull).

Gummi: Gum, resin. (1)

Gummi ammoniacum: See ammoniacum, gummi. (1)

Gummi arabicum: See arabicum, gummi. (1)

Gummi armeniacae: See armeniacae, gummi. (1)

Gummi asafoetidae: See asafoetida. (1)

Gummi copal: See copal. (1)

Gummi elasticum: India rubber. (3)

Gummi elemi, unguentum e: See arcaei, unguentum. (35)

Gummi euphorbii: See euphorbium. (1)

Gummi ghat(t)i: Same as gummi Indicum. (42)

Gummi guttae (gutti): Gamboge. (3)

Gummi hederae: See hederae, gummi. (1)

Gummi indicae, mucilago: Mucilage of Indian gum. (42)

Gummi Indicum: Indian or Ghatti gum, of *Anogeissus latifolia*, of India and Ceylon, a local equivalent to gum arabic. (42)

Gummi rubri, syrupus: See eucalypti gummi, syrupus. (42)

Gummi rubrum gambiense: See kino. (3)

Gummi sarcocollae: See sarcocolla. (1)

Gummi scorpionis; —thebaicum: Gum arabic. (3)

Gummi tacamahaca: See tacamahaca, gummi. (1)

Gummi tragacanthum: See tragacantha. (1)

Gummosa, aqua: Diluted mucilage of gum arabic (one part in sixty-four of water). (3)

Gummosa, mistura; —mixtura: See acaciae, mistura. (46)

Gummosa, pilula(e): See galbani compositae, pilulae. (40)

Gummosa, pilule: Gum pills, of myrrh and opopanax. (39)

Gummosus, pulvis: See pulvis diatragacanthae. (3) See tragacanthae compositus, pulvis. (40)

Gun cotton: See pyroxylin. (8)

Gunjah: Cannabis Indies, or Indian hemp. See apocynum (cannabinum). (3,40)

Gurjun balsam; —oil; —, oleum: An aromatic wood oil used in perfumery, from various *Dipterocarpus* species by steam distillation. (40)

Guru: See kola. (3)

Guteta, pulvis de: See gutteta, pulvis de. (1)

Gutta (*Lat*): Drop (noun), plural guttae. (1)

Gutta gamba: See gambogium. (1)

Gutta percha tissue: A thin film of gutta percha latex used as a dressing material.

Gutta percha; Gutta percha(e), liquor: The juice of *Dichopsis gutta* and related trees, a tough, flexible, plastic-like material used in making splints. The liquor consisted of gutta percha in chloroform with a small amount of lead carbonate, and could be used as an adhesive plaster base or replacement for flexible collodion. (8,42,44,46)

Gutteta, pulvis de; Guttetam, pulvis ad: Antiepileptic made from roots of peony and valerian, sometimes with other ingredients (root of white dittany, oak mistletoe, etc.). (1,39) An anti-epileptic powder of peony, valerian, dictamnus albus, hartshorn, mother of pearl, and mistletoe (viscus). Estes explains that guttetam is a Languedoc word meaning seizure. (39)

Gutti: See gamboge. (40)

Guy's pills: A pill of digitalis, squill, hyoscyamus, and mercury, for heart disorders and dropsy. (24) See digitalis compositae, pilulae. (42)

Gymnocladus: Seeds and pulp of pods of American coffee-bean tree, coffee tree, or Kentucky mahogany, *Gymnocladus canadensis*. This is not the true coffee tree, caffea. (33)

Gyno(a)cardia (, oleum): Seeds and oil of chaulmogra, *Gynocardia odorata*, "used both internally and externally in leprosy, secondary syphilis, rheumatism, scrofula, and in phthisis." (33)

Gynoacardiae, unguentum: See chaulmoograe, unguentum. (40)

Gypsum, calcined: Plaster of Paris; see calcii sulphas exsiccatus. (40)

Gypsum: Naturally occurring mineral form of calcium sulfate, $CaSO_4$. (8)

H

H.: Herba (herb), huile {*French*} (oil). (1)

Haarlem oil: See Dutch drops.

Haedera: See hedera. (1)

Haemagogum, antidotum: See antidotum haemagogum. (1)

Haematite; Haematites, lapis: Iron ore, bloodstone, red ion oxide. (3)

Haematoxyli, decoctum: Decoction of logwood, of same with cinnamon bark and water, mild astringent for diarrhea. (42)

Haematoxyli cum catechu, mistura: A mixture of tincture of catechu and aromatic sulphuric acid in decoction of logwood, a powerful astringent mixture in dysentery, diarrhea, phthisis, and internal hemmorhage of the gut. (42)

Haematoxyli liquidum, extractum: Liquid extract of haematoxylon as per BPC. Astringent. (42)

Haematoxylon; Haematoxylon, extractum; Haemat. ext.: Logwood, the heartwood of *Haematoxylon campechianum*, of Central America, or the dry extract thereof. Used as per tannic acid (tannicum, acidum). It will stain the urine and feces red. Most commonly used for gastrointestinal disorders. Figure 3-121. (8)

Haemoglobin: Red pigment of red blood cells, a protein responsible for oxygen transport. While capable of providing some value as a protein source, it was primarily used as a source of iron, although the BPC notes that absorption is probably poor. (42)

Haemoglobol; Haemol; Haemogallol: Hemoglobin combined with zinc dust or (in the latter case) pyrogallol. Use as per hemoglobin. (42)

Haemorrhoidale, unguentum: Hemorrhoid ointment, of lead acetate, hysocyamus, camphor, and crocus. (39)

Haemostasin: Trade name for adrenaline (epinephrine). (40)

Fig. 3-121 Haematoxylon or logwood.

Haffkine's prophylactic fluid: A plague vaccine. (40)

Hahnemann, soluble mercury of: A mercury solution formed by ammonia acting on the nitrate of mercury protoxide, of poorly defined composition. (44)

Hahnemann's mercury: Black oxide of mercury, see hydrargyri suboxidum. (40)

Halite: Rock salt, sodium chloride. (3)

Haliverol: Proprietary halibut liver oil fortified with vitamin D. (40)

Haller's (acid) elixir; Halleri, liquor: A solution of sulfuric acid in alcohol. Probably similar to vitriol, elixir. (3) See sulphuricum alcoholisatum, acidum. (40)

Hall's antidote: A solution of potassium iodide and quinine, to treat poisoning with mercuric chloride (hydrargyri chloridum corrosivum). (24)

Hall's dinner pills: See aloes et mastiches, pilulae. (34) This variant was of aloe, licorice extact, soap, and molasses. (46)

Hall's pills (, Marshall): See aloes dilutae, pilulae. (42)

Halowax: Proprietary non-flammable chlorinated naphthaline (primarily for pest control, i.e., mothballs). (3)

Haly ((ben) Abbas), powder of: An antitussive opium powder after Haly ben Abbas, Persia, tenth century. Of poppy, gum arabic, licorice, spodium, and starch. (39)

Hamaelidin; Hamamelin(um): These would seem to be active principals isolated from witch hazel, although no details have been located. (40,42)

Hamamel(id)is cortex: Bark of witch hazel. Astringent and local haemostatic. (42)

Hamamel(id)is foliorum, fluidextractum: Fluid extract of hamamelis leaves. Note that, while hamamelidis is the proper Latin genitive, many labels use the term hamamelis. (31)

Hamamel(id)is, extractum: Dry extract of witch hazel (BPC). (42)

Hamamel(id)is, tinctura: Simple tincture of hamamelis bark in alcohol, astringent and styptic, as a lotion or local injection for hemorrhoids. (42)

Hamamel(id)is, unguentum: Liquid extract of hamamelis in lanolin, emollient, especially for piles. (42)

Hamameli(di)s, gossypium: Absorbent cotton soaked in tincture of hamamelis and glycerin and dried. (42)

Hamamelis (Virginiana); Hamameli(di)s, fluidum, extractum; —liquidum, extractum; —, liquor; —, aqua (spirituosa); Hamamelidis: Witch hazel, the leaves of *Hamamelis virginiana*, of North America. Used as per tannic acid (tannicum, acidum). The fluid extract (same as the BPC liquor) was obtained by percolation with water, alcohol, and glycerin. A topical liquid similar to the fluid extract, and referred to as "witch hazel," is commonly used as a mild topical astringent and disinfectant following shaving or for mild skin conditions. Witch hazel water (aqua) is made by soaking twigs in water, and is said to be of no use, as it contains little of the volatile oil. A variant, actually the proper Latin genitive form—Hamamelidis—was used variably as the nominative and was preferred in the United States NF. (1,8,30,31,42)

Hamburg drops: A kind of "Swedish bitters." (3)

Hamburg tea: Identical with St. Germain tea, differently flavored. (3)

Hamdi's solution: A specimen preserving solution of sodium sulfate, salt, glycerin, and water. (24)

Hamech, confectio; —, confezione {*Italian*}**:** Purgative attributed to Arabic physician Hamech, compounded from colocynth, scammony, agaric, senna leaves, rhubarb, myrobalans, etc. (1)

Haplopappus: Herba del Pasmo, *Ericameria laricifolia*. A minor sedative. (32)

Harmala; Harmel: Wild or Syrian rue, *Peganum harmula*. Seeds used. (1)

Harmaline: Fuchsine dye. (3)

Harrington's solution: A hand disinfectant consisting of water, corrosive mercuric chloride (hydrargyri chloridum corrosivum), hydrochloric acid, and alcohol. (24)

Harrogate salts: See sal aperiens. (42)

Hartman's solution: Thymol and sulfuric ether in ninety-five percent alcohol, used to desensitize nerve roots in dental work. (24)

Hartshorn: 1. Calcium phosphate containing material extracted from stag's horn, a tonic with a wide variety of uses. 2. Aqua ammoniae (ammonia water). 3. Ammonium carbonate, a mixture of ammonium bicarbonate and ammonium carbamate in water, which produced ammonia and carbon dioxide. (39)

Hartshorn, salt of: Ammonium carbonate. (40)

Hartshorn, spirit of: A solution of ammonia; see ammoniae liquor. (40)

Hartshorn and oil: See ammoniae, linimentum. (40)

Hartshorn powder: Similar to prepared chalk, creta praeparata. (40)

Hart's solution: See hydrargyri et ammonii chloridi, liquor. (42)

Haustus sennae Co.: See sennae composita, mistura. (40)

Haustus; Haustus catharticus: A draught, a cathartic draught. General term, formula not specified. (39)

Hawkin's (Dr.) embrocation: Similar to camphorae compositum, linimentum. (40)

Hay saffron: Saffron, see crocus. (40)

Hayem's solution: Reagent used for counting red blood cells. (24)

Hayo: Coca leaves, see coca. (3)

Hay's wash: Zinc sulfate solution for ocular use. (40)

Hazeline: Distilled extract of witch hazel, see hamamelis. (40)

Hazelwort: See asarum. (39)

Hb; HB; H.B.: Variants of Herba, i.e., the whole herb.

Heal-all: 1. See scrophularia. (32) 2. See prunella. (39) 3. See collinsonia. (40)

Heberden's ink; —mixture: See ferri aromatica, mistura. (40)

Hebra's (itch) ointment: See sulphuris compositum, unguentum. (31,40)

Hebra's lead ointment: See diachylon, unguentum. (34)

Hedeoma; Hedeomae, oleum: Leaves and tops of Pennyroyal, *Hedeoma pulegiodes*, of North America, from which a volatile oil is distilled. The oil is an aromatic stimulant useful for colic, flatulence, or gastric upset. The oil has been used as an abortifacient. (8)

Hedera arboria: Ivy, *Hedera helix*. Leaves and resin used. An internal tonic used in children, a topical to keep blisters running, depilatory. Berries also said to be diaphoretic and alexipharmic. (1,39)

Hedera terrestris: Ground-ivy, *Glechoma hederacea*. Herb used as tonic, aperient, expectorant, and blood purifier. Figure 3-122. (1,39)

Hederae, gummi: Dried gum of ivy plant, *Hedera helix*. (1)

Hedychroi, trochisci: Strongly scented anti-pestilential lozenges of saffron, cassia bark, cinnamon, myrrh, opobalsam, asarabacca root, costus root, spikenard, etc. These were used to fill pomanders to protect the wearer from plague. (1)

Helcosal: Bismuth pyrogallate. (3)

Helenium: See enula. (1)

Heleny, rad., conf.: Confection of the root of heleny, i.e., that of *Inula helenium* (formerly *Elecampane inula*). No specific preparation was located. See enula. (1)

Helianthemum; Helianthemi fluidum, extractum: Frostweed, frostwort, frostplant, or rock Rose, *Helianthemum canadense*, or the fluid extract, for scrofula. (33)

Helianthi compositus, syrupus: Syrup of sunflower seed with sugar and gin. For respiratory disorders. (34)

Helianthine; Helianthinae, solutio: Methyl orange dye or a solution of same, used as a pH indicator, non-medicinal. (42)

Helianthus: Seeds of the sunflower, *Helianthus annuus*, diuretic and expectorant. (33)

Helicon: Trade name, aspirin. (40)

Helleboraster: Leaves of the bear's foot, *Helleborus foetidis*, said to be confused commonly with black hellebore. An anthelmintic. Figure 3-123. (39)

Hellebore, American; —, green: See veratrum viride. (7)

Hellebore, black; Helleborus niger; Hellebori nigri rhizoma: Black Hellebore, Christmas rRose, *Helleborus niger*. Rhizome and root used. Cathartic. Figure 3-124. (1,42)

Hellebore, white; Helleborus albus: White hellebore, *Veratrum album*. Rhizome and root used. Cathartic. (1)

Hellebori, tinctura: Tincture of hellebore, probably black hellebore. (40)

Glecoma hederacea.

Published by D. Woodville, Jan. 1. 1790.

Fig. 3-122 Hedera terrestris.

Helleborus foetidus.

Published by D. Woodville, April. 1. 1790.

Fig. 3-123 Helleboraster.

Hellebori alcoholicum, extractum: Dry alcoholic extract of black hellebore, USP. (44)

Hellebori compositum, vinum: Wine of black hellebore, of powdered hellebore, logwood chips, powdered helonias root, and sherry wine. A tonic and cathartic with a "direct influence on the female organs," useful for menstrual difficulties. (34)

Hellebori nigri, tinctura: Simple tincture of root in alcohol, cathartic and emmenagogue, and produces a digitalis-like effect on the heart. (42)

Hellenium: See helenium. (39)

Helly's fluid: A histological fixative. (24)

Helmetol: See hexamethylenamine. (32)

Helminthochorton: Corsican moss, the algae *Alsidium helmentho-chorton*, from the Mediteranian. Vermifuge. (1)

Helmitol: See formamol. (40)

Heloniadis compositum, elixir: Compound elixir of helonias, of the fluid extracts of helonias, caulophyllum, viburnum opulus, and mitchella. It is used in dysmenorrhea. (31)

Helonias; Heloniadis, fluidextractum: Helonias, blazing star, false unicorn, *Chamoelirium luteum*, rhizome and roots used, or the fluid extract therefrom. A diuretic, for kidney disorders. (7,31)

Helvetii, pulvis stipticus: See pulvis stypticum. (39)

Hemagogum, antidotum: See antidotum haemagogum. (1)

Hematites (, lapis); Hematitis (, lapis): Bloodstone, hematite, an iron oxide mineral. (1)

Hematoxylon: See haematoxylon.

Hemidesmus; Hemidesmi, syrupus: Dried root of *Hemidesmus indicus*, the Indian sarsaparilla plant, or a syrup made therefrom. It is used in India in the same manner as sarsaparilla, which probably has little or no activity in any event (see sarsaparilla). (8)

Hemisine: Trade name, adrenaline, i.e., epinephrine. (40)

Hemlock: For the classical toxin, see conium (poison hemlock). In more modern American usage, the hemlock tree, a conifer, *Balsamum canadensis*, *Tsuga canadensis*, or *Balsamum canadense*, depending on reference source.

Hemlock, emplastrum: Resin of hemlock, in this case the hemlock tree, *Pinus balsamea*, not poison hemlock. The resin was used as a plaster (discutient) as well as internally as a tonic, diuretic, and cathartic. (39)

Hemlock, poison: See conium. (39)

Hemlock, water: See cicuta. (39)

Hemlock gum, —pitch: Exudation from Canadian hemlock. (40)

Fig. 3-124 Hellebore (black).

Hemlock (oil): An extract of Canadian hemlock. Abortifacient. (39). Not related to poison hemlock (conium).

Hemlock ointment: See conii, unguentum. (40)

Hemlock pills: See conii compositae, pilulae. (42)

Hemoglobin (and related terms): See haemoglobin. (42)

Hemp agrimony: See eupatorium. (39)

Hemp resin: Resin derived from apocynum. (40)

Hemp, Canadian; Hemp, Indian: See apocynum. (8,39)

Henbane; Henban.: Henbane, see hyoscyamus.

Henna: See alkanet. (39)

Hepar: "Liver"(of sulphur, antimony, lime, etc.), generally a sulfide. (3)

Hepar antimonii (calcareum): An impure antimony and potassium sulfide. (3)

Hepar calcis: Calcium sulfide. (3)

Hepar sulphuris: Potassa sulphurata, "liver of sulphur." Now known to be a mixture of potassium sulfate and thiosulfate. (3,39)

Hepatax: A proprietary liver extract. (40)

Hepatic aloes: See aloe. (39)

Hepatica: Liverwort, *Anemone hepatica*. Herb used as demulcent and tonic. (1)

Hepatis, extractum: Extract of mammalian liver, to treat pernicious anemia (enhances B-12 absorption). (7)

Heracleum: Masterwort or cow parsnip, *Heracleum lanatum*. A minor sedative, anti-epileptic, carminative, and rubifacient. (32,39)

Herapath's salt: Quinine iodosulphate. (3)

Herb bennet: See caryophyllata. (39)

Herb christopher: See actea (spicata). (39)

Herb mastic (, Syrian): See marum syriacum. (39)

Herb mercury: See mercurialis. (39)

Herba; Herbe {*French*}**:** Herb. (1)

Herba A~G, H~M, etc.: Drawer or cabinet pull for alphabetical filing of various herbs.

Herba britannica: See lapathum. (39)

Herba regina: Queen's herb, said to be so named for curing the migraine headaches of Catherine de Medici, same as nicotiana. (39)

Herba salicariae: See lythrum. (33)

Herbarum recentium, tincturae: A term for various non-standard tinctures of fresh herbs. A generic tincture could be made with 500 grams of herb(s) of choice in 1 liter of alcohol, macerated and filtered. (34)

Hermodactylus: Hermodactyl, "Finger of Hercules," botanical of uncertain identity, thought to be the corm of a *Colchicum* species, possibly *Colchicum variegatum*. Estes indicates it may also be *Iris tuberosum. (*1,39)

Herniam, emplastrum ad: Hernia plaster, said to be a predecessor to emplastrum thuris compositium. (39)

Heroin: Diacetylmorphine, a potent derivative of morphine, see opium. (40)

Hetol: See sodium cinnamate. (40)

Hetraline: Hexamine dioxybenzene, a disinfectant. (40)

Heuchera: Alum root, American sanicle, *Heuchera americana*, an effective astringent. (33)

Hexacyanoferrate: See prussate. (29)

Hexahydropyridine: See piperadine. (42)

Hexamethylamine: See hexaminium.

Hexamethylenamine; Hexamethylenetetramine; Hexaminium: Urotropine; uritone; helmetol, hexamine, hexamethyleneamine, or methenamine, used as a urinary disinfectant or to prevent urinary infections. In acidic urine, this decomposes to release formaldehyde, which is antimicrobial. Same as adamantanamine, now used as an anti-viral. (32)

Hexamine dioxybenzene: A disinfectant. (40)

Hexamol: See formamol. (40)

Hexylresorcinol: A topical for the throat and mucous membranes, still in use for over-the-counter lozenges; see resorcin.

Hey's wash: See lotio rubra. (40)

Hiacintho, confectio de: See hyacintho, confectio de. (1)

Hibiscus: See abelmoschus. (39)

Hibiscus esculentus: Okra, gombo, bendee, *Hibiscus esculentus*. Anyone who has cooked okra will not be surprised that it is described as a "mucilagenous" emollient and demulcent. (33)

Hickery-pickery: Powder of aloes and canella. (3)

Hicra picra: See hiera picra. (3)

Hiera(,) simple: Same as hiera picra. (39)

Hiera, tinctura; Hierae, tinctura: Wine of aloes, see aloes, vinum. (3,40)

Hiera diacolocynthid[is][os]: Purgative electuary, main ingredient colocynth. (1)

Hiera logadii; Hiera logod: Purgative electuary purportedly named for Logadius of Memphis, of colocynth, aloes, agaric, scammony, squill, polypody rhizome, etc. For treatment of melancholy, seizures, and other brain disorders. (1,39)

Hiera pachii: A nonspecified purging confection. (39)

Hiera picra (, elixir or E.); Hiera p.e.: From the Greek, "sacred bitter," a purgative of Socotra aloe, saffron, cinnamon, etc. (1)

Hiera picra (in reference to powdered material): See pulvis aloes et canellae. (42)

Hiera picra, tincture of: See aloes, vinum. (40)

Hieracium: Hawkweed, veiny-leaved hawkweed, rattlesnake Weed, striped woodwort, *Hieracium venosum*, an astringent and expectorant. (33)

High bush cranberry: See viburnum opulus. (8)

Hiosciamus: See hyoscyamus. (1)

Hipericum: See hypericum. (1)

Hippo wine: See ipecacuanhae, vinum. (40)

Hippocastanum: Horse chestnut, *Aesculus hippocastanum*. A digestive stimulant related to, and used like, the Buckeye (*A. glabra*). Figure 3-125. (33)

Hippocrates: Renowned physician of ancient Greece, ca. 460–370 BCE. A multitude of *materia medica* is consequently attributed to him, correctly or otherwise. (1)

Hippocraticum, vinum: Hippocras, wine of Hippocrates. A wine flavored with cinnamon, cloves, and other spices. (1)

Hippopotamus: Hippopotamus teeth (ivory) used to construct dentures. (1)

Hippuricum, acidum: Hippuric acid, from urine of carnivorous animals, the metabolic product of benzoic acid, by condensation with glycine. Supposedly an anti-hypertensive. (42)

Hips: Rose hips, fruit of dog-rose. See rose hips. (3,8)

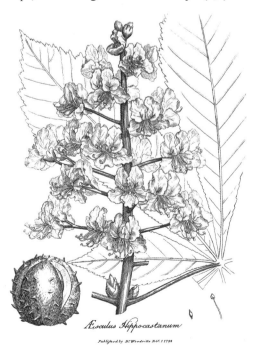

Fig. 3-125 Hippocastanum or horse chestnut.

Hircus: Goat. (1)

Hirudo (australis): See leeches. (1,8) The BPC notes an Australian variety. (42)

Hirundinum, oleum: Swallow-oil, made from the whole bird, with multiple other ingredients. (39)

Hirundo {*Latin*}: Swallow (i.e—the bird). (1)

Hissopo humida: See oesypus humida. (1)

Hissopus: See hyssopus. (1)

Histerica, aqua; Histericae, pilulae, etc.: See hysterica, aqua; hystericae, pilulae, etc. (1)

Hive powder: See hydrargyrum cum creta. (40)

Hive syrup: See scillae compositus, syrupus. (8,34)

Hoarhound: Variant of horehound, see marrubium. (8)

Hoedera: See hedera. (1)

Hoffman's anodye: See (a)etheris compositus, spiritus. (8)

Hoffman(n)'s (visceral) elixir: A mixture with gentian, absinth, mellilot, cascarilla, orange peel, and cinnamon. (39)

Hoffman(n)'s balsam of life: Proprietary tincture of balsam of Peru and other aromatic ingredients, after Friedrich Hoffman, eighteenth century. (39)

Hoffman(n)'s drops; Hoffman's anodyne (liquor): See (a)etheris compositus, spiritus. (31,39)

Hog gum: Inferior gum tragacanth. (40)

Hollandicus, syrupus: Molasses. (3)

Holocaine: Phenocaine, a local anesthetic. (40)

Holy thistle: Carduus benedictus, see carduus. (39)

Holywood: Guaiacum wood. (3)

Homalourea: Dipropyl-barbiturate, a sedative-hypnotic. (40)

Homatropinae, guttae: Eyedrops (BPC) consisting of homatropine, mydriatic. (42)

Homatropinae et cocainae, guttae: Eyedrops (BPC) consisting of homatropine and cocaine, mydriatic and anesthetic. (42)

Homatropine hydrobromide; Homatropinae hydrobromas: Homatropine hydrobromide, an isolated alkaloid prepared from atropine. See atropa. The only use of the isolated alkaloid was (and remains) the dilation of the pupil in ophthalmology. (8)

Homberg's narcotic salt of vitriol: A compound preparation of iron sulfate and borax after Dutch chemist Willem Homberg, Paris, early eighteenth century. (39)

Homberg's phosphorus: Calcium chloride, fused and exposed to sun, phosphorescent. (3)

Homberg's pyrophorus: A mixture of alum and brown sugar, or of potassium sulphide, alumina, and charcoal. (3)

Homberg's salt: See boric acid. (40)

Homo: Man. (1)

Honey of borax: A solution of borax with glycerin and clarified honey, applied to mouth ulcers and as topical disinfectant. (8)

Honey sugar: Dextrose, glucose (not obtained from honey and not entirely correct as honey contains fructose and other sugars in addition to dextrose). (3)

Honey: See mel. Aperient, detergent, and expectorant. (39)

Honthin: Albumin tannate, an antidiarrheal. (40)

Hooper's female pills: Aloes, ferrous sulphate, myrrh, extract of black hellebore, and soap, with ginger and canella flavorants. Variant of aloes et mastiches, pilulae. After Dr. John Hooper, English, ca. 1743. (34,39)

Hope's mixture: See camphorae acida, mistura. (34)

Hopi: Appears to be an orthographic variant for opium or opii. (32)

Hopogan: Trade name, magnesium peroxide. (40)

Hops: See humulus. (8)

Hordei, aqua: Barley water. A nutritive. (39)

Hordei, decoctum: Decoction of pearl barley in water, used in infant foods and as a nutritive as well as in mucous catarrh. (42)

Hordei compositum, decoctum: Compound decoction of barley, with same plus carica, licorice, and currants. Used as a nutritive for debilitated patients. (39)

Hordei praeparatus, farina: Barley flour, steamed for about 30 hours. (3)

Hordeum (decorticatum); Hordei, decoctum; —mistura: Seed of barley, *Hordeum distichon* (now *Hordeum vulgare*), or the decoction in water. A useful demulcent, especially for a dry sore throat. Decorticatum refers to removal of the husk. (8)

Hordeum (distichon): Barley, *Hordeum vulgare*. (1)

Hordeum perlatum: Pearl barley, polished grain, as one would purchase today. (39)

Horehound, water; —, wild: See lycopus and eupatorium, respectively. Horehound not otherwise specified is more typically marrubium. (39)

Horehound (, white): See marrubium. (8)

Horminum sativum: Leaves and seed of clary, *Savlia sclarea*, an antihysteric and carminative. (39)

Horse brimstone: Black sulfur. (40)

Horse chestnut: See hippocastanum. (33)

Horse radish: See armoracia. (8)

Horse salt: Glauber's salt. (3)

Horsemint: American, see monarda (this is *M. fistulosa* or *punctata)*. English, see mentha, this is *Mentha aquatica*, a close relative of other mint species. (40)

Hot drops: See capsici et myrrhae, tinctura. (31)

Hoy's salt: A cheap Epsom salt, magnesium sulfate. (39)

Huile {*French*}**:** Oil. (1)

Huile de pied de boeuf {*French*}**:** Neatsfoot oil, i.e., from calf hooves. (40)

Humulus; Humulus lupulus: Hops, *Humulus lupulus*, botanical source of lupulin. Used as a stomachic and carminative as well as a soporific. (8)

Humuli, elixir: NF elixir of the fluid extract of hops with tincture of vanilla, compound elixir of taraxacum, and aromatic elixir. (45)

Humuli, fluidextractum; —fluidum, extractum: Fluid extract of hops, used as a nerve sedative. (31)

Humuli, tinctura: Tincture of hops (humulus), by maceration and percolation, used as a sedative and bitter tonic. (31)

Hungary water: Spirit of rosemary, approximately two percent in water. (40)

Hunn's drops: See cajaputi composita, mistura. (34)

Hura brasiliensis: A Brazilian tree, juice of fruit or bark used, cathartic and emetic, as well as a topical decoction or bath derived from the bark. Unofficial, mainly homeopathic. (44)

Hurr nut: See myrobalans. (40)

Husson, eau medicinale d' {French}**:** Medicinal water of Husson, a British propietary formulation of crocus (colchicum) used for gout. (39)

Hutchinson's pills: Hydrargyri cum creta et opio, pilulae. (42)

Huxham's tincture (of bark): See cinchonae composita, tinctura. After John Huxham, England, ca. 1750. (3,34,39,40)

Hyacintho, confectio de: Composite formulation named for hyacinth, a major ingredient (apparently the botanical definition, not the gem stone). (1)

Hyacinthus (gemma)(lapis): 1. Jacinth (a gem stone). 2. Wild hyacinth, Wood Hyacinth, *Hyacinthus anglicus*, or bluebell (*Scilla nutans*). Root used. (1)

Hyd. Chlor.: May be mercuric (hydrargyri) chloride (corrosive sublimate), or chloral hydrate. The container or contents may provide an indication, as mercuric chloride is a colored solid, chloral hydrate a clear liquid. (40)

Hydr(o)iodici, acidi syrupus: Syrup of hydroiodic acid, HI, produced with potassium iodide, potassium hypophosphite, and tartaric acid in alcohol, concentrated down by evaporation and dissolved in simple syrup. (8)

Hydracetine: Acetophenylhydrazine, dye or colorant. (3)

Hydragogue powder: See podophylli compositus, resinae, pulvis. (34)

Hydragogue tincture: See sambuci, vinum. (34)

Hydragogum, electuarium: Purgative electuary, used in treatment of dropsy and sciatica. (1)

Hydrangea; Hydrangea, fluidextractum; —fluidum, extractum: Hydrangea, or seven-barks, *Hydrangea arborescens*, rhizome and roots used, or the fluid extract therefrom. A diuretic and diaphoretic, for kidney disorders. (7,31,46)

Hydrangeae et lithii, elixir: Elixir of hydrangea and lithium, of hydrangea, lithium benzoate, and lithium salicylate. (31)

Hydrargyri, emplastrum: 1. Mercury plaster, of mercury, oleate of mercury (hydrargyri, oleatum), and lead plaster (plumbi, emplastrum). (8) 2. Blue plaster, of olive oil, lead acetate, mercury, and turpentine. Resolvant and discutient (exfoliant). (39)

Hydrargyri, linimentum: There are many variants of mercury liniment, that in the BP composed of the ointment (hydrargyri, unguentum) with solution of ammonia and camphor. (40)

Hydrargyri acetica, lotio: Lotion of mercuric chloride and acetic acid in glycerin, alcohol, and rosewater. For lice. (42)

Hydrargyri, massa: Mercury mass for forming mercury pills (blue pills), blue mass. Of mercury, honey of rose, glycerrhiza, althaea, and glycerin; thirty-three percent mercury. (8) In the BPC, essentially the same, but composed of confectio rosae, licorice root, and mercury. (42)

Hydrargyri, piluli: Mercury pills or blue pills, see hydrargyri, massa. (8)

Hydrargyri (dilutum)(mite), unguentum: Mercury ointment, blue ointment. Of mercury, lard, suet, and oleate of mercury (hydrargyri, oleatum) fifty percent mercury, or dilute/weaker forms. Useful for skin conditions and to control itching. (8,42)

Hydrargyri alba, calx: Ammoniated mercury, see hydrargyri ammoniatum. (40)

Hydrargyri ammoniati, unguentum: Ointment of ammoniated mercury in paraffin ointment base. (42)

Hydrargyri ammoniatum; Hydr. ammon.: Ammoniated mercury, made from mercuric chloride. This is actually the amidochloride, below.

Hydrargyri ammonii chloridum; Hydrargyrum amidochloridum: Mercury ammonium chloride or amidochloride, $HgNH_2Cl$. A form of mercury used to lighten skin, still used in illicit ointments for this purpose in some locations today, with resulting mercury poisoning.

Hydrargyri bichloridi; —bichloridum: Mercury bichloride, i.e., corrosive sublimate. See hydrargyri chloridum corrosivum.

Hydrargyri biniodidi, injectio: Solution of mercuric and potassium iodide for antiseptic vaginal injection. (42)

Hydrargyri chloridi mitis et jalapae, pulvis: The mild chloride of mercury (calomel) and powdered jalap. (46)

Hydrargyri chloridi mitis, tabellae: Tablets of mild mercurous chloride, calomel tablets, compressed tablets containing calomel (hydrargyri chloridum mite), colored pink with carmine. (31)

Hydrargyri chloridi mitis, unguentum: Ointment of mild mercurous chloride, calomel ointment; prophylactic ointment, of thirty percent calomel (hydrargyri chloridum mite) in white petrolatum. (31)

Hydrargyri chloridi mitis; Hydrargyri chloridum mite: Mild chloride of mercury, i.e., mercurous chloride, calomel, HgCl. The term "mild" is relative to the mercuric salt, corrosive sublimate (hydrargyri chloridum corrosivum). Mercuric sulfate is rubbed with mercury to produce mercurous sulfate, which is mixed with sodium chloride and heated, with sublimation and condensation of the mercurous salt. Calomel was used as a purgative and, particularly, as a diuretic. It is highly effective at inducing diuresis, but has been replaced by less toxic alternatives. (8,39)

Hydrargyri chloridum corrosivum; Hyd. chl. cor.: Corrosive mercuric chloride, corrosive sublimate, mercuric bichloride, corrosive chloride of mercury, $HgCl_2$. This is formed by heating of mercuric sulfate and sodium chloride in the presence of manganese dioxide, which suppresses formation of the mercurous salt, with sublimation and subsequent condensation of the highly corrosive mercuric chloride; hence the name "corrosive sublimate." Corrosive sublimate is a powerful antimicrobial disinfectant mainly used for cleaning of non-metallic surfaces (mercury will deposit on metallic items). (8)

Hydrargyri compositum, unguentum: Compound mercury ointment, of mercury ointment in wax with camphor. (34)

Hydrargyri cum creta et opio, pilulae: Pill of mercury with chalk (see hydrargyrum cum creta) and compound powder of ipecac, formed with milk sugar and syrup. (42)

Hydrargyri cum creta, tablettae: Tablet of hydrargyri cum creta, sugar, starch, and theobromatis, emulsio. A children's purgative, instructed to be lightly compressed so that they can be administered as a powder by crushing with the fingers. (42)

Hydrargyri cum opio, pilulae: Pill of mercury pill mass (hydrargyri, massa) with opium. (42)

Hydrargyri cum rheo, pilulae: Mercury with rhubarb pill, of mercury pill mass (hydrargyri, massa) with compound rhubarb pill mass. (42)

Hydrargyri cyanidum: Mercuric cyanide, turpeth mineral, $Hg(CN)_2$, from potassium ferrocyanide and mercuric sulfate. (8)

Hydrargyri et ammonii chloridi, liquor: A solution (BPC) of mercuric chloride and ammonium chloride, tartaric acid, and water, Hart's solution, antiseptic. (42)

Hydrargyri et plumbi et zinci, unguentum: Unguentum metalorum, of mercurous chloride, mercuric nitrate ointment, lead acetate, zinc oxide, and soft paraffin. Stimulant and antiseptic for various skin conditions. (42)

Hydrargyri et potassii iodidum; Hydrargyri et potasii iodidi, liquor: Mercury and potassium iodide, use as per the iodide, or the liquor (solution) of same, made with red iodide of mercury, potassium iodide, and water. (42,46)

Hydrargyri et quininae chloridum: Reaction product of corrosive sublimate and quinine, believed to reduce the corrosive sublimate to the less toxic form of mercury, used orally for chronic skin disorders. Unofficial. (44)

Hydrargyri et zinci cyanidi, carbasus: Antiseptic gauze treated with mercuric and zinc cyanides and colored with a small amount of aniline violet. (42)

Hydrargyri et zinci cyanidum: Lister's salt, mercury and zinc cyanide, a powerful antiseptic and disinfectant used on gauze, lint, wool, or other dressing material. (42)

Hydrargyri flava, lotio: Lotion of yellow mercuric oxide (hydrargyri oxidum flavum), produced by addition of corrosive sublimate (hydrargyri chloridum corrosivum) to lime water (calcium oxide). (8)

Hydrargyri iodidi rubri, unguentum: Ointment of red mercuric iodide in benzoinated lard. (34)

Hydrargyri iodidi, gossypium: Absorbent cotton soaked in mercuric and potassium iodides and dried, often dyed red with eosin. (42)

Hydrargyri iodidum [flavum][viride]: Yellow or green mercurous iodide, mercury protiodide, yellow or green mercury iodide, HgI. (8,40)

Hydrargyri iodidum rubrum (, unguentum): Red mercuric iodide, mercury biniodide, HgI_2, from mercuric chloride and potassium iodide. A powerful disinfectant. The ointment was made with wax and almond oil. (8)

Hydrargyri murias: See hydrargyri chloridum corrosivum. (40)

Hydrargyri nitratis (acidus), liquor: Solution of mercuric nitrate, from action of nitric acid on mercury. Sufficiently corrosive that it is used to destroy warts and other skin lesions. (8,42)

Hydrargyri nitratis (dilutum)(mitius), unguentum: Ointment of mercuric nitrate, citrine ointment, of mercuric nitrate, made by the interaction between mercury and nitric acid, with lard and olive oil. For skin conditions, but noted to be too irritating for constant or general use. The BPC also specified a dilutum formulation of mercuric nitrate ointment mixed 1:4 with paraffin for use in eczema and other chronic skin conditions and a still more dilute mitius formulation mixed 1:7 for use in the eye or nostrils. (8, 31,42)

Hydrargyri nitrico-oxidum: See hydrargyri oxidum rubrum. (40)

Hydrargyri oleas; Hydrargyri, olea(in)tum: Oleate of mercury, twenty percent yellow oxide of mercury (hydrargyrum oxidum flavum) in oleic acid. (8, 42)

Hydrargyri oleatum, unguentum: Ointment of mercury oleate in benzoinated lard, for syphilitic lesions. (42)

Hydrargyri oxidi flavi, unguentum; Hydrargyrum oxidum flavum: Yellow oxide of mercury, HgO, from precipitation of corrosive mercuric chloride with soda, or unguent of same in ointment base of choice. Unguent used to treat topical parasites, ulcers, and other skin conditions. (8,42)

Hydrargyri oxidi rubri, unguentum: Ointment of red mercuric oxide, with ten percent of same in hydrous wool fat, water, and petrolatum. (31)

Hydrargyri oxidum [cinerium][rubrum]; Hydrargyri oxidi rubri, unguentum; Hydrarg. Oxid. Rub.; Hyd. Ox. Rub.: Red mercuric oxide, red precipitate, HgO, or ointment of same made with castor oil, red mercuric oxide, and ointment base of choice. (8,29)

Hydrargyri oxymurias: Corrosive chloride of mercury (corrosive sublimate). See hydrargyri chloridum corrosivum. (3)

Hydrargyri oxysulphatis: Mercury oxysulfate, or turpeth mineral, by boiling sulfuric acid and mercury together until dry and cooling the resulting mass in cold water. An emetic. (40)

Hydrargyri perchloridi acidi, solutio: Acid solution of mercuric chloride, of same with water and hydrochloric acid, tinted with fuchsin, a disinfectant "for excreta." (42)

Hydrargyri perchloridi, carbasus: Antiseptic gauze treated with 1:1000 mercuric chloride and dried. (42)

Hydrargyri perchloridi, gossypium: Absorbent cotton soaked in mercuric chloride solution and dried. (42)

Hydrargyri perchloridum; Hydrargyri perchloridum, liquor; —, lotio: Corrosive sublimate (see hydrargyri chloridum corrosivum) or the solution in water or the lotion (0.2 percent). (40,42)

Hydrargyri permurias: See hydrargyri chloridum corrosivum. (40)

Hydrargyri persulphas: Mercuric sulfate, non-medicinal, used in the construction of small mercury batteries per the BPC. (42)

Hydrargyri proto-ioduret: See hydrargyri iodidum flavum. (40)

Hydrargyri salicylas: Mercuric salicylate, used as a dusting powder or in ointments for syphilis, gonorrhea, or for skin infections. (42)

Hydrargyri subchloridi (compositae), tablettae: Tablet of calomel, sugar, potato starch, and etherial solution of theobroma as an excipient. The compound tablet also contained sulphurated antimony and guaiac resin. Purgative and internal antiseptic. (42)

Hydrargyri subchloridi compositi, pilulae; Hydrarg. subchlor. co., Pil.: See antimonii compositi, pillulae. (40)

Hydrargyri subchloridi compositus, pulvis: Compound calomel powder, of mercurous chloride, scammony, acid potassium tartrate, jalap, antimonial powder, and ginger. Aperient and intestinal disinfectant, used for mild febrile illness in childhood. (42)

Hydrargyri subchloridi, unguentum: Ointment of the subchloride of mercury, calomel ointment, of same in benzoinated lard. (34)

Hydrargyri subchloridi; Hydrargyri submurias: Same as mercurous chloride, or calomel, HgCl. See hydrargyri chloridi. (39)

Hydrargyri subchloridum mite; Hydrargyri submurias: Calomel, see hydrargyri chloridum mite. (40)

Hydrargyri suboxidum: A black mercury oxide, probably Hg_2O, readily soluble in water, and hence used to make lotions and solutions. See black wash.

Hydrargyri subsulphas flavus: Yellow mercuric subsulphate, $Hg(HgO)_2SO_4$. Formed by the action of sulfuric and nitric acids together on metallic mercury. This is the most powerful of the mercurial emetics. Used in venereal diseases and topically on skin sores or ulcers. (8,39)

Hydrargyri sulphas (albus): Mercury persulfate, Hg^{2+} $(S_2O_8)^{2-}$. (40)

Hydrargyri sulphas flava: Yellow mercury (oxy)sulfide, see hydrargyri oxysulphatis. (40)

Hydrargyri sulphidum nigrum: Black mercury sulfide, see hydrargyri sulphuretum cum sulphure. (42)

Hydrargyri sulphidum rubrum: Red mercuric sulfide, or cinnabar, see hydrargyrus sulphuratus ruber. (42)

Hydrargyri sulphuretum cum sulphure: Sulphurette of mercury with sulfur, see aethiops mineralis. (40)

Hydrargyri supermurias: See hydrargyri chloridum corrosivum. (40)

Hydrargyri tannas: Mercurous tannate, of the nitrate triturated with tannic acid. This is decomposed in the intestinal tract and provides a milder cathartic effect, often given as a pill with glycerin of tragacanth. (42)

Hydrargyrosi muriati mitis, piluli: Cathartic tablet of calomel, antimony sulphate, and conserve of roses. Presumably equivalent, at least in function, to hydrargyri chloridi mitis, tabellae. (39)

Hydrargyrum: Quicksilver, mercury (metal), literally "water-silver," from distillation of native cinnabar (mercury sulfide) ore and lime, which releases metallic mercury vapor. Mercury was a highly effective anti-syphilitic used both topically and systemically. Mercury exists primarily in the metallic, mercurous (1+) or mercuric (2+) states. (8) (1,8)

Hydrargyrum ammoniatum; Hyd. ammon.; Hydrargyrum ammoniatum, unguentum: Ammoniated mercury, white precipitate, ammonium mercuric chloride, NH_2HgCl, or unguent of same made with benzoinated lard. See hydrargyri ammonii chloridum. (8)

Hydrargyrum cum creta; Hyd. c. creta: Mercury with chalk, from metallic mercury, chalk, honey, and water. The metallic mercury converts to mercuric oxide over time. (8)

Hydrargyrum cum sulphure: Black mercuric sulphide HgS. (40)

Hydrargyrum nigrum, lotio: See nigra, aqua.

Hydrargyrum nitrico-oxidum, unguentum; Hydrarg. nit.-ox., unguentum: See hydrargyrum oxidum rubrum, unguentum. (40)

Hydrargyrum perchloras, tabellae; —, solv.; —, solution; —, liquor: Mercury (II) perchlorate, used primarily as a disinfectant solution, the tablets being intended for disolution in water. (40)

Hydrargyrum praecipitatum: Black mercuric sulfide HgS. (40)

Hydrargyrus acetas: Mercuric acetate. (39)

Hydrargyrus alkalisatis: Alkaline mercury, see hydrargyrum cum creta. (39)

Hydrargyrus calcinatus: Red mercuric oxide. Same as hydrargyrus praecipitatus. (3)

Hydrargyrus cum sulfure: See hydrargyrus sulphuratis niger. (39)

Hydrargyrus muriatus (corrosivus): Corrosive sublimate, i.e., mercuric chloride, $HgCl_2$. See hydrargyri chloridum corrosivum. (3, 39)

Hydrargyrus muriatus mite; Hydrargyrus muriatus praecipitatus: Calomel, see hydrargyri chloridum mitis. (39)

Hydrargyrus nitratus ruber: Red nitrate of mercury ($HgNO_3$), mainly a topical escharotic, but could be used as per calomel. (39)

Hydrargyrus oxymuras: See hydrargyri chloridum corrosivum. (39)

Hydrargyrus praecipitatus [(cinereas) (cinerius)]: Precipitated mercury, i.e., red mercuric oxide. Anti-syphilic, cathartic, diaphoretic, alterative, and cathartic, as well as emetic at high dosage. Not as powerful a purgative as calomel. (39)

Hydrargyrus purificatus: Purified mercury, i.e., the metallic form. (39)

Hydrargyrus sulphuratis niger: Black sulfur of mercury, i.e., mercuric sulfide, HgS. Per Estes, this was once thought to share the properties of calomel, but was later regarded as ineffective. (39)

Hydrargyrus sulphuratus ruber: Red sulfide of mercury, a man-made equivalent to the naturally occurring mercury ore, cinnabar or vermillion. Used for fumigations to treat syphilitic ulcers. Generally regarded as ineffective. (39)

Hydrargyrus vitriolatus (flavus): See hydrargyri subsulphas flavus. (39)

Hydrastina; Hydrastine; Hydrastinae hydrochloras; Hydrastinine; Hydrastininae hydrochloras: This is an artificial mixture of alkaloids derived from hydrastine by various oxidizing agents. Hydrastinine was used generally like natural Hydrastis (goldenseal), but was said to be especially useful for uterine hemorrhage and for general menstrual disorders (menorrhagia, metrorrhagia). (8,42)

Hydrastinae compositus, liquor: Compound solution of hydrastine, colorless hydrastine solution, contains 0.3% each of the chlorides of hydrastine (see hydrastis), aluminum, calcium and magnesium with 0.1 percent potassium chloride in a solution of glycerin and water. "It owes its activity chiefly to the hydrastine." (31)

Hydrastis (canadensis or **can.) (, pulv.); Hydrastis rhyzoma:** Goldenseal or yellow pucoon, the rhizome and roots of *Hydrastis canadensis*, containing berberine and many other alkaloids, or the powder thereof. A gastric stimulant, bitter, and diuretic. It was used topically for a variety of chronic skin conditions and for ulcers of the skin and mucous membranes as well as for uterine disorders. Topical liquid preparations were used for nasal catarrh, otorrhea, leucorrhea, gonorrhea, mouth ulcers, etc. It has been used as well for uterine bleeding either systemically or topically. (8,42)

Hydrastis (fluidum)(liquidum), extractum; hydrastis, tinctura: Solid or fluid extract and tincture of hydrastis. (8)

Hydrastis (compositum) (cum aconiti), lotio: Compound lotion of hydrastis with zinc sulphate in a strong solution of green tea, used mainly as an eyewash, but also a general irrigant. The lotion with aconite consisted of goldenseal and tincture of aconite in water and was said to be good topically for various eye conditions. Also used by injection or ingestion for various conditions, especially female difficulties. (34)

Hydrastis [r.][rad.] pulv.: Powdered hydrastis (root).

Hydrastis, glycerinum: Powder of hydrastis in glycerin, alcohol, and water. (42)

Hydrastis, glyceritum: Glycerite of hydrastis (goldenseal), a glycerin solution intended for topical use. (8)

Hydrastis composita, tinctura: Compound tincture of goldenseal, with lobelia seed, in alcohol. (34)

Hydrastis compositum, elixir: Compound elixir of hydrastis, alkaline elixir, made with fluid extracts of hydrastis, oats, and xanthoxylum with traces of ginger, gentian and sodium bicarbonate. "The most active ingredient is the alcohol." (31)

Hydrastis compositum, infusum: Compound infusion of hydrastis, of goldenseal, blue cohosh, and witch hazel, an astringent for ulcers and other conditions of the mouth and throat. (34)

Hydrastis compositum, vinum: Goldenseal root, tulip-tree bark, bitter root, prickly ash berries, sassafras bark, and capsicum in sherry wine. A tonic and stimulant, especially useful for dyspepsia. (34)

Hydrastis compositus, pulvis: Powder of goldenseal, of same with blue cohosh and helonias, a tonic and antispasmodic and for dyspepsia and chronic inflammations of mucous membranes such as aphthous ulcers. (34)

Hydric: Pertaining to the hydrogen ion, H^+. This generally pertains to an acid, i.e., the hydric chloride (hydrochloricum, acidum); acetate (aceticum, acidum); cyanate (hydrocyanidum, acidum); nitrate (nitricum, acidum); or sulphate (sulfuricum, acidum); but may also pertain to other hydrogen compounds which do not dissociate (i.e., are not acids), i.e., hydric sulphide (H_2S, hydrogen sulfide). (29)

Hydriodate: The iodide ion, I^-, generally as a sodium or potassium salt. (40)

Hydriodic ether: Ethyl iodide. (40)

Hydriodici, acidi syrupus: See hydroiodici, acidi syrupus. (8)

Hydrobromate: Bromide ion, Br^-, generally as a sodium, potassium, or lithium salt. (40)

Hydrobromic ether: See ethyl bromide. (8)

Hydrobromicum dilutum, acidum; Hydrobromic acid; Hydrobrom. D., Ac.: Hydrobromic acid, HBr, by reaction of potassium bromide and sulfuric acid, with precipitation of potassium sulfate. It is used primarily in the preparation of other materials, but could be used as a sedative, to relieve noises in the ear (tinnitus), or to treat quinine poisoning. (8)

Hydrocarbon oil: See paraffinum liquidum. (40)

Hydrochinon: See hydroquinone. (40)

Hydrochlorate: See hydrochloride. Not a chlorate salt. (40)

Hydrochloric acid; Hydrochloricum (dilutum), acidum: Hydrochloric acid, HCl, muriatic acid. Thirty-one percent or diluted (dilutum) with water to roughly half strength. (8)

Hydrochloric ether: See ethyl chloride. (40)

Hydrochlorici, acidi, unguentum: Ointment of hydrochloric acid, prepared in spermacetti. (34)

Hydrochloride: Generally a part of a longer chemical name, a hydrochloride (or hydrochlorate, incorrectly named) is formed by reacting a neutral compound with hydrochloric acid to form the positive salt of the compound with chloride, i.e., neutral cocaine reacts with HCl to form cocaine-H$^+$ Cl$^-$.

Hydrochlorophosphatum (compositum), syrupus: See phosphatum cum quinina et strychnina, syrupus. (31)

Hydrochrite; Hydrocrithe: Barley (hordeum) water. (3,39)

Hydrocotyle: Water pennywort, thick-leaved pennywort, Indian pennywort, bevilacqua, the entire plant of *Hydrocotyle asiatica*, highly toxic and used for a variety of unrelated conditions. (33)

Hydrocyani[d][c]um, acidum (dilutum)(fortius): Hydrocyanic acid, HCN, "cyanide," Prussic acid. From potassium ferrocyanide by a complex process which liberates cyanide, diluted to standard strength, typically two percent by weight. A topical anesthetic if sufficiently dilute, but of course highly toxic. Weaker (dilutum) or stronger (fortius) dilutions specified. (8,42,45)

Hydrocyanici, mistura acidi, composita: See Brompton Hospital Mixture. (40)

Hydrocyanici acidi, vapor: Vapor of dilute hydrocyanic (Prussic) acid, used to supress cough.

Hydroergotinine: A pharmacologically active component of ergot. (40)

Hydrofluoric acid; Hydrofluoricum, acidum: Hydrofluoric acid, HF, corrosive and bactericidal, but highly toxic. Etches glass, and said to account for the resistance of glassblowers to tuberculosis, and has been used by inhalation in dilute form for that disease. (42)

Hydrogen borate: See boric acid. (40)

Hydrogen borate: See boric acid. (42)

Hydrogen orthophosphate: See phosphoric acid. (40)

Hydrogen peroxide; Hydrogenii peroxidi; —, liquor: Hydrogen peroxide, H$_2$O$_2$. Used in various concentrations as a local disinfectant, mouthwash, or orally. (8)

Hydrogen, sulphurated; —, sulphret(ted): Hydrogen sulfide. (3,44)

Hydrogenii dioxidi (, aqua): See hydrogen peroxide. (8)

Hydroiodic acid; Hydroiodicum (dilutum) acidum: Hydrogen iodide solution (HI) with (in the BPC) potassium hypophosphite, tartaric acid, alcohol, and water. (42)

Hydrokinone: See hydroquinone. (40)

Hydrolapathum: See lapathum. (39)

Hydrolat {*French*}**:** A distilled water. (3)

Hydrolé {*French*}**:** An aqueous solution. (3)

Hydromel: Liquor of honey and water, which yields mead on fermentation. (1)

Hydronaphthol: Beta-naphthol, see napthol. (40)

Hydropege: Spring or hydrant water. (3)

Hydrophilous cotton: Absorbent ("water-loving") cotton. (3)

Hydropicae, pilulae: Purgative pills, used mainly for dropsy or hydrops. (1)

Hydropyrin: Proprietary lithium salt of aspirin, see acetylsalicylate. (40)

Hydroquinone: While sometimes used to lighten skin, this is primarily a photographic chemical.

Hydrosulphuret of ammonia: See ammoniae, hydro-sulphuretum. (40)

Hydrosulphuricum, acidum: Sulphuretted hydrogen, i.e., hydrogen sulfide. (40)

Hydrothionica, aqua: Sulphuretted hydrogen water, i.e., water through which hydrogen sulphide gas has been bubbled. (3)

Hydroxyquinoline sulfate: See oxyquinoline sulphate. (40)

Hyera picra: See hiera picra. (1)

Hygrophilia; Hygrophylae, decoctum: *Hygrophilia spinosa* (common name not identified). A demulcent, diuretic, and stimulant of the sexual organs. (32,42)

Hygrophilous cotton: Absorbent cotton. (3)

Hyoscinae, guttae: Eyedrops (BPC) consisting of hyoscine, 0.5-1 percent, mydriatic but less irritating than atropine. (42)

Hyoscinae et cocainae, guttae: Eyedrops (BPC) consisting of hyoscine and cocaine, mydriatic and anesthetic. (42)

Hyoscinae hydrobromas: Hyoscine hydrobromide. See hyoscyamus. (8)

Hyoscyami alcoholicum, extractum: Dried alcoholic extract of hyoscyamus leaf, USP. (44)

Hyoscyami compositae, pilulae: Compound pills of hyoscyamus, with extract of valerian, aconite, and quinine sulphate. For neuralgia, rheumatism, chorea, dysmenorrhea, etc. (34)

Hyoscyami oleum (compositum): The expressed oil of hyoscyamus. The compound oil also contained oil of peppermint, rosemary, and thyme (22) or in the NF oils of absinth, lavender, rosemary, sage, and thyme. (46)

Hyoscyami semina: Henbane seed, used as a remedy for toothache in the form of a paste or poultice, or the smoke from heating the seeds on a hot surface was directed at the tooth via a funnel or other device. The oil of the seed is noted in the BPC to have previously been used topically. (42)

Hyoscyami viride, extractum: Green extract (dry) of hyoscyamus leaves, flowers, and tops, including chlorophyll, which imparts the color. (42)

Hyoscyami, extractum; —, fluidum extractum; —, tinctura: Dried extract, fluid extract, and alcoholic tincture of hyoscyamine, respectively. (8)

Hyoscyami, succus: Fresh juice of henbane leaves (three parts), to which is added alcohol (one part) as a preservative. (34)

Hyoscyaminae hydrobromas; —sulphas: Hyoscyamine hydrobromide and sulphide. See hyoscyamus. (8)

Hyoscyamus niger

Fig. 3-126 Hyoscyamus.

Hyoscyamus; Hyoscyami folia; —semen: Henbane, *Hyoscyamus niger* or the leaves (folia) or seed (semen) thereof. The active principals, hyoscyamine and lesser amounts of hyoscine, are similar to atropine and scopolamine (see belladonna and stramonium) and are used for similar purposes. Leaves, root, and seeds used. Figure 3-126. (1,8,44)

Hyperici, tinctura; —, oleum: Tincture of St. John's wort in alcohol, or oil derived from the plant. (34)

Hypericum: St. John's wort, *Hypericum perforatum*. The herb, hung in the window on the feast of St. John (December 27), would drive away demons and spirits. Flowering tops, leaves, seeds used. For bruises and soreness. Now used for depression. Figure 3-127. (1,32)

Hyperoxymuriate of potash: See potassii chloras. (40)

Hypnal: Chloral-antipyrin, trichloraldehydphenyl-dimethylpyrazolone. A combination of antipyrin with chloral to provide sedative and pain relieving properties. (3, 8)

Hypnogen: See barbitone. (40)

Hypnone: See acetophenone. (40)

Hypo: Sodium thiosulphate, as referred to in photography. Photographic chemicals were frequently carried by apothecaries in their function as general chemists. (40)

Hypochlorite solution: Sodium hypochlorite (bleach). (40)

Hypochondrial plaster: Plaster designed to be applied to the lower abdomen. (39)

Hypocistis: Hypocist, juice of the parasitic plant *Cytinus hypocistis*. (1)

Hypophosphatum, liquor: Solution of calcium, sodium, and potassium hypophosphite and citric acid in water. (46)

Hypophosphitum, glycerinum: Compound glycerol of hypophosphites, of calcium, magnesium, potassium, iron, quinine, and strychnine hypophosphites in water and glycerin. (42)

Hypophosphitum, syrupus: A syrup of three hypophosphites, calcium, sodium, and potassium in dilute hypophosphorous acid (hypophosphorosum dilutum, acidum), with spirit of lemon, sugar, and water. (8)

Hypophosphitum (compositus), syrupus: Compound syrup of hypophosphites, of calcium, potassium, sodium and manganese hypophosphites, sodium citrate, and diluted hypophosphorous acid in a vehicle of glycerin and syrup. The compound preparation also had strychnine and quinine. "It is a widely prescribed, but useless, concoction." (31) In the BPC, the simple syrup had hypophosphites of calcium, potassium, and sodium with hypophosphoric acid, tincture of lemon, sugar, and water, and the compound form added iron hypophosphite, strychnine and quinine, and had chloroform water in place of tincture of lemon for flavor. (42)

Hypophosphitum (cum ferro), elixir: Elixir of calcium, sodium, and potassium hypophosphites, citric acid, water, glycerin, compound spirit of cardamom, and aromatic elixir. A general nutritive tonic, to which iron sulfate could be added as a hematinic. (46)

Hypophosphitum compositus, liquor: Compound solution of hypophosphites, containing quinine, strychnine and iron, with calcium, potassium, sodium, and manganese hypophosphites. (31)

Hypophosphitum cum ferro, syrupus: Syrup of hypophosphites with iron, of ferrous lactate, potassium citrate, and syrup of hypophosphites. (8)

Hypophosphorosum, dilutum, acidum: Dilute hypophosphorous acid, about ten percent $H_2(PH_2O_2)$, formed by evaporation of a solution of potassium hypophosphate and sulfuric acid. (8)

Hypophysis cerebri: Desiccated pituitary gland, for endocrine disorders, see pituitarium. (40)

Hyposulphite of soda: Sodium thiosulphate, or hypo, mainly a photographic chemical ("fixer"). (40)

Hyraceum: A secretion of the hyrax, of South Africa, used as a substitute for castor, which is derived from the beaver. Unofficial. (44)

Hyrgolum: Colloidal mercury. (40)

Hyssop, hedge: See gratiola. (39)

Hyssopus: Hyssop, *Hyssopus officinalis*. Leaves and flowering tops used. Figure 3-128. (1)

Hyssopus humida: See oesypus humida. (1)

Hysteric julep (Bate's): See moschata, mistura. Bate's julep is the same, with addition of musk. (39)

Hysterica, aqua; —, pilulae; Hystericum, electuarium; Hystericus pulvis: A medicated water, pill, electuary, or powder, respectively, used to treat uterine disorders. (1)

Fig. 3-127 Hypericum or St. John's wort.

Fig. 3-128 Hyssopus or hyssop.

I

I.: Impiastro {*Italian*} (a plaster); infusum (infusion). (1)

Iacobaea: See jacobea. (1)

Ialapium: See jalapium. (1)

Iberis: Bitter candytuft, *Iberis amara*, for treatment of enlarged, weak, or irregular heart. (32)

Ibiscus: See althaea. (1)

Ibit: Bismuth oxyiodo tannate. (3)

Ichden; Ichthammon; Ichthammonium; Ichthosan; Ichthynat; Ichthyodine; Ic(h)tham(m)ol; Ichthyol; Icthyolum: Ichthyol, or ichthamol, is obtained by treating bituminous quartz-containing fossil fish with sulfuric acid, followed by distillation and further purification. Ammonium, lithium, zinc, and sodium icthymol sulphonate salts were prepared, but the term icthymol generally refers to the ammonium salt. This rather peculiar remedy was used topically for eczema and psoriasis, often in lanolin, and a suppository was made for chronic prostatitis. (8,40)

Ichthalbin; Ichthargan; Ichthocalcium; Ichthoferrum; Ichthoform; Ichthosodium; Ichthozincum: Albumin, silver, calcium, iron, formaldehyde, sodium, and zinc ichthosulphonate, respectively. See icthamol. (40)

Ichthamolis, unguentum: Ointment of ammonium ichtholsulphonate in lanolin, for psoriasis, eczema, acne, etc. Mild dermal stimulant and antiseptic. (42)

Ichthosulphonic acid: Product of the action of sulfuric acid upon crude ichthyol. See icthamol. (40)

Ichthyol, crude: Oil from Tyrolese bituminous schist. See icthamol. (40)

Ichthyol collodion: See salicylicum compositum, collodium. (31)

Ichthyol ointment: See bituminis sulphonati, unguentum. (31)

Icthyocolla; Ichthyocollae, emplastrum: From Greek, "fish-glue." 1. A fish (esp. sturgeon) yielding isinglass. 2. Isinglass, the isolated swim bladder of fish of the genus *Acipenser*, of the Caspian and Black Seas and tributaries. It was available in sheets or rolls of pearly, iridescent, yellowish material and primarily was a source of proteinaceous gelatin used as an emollient, nutrient, and skin protectant. The plaster consisted of isinglass, alcohol, glycerin, and hot water. This was brushed on taffeta which had previously been coated on the opposite side with tincture of benzoin. (1,8) Modern isinglass, a heat resistant, translucent material used in enclosures for lamps or stoves, is sheet mica.

Iera (diacolocynthidos)(Logod, picra): See hiera. (1)

Ignatia; Ignatia amara; Ignatii semina: St. Ignatius bean, bitter ignatia (amara), the dried ripe seed of *Strychnos ignatii*. Physiological activity, much like that of strychnine. (3,42)

Ignatiae alcoholicum, extractum: Dry alcoholic extract of ignatia, USP. (44)

Ignatiae, extractum: Extract of ignatia (powdered), by exhausting the powdered drug with 75 percent alcohol, evaporating to dryness, and diluting to standard with starch. (31)

Ignatiae, tinctura: Tincture of ignatia in alcohol and water. "Its uses are similar to those of tincture of nux vomica." (31)

Ilex (Paraguariensis): Paraguay or Jesuit tea, i.e., maté, a tea of *Ilex paraguaniensis*.

Ilex opaca: American holly, *Ilex opaca*, a tonic and febrifuge. (33)

Illicium floridanum: Florida anise tree, substitute for star anise. Unofficial. (44)

Illicium; Illic.; Ilic anisat.: Star anise, the fruit of *Illicium verum*. See anise. (8)

Impatiens: Jewelweed, including balsam jewelweed, balsam weed or pale touch-me-not, *Impatiens pallida*, and speckled jewels or spotted touch-me-not, *Impatiens fulva*. An aperient and diuretic, also for jaundice. (33)

Imperatoria: Masterwort, *Peudedanum ostruthium*. Rhizome used as an aromatic. Figure 3-129. (1,39)

Imperial green: Copper acetoarsenite, Paris green. (3)

Imperiale, catartico {*Italian*}**:** Purgative electuary of scammony, cardamom seed, cinnamon, etc. (1)

Imperialis, aqua: Aromatic liquid from distillation of water and white wine spiced with cinnamon, cloves, nutmeg, lemon peel, etc. Used as a tonic and for gastric disorders. (1)

Imperialis, pilule: A cathartic pill of aloe, rhubarb, agaric, senna, cinnamon, ginger, musk, cloves, nardis indica, mastiche, and viola. (39)

Impiastro {*Italian*}**:** Plaster, i.e., the dressing referred to as a plaster. (1)

Indae ex hali, pilulae: Purgative pill of agaric, colocynth, Indian myrobalans, Indian spikenard, etc. (1)

Fig. 3-129 Imperatoria or masterwort.

India rubber: Natural rubber, from the rubber tree, *Siphonia elastica* or *Hevea guianensis*, also called caoutchouc. Can be vulcanized by heating with sulfur. Sheet rubber is used to make some types of plasters as well as bougies (for dilating strictures), pessaries, and syringe parts. Figure 3-130. (8)

Indian berry: See cocculus. (7)

Indian blistering flies: *Mylabris phalerata* and related species containing cantharidin. See cantharis. (40)

Indian cerate: Similar to plumbi acetatis, unguentum. (40)

Indian gum: Gum from India, often gum acacia, but could be other tree gums. (40)

Indian hemp: See apocynum (cannabinum). (39)

Indian nard: See nardus. (39)

Indian physic: See gillenia. (33)

Indian pink[root]: See spigelia (3)

Indian poke: Either helleborus albus or veratrum viride. (39)

Indian tobacco: See lobelia (inflata). (39)

Indian turnip: See arum. (33)

Indica lopeziana, radix: Root of eponymously named Lopez tree, *Toddalia aculeata*, after Juan Lopez Pigneiro, Portugese explorer. (39)

Indicum: See Indigo (dye). (1,3)

Indicus myrobalanus: See myrobalanus, Indicus. (1)

Indigo: Indigo, indicum, pigmentum indicum, blue dye derived from various species of the Indigo plant, genus *Indigofera*. It does not appear to have a well defined medical use. (33)

Indigo, wild: See baptesia.

Indigotin: Active compound in indigo plant, a blue dye. (40)

Indivia {*Italian*}**:** See endivia. (1)

Indum folium: Indian leaf, see malabathrum. (1)

Indum majus, electuarium; Indum minus, electuarium: Purgative electuary of turpeth root, scammony, cardamom seed, cinnamon, etc. (1)

Infantum, pulvis: Infant powder, magnesia and rhubarb, with oil of fennel, internal use as oral antidiarrheal and antacid; external use as baby dusting powder. (3,39)

Infernalis, lapis: Lunar caustic, fused silver nitrate. (3)

Infirmary plaster: Adhesive plaster (emplastrum adhaesens) on brown holland cloth. (40)

Inflammabilis, spiritus: Alcohol (whisky). (3)

Inflammable air: Hydrogen gas. (3)

Infrigidans galeni, unguentum: See refrigerans Galeni, unguentum. (1)

Infundin: Proprietary posterior pituitary extract. (40)

Infusion of tar: Tar water, see picis, aqua. (40)

Infusorial earth: See kieselguhr. (40)

Infusum; Infusa; Infusa concentrata: Infusions are generally water extracts, similar to tea. In the BPC infusia concentrata are approximately seven-fold more concentrated than standard infusions and were intended to allow storage and reconstitution in place of fresh preparation. They were noted to "have not been recieved with favour." (42)

Infusum _____: Infusion. An infusion, see _____, infusum. (1,8)

Infusum, amarum: "Bitter infusion," of gentian, orange rind, coriander, and alcoholic spirits. (39)

Ingluvin: A digestive aid extracted from the gizzard of chickens or other domestic fowl. (32)

Injectio (_____) (hypodermica): An injectable form prepared from the specified material. This would normally be done, of course, with a purified chemical material, alkaloid, or soluble extract, not with raw plant material, i.e., not "injectio opii" (opium), but rather injectio morphinae (morphine, isolated from opium). Standard USP injections included apomorphinae, ergotinae, and morphinae as of 1905. (34) These were generally small spherical pills, approximately 1/8 inch (4-6 mm) in diameter, designed to be placed in a syringe and reconstituted with water.

Injection of sulfates: See sulphatum, injectio. (42)

Injectiones hypodermicae (BPC): The BPC (42) lists numerous materials for subcutaneous injection, prepared by dissolving in freshly boiled water. These include injectio hypodermica aconitinae, apomorphinae, atropinae, betacainae (local anesthetic), cocainae, curare, ergotae, ergotininae, ergotoxinae, homatropinae, hydrargyri perchloridi, hyoscinae, morphinae et atropinae, morphinae, pilocarpinae, and strychninae. Note that these are distinct from the BPC "injectio" formulations which are for other purposes, usually injection into body orifices.

Insect flowers: See pyrethri, flores. (42)

Insect powder: Powdered flower-heads of marigold, see pyrethrum. (40)

Insufflatio: A powder or snuff for insufflation into the nasal cavity. (42)

Intybus: See endivia. (1)

Inula (helenium): Elecampane, root of *Inula helenium*. Used to treat lung disease, with no reason to believe it was effective. The "active ingredient" was believed to be inulin (alantin), a complex sugar that is used today by the intravenous route to measure renal function. Figure 3-131. (8)

Fig. 3-130 India rubber tree.

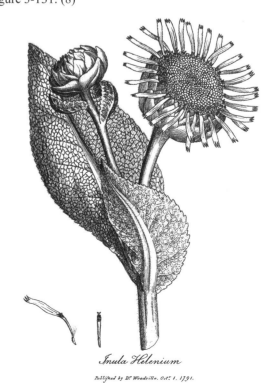

Fig. 3-131 Inula, helenium, or eecampane.

Inulae, P.; —, pulvis: Powdered inula, or possibly powdered purified inulin in later uses.

Inunctum: An inunction, i.e., an unguent or ointment. Irregularly used in place of *unguentum*. (31)

Iodantipyrin; Iodopyrin: An iodinated form of antipyrin, of the same clinical use. (8)

Iodatum, oleum: See iodipin. (40)

Iodex: A proprietary stainless iodine ointment, still commercially available. (40)

Iodhydric acid: See hydriodici, acidi. (40)

Iodi, collodium: Iodine in collodion, a topical for ringworm, chilblains, and swollen glands. (Not same as collodium iodoformi.) (42)

Iodi, glycerinum: Iodine and potassium iodide in glycerin and water, iodine formulation for injection into tumors. (42)

Iodi, linimentum: Iodine liniment, use as per iodine. The BPC indicates this is the same as iodi dilutus, liquor. (34,42) In the NF, iodine and potassium iodide, glycerin, and water and primarily alcohol base, with BP noted to be nearly identical. (46)

Iodi, unguentum: Iodine ointment, of iodine, potassium iodide, water, and benzoinated lard. (8)

Iodi, vapor: Tincture of iodine in water, an attempt to treat phthisis (tuberculosis) with iodine as an inhaled disinfectant. (42)

Iodi (, churchill), tinctura: Tincture of iodine, of iodine in alcohol. A topical disinfectant and antimicrobial applied to wounds, or used as a topical anti-parasitic, rarely as an anti-emetic, etc. (8)

Iodi (compositum), unguentum: Ointment of iodine, of iodine, potassium iodide, water and benzoinated lard. Disinfectant. (40)

Iodi (dilutus)(fortis), liquor: A standard or stronger standard solution of iodine and potassium iodide in water, disinfectant. (42)

Iodi carbolatus, liquor: See iodi phenolatus, liquor. (31)

Iodi composita, tinctura; Iodi churchill, tinctura: Two similar tinctures of iodine and potassium iodide in alcohol, variants on tincture of iodine. See iodi fortior, tinctura. (31,34)

Iodi compositus, liquor: Compound solution of iodine, Lugol's solution, of iodine, potassium iodide, and water (five percent iodine). (8)

Iodi decolorata, tinctura: Decolorized tincture of iodine, of iodine and sodium hyposulfite in water heated together, dissolved in alcohol, and decolorized by addition of ammonia water. In the BPC, of iodine dissolved in alcohol, to which was added strong solution of ammonia for a similar result. (34,42)

Iodi denigrescens, unguentum: Stainless iodine ointment, made by dissolving iodine in oleic acid (oleicum, acidum) and incorporating with a base of petrolatum and paraffin. "It represents five percent iodine although it may be questioned whether the therapeutic virtues of this are altered by the manipulations." (31)

Iodi et picis, pasta: See pigmentum picis cum iodo. (42)

Iodi et zinci phenolsulphonatis, liquor: Solution of iodine and zinc phenolsulphonate, or pyorrhea astringent, of zinc phenolsulphonate, potassium iodide, and iodine. Used topically, mainly in the mouth, and should be freshly made. (31)

Iodi etherealis, vapor: Iodine, carbolic acid, creosote, alcohol, and ether, placed on an absorbent pad and inhaled, for chronic bronchitis or tuberculosis. An attempt to treat these conditions with a disinfectant. (42)

Iodi fortior, tinctura: Stronger tincture of iodine, tincture iodi Churchill; Churchill's tincture of iodine, with 16.5 gm of iodine and 3.3 gm of potassium iodide per 100 cc of seventy percent alcohol. (31)

Iodi phenolatus, liquor: Phenolated solution of iodine, liquor iodi carbolatus, carbolized solution of iodine, Boulton's solution, French mixture. Made from compound solution of iodine, liquefied phenol, glycerin, and water. "The direction to expose it to sunlight until it is decolorized destroys much of its therapeutic value." Used externally as a disinfectant. (31)

Iodi, chloroformum: Chloroform of iodine, of same dissolved in chloroform to ten percent solution. Topical form of iodine, which stains less than tincture of iodine and produces less irritation or itching. (42)

Iodic acid; Iodicum, acidum: Iodic acid, various salts used for rheumatism, as well as topically as a disinfectant and antiseptic. (42)

Iodide of iron, tasteless syrup: See ferri citro-iodidi, syrupus. (34)

Iodidorum, tinctura: Tincture of iodides. "Although this replaces the former decolorized tincture of iodine, the formula differs importantly in that potassium iodide is used in the place of sodium thiosulphate." A solution of potassium and ammonium iodides in dilute alcohol, used externally "but is of little value." (31)

Iodine; Iodum; Iodinium: Iodine, see iodi or iodidum for salts as iodide. Obtained from seaweed. Iodine in various forms is a specific for goitre (iodine deficiency). Despite the ancient recognition that seaweed and ground sponge (which both contain iodine) were helpful for goitre, the role of iodine itself was unrecognized until about 1820. Iodine also saw use for many other conditions as a corrosive, irritant, desiccant, tonic, diuretic, emmenagogue, and diaphoretic. (8,39) In an attempt to reduce the irritancy and staining of iodine itself, there are many organo-iodine compounds, often still in use, such as iodo-pyrrol or iodo-albumin, with uses as per iodine or iodoform. However, a few such compounds (iodo-quinine, iodo-caffeine) have uses related instead to the parent compounds (quinine and caffeine, respectively).

Iodine, carbolized solution of: See iodi phenolatus, liquor. (31)

Iodine, caustic solution of: See iodi causticus, liquor. (46)

Iodine, liniment: Liniment of iodine, potassium iodide, glycerin, and alcohol, used as a counterirritant. (8)

Iodine blister (veterinary): An ointment of hydrargyri iodidi rubri. (40)

Iodine ointment, stainless: See iodi denigrescens, unguentum. (31)

Iodinii: See iodi. Iodinii is an irregular Latin genitive form of iodine.

Iodinol: See iodipin. (40)

Iodisatum, gossypium: Absorbent cotton soaked in a solution of iodine and potassium iodide in ether and dried. Disinfectant dressing. (42)

Iodo hydromal; Iodosol; Iodothymol: Thymol iodide. Disinfectant. (3)

Iodoantipyrin: Antipyrin monoiodide, anodyne. (3)

Iodo-caffeine: Sodium caffeine iodide, used as per caffeine. (40)

Iodoform albuminate: An organified iodine product consisting of albumin treated with iodine, use as per iodine as a disinfectant. (40)

Iodoform and naphthalin: See iodoformi compositus, pulvis. (34)

Iodoform aromaticum; —aromatisatum: An aromatic (pleasant smelling) formulation of iodoform with two percent coumarin. (40)

Iodoform gauze, moist; Iodoform gauze with glycerin; Iodoformi cum glycerino, carbasus: Antiseptic gauze treated with a mixture of iodoform and glycerin, similar to iodoformi, carbasus—but remains moist due to the residual glycerin. (42)

Iodoform; Iodoformum: Iodoform, CHI_3, is the iodine analog of chloroform, formed from alcohol and iodine in the presence of potassium bicarbonate. It was used as a local stimulant to the gastrointestinal tract and as a topical disinfectant and anesthetic, often in the form of a powder or in collodion. (8)

Iodoformi, collodium: Iodoform in collodion, a topical for venereal lesions. Not same as collodium iodi. (42)

Iodoformi, glycerogelatinum: Iodoform glycerogelatin, of fifteen percent glycerin and ten percent iodoform in glycerinated gelatin vehicle. (31)

Iodoformi, gossypium: Absorbent cotton soaked in iodoform in ether and dried. Disinfectant dressing. (42)

Iodoformi, injectio: Solution of iodoform and mucilage (gum) tragacanth for antiseptic injection into sinuses or bladder. (42)

Iodoformi, insufflatio: Iodoform and bismuth subnitrate for use as an antiseptic snuff in nose or ear. (42)

Iodoformi, suppositoria: Suppository of iodoform in cocoa butter, disinfectant for fissures or piles. (42)

Iodoformi, unguentum: Iodoform in benzoinated lard. A topical disinfectant. (34)

Iodoformi [sine glycerino], emulsio: Emulsion of iodoform powder in glycerin and water, or in the "sine glycerino" form, of iodoform powder in water with dried tragacanth. Used to irrigate sinuses, bladder, etc. The glycerin formulation draws water from tissue to reduce swelling, but if this is not desired the alternate form could be employed. (42)

Iodoformi compositus, pulvis: Powder of iodoform, boric acid, and naphthalene with oil of bergamot for scent. A disinfectant dressing powder. (34)

Iodoformi et acidi borici, pulvis: Powder of one part iodoform to three of boric acid, a dusting powder for wounds and ulcers. (42)

Iodoformi et eucalypti, unguentum: Ointment of iodoform and oil of eucalyptus in a mixture of hard and soft paraffin, for urethral injection in gonorrhea. (42)

Iodoformi, carbasus: Iodoform gauze, of gauze treated with iodoform in ether, and dried. Loses strength with time unless well sealed, and often colored with yellow dye to mask poor distribution of iodoform or loss of strength. (42)

Iodoformin: Iodoform-formamine complex, use as per iodoform. (40)

Iodoformogen: See iodoform albuminate. (40)

Iodo-hydrargyrate of potassium: See hydrargyri et potassii iodidum. (42)

Iodol: Tetra-iodo-pyrrol, an antiseptic iodine compound, occasionally used internally as a substitute for potassium iodide. (8)

Iodolen: Iodopyrrol albumate, an organified iodine disinfectant, used as per iodoform. (40)

Iodopin: A preparation of iodine in sesame oil, used as per iodine. (40)

Iodopyrrol; Iodopyrrolum: Tetraiodopyrrol, antiseptic, see iodol. (42)

Iodotannicus, syrupus: Syrup of iodotannin, of 0.27% iodine and 0.54% tannin. "As the iodine undergoes chemical change, the syrup does not represent the therapeutic virtue of free iodine." (31)

Iohannis de Vigo, emplastum: Plaster of Johann de Vigo, see Vigo, emplastrum de. (1)

Ipado: Coca leaves. (3)

Ipecac lozenge: See ipecacuanae, trochisci. (34)

Ipecac, American: See gillenia. (33)

Ipecacuana; Ipecacuanha; Ipecahuanhae, radix; Ipecac (, Rio) (, Brazilian): The root of the ipecac plant, *Cephaelis ipecachuana*, native to Brazil and the new world, cultivated in India. The chief active principal is emetine, a powerful emetic. Used even in modern times as an emetic for removal of toxic materials. Ipecac is a skin irritant and said to have some antimicrobial properties against skin infections, in small doses is used as a gastric stimulant and digestive aid, and may be inhaled or ingested for use as an expectorant, but in large doses reliably induces vomiting. The physiological response to vomiting also has a bronchodilating effect, and a number of treatments for asthma include the use of ipecac to induce vomiting, probably with a modicum of success despite the unpleasant side effects. Figure 3-132. (1,8,42)

Ipecacuana cum scillae, linctus (pro infantum): An antitussive and expectorant lozenge of ipecac and squill, in adult or infant (pro infantum) form. (42)

Ipecacuana cum scillae, pillule; Ipecac. c. scill., pil.: An antitussive and expectorant tablet containing ipecac and squill. In the BPC, of compound powder of ipecac, powdered squill, powdered ammoniac, and syrup. (42)

Ipecacuanae, elixir: Elixir of ipecac, of the liquid extract of same with alcohol, glycerin, simple elixir, and water. Expectorant. (42)

Ipecacuanae, trochisci: Ipecac troche or lozenge, of powdered ipecac, sugar, and gum tragacanth. Expectorant. (34)

Ipecacuanae, unguentum: Ointment of ipecac in olive oil and lard, a counterirritant and vesicant. (34)

Ipecacuanae (radix) pulvis; Ipecac r. pulv.: Powdered ipecac root.

Ipecacuanae compositus, pulvis; Ipecac co., pv.: Compound powder of ipecac with bloodroot, pleurisy root, and potassium nitrate. A diuretic and diaphoretic for febrile and inflammatory diseases. (34) In the BPC this was similar to USP pulvis ipecacuanhae et opii, but with potassium sulfate in place of milk sugar. (42)

Ipecacuanae et opii compositus, pulvis: Diaphoretic powder, of opium, camphor, ipecac, and potassium bitartrate. An anodyne and diaphoretic of "great efficacy in all febrile and inflammatory disorders"—from gout to cholera. (34)

Ipecacuanae et opii, pulvis; —, tinctura; —, syrupus: Powder, tincture, or syrup of ipecac and opium, respectively. The former, Dover's Powder, is of powdered opium and ipecac with milk sugar. The tincture (Dover's tincture) is prepared from tincture of opium and fluidextract of ipecacuana. The syrup (NF) is of tincture of ipecac and opium with spirit of cinnamon, cinnamon water, and syrup. (8, 31,42)

Ipecacuanae fluidum, extractum; —liquidum (miscibile), extractum; —, syrupus; —, vinum: The fluid extract, syrup, and wine of ipecac. The classic emetic, syrup of ipecac consists of fluid extract of ipecac, acetic acid, glycerin, sugar, and water. It rarely fails to produce results. (8) The miscible form consisted of the liquid extract washed and solubilized with acetic acid. (42)

Ipecacuanae thebaicus, pulvis: See ipecacuanae et opii, pulvis. (40)

Ipecacuanhae, acetum: Vinegar of ipecac, of the fluidextract with alcohol and vinegar. Said to be similar to the wine (vinum). (42)

Ipecacuanhae, glycerinum: Glycerin of vinegar of ipecac in glycerin. Expectorant for croup and whooping cough. (42)

Ipecacuanhae, linctus: Syrup of vinegar of ipecac with syrup of balsam of tolu, glycerin, and gum tragacanth, for cough, especially in children. (42)

Ipecacuanhae cum scilla, tablettae: Tablet of compound powder of ipecac, powdered squill, ammoniac, refined sugar, and (see) theobromatis, emulsio. (42)

Ipecacuanhae cum soda, mistura: A mixture of sodium bicarbonate, wine of ipecac, aromatic spirits of ammonia, and peppermint water, an expectorant and diaphoretic. (42)

Ipecacuanhae cum urginea, pilulae: Urginea was used in place of squill in India and the British eastern colonies, see cum scilla formulation above. (42)

Fig. 3-132 Ipecacuana oripecac.

Ipecacuanhae et opii, pulvis: In the USP, powder of ipecac and opium in milk sugar. (42)

Ipecacuanhae sine emetina, pulvis: Powder of ipecac from which emetine alkaloid has been extracted using ammoniated chloroform. Provides benefits of ipecac in reducing intestinal motility in dysentery, without concomitant vomiting. (42)

Ipomea; Ipomoea: See jalap. (7)

Ipomoea turpethum: See turpethum. (39)

Iride {*Italian*}: See iris. (1)

Iridin; Irisin; Iridinum: Powdered extract of the root of the blue flag, *Iris vesicolor*. A cholegogue that rarely "grips," useful in combination with other purgatives. (8)

Iridis rhizoma: See iris, this is the rhizome of the iris or orris plant in the BPC. (42)

Irino, oleo {*Italian*}: Liniment from iris rhizome and olive or sesame oil. (1)

Iris (florentina) (pulv.); Iris flor.; Irios {*Italian*}; **irride** {*Italian*}: Iris, Orris, *Iris florentina, Iris germanica*, and possibly related species. Rhizome used, usually as a powder (pulv.). Iris, when not otherwise specified in the US National Forumulary is *I. florentina* in some sources. (1,7) In other sources, American usage is said to be *Iris versicolor*, while European use is *Iris florentina*. Figure 3-133. (40)

Iris palustris: Strongly cathartic root of the yellow water flag, *Iris pseudacorus*. Figure 3-134. (39)

Iris (versacolor)(versicoloris); —, extractum; —fluidum, extractum; —liquidum, extractum —, oleoresina; —, tinctura: The rhizome and roots of the North American iris, *Iris versicolor*, or the extract, fluid extract, isolated oleoresin, or tincture therefrom. A cholegogue and cathartic thath rarely grips and thus can be used daily if needed for constipation, jaundice, or other liver conditions. Figure 3-135. (8,42)

Iris tuberosa: See hermodactylus. (39)

Irish moss: See chondrus. (8)

Irisin: See iridin. (40)

Iron: See ferrum (metallic), ferri (compounds). (8)

Iron, compound mixture of: See ferri cum myrrha, pilule, to which this is similar. Also may be similar to ferri composita, mistura. (39)

Iron, dialyzed: See ferrum dialysatum. (8)

Iron, proto-sulphate of: Ferrous sulfate, see ferri sulphas. (40)

Iron, sesquicarbonate of: Ferric oxide. (40)

Iron, sesquichloride of: See ferri chloridum. (40)

Iron, tartarated: From reaction of potassium tartrate with elemental iron, potassium-iron tartrate. (40)

Iron alum: See ferri et ammonii sulphas. (40)

Iron arsenate, soluble: See ferri citro-arsenias ammoniatus. (42)

Iron peptonate and manganese, solution of: See ferri peptonati (et mangani), liquor. (31)

Iron plaster: See emplastrum ferri, BP, 1885. (40)

Iron pyrolignite: Crude ferric acetate, a mordant. (3)

Iron pyrophosphate, soluble: See ferri pyrophosphas (solubilis). (40)

Iron rust: Red ferric oxide, see ferri oxidum. (40)

Isarol: See icthamol. (40)

Isatis tinctoria: Woad, a dye source. (44)

Isinglass (, stove): See icthyocolla. (8)

Isis nobilis: "Noble Isis," after the goddess Isis, later equated to Venus, and used for venereal disease, a red nitrate of mercury. See hydrargyrus nitratus ruber. (39)

Island cacao: Cocoa seeds, see theobroma. (40)

Isoamylhydrocupreine: A topical anesthetic. (40)

Isobutyl nitrate: See butyl nitrite. (40)

Isooctylhydrocupreine: A local anesthetic. (40)

Isopo {*Italian*}; **Issopo** {*Italian*}: See hyssopus. (1)

Isopus humida: See oesypus humida. (1)

Isphagula: Dried seeds of *Plantago isphagula* or *P. ovata*, used as per linseed or barley as a source of mucilage to treat dysentery or diarrhea, similar to psillium. (42)

Isphagulae, decoctum: Decoction of isphagula, a demulcent. (42)

Issue peas: Small orange berries, or round pills turned from orris root. (3) More generally, an issue pea is a small object placed in a wound or abcess to enhance suppurition, and could in fact be a pea or bean as well as a purpose-made item.

Itrol: Silver citrate. (3) See icthamol. (40)

Iuglans: See juglans. (1)

Iuiuba: See jujuba. (1)

Fig. 3-133 Iris florentina.

Fig. 3-134 Iris palustris, yellow water flag.

Blue Flag.   Iris versicolor.

Fig. 3-135 Iris versicolor.

Iulep: See julep. (1)

Iuniperus: See juniperus. (1)

Iusquiano {*Italian*}: See hyoscyamus. (1)

Iustini, electuarium: Electary of elecampane rhizome, pennyroyal leaves, juniper berries, lovage, etc. (1)

Iva arthetica; iva arthritica, Iva {*Italian*}: Ground pine, see chamaepitys. (1)

Ivivba: Orthographic variant of iuiuba, see jujuba. (1)

Ivory black: Fine bone black, carbon from ivory or bone, see carbo animalis. (40)

Ivy; Ivy, poison: See hedera for ivy, rhus for the unrelated poison ivy. (39)

I

J

Jaborandi: See pilocarpus. (8)

Jaborandi, extractum; —liquidum, extractum; —, infusum; —, tinctura: Dry extract, fluid extract, infusion, or the tincture of jaborandi in alcohol. See pilocarpus. Diaphoretic and topical to promote hair growth. (34,42)

Jacea: Wild pansy, *Viola tricolore*. Plant used. Figure 3-136. (1)

Jack-in-the-pulpit: See arum. (33)

Jack-o'lanterns: See alkekengi. (39)

Jackson's pectoral syrup: In the NF, said to be equivalent to pectoralis, syrupus. (46)

Jacobaea: Ragwort, St. James' wort, *Senecio jacobaea*. Leaves used. (1)

Jacobi, pulvis: Antimonial powder, see antimonialis, pulvis. (3)

Jaggery: Crude or raw sugar from the date palm. (3)

Jalap (, orizaba); Jalapa; Jalapium: Jalap is the root of the Mexican plant *Ipomoea* (or *Convolvulus*) *jalapa* or *I. orizabensis*. This was a powerful purgative agent used like scammony to treat constipation or to eliminate fluid by an alternative manner in the case of renal failure. See scammony. Figure 3-137. (8)

Jalap, False; —, German: See scammony. (40)

Jalap, Tampico: Tubers of *Ipomoea simulans*, use as per jalap. (40)

Jalap Rad. Pulv.; Jalapae (R.) Pulv.: Powdered jalap root. (29)

Jalapae, extractum (pulv.); —fluidextractum; —fluidum, extractum: Dry extract of jalap or jalap powder, or the fluidextract. (8,31,46)

Jalapae, resina: Resin of jalap, prepared as per resin of scammony. (8,34)

Jalapae, tinctura; —composita, tinctura: Simple tincture or compound tincture of jalap, the latter consisting of jalap and scammony with alcohol and water. (31,46)

Jalapae (et hydrargyri subchloridi) compositae, pilulae: Powder of aloes, colocynth, and jalap in soft soap with oleoresin of ginger, to which could be added mercurous chloride (calomel) for added effect. Purgative. (42)

Jalapae compositus, pulvis; Jalapa. co., pv.: 1. Compound powder of jalap, or pulvis purgans, with senna and cloves or ginger, an "excellent purgative." 2). Also refers to a related formulation in the USP and BPC of jalap and potassium bitartrate. (8,34,42)

Jalapae cum rheo, mistura: A mixture of jalap resin, compound tincture of rhubarb, tragacanth, syrup of ginger, and glycerin in caraway water, purgative. (42)

Jalapae tartaratus, pulvis: See jalapae compositus, pulvis (second item). (34)

Jalapin(um) (, false)(, German); Jalapurgin: Scammonin, active components of false jalap, i.e., scammony. (40)

Jamaica extract: Extract of the Florida sea grape, *Coccolobis uviflora*. Said by Estes to have appeared in England ca. 1790 as a dye and astringent used in admixture with valerian, and later used as a source of gum kino. (39)

Jamaica pepper: See pimento. (39)

Jamaican dogwood: See piscidia. (8)

Fig. 3-136 Jacea.

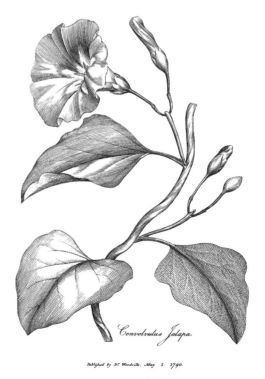

Fig. 3-137 Jalap.

Jamboo; Jambul: Jambul, jamboo, Java plum, *Syzygium jambolanum*, a stomachic, astringent, and cathartic. Useful for cicitrization of wounds. (32)

Jamestown weed: See stramonium. (39)

James' powder: See antimonialis, pulvis. (8)

Janeway's pills: See aloes et podophylli compositae, pilulae. (46)

Japan earth; Japonica terra: Catechu. (3)

Japanese aconite: See aconitum fischeri. (40)

Japanese drops: Japanese peppermint oil, from *Mentha arvensis*. (40)

Japonica, confectio: See catechu, electuarium. (39)

Japonica, tinctura: See catechu tinctura. (3,40)

Japonicum, infusum: See catechu, infusum. (39)

Jarisch's ointment: See pyrogallici, acidi, unguentum. (42)

Jasmine, yellow: See gelsemium. (7)

Jasminum: Flowers of jasmine, *Jasminum officinalis*, for female disorders, an emmenagogue and oxytocic. (39)

Jaune brilliant: Cadmium sulfide, an orange pigment, for paints. (40)

Java pepper: Cubeb. (3)

Java plum: See jambul. (32)

Jecoris aselli, oleum: See cod liver oil. (40)

Jeffersonia: Twinleaf, rheumatism root, ground squirrel pea, *Jeffersonia diphylla*. "Diuretic, alterative, antispasmodic, and a stimulating diaphoretic. Successfully used in chronic rheumatism, as a tonic in secondary or mercurio-syphilis; also used with advantage in dropsy, in many nervous affections, spasms, cramps, nervous excitability, and even during pregnancy." (33)

Jeoris aselli, oleum: See cod liver oil. (8)

Jequirity (bean)(pea): See abrus. (33)

Jera picra: See hiera picra. (1)

Jerusalem oak: See botrys (39) or gaultheria. (40)

Jervine: One of several active principals in veratrum viride. (8)

Jessamine, yellow: See gelsemium. (7)

Jesuit tea: See Ilex (Paraguariensis).

Jesuits' balsam: Copaiba. (3)

Jesuits' bark: Cinchona. (3)

Jesuits' drops: 1. Drops containing guaiacum, sarsaparilla and Peruvian balsam. 2. Synonym for compound tincture of benzoin. (3,39)

Jewelweed: See impatiens. (33)

Jews' pitch: Asphaltum. (3)

Jimson weed: See stramonium. (39)

Jodi: Orthographic variant, see iodi.

Johannes de Vigo, emplastrum: See Vigo, emplastrum de. (1)

Jonas' Salve: See ferri, emplastrum. (40)

Jordan almond: See amygdala dulcis. (8)

Jothion: A commercial form of di-iodo-isopropyl alcohol. (40)

Joviale; Jovis: Of Jupiter, i.e., made with tin. (39) Early metallurgy being limited, a number of preparations carrying this attribution later proved to involve other metals.

Joviale, diaphoreticum: Diaphoretic of Jupiter, of tin (stannum) and antimony (antimonium calcinatum). (39)

Joviale, electuarium: Electuary of Jupiter, of tin (stannum), mercury (hydrargyrum), absinth, mint, and ostrea edulis. An anthelmintic. (39)

Jovis, sal: A salt of tin, generally the nitrate or chloride, see entries for stannum. Used as a vermifuge. (39)

Judaicum, balsamum: Balm of Gilead, see gileadense, balsamum. (3)

Judas' ear: A fungus of elder-tree. (3)

Jug(u)lans; Juglandis, fluidextractum; —fluidum, extractum: Common or English walnut tee, *Jugulans regia*, nuts and leaves used, or the fluid extract therefrom. Used as a cathartic. Figure 138. (1,31,34,46)

Juglandis, lotio: Extract of walnut shells in water, used as an astringent, particularly for tonsillitis. (34)

Juglans; Juglandis, extractum: Bark of the butternut, or white walnut, *Juglans cineria*, of North America, or the fluid extract. A mild cathartic and laxative said to have been used extensively in the Revolutionary War. Nearly indistinguishable (per Woodville) from the English walnut, figure 3-138. (8)

Jujuba: Jujube Tree, *Zizyphus vulgaris*. Fruit used. (1)

Jujubae Pasta: Paste of jujuba, i.e., jujubes. This is basically a candy confection sweetened, textured, and flavored originally with jujuba fruit, but as noted by Beasley, the jujuba was often omitted. It is otherwise a typical soft candy of sugar, mucilage, and water, flavored with orange flower water (see aurantii florum, aqua). (37)

Jujubinus, syrupus: Syrup of jujube. (35)

Julap, mucilagenous; Julep, mucilagenous: See mixture, mucilagenous. (39)

Julapium; Julap; Julep: Julep, a sweet tasting drink, prepared from syrup and containing an aromatic water or essential oil. (1,34)

Julepum e moscho: Nutmeg julep, see moschata, mistura. (39)

July-flowers: See caryophyllum. (39)

Jumble beads: See abrus. (40)

Juniper oil (of); Juniperi (empyrheumaticum); Juniperi, oleum; Juniperi oxycedri (empyrheumaticum): A volatile oil distilled from the fruit of the juniper tree, *Juniperus communis*, of North America. Juniper oil was similar to pine tar (see pix liquida), but more pleasant in odor and thus preferred for topical skin disorders such as psoriasis, eczema, and pruritis, typically as an unguent in soap or ointment in wax or lard. Used for a wide variety of conditions similar to the use of turpentine (terebenthina), especially as a diuretic. (8)

Junipera co., aqua: Gin, see juniperis spiritus, compositus. (40)

Fig. 3-138 Juglans (English) or walnut.

Juniperi, baccae; Juniperi bac.: Juniper berries.

Juniperi, spiritus; —compositus, spiritus; —fluidextractum; —fluidum, extractum: The spirit of juniper, consisting of oil of juniper in alcohol, i.e., gin; or the compound tincture (spirit) consisting of the oils of juniper, caraway, and fennel in alcohol and water; or the fluidextract. A diuretic and carminative. (3,8,31,34). Estes notes that the French for juniper, Genièvre, was Anglicized as Geneva and contracted further to "gin." (39,46)

Juniperus: Common juniper, *Juniperus communis*. Fruit and wood used. Figure 3-139. (1)

Juniperus virginiana: Tops of red cedar, *Juniperus virginiana*, a stimulant, emmenagogue, diuretic, and diaphoretic, closely related to sabin. (39)

Jus: Juice, see succus. (42)

Jupiter: Ancient god associated with tin, see Joviale. (3)

Jus bovinum: "Beef juice," i.e., beef broth or tea, from boiled beef. A nutritive. (42)

Juscalum: Broth of beef, veal, turtle, etc. (3)

Jusquiamus; Jusquiame {*French*}**:** See hyoscyamus. (1,39)

Justini, electuarium: See Iustini, electuarium. (1)

Juniperus communis

Fig. 3-139 Juniperus or juniper.

K

Kaladana (resin); Kaladanae resina; —, tinctura: Seeds or resin of a vine native to India, *Ipomoea hederacea*, from which a tincture was specified in BPC for India and eastern colonies. Used as per jalap, i.e., a cathartic. (40)

Kaladanae compositus, pulvis: See jalapae compositus, pulvis. Kaladana replaced jalap as official in India and eastern British colonies. (42)

Kali (appearing alone); **Kali impuri:** See lixivia. (39)

Kali, lemon: "Sherbet," an effervescing lemon beverage of lemon juice and potassium bicarbonate. (40)

Kali; Kalium: Kalium is potassium (hence the periodic symbol, K). Kalium is nominative and kali the irregularly formed genitive. (39)

Kali aeratum: Potassium carbonate. (3)

Kali causticum: Solution of (see) potash. (40)

Kali nitratum: Potassium nitrate, see potassii nitras. (39)

Kali praeparatum: See potassii carbonas. (40)

Kali puri, aqua: Solution of (see) potash. (40)

Kali sulphuratum; —vitriolicum: Potassium sulfate, see potassii sulphas. (39)

Kali tartarisatum: See potasii tartras. (40)

Kalicum hydras: Fused potassa, hydrated potassa, which forms a mass, see potassa. (3)

Kalium aceticum: Potassium acetate, see potassii acetas. (39)

Kalium sulphuricum; —sulphuratum: Potassium sulfate. (1)

Kalmia (latifolia); Kalmiae, tinctura: Mountain laurel, *Kalmia latifolia*, or the tincture in alcohol. Per Ellingwood, "In *kalmia* we have remedy acting in a manner somewhat like *veratrum viride*, both in controlling fevers and in inflammations, as well as in its influence as an alterative, it having been successfully used both in primary and secondary syphilis. Like *veratrum* it has also been employed hypodermically in the treatment of neuralgia of the face, and sciatica." (32)

Kalmia augustifolia: Lambkill, *Kalmia augustafolia*, use similar to *Kalmia latifolia*. (39)

Kalmopyrin: Proprietary antipyretic, calcium acetylsalicylate, a variant on aspirin. (40)

Kalzana: Calcium sodium lactate. (40)

Kamala; Kameela: Glands and hairs from the capsule of *Mallotus philippensis*, a granular deep red powder with little flavor, used as an anthelmintic. (8,32)

Kamna-fuga: See acetanilidi compositus, pulvis. This was a local term in New Orleans. (34)

Kaolin: Common kaolin, a white clay.

Kaolini, cataplasma; —, unguentum: Cataplasm of kaolin, a mixture of kaolin, glycerin, boric acid, thymol and oils of peppermint and wintergreen. Used as a hot plaster or poultice, it should be "applied as hot as can be comfortably endured." The BPC unguent was of koalin with hard and soft paraffin and served also as a pill excipient for unstable or reactive materials, such as silver nitrate, potassium permanganate, or gold chloride. (31,42)

Kaolini, massa: See kaolini, unguentum. This is similar to the unguent, with reduced glycerin content, to be used as a base (massa) for pill formation. As kaolin is inert, it was useful for reactive ingredients, like silver nitrate, which react with sugar and other common organic pill bases. (40)

Kaposi's ointment: See naphthol ointment. (40)

Karabe: See carabe. (1)

Kassander: See mechoacanna. (39)

Kava; Kavae rhizoma; Kavae, fluidextractum; —fluidum, extractum; —liquidum, extractum; Kava-kava: Dried rhizome and roots of Kava kava, *Piper methysticum*, or the fluid extract. Used as a stimulant and diuretic, the plant remains in use (and abuse) as a stimulant. (3,31,42,46)

Kaylene: Colloidal suspension of the clay, kaolin. (40)

Kefir: Fermented milk, see lac fermentum. (3)

Keiri: See cheiri. (1)

Kelene: Ethyl chloride, a topical refrigerant anesthetic. (3)

Kent, powder of: Powdered crab stones. See cancrorum, lapilli. (39)

Keratin(um): Proteinaceous material derived from macerated animal horn, feathers, etc, via aggressive boiling. Used mainly as a pill, tablet, or capsule coating to resist gastric acid and allow the medication to be released in the more alkaline duodenum, which dissolves the coating. (42)

Keratini, liquor: A solution of prepared keratin in strong solution of ammonia and alcohol, to coat tablets. (42)

Kermes (grains): Kermes, red dye-stuff consisting of dried bodies of the scarlet grain insect, *Kermes*. See cochineal. (1,39)

Kermes mineralis; Kermes mineral: Kermes mineral, i.e., having the color of kermes, a red powder consisting of various sulfides of antimony. Same as vitriol antimonium, or sulphurated antimony, a crude antimony sulfate. See antimonium sulphuratum. (1,8,39)

Kerocain: Novocain, a local anesthetic. (40)

Kerosene: Paraffin oil. (40)

Kervinum, oleum: Castor oil, see ricinis. (40)

Ketopropane: Acetone. (3)

Keyseri, pilule: Keyser's pills, made with mercury acetate, see hydrargyrus acetas. (39)

Kharsivan: Arsenobenzol. (40)

Kharsulphan: Sulpharsphenamine. (40)

Kieselguhr: A nearly pure silica, finely ground, used as an adjunct to filtration. Also refers to diatomaceous earth. (40)

Kina kina: Chinchona, see peruvianus, cortex. (1)

King's (, J.) expectorant tincture: See lobeliae composita, tinctura. (34)

King's entozoic powder: See spigeliae compositus, pulvis. (34)

King's yellow: Yellow arsenic sulphide. See orpiment. (3,40)

Kino; Kino, tinctura: Inspissated juice of *Pterocarpus marsupium*, of India, or the tincture thereof. Used as per tannic acid (tannicum, acidum). (8) In the BPC, of dried kino, glycerin, and water. A "favorite remedy with bismuth or chalk mixture for diarrhea." (42)

Kino, glyceritum: Glycerite of kino, equivalent therapeutically to the tincture. (34)

Kino composita, tinctura: Tinctures of kino and opium, spirit of camphor, oil of cloves, cochineal color, aromatic spirit of ammonia, and alcohol. (46)

Kino compositus, pulvis; Kino cum opio, pulvis: Compound powder of kino, of same with cinnamon and opium. For diarrheal illness. (34)

Kino eucalypti, trochisci: See eucalypti gummi, trochisci. (40)

Kino eucalypti: Exudate from stems of various plants native to Australia, similar to eucalyptus gum. (42)

Kissingense factitium (effervescens); Kissingensis factitii effervescense, salis, pulvis: Artificial Kissingen salt of potassium chloride, sodium chloride, magnesium sulphate, and sodium bicarbonate, used to make Kissingen water. The effervescent form is made so in the usual manner, with sodium bicarbonate, tartaric acid, and citric acid. (31,46)

Knee Holly: See ruscus. (39)

Knock-out-drops: Chloral hydrate. (3)

Kola; Kolae, nuces; Kolae semina: Cola nuts, seeds of certain trees of genus *Cola*, such as *Cola acuminata*, formerly *Sterculia acuminata*. (1)

Kolae, elixir: Elixir of liquid extracts of kola and vanilla in simple syrup. Tonic and stimulant. (42)

Kolae, fluidextractum; —liquidum, extractum; —, tinctura: Fluid extract or tincture of kola, containing caffeine and used as a stimulant and for headache. (31,42)

Kolae, vinum: Kola wine, of the elixir with sherry, stimulant in headache and migraine. (42)

Kooso; Kousso: See Cusso. (8)

Krameria; Krameriae, radix: Rhatany, the root of *Krameria triandra*, of Bolivia and Peru. Krameria is a strong astringent and was used particularly for tooth powders (to suppress bleeding gums) and for nasal bleeding, for which the powder could be inhaled. See tannicum, acidum regarding use of astringents. (7,8,42)

Krameriae, extractum; —fluidum, extractum; —liquidum, extractum; —, liquor (concentratus); —, tinctura; —, infusum (concentratum); —, trochisci; —, syrupus; —fluidglyceratum: Respectively, the dry extract, fluid extract, alcoholic tincture, infusion, troche, syrup, or fluidglycerate (NF) of krameria (rhatany). The syrup was prepared from the fluid extract. The troche consisted of the dry extract, sugar, tragacanth, and stronger orange water (aurantii fortior, aqua). (8) The BPC specified a concentrated liquor as well as a standard and concentrated infusion, the latter with alcohol and chloroform water for storage and reconstitution. (42)

Kumyss: See lac fermentum. (31)

Kussander: See mechoacanna. (39)

Kyapootie oil: See cajuput oil. (40)

L

L.: At beginning or in middle of inscription: lapis (stone), lattuario {*Italian*} (electuary); lignum (wood); lilium (lily); linimentum (liniment); lohoch (lozenge). At end of inscription: lauri (laurel); lénitif {*French*}, lenitivio {*Italian*}, lenitivum (laxative electuary). (1)

L. ars. e. hyd. i(od).: See Arseni et hydrargyri iodidi, liquor.

Labarraque's solution: See sodae chloratae, liquor. (8)

Labdanum: See ladanum. (1)

Labiale, ceratum: Lip wax, i.e., lip balm. Of olive oil, spermaceti, oil of lignum rhodium, and white wax, with alkanet added if desired to produce a red color. (3,39)

Labrusca: Fox grape, *Vitus labrusca*. (1)

Laburnum: Bean trefoil, or golden chain, *Cytisus Laburnum*, extremely toxic, use variable. (33)

Lac (appearing alone): May mean milk, or alternatively shellac, see lacca. (39)

Lac fermentatum: Fermented milk, kumyss, essentially yogurt. "This well known dietetic preparation is made from fresh cows milk, compressed yeast, and sugar, properly fermented, and is used as a food for invalids." (31)

Lac magnesia(e): Milk of magnesia. (3,40)

Lac scammonii: See scammonii, mistura. (34)

Lac sublimatum; Lac sulphuris: Precipitated sulfur. See sulphur praecipitatum. (1,8)

Lac vaccinum: Cow's milk, from the Latin, vaca (cow). (7)

Lac virginal; Lac virginia: 1. See Virgin's Milk. 2. Cerussa acetata, lead acetate, see plumbi acetas. (3,39)

Lacarnol: Proprietary muscle extract. (40)

Lacca: Lac, resinous substance from the lac beatle, source of shellac. An astringent used for sore gums, as in scurvy. (1,39)

Lacca coerulea; —musica: Litmus, for pH indication, See lakmus. (3)

Laccae, tinctura: Tincture of lacca, an alcoholic solution of lacca, with myrrh and cochlearia, for bleeding gums or internally as an antiscorbutic, for leukorrhea, or for gonorrhea. (39)

Lacerta: Lizard. (1)

Lachnanthes: Lachnanthes, red root, spirit weed, root of *Lachnanthes tinctoria*, with pharmacologic action similar to atropine. (33)

Lacmus: See lakmus. (33)

Lacteol: Commercial preparation of lyophylized lactobacillus and similar bacteria. Digestive aid. (40)

Lactic acid; Lacticum (dilutum), acidum: Lactic acid, from fermentation of milk sugar, used as a topical for lesions of the mucous membranes, especially tuberculous lesions of the oropharynx, and for the preparation of many other lactate salts and formulations. (42)

Lactin; Lactis, sal: Sugar of milk, i.e., lactose. Sal usually refers to a salt, but milk sugar crystalizes out of milk and the misnomer is at least understandable. (3)

Lactobacilline: Commercial preparation of lyophylized lactobacillus and similar bacteria. Digestive aid. (40)

Lactophenin: Lactyl-para-phenetidine, identical to phenacetin except that the acetyl group is replaced by lactate. An effective analgesic and antipyretic less toxic than available alternatives at the time, but largely replaced by acetaminophen. (8)

Lactose: Milk sugar, the naturally occurring sugar in milk, consisting of glucose and galactose, adjoined. It was a useful, bland substance in triturations and as a vehicle. It was said at one time to be diuretic, and of use in dropsy. (8)

Lactuca: Garden lettuce, *Lactuca sativa*, and related species. Seeds and latex used. Said to share the antitussive, analgesic, and antidiarrheal properties of opium. (1,39)

Lactucae, aqua: Water of flowering lettuce. (40)

Lactucae, extractum: Extract of lettuce, used as a mild hypnotic and as per lactuca, above. (42)

Lactucarii, tinctura; —, syrupus: Tincture and syrup of lactucarium. Tincture is of lactucarium, glycerin, water, and alcohol. Syrup is made from the tincture with sugar and water. (8,42)

Lactucarium; Lactucarii fluidum, extractum: Lettuce-opium, concretions from the milky juice of *Lactuca virosa* or related species, or fluid extract thereof. Said to be a mild hypnotic. See lactuca. Figure 3-140. (1,8,34,39,46)

Ladani compositum, emplastrum: Plaster of ladanum, frankincense, cinnamon, oil of mace, and oil of mint. (39)

Ladanum: Aromatic gum resin of *Cistus ladanifer* or *C. creticus*, a stomachic. (39)

Lady Webster's (dinner) pills: See aloes et mastiches, pilulae. (34)

Fig. 3-140 Lactucarium.

Lady's blush: Carmine. (3)

Lady's slipper; Ladyslipper: See cypripedium. (8)

Laetificans, electuarium: Tonic electuary, from the Latin, *laetificare,* to make happy. (1)

Laevulose; Laevulosum: See levulose. (40)

Lafayette's mixture: A variant of copaibae composita, mistura. Copaiba, spirit of nitrous ether, compound tincture of lavender, tincture of opium, and mucilage of acacia. A diuretic, for gonorrhea, and for various urinary conditions. (34)

Lait virginal: Virgin's milk, see benzoini, lotio. (42)

Lakmus: Litmus, the pH indicator dye used to test for acidity. Extracted from a variety of lichens. (3)

Lambrusca: See labrusca. (1)

Lamellae _____: Small gelatin discs for placement below the eyelid to achieve various effects on the eye. Standard in the BP, these included **lamellae atropinae, homatropinae, cocainae, and physostigminae.** The first two produce dilation of the pupil, cocaine produces dilation and anesthesia, and physostigmine produces pupillary constriction. (34)

Lamii, conserva de floribus: Conserve of the flowers of dead nettle. (35)

Laminaria: The sea weed, *Laminaria cloustoni,* sometimes called sea tangles or sea girdles. The cut, dried stems were inserted into the urethra, uterine os, or other area to be dilated, and the material expanded upon rehydration. Sponge was used for similar purpose. Laminaria was more easily inserted, but more prone to accidental perforation or bleeding as it was more rigid. (33)

Lamium: Member of genus *Lamium,* ex.—Dead-nettle. Flowers used. (1)

Lamotte's drops: See ferri chloridi aetherea, tinctura. (3,31)

Lamp black: Soot, carbon.

Lana philosophica: Zinc oxide. (3)

Lanae, adeps: See lanolin. (8)

Lanain; Lanalin; Lanesin; Lanichol; Laniol: Variants for lanolin, adeps lanae. (3)

Lange's solution: Solution of colloidal gold. (24)

Lanolin: The purified fat derived from sheep's wool. The wool is washed with weak soda (sodium hydroxide) and then the oil extracted with benzine, which is evaporated and the resulting fat bleached by sunlight to a white or light-yellow color. This is adeps lanae, which can be further mixed with water and with heating will take up approximately 1¼ times its own weight in water, to form adeps lanae hydrosus, or hydrated lanolin. The latter seems to be readily taken up by the skin and is useful as a base for many ointments and unguents. It remains in use today as a topical emollient and skin protectant used, for example, to protect the nipple of a nursing mother. (8)

Lanolini, unguentum: See adipis lanae, unguentum. (42)

Lapathum: Herba Britanica, members of genus *Rumex* (Dock), esp. water dock, *Rumex hydrolapathum* or *R. aquaticus.* A cathartic and also used in mouthwashes, ointments, and as a scurvy treatment. Figure 3-141. (1,39)

Lapides cancrorum; Lapilli cancrorum: Eyestones, crab's eyes, crab stones, concretions found in stomach of European crawfish. (3)

Lapis _____: Stone or gem, see _____, lapis

Lapis amianthus: Asbestos. (40)

Lapis calaminaris: Calamine, see calamina. (1)

Lapis contrayerva: Contrayerva stone, see contrayervae compositus, pulvis. This is an herbal preparation, not a mineral, despite the name. (39)

Lapis divinus: Devine or wound stone. This appears to be a topical astringent and styptic agent. Formulations vary, but generally include silver nitrate (argenti nitras) along with copper sulfate and/or alum, formed into a stick or mass. Also called cuprum aluminatum, i.e., aluminated cupras, indicating copper sulfate and alum. See related: pulvis stypticum; aluminus composita, pulvis and cupri vitriolati composita, aqua. (40)

Lapis gancrorum: Orthographic variant, see lapilli cancrorum, crab's eye. (39)

Lapis haematitis: See haematitis, lapis. (1)

Lapis hybernicus: Irish stone, a black earth containing iron salts. Soft mineral compound used topically for bruising. (39,40)

Lapis infernalis: Infernal stone, silver nitrate, see argenti nitras. (39)

Lapis lazuli: Lapis lazuli, a blue copper-containing mineral. (1)

Lapis medicamentosus: Medical or medicated stone. 1. A mixture of astringents based on iron sulfate. 2. Sal muriaticus, i.e., common salt. (39)

Lapis mirabilis: Miraculous stone, a mixture of astringent and vulnerary materials, primarily mineral sulfates, based on vitriol. (39)

Lapis sanguineus: Blood-stone, the mineral haematite, iron oxide. (40)

Lappa; Lappae fluidum, extractum: The root of burdock, *Arctium lappa,* of northern Eurasia, naturalized in North America, or the fluid extract thereof. A diaphoretic alterative useful in skin disorders, especially psoriasis and acne. Figure 3-142. (8)

Larch: See pinus larix. (8)

Lard, benzoinated: See benzoinatus, adeps. (8)

Largin: See silver albuminate. (40)

Fig. 3-141 Lapathum.

Fig. 3-142 Lappa.

Laricis, tinctura: Tincture of larch bark, see pinus larix. (34)

Laricis composita, tinctura: Compound tincture of larch (see pinus larix), of the bark, juniper berry, prickly ash bark, wild cherry bark, seneca snakeroot, tansy, molasses, whisky, and an extract of mandrake. Technically a bitter, for a multitude of conditions. (34)

Laricis cortex: Bark of larch.

Larix: Larch, *Larix europa*, the resin of which is called Venice turpentine. Genitive form, Laricis. See pinuus larix. (1)

Larkspur: See delphinum. (7)

Lassar's paste; Lassar's (mild) resorcin paste: See pasta zinci composita and pasta resorcini, respectively. (42)

Later: Brick or tile (Latin). (1)

Lateritium (philosophorum), oleum; Lateribus, oleum e: See philisophorum, oleum. (1)

Lattuario {*Italian*}**:** Electuary. (1)

Lattuca {*Italian*}**; Lattuga** {*Italian*}**; Latuca** {*Italian*}**:** Lettuce, see lactuca. (1)

Lattucario {*Italian*}**:** See lactucarium. (1)

Laudanum: Tincture of opium, see opii, tinctura. Laudanum is also used rather haphazardly to refer to various opium preparations. (Not same as ladanum).

Laudanum, London: Tincture of about fifty-eight percent opium, with crocus, castoreum, amber oil, moschus, ambergris, and oil of nutmeg. (39)

Laudanum, Sydenham's: Sydenham's Laudanum refers to wine of opium, see opii, vinum. (1,8) Estes notes that this preparation was introduced by Dr. Thomas Sydenham, London, seventeenth century, and contained eleven percent opium with crocus, cinnamon, and clove. (39)

Laudanum, Wedel's: A concentrated opium pill, after Georg Wolfgang Wedels, Jena, seventeenth century, similar to solid panacea (see panacea, solid). (39)

Laudanum liquidum cydoniatum: Alcoholic solution of opium, with cinnamon, nutmeg, mace, and juniper. Cydoniatum means "quince" and Estes speculates that this must have been a component of the early versions of this preparation. (39)

Laudanum liquidum: See thebaica, tinctura. (39)

Laurel; Lauro {*Italian*}**:** Bay-tree, Bay Laurel, see laurus. (1)

Laurel, mountain; —, spurge: See kalmia (latifolia) and mezerium, respectively. (39)

Laurelcherry; Laurocerasus; Laurocerasi folia; Laurocerasi aqua: Cherry laurel, *Prunus laurocerasus*, of Europe, leaves used. The water of cherry laurel is made by distillation, and includes some hydrogen cyanide. It is a flavoring agent. It could be used for other purposes for which cyanide was purportedly effective, but as the hydrogen cyanide tended to volatilize, the preparation was not considered stable or reliable. Figure 3-143. (8)

Lauri, baccae; —fructis: Bay-Laurel berries (fruits). (1)

Lauri baccis, emplastrum e: Plaster of bay berries, with turpentine, frankincense, myrrh, mastich, and other ingredients, in honey. (35)

Lauri cinnamomi, tinctura: See cinnamomi tinctura. (40)

Lauri essentia, oleum: Essential (volatile) oil of bay laurel. (40)

Laurier {*French*}**:** See laurus. (1)

Laurinum, oleum: Oil of bay-laurel berries. (1,3)

Laurinum, unguentum: Bayberry unguent, or laurel ointment, of same with egg and oils of laurel, turpentine, and amber (succinum). A warm stimulant ointment said to be derived from the older unguentum nervinum (see nervinum, unguentum). (39)

Lauro, bacche di {*Italian*}**:** See lauri, bacchae. (1)

Laurus: Bay tree, *Laurus nobilis*. Leaves and berries used. (1) According to Estes, in the US this was replaced with the root bark of bayberry, *Myrica pennsylvanica*, or wax myrtle, *Myrica cerifera*. Emetic and biliary deobstruant. Figure 3-144. (39)

Laurus camphora; —cassia; —cinnamomum; —sassafras: See camphor, cassia, cinnamoma, and sassafras, respectively. (39)

Lavandula; Lavendula: Lavender, usually spike lavender, *Lavendula latiflora*. Flowers and leaves used. Tonic and antirhumatic. Figure 3-145. (1,39)

Lavandula spica: The flowering spikes of lavender. (39)

L

Fig. 3-143 Laurocerasus or cherry laurel.

Fig. 3-144 Laurus.

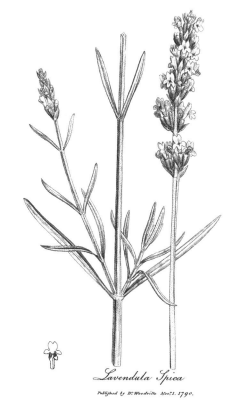

Fig. 3-145 Lavandula or lavender.

Lavandulae, aqua: Lavender water, a perfumed water scented with lavender flower petals and/or oil of lavender.

Lavandulae, spiritus: Spirit of lavender, of approximately five percent oil of lavender in deodorized alcohol. (8)

Lavandulae, syrupus: Syrup of lavender, primarily flavoring or odorant. (40)

Lavandulae composita, tinctura; Lavender, compound spirits of; Lavender drops: Compound tincture or spirit of lavender, lavender drops, consisting of oil of lavender, oil of rosemary, cassia cinnamon, cloves, nutmeg, red saunders, water, and alcohol. The material was mixed and percolated, followed by filtration to obtain the tincture. Extremely useful as a flavoring and coloring agent as well as having carminative action. (8,34,39)

Lavandulae compositus, spiritus: Compound spirits of lavender. There were many varieties of this preparation dating from ancient times, generally an alcoholic solution of lavender oil and other aromatic oils, especially orange. See lavandulae composita, tinctura. (40)

Lavatio ori: Mouth wash. "This is a sweetened aromatic solution of soap colored with fuchsin. Its therapeutic virtues are not very obvious." (31)

Lavender (flowers), oil of; Lavandulae (florum) oleum: Oil of lavender, the oil distilled from fresh flowers of *Levandula officinalis*. Lavender oil could be used like other volatile oils (see, for example, caryophyllus), but was primarily used alone or as the compound tincture as a flavoring and coloring agent and carminative. (8)

Lavender, French: See stoechas. (39) Also stated to be used as equivalent to levandula spica. (40)

Lavender, red, spirit of: See lavandulae composita, tinctura. (40)

Lavender, syrup of: See lavandulae, syrupus. (40)

Lawsonia inermis: Henna plant, the leaf of which provides henna pigment used to color or decorate hair and skin. Fruit is emmenagogue and both the fruit and the dyestuff are believed effective for leprosy and other chronic skin conditions. Unofficial. (44)

Laxativa benedicta: See benedicta laxativa.

Laxativa compositae, pilulae: In the USP, aloin, strychnine, ipecac, powdered licorice, and extract of belladonna leaf to reduce cramping, cathartic. (42)

Laxativa viennensis, aqua: Compound infusion of sienna, see black draught. (3)

Laxative pills after confinement; Laxativae post partum, pilulae: Barker's pills, for post-partum use, of compound extract of colocynth, purified aloes, extract of nux vomica, resin of podophyllum, ipecac, and extract of hyoscyamus. (46)

Laxative powder: Magnesia. (39)

Laxativus: Laxative. (1)

Lead (, red) (, white): See plumbum (metallic), plumbi (compounds). Note that red lead is the oxide, generally Pb_3O_4, and white lead is the carbonate, see plumbi oxidum and carbonas, respectively. Litharge is the simple oxide, PbO. (8)

Lead, subcarbonate of: Lead carbonate. (40)

Lead, sugar of: Lead acetate (plumbi acetata), which has a sweet taste. (39)

Lead and opium, lotion; —, wash: See plumbi et opii, lotio. (31)

Lead cerate (compound): See plumbi ceratum or plumbi compositum ceratum. (42)

Lead flake: Lead carbonate. (3)

Lead ointment, Hebra's: See diachylon, unguentum. (34)

Lead protoxide: Lead oxide, see litharge.

Leaf green: See chlorophyll. (42)

Lectisternium, unguent(um): An all-purpose ointment, a lectisternium being Latin for a celebratory feast, generally in honor of the gods. (39)

Ledum: Labrador tea, James' tea, leaves of *Ledum latifolium*, expectorant and pectoral. (33)

Leeches: Leeches, *Sanguisuga medicinalis or S. officinalis*, were used to treat bruises or to remove blood from various injuries. The live leech could be applied anywhere desired, although it is noted that a leech glass, which allows only the head to protrude, should be used when leeches are applied to the lips, rectum, or uterus. (8)

Leek: See porrum. (39)

Lee's [Windham][New London] pills: 1. Lee's pills, or Lee's Windham Pills, cholegogic pills of aloe, gamboge, niter, and heracleum, after Samuel Lee, Connecticut, ca. 1796. First medication patented in the US. 2. Unrelated version, sometimes called Lee's New London Pills, was introduced by another Samuel Lee, also of Connecticut. Originally with calomel, jalap, gamboge, and tartar emetic, later with aloe, scamonium, gamboge, jalap, rhamnus catharticus, and soap. Both were panaceas. (39)

Legno {*Italian*}**:** Wood. (1)

Leguminae; Leguminorum: Bean(s) or bean pod (s), pea(s); leguminorum being the plural genitive form, as in liquid extract of senna (pods), sennae leguminorum liquidum, extractum. (42)

Leiocom: Dextrin. (3)

Leipzig yellow: Lead chromate. (3)

Leméry's tincture: A tincture of red iron oxide and tartaric acid (or potassium tartrate), after French pharmacist Nicola Lémery, mid-eighteenth century. (39)

Lemnian earth: See bolus, this was a pale red bolus, effervescing slightly with acids, from the island of Lemnos in the Aegean. (39)

Lemon(s), acid of: Citric acid. (39)

Lemon, (essential) salt of: Misnomer for potassium oxalate as extracted from *acetosa* (rumex) species. (39,40)

Lemon, syrup of: See limonis, syrupus. (40)

Lemon; Lemonis: Lemon, see limonis. (8)

Lemon grass (, oil of); Lemon grass oil: Oil obtained from lemon grass, *Andropogon citratus*, for perfumery, but also for many medicinal purposes including insect repellent, to cure typhus, for body odor, etc. (40)

Lemonade purgative: See magnesii citratis, liquor. (42)

Lemort's extract: See opii camphorata, tinctura. This also contained licorice, sodium carbonate, and honey, after Prof. Lemort, chemist, Leyden, ca. 1700. (39)

Leniens, linctus: A soothing sucker, of gum arabic, almond oil, and water of cherries (cerasi, aqua). (39)

Leniens, unguentum: Cold cream, see rosae, aqua, unguentum. (40)

Lenitive: From the Latin, soothing or relieving pain or discomfort.

Pistacia Lentiscus

Fig. 3-146 Lentiscus or mastic tree.

Lenitive electuary: Confection of senna (sennae, confectio). (3)

Lenitivum, electuarium; Lenitivo, elettuario {Italian}; **Lénetif fin** {*French*}**:** Any electuary with mild purgative effect, typically of senna, tamarind pulp, prunes, polypody rhizome, licorice, etc. (1)

Lentiscus: Lentisk, mastic tree, *Pistacia lentiscus.* Resin used, see mastiche. An astringent, stomachic, tonic, and diuretic. Figure 3-146. (1,39)

Leo: Lion. (1)

Leonaris; Leonurus (cardiaca): Motherwort, *Leonurus cardiaca,* used for menstrual disorders and post-partum difficulties as well as for hysteria. A cure-all for various female disorders and an opium substitute. Figure 3-147. (32,39)

Leontodon [taraxacum]: Lion's tooth, same as dandelion (dent de lion), see taraxacum. (39)

Leonuri compositae, pilulae: Compound pills of motherwort, of alcoholic extracts of motherwort and unicorn-root, extract of leptandra, and resin of cimicifuga. For uterine disorders. (34)

Leopard's bane: See arnica. (32)

Leptandra; Leptandrae, extractum; —fluidum, extractum; —, tinctura: The rhizome and roots of leptandra, or Culver's root, *Veronica virginica,* of the eastern United States, or the extract, fluid extract, or tincture therefrom. A highly powerful cathartic and cholegogue, used to treat jaundice. (8)

Leptandrae compositae, pilulae: Compound pills of leptandra, with podophyllum and rhubarb. A cholegogue, for liver disorders or constipation. (34)

Leptandrae compositus, pulvis: Compound powder of leptandra, made of leptandra extract, resin of podophyllum, and sugar of milk. (34) A powerful cathartic said to be of benefit in epidemic dysentery. (34)

Lepus: Hare. (1)

Lethalis, spiritus: Carbonic acid. (3) While carbonic acid is not lethal, this is the solution of carbon dioxide in water, carbon dioxide gas being lethal in sufficient concentrations by displacement of oxygen.

Letificans, electuarium: See laetificans, electuarium. (1)

Lettuce; Lettuce opium: See lactuca and lactucarium, respectively. (39)

Leucanthemum: Whole plant of ox-eye daisy, white weed, great ox-eye, field daisy, moon daisy, maudlin daisy, white daisy, horse gowan, grande Marguerite, or goldens, *Chrysanthemum leucanthemum,* a tonic, diuretic, and antispasmodic, emetic in large doses. (33)

Leucoenus: White wine. (3)

Leucogene: Sodium bisulphite. (3)

Leucoium: See cheiri. (1)

Levant nut: *Cocculus indicus,* fish berries. (3)

Levant wormseed: See santonica. (8)

Levisticum: Lovage, *Levisticum officinale,* also called *Lygusticum levisticum.* Herb and root used. An aromatic. Figure 3-148. (1,39)

Levulose: Fructose. Fruit sugar. Also known as "diabetin" for its use as a sweetener for diabetics, having less impact on blood sugar (glucose) levels.

Liatris: Gay feather, colicrRoot, *Liatris spicata,* a stomachic. (32)

Lichen carrageenin: Gelatinous extract of lichen islandicus, below.

Lichen cen[e][i]rius terrestris: Leaves of ash colored (cenerius being Latin for ashes) ground liverwort, *Peltidea canina,* diuretic and for rabies. Figure 3-149. (39)

Lichen icelandicus; Lichen islandicus: Icelandic moss, Icelandic lichen, *Cetraria islandica.* Source of gelatinous substance, carrageenin. Figure 3-150. (1,3)

Licorice: See glycyrrhiza. (8)

Licorice, compound powder: See glycyrrhizae compositus, pulvis. (40)

Liebreich's solution: Solution of cantharidin in dilute potassium hydroxide, used for tuberculosis, pityriasis rubra, and lupus. (42)

Life-everlasting: White balsam, cudweed, or Indian posey, *Gnaphalium polycephalum.* Used for sciatica and many other purposes. (3)

Ligni: Of wood, genitive of the Latin, lignum. (1)

Ligni campechensis, extractum: See haematoxylon, extractum. (40)

Lignia nitrica: Gun-cotton, see pyroxylin. (3)

Lignorum, decoctum: Decoction of woods, same as guaiaci compositum, decoctum. (39)

Fig. 3-149 Lichen cenerius terrestris.

Fig. 3-147 Leonaris or Leonuris, the motherwort.

Fig. 3-148 Levisticum or lovage.

Fig. 3-150 Lichen islandicus or Icelandicus.

Lignum: Wood. (1)

Lignum aloes: See aloes, lignum. (1)

Lignum aspalathi: See aspalathi, lignum. (1)

Lignum campechense: See haematoxylon. (1)

Lignum camphorae: Camphor wood, i.e., the woody branches of *Cinnamomum camphora*, see camphor.

Lignum guaiaci: See guaiaci, lignum. (1)

Lignum nephriticum: See nephritcum, lignum. (1)

Lignum rhodii; Lignum rhodium: See rhodii, lignum. (1,39)

Lignum sanctum; —vitae: Guaiacum wood. See guaiaci, lignum. (3)

Lignum sandali; Lignum santali: See santalum. (1)

Lignum vitae: See guaiaci, lignum. (1,8)

Ligroin(um): Petroleum naphtha, mainly a solvent for fats and oils. (42)

Ligusticum: See levisticum. (1)

Ligustrum: Privet, Privy, or Prim, *Ligustrum vulgare*, an astringent. (33)

Lilacin; Lilacine: See terpineol. (42)

Lilium: Lily. (1)

Lilium album: White or Madonna lily, *Lilium candidum (or album)*. Flowers and root used as emollient. (1,39) Posssibly identical with *Lilium candidum*.

Lilium candidum: Meadow or white lily, *Lilium candidum*, a "mucilaginous demulcent, tonic, and astringent." Figure 3-151. (33) Possibly identical with *Lilium album*.

Lilium convallium: See convallaria. (1,8)

Lilium mineralis: Non-botanical, a mixture of tin, iron, copper, and antimony sulfides. (39)

Lilium tigrinum: Tiger lily, for various uterine conditions. (32)

Lily-of-the-valley: See convallaria. (39)

Limatura (ferri): Filings, i.e., iron filings. (1,3)

Lime: Lime or quicklime, calcium oxide, see quicklime. For the fruit, see limonis. Lemon and lime were viewed as variants, not as independent entities. (39)

Lime, milk of: Slaked lime and water in a thin cream. (40)

Lime, muriate of: Calcium chloride. See calcii chloridum. (39) For the solution, see calcii chloridi, liquor. (44)

Lime, slaked: See calcii hydras. (42)

Lime, sulphate of: Desiccated calcium sulfate. (40)

Lime tree: See tilia. See also: lime, regarding non-distinction of lemon and lime. (39)

Limonata smaragdina: A cordial of emeralds with seeds and syrup of lemon or lime. (39)

Limonis; Limonis cortex; Limonis, oleum; Limonis, spiritus: Lemon, lemon peel, or the oil expressed from fresh lemon peel, from the plant *Citrus limonum (or medica)*, originally of India. The spirit of lemon consists of lemon oil and lemon peel macerated in alcohol, followed by filtration. The oil is used primarily as a flavoring ingredient or to impart a pleasant odor, not for therapeutic purposes. Figure 3-152. (8) The compendia do not clearly distinguish lemon and lime, the two fruits being regarded as color variants. They are readily hybridized and the lime, picked green, will ripen to orange or yellow if left on the tree. Even today, the "Key Lime" is yellow and the distinction of lemon and lime is more commercial than biological.

Limonis, essentia: Essence of lemon, i.e., the essential oil distilled from the peel, often diluted with alcohol.

Limonis, sal: Potassium oxalate. See lemons, essential salt of. (40)

Limonis, syrupus: Syrup of lemon juice and peel, for febrile conditions. (34)

Limonis (fortis), tinctura: Tincture of fresh lemon peel, a flavoring. The BPC had a stronger form which was 1:1 with alcohol as opposed to 1:4. (34,42)

Limonis cum pepsino, succus: Pepsin in lime juice with glycerin, alcohol, and purified talcum, for use as a digestive aid. (34)

Limonis succus: Lemon juice, used per White's *Materia Medica* to relieve thirst, i.e., as lemonade. It is also noted that "three or four ounces of lemon juice are of great benefit daily in scurvy. Why this is, we do not certainly know. Lemon juice is probably more efficacious than citric acid." Scurvy is now known to be a deficiency of citric acid (vitamin C). Limonis is variably used in reference to lime juice as well, and in some sources, lemon and lime appear to be interchangeable or at least not fully distinguished. (8)

Limonum; Limone {*Italian*}: Lemon or citron. (1)

Linalool: A complex alcohol derived from bergamot and other essential oils, for perfumery. (42)

Linaria: Todaflex, toad flax, *Linaria vulgaris (Antirrhinum linaria)*. Herb used. Weak diuretic. Figure 3-153. (1,33,39)

Linctus: Linctus, a syrupy medication, especially one with antitussive or pectoral properties. (1)

Linctus sedativus: Syrup of morphine hydrochloride, chloroform, lemon juice, and glycerin. (42)

Lilium candidum

Published by Dr Woodville Sept. 1.1791.

Fig. 3-151 Lilium candidum.

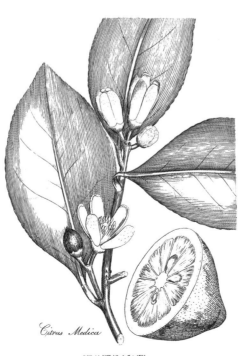

Citrus Medica

Published by W Woodville Jan.y 1. 1790.

Fig. 3-152 Limon, the lemon or limetree.

Antirrhinum Linaria

Published by Dr Woodville March 1 1790.

Fig. 3-153 Linaria or toad flax.

Linctus, simple: See scillae, linctus. (42)

Lindera: Spice bush, fever bush, wild allspice, spicewood, feverwood, or Benjamin bush, *Lindera benzoin*, from which a benzoin-like material was derived. An aromatic tonic, astringent, stimulant, and anthelmintic. (33)

Lingua avis: Seed of ash tree. (1)

Lingua cervina: See scolopendrium. (1)

Lini, cataplasma: Poultice of crushed linseed and water. Applied warm for superficial or deeper inflammation. See also kaolini, cataplasma. (42)

Lini, mucilago: Mucilage of linseed, made fresh as required for various cough mixtures and formulations of the BPC. (42)

Lini, ol[eum]: Linseed oil, see linseed, linum. (39)

Lini, oleum: Linseed oil. This is the raw oil, not the boiled oil which forms a resin-like varnish used to finish wood. It is expressed from the seed without the use of heat. It was commonly applied to burns. (8) Used in production of early composite flooring, "linoleum."

Lini (compositum), infusum: Infusion of whole linseed and licorice root, for acute respiratory disorders. (34)

Lini cum calce, oleum: See carron oil. (40)

Lini et glycyrrhizae et chlorodyni, trochisci: Troche of chlorodyne, extract of licorice, mucilages of linseed and gum acacia, and sugar. For cough. (42)

Lini farina: Crushed linseed, linseed meal. See lini, cataplasma regarding use.

Liniment, anodyne: See opii, linimentum. (34)

Liniment, simple; Linimentum simplex: Simple liniment, of four parts olive oil to one part white wax. (39)

Liniment, volatile: See ammonii, linimentum. (40)

Liniment de mino negro {*Italian*}**:** Liniment of black lead, of red lead, oxymel of squill, and wax. (39)

Linimentum: Liniment. (1)

Linimentum _____: Liniment, see _____, linimentum unless listed below. (8)

Linimentum album: See terebinthinae aceticum, linimentum. (31)

Linimentum nigrum: Black liniment, of olive oil, sulphuric acid, and turpentine, which forms a liniment spontaneously. A counterirritant. (31)

Linimentum olei; —, oleorum: Liniment of oils, specifically cedar, cajaput, sassafras, and cloves. A topical for local irritation or inflammation, rheumatism, etc. (34)

Linitivum, electuarium: See lenitivum, electuarium. (1)

Linseed; —poultice: See linum and also lini, cataplasma. (42)

Lint; Linteum: Lint, generally scraped from cotton fabric, for surgical dressing, padding, etc. (34) The BPC specifies a variety of "lints," treated with various materials for topical application including **Linteum acidi borici, acidi carbolici, acidi salicyli, eucalypti, iodoformi,** and **stypticum** (ferric chloride). (42)

Linteum salis alembroth: A gauze treated with sal alembroth, i.e., sal ammoniac, an antiseptic packing or dressing. (40)

Linum; Linosa {*Italian*}**; Linseed:** Flax seed, the seed of *Linum usitatissimum* (Latin, flax most useful). The source of linseed oil, commonly used as a demulcent or in a plaster to treat burns. Linseed tea was made with licorice, linseed, and boiling water and was used as a demulcent and a topical for sore throats due to the mucilage content and pleasant flavor. The poultice was made simply by boiling flaxseed in water, and was coated with oil prior to application to prevent sticking to the skin. Figure 3-154. (8) See also: linum catharticum.

Linum catharticum: Purging flax, a separate species, *Linum catharticum*, a mild cathartic. (39)

Linum contusum: Crushed ("bruised") linseed, to form a poultice (cataplasma lini). (42)

Lippia: *Lippia mexicana* or *L. dulcis*, for cough and respiratory disorders. (32)

Liq.; Liquor _____: Liquor, an aqueous solution, see _____, liquor. (8,31)

Liqueur de Goudron: Solution of Norwegian (pine) tar, see pix. (40)

Liqueur de Pelligrin: A caustic material made from antimony chloride and sulfur. (39)

Liquid camphor: Essential oil of camphor, see camphor for explanation re: "oil." (40)

Liquidambar; Liquidamber; Liquidambra: Sweet-gum tree, bilsted, copal gum, sweet gum, or gum wax. The balsamic exudate of *Liquidambar styraciflua*, used as per styrax, mainly as a topical for skin conditions, hemorrhoids, etc. (33,39)

Liquidamber, syrupus: Syrup of sweet-gum bark, for respiratory and gastrointestinal disturbances. (34)

Liquirita; Liquiriza {*Italian*}**; Liquorita:** Licorice, see glycyrrhiza. (1)

Liquor alkalinus: An alkaline bath salt from the BPC. (40)

Liquor antisepticus alkalinus: See aromaticus alkalinus, liquor. (31)

Liquor fowleri: Fowler's solution, see potassii arsenitis, liquor. (40)

Liquor fumanti: Fuming liquid, made of antimony, tin, and corrosive sublimate of mercury. (39)

Liquor parathyroidei: Water extract of bovine, ovine, or porcine parathyroid glands, source of parathyroid hormone, used to raise serum calcium content and to promote bone formation. (7)

Liquor stypticus: See ferri perchloridi, liquor. (40)

Liquorice: Licorice, see glycyrrhiza. (8)

Liriodendron: Bark of the tulip tree, yellow wood, white wood, poplar (American), yellow poplar, or canoe wood, *Liriodendron tulipifera*, an aromatic tonic and stimulant. (33)

Lisbon diet drink: See sarsaparillae compositum, decoctum. Antivenereal. (39)

Lister's antiseptic; —salt: A solution of mercury zinc cyanide. Despite the eponym, this is not the antiseptic for which Lister is famous, the latter being carbolic acid (phenol). See hydrargyri et zinci cyanidum. (24,40,42)

Litharge; Lithargyrus: Lead oxide (white), see plumbi oxidum. "Litharge" appears to refer to stone (lithia) and silver (argentum), or "silver-stone" an apt description for metallic lead. (8,39)

Lithargyri acetati, aqua: Water of lead acetate, see plumbi acetata. Topical for skin disorders. See plumbae subacetatis forte, liquor. (39,40)

Lithargyri acetati compositum, ceratum: See Goulard's cerate. (3)

Lithargyri cum hydrargyri, emplastrum: Plaster of white lead with mercury, see hydrargyri, emplastrum. (39)

Linum usitatissimum.
Published by D.º Woodville Nov.ª 1, 1791.

Fig. 3-154 Linum or flax, source of linseed.

Lithia (effervescens), aqua: An effervescent lithium salt, for which multiple official formulations and natural sources (spring or mineral waters) can be located in various references. (40)

Lithic acid: Uric acid. (3)

Lithii benzoas; Lithium benzoicum: Lithium benzoate. See benzoicum, acidum. (8)

Lithii bromidi, elixir: Elixir of lithium bromide and citric acid in aromatic elixir. (46)

Lithii bromidum: Lithium bromide, LiBr. From reaction of ferrous bromide with lithium carbonate. Primarily used as a sedative and for control of epilepsy. See bromine. (8)

Lithii carbonas (effervescens): Lithium carbonate, Li_2CO_3, by reaction of lithium chloride with ammonium carbonate. Used in the treatment of gout and urinary stones. Lithium carbonate remains in use for the treatment of manic-depressive illness, but the psychotropic effects of lithium were not recognized until 1949. An effervescent formula is specified in the BPC. (8,26,42)

Lithii chloridum: Lithium chloride. (42)

Lithii citra(ti)s effervescens, sal: Effervescent salt of lithium citrate, of five percent lithium citrate, made effervescent in the usual manner with sodium bicarbonate, tartaric acid, and/or citric acid and sugar. It is used as an antilithic (kidney and bladder stone preventive) and diuretic. (8,31)

Lithii citras laxativus effervescens: Effervescent mixture of lithium citrate with sodium phosphate and bicarbonate, tartaric acid, and citric acid. Diuretic, purgative, and antilithic for individuals with gout. (42)

Lithii citras: Lithium citrate. (8)

Lithii citratis, elixir: Elixir of lithium citrate in aromatic elixir. (46)

Lithii formas: Lithium formate. (42)

Lithii glycerophosphas: A little used lithium salt of glycerophosphoric acid, replacing sodium or potassium glycerophosphates when the patient also suffered with gout as lithium salts prevent stone formation. (42)

Lithii guaiacas; Lithium guaiacate: A mixture of lithium oxide and guaiac resin used in gout and rheumatoid arthritis. (42)

Lithii hydroxidum: Lithium hydroxide, used to prepare other lithium compounds. (42)

Lithii iodidi: Lithium iodide is an alternative lithium salt sometimes used in gout and rheumatoid arthritis. (42)

Lithii oxidum: Lithium oxide, used to prepare other lithium compounds. (42)

Lithii salicylas, elixir: Elixir of lithium salicylate in aromatic elixir. (46)

Lithii salicylas: Lithium salicylate. See salicylicum, acidum. (8) Particularly useful for inflammatory complications of gout, as the lithium prevents stone formation. (42)

Lithii uras: Lithium urate, an alternative lithium salt used as an antiarthritic and for gout. (42)

Lithium: Lithium, found medicinally in a variety of salt forms and historically used primarily as a uricosuric, antilithic, and as the bromide salt for sedation. The value of lithium in manic depressive illness was not recognized until the mid-twentieth century.

Lithium theobromine salicylate: This is primarily a diuretic, used for dropsy and fluid retention, despite the fact that salicylate is anti-inflammatory and theophylline also a bronchodilator. (40)

Lithontripticum, electuarium; Lithontripticus, pulvis: Electuary or powder for elimination of urinary stones (calculi), from Latin, "stone-breaker." (1)

Lithopone: A pigment consisting of mixture of barium sulfate, zinc sulfide and zinc oxide. (3)

Lithospermum: Common gromwell, *Lithospermum officinale*. Seeds used for urinary disorders and stones, but later sources note probably inactive. Figure 3-155. (1,44)

Litmus: See lakmus. (42)

Liver of sulphur: See potassii sulphurata. (8)

Liver-wort: See hepatica. (39)

Lixivia: Potash or potassium carbonate, prepared by burning vegetable material. After approximately 1790, the term is more commonly applied to caustic soda, i.e., potassium hydroxide. See potassii carbonas. (39)

Lixivia acetata: Potassium acetate, a mild cathartic, see potassii acetas. (39)

Lixivia nitrata: Sal nitri, see potassii nitras. (39)

Lixivia sulphurata: Kali sulphuricum, potassium sulfate, see potassii sulphas. (39)

Lixivia tartari[sata]: See potassii tartras. (39)

Lixivia vitriolata: Same as lixivia sulphurata, above. (39)

Lixivium saponarium: Liquor of potassium hydroxide. (3)

Lobelia: Leaves and tops of *Lobelia inflata*, Indian tobacco, and source of the nicotine-like compounds lobeline, lobelacrine, etc. Used to produce vomiting, purging, and sweating, i.e., as a purgative, and as a bronchodilator for the treatment of asthma. (8)

Lobeliae, acetum; —, Acet.: Vinegar of lobelia, of lobelia seed macerated and extracted in vinegar, then filtered. A nauseant, emetic, and decongestant, it contains nicotine and has all the expected effects of excessive tobacco intake. (33)

Fig. 3-155 Lithospermum.

Fig. 3-156 Lobelia syphilitica.

Lobelia syphilitica: Leaves of the great blue lobelia, *Lobelia syphilitica*, an emetic, cathartic, and diuretic, but not effectual for its namesake, syphilis. Figure 3-156. (39)

Lobeliae aetherea, tinctura: Same as alcoholic tincture, but made up in spirits of ether, antispasmodic and expectorant for asthma. (42)

Lobeliae composita, lotio: Lotion of bayberries, lobelia leaf and seed, and yellow-dock root in vinegar, used as a topical for various skin disorders. (34)

Lobeliae composita, tinctura: Compound tincture of lobelia, King's Tincture, of lobelia with bloodroot, skunk cabbage, wild ginger, and pleurisy roots. For cough, bronchitis, asthma, whooping cough, and convulsions. (34)

Lobeliae compositus, pulvis: Compound powder of lobelia, or emetic powder, of lobelia, bloodroot, and skunk cabbage with ipecac and capsicum. A strong emetic. (34) In the BPC, asthma powder, of lobelia, stramonium leaf, and potassium nitrate with oil of anise and powdered tea leaves. This combines the bronchodilating powers of nicotine, atropine-like compounds, nitrates and theobromine, a close relative of theophylline found in tea. (42)

Lobeliae et capsici composita, tinctura: Antispasmodic tincture, compound tincture of lobelia and capsicum, of lobelia, capsicum, and skunk cabbage root. For cramps, convulsions, and tetanus. (34)

Lobeliae fluidum, extractum; —, syrupus; —, tinctura: Fluid extract, syrup, and tincture of lobelia. The syrup was prepared from vinegar of lobelia. (8,34)

Locatelli, balsamum; Locatellus, --; Lucatelli, --; Lucatell., B.: Ointment formulated by Lodovico Locatelli, died 1657, Italian physician. Made of sandalwood, olive oil, pine resin, etc. Used in treatment of ulcers. (1)

Locco {*Italian*}; **Loch** {*Italian*}: See lohoch. (1)

Locke's solution; —, citrated; Locke-Ringer's solution: Various preparations of electrolytes used to maintain living tissue, i.e., a beating heart in a culture dish, etc. (24)

Lockyer's pills: A mixture of panacea antimonii, gum tragacanth, and sugar. Cathartic and emetic. (39)

Löeffler's pigment; —solution: See pigmentum mentholis et toluol. (42)

Logod, hiera: See hiera, logod. (1)

Logoriza (, syo. di) {*Italian*}: Licorice, or syrup of same. (1)

Logwood: See haematoxylon. (8)

Lohoch: Honey-like remedy designed to be licked. (1)

Lohoch sanum et expertum: A "sound and experienced lohoch", i.e., a reliable cure, for pulmonary and respiratory conditions. (35)

Lolium temulenticum: Lolium grass, unclear effects, possibly sedative. Unofficial. (44)

Lombrico {*Italian*}: Earthworm. (1)

London paste; Londinensis, pasta: Soda with lime, i.e., caustic soda with calcium oxide. (3,40)

Longam vitam, elixir ad; Longam vitam, tinctura ad: Modification of well-known Swedish bitters for long life. (3,42)

Longue vie, sirop de {*French*}: "Syrup of long life," made with borage, bugloss, iris rhizome, gentian root and the plant *mercurialis*. (1)

Lonicera caprifolium: Honeysuckle, *Lonicera caprifolium,* syrup of flowers used for asthma and lung conditions, juice applied to bee stings. Unofficial. (44)

Looch: See lohoch. (1)

Looch album: An emulsion of almonds and oil of almonds. (3)

Loofah: Vegetable sponge, the fibrous skeleton of a gourd. (3)

Loomis' mixture: See diarrhea mixture. (34)

Loosestrife: See lythrum. (39)

Lopez tree: See indica lopeziana. (39)

Lords and ladies: See unguent, cosmetic. (39)

Lotio _____: Lotion, see _____, lotio unless listed below. (8)

Lotio alba: White lotion, of zinc sulfate, sulfurated potash, and water, used as an astringent and skin protectant. (24)

Lotio alkalinum: Alkaline lotion, a solution of sodium carbonate. (34)

Lotio evaporans: Evaporating lotion, twenty percent alcohol in water, as a cooling dressing for sprains or bruises. (42)

Lotio flava: Yellow lotion, see hydrargyri flava, lotio. (40)

Lotio nigra: Black lotion, black wash, aqua phagedrenica nigra, made with mild mercurous chloride in lime water, the mercury being largely present as a black suboxide. It is used externally in skin diseases. (3,31)

Lotio refrigerans: A solution of salt and vinegar, used as a general cooling wash for fevers. (34)

Lotio rubra: Red lotion, an astringent solution of zinc sulfate (zinci sulphas), 1:240 in water with compound tincture of lavender (which imparts the red color). Used to treat raw or inflamed mucous membranes, gonorrhea, etc. (8)

Lotio spiritus: Lotion of spirits, one part alcohol to four parts water, used to treat sore joints or to cool the skin. (8)

Lotum (*lat adj.*): Washed.

Lovage: Lovage, lygusticum, or levisticum. See levisticum. (39)

Love-apple: Tomato. (3)

Loxa bark: Pale cinchona bark, see cinchona. (40)

Lozenge, pectoral: Pectoral lozenges or troches, i.e., essentially what we think of today as "cough drops." Generally a confection-like preparation, often with licorice, mint, or eucalyptus flavoring, these products appear to have changed little over the last several centuries.

Lozenge: Generally a troche. See dosage forms in introductory material.

Lucatelli; Lucate.: See Locatelli, balsamum. (1,35)

Lucca oil: Olive oil. (40)

Luccana, aqua; Lucii, aqua; (Sancta) Luciae, aqua: St. Lucy's water, misnamed, see Luce, eau de. (39)

Luce, eau de: Water of Luce, after eighteenth-century French pharmacist who originated the preparation, which was used like smelling salts, as an inhalant for fainting. Later called St. Lucy's water. (39)

Lucis majores, pilulae: "Pills for better vision," a treatment of eye disorders. Per Estes, this was a collyrium (eye wash) of some 37 ingredients. (1,39)

Lucius: Pike (fish). (1)

Lugol's solution: See iodi compositus, liquor. (8)

Lugo's powder: Powdered bark of cinchona. (40)

Luiula; Lujula: Wood sorrel, *Oxalis acetosella*. A diuretic, but high concentration of oxalic acid may lead to renal failure, and this fell out of use. Figure 3-157. (1)

Wood Sorrel.   Oxalis Acetosella.

Fig. 3-157 Luiula or lujula, wood sorrel.

Lumbricus; Lumbricorum, oleum: Earthworm. Infused oil of earth worms. (1,3)

Luminal: See phenobarbital. (40)

Luna: Silver. (3)

Lunar caustic: Silver nitrate, see argenti nitras fusas. Ancient philosophers associated the known metals with heavenly bodies, silver being associate with the moon, hence the term lunar caustic for this corrosive salt. (8)

Lunare, pilule: Silver pill, of recrystallized silver nitrate, a caustic, said to be milder than argentum nitratum itself. (39)

Lunaria: Uncertain, probably denoting moonwort, *Botrychium lunaria*. (1)

Lund's oil: See oleum lubricans. Also a synonym for oil of eucalyptus. (40)

Lungwort: See sticta. (32)

Lupinus: Lupin, *Lupinus albus* and related species of genus *Lupinus*. Seeds used. Anthelmintic, but said to produce severe side effects. (1,39)

Lupulin; Lupulinum: Lupulin, sticky powder derived from hops, *Humulus lupulus*. Used as a stomachic and carminative as well as a soporific. (7,8)

Lupul(in)i fluidum, extractum; —, tinctura: An official fluid extract and tincture of lupulin. (8)

Lupul(in)i, aethereum extractum; —, oleoresina: Ether extract of lupulin, which can be evaporated to the oleoresin. (8,34)

Lupul(in)i, extractum: Dry extract of hops, a bitter. (42)

Lupul(in)i, glandular: See lupulin. (40)

Lupul(in)i, infusum (concentratum); Lupulini, infusum: Infusion of hops, a convenient method of adminstering this particular remedy. (34) The BPC also specified a concentrated infusion with alcohol and chloroform water for storage and reconstitution. (42)

Lupulus: Hop plant, *Humulus lupulus*. The genitive form is irregularly used as either Lupuli or Lupulini. A bitter astringent, used as a tonic, narcotic, soporific, and antaphrodesiac. (1,39)

Lupus: Wolf. (1)

Lustron: Cellulose acetate, used to make various plastic devices. (3)

Lute[a][um][us]: Yellow. (1)

Lycetol: See dimethyl-piperazine tartrate. (40)

Lycium barbarum: Matrimony vine, unclear use. Unofficial. (44)

Lycoperdon: Powdery spores of the puffball mushroom, various *Lycoperdon* species. Applied to wounds to stop bleeding. (39)

Lycopodii, tinctura: Simple alcoholic tincture of lycopodium, for "irritability of the bladder and incontinence in children." (42)

Lycopodium hungaricum: Pine pollen from Hungary. (40)

Lycopodium: Lycopodium, or "vegetable sulphur" consists of the spores of the stag's-horn club moss, *Lycopodium clavatum*, and related species. It is useful as a base for powders and for insufflation, and also forms a good base for pills. As it is strongly water repellent, it is especially useful for compounding water-sensitive active ingredients. (8)

Lycopus (virginica): Bugleweed, *Lycopus virginica*, used to treat cardiac conditions, especially irregular rhythms. (32)

Lye: Potassium hydroxide or carbonate. See discussion for lixivia. Sometimes sodium hydroxide (caustic soda), the two not being clearly distinguished historically. A lithontryptic and antacid in dilute forms. Ley is a variant. (39)

Lysol; Lysolum: A substance of approximately fifty percent cresol by dissolving coal tar in fat and saponifying the mixture with alcohol. (8) Originally a feminine hygiene product. The current commercial cleaning products bearing this name are all disinfectant, but active ingredient varies by country.

Lythrum: Loosestrife, purple willow-herb, milk willow-herb, or herba salicariae, *Lythrum Salicaria* (or *alatum)*, a mucilagenous demulcent. Figure 3-158. (33)

Lytta vitata: See cantharis. (39)

Lyttae, tinctura: See cantharides, tinctura. (40)

Lyttae, unguentum: See cantharides, unguentum. (40)

Loosestrife.　　　Lythrum alatum.

Fig. 3-158 Lythrum or loosestrife.

M

M.: At beginning of inscription: medulla (marrow or pith); mel, miel {*French*} (honey); mirobalano, myrobalanus (myrobalan); mistura (mixture); mithridatum (see same); miva (jelly). At end of inscription: magistralis (magestral); magna (great, large); Mesuë (see same); mondo {*Italian*} (peeled, purified); Mortonii (see same); mundificativum (see same). In a prescription, misce (mix, i.e., the imperative form, thou shalt mix). (1)

M.P.: See massa pilularum. (1)

Mace; Macis: Mace is the aril surrounding the seed of nutmeg, *Myristica fragrans*. The aril, when crushed, readily gives up the volatile oil. Hence, mace is generally used intact rather than in the form of an isolated oil or extract. The oil is basically the same as oil of nutmeg (see myristica). Use as per clove and other volatile oils (see caryophyllus). (1,8)

Macidis, oleum; Macis, oleum: Oil of mace or nutmeg. (40)

Macquer's salt: Potassium arsenate. (40)

Macri, pilulae: Stomachic pills of aloes, sweet marjoram leaves, etc., after Aemilius Macer, first century BCE. Roman author, whose writings include poems regarding drugs. (1)

Macropiper: Long pepper, see piper longum. (1)

Macrotin: See cimicifugin. (40)

Madar: See calotropis. (40)

Madder: See rubia. (39)

Madreselva {*Italian*}**:** Honeysuckle. (1)

Madreselva, unguento di {*Italian*}**:** Ointment with major ingredient being honeysuckle leaves. (1)

Magendie's solution (of morphine): Injectable solution of morphine sulfate. See morphinae sulphas and morphinae hypodermicus, liquor. (24,46)

Maggiorana {*Italian*}**:** See majorana. (1)

Magisal: Magnesium acetylsalicylate, magnesium salt of aspirin, analgesic and antipyretic. (40)

Magisterium; Magistry: Magistry. 1. A substance obtained by precipitation of a metal from an acid solution, as in magisterium bismuthi. An alchemical term, generally reflecting an insoluble salt of the corresponding metal. (1,39) 2. A substance or preparation prescribed for a particular condition; see magistralis. (39)

Magisterium bismuthi; Magistry of bismuth: Magistry of bismuth, bismuth subnitrate. (3,39)

Magisterium coccionellae: Carmine. (3)

Magisterium sulphuris: Washed sulphur, see sulphur lotum. (3)

Magistery of lead: White lead oxide, see plumbi oxidum. (40)

Magistery of sulphur: See sulphur praecipitatum. (40)

Magistral(is): Medication prescribed for a particular case, i.e., for a specific individual and disorder, see appendix regarding magistral pharmacy. (1)

Magistry of (Jove or Jupiter)(Saturn)(Tartar): The acetate salts of tin, lead, or potassium, respectively. See magisterium.

Magn[a][us][um]: Large, great. Latin adjective in feminine, masculine, and neuter forms respectively. (1) Note that magnes is the term for magnet.

Magnanimitas, aqua: "Water of magnanimity," a solution of dilute formic acid made with formicae cum acervo. Aphrodisiac. (39)

Magnes arsenicalis: Magnet of arsenic or arsenical magnet, of white arsenic, antimony, and sulfur. Used topically as a mild caustic for syphilitic ulcers. (39)

Magnesia (levis); Magnesia ponderosa: When not otherwise specified, usually same as magnesia usta, the oxide of magnesium. (39) May be magnesiae carbonas levis. (40) Magnesium oxide, MgO, produced from magnesium carbonate by heating to drive off carbon dioxide. Magnesia (levis) formed in this way is "light magnesia," a fluffy powder. "Heavy magnesia," or magnesia ponderosa, is produced by trituration in alcohol to give a dense form of the powder. Light magnesia forms a gel on combination with water, but the heavy form does not do so. Magnesia is an antacid and mild laxative (i.e., today's Milk of Magnesia). (8) Other references suggest that magnesia levis is made by calcination of the light carbonate (magnesii carbonas levis) and magnesia ponderosa directly by calcination of the heavy (ponderosa) carbonate. Note that, in water, this will form magnesium hydroxide, $Mg(OH)_2$. The oxide or hydroxide is, however, invariably referred to as magnesia in Latin ("magnesii oxidi" or "magnesii hydroxidi" do not occur).

Magnesia, black; —nigra: Black manganese (di)oxide. (3)

Magnesia, calcinata: Calcined magnesia, i.e., magnesium oxide heated to drive off residual water. See magnesia levis.

Magnesia, cremor; Magnesia, milk of: See magnesium hydroxide, mistura. (40)

Magnesia alba: Magnesium carbonate. Antacid, cathartic, and antilithic. (3,39) See magnesii carbonas.

Magnesia and rhubarb; Magnesiae cum rhei: See rhei compositus, pulvis, second item. (34)

Magnesia mixture: See magnesii ammonio-sulphatis, solutio. (42)

Magnesia usta; Magn. Ust.: Calcined magnesia. See magnesia levis.

Magnesia vitriolata (, sal): Vitriol of magnesium, i.e., magnesium sulfate (Epsom salts). See magnesii sulphas. (3,39)

NOTE: Magnesiae (vs.) Magnesii: The proper genitive of *magnesium* would be *magnesii*. The term *magnesiae* properly is the genitive of *magnesia* (oxide of magnesium). Thus *trochisci magnesiae* is correct (a troche of magnesium oxide), but *magnesiae sulphas* is magnesium sulphate, not magnesium-oxide-sulphate (which does not exist) and should correctly be *magnesii sulphas*. It is clear from observation that *magnesiae* and *magnesii* are sometimes used interchangeably.

Magnesiae et asafoetidae, mistura: Mixture of magnesia and asafoetida, Dewee's carminative, of magnesium carbonate, tincture of asafoetida, tincture of opium, sugar, and water. For infantile colic. (34)

Magnesiae, emulsio: Milk of magnesia, see magnesium hydroxide, mistura. (42)

Magnesiae, lac: Milk of magnesia, see magnesium hydroxide, mistura. (42)

Magnesiae, trochisci: Troche of magnesia, of magnesium oxide, nutmeg, sugar, and gum tragacanth, for gastric acidity. (34)

Magnesic: Irregular chemical name for the magnesium ion, Mg^{2+}. For compounds see magnesii. (29)

Magnesii, trochisci: Troche of magnesia, nutmeg, sugar, and mucilage of tragacanth. Absorent and antacid.(46)

Magnesii ammonio-sulphatis, solutio: Solution of magnesium sulfate, ammonium chloride, and solution of ammonia in water, non-medicinal analytical reagent. (42)

Magnesii bicarbonas (, liquor): Same as magnesium carbonate or the liquor, below.

Magnesii borocitras: Borocitrate of magnesia, a urinary antiseptic. (42)

Magnesii borocitratis compositus, pulvis: Magnesium borocitrate and refined sugar, a urinary antiseptic and for rheumatism. (42)

Magnesii bromidi, liquor: Magnesium bromide liquor (NF) made with dilute hydrobromic acid reacted with magnesium carbonate. (46)

Magnesii cacodylas: An alternative to the sodium salt of cacodylic acid, for same purposes. (42)

Magnesii carbona(ti)s, liquor; Magnes. carb., liq.: Solution of magnesium (bi)carbonate. Antacid, laxative, and magnesium supplement. (40)

Magnesii carbonas (ponderosa) (levis): Magnesium carbonate, $MgCO_3$, from the action of sodium carbonate on magnesium sulfate. A heavy and light form (ponderosa and levis) could be prepared depending upon conditions of crystallization. See magnesia. (8,37)

Magnesii citras effervescens: Effervescent formulation of magnesium citrate, used as a laxative. From magnesium carbonate, citric acid, and sodium bicarbonate. (8)

Magnesii citratis, liquor: A solution of magnesium citrate and magnesium carbonate in citric acid, to which is added syrup of citric acid and, just prior to corkage, potassium bicarbonate. This produces a carbonated solution of magnesium citrate which effervesces when uncorked. A cathartic, still in use. (8)

Magnesii glycerophosphas: Magnesium glycerophosphate, an alternative glycerophosphate salt, see acidum glycerophosphoricum. (42)

Magnesii hypophosphis; Magnesii lactophosphas: Alternative to the calcium salts, not used for magnesium content, but as a nutritive as with other hypophosphites or lactophosphites. (42)

Magnesii peroxidum cum creta: Magnesium peroxide (magnesii peroxidum) and hard soap with menthol, oil of rose, and oil of wintergreen, in precipitated chalk (abrasive). A tooth powder. (42)

Magnesii peroxidum: A complex oxide of magnesium formed on reaction with hydrogen peroxide. It is a strong oxidizing agent and thus an intestinal disinfectant for diarrheal diseases, including phthisis and typhoid fever. (42)

Magnesii salicylas: Magnesium salicylate is an alternate form of salicylate and used for the same purposes, not for magnesium content. (42)

Magnesii sulpha(ti)s (, sol.)(, solut.): Magnesium sulfate, Epsom salts, $MgSO_4$, from naturally occurring minerals acted upon by sulfuric acid, and primary source of further magnesium containing preparations, or the solution thereof. Magnesium sulfate is a powerful laxative and cathartic still in use. (8)

Magnesii sulpha(ti)s effervescens, sal: Effervescent magnesium sulfate, Epsom salt made effervescent in the usual manner with sodium bicarbonate, tartaric acid, and citric acid. (31,42)

Magnesii sulphatis effervescens, liquor: Familiar to anyone who has had a modern "bowel prep," this is the (dreaded) effervescent solution of magnesium sulfate. This was made of magnesium sulfate, citric acid, syrup of citric acid, and water placed in a "strong bottle." One would "[t]hen add enough water to nearly fill the bottle, drop in the crystals of potassium bicarbonate, immediately close the bottle with a cork, and secure it with twine." (46)

Magnesii sulphatis, enema: Enema of magnesium sulfate, olive oil, and starch, for bowel evacuation. (42)

Magnesium and potassium carbonates, effervescing solution of: See magnesii citratis, liquor. (42)

Magnesium hydroxide, mistura; —, mixture; Mag. Hydrox., Mist.: A suspension of magnesium hydroxide in water, commonly known as milk of magnesia. Antacid and demulcent. While both mistura and mixture are noted, the Latin form for the hydroxide (hydrated magnesium oxide) is simply magnesia. "Magnesii (hydr)oxidi" is not observed.

Magnesium oxide; Magnesium oxidatum: See magnesia.

Magnetic oxide of iron: See ferri oxidum nigrum. (40)

Magnolia: Beaver tree, sweet magnolia, white bay, swamp sassafras, white or red laurel. *Magnolia glauca*. Infusion used for inflammatory conditions such as arthritis. (32)

Mahonia: See berberis (aquifolium). (32)

Mahura: See bael fruit. (40)

Maidenhair: American, *Adiantum pedatum*, English, *Adiantum Capillus-Veneris*. See capillus veneris. (40)

Maidis: See maydis. Maidis is the preferred spelling in the BPC.

Maidis liquidum, extractum: In the BPC, liquid extract of maize (corn) silks. (42)

Majorana: Sweet marjoram, *Origanum majorana*. Leaves and flowering tops used. (1)

Malabathrum: Indian leaf, aromatic leaf of plant from genus *Cinnamomum*. (1)

Malachite: Copper carbonate, naturally occuring. (40)

Malacorium: Pomegranate rind, see granatum. (40)

Malaga oil: See olivae malaga(e), oleum.

Malambo: See matias bark. (44)

Malate of iron, crude: See ferri pomatum, extractum and ferri pomata, tinctura. (31)

Male fern (oleoresin); —, oil of: See aspidium or aspidii, oleoresina. (8,34,42) The oleoresin is said to be the same as filicis maris, oleum. (42) In some sources oil of male fern is said to be a liquid extract of aspidium, presumably distinct from the oleoresin. (40)

Mallotus: See kamala. (32)

Mallow: Mallow (malvae folia), marsh mallow (althea), or common (musk) mallow (malva). (3,39)

Malonal; Malonurea; Malourea: Sedative. See barbitone. (40)

Malt; Maltum; Malti (siccum), extractum: Malt, extract of malt, i.e., the seed of barley, germinated, fermented, and crushed. Contains variable amounts of malt sugar, maltose. Malt extract is enzymatically active if fresh and will further digest other sugars, making it a particularly useful diet additive for patients with nutritional deficiency, whatever the cause. (8, 42)

Malthecode, emplastrum: A form of tar plaster, with white wax and either turpentine or pitch. (39)

Malthusian cones: Quinine pessaries. (40)

Malti cum _____, extractum (BPC): Multiple nutritive formulations of malt are noted in the BPC (42), consisting of the liquid extract with (cum):**

Malti et ferri, elixir: Extract of malt and iron phosphate in aromatic elixir. Nutritive and hematinic. (46)

Malti fluidum, extractum: Fluid extract of malt in alcohol and water, nutritive. (46)

Malti liquidum, extractum: Liquid extract of malt in water and about seven percent alcohol, mainly as a nutritive and base for related nutritive preparations above. (42)

Maltine: Extract of malt. In French use, diastase, a pancreatic enzyme. (40) See amylase. (42)

Malum: 1. Apple (when unmodified). 2. Any large fruit as per immediately below. See also: malus. (1)

Malum armeniacum: Apricot. (1)

Malum aureum: Orange (fruit). See aurantium. (1)

Malum citreum: Lemon, citron. (1) See limon.

Malum cotoneum: Quince. (1) See cydonium.

Malum granatum: Pomegranate. (1) See granatum.

Malum persicum: Peach. (1) See amygdalus persica.

Malum punicum: Pomegranate. (1) See granatum.

Malum sylvestris: Crab-apple. (1)

Malus: A large fruit-bearing tree, see listings immediately above, i.e., malus malum is an apple tree, malus or malum armeniacum is an apricot tree, etc. (1)

Malva: Common mallow, *Malva silvestris*. Flowers, leaves, root used. A cathartic and topical emolient used in enemas and cataplasms. Figure 3-159. (1,39)

Malvae flores; Malvae folia: Dried flowers or leaves, respectively, of the Mallow, *Malva sylvestris*, used to prepare emollients. Not the marsh mallow (althea). (3)

Man, oil of: Bone oil, i.e., derived from animal (or human) bone. (40)

Manaca: Manaca, or vegetable mercury, the dried root of *Brunfelsia hopeana*, a solanaceous plant containing various alkaloids, used to treat rheumatism. (3)

Manacae, fluidextractum; Manacae compositum, elixir: Fluid extract or compound elixir of manaca, the latter of manaca combined with triple salicylates (sodium, potassium, and lithium). For rheumatism. (31)

Mancona bark: See erythrophloeum. (8) See casca bark. (40)

Mandl's paint: See pigmentum iodi compositum. (42)

Mandorla {*Italian*}: Almond. (1)

Mandragora; Mandrake: Mandrake, in European use, *Mandragora officinarum* or *Atropa mandragora*, leaves and root used. A sedative and hypnotic with mild anticholinergic activity similar to atropa belladonna. In North America, this is *podophyllum*. Figure 3-160. (1,39)

Manganese: See manganum (metallic), mangani (compounds). (8) Manganesii is a common variant in place of mangani. (42)

Manganese, battery; Manganese, black oxide of; Manganese dioxide, precipitated: See mangani dioxidum. (3,42)

Manganesii _____: Variant form of mangani. (42)

Mangani chloridum: Manganese chloride, rarely used form of medicinal manganese. (42)

Mangani dioxidum: Manganese dioxide, naturally occurring black powder used for preparation of chlorine, corrosive mercuric chloride, and potassium permanganate. The precipitated form is a dense black powder used as a haematinic, but now known to be useless. (8,42)

Mangani glycerophosphas: Manganese glycerophosphate, an alternative glycerophosphate salt, see acidum glycerophosphoricum. (42)

Mangani hypophosphis: Alternative to the calcium salt of hypophosphite. (42)

Mangani peroxidum (praecipitatum): See mangani dioxidum. (42)

Mangani phosphas: Manganese phosphate, similar to and may replace iron phosphate in the preparation of various syrups. (42)

Mangani sulphas: Manganese sulfate, from action of sulfuric acid on the dioxide. Purgative and for jaundice. (8,42)

Mangifera; Mango: Mango, *Mangifera indica*, a stimulant tonic, for "gonorrhea and for gonorrheal rheumatism." (32)

Manihot: Root of tapioca, tapioca meal, or Brazilian arrow-root, *Manihot utilissima*. It is a mucilagenous demulcent as well as a major foodstuff of indigenous peoples in some regions of Latin America. (33)

Manilla elemi: See elemi. (8) See elemi gummi. (40)

Manis Christi (sic); probably also Manus Christi: Hand of Christ, see diamargaritum simplex and margaritum (pearl). (39)

Manna (gum)(ash)(flake); Manne {*French*}: The exudate or gum of *Fraxinus ornus*, of Mediterranean origin. Manna is a sugary material and dissolves easily in milk. Used as a laxative, especially in children, and in conjunction with senna in infusum senna compositum. A weak demulcent, cathartic and expectorant. Historically, this is the origin of both mannose and manitol, the latter still in use intravenously as an osmotic diuretic. (8,39,42)

Manna, alhagi and others: Exudate or gum from various species (see manna, above), including manna alhagi (*Alhagi maurorum*); briancon (*Larix Europaea*); oak (*Quercus Vallonea* or *Q. persica*); and tamarisk (*Tamarix gallica* var. *manifera*). (40)

Manna metallorum: Calomel. (3)

Manna thuris: 1. See thus. 2. A crude form of olibanum. (39)

Mannae (compositus), syrupus: Simple syrup of manna or the compound syrup of manna, senna leaf, bruised fennel, sugar, alcohol, and water, filtered. (42,46)

Mannae, syrupus: Syrup of manna, of about 12.5 percent manna with sugar, alcohol, and water. (31)

Mannite; Mannitol: Mannitol, mannite, or mushroom sugar, is a six carbon sugar alcohol used as a non-nutritive sweetener, laxative, and intravenously as a diuretic. It is commonly used today in sugar-free lozenges and gums. (40)

Fig. 3-159 Malva or common mallow.

Fig. 3-160 Mandragora or mandrake.

Manus Christi: See manis Christi.

Manus Dei: Hand of God, a plaster of myrrh, olibanum (frankincense), and gum ammoniac. (39)

Maranta (pv.): Arrow-root, *Maranta arundinacea*, usually the powder (pv.), used for nutritive value, and still in use in infant teething biscuits. (33)

Marcasit(e); Marcasita: Metallic bismuth, also a form of iron pyrite. (3,40)

Marchionis, pulvis: Marchioness' powder, see gutteta, pulvis de and guttetam, pulvis ad. (39)

Marcost ash(es): Lixivia, potassium carbonate. (39)

Margarita; Magaritae: Pearl or pearls. (1)

Margosa bark: See azadirach. (40)

Mariahuana: See cannabis (indica). (40)

Marigold: See calendula. (8)

Marina, aqua: Sea water. (3)

Marina artefacta, aqua: Artificial sea water. (3)

Marine acid: Hydrochloric acid. (3)

Marini, spiritus salis: Spirit of sea salt, i.e., hydrochloric acid. (39)

Marinum, sal: Sea salt. (3)

Marinus (hispanicus), sal: Spanish sea salt, sal muriaticus, i.e., common table salt. (39)

Maris, arte paranda, aqua: Artificial sea water, saline solution. (3)

Maris cum spiritu solis, tinctura: See ferri perchloridi, tinctura. (40) Meaning "sea (water) with spirit of the sun," this is an odd name, as the sun is associated with gold, not iron.

Marjorana: See majorana. (1)

Marmite: Yeast extract. Nutritive. (40) A similarly derived food product is available today.

Marmor (album): Marble, white marble. Powder used to furnish carbonic acid and for other chemical preparations. (34).

Maro {*Italian*}**:** See marum. (1)

Marrubium; Marrubii, syrupus: Hoarhound or horehound, the leaves and tops of *Marrubium vulgare*, of Europe, naturalized in North America. Horehound has a pleasant flavor and was used in food confections such as horehound drops. Given in a decoction or infusion as with licorice (glycyrrhiza), it was a mild diuretic and was laxative in sufficient dosage. Figure 3-161. (1,8)

Mars; Martis: Iron, associated with the planet and corresponding Roman god of war. (3) Note that in some instances, references to mars (martialis, martianum, martiatum) refer to military applications, often vulnerary ointments to be applied to wounds.

Mars, balls of; —, boules de: Mars, being the god of iron, this is a complex formulation of iron in pill form. Pills at that time being spherical, they were sometimes referred to as "balls" or "peas." (39)

Mars solubilis; Mars tartarisatus: Soluble iron, same as ferrum tartarisatum, iron tartrate. (39)

Marselles vinegar: Acetum aromaticum, but see vinaigre des quatre voleurs for the rest of the story. (39)

Marsh mallow; Marshmallow: See althae.

Marsh trefoil: See trifolium. (39)

Martial saffron: Ferri subcarbonas, i.e., iron subcarbonate. (39)

Martialis, crocus: Same as ferri rubigo, or rust. See crocus (metalurgical, not botanical). (39)

Martialis, pilulae: See chalybeatae, pilulae. (1)

Martialis, sal: Same as ferrum ammoniatum, or ammoniated iron. (39)

Martianum, unguentum; Martiatum, unguentum: 1. Soldier's ointment, a green unguent of laurel, ruta, majoram, mint, salvia, and absinthum vulgare. Martianum or martiatum in this instance does refer to the god, Mars, but is used in a military sense, not in relation to iron. (39) 2. Ointment of bay laurel leaves, sweet basil, sweet marjoram, sage, rue, olive oil, wax, etc. Used for sciatic pains. (1)

Martis, extractum: Extracted iron, same as vinum ferri, evaporated to concentrate the iron, which is in the form of soluble iron tartrate. (39)

Martis, flores; Martial flowers: Ferric chloride (3) or ferrum ammoniatum (39), depending upon reference source.

Martis, sal: Ferrous sulfate. (3)

Martis limatura preparata: Powdered iron oxide by action of moisture on powdered iron filings (limatura). (1)

Martis pomatum, extractum: Crude iron malate in the form of extract. (3)

Fig. 3-161 Marrubium or horehound.

Fig. 3-162 Marum (Teucrium marum) or cat thyme.

Marubii compositus, syrupus: Compound syrup of horehound, of red-root, elecampane root, spikenard and confrey, bark of wild cherry, leaves and tops of horehound, and bloodroot. Closely related to compound syrup of aralia, an older version of this preparation. For cough and pulmonary disorders. (34)

Marum: Term applied to labiate plants such as Herb Mastich (*Thymus mastichina*) or cat thyme (*Teucrium marum*), figure 3-162. Herb used. (1)

Massa ____: Pill mass, see ____, massa. (8)

Massa pilularum: Pill-mass from which pills are formed. (1)

Massicot: "Lead protoxide," i.e., lead oxide, see litharge. (3)

Massier's solution: A spray or paint for laryngitis, of resorcinol, menthol, glycerin, and tincture of iodine (see iodidum, tinctura). (24)

Masterwort: May be either heracleum or imperatoria. (39)

Mastic; Mastiche: The concrete resinous exudate of the pistachio tree, *Pistacia lentiscus*, of the Mediterranean. Used as a binder for tablets. (1,8)

Mastiches chloroformica composita, solutio; Mastiche et chloroformum; Mastiche cum chloroformum: Compound chloroformic solution of mastic, pulp capping varnish, a solution of mastic and balsam of Peru (Peruvinum, balsamum) in chloroform, used in dentistry. (31)

Mastichinae, pilule: A cathartic pill of mastiche, absinthum vulgare, hiera picra, and aloes. (39)

Mastichinum, oleum: Liniment made by heating mastic in a mixture of rose oil and wine. (1)

Mate: See ilex paraguariensis.

Mater metallorum: Mercury. (3)

Matias bark: Bark of South American tree, used for a variety of applications. Perhaps same as winter's bark. Unofficial. (44)

Maticae: See matico. This seems to be a primarily British variant. (42)

Maticae liquidum, extractum: Liquid extract of matico (this genitive form is preferred to matico in the BPC). (42)

Matico; Matico fluidum, extractum; —, infusum; —, tinctura: The leaves of *Piper augustafolium*, of the tropical Americas, or the fluid extract, infusion, or tincture. Little used, and said to be functionally identical to cubeb. The leaves had many fine hairs and were applied to bleeding wounds for their hemostatic properties. (1,8)

Matricaria: German chamomile, the flowering heads of *Matricaria chamomilla*. It is a typical bitter and is employed as such (see columba for details of use). Chamomile remains a popular tea used in the convalescence from various illnesses even today. Said to have powers as an antihysteric, emmenagogue, emetic, febrifuge, antiseptic, and anthelmintic. (8,39)

Matricaria (parthenium); Matricale {Italian}: The feverfew plant, *Chrysanthemum (or Matricaria) parthenium*, and possibly related plants of family *Compositae*. Herb used. Figure 3-163. (1)

Matta: The cortical portion from a variety of millet-seed, used for adulterating pepper. (3)

Matthaei, pilulae; Matthew's pills: Matthew's pills, as marketed by Richard Matthews in imitation of Pilulae Starkei. (1) Said to contain opium, iris florentina, white hellebore, black hellebore, tartaric acid, and turpentine; bound with soap. (39)

Maury's ointment: A compound rhubarb ointment. (3)

Maw-seed: Poppy-seed, see papaver. (3)

May apple: See podophyllum. (8)

Maydis, oleum; —, stigmata: Corn oil and corn silk, respectively. See zea. (Maydis is the genitive form of the Latin mays, i.e maize.) (7,32) See also: maidis.

Mayer's ointment: See plumbi compositum, unguentum. (34)

Maytee: Fenugreek seeds, see foenugraecum. (40)

Meadow saffron: Colchicum. (3)

Meadow sweet: See ulmaria. (39)

Meat biscuit: A biscuit or cake made from dried extract of meat. Nutritive. (44)

Meat extract: See carnum, extractum. (8)

Mecca, balm of: Same as balm of Gilead. (39)

Mechameck; Mechoacana (nigra): Mechoacan(a), the plant *Ipomoea jalapa*. Root used. (1) Estes states this is more often *I. mechoachana*, used in a manner similar to jalap. Purgative. (39)

Meconic acid; Meconicum acidum: An acidic moiety isolated during the preparation of morphine, which appears to lack any narcotic activity. Per BPC (1907), inactive and no longer used. (8,42)

Meconii, syrupus; Meconio, syrupus de {Italian}: Syrup of meconium, i.e., a dilute or weak syrup of poppy. A narcotic. (35)

Meconii; Meconii, tinctura: Meconii is the genitive form of meconium, i.e., juice of the opium poppy. See meconium. Tincture meconii is thus tincture of opium, see opii, tinctura. (34)

Meconium: Evaporated juice of opium poppy, *Papaver somniferum*. (1,3) The early fecal material produced by newborn infants resembles this brownish-green viscid material and is also called meconium, but has no medicinal application.

Fig. 3-163 Matricaria parthenium or feverfew.

Medeola virginica: Indian cucumber, possibly diuretic. Unofficial. Figure 3-164. (44)

Medicago (sativa): Alfalfa, Spanish clover, California clover, lucerne, *Medicago sativa*. Figure 3-165. (32)

Medicamentorum, stili: Medicated pencils, paste pencils, stili dilubiles, or unna pencils. A general formula for preparations in the form of a stick or pencil. A specified medicinal agent is incorporated into a paste of starch, dextrin, tragacanth, sugar, and water, rolled into cylinders approximately 5 mm in diameter and 5 cm long. Used in dermatological practice. (31)

Medulla (bovis) (rubra): Bone (ox, bovis) or veal marrow. (1,3)

Medulla cruris bovis: Ox-bone marrow. (1)

Medulla lactis: "Marrow of milk," i.e., butter. (3)

Medulla sassafras: Sassafras pith. (3)

Medullae rubrae, extractum: A chloroform and glycerin extract of red bone marrow, used as an iron supplement. (42)

Mel: Honey. (1)

Mel _____: Honey, a honey preparation, see _____, mel if not listed below. (1,8)

Mel acetatum: Simple oxymel, see mel simplex. (40)

Mel (a)egypticum; Mel aeruginis: Liniment of copper, made with honey and vinegar. (3,39)

Mel depuratum; Mel despumatum: Purified honey, clarified honey. Honey, from the honey bee, *Apis mellifera*. Clarified honey was prepared by heating honey in a water bath and straining, after which five percent glycerin was added to retard crystallization. (1,8)

Mel narbonense: Honey from Narbonne, Languidoc district of France, with distinctive scent. (1)

Mel simplex: Simple oxymel, i.e., a mixture of honey and vinegar, to which other materials might be added. (35)

Melagueta pepper; Meleguette pepper: See grains of paradise.

Melaleuca leucadendron: See cajaput for details and illustration. (39)

Melaleucae, oleum: See cajuput oil. (40)

Melampodia; Melampodii, tinctura: Black belle or tincture of black belle, i.e., helleborus niger. See tinctura hellebori. (3,39,40)

Melanosmegma: Soft (green) soap. (3)

Melia (azederach): See azederach. (39)

Melilotus: Clover, sweet clover, or common melilot, *Melitotus officinalis* or *M. alba*. Leaves and flowers used. An emollient, astringent, and stimulant used in clysters (enemas), ointments, and plasters for abdominal and uterine disorders. (1,32) Figure 3-166. (32)

Melimelum: A sweet conserve of cydonia malus or other apple-like fruit in honey. (39) This seems likely a corruption of *mel et malum*, honey with apple.

Melissa: Balm, the leaves and tops of lemon balm, *Melissa officinalis*, originally of Europe and Asia. Used as a flavoring agent, weak tonic, and diluent. Figure 3-167 (1,8,39)

Melissa, Indian (oil of): See graminis citrati, oleum. (42)

Melissae, aqua: Same as aqua carmelitana. (39)

Melissae, conserva; Melissa C.: Conserve of melissa. (35)

Melli optimi: Finest honey, used mainly for throat conditions and formulation of unguents. (39)

Mellis, aqua: Honey water, an aromatic formulation of honey with (in the BPC) oils of bergamot, lavender, clove, and sandalwood plus tincture of musk and saffron, rose water, orange-flower water, and alcohol. Honey constituted only about one-half percent. Used in preparation of hair washes and other toilet articles, not medicinally. (40,42)

Melo: Melon, *Cucumus melo*. Seeds used. (1)

Meloe vesicatorius: See cantharis. (39)

Melon-tree: See papaya. (32)

Menianthes: See trifolium palustre. (1)

Menispermum; Menispermi fluidum, extractum: The rhizome and roots of Canadian moonseed, *Menispermum canadense*, of North America, or the fluid extract thereof. White's *Materia Medica* describes the use as "similar to sarsaparilla," which is in turn said to be without physiological activity (see sarsaparilla). (8)

Mentha: When not otherwise specified, usually peppermint (*Mentha piperita*). May be spearmint (*Mentha viridis or spicata*), or related plants in genus *Mentha*. Herb or leaves used. (1,39)

Indian Cucumber. Medeola Virginica.

Fig. 3-164 Medeola or Indian cucumber.

Alfalfa.
Medicago sativa.

Fig. 3-165 Medicago or alfalfa.

Yellow Melilot.
Melilotus officinalis.

Fig. 3-166 Melilotus or clover.

Mentha, oleum: Oil of spearmint, see mentha viridis, oleum. (40)

Mentha cataria: Cat-mint or catnip, see nepeta. (39)

Mentha crispa; Menthae crispae, oleum: Alternate term for spearmint. See mentha viridis. (40)

Mentha peperita; Menthae piperitae, oleum: Peppermint, fresh leaves and tops of *Mentha peperita*, from which a volatile oil is distilled. Used as other volatile oils (see caryophyllus), but particularly of use topically for neuralgia due to the cool sensation resulting from the menthol component. It is an antiseptic, powerful stomachic, and carminative, but was (and still is) used extensively as a flavoring agent. Figure 3-168. (8)

Mentha pulegium: See pulegium. (39)

Mentha sativa: Cultivated mint, i.e., leaves of spearmint, see mentha viridis. (39)

Mentha viridis; Menthae viridis, oleum: Spearmint, fresh leaves of *Mentha viridis*, from which a volatile oil is distilled. Usage was as per peppermint (*Mentha peperita*). Figure 3-169. (8)

Menthae, aqua: Peppermint water. (40)

Menthae, conserva; Menthae, c.: Conserve of mint, a tonic and carminative. (36)

Menthae piperitae, aqua; Menth. pip., aq.; Menthae piperitae, spiritus: Water of peppermint, from the oil and water. Spirit of peppermint, of peppermint oil, peppermint leaves, and alcohol, by maceration and percolation. Peppermint water is a carminative and stomachic, used in conjunction with purgatives, in part to provide flavoring. (8,42)

Menthae piperitae, essentia; Menthae pip. ess.: Essence of peppermint, i.e., the essential oil distilled from leaves and stems, often diluted with some alcohol.

Menthae piperitae, tabellae: Tablets of peppermint. No specific formulation has been located, but various preparations of this type remain available for digestive upset.

Menthae piperitae, trochisci; —, trochi; Menth. pip. tr.: Peppermint troches of oil of peppermint, sugar, and mucilage of tragacanth. (8)

Menthae sativae, aqua: Spearmint water. (40)

Menthae viridae, aqua;—vir., aqua.; Menth. vir., aq(u).: Water of spearmint, by trituration of the oil with calcium phosphate in water. A vehicle, much like the similar preparation of peppermint. (8)

Menthae viridis, aqua; —, spiritus: Water of spearmint, of spearmint oil and water; or the spirit of spearmint, of the oil and leaves macerated and percolated in alcohol. (8,42)

Menthae vulgaris (, aqua): Menthae vulgaris, or common mint, is an alternate term for spearmint (or the water thereof). (40)

Menthol: A stearoptin, related to camphor, obtained by fractional distillation of peppermint oil. It is a solid at ambient temperatures. Use is essentially as per camphor. The solid itself may be drawn across the skin, or a plaster may be formulated. It may be applied locally to alleviate tooth pain and inhaled from warm water for asthma. Solutions have been painted on the pharynx to treat diphtheria, and small doses (1/10 grain, 6 mg.) may be useful for nausea and vomiting. (8)

Mentholis, aqua: Menthol water, of same with alcohol and water. A vehicle for alkaline or antiseptic nose and throat preparations or in place of peppermint water as a flavoring, carminative, and antispasmodic. (42)

Mentholis, emplastrum; Menthol plaster: Plaster of yellow beeswax, menthol, and resin, applied in neuralgia, rheumatism, lumbago, etc. (42)

Mentholis, gossypium: Absorbent cotton soaked in menthol and paraffin dissolved in ether, then dried. (42) Presumably applied topically as per the liniment on lint, below.

Mentholis, inunctum: Menthol inunction. "The necessity for the peculiar name of this ointment is not apparent. It is simply a five percent ointment of menthol in hydrous wool-fat." (31)

Mentholis, linimentum: Menthol and chloroform in olive oil, painted on or applied on lint for neuralgia, sciatica, and lumbago. (42)

Mentholis compositum, inunctum: Compound menthol inunction, of five percent menthol and ten percent methylsalicylate in hydrous wool fat, a counterirritant and local anesthetic. (31)

Mentholis compositum, pulvis: A snuff for nasal catarrh or hay fever, of menthol, ammonium chloride, boric acid and lycopodium. (42)

Fig. 3-167 Melissa or balm.

Fig. 3-168 Mentha piperita or peppermint.

Fig. 3-169 Mentha viridis or spearmint.

Mentholis et cocainae, insufflatio: Powdered menthol, cocaine hydrochloride, ammonium chloride, camphor, and lycopodium, as a snuff for coryza. (42)

Menyanthes; Menyanthis fluidum, extractum: See trifolium palustre. (1) The NF specified a fluid extract under this alternative name for buckbean. (46)

Mephite of soda: Impure sodium carbonate. (3)

Merbromin: See mercurochrome.

Mercurial balsam: See hydrargyri nitratis, unguentum. (34)

Mercurial injection: A medication formulated with one or another salt of mercury, for injection into the urethra using a penile syringe. For urethral disorders and venereal disease. (39)

Mercuriale, mel: "Honey of mercury," decoction of the plant *Mercurialis* and honey. (1)

Mercuriale, unguentum: Ointment of mercury, of which many varieties are described. See caeruleum, unguentum; enulatum cum mercurio, unguentum; neapolitanum quaduplicatum mercurio, unguentum; neapolitanum simplex, unguentum. (1) These various formulations were generally employed in the treatment of topical lesions due to syphilis. (39)

Mercuriales simplex, solutio: Simple solution of mercury, of purified mercury, gum arabic or tragacanth, kermes, and fumaria, for topical use in skin disorders. (39)

Mercuriales, pilulae; Mercurial pills: Mercurial pills, ex.—see bellostii, pilulae. (1) According to Estes (39) many varieties existed over time, nearly all for the treatment of syphilis (against which mercury does have some efficacy). Additional examples include pills of purified mercury with conserve of red roses and starch or glycerin; mercury triturated with honey to an emulsion and mixed with soap and gum ammoniac; or mercury with gum manna. Unfortunately, the term was also applied to mercurial diuretics such as calomel.

Mercurialis: Plant of genus *Mercurialis*, especially annual mercury (*M. annua*) and dog's mercury (*M. perennis*). Herb used. A mild cathartic used by enema. (1,39)

Mercuric ammonium chloride: See hydrargyri ammonii chloridum. (40)

Mercuric bichloride: See hydrargyri chloridum corrosivum.

Mercuric chloride soluble tablets (strong): See solvellae, specifically hydrargyri perchloridi (fortes). (42)

Mercuric oxide, red; Mercurous oxide: See hydrargyri oxidum rubrum. (40)

Mercuric precipitate (rubrum)(, red): Red mercuric oxide, a corrosive escharotic. (39)

Mercuric sublimate: See corrosive sublimate. (39)

Mercurii cinereus, pulvis: Same as hydrargyrus praecipitatus. (39)

Mercuris corrosivus albus: Corrosive sublimate, see hydrargyri chloridum corrosivum. (40)

Mercuris dulcis praecipitatus: Calomel. See mercurius dulcis below. (40)

Mercuris sublimatus corrosivus: Corrosive sublimate, see hydrargyri chloridum corrosivum. (40)

Mercurius alkalisatis: A preparation of purified mercury and cancrorum lapilli, much like hydrargyrum cum creta. (39)

Mercurius corallinus: Red oxide of mercury, see arcanum corallinum. (1)

Mercurius dulcis (precipitatus albus): Sweet mercury, sweet white mercury precipitate, i.e., calomel, mercurous chloride. See hydrargyri chloridi mitis. (1,3)

Mercurius dulcis mortis; —vitae: Antimony oxide. (3)

Mercurius liquidus: "Liquid mercury," not the metal, but rather metallic mercury dissolved in nitric acid (i.e., mercury nitrate), a topical for skin sores. (39)

Mercurius praecipitatus ruber: Red precipitate of mercury nitrate. (39)

Mercurius vitae: A recrystallized and purified antimonium muriatum (antimony chloride), but in fact antimony oxychloride, SbOCl. See Algaroth, powder of. (39)

Mercurius; Mercurio {*Italian*}**:** Mercury. (1)

Mercurochrome: Mercurochrome or merbromin, dibromohydroxymer-curifluorescein, a complex of mercury and fluorescein dye, introduced into clinical use as an antiseptic in 1919 by Dr. Hugh Young of Johns Hopkins Hospital. The one percent solution used to treat wounds has largely fallen into disuse due to concerns regarding mercury toxicity.

Mercury: See hydrargyrum (metallic), hydrargyri (compounds). (8)

Mercury, alkalised: See hydrargyrum cum creta. (40)

Mercury, calcined: Red mercuric oxide; see hydrargyri oxidum rubrum. (40)

Mercury, chloramide: Ammoniated mercury, more properly mercury amidochloride, below.

Mercury, coagulated: Red oxide of mercury. (3)

Mercury, compound ointment of: See hydrargyri compositum, unguentum. (40)

Mercury, Hahnemann's soluble: Black mercury oxide. (3)

Mercury, proto-chloride of: Calomel, see hydrargyri chloridi mitis. (40)

Mercury, proto-iodide of: See hydrargyri iodidum flavum. (40)

Mercury, subiodide of: See hydrargyri iodidum flavum. (40)

Mercury, subsulphate of: Turpeth mineral. See hydrargyri subsulphas flavus. (40)

Mercury amidochloride; Mercury ammonium chloride: $HgNH_2Cl$, a form of mercury used to lighten skin, still used in illicit ointments for this purpose in some locations today, with resulting mercury poisoning.

Mercury resorbin: One part mercury in two of resorbin. (40)

Mercury suboxide: See hydrargyri suboxidum.

Mescal buttons: See anhalonium. (40)

Mesembryanthenmum crystallinum: Ice plant, demulcent and diuretic. Unofficial. (44)

Mesenna: A vermifuge bark derived from a poorly defined tree in Abyssinia. Unofficial. (44)

Mespilus: Common medlar, *Mespilus germanica*. Fruit and seed used. (1)

Mesquite gum: Gum of *Algarobia glandulosa*, of Southern US and Mexico, said to be equivalent to gum arabic. Unofficial. (44)

Mesuë: Medieval physician, believed to be fictitious. Said to have authored *Grabadin*, one of the earliest textbooks of *Materia Medica*. (1)

Metabisulfite: The bisulfite ion, or sulfite ion is HSO_3^-, while metabisulfite, or pyrosulfite is $S_2O_5^{2-}$; both being reducing agents and antioxidants.

Meta-dihydroxy-benzene: See resorcin. (40)

Metallic pills, bitter: See metalorum, pilulae. (46)

Metallicum, sal: See lilium minerale. (39)

Metallorum, aqua: "Water of metal," i.e., mercury. (3)

Metallorum, unguentum: Metallic unguent, an ointment of zinc oxide, lead acetate, and dilute mercuric nitrate used to treat sores, eczema, ulcers, and other skin conditions. (8) In the BPC hydragyri et plumbi et zinci, unguentum. (42)

Metalorum (amarae), pilulae: Metallic or bitter metallic pills, of reduced iron, quinine sulfate, strychnine, and arsenous acid. (46)

Metaphosphoric Acid; Metaphosphoricum, acidum: Glacial phosphoric acid, see phosphoric acid. Technically this is the anhydride, $(HPO_3)_n$ and exists in polymerized form. (40)

Metaphosphoricum dilutum, acidum: Glacial phosphoric acid diluted 10:1 with water. (46)

Metarsenobillon: Sulpharsphenamine, an arsenical antibiotic, for syphilis. (40)

Metasulphite of potash: Potassium metabisulphite. (40)

Metchnikoff's calomel ointment: See hydrargyri subchloridi, unguentum (this is the "forte," or stronger, version from the BPC). (40)

Methacetine: Para-acetanisidine, an antipyretic. (3)

Methanilid: See exalgin. (3)

Metheglin: Honey wine, mead. (3)

Methenamine; Methylaminium hydrochloridum: See hexaminium.

Methonal: Dimethylsulphone-dimethylmethane (sic), an unofficial sedative-hypnotic. (3)

Methyl aldehyde: Formaldehyde. (40)

Methyl benzol: Toluol, toluene. (3)

Methyl chloride: Monochloromethane, highly volatile solvent, a refrigerant topical anesthetic and, in the vapor form, an inhalational anesthetic as well. (42)

Methyl disodium arsenite: See sodii metharsenis. (42)

Methyl orange (solution): See helianthine. (42)

Methyl salicylate: Oil of wintergreen, see gaultherium. A very similar oil is derived from birch (betula). (42)

Methyl salicylate; Methyl(is) salicylas: This is equivalent to oil of wintergreen (gaultherium) or sweet birch (betulae). Methyl salicylate has antipyretic and anti-inflammatory effect similar to salicylate salts. (8)

Methyl sulphonal: Trional, a sedative-hypnotic. (40)

Methylacetal: Acetone. (3)

Methylacetanilide; Methylacetanilidum: An analgesic related to paracetamol or acetaminophen. See exalgin. (8,42)

Methylamine; Methylaminae, liquor: Methylamine or a solution of same, non-medicinal reagent. (42)

Methylbenzene: Toluene, an aromatic solvent. (40)

Methyl-benzoyl-ecgonine; Methyl-benzyl-ecgonine: Cocaine, see coca. (40)

Methylene blue: A blue coal tar dye used to treat rheumatism and intermittent fevers. It remains available for intravenous injection, but only for the treatment of a rare hematological condition, methemoglobinemia. (8)

Methylene chloride; Methylene bichloride; Methylenum dichloridum: Methylene chloride, dichloromethane, CH_2Cl_2. Used as an anesthetic, but explosive due to impurities, and associated with several deaths. It is now used primarily as a paint remover and is known to cause fatalities via metabolism to carbon monoxide. (8)

Methyl(ene) ditannin: Condensation product of formaldehyde and tannic acid, a non-irritating antiseptic dusting powder. (42)

Methylis salicylatis compositum, unguentum: Compound ointment of methyl salicylate, of wintergreen oil, menthol, oil of eucalyptus, essential oil of camphor, lanolin, and paraffin ointment base. Topical analgesic in rheumatism, sciatica, or lumbago. (42)

Methylis salicylatis, unguentum: Oil of wintergreen in lanolin, rubbed over rheumatic joints, as with similar formulations today. (42)

Methyl-morphine: See codeine. (40)

Methyl-phenyl-acetamide: Methylacetanilide, see exalgin. (40)

Methylrosanaline; Methylrosanilinum: Methyl violet, an aniline dye for topical or internal treatment of tumors, also for dropsy and a local topical treatment of diphtheria. A dusting powder with boric acid is also noted. (42)

Methylsulfonal(um): Sedative-hypnotic derivative of sulfonal. (42)

Methyl-theobromine: Caffeine, see caffea and caffeina. (40)

Methylthioninae hydrochloridum; Methylthionine hydrochloride: See methylene blue. (40)

Metol: Salt of monomethyl-para-amidometacresol, developer for photographic use. (3)

Metozin: Expressed oil of almonds. (3)

Metozin; Metpozin: Antipyrin. (3)

Metramine: See hexaminium. (40)

Metrenchyta: Vaginal injection or a vaginal syringe. (3)

Meum: Spignel, Baldmoney, *Meum athamanticum*. Root used as aromatic stimulant and carminative. (1,39)

Mexican tea: See chenopodium. (40)

Mexico seeds: Castor seeds, see ricinus. (40)

Mezerei (aethereum), extractum: Aetherial extract of mezerium in the BPC, of bark extracted in alcohol and methyl ether. (42)

Mezerei, unguentum: Mezereum ointment of the fluid extract in wax and lard. An irritant, applied to chronic skin ulcers and wounds to stimulate suppuration (believed to enhance healing). (34)

Mezereum; Mezerion; Mazerei cortex; Mazerei, extractum; —, fluidextractum; —, fluidum, extractum: The bark of *Daphne mezereum*, from which is extracted (with alcohol) an oil similar to other volatile oils. For use, see caryophyllum. (8,31,42,46) In American usage, may be *Dirca palustris*. Figure 3-170. (40)

Mica panis; Mica panio: Bread crumbs. Used as a pill base. (3,8,39)

Mica thuris: Crumbs of thus, i.e., olibanum, (frankincense), thuris being the genitive form. (39)

Micleta, electuarium: Composite preparation used to control hemorrhage. (1)

Microcidin: Trade name for sodium betanaphthol, sodii naphtholas. Antiseptic. (3,42)

Microcosmic salt; Microcosmicum, sal: Salts of urine (mostly phosphates), i.e., a salt mixture reflecting the "internal environment." A mixture of sodium and ammonium phosphates. (3)

Midolla {*Italian*}**:** See medulla. (1)

Miel de Narbonne {*French*}**:** See mel Narbonense. (1)

Miel {*French*}**; Miele** {*Italian*}**:** Honey. (1)

Migrainine: Antipyrine and caffeine citrate, similar to today's acetaminophen with caffeine, for migraines. (40)

Mikozone: Hypnotic and sedative, a variety of chlorodyne. (3)

Mild chloride of mercury: See hydrargyri chloridum mite. (8)

Milium: Millet, *Panicum miliaceum*. Seed used. (1)

Milium solis: See lithospermum. (1)

Daphne Mezereum

Publish'd by Dr Woodville. May. I. 1790.

Fig. 3-170 Mezereum.

Milk; Milk of ____: May refer to milk, usually of the cow or other species serving as a source of materials, i.e., milk sugar (lactose). More commonly refers to an emulsion of an oily substance of oil in water, produced by trituration. For example see Milk of Almond, amygdalae, emulsum. For milk of ____, see ____, emulsum if not listed below. (8)

Milk, virgin's: Rose water rendered milky by the addition of tincture of benzoin. (3)

Milk of asafetida: See asafoetidae, emulsum. (8)

Milk of sulphur: Precipitated sulfur (strictly, that precipitated by sulfuric acid). See sulphur praecipitatum. (3,8)

Mille florum: Water of one thousand flowers. Same as florum omnium, aqua. (39)

Millefolium: Yarrow, milfoil, *Achillea millefolium*. Leaves and flowering tops used. Also medicinally called achillea, an astringent. Figure 3-171. (1)

Millepeda: Dried and powdered wood lice, a diuretic and deobstruent. Evidently a conserve was made and was used for children. (39)

Millon's reagent: A test reagent consisting of murcuric and mercurous nitrate in nitric acid, by dissoluion of metallic mercury in the latter. It forms a white precipitate in the presence of protein. (24,29)

Mimosa catechu: See catechu. (39)

Mimosa nilotica: Gum arabic, see acacia (vera) for details and illustration. (39)

Mimulus: Hairy monkey-flower, *Mimulus pilosus*, a small plant native to California, said to be useful in rheumatism and in various local inflammations, including skin disorders. (33)

Mindereri, liquor; —, spiritus; Mindererus, spirits of; __, tincture of; —, spiritus; —, tinctura: Solution of ammonium acetate similar to aqua ammoniae acetatae, after Raymond Minderer, physician, Augsburg, ca. 1610. (3,39)

Mineral gum: Soluble glass; sodium or potassium silicate. (3)

Mineral solution: See arsenici, solutio mineralis and also potassii arsenatis, liquor. (40)

Mineral syrup: Liquid paraffin, mineral oil. (40)

Mineral wax: Ceresin or ozokerite, crude paraffin. (3)

Mineralis, aqua: Mineral water. (3)

Minium: Red lead oxide, plumbi oxidum rubrum. (1,3)

Minium graecorum (purum): Red mercuric sulphide (pure). (3)

Achillea Millefolium.

Fig. 3-171 Millefolium.

Mint: See mentha. (39)

Mint, horse: See monarda. (39)

Mint balm: See melissa. (39)

Mint water: See menthae viridis, aqua. (40)

Mirabile glauberi, sal; Mirabile (perlatum), sal: Glauber's miraculous salt, sodium sulphate. See sal catharticus glauberi. (1,3,39)

Mirabilito: A naturally occurring crude Glauber's salt, sodium sulfate. (3)

Miraculum chemicum: Magnesium carbonate. (3)

Mirandolae, pulvis principis: Powder of Prince Mirandola, Giovanni Pico, fifteenth century. A gout cure said to be similar to (see) Portland, gout powder of Duke of. (39)

Mirbane, oil of: See nitrobenzene. (42)

Mirobilano {*Italian*}**:** See myrobalanus. (1)

Mirra {*Italian*}**; mirrha** {*Italian*}**:** See myrrha. (1)

Mirtillo {*Italian*}**:** Bilberry, whortlebery, see myrtillus. (1)

Mirto: Common myrtle, see myrtus. (1)

Mist. ant. chol.: Probably mistura anticholerae, an anti-cholera mixture used to treat dysenteric illness. No specific formulation has been identified.

Mistletoe (, fluid extract): See viscum album. American usage may be *Phoradendron flavescens*. (40)

Mistura; Mist.: Mixture. (1)

Mistura ____: Mixture, see ____, mistura. (8)

Mistura acaceae: Mucilage of gum arabic, variable strength. (3)

Mistura alba: White mixture, a mixture of magnesium carbonate and sulphate in water, a saline cathartic. (42)

Mistura ammon. acet.: See ammonii acetatis, liquor. (40)

Mistura antiperiodica; Mist. antiperiodica: An antiperiodic mixture, i.e., one used to treat periodic fevers as seen in malaria. No specific formulation has been identified, but after discovery of the New World, one assumes most such mixtures contained quinine (cinchona).

Mistura camphore: Camphor water, see camphorae, aqua. (40)

Mistura diaphoretica: Per Estes, a "saline julap," presumably a saline julep, or sweetened beverage containing salts and intended to produce sweating. (39)

Mistura nostra: See Begbie's mixture. (40)

Mistura oleoso-balsamica: Alcoholic solution of Peru balsam, oil of amber, and various volatile oils. (3)

Mit.; Mite; Mitis (*lat adj.*)**:** Mild, mitis is feminine and masculine, mite is neuter gender. (29)

Mitchella; Mitchellae, fluidextractum: Mitchella, squaw vine, or partridge berry, *Mitchella repens*, whole dried plant used, or the fluid extract therefrom. A diuretic and emmenagogue. (7,31)

Mitchellae compositus, syrupus: Compound syrup of partridgeberry, of the berry with helonias root, highbush cranberry bark, blue cohosh, and brandy. For female and gestational disorders. (34)

Mitchell's fluid: A solution of sodium chloride, bromine, hydrochloric acid, and water, through which an electric current has been passed, used to treat tuberculosis. (24)

Mithridate: See confectio Damocratis. (3)

Mithridatium; Mithridatum Andromachi; Mithridatum Damocratis; Mithridatum; Mithridato {*Italian*}**:** Polypharmaceutical preparation related to theriac (see theriaca), devised by Mithridates, King of Pontus, 131-64 BCE as a universal antidote to poisons. Later modifications attributed to Andromachus and Damocrates. (1)

Mithridatum (, electuarium): Electuary of mithridatum. (35)

Mitridatum: See mithridatum. (1)

Miva: Jelly or jam, a preserve, especially of quince. (1)

Mixa: See sebesten. (1)

Mixtura: Mixture. (1)

Mixture, mucilagenous: A mixture of gum arabic and conserve of roses and/or marshmallow in hot water, as a remedy for sore throat. (39)

Moerbei {*Dutch*}: See morus. (1)

Mohr's salt: Ferrous ammonium sulfate. (3)

Molasses: See treacle. (40)

Molle: Soft. Latin adjective. (8)

Mollin: Proprietary potash coconut oil soap. (3)

Molybdos: Lead, a Greek term for a mineral thought to be lead ore, found to be a new element, molybdenum, in 1778. (3)

Momordicin: See elaterinum. (42)

Monarda: Horsemint, *Monarda punctata*, a stimulant, carminative, diaphoretic, and antiemetic. (39)

Monardae, oleum: Oil of horsemint, or wild bergamot (not related to true bergamot), an oil derived from various members of the North American genus *Monarda*. (29)

Mondificatif, onguent {*French*}: See mundificativum, unguentum. (1)

Mondificatif d'ache, onguent {*French*}: See mundificativum de apio, unguentum. (1)

Mondo {*Italian*}: Peeled, purified. (1)

Monesia: See chrysophyllum. (33)

Monkshood; Monk's hood: See aconite. (32)

Monoglycerylphosphoric acid: See glycerophosphoric acid. (40,42)

Monopotassium orthophosphate: Potassium pyrophosphate, see discussion under phosphoricum, acidum. (40)

Monosodium orthophosphate: Sodium pyrophosphate, see discussion under phosphoricum, acidum. See sodii diphosphas. (40,42)

Monotropa: The root of Indian pipe, ice plant, bird's nest, fit plant, ova-ova, or pipe plant, *Monotropa uniflora*. A "tonic, sedative, nervine, and antispasmodic." (33)

Monsel's salt; Monsel's solution: See ferri subsulphatus, liquor. (8)

Montau wax: A waxy substance obtained from European lignite. (3)

Moogrol: "Ethyl chaulmoograte" derived from (see) chalmoogra oil. (40)

Moore's ointment: Similar to resinae, unguentum. (40) This would seem to be the British form. Mention is made in various Canadian citations to an ointment with sulfur and green iodide of mercury using the same eponym.

Mora {*Italian*}: See morus. (1)

Mordant salt: Tartar emetic. (3)

Mori succus; Mori, syrupus: The juice of the mulberry, *Morus nigra*, of Britain, was used as a flavoring and coloring agent much as the raspberry was used in North America. A syrup was prepared with rectified spirits, water, and sugar. (8)

Moro's ointment: A (see) tuberculin ointment, for diagnosis of tuberculosis. (40)

Morphacetin: Acetyl-morphine, i.e., heroin. (40)

Morphia; Morphiae: Variant of morphine; see morphinae. (44)

Morphiae (et ipecacuanhae), trochisci: Troches of morphine, with or without ipecac, with sugar, balsam of tolu, and gum arabic. (44) This is similar to but not identical to morphinae et ipecacuanae, trochisci, below.

Morphina; Morphine: Morphine, from Morpheus, god of dreams. Crystallized from opium by extraction with alcohol and addition of ammonia. Morphine is an alkaloid (a nitrogen containing compound) and can bear a positive charge. Soluble forms of morphine for therapeutic use are invariably salts, i.e., hydrochloride, acetate, sulfate. See also: opium. (8)

Morphinae, ole(in)atum: Morphine in oleic acid, a readily absorbed topical for pain. (42)

Morphinae, suppositoria: Suppository of morphine hydrochloride in cocoa butter, for systemic relief of pain and for sedation. (42)

Morphinae acetas; Morphinae acetatis, liquor: Morphine acetate, from morphine precipitate and acetic acid, or the solution of same in dilute acetic acid. (8,42) This is a salt, distinct from (di)acetyl morphine, or heroin.

Morphinae acidus, linctus: See linctus sedativus. (42)

Morphinae bimeconatis, liquor: A preparation of morphine by precipitation with ammonia, which results in co-precipitation of meconic acid. (8)

Morphinae citratus, liquor: Solution of morphine, citric acid, alcohol, water, and cochineal colorant (red). Unsuitable for storage, it was prepared when needed. (46)

Morphinae compositus, pulvis: Powder of morphine, Tully's powder, of morphine sulphate, camphor, glycyrrhiza, and calcium carbonate. For pain. (34,42)

Morphinae compositus, syrupus: Compound syrup of morphine, from fluid extracts of ipecac, senega, and rhubarb, morphine sulfate, and oil of sassafras in simple syrup. (46)

Morphinae et ipecachuanae, trochisci: Troches of morphine sulphate, ipecac, sugar, oil of gaultheria, and mucilage of tragacanth. For cough. (8,34)

Morphinae hydrochlora(ti)s; Morphinae murias; Morphinae hydrochloridi, liquor: Morphine hydrochloride (or muriate, muriatic acid being a trivial name for hydrochloric acid), by extraction of opium solution using calcium chloride, evaporation, and decolorization with charcoal, or the solution of same in dilute hydrochloric acid and alcohol. (8,42,44)

Morphinae hypodermicus, liquor (NF): A 3.5 percent solution of morphine sulfate in distilled water. The NF notes that chloroform water could be added to prevent microbial growth. See also: morphinae sulphatis, liquor. (46)

Morphinae murias: See morphinae hydrochloras. (40)

Morphinae sulphas; Morphinae sulphatis, syrupus: Morphine sulfate, from a solution of morphine in boiling water, to which sulfuric acid is added. Morphine sulfate precipitates out on cooling. A syrup or liquor was commonly used. (8,34)

Morphinae sulphatis, liquor (USP): This is similar to morphinae hypodermicus, liquor, but was specified at one grain per fluid ounce. (46)

Morphinae tartras; Morphinae tartratis, liquor: Morphine tartrate or a solution of morphine tartrate in alcohol and water. (42)

Morrhuae, olei, emulsio: An emulsion of cod liver oil. Many variants existed, all to the same purpose, i.e., a lubricant laxative. According to King's Dispensatory, "Emulsion of cod-liver oil may also be prepared by any other method capable of emulsifying oil…," and cites examples of emulsions stabilized with gum acacia and syrup of tolu, with glycerite of egg, and with mucilage of Irish moss. In the BPC, of cod liver oil, gum acacia, syrup, oil of bitter almond, and water. In the NF, cod liver oil with acacia powder, syrup of tolu, flavoring as desired, and water; but four alternative formulations are presented. (33,42,46)

Morrhuae, oleum cum calcii et sodii phosphatibus, emulsio: Same components as NF emulsion above, but with addition of sodium and calcium phosphates. (46)

Morrhuae, oleum cum calcii lactophosphate, emulsio: NF emulsion above, with addition of calcium lactate and phosphoric acid. (46)

Morrhuae, oleum cum calcii phosphate, emulsio: Same components as NF emulsion above, but with addition of calcium phosphate. (46)

Morrhuae, oleum cum extracto malti, emulsio: Of cod liver oil, mucilage of dextrin, and malt extract. (46)

Morrhuae, oleum cum hypophosphite, emulsio: Same components as NF emulsion above, but with addition of any of the hypophosphites (sodium, calcium, potassium, etc.). (46)

Morrhuae, oleum cum pruno virginiana, emulsio: Same components as NF emulsion above, but with addition of fluid extract of wild cherry (*Prunis virginiana*) for flavoring. (46)

Morrhuae, oleum: See cod liver oil. (8)

M

Morrhuae composita, olei, emulsio: Compound emulsion of cod liver oil in the BPC. Of same with egg yolk, tragacanth powder, saccharin, tincture of benzoin, spirit of chloroform, essential oil of bitter almonds, and water. This is sugar free, i.e., suitable for diabetics. (42)

Morrhuae olei (cum hyphosphitibus) (cum malto) (cum vitello), emulsum: Emulsion of cod liver oil with calcium, sodium, and potassium hypophosphites, malt, or egg, respectively. The malt formulation affords "one of the most acceptable preparations of cod liver oil." The egg emulsion contained glycerite of egg yolk, syrup of tolu, and flavoring, and was used as a tonic. (31)

Morrhua(e) pancreaticus, cremor (olei); Morrhuae pancreatici (cum chondro), emulsio olei: A cream or emulsion of cod liver oil as specified in the BPC. Of glycerins of pepsin and pancreatin, cod liver oil, mucilage of Irish moss (chondro), syrup of tolu, alcohol, oil of almond (flavoring) and water. It is an emulsion of about fifty percent cod liver oil, intended to be less unpleasant. (40) A later version of the BPC lists ingredients as glycerin of pancreatin and pepsin, cod liver oil, gluside (saccharin), potassium hydroxide, powdered tragacanth and gum acacia, oils of cassia and bitter almond, and water. (42)

Morrhuae pancreatica cum byno, emulsio: Pancreatized emulsion of cod liver oil with malt extract; of glycerin of pancreatin, cod liver oil, gums of acacia and tragacanth, saccharated solution of lime, and malt extract. A more nutritive form of cod liver oil emulsion. (42)

Morsus diaboli: Devil's bit, *Scabiosa succisa*. Leaves, flowers, and root used. (1)

Mort(e): Fresh lard. (40)

Mortonii, pilules; Morton, pilules de {*French*}: See balsamicae, Mortonii, pilulae. (1)

Morton's fluid: A solution of iodine, potassium iodide, and glycerin, injected for spina bifida (presumably locally into cystic lesions to scar down the area). (8)

Morus: Mulberry tree, *Morus nigra*, or red mulberry (nearly identical save for color), *M. rubra*. Fruit, bark, root used primarily for flavoring, see syrupus diamoron. Figure 3-172. (1,33)

Moscata, noce; Moschata, nux: Nutmeg, see noce moscata. (1)

Moschata, mistura: Nutmeg (nux moschata) mixture, made with nutmeg, gum arabic, sugar, and rose water. Bate's Hysteric Julep, a similar proprietary product, also contains musk. (39)

Moschata, oleum: Oil of mace. (40)

Moschatae, trochisci galliae: See galliae moschatae, trochisci. (1)

Fig. 3-172 Morus nigra or mulberry.

Moschus; Moschi, tinctura: Dried secretions of the musk gland of the musk ox, *Moschus moschiferus*, of Central Asia, or an alcoholic tincture of musk. Musk is a powerful "diffusible stimulant," i.e., one that effectively travels through the body and is effective on the heart and nervous system. (1,8) Alternatively, may be seeds of the aromatic plant, *Hibiscus esculentus*. (39)

Moss (, Irish)(, Icelandic): A moss-like material, most commonly Irish moss (a seaweed, see chondrus) or Icelandic moss (a lichen, see cetraria). These were primarily boiled in water to produce a mucilaginous material used as a demulcent or as a component of other preparations. (8)

Mostarda {*Italian*}: Mustard, see sinapis. (1)

Mother of pearl: Iridescent lining material of various mollusk shells, used as a cephalic, cordial, analeptic, pectoral, and styptic. (39)

Mother of thyme: See serpyllum. (39)

Mother plaster, camphorated: See fuscum camphoratum, emplastrum. (31)

Mother's cordial: See mitchellae compositus, syrupus. (34)

Mother's ointment: Ointment of white lead in suet, pork fat, and butter. (39)

Mother's salve: See fuscum, unguentum. (31)

Motherwort: See leonurus. (32)

Moult's (bitter purging) salts: Proprietary preparation of Epsom salts, magnesium sulfate. (39)

Mountain balm: See eriodictyon. (8)

Mountain fat: Paraffin. (3)

Mountain laurel: See kalmia. (32)

Mountain tea: See gaultheria. (40)

Mountain tobacco: See arnica. (40)

Mouse's ear: See marrubium. (40)

Moxa: Downy covering of the leaves of various wormwoods of Eastern Asia, esp. *Artemesia moxa*, used for burning on skin in the treatment of gout (i.e., moxibustion). (1) Small mass of combustible material burnt in contact with skin to produce a burn. Originally from Chinese practice, moxibustion involved leaf material from plants of the genus *Artemesia*. In later times and other places, different materials served, including linen, cotton, pith of sunflower, etc. (44)

Moynahan's cream: Bismuth carbonate mixed with a 1:1000 solution of mercuric iodide (see hydrargyri iodidum rubrum) to form a paste, used as a wound dressing. (24)

Mucago; Mucilago: Mucilage. (1)

Mucilages, oil of: Olive oil boiled with decoction of marshmallow root (malvus), linseed, and fenugreek seeds. (40)

Mucilago _____: Mucilage, see _____, mucilago. (8)

Mucuna: Cowhage or cowage, hairs from the pods of *Mucuna pruriens*. An anthelmintic, supposedly by mechanical action. (33)

Mudar: See calotropis. (40)

Mugwort: See artemesia. (39)

Mulberry; Mulberry juice: See morus and mori succus. (8)

Mullein: See verbascum. (39)

Mummy: Ground Egyptian mummy, a restorative. (39)

Mundificativum, unguentum: From mundus (*Latin*), "to clean," an ointment for cleansing wounds. The chief ingredient was either smallage (unguentum mundificativum de apio) or a resin (unguentum mundificativum resina). (1,39)

Muria; Murias: When alone, sal muriaticus, the salt of muriatic (hydrochloric) acid, i.e., common salt. (39)

Murias ammoniae et ferri: Crude ammoniated iron, see ferrum ammoniatum. (39)

Murias ammoniae: Ammonium chloride, sal ammoniac. (39)

Murias barytae: Barium chloride, see barii chloridum. (39)

Murias calcis: Calcium chloride; calcii chloridum. (39)

Murias hydrargyri: Mercurous chloride, specifically calomel, HgCl. (39)

Murias sodae: Sodium muriate, i.e., sodium chloride, common salt. (39)

Muriated tincture of iron: See ferri chloridi, tinctura. (34)

Muriatic acid; Muriaticum, acidum: Hydrochloric acid, see hydrochloricum, acidum. (8)

Muriatico-ethereus martiatus, spiritus: Etherial tincture of ferric chloride. (3)

Muriaticum, acidum; Ac. Muriatic.: A crude hydrochloric acid.

Muriaticum oxygenatum, acidum: Chlorine. (3)

Muriaticus, sal: Sea salt, sodium chloride. (39)

Muride; Murina: Bromine. (3)

Mus agrestis; Mus rusticus: Field mouse. (1)

Mus alpinus; Mus montanus: Marmot. (1)

Mus: Mouse, rat. (1)

Musa aenea: Copper muse, an opium containing remedy. (39)

Musc: See moschus.

Muscarine; Mascarina: An alkaloid from *Amanita muscaria*, the fly agaric (the classic red mushroom with white spots, of fairy-tale fame). Muscarine is much like the calabar bean (physostigma), antagonizing atropine and causing pinpoint pupils and an increase in bowel and bladder function, slowing of the heart, paralysis, and death in excess. It was little used, but useful for atonic gut to increase motility, and supposedly for pulmonary hemorrhage. Of note, later research demonstrated that the parasympathetic nervous system is mediated via acetylcholine receptors identified as binding muscarine, as opposed to nicotine, and thus referred to as muscarinic. (8)

Muscus: Moss (Icelandic, Irish, etc.). (3)

Mushroom sugar: See mannitol. (40)

Musk mallow; —seed: Musk mallow, *Malva moschata*. Same uses as common mallow, see malva. (40)

Musk root: See sumbul. (8)

Musk: See moschus (animal derived musk) and abelmoschus (the musk plant). (8)

Mustard; Mustard oil: See sinapi or sinapis, oleum respectively.

Mustard bran: Mustard seed husks ground with a small proportion seed, see sinapis. (40)

Mustard poultice: See sinapis, cataplasma. (42)

Mustard, flour of: Ground mustard, see sinapis. (40)

Muthu's inhalant(s): See Formaldehydi, nebula. (40)

Mylabrides, acetum: Vinegar of mylabris, with water and acetic acid, similar to cantharidis, acetum. (42)

Mylabridis, emplastrum: See cantharidis, emplastrum, mylabris being a replacement for cantharides. (42)

Mylabridis, unguentum: Mylabridis in benzoinated lard, equivalent to ointment of cantharidis. (42)

Mylabris: A beetle native to Asia, *Mylabris phalerata*, used as per cantharidis. (40)

Mynsicht: Adrianus van Mynsicht, 1603-1638, German physician, introduced the use of tartar emetic. (1)

Mynsicht's aperative martial magestry: A fancy name for an aperient iron-containing specific used as a tonic and deobstruent. Of tamarind and purified iron filings (ferri limitura purificata). (39)

Mynsicht's blistering plaster: Blistering plaster with cantharides, ginger, and pepper (piper longum). (39)

Mynsicht's cicera tartari: Peas (cicera, small round tablets) of tartar. Tablets of tartaric acid, with turpentine, violet water, niter, and iris florentina. Deobstruent. (39)

Mynsicht's elixir (of vitriol): Similar to acidum vitrioli aromaticum, or aromatic sulphuric acid, but with many more aromatic materials. (39)

Myosalvarsan: See salvarsan. (40)

Myoston: A proprietary muscle extract, nutritive. (40)

Myrcia; Myrcis acris: West Indian bay or bay rum tree. A volatile oil (below) is distilled from the leaves.

Myrcia(e), spirit of; —spiritus: Spirits of bay rum, topical cologne and astringent, of oil of myrcia, orange peel (aurantia cortex, oleum), and pimento. (40)

Myrciae compositus, spiritus: Compound spirit of myrcia, a water and alcohol solution of oils of bay (myricae, oleum), orange (aurantii cortex, oleum), and allspice (pimenta), resembling bay rum. (31)

Myrciae, oleum; —, Ol.; —, spiritus: Volatile oil distilled from *Myrcia acris*, of the West Indies. Spirit of bay consisted of bay oil, orange-peel oil, oil of pimenta, alcohol, and water. The latter was referred to as "bay rum." The oil was used as a perfume, the spirit as a flavoring. (8)

Myrepsus: See requies nicoli. (39)

Myrica cerifera (humilis): American laurel, i.e., bayberry. (39)

Myrica: Bay berry, wax myrtle, candle berry, wax berry, *Myrica cerifera*. It is, per Ellingwood, "a remedy for those conditions where the vital powers are at low ebb. It aids the nutrition, stimulating the absorption of food, and promotes the restoration of depraved blood. It is considered a valuable alterative." (32)

Myricae compositu[m][s], unguentum: Compound ointment of bayberry, of bayberry-tallow and sweet gum, for various skin conditions, including tinea. (34)

Myricae compositus, pulvis: Compound powder of bayberry, cephalic or composition powder, a headache cure used alone or with common snuff, of equal parts bayberry bark and bloodroot. For disorders of the nasal mucosa. Also a variant with bayberry, ginger, and capsicum. (34)

Myricalis, pulvis: Powder of tamarisk (in Latin, myrica), an appetite stimulant. (39)

Myristica; Myristicae, nuclei; Myristicae, oleum; Myristicae, spiritus: Nutmeg, the seed of *Myristica fragrans*, of the Molucca Islands, from which a volatile oil can be distilled. The spirit, or essence, of nutmeg consists of equal parts oil and alcohol. Figure 3-173. (1,8)

Myristicae adeps: Oil of nutmeg. (40)

Myrobalani (cum opio), unguentum: Powdered myrobalan in benzoinated lard or suet, BPC equivalent in India and Eastern Colonies to unguentum gallae (cum opio). (42)

Myrobalani; Myrobalanus bellericus: Belleric myrobalan, bastard myrobalan, *Terminalia bellerica*. Fruit used as astringent cathartic. (1,39)

Myrobalans; Myrobalanus chebulus: Chebulic myrobalan, *Terminalia chebula*. Fruit used. (1)

Myrobalanus citrinus: Yellow myrobalan, *Terminalia citrina*. Fruit used. (1)

Myrobalanus emblicus: Emblic myrobalan, *Phyllantus emblica*. Fruit used. (1)

Fig. 3-173 Myristica or nutmeg.

Myrobalanus indicus: Indian myrobalan, a variety of chebulic myrobalan, above. (1)

Myroxylon (balsamum): Same as syrup of tolu. (39)

Myroxylon Pereirae; —Peruifera: Balsam of Peru. (39)

Myrrh; Myrrha: A gum-resin obtained from myrrh, *Commiphora myrrha*, of Africa and near-African Middle East. Use as per clove oil (see caryophyllus), especially for genito-urinary and menstrual disorders, or as a mouthwash in combination with borax and simple syrup. (1,8)

Myrrha[e][:] co., pilula(e): See galbani compositae, pilulae. (40)

Myrrhae composita, lotio: A lotion of powdered myrrh with lead and zinc acetate, used particularly for eye conditions, but also a general irrigant. (34)

Myrrhae composita, tinctura: In American use see capsici et myrrhae, tinctura. (34) In the BPC, of myrrh and aloe powder, water, and alcohol and noted to be used in veterinary practice for wounds. (42)

Myrrhae compositum, elixir; Myrrh. Co. Elix.: See sabinae composita, tinctura. (39)

Myrrhae compositus, pulvis: Compound powder or myrrh, with savin, ruta, and castor, an emmenagogue. (39)

Myrrhae et boracis, tinctura: A mouthwash concentrate diluted 1:20 with water for use, of the tincture of myrrh, oils of bergamot, lemon, orange, neroli, and rosemary, powdered borax, glycerin, and alcohol. (42)

Myrrhae, gargarisma: Gargle of the tincture of myrrh and honey in the acid infusion of roses. Astringent for pharyngitis and ulcerations of the throat. (42)

Myrrhae, tinctura: Alcoholic tincture of myrrh. (8)

Myrrhae, unguentum: An ointment base consisting of one part myrrh and ten parts wax melted together with oats. (3)

Myrrhis: Sweet cicely, *Myrrhis odorata*. Herb and seed used. (1)

Myrtillus: Bilberry, whortleberry, *Vaccinium myrtillus*. Fruit and leaves used. (1)

Myrtinus, syrupus: Syrup of myrtleberries, pomegranates, medlars, quince, etc. (1)

Myrtle; Myrtus: Common myrtle, *Myrtus communis*. Leaves and berries used internally as an astringent, antiseptic, and sedative. Topical stimulant and antiseptic. (1)

Myrtle, wax: American laurel, i.e., bayberry, see myrica. (39)

Myrtus pimenta: See pimento. (39)

Myva: See miva. (1)

Myxa: See sebesten. (1)

N.: At end of inscription: nero {*Italian*} (black); Nicolai, Nicolao (see Nicolao); niger (black). (1)

N.A.B.: See neoarsphenamine. (40)

Nabalus: Lion's foot, rattlesnake root, white lettuce, gall of the earth, or cancer weed, *Nabalus albus*, for treatment of venomous snake bites. The sap was taken internally while the leaves were boiled and the liquid applied topically. (33)

Nabee: See bikh. (40)

Naegeli's solution: Solution of zinc chloro-iodide. (3)

Naftalan: According to Hughes (40), a mixture of dry soap and mineral naphtha. Naftalan, a city in Azerbaijan, was an ancient source of a petroleum oil also known as Naftalan, source of the term naphtha.

Nancic acid: Lactic acid. (3)

Nancy, balls of; —, boules de: Balls of Nancy, see mars, balls of. (39)

Napellum: See aconitum. (39)

Naphae flores (aqua); Naphae, aqua: Orange flower (water), see aurantia flores, aqua. (3)

Naphtalinum; Naphtalin; Naphthalene: Naphthalene, a bicyclic aromatic hydrocarbon derived from coal tar, $C_{10}H_8$. Used as an antiseptic for the gastrointestinal tract, as it is poorly absorbed. (8) Most familiar today in the form of mothballs.

Naphtha, coal tar; —, petroleum: Benzine, petroleum ether. (3)

Naphtha, Hasting's: Wood alcohol, i.e., methyl alcohol. (40)

Naphtha aceti: See ether aceticus. (40)

Naphtha vitroli: See ether, vitriolic. (40)

Naphthamine: See hexaminium. (40)

Naphthol (, beta-); Naphtol; Naphthalol; Naphthosalol; Naphthyl: The alcohol of naphthalene, beta-naphthol, $C_{10}H_7OH$. It was used as a topical disinfectant and to kill parasites of the skin (scabies, etc.), as well as an intestinal disinfectant. (3,8)

Naphthol ointment; Naphtholis, unguentum: There are multiple variants of naphthol, or Kaposi's, ointment with napthol in lard, soap, and chalk, with or without flowers of sulphur, etc. Generally used for tinea (fungal) infections of the skin and for infestations of lice. (40,42)

Naphthol salicylate; Naphthosalol: A salicylate compound said to remain undissolved in the stomach and dissociate in the intestine. Used as an intestinal disinfectant, as per naphthol. (40,42)

Naphtholis benzoas: Naphthol benzoate, used as per naphthol, dissolving in the intestine and acting there as a disinfectant. (42)

Napi, oleum: Rapeseed (napus) oil. (3)

Napolitain quadruple de mercure, onguent {*French*}**; Napolitain simple, onguent** {*French*}**:** See Neapolitan ointment. (1)

Napus: Rape (i.e., oilseed rape), *Brassica napus*. Seeds used. (1) The oil known as canola is a variety of rapeseed oil.

Narancia {*Italian*}**; Narancio** {*Italian*}**:** Orange (fruit) and orange tree, respectively. (1)

Narbonense, mel; Narbonne miel de {*French*}**:** See mel Narbonense. (1)

Narceine: An alkaloid derived from opium, and used for the same purposes (see opium). (8)

Narcoticus aethiopicus: See aethiops narcoticus. (39)

Narcotine: An alkaloid derived from opium, but without narcotic action, initially sedative, then followed by spinal stimulation as with strychnine, rarely used as per quinine as an antiperiodic. (42)

Nard, Indian; Nardus indica: Indian spikenard, root of *Nardostachys jatamansi*. A stomachic, carminative, diuretic, alexipharmic, and emmenagogue. (1,39)

Nardus (, oleum); Nardinum, oleum: Spikenard, nard, various species of valerianaceous plants and balsamic substances or the oil obtained from them. (1)

Nardus celtica: Celtic spikenard, probably the root of *Valeriana celtica*. (1)

Nargol: See silver nuleinate. (40)

Narium, oleum: Liniment of spikenard heated in a mixture of wine and sesame or olive oil, for treatment of palsy and nervous conditions. (1)

Nasturtium aquaticum: Water-cress, *Nasturtium officinale*. Herb used as aperient and antiscorbutic. Figure 3-174. (1,39)

Nasturtium hortense: Garden-cress, *Lepidium sativum*. Leaves and seeds used. (1)

Nat. bicarb.: Sodium bicarbonate, see sodii bicarbonas.

Nataloin: Aloin from natal aloe, not clearly distinct from aloe, but said to be from *Aloe bainsii*. (40)

Natr. biboric: Sodium borate.

Sisymbrium Nasturtium

Published by D.ʳ Woodville Oct.ʳ 1.1790.

Fig. 3-174 Nasturtium aquaticum or watercress.

Natrium; Natron; Natr.; Nat.: Sodium, especially in homeopathic use. See sodii. Natrium can also refer to natron, i.e., a mixture of sodium carbonate and bicarbonate, a naturally occuring mineral, "soda" from which sodium acquires both its name and symbol, Na. (39)

Natrium sodium; Natron: Sodium carbonate. (3)

Natrium sulphuricum: Sodium sulfate. (1)

Natro-kali tartaricum: Rochelle salt, see potassii et sodii tartras. (3)

Natron vitriolatum: Sodium sulfate, see sodii sulphas. (40)

Natrum: See natron. (40)

Neapolitan ointment; —unguent; Neapolitanum quadriplicatum mercurio, unguentum: Quadruple mercury ointment of Naples, a mercurial ointment used for treatment of venereal disease, named after *mal de Naples*, a French term for syphilis. (1,3,39)

Neapolitan opiate: A sedative formulation which did not, in fact, contain opium, but rather senna, sarsaparilla, sassafras, and hermodactyl in honey. (39)

Neapolitanum simplex, unguentum: Mercurial ointment used to treat parasites. (1)

Neat('s) foot oil; Neatsfoot oil: See bubulum, oleum. (39)

Neatsfoot oil, factitious: A mixture of lard and rapeseed oil. (40)

Nebula; Nebulae (plural): A spray, i.e., from a nebulizer. (40)

Nebulae (BPC): Medications applied to the nose and throat via atomizer. Generally contained compounds for: relief of pain (cocaine); vasoconstriction (cocaine, adrenalin); astringency (tannic acid, ferric chloride); and/or disinfection (iodine, carbolic acid, guaiacol, thymol), although some were simply soothing liquids. The BPC (42) indicates:

- **Acidi tanici**—with glycerin and tannic acid in water.
- **Adreninae (cum cocainae)**—adrenine hydrochloride in chloroform water, optionally with cocaine.
- **Alkalina composita**—sodium bicarbonate, borax, carbolic acid, and glycerin in water.
- **Antiseptica alkalina**—sodium bicarbonate, borax, sodium benzoate, sodium salicylate, eucalyptol, thymol, menthol, and gaultheria (wintergreen) oil in water.
- **Benzoini composita (cum cocaina et quinina)**—oils of pine, eucalyptus and cassia with menthol and glycerin in water, alone or as a base for the more complex formulation with cocaine, camphor, quinine, and antipyrine.
- **Eucalypti (et mentholis et cocainae) (et pini)**—oil of eucalyptus in liquid paraffin, alone or as a base for added cocaine, menthol, and camphor (for cough, asthma or bronchitis) or with added oil of pine.
- **Ferri perchloridi**—of ferric chloride in water.
- **Guaiacolis et mentholis**—with guaiacol and menthol in liquid paraffin, disinfectant for tuberculosis.
- **Iodi composita**—of iodine and carbolic acid in liquid paraffin.
- **Iodi et mentholis**—of iodine and menthol in liquid paraffin.
- **Iodoformi**—iodoform in ether, a deodorant and detergent for nasal conditions.
- **Mentholis**—of menthol in liquid paraffin.
- **Mentholis aetherea**—of menthol and chloroform in ether, used to produce topical and refrigerant anesthesia.
- **Mentholis composita**—of menthol, cocaine, tincture of benzoin, and glycerin.
- **Mentholis et cocainae**—of menthol and cocaine in a mixture of almond oil and liquid paraffin.
- **Sodii chloridi composita**—of sodium bicarbonate and chloride with borax in water, for irrigation.

Nectandra; Nectandrum: See bebeeru. (8)

Neem bark: See azadirach (Indian). (40)

Nembutal: Pentobarbital sodium, barbiturate sedative, still in use. (40)

Nenufaro: Water lily, see nymphacea. (1)

Nenupharinum, mel: Honey of water lilies, a decoction of lily flowers and honey, see nymphacea. (1)

Neoarsphenamine: An arsenical antimicrobial related to arsphenamine. For syphilis and yaws. (40)

Neogale: Fresh milk. (3)

Neokharsivan: See neoarsphenamine. (40)

Neoquinophan: A synthetic analgesic. (40)

Neosalvarsan: See neoarsphenamine. (40)

Nepenthes: Laudanum. (39)

Nepeta: Cat-mint, Cat-nip, *Nepeta cataria*. Herb used as tonic, antispasmodic, emmenagogue, and for toothache. (1,39)

Nephedrine; Nephridine: See adrenaline. (40,42)

Nephritica, aqua: Kidney water, spirit of nutmeg with hawthorn flowers, for urinary disorders. (39)

Nephriticum, decoctum ad: Decoction for kidneys, specifically for renal colic (kidney stones) of althea with carica, linseed, licorice, and daucus sylvestris, and root of the restharrow. (39)

Nephriticum, lignum: Nephritic wood, allied to sandalwood, an infusion of which was used to treat kidney disease. (1)

Nero {*Italian*}: Black. (1)

Neroli, oleum: See aurantii florum, oleum. (40)

Nerprun {*French*}: Buckthorne, see rhamnus. (1)

Nerv(in)um, oleum: Neat's-foot oil. (3,40)

Nerve oil; Nerves, oil of: See neat's-foot oil. (40)

Nerve powder: See cypripedii compositus, pulvis. (34)

Nervinis camphoratus, spiritus: See saponis viridis, tinctura.

Nervinum, unguentum: 1. Ointment used to fortify the nerves (1). 2. Compound ointment of rosemary. (3) According to Estes, one formulation included neatsfoot oil, wine, and turpentine. (39)

Nessler's reagent: Solution of potassio-mercuric iodide, for detection of ammonia. (40)

Nettle (common): See urtica. **(39)**

Neuralgia pills: See pilulae antineuralgicae. (46)

Neurotropine: See formamol. (40)

Neutral mixture: Same as potassae citratus, liquor. (39)

Neutralizing cordial: See rhei et potassae compositus, syrupus. (34)

Niccolum: Nickel, metallic. (40)

Nicolao; Nicolas; Nicolaus; Nicolo {*Italian*}: 1. Nicolas Myrepsus, physician of thirteenth century Byzantium, formulated requies magna ("great rest," see requeis Nicoli), an opiate in use until the close of the eighteenth century. 2. Nicolas Salternitanus (Nicholas of Salerno), presumed author of *Antidotarium Nicoli*, a dispensatory of high repute in the middle ages. (1)

Nicoli, requies: See requies Nicolai, and Nicolao, above. (1)

Nicotiana (tabacum): Tobacco plant, *Nicotiana tabacum*. See tabacum. (1,8)

Nicotiana, vin: Tobacco or nicotine wine, of tobacco steeped in wine, and used as a diuretic, expectorant, or laxative, including via enema, but potentially highly toxic. (39)

Nicotina; Nicotinae tartras: Nicotine, nicotine tartrate. Due to complex physiological effects (both sympathetic and parasympathetic, as well as muscular) and high toxicity, nicotine found use primarily as an insecticide. Used to reduce spasm in tetanus and as an antidote to strychnine, in both cases due to action at the neuro-muscular junction, but with risk of temporary paralysis. (42)

Nigella: 1. Fennel-flower, *Nigella sativa*. Seeds used. (1) 2. Roots of goldenthread, *Coptis groenlandia*, used as tonic, astringent, and digestive. (39)

Niger; Nigra; Nigrum: Black (adjective), the masculine form being niger, not "nigrus." (1)

Night-blooming cereus: See cereus grandiflora. (8)

Nightshade (, American): May refer to either belladonna or dulcamara species. For American nightshade see phytolacca. (39)

Nigramentum: Black ink. (3)

Nigrosine: Class of blue or black dyes of coal-tar origin. (3)

Nihil(i) album; —griseum: Crude zinc oxide. (3) Nihil also means "nothing" in Latin, as in "NPO," *nihil per os*, or "nothing by mouth."

Nil: See nihil. (40)

Nimphaea; Ninfea {*Italian*}**:** See nymphaea. (1)

Nitrae, spiritus; Nitrae sp.: Spirits of nitre, i.e., nitric acid.

Nitras argenti; Nitratum argentum: Silver nitrate, see argenti nitratum. (39)

Nitras potassae: Potassium nitrate, saltpeter. (39)

Nitras: Any salt of nitric acid, a nitrate salt. (39)

Nitrata, charta: Nitre paper; see potassii nitratis, charta. (40)

Nitratine: Sodium nitrate. (3)

Nitre, cake: Acid sodium sulfate. (3)

Nitre, Chili; —, cubic: See sodii nitras. (40)

Nitre, rough: Magnesium chloride. (3)

Nitre, spirit of: Nitric or nitrous acid, or sometimes sweet spirits of niter. There is often confusion or ambiguity in textbooks regarding these materials. See nitri dulcis, spiritus (sweet spirits) and nitri spiritus glauberi below.

Nitre balls: See nitrum, tabulatum. (40)

Nitre paper: See potassii nitratis, charta. (40)

Nitri, sal; Nitrum: Ancient term applied to various compounds of sodium or potassium—soda (sodium carbonate), potash (potassium carbonate), etc. In more modern uses, nitre or saltpeter, potassium nitrate. (1)

Nitri dulcis, spiritus; Nitri dulcis duplex, spiritus; —fumans: Sweet spirits of nitre. This is ethyl nitrate, which is a sweet, ether-like material. It is made by dissolving nitric acid in wine or other alcohol solutions and may be purified by distillation therefrom. (3)

Nitri glauberi, spiritus; Nitri spiritus; —glauberi: Nitric acid, HNO_3. (3), or more properly per Estes (39), actually nitrous acid, HNO_2, made of sal niter (saltpeter) in vitriol (sulfuric acid).

Nitric acid: See nitricum, acidum. (8)

Nitric oxide of mercury: See hydrargyri oxidum rubrum. This is prepared by oxidation of mercury in association with nitric acid, but is not the nitrate salt. (40)

Nitrico-aethereus, spiritus: Sweet spirit nitre. See nitri dulcis, spiritus. (3)

Nitrico-nitrosum, acidum: Fuming nitric acid. (3)

Nitricum (dilutum), acidum: Nitric acid, HNO_3, from distillation of potassium nitrate and sulfuric acid. The dilute form is approximately ten percent nitric acid in water. Antiphlogistic, tonic, antiseptic, and antisyphilitic. (8,39)

Nitriti, unguentum: A vulnerary (wound ointment) of saltpeter. (39)

Nitrobenzene; Nitrobenzol: Highly poisonous, used mainly in soap and perfume production for its almond-like odor. (42)

Nitro-erythrite: See erythritol tetranitrate. (40)

Nitrogenii moxoxidum: Nitrogen monoxide, nitrous oxide, i.e., laughing gas, discovered by Priestly in 1776, liberated from ammonium nitrate. (34)

Nitroglycerin: See glonoini, spiritus. (8)

Nitroglycerini, tablettae: Tablet of solution of trinitrin (nitroglycerin), cocoa, sugar, gum acacia, and (see) theobromatis, emulsio. (42)

Nitro-hydrochloric acid; Nitrohydrochloricum, acidum (dilutum): Nitrohydrochloric acid, Aqua Regia, nitromuriatic acid, a mixture of nitric and hydrochloric acids, diluted, if desired, with water. (8,29)

Nitromuriaticum, acidum (dilutum); Nitromuriatic acid: See nitrohydrochloricum, acidum. (8)

Nitrous acid; Nitrosum, acidum: See nitre, spirits of. (39)

Nitrum (unspecified); Nitrum, sal: Unspecified, this is usually sal niter, potassium nitrate. (3)

Nitrum flammans: Ammonium nitrate. (3)

Nitrum saturninum: Lead nitrate. (3)

Nitrum stibiatum: Said to be the same as antimonium calcinatum (39). The former should properly be a tin (stibium) salt but several alchemical sources suggest that this material was made by heating antimony with nitric acid. Alchemical names were based more on physical characteristics than chemistry, so this discrepancy is less than surprising.

Nitrum tabulatum: Balls (pills) formed of pure nitre (potasii nitras) by heating. Diuretic and sedative, use as per niter. Also noted to be a veterinary diuretic, so that some such "pills" were rather large, with equine doses on the order of 1 oz. (40)

Nitrum vitriolatum: Sulfate of potassium or sodium. (1) See sodii sulphas. (40)

Nivalis, aqua: Snow water, i.e., melted snow. (3)

Nix zinci: Zinc oxide. (3)

Nizin: See zinci sulphanilas. (40)

Noce {*Italian*}**:** Nut, walnut. (1)

Noce moscata {*Italian*} Nutmeg. See myristica. (1)

Noir {*French*}**:** Black. (1)

Noli me tangere {*Italian*}**:** Touch-me-not, yellow balsam, *Impatiens noli tangere*. (1)

Norit: Proprietary animal charcoal used for decolorizing and/or deodorizing preparations. (3)

Norsulfazolum: Norsulfazole, an early sulfa antibiotic.

Norwood's tincture (of veratrum): A formulation of veratrum with nearly twice the strength of the official USP formulation. See veratrum viride. (8)

Nosophen: Iodo-phenolphthalein, a radiologic contrast material. (40)

Nouffer's tapeworm cure: Powder of filix, with addition of several cathartics, first introduced ca. 1755 by the widow of a Swiss surgeon. (39)

Novargan: See argein. (40)

Novarsan; Novarsenobenzene; Novarsenobenzol: See neoarsphenamine. (40)

Novaspirin: See citrosalic acid. (40)

Novatophan: See neoquinophan. (40)

Nuc; Nuc.; Nuces: Nut, proper Latin singular nux, plural nucis. Nuc may be an orthographic variant of nux or abbreviation for nucis, see nux. (1)

Nucis, oleum: Nut oil from arachis, i.e., peanut oil. (40)

Nucis moschatae, oleum; Nucistae, oleum: Fixed or volatile oil of nutmeg. (3)

Nucis vomicae alcoholicum, extractum: Dry alcoholic extract of nux vomica, USP. (44)

Nucis vomicae, extractum; —, fluidum extractum; —, tinctura: Dried extract, fluid extract, and tincture of nux vomicae, i.e., strychnine. (8)

Nucistae, balsamum: Ointment with volatile and fixed oils of nutmeg. (3)

Nuclein; Nucleinic acid; Nucleicum, acidum: Nuclear cellular material, i.e., DNA, not in a purified form. The structure and function would not be recognized until 1953. (42)

Nucleogen: Nuclein combined with iron and arsenic. (40)

Nucleus pini: See pini, nucleus. (1)

Nuffer's…: See Nouffer's. (39)

Nulomoline: Proprietary invert (hydrolyzed fruit) sugar. (3)

Nuremburg cerate: An astringent and resolvent plaster of rosemary oil, camphor, and minium (white lead), which must have had a quite pleasant odor. (39)

Nursery hair lotion: See staphisagriae, lotio. (42)

Nut, purging; —, physic; —, Barbadoes: See curcas purgans. (33)

Nut oil: Castor (bean) oil, see ricinis. (39) Alternatively, may be arachis (peanut) oil. (40)

Nutgall: See galla. (8)

Nutmeg butter: Oil of nutmeg, see myristica. (40)

Nutmeg: See myristica. (8)

Nutrientia, suppositoria: Nutrient suppository of beef peptone and gelatin, for rectal alimentation. (42)

Nutritum, unguentum: 1. See tripharmacum, unguentum. (1) 2. A nourishing ointment made with cerussa (lead acetate). (39)

Nutrose: Proprietary sodium caseinate, the latter being milk protein, nutritive. (40)

Nux: Nut, plural nuces, genitive nucis. (1)

Nux aromatica: Nutmeg. See myristica. (3)

Nux colae: Cola nut, see kola. (1)

Nux cupressi: Galbulus, seed producing cone of a cypress tree. (1)

Nux juglans: Walnut. (1)

Nux metella: Nux vomica. (3)

Nux moschata; —nucista; —myristica: Nutmeg. See myristica. (3,39)

Nux pistachia: Pistachio nut, *Pistachia vera*, used as an analeptic. (39)

Nux vomica; Nux vomicus: The seed of *Strychnos nux-vomica*, Dog nut, poison nut. Plural is nuces, genitive nucis. Primary use was as a stomachic and general stimulant, but in excessive dose causes seizures arising from the spinal cord level. Stimulates the heart, raises blood pressure, and stimulates respiration. Nux vomica, or "imprinted nut" refers to a thumbprint-like marking, said to be of divine origin. This is the source of strychnine and also contains lesser amounts of brucine. Figure 3-175. (1,8)

Nymphaea: Water lily, *Nymphaea alba*. Flowers and root used. Astringent and narcotic. (1)

Nytro... (*orth. var.*): See Nitro.... (8)

Fig. 3-175 Nux vomica, source of strychnine.

O

O.: At beginning of inscription: oleum, olio {*Italian*} (oil); onguent {*French*} (unguent); opiatum (opiate). At end of inscription: opium (opium). (1)

O.O.O.: Finest olive oil, oleum olivae optimum. In modern usage may refer to ozonated olive oil.

Oak: See quercus.

Oats: See avena. (7)

Oca {*Italian*}**:** Goose. (1)

Ocher; Ochre: Iron oxide, yellow, red or brown, used as a pigment. (3)

Ochra: Ocher (Latin), yellow oxides of iron. (39)

Ocimum: See ocymum. (1)

Oculi cancrorum: See cancrorum, oculi. (39)

Oculis, unguentum de tutia pro: See tutia pro oculus…. (1)

Ocymum: Sweet basil, *Ocymum basilicum*. Herb and seeds used. (1,44)

Odoratus, spiritus: Perfumed spirit, Cologne water, aqua Colognensis, a water and alcohol solution of oil of bergamot, lemon (citrus), rosemary, lavender (lavandula), orange flowers (aurantii florum, oleum), and acetic ether (ether, aceticus). Used as a perfume. (31)

Oellet {*French*}**:** Clove-scented pink, see tunicae, flores. (1)

Oenanthe (crocata): Water dropwort, *Oenanthe crocata*. A minor sedative and emetic. Figure 3-176. (32)

Oenanthe phellandrium: Fine-leaved water-hemlock, *Phellandrium aquaticum*, similar to conium, and used for a variety of conditions as a volatile oil or as the seed. Unofficial. Figure 3-177. (44)

Oenanthic ether: Artificial oil of cognac. (3) Modern sources indicate that it is a mixture of ethyl esters of various medium chain fatty acids (7-10 carbons) with a wine or cognac-like odor.

Oenothera: Evening or tree primrose. Root, bark, leaves, and twigs of *Oenothera biennis*, used to prepare a topical ointment for skin disorders, especially in infants, and used systemically for various illnesses, particularly female complaints. (33)

Oesipus; Oesypus (humida): Wool fat, lanolin. (1) Impure wool fat. (3)

Oestrin: Ovarian hormone, i.e., estrogen. (40)

Oglio {*Italian*}**:** See olio. (1)

Oil, boiled: Generally linseed oil, in the BPC of 1923 this referred specifically to linseed oil boiled with litharge, used as a liniment. (40)

Oil, camphorated: See oleorum camphorata, mistura. (34)

Oil, fermented: Oil from fermented olives. (40)

Oil, hardened: Hydrogenated oil of any type. (3)

Oil, ioduretted: A solution of iodine in almond oil. (40)

Oil, oxygenated: Olive oil through which chlorine (other sources suggest oxygen) gas is bubbled for an extended time. (40)

Oil, Provence: Finest olive oil, from French Provence. (40)

Oil, Sicily; Oil, Spanish: Inferior olive oil. (40) One assumes the Sicilians and Spaniards would beg to differ.

Oil, sulphurated: See sulphuratum, oleum. (39)

Oil, train: Whale oil, of various species. (40)

Oil (of) _____: Oil, see _____, oil (of) if not listed immediately below. (8)

Fig. 3-176 Oenanthe crocata or water dropwort.

Fig. 3-177 Oenanthe phellandrium.

Oil and hartshorn: See ammoniae, linimentum. (40)

Oil of ben; —behen; —been; —behn: Oil of the ben-oil or horseradish tree, *Moringa oleifera*, not same as oil of bene, which comes from sesame (sesamum). (3) A stable and pleasant-tasting oil used in perfumery or machine lubrication as well as in medicine for a vast array of conditions. Source of behenic acid, a very long chain (22 carbon) fatty acid.

Oil of cassia, artificial: Cinnamic aldehyde. (3)

Oil of cuscus: See vetiver, oil of. (40)

Oil of eggs: Oil expressed from hardboiled egg yolks. (3)

Oil of niobe: Methyl benzoate. (3)

Oil of smoke: Creosote. (3)

Oil of spike: See stoechas, oleum. (40)

Oil of tar (mixture): See pitch oil (pix) and olei picis, mistura respectively. (34)

Oil of tartar: Solution of potassium carbonate. (3)

Oil of three ingredients: Mixture of the oils of turpentine, lavender, and bricks (see philosophorum, oleum), in equal parts. (40)

Oil stone: A sundry item carried by pharmacists, or for their own use. A sharpening stone or soapstone used to sharpen knives, implements, etc.

Oil-sugar: See oleosacchara. (46)

Ointment, golden: See hydrargyri oxidi flavi, unguentum. (40)

Ointment, green: Elder ointment, details not specified, but see for example sambuci, unguentum. (40)

Ointment, simple: See liniment, simple. (39)

Okra: See hibiscus esculentus. (33)

Ol.: Oleum, i.e., oil. Olive oil if not otherwise specified.

Ole(in)atum (_____); Oleate: An oleinate, i.e., a material mixed in oleic acid (the primary fatty acid in olive oil), generally for topical use; see _____, oleanatum. (42) Oleinatum is proper, but oleatum is very commonly seen as a variant.

Olea: Olive tree, *Olea europaea (or europoea)*. Leaves, fruit, and oil used. Figure 3-178. (1)

Olea fixa: Fixed oils, or expressed oils, from application of pressure to seed or other material, often mildly heated to aid release of oil (but not to the point of distillation, which creates volatile oils). (44)

Olea infusa: An infusion in oil. Primarily used to extract oil-soluble components from various herbs in the making of other preparations, occasionally used directly. See underlying name of herb or plant material. (34) In the NF, 200 grams dry herb infused in 150 gm alcohol, 4 gm water of ammonia, and 500 gm each lard oil and cottonseed oil.

Olea volatilia: Volatile or essential oils, by distillation of material or from solutions or extracts of material. (44)

Oleae foliorum, extractum: Extract of olive leaves, of fresh leaves extracted in alcohol, a tonic. (42)

Oleae foliorum, tinctura: Tincture of olive leaf in alcohol, a bitter tonic, antiperiodic, and febrifuge. (42)

Oleae, folia: "Oil leaves," i.e., olive leaves, used in a small number of formulations, allegedly a tonic and febrifuge. A decoction could be used in place of quinine. (42)

Oleander: Oleander, the leaves of *Nerium oleander* are highly toxic and contain a compound similar to digitalis, used in the treatment of heart failure and dropsy to increase the strength and decrease the rate of cardiac function. (33)

Olefiant gas: Ethylene gas, C_2H_4. (40)

Olei picis, mistura: Mixture of oil of tar, tar mixture, mistura picis liquidae. A mixture of purified extract of licorice, sugar, oil of peppermint, chloroform, alcohol, and water. An expectorant. (34,46)

Olei picis: Pitch oil, see pix. (34)

Olei volatilis, spiritus: Any volatile oil made into a spirit not otherwise defined in the formulary. Typically, in the USP, by combining 65 parts of oil to 935 parts deodorized alcohol. This is a five percent by weight solution, given that oil has a density of about 0.9. (34)

Oleicum, acidum; Oleic acid: A fatty acid (18 carbons) derived from various fats. The primary fatty acid in olive oil. Oleic acid was used as a vehicle for skin preparations, as it tends to help with penetration of the skin. (8)

Oleite: Sodium sulphoricinoleate. Sodium salt of sulphoricinoleic acid, i.e., ricin or castor oil treated with sulphuric acid. Ointment base. (3)

Oleo mixture: See oleosa simplex, emulsio. (39)

Oleo-balsamica, mistura; Oleoso-balsamica, mixtura: Oleo-balsamic mixture, Balsamum vitae Hoffmanni; of alcohol, balsam of Peru, and oils of lavender, thyme, lemon, mace, orange flowers, clove, and cinnamon. (46)

Oleogen: See parogen. (40)

Oleoresina, ____: An oleoresin, see ____, Oleoresina. (8)

Oleorum camphorata, mistura: Camphorated mixture of oils, a mixture of oils of clove, cajaput, and amber (rectified) with camphor in equal parts, used for toothache. (34)

Oleorum composita, mistura: Compound mixture of oils, or vermifuge oil, a mixture of castor oil, wormseed oil, turpentine, and oil of anise. An effective vermifuge. (34)

Oleorum volatilium, spiritus: Spirits of volatile oils. "Any spirit of a volatile oil for which no specific formula is provided may be prepared by dissolving 6.5 parts of the oil in 93.5 parts of alcohol." This is a five percent solution by weight. (31)

Oleosa simplex, emulsio; Oleosa volatilis, emulsio: "Emulsion of simple or volatile oils," of almond oil with marshmallow (althaea) and gum arabic. (39)

Oleosa volatilis, emulsio: Volatile oil emulsion, same as emulsio oleosa simplex, above, but with spirits of ammonia. (39)

Oleosacchara: A dose form consisting of a drop of any essential oil triturated with two grams of sugar. (34,46)

Oleum; O.; Ol.: Oil, generally olive oil if not otherwise specified. (1) Oleum is also used to refer to fuming sulphuric acid. (40)

Oleum, _____: See _____, oleum if not listed immediately below.

Oleum adipis: Oil derived from fat, lard oil. (34)

Oleum badiani: See anisi, oleum. (40)

Oleum carbolatum: Carbolized oil, i.e., carbolic acid in cottonseed oil. (34)

Fig. 3-178 Olea europoea or olive tree.

Oleum lubicans: Catheter or lubricating oil, of five percent carbolic acid (disinfectant) in a mixture of castor and almond oil. (42)

Oleum pedum tauri: Oil of bull's foot, see bubulum. (34)

Oleum rusci: Oil of white birch.

Oleum terrae: Crude petroleum. (3)

Olibani, gummi; olibanum: Oilbanum, or frankincense, oleoresin of trees of genus *Boswellia*. (1)

Olibanum, American: Oleoresin from a juniper species, as a replacment for true olibanum, i.e., frankincense. (40)

Olio {*Italian*}: Oil, olive oil. (1)

Oliva, Ol.; Olivae, oleum: Olive oil, the fixed oil derived from the fruit of *Olea europaea*. (8,39)

Olivae Malaga(e), Oleum: A low grade or imitation olive oil, named for the region of Malaga, Spain.

Olivae, olei, enema: Enema of olive oil, used for impacted feces. (42)

Oliveri, cortex; Oliver's bark; Oliveri corticis, tinctura: See cinnamomum oliveri. A simple tincture was specified in the BPC. (40,42)

Omal: Trichlorophenol. (3)

Omnopon; Omnoponum: Omnopon is a trade name for a proprietary mixture of opium alkaloid salts, pseudo-Latinized to Omnoponum. See opium. (40)

Omotribes: Oil expressed from unripe green olives. (39)

Omphacinum (, oleum): Crude olive oil. (3) Oil of unripe olives. (1,39)

Omphacium: Juice of unripe grapes. (1)

Onguent {*French*}: Unguent, ointment. (1)

Onion: See allium. (44)

Ononis: See anonis. (1)

Onosmodium: Root and seeds of False Gromwell, Gravel Weed, or Wild Job's tears, *Onosmodium virginianum*, a tonic and diuretic, said to dissolve renal stones, hence the name Gravel Weed. (33)

Ophthalmic balsam (Pettit's): See zinci oxidi compositum, unguentum. (34)

Ophthalmic spirits; Opthalmicus, spiritus: Oils of lavender and rosemary in alcohol. (46)

Ophthalmic unguent; Ophthalmicum, unguentum: 1. A mild ointment of mercuric oxide. (3) 2. Zinc oxide ointment for treatment of eye disorders. See also tutia pro oculis, unguentum de. (1,39)

Ophthalmicum rubrum, balsamum: Ointment of red precipitate (hydrargyri oxidum rubrum). (3)

Opiata, confectio: A weak narcotic preparation said to be derived from theriac, with opium, piper longum, ginger, carum, and syrup of white poppies. (39)

Opiata salomonis: Composite remedy for treatment of infectious diseases and helmintic infestations. (1)

Opiatum: Opiate. (1)

Opiatum, electuarium: A weak narcotic preparation said to be derived from theriac, with opium, pulvis aromaticus, and serpentina. (39)

Opiatum, linimentum; —, unguentum: A mixture of opium, wine, rosemary oil, and soap, usually as a topical analgesic. (39)

Opiatus, pulvis: Powdered opium, actually a mixture of opium powder ground with chalk (creta). (39)

Opiatus, pulvis: See cretae compositus (cum opio), pulvis. (40)

Opifer que (per) orbem dicor: "Spoken of around the world as healer." Motto of the Worshipful Society of Apothecaries (London), formed in 1617. May be found on apothecary wares of Britain from that time onwards. (35)

Opii, acetum: Official vinegar of opium, black drop, in BPC of opium, nutmeg, sugar, and dilute acetic acid. Narcotic. A similar formulation with less acetic acid is found in the USP. (8,42)

Opii, confectio: Confection of opium in honey and aromatic powder. (44)

Opii, emplastrum: Opium plaster, of extract of opium, Burgundy pitch, lead plaster, and water. Applied locally for pain, although the BPC notes that location is probably moot as the opiates act via absorption and effect on the central nervous system. (8,42)

Opii, enema: Enema of tincture of opium and mucilage of starch, a sedative and inhibitor of intestinal motility. (42)

Opii, extractum: Extract of opium, by trituration and extraction of opium with water and milk sugar (lactose) followed by evaporation. (8)

Opii, linimentum: Simple liniment of opium, or anodyne liniment. (See also: opii compositum, linimentum). A topical method of opium delivery. (34)

Opii (compositae), pilulae; Opii co., pil.: Opium pills, of powdered opium and soap. (8,4)

Opii, pulvis: Powdered opium. See also opiatus, pulvis. (8)

Opii, tablettae: Opium tablet, of same with sugar and (see) ethereal solution of theobroma. (42)

Opii, tinctura (simplex): Tincture of opium, laudanum. Of powdered opium, alcohol, and water, macerated with calcium phosphate and percolated. (8)

Opii [acetata] [muriatica], tinctura: Variants on the tincture of opium, using material extracted from raw opium using either acetic acid (vinegar) or hydrochloric (muriatic) acid. (34)

Opii, vinum: Wine of opium, Sydenham's laudanum. Of powdered opium, cassia cinnamon, cloves, alcohol, and white wine, by maceration and filtration. (8)

Opii alkalina, mistura: See sassafras et opii, mistura. (34)

Opii ammoniata, tinctura: Ammoniated tincture of opium, with opium, flowers of benzoin, saffron, anise, and spirits of ammonia. (39)

Opii ammoniatum, linimentum: Liniment of soft soap, of strong solution of ammonia, compound camphor liniment, tincture of opium, and liniment of belladonna (BPC). (42)

Opii camphorata, tinctura; Opii cam., tr.: Camphorated tincture of opium, or paregoric. This extremely popular remedy is prepared from powdered opium, benzoic acid, camphor, oil of anise, glycerin, and alcohol. (8,29) In the BPC (42), same as camphorae composita, tinctura.

Opii compositum, linimentum: Compound liniment of opium, Canada liniment, of tincture of opium, oil of turpentine (terebinthinae, oleum), and ammonia water, with camphor, alcohol and oil of peppermint, made into a somewhat permanent emulsion with fresh egg albumen. It is used as a stimulating anodyne. (31)

Opii compositus, pulvis: Compound powder of opium, with black pepper, ginger, caraway fruit powder, and tragacanth. Use as per opium. (34,42)

Opii crocata, tinctura: Tincture of opium with saffron, Sydenham's laudanum (see also opii, vinum). A tincture made from granulated opium, saffron (crocus), cinnamon, and clove (caryophyllum), by maceration and percolation with diluted alcohol. For pain. (31)

Opii crocatum, acetum: Black drop, an opium preparation four times the strength of laudanum (opii, tinctura). (8)

Opii deodorati, tinctura; Opi. deod., tinct.: Deodorized tincture of opium, or "D.T.O.," made with powdered opium, ether, alcohol, and water. The mixture is macerated with precipitated phosphate, percolated, and then evaporated to drive off the ether to leave an alcohol solution of opium. (8)

Opii et camphorae, pilulae: Pills of opium and camphor. (34)

Opii et gambir composita, tinctura: Compound tincture of opium and gambir, tinctura pectoralis, guttae pectorales, pectoral drops, or Bateman's pectoral drops. Made with tincture of opium, compound tincture of gambir and diluted alcohol, it is also for infantile colic. (31)

Opii et plumbi, pilulae: Pills of opium and lead, of powdered opium and lead acetate. Astringent and anodyne in bowel and bronchial disorders. (34)

Opii sedativus, liquor: An unofficial preparation of opium, approximately twice the strength of laudanum (see opii, tinctura). (8) A solution (BPC) of opium in calcium hydroxide, alcohol, sherry, and water. (42)

Opii venalis, tinctura; Opi. venalis, tinct.: No specific formulation has been located, but as "venalis" indicates "prepared for commercial sale," this must presumably be a commercial preparation of tincture of opium. See opii (simplex), tinctura.

Opio {*Italian*}: Opium. (1)

Opio, confectio: In the BPC, twenty-five percent powdered opium in simple syrup, for diarrhea without inflammation or for flatulent colic. (42)

Opium; Oppio {*Italian*}: Dried, milky exudate obtained by incising the capsule of unripe opium poppy, *Papaver somniferum,* yielding predominantly morphine, with codeine, and a variety of other compounds. Opium and related narcotics are of course used for control of pain, but also suppress motility of the gastrointestinal tract (to treat cramping or diarrhea), suppress respirations, and served as sedatives, sleep aids, and anxiolytics. White's *Materia Medica* notes that children are particularly susceptible to overdose and should be dosed with care. Morphine is noted to act more quickly and be suitable for subcutaneous injection, whereas opium and various opium compounds are more prone to suppressing GI motility. Hence, paregoric or deodorized tincture of opium were commonly used for GI disorders. (1,8)

Opium colatum: Extract of opium. (40)

Opium deodoratum; Opium denarcotisatum: Deodorized or "de-narcotized" opium. Powdered opium is extracted with ether to mobilize and remove the active principals (morphine, etc.), then evaporated to dryness and triturated with milk sugar. (8)

Opium enema: Opium in a "domestic enema" (see enema, domestic). This reduces cramping and serves as both a local and systemic analgesic as well as a sedative. (39)

Opium lozenge: See glycyrrhizae et opii, trochisci. (34)

Opium purificatum: Extract of opium. (40)

Opium, Trebizond: Persian opium. (40)

Opobalsamum: Opobalsam, balm of Gilead, balm of Mecca. Oleoresin from the tree *Commiphora opobalsamum.* (1)

Opodeldoc; Opodeldoc, liquid: Soap liniment used to treat sprains and bruises. See saponis viridis, tinctura. (1,34) According to Estes (39) the term opodeldoc was applied by Paracelsus to various plasters, but over time this became a soap liniment. See also Steers' opodeldoc. Term also used in patent medicine to indicate a panacea.

Opodeldoc, solid: See saponato-camphoratum, linimentum. (31)

Opopanax: 1. Opopanax, gum resin from the root of *Opopanax chironium (*formerly *Pastinaca opopanax)*. This was a mild cathartic, deobstruant, antispasmodic, and emmenogogue. Figure 3-179. (1,39) 2. Juice of lygusticum. (39)

Opt.; Optim[a][us][um]: Best or finest (Latin).

Opthalmia, aqua: Eye water, any eye wash. (39)

Opthalmicus, lapis: Eyestones (concretions found in stomach of European crawfish). (3)

Opticae, pilulae: See lucis majores, pilulae. (1)

Orange: See aurantii. The peel (aurantii cortex) is used in several preparations. This may refer either to the bitter orange (aurantii amari) or sweet orange (aurantii dulcis). (8)

Orange berries: See issue peas. (40)

Orange flower water (, triple): See aurantii florum, aqua. "Triple" refers to the stronger dilution, or aqua aurantii florum fortior. (8)

Orange flower, oil of: See aurantii florum, oleum. (40)

Orchid; Orchis: See satyrion and associated Figure 3-236. (1,39)

Orchil: See lakmus. (40)

Ordeal Bark; —, Bean: See erythrophloeum. (8)

Ordeum: See hordium. (1)

Orellans; Orleana; Orleans: Annatto, a yellow colorant. (3,40)

Organs: See pulegium. (40)

Organum: Observed, probably a variant of oreganum.

Organy: Usually pennyroyal (pulegium); also can be origanum. (40)

Origanum (Oleum); Origano {*Italian*}: Origano, from wild marjoram, *Origanum vulgare* or the oil (oleum) therefrom. Leaves and flowering tops used. Figure 3-180. (1)

Origanum creticum: See dictamnus creticus. (1)

Origanum majoram; Oreganum majorana: Marjoram, from the plant *Origanum majoram,* or pot marjoram. This is closely related to wild oregano, *O. vulgaris*, and it is unclear how carefully this distinction was made in practice. Figure 3-181. (3,39)

Oriza: See oryza. (1)

Fig. 3-179 Opopanax.

Fig. 3-180 Origanum vulgare or origano (oregano).

Fig. 3-181 Origanum majoram or marjoram.

Orobanche: Broom rape, chokeweed, a member of the genus *Orobanche*. (1)

Orobranche virginiana: Beech drops or cancer root, *Epifagus Americanus*, allegedly for cancers. Unofficial. (44)

Orobus; Orobo {*Italian*}: Probably denotes tuberous pea, *Lathyrus macrorrhizus*. (1)

Orphol: See bismuth naphtholate. (40)

Orpiment: A bright yellow-arsenic trisulfide, used as a pigment and pharmaceutical. (39)

Orris (root); Orris rt. po.: Powdered orris (iris) root. See iris. (7)

Orr's white: See lithopone. (3)

Orso {*Italian*}: Bear. (1)

Ortho-oxycinnamic acid: See coumarin. (40)

Orthoboric acid: Boric acid. (3)

Orthobromocamphor: See camphor monobromata. (40)

Orthoform (, new): A local anesthetic. (40)

Ortica {*Italian*}: See urtica. (1)

Orvietanum; Orviétan {*French*}: Electuary used as antidote against poisons, to prevent pestilence or smallpox, and as a tonic. Supposedly originated by Christophoro Contugi of Ovieto. (1)

Oryza: Rice, *Oryza sativa*. (1,3)

Orzo {*Italian*}: Barley, see hordeum. (1)

Os: Bone. (1)

Os cordis cervi: Stag's heart bone (anatomically mythical, or perhaps the sternum). (1)

Os sepiae: Cuttlefish bone. A source of calcium carbonate, from the cuttlefish, a mollusk, *Sepia officinalis*. Used primarily in ground form as a dentrifice. Said to be sold under the names "Sys. Specific" and "Pulvis Bataviae Compositus" for this purpose. (5,30)

Os ustum: Burnt bone, i.e., bone charcoal.

Osatum, unguentum: Lip salve (Latin, "of mouths"), of alkanna root (red colorant), beeswax, oil of rose, and lard. This is essentially red lipstick. (42) Although verified in the original reference, this seems likely to be a corruption of the older rosatum, unguentum.

Osipo {*Italian*}: Wool-fat, lanolin. (1)

Osmo kaolin: Proprietary colloidal kaolin. (40)

Osmorrhiza: The root of sweet cicely, *Osmorrhiza longistylis*. King's notes that the "real" sweet cicely is *Myrrhis odorata*, a European plant. An aromatic, stomachic, carminative, and expectorant. (33)

Osmunda: Buck thorn or buckhorn brake, royal flowering fern, *Osmunda regalis*. The extract is mucilagenous and used to treat bone disorders such as rickets as well as diarrhea and dysentery. (32,33)

Ossa sepiae: See os sepiae. (1)

Ossium, acidum: Glacial phosphoric acid, "bone acid." (3)

Ossiurn, sal: Ammonium carbonate. (3)

Osso {*Italian*}: Bone. (1)

Ostrea (edulis): Powdered shell of the oyster (*Ostrea* spp.), an antacid and, like other shells, roasted as a source of quicklime. (The roasting of shells, calcium carbonate, drives off carbon dioxide to leave calcium oxide, quicklime). (39)

Ostrya: The inner wood and bark of ironwood, hop hornbeam, or leverwood, *Ostrya virginica*, a tonic and alterative used in the treatment of periodic fevers (i.e., malaria). (33)

Otto: Oil or attar of roses. (40)

Ouabain; Ouabainum: A glucoside probably obtained from the root of *Carissa schinperi*, of Africa. Said to be a local anesthetic more powerful than cocaine, and useful for whooping cough. Ouabain is now known to be closely related to digitalis, and unless there is some confusion regarding identity, these purported actions seem unlikely to be anything but mythical. (8)

Ourari: See curare. (40)

Ovarium: Dried bovine, ovine, or porcine ovary, a crude source of female hormones, for menopause and various gynecological conditions. (7)

Ovi albumen: See albumen (egg). (8)

Ovi vitellus: Egg yolk. (40)

Ovi, ol(eum): Egg oil, oil expressed from fried eggs, used to treat diarrhea and as a topical styptic. (39)

Ovillum, sevum; —, unguentum: Sheep or mutton fat, prepared mutton suet. (The term suet derives from the Latin sevum or seuum.) (39)

Ovis (aries): Sheep, ewe, or often mutton suet. (1)

Ovo, electuarium de: Antipestilential electuary of eggs and other ingredients. (1,35)

Ovolecithin: Lecithin, a fatty material derived from eggs, used as an emulsifier. (40)

Ovum: Egg, hen's egg, white or yolk used in various preparations. Whites used as an antidote, especially for metal salts, and yolk used in jaundice due to the yellow color (as per the doctrine of signatures). Egg shells, like mollusk shells, can be burned to make quicklime (see ostrea). (39)

Oxalicum, acidum: Oxalic acid, chemically derived from a number of sources, it is highly corrosive and, according to King's, "This article, unless in great attenuation, is an unfit agent for internal administration…" (33)

Oxalis (acetosa): See acetosa. (39)

Oxalis (acetosella): Wood sorrel, *Oxalis acetosella*, used as a refrigerant and diuretic. Figure 3-182. (33,39)

Oxalium: Potassium (bin)oxalate. (3)

Oxgall; Ox gall; Ox bile: See fel bovis. (8)

Oxidum antimonii cum sulphureticum, per nitratum potassae: See crocus antimonii. This name is a description of the process by which the substance is made. (39)

Oxidum antimonii vitrificatum cum cera: See antimonii vitrum ceratum. (39)

Oxidum antimonii: See crocus antimonii. (39)

Oxidum antimonium cum phosphate calcis: See antimonialis, pulvis. (39)

Oxidum antimonium cum sulphure, vitrificatum: See antimonium vitrificatum. (39)

Oxidum arsenici: Arsenic oxide, white arsenic. (39)

Oxidum ferri nigrum purificatum: Purified black iron oxide, similar to ferri limatura purificata, purified iron filings. (39)

Fig. 3-182 Oxalis acetosella or wood sorrel.

Oxidum (ferri) rubrum: Red oxide. Unspecified (without ferri), this is generally the red oxide of mercury (hydrargyrum oxidum rubrum) as specified in the USP. When specified as iron (ferri) and perhaps in some instances when unspecified, this is red lead oxide, oxidum ferri rubrum. (39)

Oxidum hydrargyri cinereum: See hydrargyrus praecipitatus. (39)

Oxidum hydrargyri et ammoniae: White precipitate, see hydrargyrum ammoniatum. (39)

Oxidum hydrargyri ruber: Red precipitate of mercuric nitrate, see hydrargyri nitratus (liquor). (39)

Oxidum plumbi rubrum: Red oxide of lead, see plumbi. (39)

Oxidum plumbi semivitreum: Partially vitrified white lead oxide. (39)

Oxidum zinci (impurum): Calcined zinc oxide, zincum ustum. (39)

Oxim.; Oximel (*orth var.*)**:** See oxymel. (1)

Oxitriphyllon: See luliula. (1)

Oxizaccara {*Italian*}**:** See oxysacchara. (1)

Oxone: Sodium peroxide. (3)

Oxy-di-methyl-chinizin: Antipyrin. (3)

Oxycantha: Hawthorn, Whitethorn, *Crataegus oxyacantha*. Also referred to medicinally as cretaegus. Berries, leaves, flowers used to treat cardiac conditions. (1)

Oxycantha Galeni: See berberis. (39)

Oxycratum Saturni: See virgin's milk. (39)

Oxycroceum, emplastrum: Poultice of saffron, yellow wax, vinegar, myrrh, frankincense, mastic, and other resins. Used for relief of muscular pains. (1)

Oxydendron; Oxydendrum: Sour wood, Sorrel tree, Elk tree, *Oxydendrum arboreum*, for dropsy and urinary difficulties. (32,33)

Oxydum: Variant of oxidum, see oxidum.

Oxygenated paraffin: See parogen. (40)

Oxygenated tooth powder: See magnesii peroxidum cum creta. (42)

Oxymel (simplex); Oxym.; Oxim.: A potion prepared by evaporating a mixture of honey and vinegar to a syrup. (1)

Oxymel aeruginis: Honey with copper acetate. (3)

Oxymuriate: A chlorate salt or compound. (40)

Oxymuriate of soda: See sodae chlorinatae, liquor. (40)

Oxyneurine: See betaine. (40)

Oxyquinoline sulphate: Oxy- or hydroxy-quinoline is a topical disinfectant, bacteriostatic, and fungicide, still used in cosmetic formulations. (40)

Oxyquinotheine cachets: Oxyquinotheine is a pain reliever, and the cachets were used for the treatment of migraine. It appears to be a combination or chemical reaction product of quinine and antipyrene. (40)

Oxyrhodanum: A mixture of vinegar and oil of roses. (39)

Oxysaccara; Oxysaccharum: Syrup made by evaporating a mixture of sugar and vinegar, sometimes with pomegranate juice. (1)

Oxysulphuret of calcium, solution of: See calcis sulphurata, liquor. (31)

Oxytriphyllon: See luliula. (1)

Ozokenite: Earth-wax; an impure paraffin. (3)

P

P.: At beginning of inscription: pilulae (pills); pinguedo (grease, fat); pommade {*French*} (pomade); pulpa (pulp); pulvis (powder). At end of inscription: precipitatus (precipitated); praeparatus (prepared). (1)

Pacific pill: See thebaic pill, with added pimento. (39)

Pacifick pill (Bate's): Primarily opium (thirty percent) with a soap base, crocus, anthenum, and tartaric acid. (39)

Paeonia: Common peony (rarely seen as Piney), *Paeonia officinalis*. Petals, root, seeds used. A minor sedative and antispasmodic. Figure 3-183. (1,32)

Paeonia albiflora: A variety of peony native to eastern Russia and the Orient.

Paeonia composita, syrupus; Paeon. com. s.: Compound syrup of peony, with white wine, contrayerva, lovage, rosemary, hyssop, and many other ingredients. Often used to sweeten other preparations, or in nervous disorders. (35)

Pagenstecher's ointment: Ointment of yellow mercuric oxide. See hydrargyri oxidi rubri, unguentum. (24,40)

Paint: As a therapeutic, see pigmentum. (42)

Palacetyrus: Old cheese. (3)

Palm butter: Palm oil, see palmae, oleum. (40)

Palm spirit: See arrack. (40)

Palma; Palmae, oleum: 1. Date palm, see dactylus. Fruit used. 2. Coconut palm. Fruit used. 3. Palm-oil tree. Oil (oleum palmae) expressed from kernels of fruit. (1)

Palma, white powder of the Count of: See magnesia alba. (39)

Palma christi (, oleum); Palmi christi: Castor oil plant, *Ricinus communis*. Seeds (castor bean) or the oil therefrom used. The five-lobed leaf of this plant resembles a human hand, hence "palm of Christ." (1,3)

Palma rosae, oleum; Palmarosa, oil of; Palmarosae, oleum: Aromatic oil obtained from leaves of *Andropogon schoenanthus*, the Indian or Turkish geranium, which contains compounds similar to rose oil. (40)

Palsy drops: See lavendulae composita, tinctura. (3)

Panacea: 1. A cure-all. 2. Alchemical term, any substance prepared via a chemical process as opposed to naturally occurring, as in panacea mercurii rubra (red oxide of mercury). (1)

Panacea, liquid: Any liquid formulation of opium, typically twenty to twenty-five percent . (39)

Panacea, solid: A powerful pill of opium in soap. (39)

anacea antimonialis; —antimonii: 1. An evaporated mixture of sal tartari and antimonium muriatum (tartaric acid and antimony chloride or oxychloride). 2. A mixture of antimony, sal niter, salt, and powdered wood charcoal. Both items being used as a cathartic and emetic.

Panacea cinnabarina sive mercurius diaphoreticus: "Panacea of cinnabar or sweating mercury," presumably in reference to the ability of heated crude cinnabar to "sweat" metallic mercury. See Thompson's panacea. (39)

Panacea holsatica: "Sea kale" panacea, same as kali sulphuratum, potassium sulfate. (39)

Panacea mercurialis violacea: Purple mercury panacea, of calomel with sulfur and sal ammoniac. (39)

Panacea mercurialis: Calomel or calomel in spirits of wine. (3,39)

Panada; Panado: Bread boiled to a cereal in water, flavored to taste. A nutritive. (39)

Panarolis' Medicine: Ointment after Dr. Domenico Panarolis, Rome, ca. 1650, of sulfur and lemon juice combined in lard. (39)

Panax: *Panax ginseng*, see ginseng. (32)

Fig. 3-183 Paeonia or common peony.

Panax quinqefolia; Panax quinq.: *Panax quinquefolia* is Amerian ginseng, used interchangeably with Asian Ginseng. A panacea. Figure 3-184. (32)

Panchrestum, sal: Potassium tartrate. (3)

Panchymagogue; Panchymagogum: A medication purging all humors, pan (all) + chima (fluid) + agogus (to lead out).

Panchymagogum crollii, extractum: Compound extract of rhubarb, one of a range of laxative preparations containing rhubarb. (3)

Panchymagogum minerale; Panchymagogum minerali; — Quercetani: Calomel, or calomel as prepared by (see) Quercetanus. See hydrargyri chloridi mitis. (3,40)

Panchymagogum, extractum: Purgative preparation of colocynth pulp, agaric, scammony, aloes, black hellebore, etc. (1)

Pancreatic solution; Pancreaticus, liquor: See pancreatini, liquor. (31)

Pancreaticus, liquor; Pancreatini, liquor: Solution of pancreatin, liquor pancreaticus, pancreatic solution, made from pancreatin, sodium bicarbonate, glycerin, compound spirit of cardamom, alcohol, purified talc, and water, used as a digestive. (31) A simpler form comprised of glycerin of pancreatin, sodium bicarbonate, glycerin, alcohol, and water is specified in the BPC. (42)

Pancreaticus compositus, pulvis: Peptonizing powder, of pancreatin and sodium bicarbonate. This was generally added to foods, usually milk, to pre-digest. (42)

Pancreatin; Pancreatinum: A mixture of enzymes derived from animal pancreas, usually from swine. For use, see pepsin. (8)

Pancreatini, elixir: Elixir of pancreatin in sodium bicarbonate, alcohol, water, and aromatic elixir. Digestive aid. (42)

Pancreatini, glycerinum: Glycerin of pancreatin in glycerin, simple elixir, and water. Digestive aid. (42)

Pancreatis, liquor: A solution of fresh pig pancreas in alcohol specified in the BPC, distinct from liquor pancreaticus, mainly used to prepare "peptonized" or pre-digested foods. (42)

Pandeleon: An opium electuary. Pectoral. (39)

Pane's or Panne's serum: Anti-pneumococcal serum, for treatment of pneumonia. (40)

Panis: See panus.

Panis regius: Royal or king's bread, a cordial, stomachic, and pectoral electuary. Composition unclear. (39)

Pansecretin: A duodenal enzyme preparation, digestive aid. (40)

Pantopon: See papaveretum. (40)

Panus: Corruption of the Latin, *panis*, meaning bread. The incorrect form seems to appear more often than the correct. Panus properly refers to a rag or a patch.

Panus, emplastrum de crusta: See crusta panis, emplastrum de. (1)

Panus azymus: Unleavened bread ("a-zymus," without yeast), used as a pill coating. (39)

Papaber(is): Variant, see papaver(is).

Papain; Papainum: A strong proteolytic enzyme obtained from papaya, similar to pepsin, used as a digestive aid, applied topically to digest dead tissue or diphtheritic membranes, and injected to destroy tumors. (42)

Papaini, elixir: Elixir of papain in alcohol, water, and aromatic elixir. Digestive aid. (42)

Papaini, glycerinum: Glycerin of papain in glycerin, simple elixir, and water. Digestive aid. (42)

Papaini et iridini, liquor: A solution of papain and iridin in alcohol, water, and glycerin, a digestive aid. (42)

Papalis, confectio: Papal electuary, tablets of (see) althea. (39)

Papaver album: 1. Opium poppy (white), *Papaver somniferum (var. album)*. Leaves, seeds, flowers, capsules, and dried latex (opium) used. (1): 2. Extract of the seed pod of the white variety of poppy, but excluding the exudate from which opium is produced. Being less potent, it was felt appropriate for children. Figure 3-185. (39)

Papaver erratico, syrupus de; Papav Err. S.: Syrup of wild poppy. (35)

Papaver erraticum; Papav. Err.: wild poppy, red poppy. See papaver rhoeas. (1)

Papaver nigrum: Probably the black-specked opium poppy, *Papaver somniferum var. nigrum*. A variant of papaver album, Figure 3-185. (1)

Papaver rhoeas; Papaver rubrum: Red, field, or corn poppy, *Papaver rhoeas*. Petals used. Figure 3-186. (1)

Papaver somniferum: Opium poppy. See opium. (8)

Papaver(is) capsulae; —, syrupus (variant, papaberis, noted): Poppy capsules, see opium, or the syrup made therefrom. (33)

Papaveretum: A preparation of hydrochloride salts of poppy alkaloids. (40)

Papaveris, decoctum: Decoction of poppy, as adjunct to astringent injections (presumably to assist in diarrhea and cramping) and as a topical fomentation to treat pain of abscesses. (42)

Papaveris (liquidum), extractum: Dry or liquid extract of poppy (from capsules, free of seeds). (42)

Fig. 3-184 Panax quinquefolium or American ginseng.

Fig. 3-185 Papaver album or P. somniferum, opium poppy.

Fig. 3-186 Papaver rhoeas, red or field poppy.

Papaveris, syrupus: Simple syrup with tincture of poppy. (46)

Papaveris, tinctura: Tincture of poppy, a crude tincture of opium made of dried poppy capsules, glycerin, and alcohol. (34)

Papaya: Papaya, pawpaw, melon-tree, *Carica papaya*, a stomachic. See papain. (32)

Papayotin: Papain, a protein digesting enzyme, from the papaya. (40)

Paper, oil of: Oil obtained by burning paper on a tin plate. (40)

Papoose root: See caulophyllum. (40)

Para-thor-mone: Proprietary parathyroid hormone extract. (40)

Paracelsi specificum purgans: Specific purgative of Paracelsus, kali sulphureticum, i.e., potassium sulfate. (39)

Paracelsus, sympathetic ointment of: See unguentum armarium. (39)

Paracoto bark; Para coto cortex: See coto. (40)

Paracotoin: An active principal derived from coto bark. (8)

Paraffin dressing; —film: See curatio paraffini (31)

Paraffin scale: Paraffin flakes. (3)

Paraffini, emulsio: Emulsion of paraffin (BPC) or aseptic shaving cream; of hard paraffin, suet, soft soap, powdered tragacanth, glycerin, oil of lavender, and boiling water. This was recommended as a pre-surgical shaving cream and leaves a residue of paraffin on the skin. Not for general shaving. (42)

Paraffini, massa: Pill mass of mixed hard and soft paraffin, ratio adjusted to desired consistency, as an excipient for pills of silver nitrate, gold chloride, potassium permanganate, or other materials that are unstable in the presence of the water present in most pill masses. (42)

Paraffini, unguentum; Paraffin ointment base: A mixture of hard and soft paraffins. The relative proportions of hard and soft paraffins could be varied as desired to get anything from a soft eye ointment to a firm liniment. (42)

Paraffinum (molle)(flavum)(album): Paraffin, soft, yellow, or white.

Paraffinum carbolisatum: Carbolized paraffin, i.e., with phenol, a disinfectant used in wounds and as a lubricant for catheters, etc. (42)

Paraffin(um) chlorinatum: Chlorinated paraffin, no clear therapeutic use identified.

Paraffinum durum: Hard paraffin. (42)

Paraffinum liquidum: "Liquid paraffin," i.e., mineral (petroleum) oil. See petrolatum, liquidum. (40)

Paraform; Paraformaldehyde; Paraformum; Paraformic aldehyde: A polymerized formaldehyde used as a disinfectant, fungicide, and fumigant. (4,40)

Paragoric (elixir); Paragoricum, elixir: From the Latin, meaning "soothing." Alcoholic tincture of opium, flavored with aniseed oil and other ingredients. For relief of cough. (1) Estes (39) indicates a tincture of 0.2 percent opium with benzoin, camphor, licorice, anise oil, and honey, but also directs the reader to opii camphorata, tinctura, the camphorated tincture of opium. In the BPC, see camphorae composita, tinctura. (42)

Paraguay tea: See ilex (paraguariensis). (40)

Paraldehyde; Paraldehydum: Paraldehyde, $C_6H_{12}O_3$, is a condensation product formed from acetaldehyde (ethylic aldehyde, C_2H_4O). It is a pungent liquid used as a sedative hypnotic by the oral route, although the unpleasant odor must be masked in syrup, typically with tincture of orange peel. Paraldehyde is also used rectally, and is currently used to control intractable seizures when other agents fail. (8)

Paraldehydi, elixir: Elixir of paraldehyde in glycerin, alcohol, tincture of cardamom, oils of orange and cinnamon, and aromatic elixir. (46)

Paralysis (plant); Paralysis, syrupus: Cowslip, paigle, palsywort, *Primula officinalis*. Flowers and root used. Syrup of cowslip and other ingredients. Used to treat nervous disorders. Although Drey (1) lists "paralysis" as a botanical name, this is the only such occurrence noted.

Paralyticos, unguentum ad: Ointment for treatment of palsy. (1)

Paramorphine: See thebaine. (8)

Paranephrin: See adrenaline. (40)

Paraphakin: An evidently ineffective treatment for senile cataracts in the early twentieth century. (40)

Paraphthalein: Proprietary preparation of phenolphthalein. (40)

Paregoric: See opii camphorata, tinctura. (8)

Paregoric, Scotch: See opii ammoniata, tinctura. (40)

Pareira (brava); Pareira radix; Pareirae fluidum, extractum; —liquidum, extractum: Pareira brava, root of *Chondrodedron tomentosum*, of Brazil, or the fluid extract obtained by percolation with alcohol, water, and glycerin. It was used as a diuretic, urinary anti-inflammatory, and, at one time, for the treatment of kidney stones. (1,8) Although it has little activity orally, this is the botanical origin of curare, the paralytic toxin used on poison arrows and darts, active via injection. (39,42)

Pareirae, decoctum: Decoction of pareira root, for catarrhal diseases of the genitalia, i.e., venereal diseases. (42)

Parenol, liquid: Liquid paraffin; white beeswax and distilled water; a base for ointments. (40)

Parenol (solid): Soft paraffin with lanolin and distilled water; base for ointments and plasters. (40,42)

Parietaria; Parietar fol.: Pellitory of the wall, *Parietaria officinalis*, or leaves (folia) thereof. Herb used as emollient and diuretic. A source of potassium nitrate. Figure 3-187. (1,39)

Paris black: Animal charcoal, carbo animalis. (3)

Paris green: Copper arsenoacetate (copper acetoarsenite). (3) A pigment and insecticide.

Paris red: Vermillion dye. (40)

Paris white: Calcium carbonate. (3)

Paris yellow: Lead chromate. (3)

Parisen's vegetable specific: See oleorum camphorata, mistura. (34)

Parkesine: Celluloid, for forming pessaries and other items. (3)

Parodyne: Antipyrin. (3)

Parogen (, liquid)(, thick); Parogenum (spissum): Mixture of hard paraffin, liquid paraffin, oleic acid, and ammoniated alcohol. Ointment or ointment base. Liquid or thick (spissum) variants existed. (40)

Parogen cold cream: See refrigerans Galeni, ceratum. A variant using parogen. (40)

Parietaria officinalis

Published by D.? Woodville, May 1, 1792.

Fig. 3-187 Parietaria or wall pellitory.

Parogenum _____ (BPC): A parogen preparation (42) consisting of parogen and other ingredients, and used topically, including:

- **Chloroformi camphoratum**—with camphor and chloroform, a rubifacient and counterirritant.
- **Creosoti**—with creosote, for topical treatment of parasitic infestations, chronic eczema, or psoriasis.
- **Empyreumaticum**—with oil of cade, antiseptic, antipruritic for eczema and psoriasis.
- **Eucalyptolis**—with eucalyptol, antiseptic and mild rubifacient counterirritant.
- **Guaiacolis**—with guaicol, antiseptic and antiparasitic, for orchitis and phthisis.
- **Hydrargyri**—with mercury and lanolin (wool fat) in thick parogen, topical for syphilis and parasitic skin infestations and as a general replacement for older mercury ointments.
- **Ichthamolis**—Ammonium ichthosulphonate in parogen, for eczema and psoriasis.
- **Iodi (dilutum)**—with iodine, oleic acid, and ammoniated alcohol, a non-staining topical iodine preparation. The diluted form (sixty percent) was used for topical iodine when counter-irritancy was not desired.
- **Iodoformi (deodoratum)**—with iodoform, for injection in tuberculous abcesses. The deodorized form contained eucalyptol.
- **Mentholis**—with menthol, topical for local pain.
- **Naphtholis**—with naphthol, scabicide and for eczema and psoriasis.
- **Picis**—with tar (pine pitch), antiseptic and for psoriasis and eczema.
- **Salicylatum**—Ten percent salicylic acid in parogen, to clean foul ulcers and for eczema and psoriasis as well as applied to painful joints.
- **Sulphuris**—with sublimed sulfur and linseed oil, anti-parasitic.
- **Terebinthinae**—with turpentine, stimulant and rubifacient.

Paroidin: Proprietary parathyroid extract, hormonal (calcium regulation). (40)

Parrish's camphor mixture: See camphorae aromatica, mistura. (46)

Parrish's syrup: See ferri phosphatis compositus, syrupus. (42)

Parsley: See petroselinum. (39)

Parsley piert: See alchemilla, this is *A. arvensis*. (40)

Parsnip; Parsnip, water: See pastinaca or, for water parsnip, sium. (39)

Parthenium: Feverfew or featherfew, *Pyrethrum parthenium*. According to King's, "Tonic, carminative, emmenagogue, vermifuge, and stimulant. This agent is one of the pleasantest of the tonics, influencing the whole intestinal tract, increasing the appetite, improving digestion, and promoting secretion, besides having a decided action upon the renal and cutaneous functions." (33)

Partridge berry, oil of: Wintergreen, see gaultheria. For the oil, see gaultherium. (40)

Parturient balm: A balm for disorders of labor, of blue cohosh, spikenard, black cohosh, partridgeberry, queen-of-the-meadow, ladies' slipper, and comfrey. (34)

Pas d'âne {*French*}: Coltsfoot, see tussilago. (1)

Pasqueflower: See pulsatilla (nigricans). (39)

Passiflora; Passiflorae, tinctura: The passion flower, or passion vine, *Passiflora incarnata*, or the tincture thereof. Applied to hemorrhoids, used to treat skin burns or erysipelas, or internally for neuralgia. (3,31)

Passion flower, —vine: See passiflora.

Passula; Passula solis: Raisin, raisin of the sun, i.e., a sun-dried raisin. (1)

Passulae solis, lohoch e: Lohoch of (sun dried) raisins. (35)

Passuli; —minores: Raisins or Corinthian raisins (currants) respectively. (3)

Pasta: Paste, which could be made from water and a variety of dried ingredients. The term was not extensively used in American apothecary. This could be a topical dermatologic or ocular preparation, but often was a troche, pastille, or equivalent confection for oral use. Beasley lists a variety of "pastas," many of which are confections (pasta caracara, fig paste; pasta jujubae, jujubes; glycyrrhizae, licorice candy, etc.). Other examples are a good bit more sinister-sounding dermatologicals such as pasta escarotica arsenicalis (escharating arsenic paste) or pasta epliatoria (depilatory paste, of lye). (37)

Pasta _____ (BPC): A paste preparation in the BPC (42) including:

- **Hamamelidis**—stearic acid, sodium carbonate, glycerin, solution of hamamelidis (witch hazel), and water, a cleansing preparation for skin.
- **Ichthamolis**—ammonium ichthosulphonate, gelatin, glycerin, and water, for various skin conditions.
- **Ichthamolis composita**—ammonium ichthosulphonate, carbolic acid, starch, and water, for acne rosacea.
- **Iodi et amyli**—starch and glycerin with diluted solution of iodine and water, topical for syphilitic sores.
- **Lubricans**—carbolic acid, glycerin, tragacanth, and water. A catheter lubricant that is water soluble and does not damage rubber (unlike catheter oil).
- **Potassae et calcis; Potassae cum calce**—Potassium hydroxide and calcium hydroxide in alcohol. A caustic or corrosive for tumor destruction.
- **Resorcini (mitis)**—Resorcin paste in zinc oxide, starch, and liquid paraffin, for acne, eczema, and psoriasis, twenty percent resorcinol, or ten percent in the mild (mitis) form.
- **Theobromatis**—cocoa paste, i.e., chocolate, cocoa nibs triturated with sugar and vanilla. Flavoring and component of certain tablets.
- **Zinci composita**—of zinc oxide, starch, salicylic acid, and soft paraffin, for inflammatory skin diseases.
- **Zinci et gelatini**—glycerin, water, zinc oxide, and glycerin, for eczema.
- **Zinci et ichthamolis**—as immediately above, but with ichthamol.

Pasta bixas: See annatto. (40)

Pasta caustica: Vienna paste, see potassa cum calce. (40)

Pasta gummi: Marshmallow paste. See althea. (40)

Pastille fumigatus; Past. Fumigat.: Fumigating pastille, consisting, in general, of activated charcoal or powdered saunders treated with various essential oils, volatiles, or other perfumes to provide a pleasant scent or at times to prevent infestation, usually by insects. Dozens of variants exist.

Pastilles de Guimauve: Marshmallow paste. See althea. (40)

Pastillus _____ (BPC); Pastilli {plural}: Pastilles, as per the BPC (42) were formulated with glyco-gelatin, a mixture of glycerol and gelatin mixed hot and cooled in a tray, then cut to size. The hardness was controlled by increasing (softer) or decreasing the glycerol. Often contained acetomorphine (i.e., heroin). These were numerous and included:

- **Acetomorphinae**—acetomorphine, for pain.
- **Acetomorphinae compositus**—acetomorphine, ammoniated glycyrrhizin, and pine oil.
- **Acidi borici**—boric acid.
- **Acidi carbolici**—carbolic acid (phenol), as in modern throat lozenges.
- **Aconiti**—tincture of aconite (topical anesthetic).
- **Ammonii bromidi**—ammonium bromide, a bromide sedative.
- **Apomorphinae et codeinae**—apomorphine and codeine, for cough and expectorant properties.
- **Betacainae**—with betacaine (local anesthetic).
- **Bismuthi**—with bismuth carbonate.
- **Bismuthi et morphinae**—bismuth carbonate and morphine.
- **Boracis**—borax.
- **Cascarae sagradae**—with cascara sagrada (laxative).
- **Cocainae**—with cocaine for topical anesthesia.
- **Cocainae et morphinae**—cocaine and morphine, for cough.
- **Tussis**—see cocainae et morphinae.
- **Codeinae**—with codeine for cough.
- **Eucalyptolis**—eucalyptol, common in modern throat lozenges.
- **Eucalyptolis et cocainae**—with eucalyptol and cocaine.
- **Iodoformi**—with iodoform disinfectant.
- **Mentholis (et cocainae)(et codeinae)(et eucalyptolis)**—with menthol (cooling) to which cocaine, codeine, or eucalyptol could be added.
- **Morphinae**—with morphine.
- **Pepsinae**—with pepsin, a digestive aid.
- **Pini et terpini et acetomorphinae**—with pine oil, terpin hydrate (sedative) and acetomorphine.
- **Sulphuris compositus**—with precipitated sulfur and acid potassium tartrate.
- **Terebeni**—with terebene (from turpentine).
- **Terpini et acetomorphinae et mentholis**—with terpin hydrate (sedative), acetomorphine, and menthol.
- **Thymolis**—with thymol, disinfectant.

Pastinaca: Seeds of parsnip, *Pastinaca sativa*, used as an aromatic. Figure 3-188. (39) For rough parsnip, *Pastinaca opopanax*, see opopanax

Pate de Guimauve: Marshmallow paste. See althea. (40)

Patent mixture: See (a)etheris cum ammonia, mistura. (42)

Patiens, radix; Patien:, rad.: This is probably the root of patience, i.e., patience dock, *Rumex patientia*.

Patrum, pulvis: "Father's powder" (presumably in reference to clergy), see cinchona, this is the powdered bark. (40)

Paullinia: See guarana. (44)

Pavot {*French*}: See papaver album. (1)

Pawpaw: See papaya. (32)

Peach: See persica. (39)

Peachwood: See Brazil wood. (40)

Peacock's stomachic mixture: See sodae composita, mistura. (42)

Pear oil; Pear oleum: Amyl acetate. (3)

Pearl ash: Crude potassium carbonate. See lixivia. (39) This is wood ash with a pearlescent hue, not obtained from pearls.

Pearl barley: See hordeum (perlatum). (39)

Pearl moss: See chondrus. (3)

Pearl white: Bismuth subnitrate or subcarbonate. (3) Bismuth oxychloride or zinc oxide. (40)

Pearlash: See pearl ash. (3)

Pearly everlasting: See Life Everlasting. (33)

Pearson's (arsenical) solution: See sodii arsenatis, liquor. Pearson's solution is a 1:10 dilution of the USP formulation. (8,40)

Pearson's cerate: See plumbi, ceratum. (42)

Pece {*Italian*}: Pine tar, pitch, rosin. (1)

Pêche {*French*}; **Pêcher** {*French*}: Peach, see persica. (1)

Pectoral decoction.: See hordei, mistura. (40)

Pectoral drops; Pectoralis, tinctura; —, guttae: See opii et gambir composita, tinctura. (31)

Pectoral powder: See glycyrrhizae compositus, pulvis. (40)

Pectorale, electuarium; —, emplastrum; —, unguentum: Electuary, poultice, or ointment used for treatment of disorders of the chest. (1)

Pectorale, elixir: Compound ammoniated elixir of liquorice with oils of fennel and anise. (3)

Pectoralis, mistura: Stokes' Expectorant, senega and squill cough mixture with ammonium carbonate. (31)

Pectoralis, syrupus: Jackson's pectoral syrup, syrup of acacia with oil of sassafras and morphine hydrochloride. (46)

Pectorialis kurelte, pulvis: See glycyrrhizae compositus, pulvis. (40)

Pediculos, unguentum contra: "Ointment against lice," of sulfur, stavesacre seeds, etc. Used to control parasites of the hair. (1)

Pedis cati: Cat's foot, mountain cudweed, *Antennaria dioica*. Flower heads used. (1)

Peganum: See harmula. (1)

Pelargonium, oil of: Oil of geranium. (40)

Pelletierine; Pelletierina; Pelletierinae tannas: Brown alkaloid (or tannate salt) obtained from pomegranate bark or root, see granatum. Anthelmintic. (40,42)

Pellitory (Spanish); Pellitory, bastard or wild; Pellitory of the wall: See pyrethrum, ptarmica, or parietaria, respectively. (8)

Pellitory root: Root of pyrethrum. (40)

Pelosine: Beberine, see beeberu bark. (40)

Pelvis: Uncommon variant for powder, i.e., pulvis. (32)

Pencil, styptic: A pencil or stylus of silver nitrate (see argenti nitras fusas) or other common styptic agents, alum and/or copper sulphate. See related: lapis divinus.

Pencils, paste; —, unna: See medicamentorum, stili. (31)

Penidia; Penidiae; Penidium: See saccharum penidiatum. (1,39)

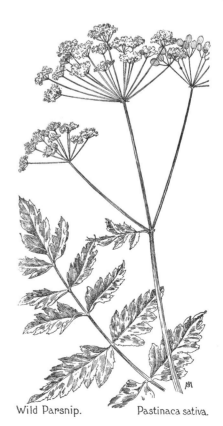

Wild Parsnip.   Pastinaca sativa.

Fig. 3-188 Pastinaca or parsnip.

Pennickwater {*Dutch*}: Pennyroyal water, i.e., liquor distilled from leaves of pennyroyal, see pulegium. (1)

Pennyroyal: American usage, see hedeoma. In British use, see pulegium. Either was abortifacient. (8,40)

Pennyroyal, American: See hedeoma. (40)

Pennyroyal, oil of: Oil of pulegium. (40)

Pental; Pentene; Pentalum: Trimethylethylene, or beta-isoamylene; a pentene isomer obtained from amylic alcohol, and used as an inhalational anesthetic. Said to be as effective as nitrous oxide. See amylene. (8,40)

Pentaphyllum: Cinquifoil, five fingers, *Potentilla reptans*. Herb and root used as weak astringent. Figure 3-189. (1,39)

Penthorum: Virginia stonecrop, *Penthorum sedoides*, for respiratory conditions. (32)

Peonia {*Italian*}; **Peony:** See paeonia. (1,32)

Pepe {*Italian*}: Pepper, see piper. (1)

Pepo; Peponis semen: Pumpkin, pumpkin seed. The seed of the pumpkin, *Cucurbita pepo*, was directly administered as an emulsion to treat tapeworm. It is said to be among the most effective and least harmful agents for this purpose. (1, 8)

Pepper: See piper (black pepper) or capsicum (cayenne or African pepper). (8)

Pepper bark: See winteranus, cortex. (40)

Pepper, red: See capsicum. (40)

Pepper, water: See persicaria. (39)

Pepperette: Olive pits (used to adulterate pepper). (3)

Peppermint: See mentha piperita. (8)

Peppermint (oil), Japanese: Japanese peppermint, *Mentha arvensis*, or the oil therefrom. (40)

Pepsin; Pepsina; Pepsinum; Pepsinum saccharatum; —, glyceritum: Pepsin, a proteolytic enzyme generally obtained from the glandular (inner) layer of pig stomach and dried to a fine powder. Saccharated pepsin consists of ninety percent lactose and the remainder pepsin, combined by trituration. The glycerite is in water and glycerin. Pepsin was used to assist digestion or to pre-digest proteins for oral or rectal administration to debilitated patients. For example, pepsinized meat suppositories could be made with extract of pepsinized beef and cocoa butter. (8,31)

Pepsinae, tablettae: Tablet, of powdered pepsin with sugar and ethereal solution of theobroma. Digestive aid. (42)

Pepsini, elixir: Elixir of pepsin. Made from glycerite of pepsin, hydrochloric acid, and aromatic elixir. "It is improbable the pepsin retains its enzymic activity in the presence of so much alcohol. It affords, however, a useful vehicle for certain salts, as the iodides or bromides." (31) In the BPC, of pepsin in alcohol, water, and simple elixir. (42)

Pepsini, essentia; Pepsin, essence: See pepsini, elixir. (42)

Pepsini (fortius), glycerinum: Glycerin of pancreatin in glycerin, hydrochloric acid, and water. Digestive aid. The stronger form contained simple elixir and additional pepsin. (42)

Pepsini (aromaticus), liquor: Solution of pepsin, of glycerite of pepsin, hydrochloric acid, glycerin, and water. One cc of solution will digest 10 gm of egg albumen. "It is too weak to be of therapeutic value." See pepsini antisepticus, liquor. (31) The NF and USP of 1880 specified a solution of saccharated pepsin, hydrochloric acid, glycerin, and water; and the NF also specified an aromatic form containing pepsin, oils of cinnamon, clove, and pimenta, alcohol, hydrochloric acid, glycerin, and water. (46)

Pepsini, pulvis: Powdered pepsin, digestive enzyme, as a digestive aid. (40)

Pepsini, vinum; Pepsin., vin.: Pepsin, hydrochloric acid, glycerin, and purified talcum in sherry wine. A digestive aid. (34)

Pepsini antisepticus, liquor: Antiseptic solution of pepsin, of five percent pepsin with traces of menthol, eucalyptol, and methyl salicylate. It is much stronger than the preceding (pepsini, liquor), as 1/10 cc will digest 10 gm of egg albumen. "It is used externally in the treatment of old sores to assist their healing." (31)

Pepsini aromaticus, liquor: See pepsini (aromaticus), liquor above.

Pepsini composita, mistura: A mixture of stronger glycerin of pepsin, solution of strychnine, diluted nitro-hydrochloric acid, glycerin, and water, colored with cudbear, a digestive aid for wasting diseases. (42)

Pepsini compositum, elixir: Compound elixir of pepsin, compound digestive elixir. The main difference between this and elixir of pepsin are the color and flavor, as it contains lactic acid, glycerin, alcohol, and oil of orange, and is colored with cudbear (see persio) "It is a pleasant vehicle." (3,31)

Pepsini compositus, pulvis: Digestive powder (NF) of saccharated pepsin, pancreatin, diastase, lactic acid, hydrochloric acid, and lactose; a digestive aid. (46)

Pepsini cum byno, mistura: A mixture of stronger glycerin of pepsin with malt extract and alcohol, nutritive and digestive aid. (42)

Pepsini et bismuthi cum ferro, elixir: Elixir of pepsin and bismuth with iron, of the stronger glycerin of pepsin, bismuth and ammonium citrates, iron and ammonium citrates, alcohol, and simple elixir. A sedative and tonic said to be useful for dyspepsia accompanied by anemia. (42)

Pepsini et bismuthi cum podophyllino, elixir: Elixir of pepsin and bismuth with podophyllum, of the stronger glycerin of pepsin, bismuth and ammonium citrates, podophyllum resin, aromatic spirit of ammonia, cochineal for color, and simple elixir. Said to be useful for dyspepsia accompanied by liver congestion. (42)

Pepsini et bismuthi cum strychnina, elixir: Elixir of pepsin and bismuth with strychnine, of the stronger glycerin of pepsin, bismuth and ammonium citrates, solution of strychnine hydrochloride, alcohol, and simple elixir. Said to be useful for "atonic" dyspepsia not accompanied by anemia (i.e., no need for iron, see the cum ferro version, above). (42)

Potentilla reptans

Published by Dr Woodville Decr 1. 1790.

Fig. 3-189 Pentaphyllum.

Pepsini et bismuthi et strychninae cum ferro, elixir: Elixir of pepsin, bismuth and strychnine with iron, of the stronger glycerin of pepsin, bismuth and ammonium citrates, iron and ammonium citrates, solution of strychnine hydrochloride, alcohol, and simple elixir. For "atonic" dyspepsia accompanied by anemia. (42)

Pepsini et bismuthi, elixir: Elixir of pepsin, bismuth and ammonium citrates, water of ammonia, glycerin, alcohol, syrup, compound elixir of taraxacum, purified talcum, and water. Digestive aid. (46) Elixir of pepsin and bismuth, made of pepsin and the glycerite of bismuth. Primarily a vehicle. (31)

Pepsini et ferri, elixir: Elixir of pepsin and tincture of citro-chloride of iron. Digestive aid. (46)

Pepsini et quininae [cum ferro], elixir: Elixir of pepsin and quinine, with or without iron, of the stronger glycerin of pepsin, quinine (hydrochloride), alcohol, and simple elixir, as well as iron and quinine citrates in the iron containing (cum ferro) form. A digestive and bitter tonic, and for concomitant anemia if with iron. (42)

Pepsini et rennini compositum, elixir: Compound elixir of pepsin and rennin. This elixir contains pepsin, rennin, and lactic acid. It is used chiefly as a vehicle. (31)

Pepsini, bismuthi et strychninae, elixir: Elixir of pepsin, bismuth, and strychnine, containing strychnine, pepsin, and glycerite of bismuth. "It is an irrational combination." (31)

Pepsinum aromaticum: A dry aromatic pepsin, digestive aid, of saccharated pepsin, tartaric acid, sodium chloride, and a small amount of aromatic fluid extract (USP). (46)

Peptenzyme (, elixir): A preparation of pancreatic digestive enzymes, intended to assist in dyspepsia and indigestion. A number of proprietary products were marketed. A particular US product by Reed and Carnrick was packaged in cobalt glass bottles and seems to be popular among collectors.

Pepticus, liquor: A solution of stronger glycerin of pepsin in hydrochloric acid, water, alcohol, and glycerin, a digestive aid. (42)

Peptonata, suppositoria: Nutrient suppository of peptone in cocoa butter, for rectal alimentation. (42)

Peptone (paste); Peptonum (bovinum): A water soluble protein hydrolysate (if beef, bovinum) providing amino acids. A nutritive. Various proprietary products have been marketed under these names, all of similar general composition, but protein sources vary. (40)

Peptonized iron solution: See ferri peptonati, liquor. (40)

Peptonizing powder: See pancreaticus compositus, pulvis. (42)

Peptonizing tablets: Pancreatin, i.e., pancreatic enzyme tablets, derived from livestock, as a digestive aid added to foods or taken orally. (40)

Pera {*Italian*}: Pear. (1)

Perborin: Sodium perborate. (3)

Perchloride of iron, tincture: See ferri chloridi, tinctura. (34)

Perfoliata: Hare's ear, thoroughwax, *Bupleurum rotundifolium*. Herb used. (1)

Perlatum, sal: Sodium phosphate. (3)

Permanent white: Barium sulfate (paint pigment). (3)

Permutit: Artificial zeolite used for water softening and purification. (3)

Peronin: Benzylmorphine hydrochloride, see morphine. (40)

Perpetua, pilule: See pills, eternal. (39)

Persian powder: Powdered flower-heads of marigold, see pyrethrum. (40)

Persica; Persicus: Peach tree, *Amygdalus persica*. Peach is a mild cathartic and said be sedative and anthelmintic. Note that flowers, leaves, and seed (stones) of the peach were utilized, not the fruit. (1,39)

Persica malus: See persicus. (1)

Persicaria: Water pepper, smartweed, *Polygonium hydropiper*. Herb used as tonic, diuretic, antiscorbutic, and discutient. (1)

Persicorum: "Of peach," in reference to *Prunus persicorum*. See prunus.

Persicorum, syrupus de floribus; Persicor s.f.: Syrup of peach blossoms. (1)

Persicum, philonium: See philonium persicum. (1)

Persimmon: See diospyros. (39)

Persio: Cudbear, a red to purple dried lichen of various species (*Rocella, Lecanora*, etc.), used as a coloring agent. (31)

Persionis (composita), tinctura: Tincture of cudbear, made of cudbear (persio), in alcohol and water; it was used as a bright red coloring agent. The compound tincture (composita) contained caramel and was used as a reddish-brown coloring agent. (31)

Peru, apple of: See stramonium. (39)

Peru, balsam of; Peruvinum, balsamum: Balsam of Peru, extruded from the trunk of the tree *Myroxylon pereirae*. (1)

Peru, rhubarb of: See mechoacanna. (39)

Peruvian bark; Peruvianus cortex; Peruviani cortex: Peruvian bark, cinchona bark, Jesuit's bark, dried bark of trees of the genus *Cinchona*. Source of quinine, used to treat recurrent fevers, especially malaria. (1) For preparations of Peruvian bark see cinchonae. While the bark is usually labeled Peruvianus cortex, preparations are more frequently labeled cinchonae.

Peruvianus, unguentum: Ointment of balsam of Peru, parasiticide. (42)

Pervinca: Periwinkle, plant of the genus *Vinca*. Herb used. (1)

Pesca {*Italian*}: Peach. (1)

Pessary; Pessaries; Pessi: A pessary is a medicated ring for vaginal insertion, of cocoa butter and glycerin, incorporating dissolved or suspended ingredients.

Pessus _____ (BPC): Pessaries of the BPC (42) include:
- **Acidi borici**—boric acid.
- **Acidi carbolici**—carbolic acid (phenol).
- **Acidi tannici**—tannic acid, astringent.
- **Aluminis et zinci**—alum and zinc sulfate, astringent.
- **Aluminis**—alum, astringent.
- **Belladonnae**—alcoholic extract of belladonna.
- **Cocainae**—cocaine.
- **Coniinae**—coniine.
- **Hydrargyri**—mercury ointment.
- **Hydrastis**—liquid extract of hydrastis.
- **Ichthamolis**—ammonium ichthosulphonate.
- **Iodoformi**—iodoform (disinfectant).
- **Plumbi iodidi**—lead iodide.
- **Quininae**—quinine hydrochloride.
- **Zinci oxidi**—zinc oxide.

Pestacchio {*Italian*}: Pistachio. (1)

Pestim, pilulae contra; Pestilentiales, pilulae: Antipestilential pills of aloe, myrrh, saffron, etc. See also pilulae Rufi. (1)

Pesto {*Italian*}: Crushed, ground. (1)

Petasites: Butterburr, member of genus *Petasites*. Root used as aperient, deobstruent, and aromatic. (1)

Peter, oil of: Presumably a corruption of *petrae oleum*, or "rock oil," i.e., petroleum. (39)

Peter's drops: See benzoini composita, tinctura, this version is flavored with oil of origanum. (40)

Peter's pills: Proprietary cathartic of aloes, calomel, gamboge, jalap, and scammonium; nineteenth century. (39)

Petitgrain, oil of: See aurantii amari florum, oleum. (40)

Petrae, oleum; Petre, oleum: Crude petroleum. (3,40)

Petrae, sal: Peter's salt, saltpeter, i.e., potassium nitrate. (3)

Petrolati, emulsum; Petrolei, emulsum: Emulsion of petrolatum containing about twenty-two percent each white petrolatum and expressed oil of almond (see amygdalae (expressum), oleum) with acacia, tragacanth, syrup, tincture of lemon peel, and water. (31)

Petrolatum (liquidum) (molle) (spissum): Petrolatum is obtained from petroleum by distillation to varying degrees to drive off lighter and more liquid components. By raising the distillation temperature, one can thus obtain liquid, soft (molle), and then hard (spissum) petrolatum. In the preparation of ointments, the forms can be mixed in various proportions to obtain a desired consistency. Petrolatum is familiar to most in the form of "petroleum jelly." (8)

Petrolatum, oleum: See petrolatum, liquidum. (40)

Petrolatum; Petroleum jelly: Soft paraffin, as available today. (40)

Petrolei, plasma: Plasma of petroleum oil with glycerin and starch. A topical for skin disorders, and for hemorrhoids. (34)

Petrolei compositum, linimentum: Liniment of petrolatum, ammonia water, and tinctures of opium and camphor. A counterirritant and analgesic. (34)

Petrolei cum glycerophosphatibus, emulsio: Emulsion of petroleum with glycerophosphates, of liquid paraffin, with calcium, magnesium, potassium, and sodium glycerophosphates, citric acid, gums of acacia and tragacanth, oil of cinnamon, elixir of gluside (saccharin), and water. A nutrient intended for phthisis, but said to be of highly questionable value. (42)

Petrolei cum hypophosphatibus, emulsio: Emulsion of petroleum with hypophosphites, of liquid paraffin, with calcium and sodium hypophosphites, citric acid, gum acacia, spirit of chloroform, tincture of lemon, elixir of gluside (saccharin), and water. A nutrient intended for phthisis, but said to be of highly questionable value. (42)

Petroleum (, crude)(, rectified)(barbadense): A general term for "rock oil," i.e., natural petroleum and its various distillates. Used as a liniment as well as a cathartic and anthelminthic, diaphoretic, and expectorant. (39)

Petroleum, Stockholm: Stockholm tar, i.e., petroleum or bituminous tar. (40)

Petroleum ether: See benzine. (8)

Petroleum naphtha: Ligroin, a petroleum distillate heavier than benzine. (40)

Petrolone: Asphalt. (3)

Petroselini radicis fluidum, extractum: Fluid extract of parsley root. (46)

Petroselinum; Petroselini, oleum: Parsley, *Petroselinum sativum.* Root, herb, and fruit (seed) used; or the oil (oleum) from seed. Carminative, aperient, diuretic, and emmenagogue. Figure 3-190. (1)

Petrosulfol: Synthetic ammonium ichthosulphonate. See icthamol. (40)

Petum: Tobacco. (1)

Fig. 3-190 Petroselinum or parsley.

Peucedanum: Hog's fennel, sulphurwort, *Peucedanum officinale.* Rhizome used. (1)

Peyote: See anhalonium. (32)

Pfeiffer's vaccine: An influenza vaccine. This was created using a bacteria, *Haemophilus influenza*, mistakenly believed to be the cause of influenza. (40)

Phagedrenic(a): Archaic term, of or related to ulcers, especially cutaneous ulcers as may occur in venereal disease, but may refer to gums or elsewhere.

Phagedrenica flava, aqua: See flava, lotio. (31)

Phagedrenica nigra, aqua: See nigra, lotio. (31)

Phalaris: Canary seed; see canariensis, semen et flora. (3)

Pharbitis nil; Pharbitisin: See kaladana. (40)

Pheasant's eye: See adonis. (32)

Phellandrium: Water hemlock, cowbane, *Cicuta virosa,* now *C. maculatum.* See cicuta virosa for comment. Herb used. (1)

Phenacaine: A local anesthetic. (40)

Phenacetin; Phenacetinum: Phenacetin, a synthetic antipyretic, para-acetylphenetidine. It is closely related to the modern acetaminophen, and safer than the predecessors, acetanilid or antipyrin. (8)

Phenacetini, tablettae: Tablets of phenacetin, glucose, potato starch, and (see) theobromatis, emulsio. (42)

Phenamine: See phenocoll hydrochloride. (40)

Phenates: Carbolates, i.e., carbolate (phenol) salts of metals, sodium carbolate. (3,40)

Phenazone; Phenazonum: See antipyrin. (8)

Phenetol: Ethyl phenate. (3)

Phenic acid; —alcohol; Phenicum, acidum; Phenylicum, acidum: Carbolic acid, see phenol. (3,40)

Phenobarbital; Phenobarbitone: A sedative and major anticonvulsant, still in use.

Phenocain: A local anesthetic. (40)

Phenocoll salicylate: Analgesic, see phenocol and salicylate. (40)

Phenocoll; Phenocol(l) hydrochloride; Phenocolli hydrochloridum: Amidoaceto-paraphenetidine, a mixture of phenetidine with glycocol, or amido-acetic acid, used as an antipyretic and analgesic. (3,8,42)

Phenol (cryst.): Phenol (crystalline), carbolic acid, the alcohol of benzene C_6H_5-OH.

Phenol, iodized: Iodine in phenol, 1:4. Disinfectant. (40)

Phenol bismuth: See bismuth phenate. (40)

Phenol cum camphora; Phenol camphor: Phenol (twenty-five percent) in camphor, topically for toothache. (42)

Phenol gauze: See carbolici acidi, carbasus. (42)

Phenol iodatum: Iodized phenol, antiseptic douche for midwifery. (42)

Phenolata, aqua: Phenolated water, a two percent solution of phenol in distilled water, used as a lotion, gargle, or general topical. (31)

Phenolax: Proprietary preparation of phenolphthalein laxative. (40)

Phenolin: Mixture of soap with cresol. (3)

Phenolis, glyceritum: See acidi carbolici, glycerinum. (42)

Phenolis soluto: See phenolata, aqua. (31)

Phenolphthaleine; Phenolphthaleini, tabellae: Phenolphthalene is a common laxative today, tablets were flavored with cinnamon and cocoa. (31)

Phenolphthaleini, solutio: Solution of phenolphthalein in alcohol and water, a pH indicator. (42)

Phenolphthaleini, trochisci: Purgative lozenge of phenolphthalein in chocolate. (42)

Phenolphthaleini compositae, tablettae: Tablet of phenolphthalein, green extract of belladonna, strychnine, starch, milk sugar, and (see) theobromatis, emulsio. Laxative. (42)

Phenoquin: See chincophen. (40)

Phenyl hydrate: See phenol. (40)

Phenyl methyl ketone: See acetophenone. (40)

Phenylacetamide: See acetanilid.

Phenylamine: Aniline. (40)

Phenyl-aspriodine: Acetyl-iodo-salol, analgesic derivative of salol. (40)

Phenylformic acid: Benzoic acid. (3)

Phenylhydrazinae hydrochloridum; Phenylhydrazine (hydrochlo-ride): An analytical reagent used to test for glucose, not therapeutic. (42)

Phenylic acid: Carbolic acid. (3)

Phenylii salicylas; Phenylsalicylate: See salol.

Phenylone: Antipyrin. (3)

Phenyl-sedaspirin: Acetyl-bromo-salol, analgesic derivative of salol. (40).

Phenylurethanum; Phenylurethane: Analgesic similar to phenacetin, but also claimed to have anti-inflammatory properties. (42)

Pheonigmus: A plaster of mustard, see sinapis. (39)

Philonium londonense; —Persicum; —Romanum; Ph. londin; etc.: Composite preparation containing opium. Used to relieve pain and induce sleep. Named after Philon of Tarsus, first century BCE. physician. (1) These were complex formulations, as indicated by Estes for Persian (opium, piper album, white hellebore, lemnian earth, hematite, crocus, camphor, and conserve of roses) or Roman (piper nigrum, white hellebore, cassia wood, parsley, sweet fennel, daucus creticus, crocus, and honey) phelonium. (39)

Philosophorum, oleum: Philosopher's oil, oil of bricks, oleagenous liquid obtained by distillation of a mixture of powdered brick or tile with olive oil. The name is an allusion to brick furnaces used in alchemical (philosophical) operations (1), or simply olive oil distilled over hot bricks. (3) See also brick oil.

Phloridzin(um); Phlorizin: Glycoside from the roots of fruit trees (genus usually *Prunus*—i.e., peach, cherry, etc.) that has anti-diabetic activity. (40)

Phloroglucin; Phloroglucinol; Phloroglucol: An isomer of pyrogallol. Analytical reagent for aldehydes. (40,42)

Phoenix dactylifera: See dactylus. (39)

Phosgene: Carbonyl chloride. (3)

Phosote: Creosote phosphate, see creosote. (40)

Phosph. co., syrupus: See ferri phosphatus, syrupus (approx). (40)

Phosphas calcis: Calcium phosphate, see calcii phosphas. (39)

Phosphas sodae: Sodium phosphate; see sodii phosphas. (39)

Phosphate mixture: A mixture of hartshorn (calcium phosphate) and sodium phosphate, for rickets. (39)

Phosphatica, emulsio; Phosphatica, mistura: An emulsion of cod liver oil, glycerite of egg yolk, diluted phosphoric acid, oil of bitter almond, rum, and orange flower water. Presumably a nutritive. (46)

Phosphatum acidus, liquor: Acid solution of phosphates, by dissolving calcium and magnesium carbonate in phosphoric acid and water. (31)

Phosphatum compositus, liquor: Compound solution of phosphates, "a polypharmacal preparation containing the phosphates of ammonium, calcium, iron, potassium, and sodium held in aqueous solution by the use of glycerin and citric acid. It is used for making the compound syrup of phosphates" (immediately below). (31)

Phosphatum compositus, syrupus: Compound syrup of the phosphates, "chemical food." With fifty percent compound solution of the phosphates (phosphatum compositus, liquor) in a vehicle of glycerin and syrup colored with cudbear (persio). "The apparently grandiose synonym is not so fanciful as it would seem for the composition contains the essential bases, calcium, potassium, sodium, and iron, as well as the equally essential phosphoric acid radical. As, however, it is difficult to conceive of a condition, short of actual starvation, in which there would be a lack of all of these mineral elements, the composition is not one which seems to us to be scientifically desirable." (31)

Phosphatum cum quinina et strychnina, syrupus: Syrup of phosphates with quinine and strychnine, compound syrup of hydrochlorophosphates, or hydrochlorophosphatum (compositum), syrupus; of quinine hydrochloride and strychnine nitrate in compound solution of phosphates (phosphatum compositus, liquor). (31)

Phospholutein: Lecithin, phospholipid emulsifier derived from fats and oils. (40)

Phosphorated oil; Phosphoratum, oleum: Oil of phosphorus, phosphorated oil, by dissolving elemental phosphorus in hot almond oil. (8)

Phosphorated soda: Sodium phosphate; see sodii phosphas. (39)

Phosphori [compositum], elixir: Elixir of phosphorus, consisting of spirit of phosphorus (phosphori, spiritus) with oil of anise, glycerin, and aromatic elixir. (8) In the BPC, the simple elixir is of compound tincture of phosphorus plus glycerin and the flavored version with anise oil is the compound (compositum) form. (42)

Phosphori, liquor: Solution of phosphorus, Thompson's solution of phosphorus, made from phosphorus, dehydrated alcohol, spirit of peppermint and glycerin, and used as a tonic and stimulant in nervous diseases. (31)

Phosphori, pilulae: Pills consisting of phosphorus dissolved in chloroform, to which is added althea, acacia, water, and glycerin. (8) In the BPC, of phosphorus in equal parts beeswax, lard, and kaolin, bound with gum acacia and carbon disulfide. (42)

Phosphori, spiritus; —, tinctura; —, elixir: Spirit of phosphorus. Tincture of phosphorus, by dissolving elemental phosphorus in absolute alcohol. Used to produce elixir phosphori. The elixir consists of the tincture plus spirit of orange (aurantii, tinctura) and oil of anise (anisi, oleum). (8,31)

Phosphori, syrupus; Phosphorus, syrup of: See phosphori compositum, elixir. (42)

Phosphori composita, tinctura: Tincture of phosphorus (about 0.2 percent) in chloroform and alcohol. Used in place of phosphorated oil. (42)

Phosphori compositae, pilulae: Pill of phosphorated suet, quinine sulfate, reduced iron, and strychnine, bound with compound powder of tragacanth, mucilage of acacia, and chloroform. (42)

Phosphori cum quinina, pilulae: Pill of phosphorated suet and quinine sulfate, bound with compound powder of tragacanth, mucilage of acacia, and chloroform. (42)

Phosphori et nucis vomicae, elixir: Elixir of phosphorus and nux vomica, of tincture of nux vomica (see nucis vomicae, tinctura) and phosphorus. (31)

Phosphori pentoxidum: Phosphorus pentoxide is a dehydrating agent for gasses. Not therapeutic. (42)

Phosphoric acid, syrupy; Phosphoric anhydride: See metaphosphoric acid. (40)

Phosphoric acid; Phosphoricum (dilutum), acidum: Phosphoric acid, ortho-phosphoric acid, H_3PO_4, from oxidation of phosphorus by nitric acid, of approximately eighty-five percent strength, or diluted to approximately ten percent. (8) First isolated from bones ca. 1640, used as a tonic, refrigerant, analgesic, antispasmodic, aphrodisiac, and antilithic. (39)

Phosphorici compositus, liquor acidi: Compound liquor of phosphoric acid, from bone ash and sulphuric acid. Use as per phosphoric acid. (34)

Phosphoricum concentratum, acidum: See metaphosphoric acid. (40)

Phosphorus: Elemental phosphorus, for use in preparation of other materials, from bone ash or lime phosphate treated with sulfuric acid and heated to form calcium metaphosphate, which is heated with charcoal to reduce phosphorus to the elemental form. This is white or yellow phosphorus, which is a waxy solid and bursts into flame on exposure to air. Treatment with hydrogen results in the less reactive red phosphorus. (8) Estes (39) notes that as this material produced light (phosphorescent), it was assumed to be the equivalent of combustive processes and thus useful as a tonic. It is, however, highly toxic. Ironically, we now know that cellular energy is in fact stored largely in the form of phosphates, i.e., adenosine triphosphate, or ATP.

Phosphorus, red: Amorphous elemental phosphorus. See discussion immediately above. (40)

Phosphorus salt: See sodii et ammonii phosphas. (40)

Photophor: Calcium phosphide. (3)

Photoxylin: Similar to guncotton, but made from wood pulp. (3)

Phu: Probably the plant *Valeriana phu*. Root used. (1)

Phyllis amara: Bitter almond bran. (3)

Phylonium: See philonium. (1)

Physalis (alkengi): Ground cherry, or yellow henbane, the berries of *Physalis viscosa*, a tonic, diuretic, laxative, and possibly sedative. (33,44)

Physeter macrocephalus: Whale oil, spermaceti, from the sperm whale, *Physeter macrocephalus*. (39)

Physic nuts: See Barbados nuts. (44)

Physostigma (venenosum): Physostigmine, also called eserine, derived from *Physostigma venenosum*, the calabar or ordeal bean. Consumption of the bean to produce hallucinations was a ritual of the natives of Old Calabar. Physostigmine is a direct antagonist of atropine and the other belladonna alkaloids (see belladonna). Used to increase oral secretions, enhance motility of the GI tract, and slow the beating of the heart, as well as for the treatment of glaucoma and to constrict the pupil. Used in the treatment of tetanus, although presumably with little effect. (8)

Physostigmata semina: Seed or "bean" of physostigma, i.e., calabar bean. (42)

Physostigmatis, extractum; —, tinctura: Dried alcoholic extract or alcoholic tincture of physostigmine, respectively. (8)

Physostigminae, guttae: Eyedrops (BPC) consisting of physostigmine, miotic. (42)

Physostigminae et cocainae, guttae: Eyedrops (BPC) consisting of physostigmine and cocaine, miotic and anesthetic. (42)

Physostigminae salicylas; —sulphas: Physostigmine (eserine) salicylate and sulfate respectively. (8)

Phytolacca (radix); Phytolaccae (fructis)(bacca): The fruit (fructis), i.e., berry (bacca) or root (radix) of pokeweed, *Phytolacca decandra*. An emetic and purgative. (8)

Phytolaccae compositae, pilulae: Compound pills of pokeweed, of extracts of pokeweed, stillingia, and stramonium. For bone pain, rheumatism, scrofula, and syphilis. (34)

Phytolaccae compositum, vinum: Compound wine of pokeberry, rheumatic liquid, of pokeberry juice, white turpentine, and sherry wine, for rheumatism and venereal disease. (34)

Phytolaccae compositus, syrupus: Compound syrup of poke, of pokeroot, American ivy, black cohosh, and sheep laurel. For syphilis, scrofula, and rheumatism. (34)

Phytolaccae (radicis) fluidum, extractum; —, tinctura: Fluidextract or alcoholic tincture of phytolacca (pokeweed) root. (8)

Phytolaccae, unguentum: Ointment of poke, of poke leaves, lard, and wax. For various skin conditions including tinea capitis. (34)

Piantaggine {*Italian*}: Plantain, see plantago. (1)

Pice; Piceae; Piceae: Pitch or tar. The singular nominative form is pix, genitive picis, although the ablative pice is also seen as are the improper genitive forms, piceae or piceum.

Pice, unguentum e; Piceum, unguentum: Ointment of tar. Used to treat skin disorders. Tar is still used to treat psoriasis in modern medicine. See pix. (1)

Picea, charta: Poor man's plaster, an inexpensive plaster of paper impregnated with pine resin or a slightly more sophisticated version with pine resin, pitch, and wax. Note that there are citations to "poor man's plaster" as relates to a finish for walls, not to be confused with the apothecary version. (40)

Piceae, pilule: Tar pill with pix liquida and enula. (39)

Picea excelsa: Spruce fir tree.

Piceum, emplastrum: A tar plaster. Estes notes that this was used for tinea capitis as it would exfoliate the hair at the root when removed. (39)

Pichi: Branches of the shrub *Fabiana imbricata*, of Peru and Chile, from which a non-standard fluid extract can be prepared. It is diuretic and has anti-inflammatory activity in the bladder, especially if given in combination with alkali such as sodium carbonate. (8)

Pichurim beans: Seed of uncertain tree from Brazil and region, a possible substitute for nutmeg, oil and bark used. Unofficial. (44)

Picis (burgundicae), emplastum: Plaster of Burgundy pitch (see pix burgundia), of Burgundy pitch, yellow wax, and olive oil. (8)

Picis alkalinus, liquor: A solution of tar and potassa (potassium hydroxide) in water. (46)

Picis burgundicae, emplastrum, compositum: Composite plaster of Burgundy pitch, emplastrum cephalicum. Prepared from Burgundy pitch, laudanum, mace oil, turpentine, and white wax. (39)

Picis canadensis, emplastrum: Pitch plaster of Canadian pitch in yellow wax. (46)

Picis cantharidatum, emplastrum: Cantharidal (burgundy) pitch plaster (see pix burgundia), of cerate of cantharides and Burgundy pitch. Also called a "warming plaster." (8)

Picis carbonis (compositum), unguentum: Ointment of coal tar in soft paraffin, with ammoniated mercury as well in the compound ointment. (42)

Picis carbonis, liquor: Coal tar solution, liquor carbonis detergens, made by digesting coal tar and soap bark with alcohol, used externally in skin diseases. (31)

Picis carbonis alkalina, lotio: Lotion of coal tar solution with sodium bicarbonate and water, for eczema. (42)

Picis compositum, elixir: Syrup of wild cherry, syrup of tolu (from pitch), morphine sulfate, methyl alcohol, water, and wine of tar. (46)

Picis compositum, unguentum: Compound tar ointment, of four percent oil of tar, tincture of benzoin, and zinc oxide in a base of yellow wax, lard, and cotton-seed oil. (31)

Picis cum canthaide, emplastrum: In the US, essentially picis cantharidatum, emplastrum above. The British form was prepared from coarse cantharides, water, oil of nutmeg, yellow wax, resin, soap plaster, and resin plaster. (44)

Picis liquidae, aqua; Picis liq., aqua: Pitch or tar water, a solution derived from water and tar containing the water soluble components of tar, and with a similar odor. Used internally, mainly for chest disorders. (33)

Picis liquidae, glyceritum: See picis pini, glyceritum. (46)

Picis liquidae, mistura: See olei picis, mistura. (34)

Picis liquidae, plasma: Plasma of tar in starch and glycerin. (34)

Picis liquidae, syrupus; —, unguentum; —, oleum: These are, repectively, the syrup of liquid pitch or tar (tar, water, glycerin, and sugar); the unguent (tar with yellow wax and lard), and the distilled, purified oil. For usage, see pix liquida (picis is the possessive form of pix). (8)

Picis liquidae compositum, emplastrum: Plaster of resin, tar, podophyllum, phytolacca root, and sanguinaria. (46)

Picis pini, glyceritum: Glycerite of tar, glyceritum picis liquidae, of tar, magnesium carbonate, glycerin, alcohol, and water. (31)

Picis, emplastrum: See picis burgundicae, emplastrum.

Picis, vinum: Wine of tar, containing tar, pumice, and stronger white wine (vinum album fortior). Used internally as a tonic or topically for skin disorders. (34)

Pickling acid: Sulfuric acid. (3) Acetic acid, vinegar. (40) The metal cleaning process called "pickling" is typically performed with sulfuric acid, the preserving process for foods with vinegar.

Picrasma (excelsa); Picrasmin: See Quassia.

Picric acid; Picricum acidum: Picric acid, or trinitrophenol, is a poison. It appears to have limited if any use in classical apothecary products, but is a part of the homeopathic arsenal, used to treat phthis (tuberculosis) and various cognitive and neurological disorders. Primary medical use was as a reagent in the test for protein in urine.

Picrici, acidi, lotio: Picric acid prepared at one percent in water and diluted further and applied to burns or wounds or topically for inflammatory skin conditions. (42)

Picronitric acid: See picric acid. (40)

Picrorhiza; Picrorhizae liquidum, extractum; —, tinctura: Dried rhizome of *Picrorhiza kurroa*. Picrorhiza was official in India and British colonies, a bitter and antiperiodic, used as the liquid extract or tincture. (42)

Picrotoxin; Picrotoxinum: Picrotoxin is a specific material derived from *Anamirta paniculata* (now *A. cocculus* in some sources), of India by exhaustive extraction with alcohol followed by evaporation, crystallization, and purification by recrystallization after decolorizing with charcoal. It was used as a topical antiparasitic. Picrotoxin is an excitatory nervous toxin and could cause serious toxicity if ingested or if excessively applied, especially to broken skin. It is also noted to be expensive. Small doses given systemically by injection (1/100 of a grain, or 0.6 milligrams) were thought to help the night sweats of tuberculosis. (8)

Pied-de-chat {*French*}**:** Cat's-foot, see pedis cati. (1)

Piermont water: Water from Pyrmont, Germany, considered a tonic due to iron content as well as a cathartic due to magnesium and sodium salts. (39)

Pigeon berry: See phytolacca. (40)

Pigmentum _____ (BPC); Pigmenta {*plural*}**:** "Paints," or therapeutic pigments, a series of unrelated liquid formulations of the BPC (42) designed to be applied to the skin (or sometimes throat) with a brush or other device. These included:

- **Calaminae**—of calamine, zinc oxide, glycerin, and rose water, soothing and astringent.
- **Chrysarobini**—of chrysorobin in solution of gutta percha, a non-staining ointment.
- **Iodi**—iodine and potassium iodide in water, for fungal infections and as a counterirritant similar to liquor iodi fortis.
- **Iodi carbolisatum**—Iodine, potassium iodide, phenol, glycerin, and water, an antiseptic for the throat.
- **Iodi compositum**—Iodine, potassium iodide, oil of peppermint, and glycerin, for the throat.
- **Iodi et olei picis**—see picis cum iodo in this entry.
- **Iodoformi compositum**—benzoin, prepared storax, balsam of tolu, socotrine aloes, and iodoform in methylated ether, as a surgical dressing for open surfaces, especially on the tongue.
- **Mentholis compositum**—menthol, thymol, and oil of eucalyptus in liquid paraffin, for nasal application in hay fever and catarrh.
- **Mentholis et toluol**—menthol, alcohol, ferric chloride, and toluene, antiseptic for diphtheritic membrane of the throat.
- **Picis cum iodo**—iodine in rectified oil of tar, for ringworm.

Pigmentum indicum: See indigo. (33)

Pigmentum picis cum iodo: A mixture of wood pitch or wood oil and iodine. Painted on skin for ringworm. (40)

Pilewort: See chelodonium (minus). (39) According to Hughes, American use is *Scrophularia marilandica* and British is *Ranunculus ficaria*. (40)

Pill coating solution: See acaciae composita, mucilago. (42)

Pill unique: A proprietary cathartic with mercury and antimony. (This is the correct word order, i.e., no comma was omitted.) (39)

Pill varnish: See sandarach solution. (42)

Pillola {*Italian*}**:** See pilula. (1)

Pills, eternal; —, everlasting; —, perpetual: "Pills of metallic antimony, about 15 grains each, which were recovered from the stool after use, washed, and re-used." (3) Economical—if somewhat unappealing—but probably did deliver a small dose of antimony with each use due to action of stomach acid on the pill.

Pillulae ante cibum: "Pills (for) before meals," generally a stomachic or digestive aid, typically of aloes. (39)

Pillulae aperientes: Aperient (i.e., laxative) pills. There were many variations, often containing rhubarb or aloe in combination with other ingredients, including vegetable laxatives or even cod liver oil.

Pillulae aromaticum: Aromatic pills, generally of aloe and guaiac. (39)

Pillulae benedictae: Blessed pills (not eponymously named), many variants, for various mental and internal conditions. (35)

Pilocarpi, elixir: Elixir of the fluid extract of pilocarpus with syrup of coffee, tincture of vanilla, and compound elixir of taraxacum. (46)

Pilocarpi fluidum extractum: Fluid extract of pilocarpus. (8)

Pilocarpinae, guttae: Eyedrops (BPC) consisting of pilocarpine, miotic. (42)

Pilocarpine hydrochloras; Pilocarpinae hydrochloridum; —nitras; —salicylas: Pilocarpine hydrochloride, nitrate, or salicylate from extraction of pilocarpus. (8)

Pilocarpus: Leaflets of *Pilocarpus selloanus* and *P. jaborandi*, both native to Brazil. Source of pilocarpine and lesser amounts of jaborine. Pilocarpine is a powerful cardiac depressant and miotic, increases salivary and gastric secretion and GI motility, and induces profuse sweating. Primary therapeutic use was as a sudorific. It is a pharmacologic antagonist of atropine and related belladonna alkaloids (see also physostigmine) and has been used as an antidote. (8)

Pilosella: Hawkweed, mouse-ear, *Hieracium pilosella*. Herb used. (1)

Pilula; Pillula: 1. Pill, plural: pilulae. 2. Pill mass, see massa pilulae. (1) The two "l" variant is common.

Pilula triplex; Pilulae triplicates; —triplices: See triplex pill. (34)

Pilulae ad prandium: See dinner pills. (34)

Pilulae antidyspepticae: Pills of strychnine, ipecac, and belladonna in mercury pill mass with extract of colocynth. For dyspepsia. (34,46)

Pilulae antineuralgicae: Antineuralgic pills of quinine and morphine sulfate, strychnine, arsenous acid, and extract of aconite leaf. (46)

Pilulae antiperiodicae: Warburg's, or antiperiodic pills, for fever, of rhubarb, angelica seed, elecampane, saffron, fennel, zedoary, cubebs, myrrh, white agaric, camphor, quinine sulfate, and extract of gentian; with or without aloes. (46)

Pilulae quadruplices: Quadruplex pills, pilulae ferri et quininae compositae, of iron sulphate, quinine sulphate, aloes, nux vomica, and extract of gentian. Cathartic. (34)

Pilulae sine quibus esse nolo: See sine quibus esse nolo, pilulae. (1)

Pilule {*French*}**:** See pilula. (1)

Pimenta; Pimentae, oleum; Pimento: Allspice fruit, Jamaica pepper, *Pimenta officinalis* (formerly *Myrtus pimenta*) from which a volatile oil can be distilled. It is used in the manner of clove oil (see caryophyllus) as a tonic and carminative. Figure 3-191. (1,8,39)

P

Fig. 3-191 Pimenta or pimento.

Pimentae, aqua: Pimento water, of the fresh material or the expressed oil in water. For flatulence and digestive disturbances. (33)

Pimentae, spiritus: See myrciae, spiritus and note relative to pimenta foliae, below. (42)

Pimentae foliae, oleum: *Pimenta acris* is a synonym for *Myrcia acris*. This is a synonym for myrciae, oleum, or oil of bay (leaf), not pimento. (42)

Pimpernel: See anagallis. (39)

Pimpinella; Pimpinellae, tinctura: Probably burnet saxifrage, *Pimpinella saxifraga*, or the tincture therefrom. Root used for many purposes: emollient, stomachic, resolvent, detergent, expectorant, diuretic, diaphoretic, febrifuge, alexipharmic, and antiscorbutic. Figure 3-192. (1,39)

Pimpinella anisum: See anisum. (39)

Pimpinellie, oleum: See anisi, oleum. (40)

Pinckneya pubens: A shrub in Southeastern US with bark said to be similar to cinchona. Unofficial. (44)

Pine tar: See pix liquida. (8)

Pinea: See pinus. (1)

Piney: A coruption of peony, see paeonia. (32)

Pinguedo: Fat, grease. (1)

Pinguedo: Lard. (3)

Pinguoleum: Fixed oil, i.e., not volatile, a fat. Usually lard. (3):

Pinus picea: Silver fir, alternative source of pitch (see pix burgundia) or turpentine (see terebinthina). Figure 3-193.

Pini, nucleus: Pine-kernel, pine-seed. (1)

Pini, oleum: Pine oil. See abietis, oleum. (40)

Pini, resina: Turpentine (solid, hard). (3)

Pini, syrupus: Syrup of oil of pine, alcohol, tincture of saffron, glycerin, magnesium carbonate, and simple syrup. A pulmonary antiseptic. (42)

Pini, turio: Pinecone. (1)

Pini, vapor olei: Oil of pine and magnesium carbonate in water, mixed with hot water and inhaled as a mild antiseptic in respiratory catarrh. (42)

Pini albae compositus cum morphina, syrupus: Compound syrup of white pine with morphine, by dissolving morphine sulphate in compound syrup of white pine (below). "It is an undesirable preparation as being not only of little therapeutic value but of encouraging the improper use of morphine." (31)

Pini albae compositus, syrupus: Compound syrup of white pine, syrupus pini Strohi compositus. This syrup is made from white pine bark, wild cherry bark (*Prunus virginiana*), aralia, balsam poplar buds (populus), sanguinaria, sassafras, cudbear (persio), chloroform, oil of sassafras, sugar, alcohol, water, and syrup. (31)

Pini canadensis cortex, pilulae: Bark of the Canadian hemlock spruce, *Pinus canadensis* or *P. abies*. Astringent that can be used as a pill, a powder for topical use, a liquid extract for oral use in diarrhea or hemoptysis, or injected (urethral) for leucorrhea. (42)

Pini canadensis liquidum, extractum: In the BPC, extract of pine bark in alcohol. Astringent for leucorrhea and gonorrhea. (42)

Pini empyreumatica, resina: See pix nigra. (33)

Pini et terpini et acetomorphinae, elixir; —, linctus: Elixir or linctus of pine with terpin hydrate and acetomorphine (heroin), of oil of pine, terpin hydrate, acetomorphine hydrochloride, alcohol, tincture of saffron (color), glycerin, light magnesium carbonate (to triturate the oil in formulation) and simple syrup. For cough and respiratory congestion. (42)

Pini strohi compositus, syrupus: See pini albae compositus, syrupus. (34)

Pini sylvestris, oleum; Pini sylvestris olei, vapor: Fir tree oil, by distillation from fresh leaves of the fir tree, *Pinus sylvestris*, Figure 3-194. Used as per turpentine (terebinthina), but the vapor produced by addition to heated water was much more pleasant to inhale as an expectorant. (8)

Pink salt: Stannic chloride. (3)

Pinkroot (, Carolina): See spigelia. (8,39)

Pino, lohoch de: Antitussive and antiasthmatic remedy from pine kernels and other components. (1)

Pinus; Pinus albus: Member of genus *Pinus*, pine, or the white (albus) pine. (1)

Pinus abies: See balsam, Canada (*Balsamum canadense*) and for details and illustration, Terebinthina canadensis. (39)

Pinus balsamea: Probably the same as pinus abies, i.e., *Balsamum canadense*. (39)

Pinus larix: Bark of the larch, *Pinus larix*, collected in spring, from which a tincture is prepared in alcohol. Sometimes referred to as tamarac. It is essentially an alternative source of turpentine (see terebinthina venata for details and illustration). Genitive form is laricis. (8)

Pinus pendulae composita, tinctura: See laricis composita, tinctura. (34)

Pinus sylvestris: Scotch fir, *Pinus sylvestris*, figure 3-194. See entries for Pini sylvestris, above.

Piombo {*Italian*}: Lead (metal). (1)

Fig. 3-192 Pimpinella.

Fig. 3-193 Pinus picea, pitch pine or silver fir.

Fig. 3-194 Pinus sylvestris, Scotch fir.

Piombo, unguento di {Italian}: See plumbo, unguentum de. (1)

Piony: Variant of peony, see paeonia. (35)

Piper (nigrum); Piperis, oleoresina: When unspecified, black pepper, the unripe fruit of *Piper nigrum*, of Indian origin, from which an oleoresin can be extracted using ether, which is then evaporated away. The oleoresin or pepper itself can be used like other volatile oils (see caryophyllus), and was thought to be a mild antipyretic. It remains in use as a condiment, and could also be given in the form of a confection. Stimulant and carminative. Figure 3-195. (1,8)

Piper alba: White pepper, the source is *Piper nigrum* (below), the colored husk of the seed being removed prior to grinding. (39)

Piper indicum: Cayenne pepper, bird pepper, *Capsicum frutescens*, stimulant and digestive. (39) See capsicum annuum.

Piper longum: Long pepper, the fruit or distilled oil. Introduced to Europe from the West Indies in the mid-1500s. Stimulant and carminative. Figure 3-196. (39,42)

Piper nigrum; Piperis nigri; Piper nig.: Black pepper, see piper (nigrum) above.

Piperadine; Piperidinae tartras; —citras: Hexahydropyridine, by distillation from piperine, in turn derived from pepper, used as tartrate or citrate salt. Said to have weak activity similar to coniine, rarely used for rheumatism and gout. (42)

Piperazidine; Piperazine, Piperazinum (effervescens): Piperazine, injected subdermally in gout and rheumatism, although the benefit was evidently disputed. The BPC had an effervescent formulation of piperazine with sodium bicarbonate, tartaric and citric acids, and refined sugar. (8,40)

Piperin; Piperina: A crystalline material derived from an alcohol extract of black pepper, *Piper nigrum*, and responsible for much of the flavor. The purity and identity of this material is not terribly clear, but it is said to be a febrifuge, antiperiodic, carminative, and stomachic and to be useful in conjunction with quinine. See piper. (29,42)

Piperis, confectio: A confection of pepper (BP), of ground pepper, caraway, and honey, used particularly for relief of hemorrhoids, rectal ulcers, and anal fissures. (8)

Piperis, oleum: Oil of (black) pepper.

Piperis nigri, unguentum: Ointment of black pepper, of same in lard with suet and tar. For tinea capitis. (34)

Piperyl-piperidine: See piperine. (40)

Pipsissewa: See chimaphila. (8)

Pirethrum: See pyrethrum. (1)

Pirum: See pyrum. (1)

Piscarol: Ammonium ichthosulphonate. See icthamol. (40)

Piscidia: Bark of the root of Jamaican dogwood, *Piscidia erythrina*, from which a non-standard extract was prepared. Said to be a narcotic, constricting the pupil and reducing pulse rate, valuable as a local anodye in toothache, and used as well for neuralgia, nervous insomnia, and in combination with viburnum for dysmenorrhea. (8)

Piscidiae liquidum, extractum: Liquid extract of piscidia in alcohol. (42)

Pisilio: See psilio. (1)

Pisselaeum indicum: Petroleum. (3)

Pistachia (vera), nux; Pistacia; Pistachio: Pistachio. See nux pistachia. (1,39) Pistachia can also refer to mastiche. (39)

Pistacia terebinthus: See chian turpentine. (40)

Pitch: See pix. (8)

Pitch, white: Burgundy pitch, see pix burgundia. (40)

Pitcher plant: See melilotus. (32)

Pitibulin; Pituglandol; Pituitrin: Various proprietary posterior pituitary hormone extracts. (40)

Pitimo: See epitemo. (1)

Pituitarium totum, —anterior; —, posterior: Dried whole or partial pituitary gland of cow, pig, or sheep. For endocrine disorders. The entire gland could be used to contract the uterus (oxytocin, vasopressin), to treat diabetes insipidus (antidiuretic hormone), to promote sexual development, or to enhance growth (growth hormone). Anterior pituitary was used to control uterine bleeding, reverse diabetes insipidus, or to retain fluid in shock. The posterior, for dysmenorrhea or hypermenorrhea, to promote sexual development or ovarian function, and for growth. The disadvantages of the mixed preparations are obvious, and this has been replaced by growth hormone, other purified pituitary hormones, or hormones produced by end organs in response to pituitary stimulation (estrogens, progestins, androgens, corticosteroids, etc.). (7)

Pivoine {French}: See paeonia. (1)

Pix: Pine tar, pitch, rosin. (1) Note—the genitive form of pix is picis, although the variant piceae and the ablative pice are often seen in place of picis.

Pix abies; Pix abretina; Pix alba: See pix burgundia. (39,40)

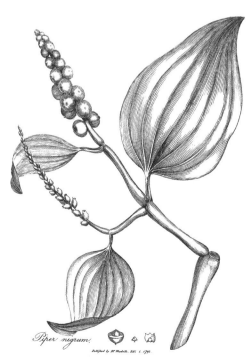

Fig. 3-195 Piper (nigrum) or black pepper.

Fig. 3-196 Piper longum.

Pix burgundia: Burgundy pitch, prepared from the conifer, *Abies excelsior*, of Southern Europe (Burgundy). This is described as a hard and brittle pitch, which was nonetheless slightly plastic, "gradually taking the form of the vessels in which it is kept." (1,8) Not always distinguished clearly from pix canadensis (below), derived from a closely related North American species.

Pix canadensis: Same as balsamum canadensis, see terebinthina canadensis. (39)

Pix carbonis praeparata: Prepared coal tar, of crude coal tar heated and stirred at 49° C for one hour to drive off volatile components. To prepare liquor picis carbonis. (42)

Pix carbonis; Picis carbonis (, aqua): Coal tar and coal tar water, used in a manner similar to picis liquida. (33)

Pix liquida: "Liquid pitch," pine tar derived by destructive distillation of pine species, i.e., at temperatures high enough to cause blackening of the material. Pitch was a complex mixture of cresols, phenol, and other partially oxidized and non-oxidized hydrocarbons. Use was as per turpentine (terbenthina), but it is said to be less potent and more prone to upsetting the digestion. Note that preparations using pix liquida may be found under the possessive form, picis. (8)

Pix mineralis: Asphaltum, butiminous tar. (40)

Pix nigra: Black pitch, the dark residue left after distillation of pitch to produce pitch oil (see picis, oleum). Used topically for skin disorders. (33)

Pix solida: See pix nigra. (33)

Pix vegetabilis: Black pitch, plant matter derived. (40)

Placent(a): A flat cake or pancake in Latin, refers to a small cake or wafer of material, as in cera alba placent(a), small cakes of white wax.

Planche's purgative: See scammonii, lac. (40)

Planocaine: Novocain, a local anesthetic. (40)

Plantaginus semen; Plantago psyllium; Plant. ps., sem.: Psyllium seed, seed of *Plantago psyllium*, see psyllium. (7)

Plantago: Greater plantain, *Plantago major*, and related species. Herb used. Astringent and to treat envenomations of snakes, spiders, and insects. Figure 3-197. (1,39)

Plantains: Term evidently used irregularly to refer to plantago (the modern usage), psyllium, or satyrion. (39)

Plasma: Glycerite of starch, or a topical plaster-like or unguent-like material made with glycerin and starch. (3,34)

Plasmochin; Plasmoquin: A synthetic antimalarial. (40)

Plaster, adhesive: Per the BPC, an alternate name for resinae, emplastrum. However, also see emplastrum adhaesans. (42)

Plaster, Nuremberg: Brown plaster, mother plaster, see fustum, emplastrum. (3)

Plaster, strengthening: See ferri, emplastrum. (40)

Plaster of Paris: See calcii sulphas exsiccatus. (8)

Platini chloridi, solutio: Analytical solution, non-medicinal, of platinum foil in hydrochloric and nitric acids. (42)

Plenk's solution: See mercurialis simplex, solutio. (39)

Pleres arconticon: A cephalic mixture, otherwise unspecified. (39) Probably related or identical to pleres arconticum, below.

Pleres arconticum, electuarium; Pliris aconitum, electuarium: Electuary of pearls, red coral, musk, aloe-wood, cinnamon, cloves, nutmeg, roses, violets, etc. Used as a tonic and in treatment of melancholy. (1)

Pleurisy root: See asclepias. (8)

Pll.: {*Italian*}: Pillole, pills. (1)

Plum, java: See jambul. (32)

Plum stones, oil of: Oil from plum (prunis) kernels. (40)

Plumbago: Black lead ore. In the USP, plumbago refers to lead ore, but the term is also used for similar looking materials, especially graphite. Further, the genus *Plumbago* is a common flowering ornamental herb and *P. zelonica* and other species were used as medicinal plants by indigenous peoples and can be found in American herbal texts. (3)

Plumbago europea: Leadwort or dentillaria, root chewed to relieve toothache. Unofficial. (44)

Plumbi, aqua: See plumbi subacetatis dilutus, liquor. (40)

Plumbi, ceratum: Lead plaster (plumbi, emplastrum) with yellow beeswax and almond oil, a soothing material for eczema and irritated skin conditions. (42)

Plumbi, emplastrum: Lead plaster, or oleate of lead, sometimes called diachylon plaster. Formed by boiling lead oxide and olive oil in water, which forms the lead salt of fatty acids, liberating glycerol. The resulting mass is kneaded to remove the glycerol and divided into rolls or masses of desired size. Frequently used as a base material for plasters containing additional ingredients. (8)

Plumbi, liquor: See plumbi subacetatis dilutus, liquor. (40)

Plumbi (cum opio), lotio: Lotion of 1.25 percent lead acetate in water, "astringent and sedative" lotion for sprains and bruises, as well as for inflammatory skin conditions. Five percent tincture of opium could be added. (42)

Plumbi, olea(ti)s; —, oleatum: Lead oleate, obtained by reaction of hot alkaline oleic acid with lead acetate. (42)

Plumbi, unguentum: See plumbi carbonatis, unguentum. (40)

Plumbi acetas (pura)(liquor): Lead acetate, $Pb(C_2H_3O_2)_2$, cerussa acetata, album Rhazes, or sugar of lead due to the sweet taste of this compound, by dissolution of metallic lead in acetic acid. May be described as pure or as a "liquor" (aqueous solution). Primarily used in preparation of remedies containing lead subacetate. (8)

Plumbi acetatis, lotio: Lotion of lead acetate and dilute acetic acid in water, essentially same as lotio plumbi. (42)

Plumbi acetatis, unguentum; Plumb. ac., ung.: Ointment of lead acetate, of same in benzoinated lard or, in the BP, paraffin. For skin conditions and wounds. (34)

Plumbi carbonas; Plumbi carbonatis: Lead carbonate, usually a mixture of carbonate ($PbCO_3$) and hydrate ($Pb(OH)_2$), formed by exposing lead to a mixture of acetic acid vapor and carbon dioxide. (8)

Plumbi carbonatis, unguentum: Lead carbonate (plumbi carbonas) in benzoinated lard. (8)

Plantago major

Fig. 3-197 Plantago or greater plantain.

Plumbi composita, suppositoria: Suppository of lead acetate and opium powder in cocoa butter, astringent for hemorrhoids. (42)

Plumbi compositum, ceratum: A cerate of yellow beeswax with olive oil, camphor, and solution of lead subacetate (plumbi subacetatis), for inflamed surfaces, chilblains, and other skin conditions. (42)

Plumbi compositum, unguentum: Compound lead ointment, Mayer's ointment, of olive oil, turpentine, beeswax, butter, red lead, honey, and powdered camphor. For skin conditions and wounds. (34)

Plumbi cum opio, pilulae: Pills of lead acetate and opium powder bound with syrup. (42)

Plumbi cum opio, tablettae: Tablets of lead acetate, powdered opium, sugar, and ethereal solution of theobroma. (42)

Plumbi diacetatis, liquor: See plumbi subacetatis forte, liquor. (40)

Plumbi et opii, lotio: Lotion of lead and opium, lead and opium wash, of lead acetate and tincture of opium, used as an astringent and sedative by external application. (31)

Plumbi evaporans, lotio: Essentially same as lotio plumbi, but with twenty percent alcohol, which evaporates and cools the skin. (42)

Plumbi fortis, liquor: See plumbi subacetatis forte, liquor. (40)

Plumbi hebrae, unguentum: Lead ointment of the Hebrews, see diachylon, unguentum. (34)

Plumbi iodidi, emplastrum: Plaster of lead iodide in lead plaster (plumbi, emplastrum) and resin, for joint pains, swollen glands, and as a minor counterirritant for pain. (42)

Plumbi iodid(i)(um), unguentum: Unguent of lead iodide in benzoinated lard. Said to be useful for glandular enlargements. (8,34)

Plumbi iodidum: Lead iodide, PbI_2. A bright yellow powder formed by reaction of sodium iodide with lead nitrate. (8)

Plumbi nitras: Lead nitrate, $Pb(NO_3)_2$, from action of nitric acid on lead. (8)

Plumbi oleatis, unguentum: Ointment of lead oleate. See plumbi, emplastrum above for details and also diachylon, unguentum. Note that the "oleate" is formed by reaction of lead with oil (oleum), specifically with the fatty acids, oleic acid among them. (40)

Plumbi oxidum rubrum: Red lead is lead oxide, Pb_3O_4. (8)

Plumbi oxidum: White lead oxide, PbO, or litharge, from roasting of metallic lead in air. Primarily for preparation of further remedies.

Plumbi subacetatis (dilutus), liquor: Solution of lead subacetate (see plumbi subacetatis) and lead oxide in water, Goulard's extract. It is used topically. Various dilute forms were specified over time in the BP and USP. (8,44) The dilute solution is said to be "too weak to be of any real value." (31)

Plumbi subacetatis forte, liquor; Plumb. Subacet. Fort., Liq.: A strong solution of lead subacetate, lead water. See the "dilutis" form above. (40)

Plumbi subacetatis, [glycerinum] [glycerita] [glyc.] [unguentum]: Glycerite of lead subacetate in glycerin and water, also referred to as an unguent (but see also unguentum glycerini, below) and generally used as a base for the preparation of topical ointments. (42)

Plumbi subacetatis, ceratum: Cerate of lead subacetate, a mixture of lead subacetate with camphor cerate. (8)

Plumbi subacetatis, linimentum: Liniment of lead subacetate in cottonseed oil used for chapping and skin irritation. (8)

Plumbi subacetatis, unguentum glycerini: Ointment from glycerin of lead subacetate in paraffin ointment base. (42)

Plumbi subacetatis; —, linimentum: Lead subacetate (see plumbi acetas), $Pb_2O(C_2H_3O_2)_2$ formed from lead acetate, or a liniment of same in cottonseed oil used for chapping and skin irritation. (8)

Plumbo, unguentum de: Ointment of calcined lead, litharge, ceruse, antimony, rose oil, turpentine, and yellow wax. Used in treatment of ulcers. (1)

Plumbum: Lead. Various compounds of lead were used primarily as topical treatments for skin conditions and to treat oral ulcers. Lead salts were used internally as astringents and haemostatics, but were substantially toxic, limiting their utility. (1,8) See entry above lead compounds (plumbi).

Plumbum album: "White lead," acually a term for tin when referring to a metallic form, not the white lead oxide. (3)

Plumbum scyto(-)depsic[um][i] (, unguentum): Moist lead tannate. (3,40)

Plummer's pills: See antimonii compositi, pilulae. (8) Said to originally contain golden sulphurette, calomel, and gentian with soap, later the mild mercurial pill, hydrargyri chloridi mitis. After Dr. Andrew Plummer, Edingurgh, ca. 1733.

Plunkett's remedy: Arsenic. (39)

Plutonium: Barium (name later assigned to the unrelated element plutonium). (3)

Pluvialis, aqua: Rain water. (3)

Po.: Powdered or pulverized.

Pocula emetica: Emetic cup, same as cuppa emetica. (39)

Pod pepper: See capsicum. (40)

Podalyria tinctoria: Dye of Podalirius (son of Aesculapius), see sophora, tinctoria. (39)

Podophylli, extractum; —fluidum, extractum; —, resina; —, tinctura: The dry extract, fluid extract, resin or tincture extracted from the root of May apple. (8)

Podophylli, resinae, trochisci: Troches of podophyllum resin, of same with oil of sassafras, sugar, and gum tragacanth. A cholegogue and alterative for constipation, hepatic disorders, dysentery, etc. (34)

Podophylli (ammoniata), tinctura: Simple alcoholic tincture of podophyllum resin, purgative and cholegogue. Alternatively prepared in aromatic spirits of ammonia. (42)

Podophylli compositae, pilulae: Purgative pill of podophyllum resin and calomel, with alcoholic extract of belladonna to reduce cramping, bound with milk sugar and syrup. (42)

May Apple. Podophyllum peltatum.

Fig. 3-198 Podophyllum or mandrake.

Podophylli compositae, resinae, pilulae: Compound pills of podophyllum resin, with scammony, gamboge, and soap. Useful for hepatic disorders and as a cathartic. (34)

Podophylli compositae, tablettae: Tablet of podophyllum resin, mercurous chloride (calomel), alcoholic extract of belladonna, and (see) theobromatis, emulsio. Purgative with belladonna to reduce cramping. (42)

Podophylli compositus, pulvis: Powder of podophyllum with bitter root, swamp milkweed, and bloodroot. For severe constipation, hepatic conditions, dyspepsia, worms, scrofula, rheumatic diseases, syphilis, etc. (34)

Podophylli compositus, resinae, pulvis: Compound powder of resin of podophyllum, hydragogue powder, of the resin and potassium bitartrate. For dropsy and obstructed menstruation. (34)

Podophylli (et) belladonnae et capsici, pilulae: Squibb's compound pills of podophyllum, belladonna, and capsicum, with milk sugar, acacia, glycerin, and syrup. A laxative and cathartic. (34)

Podophylli et belladonnae et nucis vomicae, pilulae: Podophyllum resin and extracts of nux vomica and Barbados aloes, with alcoholic extract of belladonna to reduce cramping. Purgative. (42)

Podophyllum indicum; Podophylli indici [resina][rhizoma]; —, tinctura: Indian podophyllum (*P. emodi*) was used as per podophyllum in India and eastern British colonies and was official in the BPC. A simple alcoholic tincture of the resin was specified. (42)

Podophyllum; Podophylli resina; —rhizoma: The rhizome and roots of American mandrake, *Podophyllum peltatum*, also called the May apple of North America, from which an active resin can be derived. (For Asiatic mandrake, see mandragora.) It is both a cholegogue (increasing bile secretion) and purgative, "especially suitable for hepatic disorders." As it causes significant gripping, it is recommended that it not be used alone, but with other cathartics such as calomel and with anticholinergics, like hyoscyamus or belladonna (as above) to reduce cramping. Figure 3-198. (8,42)

Poison berry: See melia azaderach. (39)

Poison hemlock: See cicuta. (39)

Poison ivy; Poison oak: See rhus toxicodendron. (8)

Poison nut: Nux vomica. (3)

Poison parsley: See conium, this is poison hemlock. (3)

Poison tobacco: Hyoscyamus. (3)

Poivrette: Olive pits (ground); adulterant of pepper. (3)

Pokeberry; Pokeweed: See phytolacca. (8)

Pokeroot: Irregularly used for helleborus albus, phytolacca (pokeweed), and veratrum viride. (39)

Polemonium: American Greek valerian, sometimes blue bells or Jacob's ladder, *Polemonium reptans*; an alterative, diuretic, and astringent. (33)

Polmone di volpe, loch di {*Italian*}**:** Lohoch of fox's lung, see pulmone vulpis, lohoch de. (1)

Polvere {*Italian*}**:** Powder. (1)

Polychreste; Polychrestum, sal (glaseri); Polychristum, balsam (glaseri); Polychris: From the Greek, "much useful," i.e., treats many conditions. Also known as sal polychrestum Glaseri after Christopher Glaser, seventeenth-century apothecary to the king of France, who introduced it. Consists of potassium sulfate (see arcanum duplicatum). (3,39)

Polychrestum seignetti, sal: Seignette salt, Rochelle salt, potassium sodium tartrate after Elie Seignette, b. 1632, France. See potassii et sodii tartras. (1,3,39).

Polychrestum stibiale, sal: Antimony salt of many virtues or many uses, antimony panacea, an unspecified mixture of antimonial compounds. (39)

Polychrestus, sal: Potassium sulfate. (3)

Polychroit: Colored material derived from saffron, see crocus. (40)

Polygala: Common milkwort, *Polygala vulgaris* or *P. rubella*. Herb used as a tonic and in large doses a laxative and diaphoretic. (1,44)

Polygala senega: See senega. (39)

Polygonatum: See convallaria. (39)

Polygoni, tinctura: Tincture of polygonum. For menstrual disorders. (34)

PPolygonum: Knot-grass, knot-weed, water-pepper, *Polygonum aviculare*. Herb used. (1)

olygonum bistorta; —hydropiper: See, respectively, bistorta or persicaria. (39)

Polygonum compositae, pilulae: Compound pills of water-pepper, with iron sulphate, resin of cimicifuga and iris, and extract of water pepper. An emmenogogue and for menstrual and other female disorders. (34)

Polymnia: Bearsfoot, leaf-cup, yellow leaf-cup, *Polymnia uvedalia*, a powerful emetic and cathartic. (32)

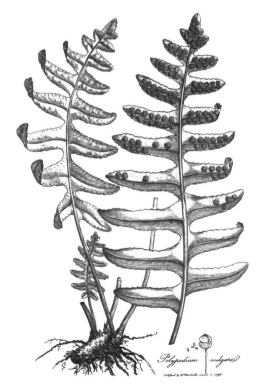

Fig. 3-199 Polypodium.

Fig. 3-200 Polytrichum.

Polypodium: Common polypody, *Polypodium vulgare*. A fern, rhizome used as astringent, antiscorbutic, and styptic. Figure 3-199. (1,39)

Polypodium filix mas: See filix. (39)

Polytrichum: Probably maidenhair spleenwort, *Asplenium trichomanes*. Leaves used. (1) In American usage *Polytricum juniperinum* is said to be the hair-cap moss or robin's rye, a moss native to New England, from which a tea is made as a diuretic and for dysuria. Figure 3-200. (44)

Pom: See also, pommade

Poma aurantii; —aurantiorum: Orange buds. (3) This may possibly also refer to the fruit as this is literally "apple of orange."

Pomatum saturni: See plumbi acetatis, unguentum. (40)

Pomegranate: See granatum. (8)

Pomfolice {*Italian*}**; Pomfolige** {*Italian*}**:** Crude zinc oxide, see pompholyx. (1)

Pomis compositus regis saporis, syrupus de; Pomis r.s., syrupus de: Purgative syrup of senna leaf, borage, apple juice, etc. Supposedly named after Sabur Ben Sahl, Persian physician, ninth century. (1)

Pomis magistralis, syrupus de; Pom. mag. s.d.: Magistral syrup of apple, a complex purgative used for mental disorders. (35)

Pomis purgans, syrupus de; Pomis purg. s.d.: Purging syrup of apple, of apple juice with borage, bugloss, senna, anise seed, saffron, and sugar. A purgative, said to be relatively gentle and to be good for mental disorders. (35)

Pommade {*French*}**:** Pomade, scented ointment. (1)

Pom(mad(e)) divin(e): A hair dressing of Victorian origin, variable in composition. Later a brand-name product of Butler & Co., UK, and a common household item for which various display jars were made.

Pommade en creme: Cold cream, see rosae aquae, unguentum. (40)

Pomme {*French*}**:** Apple. (1)

Pommes composées r.s., sirop de {*French*}**:** See pomis compositus.... (1)

Pomo {*Italian*}**:** Apple. (1)

Pomo arancio {*Italian*}**:** Orange (fruit). (1)

Pomo granato {*Italian*}**; Pomo punico** {*Italian*}**:** Pomegranate, see granatum. (1)

Pompholix; Pompholyx: Crude zinc oxide, tutty. See zinci oxidum. (1,3,40)

Pompilion, factitious, oil of: Green elder ointment, mimicking the ointment of poplar buds, see populeum, unguentum. (40)

Pompilion, oil of: Ointment of poplar buds, see populeum, unguentum. (40)

Pomum: Apple. (1)

Pond.; Ponderosa (*lat adj.*)**:** Heavy.

Pondicherry oil: Castor oil, see ricinis. (40)

Poor man's plaster: See picis emplastrum, pitch plaster, or for those in still more dire economic straits, consider picea, charta. (40)

Poplar, American: Same as *Liriodendron tulipifera*. (39)

Poplar, Carolina: See tacamahaca. (39)

Poppy petals: Petals of red poppy, rhoeados petala, were used to make a syrup used only as a colorant. (8)

Poppy, white: See papaver. (39)

Poppy: See papaver (various entries) and opium.

Populeum, unguentum; Populeon, unguento {*Italian*}**:** 1. Ointment of poplar buds, black nightshade, henbane leaves, etc. Used as emollient and treatment of burns. (1) 2. Poplar ointment, of same with opium, mandrake, lactucca, bardana, viola, and other ingredients in lard. (39)

Populi, oleum: Olive oil in which the buds of poplar have been digested. (40)

Populus (candicans): Poplar, black poplar, *Populus niger*, and perhaps other species. (1) In North American usage, may be *Populus niger* (black poplar), *P. candicans*, or *P. balsamifera*. Buds used, i.e., balm of Gilead refers to poplar buds. (3)

Populus tremula: Trembling or quaking poplar, i.e., the Aspen tree, *Populus tremula*. Use generally as per populus, above.

Porcelain clay: Kaolin. (40)

Porcus: Hog, pig. (1)

Porrum: Leek, *Allium porrum*. (1)

Portense, vin(um): See vinum portense.

Porter: Strong beer, used as an astringent and tonic. (39)

Portland, gout powder of the Duke of: Said by Estes to be an "ancient remedy that was resurrected by a mid-eighteenth-century English nobleman," consisted of aristolochia, gentian, chamaedrys, chamaepithys, and centaurium minus. For gout. (39)

Portugal, oil of: See aurantii corticus, oleum. (40) May also refer to oil of bergamot as per next entry.

Portugallicum, oleum: Oil of bergamot. (3)

Portulaca: Purslane, *Portulaca oleracea*. Herb and seeds used. Soothing diuretic and anthelmintic. (1,44)

Potash; Potashes: 1. Historic name for potassium hydroxide, KOH, remaining in the ash of roasted organic material, thus pot-ash; source of the element name, potassium. Often used in reference to potassium salts, i.e., "chlorate of potash" is potassium chlorate. (8) 2. Per Estes, prior to 1790 this referred more commonly to potassium carbonate, prepared in a similar manner. (39) As the hydroxide can be prepared by heating of the carbonate (releasing carbon dioxide), and as the preparation process involves heat, it is not surprising that the two potassium compounds were not clearly distinguished before the advent of modern chemistry.

Potash, caustic: This is almost always potassium hydroxide, not potassium carbonate, see discussion under potash.

Potash, dry: Same as potassii acetetas, potassium acetate. (39)

Potash, red chromate of: Potassium bichromate. (40)

Potash, subcarbonate of: Potassium carbonate. (40)

Potash and lime paste: See pasta potassae et calcis. (42)

Potash lozenges: See potassii chloratis, trochisci. (40)

Potash pellets: See potassii chloridi, tabellae. (40)

Potasii biboras: Potassium borate. (40)

Potassa; Potassium hydrate; Potassa caustica: Potassium hydroxide, KOH, caustic soda, see discussion under potash. (8,44)

Potassa cum calce: Potash with calcium, equal parts of potassa (potassium hydroxide) and lime (calcium oxide). (8)

Potassa fusa: "Fused" or melted potash. This is almost always potassium hydroxide, not potassium carbonate, see discussion under potash. (40)

Potassa sulphurata: Sulphurated potash, liver of sulfur, a mixture containing mainly potassium hyposulfite ($K_2S_2O_3$) and the sulphide, K_2S_3, from heating of sublimed sulphur (see sulphur sublimatum) and potassium carbonate (see potassa carbonas). (8)

Potassae _____: NOTE: Potassium can be designated *potassae* (feminine genitive form of *potassa*), or as *potassii* (neuter genitive form of *potassium*). Be sure to check for listings in both variants. While potassa is properly potash, not elemental potassium, the various salts can be formed from potash and the feminine variant seems to occur almost as often as the masculine in some sources.

Potassae, aqua: A solution of potassium hydroxide, ingested as an antacid, used as a bladder irrigation to dissolve stones, topical corrosive when used in concentrated form. See potash. (39)

Potassae, liquor: Solution of potassium hydroxide (see potassa), approximately five percent by weight. This and lesser concentrations were used primarily as a topical to cleanse skin, remove fatty residue, remove skin lesions, dissolve ingrown nails, etc. It is generally too corrosive to use systemically. (8)

Potassae bitartras: Cream of tartar. (39)

Potassae carbonas impuris: See lixivia. (39)

Potassae chlor(in)atae, liquor: Similar to the solution of potassium chlorate, the NF specified a solution of potassium carbonate and chlorinated lime in water. (46)

Potassae citratis, liquor; —, mistura: A solution of potassium citrate in soda (carbonated) water. A refrigerant, diaphoretic, and "gastric sedative." (39) In the USP, the liquor is of citric acid and potassium bicarbonate in water, the mixture is of lemon juice and potassium bicarbonate, resulting in a very similar result. (44)

Potassae effervescens, aqua: An effervescent form of potash water. See potassae, aqua and also potash. (40)

Potassae et sodae tartras: A "double salt" of potassium carbonate and sodium tartrate, or tartarized soda. (44)

Potassae hydras: Caustic potash, potassium hydroxide. (40)

Potassae hydriodas: See potassii iodidi. (40)

Potassae hydrobromas: See potassii bromidum. (40)

Potassae nitratis, fumus: See nitre paper. (40)

Potassae prussias [flavus][ruber]: See potassii ferrocyanidum. (40)

Potassae subcarbonas: See potassii bicarbonas. (40)

Potassae sulphurata, unguentum: Potassium sulphurate (potassa sulphurata) in paraffin, for ringworm and other skin diseases. (34)

Potassae supersulphas: See potassii bisulphas. (40)

Potassae(,) super-carbonatis aqua: A solution of lixivia (crude potassium carbonate and bicarbonate) saturated with carbon dioxide, primarily a lithontriptic. (39)

Potassae(,) super-carbonatis: Potassium bicarbonate. (39)

Potassae(,) super-tartras: Potassium tartrate, cream of tartar. (39)

Potassic _____: A potassium salt, K+ in conjunction with a negative ion, see potassii _____. (29)

Potassii _____: NOTE: Potassium can be designated *potassae* or *potassii*. Be sure to check for listings in both variants. (See note regarding potassae.)

Potassii acetas; —acetis: Potassium acetate, $KC_2H_3O_2$, by action of acetic acid on potassium carbonate or bicarbonate. Used as per potassium citrate. (8)

Potassii acetatis (et juniperi), elixir: Elixir of potassium acetate in aromatic elixir, optionally with fluid extract of juniper. (46)

Potassii arsenatis et bromidi, liquor: A solution of arsenious acid and potassium bicarbonate in water with 0.5 percent bromine (BPC), for diabetes and epilepsy. (42)

Potassii arsenitis, liquor: Solution of potassium arsenite, Fowler's solution, of arsenous acid (acidum arsenosum), potassium bicarbonate, and compound tincture of lavender. (8)

Potassii benzoas: Potassium salt of benzoic acid, used for same purposes as bonzoate, i.e., cystitis, gout, and rheumatism. (42)

Potassii bicarbonas: Potassium bicarbonate, $KHCO_3$, by action of CO_2 on potassium carbonate. Used as a gastric stimulant and antacid, diuretic, leavening agent (baking powder), in effervescent formulations as a source of CO_2, and in the preparation of other potassium compounds. (8)

Potassii bichromas: Potassium bichromate, potassium dichromate, $K_2Cr_2O_7$. Rarely used internally for gastric ulcer or dyspepsia. (8)

Potassii bisulphas: Potassium bisulfate.

Potassii bitartras; Pot. bitart. Potassium bitartrate. Potassium acid tartrate, or cream of tartar. From crude tartar, which deposits in wine casks during fermentation. Used as a diuretic and refrigerant, or to alkalinize the urine. (8) See tartar, cream of.

Potassii bromidi effervescens ([compositum, sal][(cum caffeina), pulvis]): Effervescent powder ("salt") of potassium bromide or the compound powder with lithium carbonate, to which caffeine could be added. The latter contained potassium bromide, lithium carbonate, and caffeine and was made effervescent in the usual manner, with sodium bicarbonate, tartaric acid, and citric acid. (31, 46)

Potassii bromidi, elixir: Elixir of potassium bromide, containing about 10 grains of potassium bromide in each fluidrachm, and used as a sedative. See bromine. (31)

Potassii bromidi, tablettae: Tablets of compressed, heated potassium bromide alone, dissolved in water before consuming. Sedative. (42)

Potassii bromidum (, sol.)(solut.)(effervescens): Potassium bromide (solution), KBr. From addition of bromine to a solution of potassa (potash, KOH). Primarily used as a sedative and for control of epilepsy. An effervescent solution was specified in the BPC. (8)

Potassii carbonas (impuras) (puras): Potassium carbonate, K_2CO_3 from pearl ash (wood ash) extraction with water and evaporation. Used primarily in the preparation of other carbonate salts. Wood ash would be the impure form, and the extracted and recrystallized form pure (puras). See discussion of potash. (8)

Potassii chloras (, sol.)(, solut.); Potassii chloratis (, sol.)(, solut.): Potassium chlorate, chlorate of potash, $KClO_3$, by action of chlorine on potassium carbonate, or the solution thereof. Used as a topical for disorders of the mouth, throat, and stomach. (8)

Potassii chloras, glyceritum: A glycerite of potassium chloride, used as a topical disinfectant and for treatment of irritation or inflammation of the various mucous membranes. (34)

Potassii chloratis (et boracis (cum cocainae)), tablettae: Tablets (troches) of compressed, heated potassium chlorate, which may include borax or both borax and cocaine. These were sucked for inflamed or ulcerated throat or for stomatitis. (42)

Potassii chloratis, gargarisma: See chlori, gargarisma. (42)

Potassii chloratis, mistura: A mixture of potassium chlorate and dilute hydrochloric acid in water, for stomatitis, tonsillitis, pharyngitis, or cystitis; essentially a weak chlorine solution. (42)

Potassii chloratis, trochisci: Troches of potassium chlorate with sugar, gum tragacanth, and lemon spirits. (8)

Potassii chloridi, tabellae: Tablets of potassium chloride, as a potassium supplement. No standard apothecary formula was found.

Potassii chloridum: Potassium chloride.

Potassii citras (neutralis); —citratis: Potassium citrate, by action of citric acid on potassium carbonate. Used as a diuretic and to alkalinize urine in order to dissolve or prevent stone formation, and as a diaphoretic. Said to be antiscorbutic, although the latter is now known to be due to ascorbate (vitamin C) deficiency. (8,39)

Potassii citras effervescens: Effervescent mixture of potassium citrate, sugar, and potassium bicarbonate. (8)

Potassii citratis effervescens, mistura: A mixture of potassium bicarbonate and citric acid mixed immediately in water, forming an effervescent tonic, said to be a febrifuge. An effervescent base for administering other materials. (42)

Potassii cyanidi, unguentum: Ointment of potassium cyanide, of same with oil of almond and cold cream. For local neuralgia. (34)

Potassii cyanidum; Pot. Cyanid.: Potassium cyanide, KCN, highly toxic, source of cyanide gas (HCN) if acidified. (8)

Potassii dichromate: See potassii bichromas. (8)

Potassii diphosphas: Potassium dihydrogen phosphate, the mono-potassium salt of phosphoric acid; diuretic and urinary acidifier. (42)

Potassii et sodii tartras: Potassium and sodium tartrate, Rochelle salt. Primarily for gastric upset. (8)

Potassii ferricyanidum: Potassium ferricyanide, $K_3Fe(CN)_6$. (Differs from ferrocyanide in the charge carried by the ion complex, 3+ vs. 4+, immediately below).

Potassii ferrocyanidum; Potassii ferocyanuretum: Potassium ferrocyanide, yellow prussate of potash, $K_4Fe(CN)_6$. (8,39)

Potassii floridum: Potassium fluoride, non-medicinal reagent. (42)

Potassii formas: Potassium formate, used as per sodium and other formates. (42)

Potassii glycerophosphas: Used as per other glycerophosphates or in combinations such as glycerinum glycerophosphatum compositum. (42)

Potassii guaiacosulphonas: Potassium guaiacol-sulphonate was a readily soluble form of guiacol used to treat intestinal catarrh and phthisis. (42)

Potassii hippuras: Potassium hippurate, used as per the sodium salt. (42)

Potassii hydroxidi, liquor: See potassae, liquor. (42)

Potassii hydroxidum: See potash. (42)

Potassii hypophosphis: Potassium hypophosphate, KPH_2O_2. (8)

Potassii iodidi alkalina, mistura: Alkaline mixture of potassium iodide and bicarbonates, ammonium carbonates, and camphor water. Expectorant and diuretic. (42)

Potassii iodidi cum sapone, linimentum: 1. Potassium iodide and soap liniment, for administration of systemic iodine. (34) 2. Liniment (BPC) of curd soap, potassium iodide, glycerin, oil of lemon, and water. More solid than linimentum potassii iodidi. (42)

Potassii iodidi et stramonii, mistura: A mixture of potassium iodide, tincture of stramonium, chloroform emulsion, liquid extract of licorice, and water, as a mild sedative and antispasmodic for asthma (due to anticholinergic activity of the stramonium). (42)

Potassii iodidi, [liquor][sol.][solut.]: Solution of potassium iodide, saturated solution of potassium iodide, "SSKI." An aqueous solution containing not less than 97 gm and not more than 103 gm of KI in each 100 cc. (31)

Potassii iodidi, linimentum: Liniment (BPC) of soft soap with potassium iodide, glycerin, and oil of lemon. (42)

Potassii iodidi, plasma: Plasma of potassium iodide in glycerin and starch; an antimicrobial unguent for scrofula, skin infections, and tumors. (34)

Potassii iodidi, unguentum: Ointment of potassium iodide and sodium hyposulphite dissolved in hot water and mixed with benzoinated lard. Rubbed over synovia (capsules) of enlarged rheumatic joints. (8,42)

Potassii iodidum: Potassium iodide, KI, from iodine and potassium hydroxide, dried and heated with carbon to convert the resulting potassium iodate (KIO_3) to iodide. For syphilis. (8)

Potassii lactas: Potassium lactate, for gout, rheumatism, and to alkalinize plasma or urine. (42)

Potassii nitras: Potassium nitrate, KNO_3, saltpeter, from native saltpeter. Used as a cardiac depressant and diuretic. Burning paper treated with this material (immediately below) produces smoke therapeutic for asthma. (8)

Potassii nitratis, charta; —, fumus: Potassium nitrate paper, made by saturating unsized paper in a strong solution of potassium nitrate and drying. It is burned and the smoke inhaled for asthma. (31,40)

Potassii permanganas, gargarisma: Gargle of dilute potassium permanganate; a disinfectant and deodorant gargle. (42)

Potassii permanganas; Potassii permanganatis, liquor: Potassium permanganate from oxidation of manganese oxide (mangani dioxidum) by potassium chlorate and potassium hydroxide. Dilute solutions (the one percent liquor, for example) used as an astringent. Concentrated solutions (ex.—Condy's solution) used for a surface disinfectant, antiseptic, and deodorant for bedpans, instruments, etc. Used to treat anemia, although probably without effect. Rapidly oxidizes many materials, and may cause explosion if formulated with organic materials in solid form. White's *Materia Medica* warns that one should formulate pills using kaolin (clay, in place of organic materials, like sugar) "or an explosion will likely take place." (8,42)

Potassii phosphas: Potassium phosphate, the dipotassium salt of phosphoric acid (see also potassii diphosphas). Saline purgative. (42)

Potassii salicylas: Potassium salt of salicylate, used for same purposes. (42)

Potassii sulphas [cum sulphure][sulphuretum]: Kali sulphuratum, sulphurette of potassium, poorly characterized. (39,40)

Potassii sulphas: Potassium sulfate, K_2SO_4. A cathartic and diaphoretic as well as topical for skin disorders. Forms insoluble salts with mercury and other heavy metals, and thus used as an antidote for poisoning with same. (8,39)

Potassii tartras acidus: The acid, or monopotassium salt of tartaric acid. Same use as the dipotassium salt. (42)

Potassii tartras: Potassium tartrate, saline cathartic. This was also called "normal" potassium tartrate and was the dipotassium salt. (42)

Potassii uras: Potassium urate, non-medicinal reagent. (42)

Potassio-cupri tartratis, solutio: Fehling's solution, one part consisting of copper sulfate and sulphuric acid in water, the other of sodium potassium tartrate and sodium hydroxide in water, the two being mixed immediately upon use. For detection of glucose in urine. (42)

Potassio-hydrargyri iodidi, solutio: Nessler's reagent, of potassium iodide, mercuric chloride, and sodium hydroxide in water, analytical reagent for detection of ammonia. (42)

Potassio-mercuric iodide: Mixture of mercury and potassium iodides. See hydrargyri et potassii iodidum. (40,42)

Potassio-tartrate of iron: See iron, tartarated. (40)

Potassium: Potassium compounds can be designated potassae (feminine genitive form of potassa), or as potassii (genitive neuter form of potassium). Check for listings in both variants. While potassa is properly potash, not elemental potassium, the various salts can be formed from potash and the feminine variant seems to occur almost as often as the masculine in some sources.

Potassium bromide with caffeine, effervescent: See potassii bromidi effervescens compositum, sal. (31)

Potassium creosote sulphonate: Potassium salt of creosote sulfonate, disinfectant. (40)

Potassium diarsenate: Potassium arsenate. (40)

Potassium dihydrogen phosphate: Potassium phosphate. (40)

Potassium diphosphate: Potassium pyrophosphate, see discussion under phosphoricum, acidum. (40)

Potassium guaiacol sulphonate: A mucolytic, similar to guiafenisin. For congestion, commonly in conjunction with a narcotic cough suppressant. (40)

Potassium hydrate: See potassae, liquor. This is a trivial name for potassium hydroxide.

Potassium hydriodate: Potassium iodide. (3)

Potassium hyperoxymuriate: Potassium chlorate. (3)

Potassium iodide, saturated solution of: See potassii iodidi, liquor. (31)

Potassium iodo-hydrargyrate; Potassium mercurio-iodide: Mixture of mercury and potassium iodides. See hydrargyri et potassii iodidum. (40,42)

Potassium metabisulphite: See metabisulfite.

Potassium pyroborate: Potassium borate. (40)

Potassium rhodanate: Potassium sulphocyanide. (3)

Potato oil; —spirit: Fusel oil. (3,40)

Potentilla: See argentina. (1)

Poterii, antihecticum: Treatment for hectic fevers made by heating antimony, tin, and nitre, per Pierre Potier (Petus Poterus), French seventeenth-century chemist. (1)

Poterii, stomachicum: Stomachic of Poterius, same as diaphoreticum solare, with added gum tragacanth, after Pierre Potier (Petus Poterus), French seventeenth-century chemist. (39)

Potio rivierii: "River potion," see sodii citratis, liquor or mistura. (31)

Potpourri: "Fumigating species, mostly flowers, generally preserved with salt." (3)

Potstone: Talc, talcum. (3)

Pottage's tincture: Tincture of acteae. (40)

Potus excitans: Exciting or stimulating drink, a stimulant created by Dr. Joseph Frank Pavia, Italy, ca. 1800, as a part of a therapeutic trend called "Brunonian," of alcohol, honey, water, sugar, eggs, and nutmeg. (39)

Potus: Latin, a drink, draught. (39)

Poudre {*French*}**:** Powder. (1)

Poudre savory: See effervescens compositus, pulvis. (40)

Pounce: 1. Gum obtained from the common juniper tree. (39) 2. Powdered sandarac, see sandaraca. (40)

Pourpier {*French*}: See portulaca. (1)

Powder, digestive: Compound powder of pepsin. (3)

Powder, Prussian: See glycyrrhizae compositus, pulvis. (40)

Powder, sympathetic: A powder believed to cure an injured person if soaked with the blood of that individual, possibly zinc sulfate, which must be prepared by placing in the sun under the sign of Leo during July. (39)

Powder, testaceous: Any powder of, or made up in, crushed oyster shell, testaceous meaning shelled. (39)

Powder of algaroth: Antimony oxide. (3)

Powder of Mars (, Della Lena's): Mars is the symbol for iron. Proprietary product ca. 1800, with iron tartrate. (39)

Praecipitatum albi, unguentum: See hydrargyrum ammoniatum, unguentum. (40)

Praecipitatum flavum: Yellow precipitate, i.e., of mercury, the yellow mercury sulfate, hydrargyrus vitriolatus. (39)

Praecipitatum rubrum (, unguentum, etc.): Red precipitate is red mercuric oxide, see hydrargyri oxidum rubrum and associated entries. (34)

Praecipitatus: Precipitate, precipitated. (1)

Praecipitatus _____: A precipitate, see _____ praecipitatus. (8)

Praeparat[a][us]: _____: Prepared, see _____ praeparata. (8)

Praeparatio: Preparation, substance prepared for medicinal use. (1)

Prassio; Prassio, syrupus de: Syrup of horehound, see marrubium. (35)

Prassium: See marrubium. (1)

Prayer beads: See abrus (seeds). (40)

Precipitatus _____: A precipitate, see _____ precipitatus. (8)

Précipité blanc {*French*}: In French prescriptions for internal use, calomel, for external use generally white precipitate (see hydrargyrum ammoniatum). (3)

Prenanthes serpentaria: A decoction of lion's foot root claimed to treat rattlesnake envenomation. Unofficial. (44)

Preparata _____: Prepared, see _____ preparata. (8)

Preparing salt: Sodium stannate. (3)

Preservaline: Proprietary food preservatives including formaldehyde, sulphites, borax, etc., "all of which are illegal" (as of 1926). (3)

Preston's salts: Ammonium carbonate. (3)

Prickly ash bark: See xanthoxylon. (8) According to Estes (39), in Europe this is aralia, in North America, xanthoxylum. Stomachic, antirheumatic, and diaphoretic.

Prickly poppy: See argemone. (33)

Pride of China; Pride of India: See melea azedarach. (39)

Primula officinalis: Cowslip, *Primula officinalis*, see paralysis syrup.

Primula veris: Primrose, *Primula vulgaris*. Herb and root used. (1)

Prince's pine: See chimaphila. (8)

Prinos: Bark and berries of black alder, winterberry, or feverbush, *Prinos verticillatus*, a tonic, alterative, and astringent. (33)

Prinus sylvestris: Blackthorn, *Prunis spinosa*. Fruit, referred to as sloe, used. (1)

Privet; Privy: See ligustrum. (33)

Pro: For (Latin preposition).

Pro dolore (moderata): For (moderate) pain. Commonly seen on promotional containers of Darvon or Darvocet created bu Eli Lilly and Co., ca. 1970; older occurences not observed.

Pro infantum: For infants, i.e., an infant dosage form.

Probilin: Proprietary phenolphthalein laxative. (40)

Procainae hydrochloridi, liquor: Solution of procaine hydrochloride, two percent, with thymol preservative. Local anesthetic. (31)

Propanone: Acetone. (3)

Propenal: Acrolein. (3)

Propenyl alcohol: Glycerin. (40)

Propenyl trinitrate: See glonoini, spiritus. (8)

Prophylactic ointment: See hydrargyri chloridi mitis, unguentum. (31)

Proponal: Dipropyl-barbiturate, a sedative-hypnotic. (40)

Proprietatis (Paracelsi), elixir: "His own elixir," in reference to Paracelsus, see aloes composita, tinctura. (39)

Propylami(n)a: This appears to be dipropylamine, derived from herring. For rheumatism and a variety of painful conditions as well as paralysis. Unofficial. (44)

Protargol: See argein. (40)

Protochloride of mercury: Calomel, HgCl. (39)

Proto-oxide of azote: Nitrous oxide, laughing gas. (39)

Proxy: A hydrogen peroxide solution. (40)

Prune; Prunum: Prune, fruit of *Prunus domestica*, see prunus, below. Used whole as a mild laxative. Figure 3-201. (8)

Prunella: Self-heal, *Prunella vulgaris*. Herb used, mainly as a vulnerary. (1,39)

Prunella (balls), sal; Prunellae, globuli: Sal prunella was saltpeter (potassii nitratis), which could be fused with heat into small balls or lozenges used for sore throat. See nitrum, tabulatum. (40)

Fig. 3-201 Prunus domestica or prune.

Fig. 3-202 Prunus sylvestris.

Prunellae, sal: 1. A crude potassium sulfate, evidently named for the similarity in color to the fruit of blackthorn, *Prunis sylvestris*. (39) 2. Potassium nitrate, fused. (1,3)

Prunellorum, conserva; Prunello, C.: Conserve of sloes. To "tye the bowels"—i.e., used to treat diarrhea or looseness of the stools. (35)

Pruni virginianae (ferratum), vinum: Wine of wild cherry, of wild cherry powder, sugar, and talcum in wine of angelica. A tonic and sedative. (34) In the NF, tincture of citro-chloride of iron (ferratum) could be added.

Pruni virginianae, syrupus: Syrup of wild cherry, primarily a flavoring. (34)

Pruni virginianae, tinctura: Simple tincture of wild cherry bark in alcohol and water, mild sedative for cough and for bronchitis. (42)

Prunus (domestica) (gallica): Plum, prune, the common plum tree, *Prunus domestica.* (1)

Prunus amygdalus: See amygdalus, refers to almond, not prune. (39)

Prunus cerasifera: See myrobilans. (39)

Prunus cerasus: The sour cherry, the syrup of which (syr. cerasi) is used as a flavoring. (7) Estes (39) indicates that this is the same as Prunus virginianus, below.

Prun[us][ellorum] sylvestris: 1. Forest plum, sloe, or acacia plant. Fruit used. Figure 3-202. (35) 2. Fruit of buckthorn or sloe, *Prunus spinosa*, a mild astringent. (39)

Prunus virginian(a)(us); Pruni virginianae fluidum, extractum; —liquidum, extractum; —, infusum; —, syrupus: Bark of the wild cherry, *Prunus serotina*, of North America, or the fluid extract, infusion, or tincture thereof. The fluid extract was obtained by percolation of macerated bark with water, glycerin, and alcohol; the infusion was made similarly with water only; and the syrup by maceration and percolation with water, sugar, and glycerin. It was used primarily for treatment of cough. Activity was attributed to the presence of hydrocyanic acid (i.e., hydrogen cyanide), found in the seed and bark of many *Prunus* species, although this is probably incorrect. The syrup is noted to be a good general vehicle for other drugs, particularly digitalis, which is less likely to cause gastric disturbance when administered in this fashion. (8,42)

Prussate; Prussate of potash, etc.; Prussic acid: Prussic acid is invariably hydrogen cyanide (HCN), see hydrocyanicum, acidum. "Prussate" is technically the cyanide ion (CN-), but often refers instead to hexacyanoferrate (ferrocyanide) ion, $Fe(CN)_6{}^{4-}$, as in Prussian blue. (8)

Prussian blue: A blue ink, iron hexacyanoferrate.

Psoralea: Psoralea, root and leaves of *Psoralea melilotoides*, a bitter tonic. (33)

Psyllium; Psillio {*Italian*}**:** Fleawort, *Plantago psillium*. Seeds (plantaginus semen) used. Psyllium is derived from the Greek for flea, in reference to the tiny seed. The seed husk is the source of psyllium fiber commonly available today. (1)

Ptarmica: Roots or leaves of sneezewort, or bastard or wild pellitory, *Achilla ptarmica*, a sialogogue and errhine (snuff). (39)

Ptelea; Pteleae, oleoresina: Wafer ash, *Ptelea trifoliata*, or the extracted oleoresin, a stomachic. (32,34)

Pteris: Pteris, the plant *Pteris atropurpurea,* an astringent and effective anthelmintic. (33)

Pterocarpi lignum: See santalum rubrum. (39)

Pterocarpus marsupium; —santolinas: See gum kino and santalum rubrum, respectively. (39)

Ptisan; Ptisana: Originally hordeum, aqua. Later referred to any herbal infusion or tea. (39)

Ptychotis, oil of: See ajowan, oil of. (40)

Puccoon: See sanguinaria canadensis. (40)

Pudding pipe; —, stick: Cassia fistula. (3)

Puerorum, pulvis: "Children's powder," see pulvis infantum (internal use). (3)

Pulegi; Pulegium: Pennyroyal, *Mentha pugelium*. Leaves used. (1) Estes (39) indicates European pennyroyal is *Mentha pulegium* while American pennyroyal is *Hedeoma puligioides*. Interchangeably used as aperient, carminative, deobstruant, diaphoretic, antihysteric, and emmenagogue. Used also (and still used today) as an abortifacient. Figure 3-203. (39)

Pulicaria: Probably small fleabane, *Inula pulicaria*. Seeds used.

Puligii, essentia: Essence of pennyroyal, of the oil in alcohol, on sugar or in hot water as emmenagogue. (42)

Pulmentum: Gruel, this is a Latin term for any grain mush or porridge. Latin dictionaries indicate a somewhat broader definition of a condiment or dip eaten with bread, but in medicinal use the term seems to be restricted to gruel. (40)

Pulmonaria: Lungwort, *Pulmonaria officinalis*. Leaves used, for pulmonary conditions. Figure 3-204. (1)

P

Fig. 3-203 Pulegium or pennyroyal.

Fig. 3-204 Pulmonaria or lungwort.

Pulmone vulpis, lohoch e; E. PULM. VVLP. L.: Lohoch of fox's lungs. In early references this appears to have been prepared from lungs of the stated animal and was used to treat pulmonary disorders. (1,35) Perhaps equivalent to syrup of poppies, rhoeados syrupus. (40) There are myriad stories of pharmacists or physicians named Fox, herbs called Fox's lLung, etc. in the literature and the true origin of the term is probably lost.

Pulp capping varnish: See mastiches chloroformica composita, solutio. (31)

Pulpa: Pulp (of fruit). (1)

Pulsatilla (nigricans); Pulsatilae, tinctura: The herb, *Anemone pulsatilla*, of European origin, Pasque-flower, Pasque-anemone, or the tincture therefrom. It is said to be therapeutically similar to senega. (1,8,31) American usage is said to be *Anemone patens, var. Nuttalliana;* British usage *A. Pulsatilla* or *A. pratensis*. (40)

Pulv. sal. carol. fact. eff.: Pulvis sal carolinum factitium effervescens; see carolinum factitium (effervescens), sal.

Pulvis: Powder. (1)

Pulvis _____: Powder of, see _____, pulvis if not listed immediately below. (8)

Pulvis antacidus: See rhei compositus, pulvis, second item. (34)

Pulvis anticatarrhalis: Catarrh powder of morphine hydrochloride, acacia, and bismuth subnitrate. (34)

Pulvis antilyssus: A powder to cure rabies (ineffectual, no doubt). (39)

Pulvis aromaticus compositus: Compound aromatic powder of cinnamon bark, nutmeg, saffron, cloves, and cardamom in refined sugar. This was identified as pulvis aromaticus in the BP, one of the many variants noted immediately below. (42)

Pulvis aromaticus; Pulvis aromaticum fluidum, extractum: Aromatic powder consists of 35 parts cinnamon, 15 cardamom, 35 ginger, and 15 nutmeg. There are many reported variants. It is macerated and percolated with alcohol to produce the fluid extract of aromatic powder. (8,39) See also the compound powder below.

Pulvis basilicus: See hydrargyri subchloridi compositus, pulvis. (42)

Pulvis catharticus: See jalapae compositus, pulvis (second item). (34)

Pulvis contra insectos: Insecticidal powder, variable composition. This is among the sundries carried by many apothecaries.

Pulvis e. bolo compositus sine opio: See cretae compositus, pulvis. (40)

Pulvis fulminans: Fulminating or exploding powder, similar to gunpowder (which also contains charcoal), of niter, potassium tartrate, and sulphur, which detonates on exposure to flame. See also pulvis tormentorius. (39)

Pulvis fumalis; Pv. fumalis: "Smoking powder," a balsamic or resinous combination that was burnt in the sick room as a treatment for congestion and cough. This could consist of benzoin alone, or of other resinous materials, including olibanum, mastic, amber, styrax, and laudanum (opium)—the latter to suppress cough. Similar aromatic mixtures remain in use, but are usually vaporized using steam.

Pulvis infantum: See rhei compositus, pulvis, second item. (34)

Pulvis nigrum: Black, or emmenagogue, powder. Of flowers of sulphur, myrrh, steel filings, sugar, and white wine, evaporated dry and pulverized. A "not very scientific compound" of use in amenorrhea, chlorosis, and several skin disorders. (34)

Pulvis purgans: See jalapae compositus, pulvis. (34)

Pulvis (Helvetii) stipticus: Styptic powder of Helviticus, of alum, gum kino, and sanguis draconis, after Adrien Helvetius, France, seventeenth century. (39)

Pulvis stypticum: Styptic powder, of iron sulphate and alum, heated to fusion, cooled, and pulverized. A topical for hemorrhage, occasionally used internally (by mouth) for bleeding of the lung or uterus. (34)

Pulvis tormentorius: "Artillery powder," i.e., gunpowder, of charcoal, niter (saltpeter), and sulfur. See also pulvis fulminans. (39)

Pumice; Pumex; Pumicus (pulvis): Pumice, generally powdered. A common sundry, abrasive. (1)

Pumpkin: See pepo. (8)

Pumpkin seed: See cucurbitae semina praeparata. (42)

Punica (malus)(granatum): Pomegranate tree, *Granata malus*. See granata. (1,39)

Punicine: Brown alkaloid obtained from pomegranate bark or root, see granatum. Anthelmintic. See pelletierene. (40,42)

Pur(a)(um)(us); Pur.: Pure, from the Latin.

Pura, aqua: Distilled water. (3)

Purgans, elixir: See jalapae composita, tinctura. (3)

Purgans, pulvis: Purging powder, see jalapae compositus, pulvis. (8)

Purgans cum scammonia, emulsio: See scammonii, mistura. (34)

Purgatol; Purgatin: See anthrapurpurin diacetate. (40)

Purgella; Purgen; Purgo; Purgolade; Purgylum: Various proprietary preparations of phenolphthalein laxative. (40)

Purging cassia: See cassia. (8)

Purging nuts: Croton seeds, see croton oil. (40) See barbados nuts. (44)

Purified aloes: See aloes, extractum. (40)

Purple coneflower: See echinacea.

Purple of Cassius: Gold precipitated from solution by tin chloride. (3) Gold stannate. (40)

Purple oxide: Ferric oxide. (3)

Pussy willow (bark): See salicis nigrae, cortex. (42)

Putty powder: Commercial oxide of tin, a fine abrasive. Sundry item for use as a metal polish. (40)

Pycnanthemum: Pycnanthemum, basil, or wild basil, *Pycnanthemum pilosum*, a diaphoretic, stimulant, antispasmodic, carminative, and tonic. (33)

Pyoktanin: Trade name for methylrosaniline. (42)

Pyorrhea astringent: See iodi et zinci phenolsulphonatis, liquor. (31)

Pyracine: Antipyrin. (3)

Pyraloxin: Oxidized pyrogallic acid. (40)

Pyrene: Fire extinguishing fluid, i.e., carbon tetrachloride. (3)

Pyrethri flores: Powdered flowers of chrysanthemum, *Pyrethrum cinerariaefolium* or *Crysanthemum roseum*, source of pyrethrum insecticide. (42)

Anthemis Pyrethrum

Published by B.C. Woodville, Sep.t 1, 1791.

Fig. 3-205 Pyrethrum.

Pyrethri florum, tinctura: A preparation of 25 parts pyrethrum flowers in alcohol, diluted 1:20 with water and used as an insect repellent lotion. (42)

Pyrethrum; Pyrethri, radix; Pyrethri, tinctura: The root of pellitory of Spain, *Anacyclus (or Anthemis) pyrethrum*. A tincture derived from this root contains an essential oil. It is a powerful sialogogue and causes burning of the mouth, but small amounts are said to give a pleasant taste to tooth powders. Could be used like other volatile oils (see caryophyllus), but not often employed for these purposes. Figure 3-205. (8)

Pyrethrum ros. pulv.: Probably powdered red (rosae) pyrethrum (*Pyrethrum cinerariaefolium*, also known as *Crysanthemum roseum*), i.e., chrysanthemum flowers. For use in insecticidal powder. See pyrethri flores.

Pyridine; Pyridinum: Pyridine, distilled from bone oil following the action of sulfuric acid. Administered by inhalation for asthma, White's *Materia Medica* notes that its "persistant and abominable odor is a great obstacle to its use." (8)

Pyrmont water: See Piermont water. (39)

Pyro: See pyrogallic acid. (40)

Pyroacetic spirit: Acetone. (40)

Pyroalcohol: Methyl alcohol. (3)

Pyrocatechin: See catechol. (40)

Pyrodine: Acetophenylhydrazine. (3)

Pyroenus: Alcohol (presumably ethyl). (3)

Pyrogallici compositum, acidi, unguentum: Ointment of pyrogallic acid, ammonium ichthosulphonate, and salicylic acid in soft paraffin, for psoriasis and chronic eczema. (42)

Pyrogallici, acidi, unguentum: Pyrogallic acid in lard, for psoriasis. (42)

Pyrogallol; Pyrogallic acid; Pyrogallicum, acidum: Pyrogallic acid is obtained by the dry distillation of gallic acid and is related to phenol, having three hydroxyl (OH) groups on a six-membered benzene ring. It is an astringent (see tannicum, acidum for uses), but also possesses significant antiseptic properties and could be used to treat topical parasites or fungi such as ringworm. It can be applied in flexible collodion or as an ointment in lard (Jarisch's ointment). (8)

Pyrogallol disalicylate: Reaction product of salicylic acid and pyrogallol. Insoluble in water, a solution in acetone was used to treat eruptive skin conditions, like eczema or psoriasis.

Pyrogallol oxide; Pyrogallol oxidi, unguentum: Oxidized pyrogallic acid, potassium carbonate, water, and benzoinated lard, claimed to be active in leprosy. (40,42)

Pyrola: Plant of genus *Pyrola*, wintergreen or shinleaf. Herb used as a diuretic, digestive, and topical discutient and rubifacient. Oil of wintergreen (see gaultherium) remains in use for the latter purpose today. (1,39)

Pyroligneous acid; Pyroligneum, acidum; Pyrolignosum, acidum: Pyroligneous acid is an acid derived from the water soluble fraction of destructive distillate of wood (pyro = fire, lignos = wood), the water insoluble fraction being creosote. It contains mainly acetic acid with various other compounds. Used as a topical disinfectant and internally for a variety of disorders.

Pyroligneous spirit: Wood alcohol, i.e., methyl alcohol. (40)

Pyrophorus: Adjective (*Latin*), a substance that ignites spontaneously on exposure to air. (3)

Pyrosulfite; Pyrosulphite of potash: Potassium metabisulphite, see discussion of metabisulfite. (40)

Pyroxylicus, spiritus; Pyroxylic spirit; Pyroxilicus rectificatus, spiritus: Wood spirits, methyl alcohol, see pyroligneous spirit. (3,40,44)

Pyroxylin; Pyroxylinum: Pyroxylin (caloxylin) is made from nitrated cotton, or gun cotton. The latter is made by treating cotton fiber with a mixture of concentrated sulfuric and nitric acid. The gun cotton is then dissolved in a small volume of ether and alcohol. Used to produce collodion. (8)

Pyrozone: See ether, ozonic. (40)

Pyrum: Pear. (1)

Q

Quadruplex pills; Quadruplices, pilulae; Quatuor pills: See ferri et quininae compositae, piluli. (34,46)

Quaker button: Nux vomica. (3)

Quaker's black drop: Vinegar of opium, see opii, acetum. (3)

Quassation: "The act of reducing roots and tough barks to morsels." (3)

Quassia; Quassiae lignum: Quassia, bitter wood, stem-wood of the tree *Picrasma excelsa*, native of West Indies, or *Quassia amara*, indigenous to South America (Figure 3-206), or the fluid extracts thereof. It is a typical bitter and is employed as such (see columba for detail of use). (1,8,42)

Quassia simarouba: See simarouba. (39)

Quassiae, extractum; —fluidum, extractum; —, infusum (concentratum); —concentratus, liquor; —, tinctura: The extract, fluid extract, infusion, concentrated liquor (BPC) and alcoholic tincture of quassia. The BPC also specified a concentrated infusion with alcohol and chloroform water for storage and reconstitution. (8,34,42)

Quassin: Bitter alkaloid derived from quassia, said to be among the most bitter substances known. (40)

Quebracho; —, tinctura: See aspidosperma. (8) In the BPC a simple tincture was specified, for use as a bitter and febrifuge. (42)

Queen Anne's lace: See daucus sylvestris. (39)

Queen of Hungary water: Rosemary distilled in wine, after Elizabeth of Hungary, ca. 1235, antispasmodic. (39)

Queensland fever bark: Bark of (see) alstonia. (40)

Queen's delight; Queen's root: See stillingia. (8,40)

Quercetanus: Latinized form for Joseph du Chesne, from chĕne {*French*} + quercus (Latin, oak), French chemist, 1544–1609, introduced calomel to medicine. See tartareae quercitanus, pillulae. (1)

Quercinum, unguentum: Soft (moist) lead tannate. (3)

Quercinum, viscum: See viscum quercinum. (1)

Quercitanus' extract of opium: Opium extracted in vinegar, ascribed to Quercitanus. (39)

Quercitanus, stomachic powder of: Powder of arum, calamus, pimpinella, lixivia (potassium carbonate, an effective antacid) and crab's eyes (see cancrorum lapilli). (39)

Quercitron bark: Bark of quercus, specifically, this is *Q. tinctoria*. (40)

Quercus; —, fluidextractum: Oak tree. Bark, buds, and acorns used. The fluid extract is said to be rarely used internally. (1, 31)

Quercus alba; —rebra; —robur, —tinctoria; Quercus cortex: Bark (cortex) of the white oak, *Quercus alba*, red oak, *Q. rubra*, or black oak, *Q. tinctoria* of North America. An astringent, used in a manner similar to tannic acid (see tannicum, acidum). (8,44) Per Estes, these were substitutes in North America for the English oak, also formerly called *Quercus tinctoria*, now *Q. robur*, Figure 3-207.

Quercus (albae), decoctum: Decoction of (white) oak bark, a strong astringent, used by urethral injection for gonorrhea and leucorrhea, and as a gargle for sore throat. (42,44)

Fig. 3-206 Quassia.

Fig. 3-207 Quercus robur.

Quercus cerris: See galla. (39)

Quevenne's iron: Reduced (i.e.-metallic) finely divided iron. (40)

Quickgrass: See gramen. (39)

Quicklime: Calcium oxide. An astringent, tonic, and topical escharotic. (39)

Quicksilver: Mercury, see hydrargyrum (metallic), hydrargyri (compounds). (8)

Quickwater: Solution of mercuric nitrate. (3)

Quillain; Quillaic acid: Saponin, complex chemical derived originally from various saponaria (soap-forming) plants. Used as a frothing agent to maintain foams, not medicinal. (40)

Quillaja (cortex)(bark); Quillaia; Quillajae, fluidum, extractum; —tinctura; Quillian.: Soap bark, the inner bark of *Quillaja saponaria*, of Chile and Peru, or the fluid extract or alcoholic tincture thereof. This imparts a soapy character to water, although it actually consists primarily of soluble glycosides, not true fatty soaps. It is a useful emulsifier for incorporating oils and oily substances into aqueous preparations. (8,46)

Quinalgen; Quinalgen: Benzoylamino-ethoxy-quinoline; or analgen, an analgesic. (40)

Quince: See cydonia. (39)

Quince, (Bengal)(Indian): See belae fructus. (33)

Quinetum: Mixture of cinchona derived alkaloids. (40)

Quiniae composita, tinctura: Quinia, i.e., quinine, in tincture of orange peel, use similar to the compound tincture of quinine. (44)

Quinic anhydride: This is a purported uricosuric, for gout. (40)

Quininae, mistura: A mixture of quinine sulfate, dilute sulfuric acid, tincture of orange, and water, appetite stimulant, especially following debilitating illness. (42)

Quininae, ole(in)atum: Quinine in oleic acid, a readily absorbed topical form. (42)

Quininae, tablettae: Tablet of quinine, gum acacia, glucose, potato starch, and (see) theobromatis, emulsio. (42)

Quininae, vinum; Quinine wine: Quinine wine, of quinine hydrochloride and orange wine (vinum aurantii). A pleasant way to take the bitter alkaloid, quinine. (31)

Quinidinae, syrupus; Quinidine, bitterless syrup: Syrup of quinidine, made of quinidine (quinidinae sulphas), oil of orange (aurantii cortex, oleum), and syrup. (31)

Quinidinae sulphas: The sulfate of quinidine, a lesser alkaloid derived from cinchona to treat fever and malaria. (8) This is a stereoisomer of the modern cardiac antiarrhythmic.

Quinina, Quinine: Quinine, a purified alkaloid from cinchona. (8)

Quininae arsenas: Quinine arsenate, an antiperiodic for malaria. (42)

Quininae (ammoniata), tinctura: Simple quinine tincture, in the BPC of quinine sulphate and tincture of orange. The ammoniated form was made up in ten percent strong solution of ammonia in alcohol. (42)

Quininae ammoniatum, elixir: Ammoniated elixir of quinine, of quinine sulphate, ammonium carbonate, alcohol, carmine solution (color), elixir of orange (flavor), and water. More palatable form of ammoniated quinine for influenza and catarrh. (42)

Quininae ammoniatus (, liquor)(, tabellae); Quin. Ammon. Liq.: Solution of ammoniated quinine, of quinine dissolved in ammonia water (liquor ammoniae). A dry powder product could be obtained, and unofficial tablets of ammoniated quinine are noted. (42)

Quininae benzoas: Little used salt form of quinine. (42)

Quininae bisulphas: See quininae sulphas. (42)

Quininae cacodylas: Little used salt form of quinine with cacodylic acid. (42)

Quininae citras (effervescens): Convenient salt form of quinine for pills, liquids, or effervescent formulations, for which it is combined with sodium bicarbonate, tartaric and citric acids, and refined sugar. (42)

Quininae composita, tinctura: Compound tincture of quinine, ague bitters, of quinine, cream of tartar, cloves, and alcohol. For intermittent fevers. (34)

Quininae compositae, pilulae: Compound pills of quinine (sulphate), extract of cornus and black cohosh, and tartaric acid. For intermittent and recurrent fevers. King's notes a variant with quinine, berberine, podophyllum, and nux vomica. (34)

Quininae compositum, elixir: In the later NF, of aromatic elixir containing quinine, cinchonidine, and cinchonine sulfates. A substitute of the earlier elixir cinchonae. (46)

Quininae compositus, pulvis: Compound powder of quinine, of quinine sulphate and iron ferrocyanide. A tonic and febrifuge. (34)

Quininae cum ferro, mistura: A mixture of quinine sulfate with solution of ferric chloride and water, a general tonic aperient (see quininae, mistura) with additional benefits of iron. (42)

Quininae cum ferro, pilulae: Tonic pills of quinine sulfate, exsiccated ferrous sulfate, milk sugar, and syrup. (42)

Quininae et ferri, tablettae: Quinine and iron tablets, of quinine and ferrous sulfates, sugar, and (see) theobromatis, emulsio. (42)

Quininae et phosphatum compositum, elixir: Elixir of quinine sulfate, phosphate of iron, potassium citrate, syrup of calcium lactophosphate, and aromatic elixir. (46)

Quininae et strychninae, liquor: A solution of quinine sulfate and strychnine in water and phosphoric acid, for preparation of other formulations, especially syrupus ferri phosphatis cum quinina et strychnina. (42)

Quininae ethylcarbonas: Less used salt form of quinine, which is not bitter. (42)

Quininae formas: Quinine formate, a readily soluble form of quinine for solutions or cachets. (42)

Quininae glycerophosphas: Quinine glycerophosphate, a form of quinine used in cachets or capsules. (42)

Quininae hydrobromidum (acidum): Bromide salts of quinine, allegedly less prone to causing quinine toxicity. (42)

Quininae [hydrochloridi][hydrobromidi], syrupus: Syrup of quinine hydrochloride or hydrobromide in simple syrup. (42)

Quininae hydrochloridum (acidum): Hydrochloric acid salts of quinine, used in place of the sulfate and said to be better absorbed. (42)

Quininae hydrofluoridum: Quinine hydrofluoride has been used along with iron fluoride in rickets to assist in hardening bone. (42)

Quininae hydroiodidum (acidum): Quinine hydroiodide, used as a disinfectant for chronic tuberculosis and also for rheumatism. The acid form was crystallized out of sulfuric acid instead of water, but was essentially equivalent. (42)

Quininae hypophosphis: Quinine hypophosphite, used with other phosphites in phthisis and neurasthenia. (42)

Quininae iodidum: See quininae hydroiodidum. (42)

Quininae lactas: Quinine lactate, a soluble form employed hypodermically or for local (urethral) injection in gonorrhea. (42)

Quininae salicylas (effervescens): Salt of quinine used occasionally in acute rheumatism and gout, in typhoid fever, and as an analgesic in neuralgia. An effervescent form with sodium bicarbonate, tartaric and citric acids, and refined sugar was noted in the BPC. (42)

Quininae sulphas (acidus); —bisulphas: These are the soluble salts of quinine used to the treatment of malaria and fever. The sulphate has two quinine molecules for each sulfate, the bisulphate (acidus) has a 1:1 ratio and was precipiated from an acid soluton. The forms are essentially interchangeable. (8,42)

Quininae sulphas, glyceritum: Glycerite of quinine sulfate, used as per quinine itself. (34)

Quininae sulphatis compositae, pilulae: Quinine sulfate, reduced iron, arsenious anhydride (arsenic trioxide) and strychnine, with extract of gentian. (42)

Quininae sulphatis, pilulae; Quin. Sulph., Pil.: A simple pill of quinine sulphate wet with aromatic sulphuric acid. It is recommended that it be coated with sugar or gelatin. (34) In the BPC, of the sulfate with tartaric acid powder, tragacanth powder, and glycerin. (42)

Quininae tannas: Tannic acid salt of quinine, usable by injection. (42)

Quininae valerianas: Quinine valerianate, used with other valerianates in formulations for neurotic conditions and hysteria. (42)

Quininae valerianatis et strychninae, elixir: Elixir of quinidine valerianate, strychnine sulfate, compound tincture of cudbear, and aromatic elixir. (46)

Quinine acetosalate: Quinine acetylsalicylate, an antipyretic and antirheumatic compound formed from aspirin and quinine. (40)

Quinine bisulphate; Quinine disulphate: Quinine sulfate, see quininae sulphas. (40)

Quinine fluoride; —iodide; —periodide: Quinine hydrofluoride (see quininae hydrofluoridum, above), or the hydriodide and iodohydriodide, immediately below. (40)

Quinine hydriodide, iodized; Quinine iodo-hydriodide; Quininae iodohydriodum: An iodized form of quinine, forming the hydro-iodide salt but also containing elemental iodine. Used for syphilis and rheumatological disorders. (40)

Quinine salacetate: Quinine acetylsalicylate, an antipyretic and antirheumatic compound formed from aspirin and quinine. (40)

Quinine sulphate basic; —, soluble: See quininae sulphas. (40)

Quinine sulphate, neutral: This is the bisulfate, see quininae sulphas. (42)

Quinine valerate: See quininae sulphas, above.

Quinine, muriate of: See quininae hydrochloridum. (42)

Quinoidine: Amorphous (non-crystalline) quinine. See quininae sulphas. (40)

Quinol: See hydroquinone. (40)

Quinoline bismuth salicylate: Probably an antidiarrheal. (40)

Quinophan: See chincophan. (40)

Quinosol: Potassium salt of (see) oxyquinoline sulphonate. (40)

Quinque radicibus, syrupus de: Syrup from the roots of five plants—butcher's broom (ruscus), smallage (apium), fennel, parsley, and asparagus. (1)

Quinquefolium: See pentaphyllum. (1) For ginseng, *Panax quinquefolium*, see panax.

Quinquina: See peruvianus cortex. (1)

Quodit: See conditum. (1)

R

R.: At beginning of inscription: racine {*French*}, radice {*Italian*}, radix, raíz {*Spanish*} (root). At end of inscripton: Rhazes (of Rhazes); rheum (a plant, see rheum); romanum (of Rome); rosatum (of roses); ruber (red). (1)

R.S.: Rex Sapor, see pomis compositus Regis Saporis, syrupus de. (1)

Rabarbaro {*Italian*}: See rhazes. (1)

Rabelli, aqua: Water of Rabelli, a three-to-one solution of alcohol and sulfuric acid. (40)

Racine {*French*}; **Radice** {*Italian*}: Root. (1)

Radcliff's (purging) elixir: Multiple formulations after Dr. John Radcliff, London, ca. 1700. Like most remedies of the era, primarily a purgative, as most versions contained aloe, jalap, gentian, scammonium, and senna. (39)

Raddle: See bolus armenia (rubra). (40)

Radical vinegar: Glacial (concentrated anhydrous) acetic acid.

Radicibus, syrupus de duabus: See duabus radicibus, syrupus de. (1)

Radicibus, syrupus de quinque: See quinque radicibus, syrupus de. (1)

Radiostol: Irradiated ergosterol, i.e., vitamin D produced from ergosterol by ultraviolet light. (40)

Radix; Radicis; R.; Rad.: Root (plural is radices, genitive is radicis). (1)

Radix _____ : See _____ , radix.

Radix A~G, H~M, etc.: Drawer or cabinet pull for alphabetical filing of various roots.

Radumine: Proprietary synthetic oxalic acid, non-therapeutic. (3)

Rafanus: See raphanus. (1)

Rag oil: See paper, oil of. (40)

Ragia {*Italian*}: Venice turpentine, see terbinthena veneta. (1)

Ragweed: In American usage, ambrosia (*Ambrosia artemisiaefolia*); in British usage, see senecio. (40)

Raisins: Dried grape, used as a sweetening agent and demulcent. (8)

Raisins, Corinthian: Grocers' currants. (3)

Raiz {*Portuguese*}; **Raíz** {*Spanish*}: Root, see radix. (1)

Raleigh, confectio; Raleighana, confectio; Raleigh, Great cordial of Sir Walter: Raleigh's Confection, Raleigh's Cordial. A complex (composite) cordial purported to have been the invention of Sir Walter Raleigh during his imprisonment in the Tower of London, 1603–1616. (1,39)

Ramenti ferri: Iron filings. (3)

Ramich trochisci: Tonic lozenges of rose petals, cloves, nutmeg, yellow sandalwood, gum arabic, etc. (1)

Ramno {*Italian*}: See rhamnus. (1)

Ramolaccio {*Italian*}: Horseradish, see raphanus rusticanus. (1)

Randall's solution: Solution of potassium citrate, acetate, and bicarbonate used to treat potassium deficiency. (24)

Rangoon oil: Heavy petroleum oil. (40)

Ranich, trochisci: See ramich, trochisci. (1)

Ranis, emplastrum de: Frog plaster, see vigonium, emplastrum. (39)

Ranunculae ficariae, suppositoria: Suppository of pilewort, for hemorrhoids. See cheladonium minus. (42)

Ranunculi (ficarii), unguentum: Ointment pilewort and lard, for hemorrhoids, see cheladonium minus. (42)

Ranunculus: Fresh bulbous base and flowering tops of *Rununculus* species, including crowfoot, bulbous crowfoot, or buttercup, *Ranunculus bulbosus* and *R. acris*, Figure 3-208. Said to be "too acrid" to be taken internally, it was a rubifacient and epispastic. (33,39)

Ranunculus ficaria: Pilewort, see cheladonium minus. (42)

Rapae semen (radix, syrupus); Rape oil: Rape, colza, or oilseed rape seeds (commonly known Canadian variety is canola). Source of rapeseed or canola oil. A syrup was evidently prepared from the root and utilized for digestive disorders and flatulence. (40)

Raphani co., aqua; Raphani, spiritus: See armoraciae compositus, spiritus. (40)

Raphani compositus, spiritus: Compound spirits of horseradish, of same with orange peel, cochlearia, nutmeg, and alcoholic spirits, with or without arum, an antiscorbutic. (39)

Raphanus hortensis: Garden radish. (1)

Raphanus rusticacia; Raphanus rusticanus: Horse radish or horseradish, *Armoracia rusticana* or *A. lapathifolia*. Contains a mustard-oil-like volatile oil, a tonic, diaphoretic, and diuretic. See armoracia. (1,39)

Rapontico {*Italian*}: See rhaponticum. (1)

Rases: See Rhazes. (1)

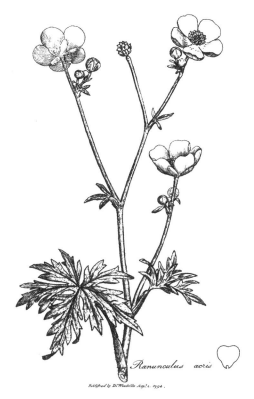

Fig. 3-208 Ranunculus (acris).

Raspail's solution: See ammoniacalis camphorata, lotio. (40)

Raspberry; Raspberry syrup: See rubus idaeus. (8)

Rasura: Shavings, filings. (1)

Rasura eboris: Ivory shavings, rasped ivory. (1)

Ratafia: Essence of almonds, see amygdalae, oleum. (40)

Ratsbane: See nux vomica. (40)

Rattlesnake root: See senega. (39)

Razes: See Rhazes. (1)

Rea: See rhea. (1)

Realgar: Realgar, red sulfide of arsenic, arsenic disulfide. (1,3)

Recens: "Recent," i.e., fresh, as in ovi vitellum recens, fresh egg yolk. (7)

Rectificatus, spiritus: Rectified (distilled) spirits of approximately eighty-four percent alcohol. (8)

Red blister: See hydrargyri iodidum rubrum, unguentum. (40)

Red bottle: See Whitworth's red bottle. (40)

Red cerate: Calamine cerate (calamine wax). (3)

Red crocus: Ferric oxide, red iron oxide. (40)

Red drops: See lavandulae composita, tinctura. (40)

Red gum; —, liquid extract of; —, syrup of; —, tincture of; —, troches of; —lozenges: For red gum, see eucalyptus. Otherwise see respectively eucalypti gummi (rubri) liquidum, extractum; eucalypti gummi, syrupus; eucalypti gummi, tinctura, or—for the lozenges or troches—eucalypti gummi, trochisci. (8,31,42)

Red lavender: See lavandulae composita, tinctura. (40)

Red lead: The red tetroxide, Pb_3O_4, used as a topical for skin disorders. See plumbi oxidum rubrum. (39,40)

Red liquor: Aluminum acetate solution. (3)

Red lotion: See lotio rubra. (8)

Red oil: Crude oleic acid. (3) Liquid paraffin colored with alkanet. (40)

Red precipitate (ointment): See hydrargyri oxidum rubrum, unguentum. (8) According to Estes (39) this was the mercuric oxide in later use, and earlier had been the red precipitate of mercuric nitrate, hydrargyrus nitratis ruber.

Red prussiate of potash: See potassii ferrocyanidum. (40)

Red raddle: Red ochre, a bole. (40)

Red rub: See Whitworth's red bottle. (40)

Red rudd: See bolus armenia. (40)

Red saunders: See santalum rubrum. (8)

Red sin: See potassii permanganas. (40)

Red sulphuret(um) of quicksilver: See hydrargyrus sulphuratus ruber. (39)

Red tartar: See tartar. (3)

Red water bark: Sassy bark. See erythrophloeum. (40)

Reddle: Red chalk. (3) See bolus Armenia. (40)

Refrigerans Galeni, ceratum; Refrigerans, unguentum: Galen's refrigerant cerate, or wax, compounded from oil of roses or sweet almonds, white wax, and chilled water. Used as emollient and to treat inflammations. (1,40) This is essentially cold cream, see rosae aqua, unguentum.

Refrigerant counterirritant: See dentilinimentum aconiti et iodi compositum. (31)

Réglisse {*French*}; **Regolitia** {*Italian*}: Licorice, see glycyrrhiza. (1)

Regius, syrupus: "Royal syrup," syrup made from rose-water. (1)

Regnauld's anaesthetic: Chloroform and methanol, 4:1. General anesthetic. (40)

Regulin: Agar gelatin preparation. (Current trade name for antihypertensive drug, bethanidine). (40)

Regulus: A pure metal when separated by fusion, i.e., regulus antimonii is pure antimony. (3)

Remijia (bark): A substitute for cinchona. (40)

Renaglandin: Proprietary extract of suprarenal glands. (40)

Renalina; Renoform: See adrenaline. (40)

Renninum: Bovine derived rennin, used as a digestant and as an agent to curdle milk (i.e., cheese manufacture). (7)

Renostypticin; Renostyptin: See adrenaline. This was used as a vasoconstrictor for topical use to control bleeding. (40)

Requies (magna) Nicolai; Requies Nicoli: "Nicoli's rest," "Nicolas' repose," a somifacient made with opium, hyoscyamus, and mandragora, after Nicoli Myrepsus, thirteenth century, Nicea. see Nicolao. (1,39)

Reseda luteola: Weld or dyer's weed, dye source, but also diuretic and diaphoretic. Unofficial. (44)

Residuum ovarii: Ovarian residue, dried and powdered, from bovine, porcine, or ovine sources. (7)

Resin; Resinsa; Resina ____: Resin, or rosen, for formulations see ____, resina, for resin itself, see colophony. (1,42)

Resina alba: White pine resin, terebentha veneta. (39)

Resina cannabis: Extract of Indian hemp. See apocynum (cannabinum). (40)

Resina carbolisata: Carbolized resin, of resin with carbolic acid and chloroform, a topical for decayed tooth or to treat toothache. (42)

Resina flava: Yellow pine resin, terebentha vulgaris. (39)

Resina nigra: See pix nigra. (33)

Resina pini: See pix burgundia. (1)

Resinae, ceratum: Cerate of resin (rosen) with beeswax and lard. (30)

Resinae, emplastrum: A plaster of resin, soap, and lead plaster, combined. (30)

Resinae, unguentum: An ointment of resin, beeswax, and olive oil; see basilicon, unguentum. For chronic sores and ulcers. (30,42)

Resinae chloroformica, solutio: Chloroformic solution of rosin (resin), of rosin in chloroform, preserved in amber-colored, cork-stoppered bottles, used as a dental varnish. (31)

Resinae compositum, ceratum: Compound cerate of resin with wax, suet, turpentine, and linseed oil. (30)

Resinae compositum, unguentum: Compound ointment of resin, with eucalyptus oil, paraffin, and resin. (30)

Resorbin: A prepared substitute for lard, of almond oil, a glue or soap solution, and wax, with or without lanolin. For preparation of ointments, plasters, etc.

Resorcin; Resorcinum; Resorcinol: Resorcinol, the di-alcohol of benzene, $C_6O_2H_6$. A modest antipyretic, replaced by the more effective acetanilide. Used topically in glycerin to remove scales of chronic skin disorders, and helpful with dyspepsia. (8)

Resorcini, lotio: Ten percent resorcin(ol) in water, applied to psoriasis, eczema, and as an antiseptic for syphilitic sores. (42)

Resorcini, spiritus: Resorcin(ol), castor oil, and Cologne spirits (Coloniensis, spiritus) in alcohol. Used topically for dandruff and alopecia. (42)

Resorcini, unguentum: Unguent of resorcin, glycerin, lanolin, and soft paraffin, antiseptic and antipruritic. (42)

Resorcini compositum, unguentum: Similar to resorcinolis compositum formulation below, this BPC formulation was of resorcin, water, oil of white birch (betula), zinc oxide, paraffin, and lanolin. Antiseptic and antipruritic for acne rosacea, eczema, etc. (42)

Resorcini cum amylo, unguentum: Ointment or resorcin with starch, zinc oxide, lanolin and soft paraffin. (42)

Resorcinol ointment, compound; Resorcinolis compositum, unguentum: Compound resorcinol ointment, with resorcinol (resorcin), zinc oxide (zinci oxidi), bismuth subnitrate, and rectified oil of birch tar (betulae volatilae, oleum), with a base of petrolatum, anhydrous wool fat (lanolin), and glycerin. (31)

Restharrow: Restharrow or cammock plant, *Ononis arvensis*. See nephriticum, decoctum ad. (39)

Resumptivum, unguentum: From Latin meaning "restorative," ointment of fenugreek, oil of violets, oil of sweet almonds, chamomile oil, yellow wax, etc. Used to treat asthma or pleurisy. (1)

Retinol: Rosin oil, rosinol. (3) In modern biochemistry, a form of vitamin A.

Rex metallorum: King of metals, i.e., gold. (3)

Rhabarbarum (, syrupus de); Reubarbaro {*Italian*}**:** Rhabarbarum is a variant of rhubarb, see rheum and rhei, syrupus. (35)

Rhamni, succus: Buckthorn juice, liable to fermentation and little used except to prepare formulations such as syrup, below. (42)

Rhamni, syrupus: In the BPC, of fresh buckthorn juice, tincture of ginger, oil of pimento, alcohol, sugar, and water. A purgative. (42)

Rhamni catharticae, fluidextractum: Fluid extract of *Rhamnus cathartica*, used as a cathartic. (31)

Rhamni catharticae, syrupus; Ramn. cath, S. de: Syrup of rhamnus cathartica, syrup of buckthorn berries; syrupus spinae cervinae. Twenty percent fluid extract of buckthorn berries (rhamnus) with oils of fennel (foeniculi, oleum) and cinnamon, in syrup. (31)

Rhamni frangulae (liquidum), extractum: The solid or liquid extracts of *Rhamnus frangula*. (42)

Rhamni purshianae (compositum), elixir: See cascarae sagradae (compositum), elixir. (31) Fluid extract of cascara as well as senna and juglans in compound elixir of taraxacum. (46)

Rhamni purshianae fluidum aromaticum, extractum: Aromatic fluid extract of cascara powder, with licorice, magnesia, glycerin, compound spirit of orange, alcohol, and water. Laxative. (46)

Rhamni purshianae fluidum, extractum; —, elixir: Fluid extract of *Rhamnus pursiana*, i.e., cascara sagrada. The elixir was of the fluid extract plus compound elixir of taraxacum. (8,46)

Rhamnus (cathartic[a][us]): Buckthorn, *Rhamnus cathartica*, or bacccae spinae cervinae, fruit used as a strong cathartic, sometimes as a tonic, astringent, or antiseptic. Figure 3-209. (1,7,39)

Rhamnus frangula: Lesser used cathartic bark of species related to *R. cathartica*, the Glossy Buckthorn, *Rhamnus frangula*. (40)

Rhamnus purshiana: See cascara sagrada. (8)

Rhaponticum: Rhapontic or monk's rhubarb, *Rheum rhaponticum*. Rhizome used, a less potent cathartic than rheum. (1)

Rhases; Rhazes: Persian physician and author, 865-925 CE. (1)

Rhatany: See krameria. (8)

Rhatany; Ratanhia: Rhatany, South American shrub *Krameria triandra*. An astringent, root used. (1)

Rhatany, extract of: See Krameria, extractum. (40)

Rhea: Poppy. (1)

Rhei: Singular posessive of rheum, i.e., rhubarb. See rheum.

Rhei, elixir: Elixir of rhubarb; of the powdered root (extracted to produce the elixir), fennel fruit, refined sugar, glycerin, alcohol, and water. (42)

Rhei, extractum; —fluidum extractum; —tinctura; —, fluidglyceratum: The dry extract, fluid extract, alcoholic tincture, or fluidglyrerate (NF) of rhubarb. The tincture contains cardamom and glycerin. A purgative and stomachic. (8)

Rhei, infusum: An infusion of rhubarb in water, as a stomachic and aperient. The BPC also specified a concentrate with alcohol and chloroform water for storage and reconstition. (42)

Rhei, pilulae: Pills of rhubarb and soap. Laxative. (8,34)

Rhei, syrupus: Syrup of rhubarb root, coriander fruit, sugar, alcohol, and water, a purgative for children. (42)

Rhei, tinctura: See rhei composita, tinctura. (40)

Rhei, vinum: Wine of rhubarb, of powdered rhubarb and calamus in stronger white wine (vinum album fortior). A laxative and carminative. (34)

Rhei alcoholicum, extractum: Dry alcoholic extract of rhubarb, USP. (44)

Rhei aquosa (tinctura): Aqueous tincture of rhubarb, of rhubarb (rhus) with potassium carbonate, cinnamon water (cinnamomi, aqua), alcohol, and water. Purgative and stomachic. (31,34,42)

Rhei aromatica, tinctura: Aromatic tincture of rhubarb with cassia cinnamon, cloves, nutmeg, glycerin, and alcohol. (8)

Rhei aromaticum, fluid extract: Aromatic fluid extract of rhubarb, from rhubarb, cinnamon, cloves, and nutmeg. (29)

Rhei aromaticus, syrupus; Rhei syr. ar.: A syrup made with syrup of rhubarb and aromatic tincture of rhubarb (rhei aromatica tinctura). (8)

Rhei chinensis (,(radix) (pulv.)): Chinese rhubarb (see rheum) root (radix), generally powdered (pulv.).

Rhei composita, mistura: Compound mixture of rhubarb, or Squibb's rhubarb mixture, of fluid extracts of rhubarb and ipecac, sodium bicarbonate, glycerin, and peppermint water. Purgative and carminative. (34,46)

Rhei composita, tinctura: Compound tincture of rhubarb, with bitter root, goldenseal, gentian, prickly ash berry, sassafras, cardamom, and alcohol. A tonic for intestinal and hepatic disorders. (34) In the BPC, of powdered rhubarb root, cardamom seed, coriander fruit, glycerin, and alcohol. (42)

Rhei compositae, pilulae; Rhei compositus, pulvis: 1. Compound pills or powder of rhubarb, purified aloes, myrrh, and oil of peppermint. 2. Compound powder or pills of rhubarb, with magnesia and ginger, Gregory's powder. A laxative. (8,34,42)

Rhei compositus, pulvis: Neutralizing powder, compound powder of rhubarb, of same with potassium bicarbonate and peppermint leaf. For gastrointestinal complaints, especially heartburn and infantile colic. A variant specified in the BPC, also called Gregory's powder, was of rhubarb and magnesium carbonate and flavored instead with ginger powder. (34,42)

Rhei concentratus, liquor: A concentrated solution extracted from rhubarb root with alcohol. For preparation of other mixtures. (42)

Rhei cum hydrargyro (et soda), pulvis: Powdered rhubarb root and mercurous chloride (calomel) with powdered ginger, optionally with sodium bicarbonate. Purgative. (42)

Rhei cum magnesia, pulvis: Improved Gregory's powder. See rhei compositus, pulvis as described in the BPC. (42)

Rhei cum soda(e), mistura: A mixture (BPC) of powdered rhubarb root and sodium bicarbonate in caraway water, mild laxative, antacid, and stomachic. In the USP, it is made with sodium bicarbonate, liquid extract of rhubarb, liquid extract of ipecac, glycerin, and spirits of peppermint. (42)

Rhei cum soda, pulvis: Rhubarb root in sodium bicarbonate powder, laxative. (42)

Rhei darelii, elixir: See tinctura rhei dulcis. (3)

R

Rhei dulcis, liquor: See rhei, elixir. (42)

Rhei dulcis, tinctura: Sweet tincture of rhubarb, with licorice (glycyrrhiza), anise, cardamom, glycerin, and alcohol. (8)

Rhei et colocynthidis et hydrargyri, pilulae: Purgative pill composed of the masses of compound rhubarb pill, colocynth pill, and mercury pill (blue pill), combined. (42)

Rhei et gentianae, tinctura: Tincture of rhubarb (rhus) and gentian. (31)

Rhei et magnesiae (acetatis), elixir; Rhei E. Mag., El.: An elixir of rhubarb and magnesium acetate in aromatic syrup, used as a laxative.

Rhei et magnesiae anisatus: A powder of magnesium bicarbonate, rhubarb, and anise powder, used as per rhei compositus, pulvis. (34)

Rhei et nucis vomicae, pilulae: Purgative pill of compound rhubarb pill mass with added extract of nux vomica and alcoholic extract of belladonna to reduce cramping, in milk sugar. (42)

Rhei et potassae (compositus), syrupus: A syrup of rhubarb powder, potassium bicarbonate, cinnamon, goldenseal, brandy, water, and sugar. For gastric upset or acidity, also called neutralizing cordial. (34)

Rhei et potassae, trochisci: Troches of rhubarb, potassium bicarbonate, oil of peppermint, sugar, and gum tragacanth. For heartburn, diarrhea, or acute gastrointestinal conditions. (34)

Rhei et sennae, syrupus: Syrup of rhubarb and senna. Laxative.

Rhei et sodae, mistura: Mixture of rhubarb and soda, of sodium bicarbonate, extract of rhubarb, fluidextract of ipecac, glycerin, spirit of peppermint, and water. A purgative and carminative and for infantile colic. (8,34)

Rhei et sodae, tablettae: Tablet of powdered rhubarb root, sodium bicarbonate, ginger powder, gum acacia, and (see) theobromatis, emulsio. (42)

Rhei hemm, syrupus; Rhei hemm, Syr.: Syrup of rhubarb as made according to Hemm, who produced this syrup by extraction of rhubarb with alcohol, followed by distillation of the alcohol and replacement with water. (39)

Rhei radix (p. or pulv.): Powdered rhubarb root.

Rhei salinus, pulvis: See rhei compositus, pulvis. (40)

Rhei vinosa, tinctura: Vinous (wine-based) tincture of rhubarb, of the fluid extract with fluid extract of bitter orange peel, cardamom, sugar, and sherry wine. (34)

Rheum: Rhubarb root, the root of *Rheum officinalis*, Chinese rhubarb, *Rheum palmatum* and related species. Rhizome used as a moderate laxative in a large number of formulations, and as a purgative in high dosage. Note the posessive is *rhei*. Figure 3-210. (8)

Rheum; Rheum palmatum; Rheum undulatum: Rhubarb, genitive Rhei. See detailed entry and illustration before the entries for rhei. (39)

Rheumatic weed: See chimaphila. (39)

Rhodallin: See thiosinamina. (42)

Rhodeoretin: See jalapin. (42)

Rhodia radix: Rose-root, rose-wort, plant of genus *sedum*. Root used. (1)

Rhodii, lignum; Rhodium: Rosewood. (1)

Rhodii, oleum; Rhodium oil; Rhodium, oil of: 1. Oil of Rhodium, an oil extracted from the root of the shrub *Rhodeola rosea* or *Lignum rosae*, i.e., rosewood. Used in perfumery to confer the smell of roses. No pharmaceutical use identified, but apothecaries regularly prepared perfumes, fumigating pastilles, etc. 2. Aromatic oil from root of *Genista canariensis*. (40)

Rhodinol: See geraniol. (42)

Rhodinum: A mixture of rosemary oil and vinegar. (39)

Rhodium, factitious, oil of: Mixture of sandalwood (santalum) oil and oil of rose or rose geranium. (40)

Rhododendron: Yellow-flowered rhododendron, rosebay, snow rose, *Rhododendron chrysanthum* (not the large rhododendron generally familiar in the eastern US). Said to be a stimulant and narcotic and used for acute muscular pain. Figure 3-211. (33)

Rhodomel: See rosa, oxymel. (40)

Rhodosaccharum: See rosae, syrupus. (40)

Rhoeados petala; Rhoeados syrupus: Red poppy petals, see poppy petals (official as such in the British Pharmacopoeia). (1,8,33)

Rhoeas: Wild poppy, see papaver erraticum. (39)

Rhois glabra fluidum, extractum: Fluid extract of *Rhus glabra* with glycerin and alcohol. (8)

Rhubarb: See rheum, rhei. (8)

Rhubarb, sweet essence of: See rhei, elixir. (42)

Rhubarb and magnesia, elixir: See rhei et magnesii acetatis, elixir. (46)

Rhubarb of Peru: See mechoacanna. (39)

Rhubarbitate: "Of rhubarb" (rheum), see rhei. (39)

Rhus: See sumach. (1)

Rhus aromatica: Bark of the root of sweet or fragrant sumach, *Rhus aromatica*. Said to be an exceedingly valuable medication, particularly for diabetes, the list of other uses is both long and, to the modern clinician, utterly perplexing. (33)

Rhus copallina: Source of the resin referred to as copal, *Rhus* or *Toxicodendron copalina*. (39)

Fig. 3-210 Rheum or rhubarb.

Fig. 3-211 Rhododendron.

Rhus glabra; Rhus glabrum: This is the fruit of the sumach (sumac) tree, *Rhus glabra*, of North American origin. It was used as an astringent (see tannicum, acidum for uses), most particularly for the oral cavity and pharynx, often as a gargle. (Preparations are under the possessive form, rhois.) (8)

Rhus radicans: Poison ivy, use as per rhus toxicodendron. (39)

Rhus toxicodendron: Referred to in White's *Materia Medica* as *Rhus radicans*, this could be the leaf of either poison ivy (*Rhus toxicodendron,* now *Toxicodendron radicans*), or poison oak (now *Toxicodendron diversilobum)*, or possibly other related species, all of which contain a volatile oil well known to result in skin eruptions. The same source notes that this was used in dilute form for bruises and burns and internally for paralysis, nocturnal incontinence, and various skin diseases, but that the "remedy is dangerous and, probably, an (*sic*) useless one, for these purposes." For the tincture and other formulations, see toxicodendri. (8)

Rhus typhinum: Berries of staghorn Sumac, *Toxicodendron* or *Rhus typhina*. Astringent. (39)

Rhus vernix: Leaves of poison sumac, *Toxicodendron vernix*. Similar to *Rhus toxicodendron*. (39)

Ribes; Ribesia; Ribe {*Italian*}**:** Red currant (*Ribes rubrum*) or sometimes black currant (*Ribes nigrum*). (1) Not same as Rubis species, the raspberry and blackberry. Figures 3-212 and 3-213.

Ricini, olei, emulsum: Emulsion of castor oil, containing thirty-five percent castor oil, tincture of vanilla, syrup and water. Used as a cathartic. (31,46)

Ricini, olei, mistura: A mixture of castor oil, gum acacia, orange flower water, and cinnamon water, a pleasant form of castor oil. (42)

Ricini, semina: Castor beans. (42)

Ricini aromaticum, oleum: Aromatic castor oil, of the latter with small amounts of alcohol, amyl acetate, and gluside (saccharin). A castor oil "specially suitable for administration to children." (42)

Ricini cum sapone, olei, enema: Enema of castor oil with soap and water, for bowel cleansing. (42)

Ricinus; Ricini, oleum; —, Ol.; Ricinus: Oil derived from the castor bean, *Ricinus communis*. Castor oil is relatively inert topically and can be used to prepare ointments or eyedrops. Internally it is a moderate laxative, and is said to be a galactogogue if applied locally to the breast. Figure 3-214. (1,8) Castor bean also contains the highly toxic protein ricin, but this is not contained in the oil.

Ringer's solution: An electrolyte solution used to maintain living tissue in culture and also as an intravenous solution for dehydration. (24)

Riso {*Italian*}**:** Rice. (1)

Rizine: Rice, steamed. (3)

Rob; Roob: Juice of fruit, often sweetened and concentrated to a syrup. (1) An inspissated juice (of elderberry, carrot, juniper berries, etc.). (3)

Robinia: Bark and leaves of the Locust tree, black locust, yellow locust, or false acacia, *Robinia pseudacacia*, quite toxic, it is an emetic and cathartic. (33)

Roborans Whyttii, elixir: A compound tincture of cinchona, containing saffron. (3)

Rochdale salt; Rochelle('s) salt: See potassii et sodii tartras. (8,40)

Roche alum; Rochi gallis: Rock, Roche, or iron alum. The chemical and mineralogical definitions of this salt are highly variable. (40)

Roche's embrocation: A mixture of oils consisting of oils of alnus, chamaemelum, carum, and rosemarinum, with cochineal and alkanet, ca. 1800. (39)

Rock ammonia: Ammonium carbonate, see ammonii carbonas. (40)

Rock oil: Petroleum. (3)

Rock salmon: See scillae, oxymel. (40)

Rock salt: Native sodium chloride. (3)

Rocket: See eruca. (39)

Rodagen: Dried antithyroid preparation obtained from goats whose thyroid has been removed, said to be effective for goitre. (40)

Roffo's pill: Correct and original name for Rufus' Pill, see Rufi, pilulae. (39)

Rohan tree: See soymida. (39)

Roman ointment: A mixture of extracts of opium and belladonna with glycerin and resin (pitch) ointment. (40)

Roman vitriol: Copper sulphate (cupri sulphas). (3)

Romanum, philonium: See philonium romanum. (1)

Romarin {*French*}**:** See rosmarinus. (1)

Rongalite: Proprietary bleaching compound of sodium hydrosulphite. (3)

Root, bitter: Gentian. (3)

Ros solis: Sundew, round leaved sundew, *Drosera rotundifolia*. Herb used. (1)

Ros., syr. di sec^^he: Observed, probably Italian, syrup of dried rose (rosa seccar(h)e).

Rosa: Rose. Note that the singular possesive is rosae, but one often sees the plural posessive ("of roses") rosarum.

Fig. 3-212 Ribes rubrum or red currant.

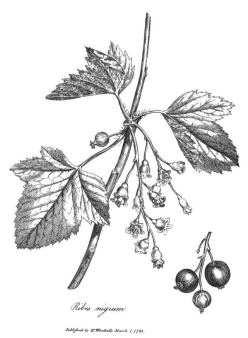

Fig. 3-213 Ribes nigrum or black currant.

Fig. 3-214 Ricinus communis or castor bean.

Rosa; Rosa galica; Rosa centifolia: The red rose, *Rosa gallica*, figure 3-215, was used extensively as a perfuming and flavoring agent. It had no therapeutic use. The pale rose (*R. centifolia*), Figure 3-216, was similarly employed. (8)

Rosa, mel; Rosa, oxymel: Honey of roses, clarified honey with acetic acid and rose water. An emollient.

Rosa (alba)(gallae), essentia: Essence of (white)(red) rose, i.e., the distilled essential oil, often diluted with some alcohol. See rosa (alba).

Rosa (alba)(centifolia) (gallica): White, pale, or red rose, respectively. Petals used. (1)

Rosa cana; Rosa canina: Dog rose, see cynorrhodon. Figure 3-217. (1,33)

Rosa damascena: Damask rose. (1)

Rosa hiericontea: Rose of Jericho, *Anastatica hierochuntica*. (1)

Rosa pallida: Pale (pink) rose. (1)

Rosa provincialis: Rose grown at Provins, east of Paris. Petals used. (1)

Rosa rubra: Red rose. (1)

Rosaceum, unguentum: See rosatum, unguentum. (1)

Rosaceus solutivus, syrupus: See rosatus solutivus, syrupus. (1)

Rosae, aqua; Rosae fortior, aqua; Rosae aquae, unguentum: Prepared from rose oil. Rose water, stronger rose water, and rose water ointment, respectively. The strong rose-water was a saturated solution of water and rose oil (rosae, oleum); with rose water being a fifty percent dilution of the saturated solution. The ointment, commonly known as cold cream, consisted (historically) of spermaceti (whale oil), white wax, expressed oil of almond, stronger rose water, and sodium borate. A non-pharmacopoeial infusion of rose water, used as a topical astringent, contained dried rose petal, dilute sulphuric acid, and sodium borate. (8)

Rosae, confectio; Rosae, fluidum, extractum; Rosae, mel; Rosae, syrupus: Confection of rose consisted of rose petals, sugar, clarified honey, and stronger rose water. The fluid extract was prepared by maceration with water and glycerin and was further used to prepare the honey of rose (fluid extract plus clarified honey) or the syrup (fluid extract with simple syrup). (8)

Rosae, mel: Honey of roses, decoction of rose petals in honey. (1,42)

Rosae, trochisi: See rosae, confectio.

Rosae [centrifoliae][gallicae] petala: Petals of pale (pink, *Rosa centifolia*) or red (*R. gallica*) rose, respectively. (42)

Rosae acidum, infusum: An infusion of rose petals in water with dilute sulphuric acid, as a base for astringent gargles. The BPC also specified a concentrate with alcohol for storage and reconstitution. (42) See rosarum (acidum) infusum. (40)

Rosae caninae: See rose hips. (8)

Rosae compositum, infusum: Compound infusion of rose, made from red rose, diluted sulphuric acid, sugar, and water. It is used as a vehicle or mild astringent. "[D]eserves a larger use on account of its pleasant flavor and beautiful color." (31)

Rosae compositus, pulvis: Compound rose powder of oil of rose, gum acacia, and refined sugar as well as carmine solution for red color. A diluent for other unpleasant powders such as calomel. (42)

Rosae fluidextractum; Rosae liquidum, extractum: Liquid extract of red rose petals, in alcohol with ten percent glycerin. A coloring. (42)

Rosae gallicae, confectio: See rosae, confectio. (42)

Rosae oleum: Rose oil, distilled from the flowers of the red rose, *Rosa damascena*, used in the preparation of other materials. (8)

Rosae pallidae, confectio flores; Ros: pall:, c. fl.: Confection of flowers of the pale rose, similar to rosae, confectio, above.

Rosarum (acidum), infusum; —, tinctura: A water extract of dried rose buds combined with dilute vitriol, used as a refrigerant, astringent, and gargle. (39)

Rosarum (Damascena) (rubrarum), conserva: Conserve of Damask or red roses, respectively. A jelly made of roses, vitriol, and sugar, for use as a gargle. Used to counteract the irritancy of calomel. (35,39)

Rosarum cum agarico, syrupus; S. Rosar. c. ag.: Syrup of roses with agaric (mushroom). A purgative. (35)

Rosarum rubrarum, tinctura: See rosarum (acidum) infusum. (40)

Rosarum solutiv(a)(um), syrupus: See rosatus solutivus, syrupus. (1,35)

Rosarum, tabellae de succo: Tablets of rose "juice," a cathartic and cholegogue of rose water. (39)

Rosary bean; Rosary pea: See abrus. (33)

Rosatum perlatum: Pearled rose, see diamargaritum simplex. (39)

Rosatum, mel: Honey of roses, decoction of rose petals in honey. (1,42)

Rosatum, unguentum: Ointment of rose petals or rose water and other ingredients. Used as emollient. (1) This is essentially modern cold cream, which originally consisted of spermaceti, white wax, almond oil, and rose water.

Fig. 3-215 Rosa galica or red rose.

Fig. 3-216 Rosa centifolia or pale rose.

Fig. 3-217 Rosa canina or dog rose.

Rosatus solutivus, syrupus: Aperient syrup prepared by infusing rose petals in water, followed by straining, adding sugar, and evaporating the product to a syrup. (1)

Rose: See rosa. (8)

Rose hips; Rosae caninae, confectio: Ripe fruit of the dog rose, *Rosa canina*, and related species, or the confection of rose hips and sugar. The confection was a pleasant base for pills. (8)

Rose mouth wash; Rose mouth W.: Rose water mouthwash, generally of rose water and glycerin.

Rose ointment; Rose lip salve: See rosatum, unguentum and also osatum, unguentum. (42)

Rose pink: Whiting colored with decoction of Brazil wood and pearl ash. (3)

Roseine: Fuchsin, a red dye. (40)

Rosemary, marsh: See statice limonium. (39)

Roses, honey of: See rosa, oxymel. (40)

Rosewood: See rhodium, lignum. (39)

Rosin: See colophonia. (7)

Rosinol: Rosin (resin) oil. (3)

Rosis siccis, syrupus de; Rosaris siccis, syrupus de; Rosar. Sic. S.D.: Syrup of dried roses. (35)

Rosmarinae, aqua: Water of rosemary. (40)

Rosmarini, spiritus: Spirits of rosemary, from the oil in rectified spirits (alcohol). For "hysterical affections." (34)

Rosmarinum; Rosemary, oil of; Rosmarini, oleum: Volatile oil distilled from Rosemary, *Rosmarinus officinalis,* of the Mediterranean basin. It is commonly used to provide a pleasant scent to lotions or other topical formulations, soaps, etc. It may also be used in a manner similar to other volatile oils such as clove (see caryophyllus). Figure 3-218. (8)

Rosmarinus; Rosmarini, flores: Rosemary, *Rosmarinus officinalis*. Leaves and flowering tops (flores) used. (1)

Rosse, oleum: See rosae, oleum. (40)

Rossolis: A febrifugal formula of tincture of cinchona, coriander, canella, and sugar. (39)

Rothera's crystals: See sodium nitroprusside. (40)

Rottenstone: A common sundry, abrasive. (44)

Rottlera: See kamala. (8)

Rotula: Irregularly shaped lozenge. (1)

Rouge: Red ferric oxide. (3)

Rouge, jewellers'; Rouge, mineral: Fine calcined ferric oxide, a sundry, used as an abrasive polish. (40)

Rouge, toilet vegetable: Diluted carthamin, in chalk or other powder. Cosmetic. (40)

Rouge, toilet: Chalk colored red, usually with carmine. Cosmetic. (40)

Ruber; Rubra; Rubrum: Red (masculine, feminine, neuter), Latin. (1)

Rubi, syrupus: Blackberry syrup, syrup et rubus. This contains twenty-five percent fluid extract of rubus in simple syrup, and was used as an astringent. (31)

Rubi, vinum: Raspberry wine, i.e., the wine of the fruit of *Rubus idaei.*

Rubi aromaticus, syrupus: Rubus (blackberry root), cinnamon, nutmeg, clove, allspice, sugar, alcohol, and blackberry juice. A flavoring. (46)

Rubi compositum, elixir: Similar to the cordial, a flavoring of blackberry juice with blackberry root, galls, cinnamon, cloves, mace, ginger, syrup, glycerin, and alcohol. (46)

Rubi fructus, cordale: Blackberry cordial (NF), of the juice, syrup, alcohol, cinnamon, clove, and nutmeg, a flavoring. (45)

Rubi fructus, cordiale; Rubi villosi, cordiale; Rubi Vill., Cord.: Cordial, i.e., syrup of blackberry. Of the juice, cinnamon, clove, nutmeg, alcohol, and simple syrup. A flavoring. (46)

Rubi idaei, acetum: Raspberry vinegar. (40)

Rubi idaei, syrupus: Syrup of raspberry (rubus idaei), made with raspberry juice and sugar. It is heated to the boiling point and filtered while hot. Used as a flavoring agent. (31)

Rubia tinctorum: Madder, *Rubia tinctorum*. Root used. A source of commercial red dye. Figure 3-220. (1)

Rubidium; Rubidii carbonas; —iodidum: Elemental rubidium or the carbonate or iodide salt. Noted to be rarely used in clinical medicine. (42)

Rubigo ferri: Iron rust. (3)

Rubina antimonii: Probably similar to magnesia opalina, an unknown compound of antimony. (39)

Rubini's essence of camphor: A concentrated spirit of camphor, see camphorae, spiritus. (40)

Rubramentum: Red ink. (3)

Rubrum, balsam: A plaster of red lead. (39)

Rosmarinus officinalis

Fig. 3-218 Rosmarinum or rosemary.

Rubus idaeus

Fig. 3-219 Rubus idaeus or raspberry.

Rubia tinctorum

Fig. 3-220 Rubia tinctorum or madder.

Rubrum des(s)icativum, unguentum; Rubrum, unguentum: Ointment of lead oxide, lead carbonate, calamine, Armenian bole, etc. Used to promote healing of wounds, especially chapping and chilblains. (1)

Rubus idaeus; Rubi idaei, syrupus; —, fluidextractum (NF): Raspberry, *Rubus idaeus*, or the American variety *R. strigosus*. Fruit and leaves used. Filtered raspberry juice and sugar were used to make raspberry syrup. Used for flavoring purposes and as a diaphoretic, tonic, and refrigerant. Figure 3-219. (1,8,31,39)

Rubus niger: Fruit of the brambleberry or blackberry, *Rubus fructicosus*, a flavoring and mild astringent. (39) Appearance, save for color, very similar to *Rubus idaea*, or raspberry, above and figure 3-219.

Rubus villosus; —vill.: The bark of the root of blackberry, *Rubus villosus, canadensis,* or *trivialis*. Used as per tannic acid (tannicum, acidum). The fluid extract was obtained by percolation with water, alcohol, and glycerin. Blackberry was mainly used in diarrhea. (8)

Ruddle: A kind of red chalk, reddle. (3)

Rudii, pilulae: Pills of Rudius, purgative pills of Socotra aloe, colocynth, scammony, black hellebore root, etc. Used to treat quartan fever, melancholy, or lethargy. (1) Per Estes (39) after Rudius or Rudiae, a town in southern Italy. Approximately same as colocynthidis compositae, pilulae. (40)

Rue; Rue oil: See rutae, oleum. (8)

Rufi, pilulae; Rufus's pills: Anti-pestilential pills of Socotra aloe, myrrh, and saffron, after Rufus of Ephesis, first century CE anatomist and physician. (1,3) Per Estes (39), these were correctly Roffo's pills. In the BPC, see aloes et myrrhae, pilulae. (42)

Ruge's solution: A tissue stain for microscopy. (24)

Rumex (crispus); Rumicis fluidum extractum: The root of yellow dock, *Rumex crispus,* of Europe, but naturalized in North America. Used as per tannic acid (see tannicum, acidum). The fluid extract was obtained by extraction with alcohol. Rumex is a mild astringent and was used in syphilis, scorbutic disorders (scurvy), and skin disorders including skin cancers. Figure 3-221. (8,39)

Rumex acetosa: See acetosa, but arguably same as *Rumex crispus* above.

Rumex acutus: Narrow-leaved dock, used as per *Rumex crispus*. (39)

Rumex aquaticus; —Britannica: Same as lapathum. (39)

Rumex obtusifolius: Broad-leaved dock, bitter dock; an astringent and laxative. (39)

Rumex patiens: See patiens, radix.

Rumicis compositus, syrupus: Syrup of yellow dock with bittersweet, American ivy, figwort, and sugar; an alterative and anti-scrofulous medication. See acetosa. (34)

Rupellenis, sal; Rupellensis, sal: Same as Rochelle's salt, cream of tartar, sodium potassium tartrate. See potassii et sodii tartras. (3,39)

Ruperti, herba: See gratia dei. (1)

Rusci, oleum: Empyreumatic oil of birch (oil of Russia leather). (3)

Rusci (pyroligneum), oleum: See betulae, oleum. (42)

Rusci compositum, unguentum: See resorcini compositum, unguentum. (42)

Ruscus: Butcher's broom, *Ruscus aculeatus*. Root used as deobstruent, diuretic, and diaphoretic. Figure 3-222. (1,39)

Ruta; Rutae herba: Rue, herb of grace, *Ruta graveolens*. Herb used. Rue was a strong tonic, attenuant, detergent, deobstruent, diuretic, diaphoretic, antihysteric, emmenagogue, antispasmodic, circulatory stimulant, and topical skin irritant and vesicant. Figure 3-223. (1,39,42)

Ruta capraria: Goat's rue, *Galega officinalis*. Capra being Latin for goat. See galega. (1)

Ruta muraria: Wall-rue, white maidenhair, *Asplenium ruta-muraria*. (1)

Rutae, confectio: Confection of rue, of powdered rue (ruta), bay laurel berries, black pepper, caraway fruit, and sagapenum, in clarified honey and distilled water. Antispasmodic and carminative, or an enema for infantile convulsions. (42)

Rutae, conserva: Conserve of rue. (35)

Rutae, enema: Enema of confection of rue and decoction of barley, anthelmintic. (42)

Rutae, oleum: Oil of rue, distilled from the fresh herb, *Ruta graveolens*, of Britain. A typical volatile oil, it was used as an irritant and vesicant both topically or by ingestion. It was said to be particularly effective for inducing menstrual flow. Due to the ability to induce menses, it has been tried in larger doses as an abortifacient, sometimes with fatal results for the mother and child. (8)

Rye: See secale (cornutum). (39)

Fig. 3-221 Rumex crispus or yellow dock.

Fig. 3-222 Ruscus or butcher's broom.

Fig. 3-223 Ruta or rue.

S.: At the beginning or middle of inscription: sal, sel {*French*} (salt); sciroppo {*Italian*}, sirop {*French*}, siropo {*Italian*}, syropo {*Italian*}, syrupus (syrup); seme {*Italian*}, semen (seed); sine {*Latin*} (without); species (see species); spiritus (spirit); succus (juice). At middle or end of inscription: Salomonis (of Solomon); semplice {*Italian*}, simplex (simple, i.e., not composite); siccus (dry); solutivus (aperient); Sylvius (see Sylvius). (1)

S.5 Radicum; S. V Radicum: Syrup of five roots, see syrupus de quinqe radicibus.

S.A.: At end of inscription: sine agarico (without agaricus), as in confectio Hamech s.a. (1)

S.C.: Syrupus corticus, bark syrup. (1)

S.D.: Syrupus de; syrup of.

S.E. Cort. Citr.: See citronum, syrupus e corticum.

S.O.: At end of inscription: sine opio, without opium. (1)

S.S.: Syrupus simplex, simple syrup. See syrupus. (1,8)

Sabadilla: Sabadilla or cevadilla (latter is official term in BPC), *Schoenocaulon officinale.* Seeds were used as a vermifuge and topical antiparasitic, but the irritancy and "drastic properties" (emetic and cathartic effects) limited use. (33)

Sabadillin(e): Active material extracted from sabadilla. See veratrine. (40)

Sabal: Saw palmetto berry, *Serenoa serrulata,* a diuretic and stimulant of the mucous membranes used in cystitis, urethritis, and other genitourinary conditions. Used today for treatment of prostate enlargement. (7,31)

Sabal, fluidextractum: Fluid extract of sabal. (31)

Sabal et santali, tinctura: Tincture of saw palmetto and santal. (31)

Sabal et santali compositum, elixir: Compound elixir of sabal and sandalwood, compound elixir of saw palmetto and sandalwood, of sabal, triticum, and corn-silk, with fluid extract of sandalwood (santalum). Used in cystitis. (31)

Sabbatia (ang.)(angularis): American Centaury, or Rose-pink, *Sabbatia angularis,* a mild tonic. (33)

Sabin; Sabina (cacumina); Sabinae, oleum; —fluidum, extractum; —, tinctura; —, unguentum: Tops of Sabin, Savin, or Savine, *Juniperus sabina,* from which an oil can be distilled, or an alcoholic tincture or a fluid extract prepared. The unguent consists of fresh sabine tops in lard and yellow wax and was employed as a topical irritant, sometimes following that induced by cantharides. It is said to be identical in use to turpentine (terebenthina), but more powerful, especially in its action on the skin and on the ovaries and uterus, where it is said to accelerate menstruation and also induce contractions of the pregnant uterus (an ecbolic). Figure 3-224. (1,8,42)

Sabinae, ceratum; Sabinae, unguentum: Savine ointment, of savin tops in yellow wax and lard. An irritant, as per cantharide. (34)

Sabinae composita, tinctura; Sabinae compositum, tinctura: Compound tincture of sabine, with castor and myrrh, in alcohol. An emmenagogue. (39)

Sabinas cacumina: Sabin. (40)

Sacchari, acidum: Oxalic acid. (40)

Sacchari, spiritus: Sugar spirits, i.e., rum, fermented molasses. (3)

Sacchari faex; —foex: Treacle, molasses. The Latin faex refers to dregs or remnants, molassess being the residue of sugar production. (3,40)

Saccharin(i), elixir; —, liquor: Elixir or liquor of saccharin (about four percent) in alcohol, water, and sodium bicarbonate. Added at about one percent volume as a sweetener when sugar was not desired or compatible. (42)

Saccharin; Saccharinum: Saccharin, the artificial sweetener derived from coal tar, still in use. Primarily used as a sweetener in preparations to be used by diabetics, when sugar was not tolerated. (8)

Saccharolé {*French*}: Any liquid preparation (except syrup) containing large amounts of sugar. (3)

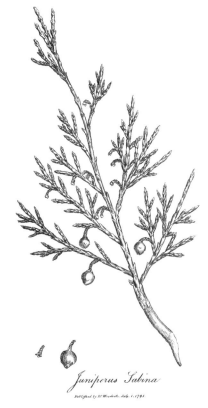

Juniperus Sabina

Fig. 3-224 Sabin or savin.

Saccharum (album)(purificatum); Saccaro {*Italian*}: Sugar (white or purified), typically cane (*Saccharum officinarum*) sugar (figure 3-225) , but could be obtained from beet (*Beta vulgaris*) and other sources. (8,39)

Saccharum acerinum; —, canadense: Maple sugar. (3)

Saccharum candidum; —candum; —candisatum; —cantum (album)(rubrum): Rock candy, or candy sugar, which could be either white (album) or brown (rubrum, which means red). (3)

Saccharum hordeatum: Barley sugar. (1)

Saccharum lactis: Milk sugar, see lactose. (8)

Saccharum nonpurificatum: Unpurified sugar, i.e.—brown sugar. (39)

Saccharum officinarum: Cane sugar, or sometimes molasses. (39)

Saccharum penidi(at)um: Twisted sugar, said to be an anodyne mixture. Confection made by melting sugar over low heat, then drawing out the product in strands. (39) Hughes (40) states this is a synonym for barley sugar, but references almost always provide the former definition.

Saccharum saturni: Sugar of lead (lead acetate), Saturn being the planet associated with lead. (3)

Sacra, tinctura: See aloes, vinum. (40)

Sacred bark: See cascara sagrada. (8)

Sacred elixir: A compound tincture of rhubarb. (3)

Sacred tincture: See aloes, vinum. (39)

Safflower: See carthamus. (40)

Saffran de Mars apéritif {*French*}: Red iron oxide by action of moisture on iron, see crocus martis and martis limatura preparata. (1)

Saffron (, Spanish)(, meadow,)(wild): See crocus. (8)

Safrol; Safrolum: A chief component of oil of sassafras, but found in other fragrant oils. For perfumery. (42)

Sagapenum: Gum resin of *Ferula persica* and related *Ferula* genus. A stimulant aperient, deobstruent, antispasmodic, antihysteric, emmenagogue, and expectorant. (1,39)

Sage; Sage water: See salvia. (3,8)

Sago (perlata): Sago, a prepared farinous (starch-like) material from the heart of the sago palm, *Metroxylon rumphii* or *Cycas revoluta*, and other similar palm species. Used as a nutritive in the invalid, and occasionally as a demulcent. (33,39)

Sailor's pepper: See cubeb. (40)

Saim: Adeps, i.e., fat. (3)

Sal: A solid substance, usually inorganic, a salt. (1)

Sal absinthii: Residue from calcination of wormwood (see absynthium). (1)

Sal alembroth, carbasus: Antiseptic gauze treated with sal alembroth (sal ammoniac), distilled water, and aniline blue dye. (42)

Sal alembroth, gossypium: Absorbent cotton soaked in sal alembroth and dried, usually dyed blue with aniline dye. (42)

Sal alembroth: See ammonio-mercuric chloride. (8)

Sal ammoniacum; Sal armeniacum: Sal ammoniac, ammonium chloride. (1)

Sal aperiens: Aperient salt, of acid potassium tartrate, sulphurated potash, and exsiccated magnesium sulphate, a purgative for gout and rheumatism. (42)

Sal c:c: Either sal carbonas calcii (calcium carbonate) or sal cornu cervi, hartshorn (crude calcium phosphate). (39)

Sal catharticum amarus: Bitter cathartic or purging salts, prepared from the residual salts present after common salt has precipitated from evaporated sea water. A cheap replacement for Epsom salts. A mild purgative. (35)

Sal catharticus glauberi: Sodium sulfate, Glauber's Salt, after Johann R. Glauber, 1604–1670, German chemist who introduced this material into medical use. (1)

Sal commune; Sal communis: Common salt, i.e., table salt, sodium chloride. (1,8)

Sal de duobus; Sal duobus; Sal duplicatum: See arcanum duplicatum. (1)

Sal gemmeum: "Gem" salt, i.e., rock salt. (1)

Sal mirabile: See sal catharticus Glauberi. (1)

Sal nitri; Sal nitriti: Potassium nitrate, see potassii nitras. (39)

Sal pepsinae: Three parts pepsin in salt, used in the place of table salt to assist in digestion. (42)

Sal petrae: Salt of Peter, saltpeter, i.e., nitre. (1)

Sal polychrestum: See polychrestum, sal. (1)

Sal prunellae: See prunellae, sal. (1)

Sal sodae: Soda salts, sodium carbonate, used as an antacid.

Sal tartari: Salt of tartar, impure potassium carbonate, residue obtained via calcination of cream of tartar. (1)

Sal vitrioli: See vitriolum album. (1)

Sal volatile: "Volatile" salts, i.e., smelling salts. See ammoniae aromaticus, spiritus. (8)

Salacetici, acidi, tablettae: Tablets of salacetic acid (aspirin), gum acacia, potato starch, and (see) theobromatis, emulsio as excipient. (42)

Salacetin; Salaceticum, acidum: Acetylsalicylic acid, i.e., aspirin. (40)

Salamander's blood: Fuming nitric acid. See sang de salamandre. (3,39)

Salazolon: Antipyrine salicylate, analgesic, see antipyrine and salicylate. (40)

Salep, mucilago: Mucilage of powdered salep in water, used as per salep. (34)

Salep: Salep, tuber of various plants of the orchid genus *Orchis*, used as a nutritive and demulcent. (33)

Salep radix, Pulv.; Salep r.,p.: Powdered salep root.

Saleratus: See potassii bicarbonas. (40)

Saletin: Acetylsalicylic acid, i.e., aspirin. (40)

Salicin; Salicinium; Salicinum: A neutral principal obtained from various species of *Salix* (willow) and *Populus* (poplar). Structurally related to salicylic acid. (8)

Salicinum effervescens: An effervescent preparation of salicin, with sodium bicarbonate, tartaric and citric acids, and refined sugar. (42)

Salicis, cortex: Willow bark, a bitter and astringent, and source of salicin. (42)

Salicis nigrae cortex: Black willow bark. Liquid extract used for gonorrhea, ovarian pain, and miscellaneous disorders associated with the reproductive organs of either sex. (42)

Salicis nigrae liquidum, extractum: Liquid extract of black willow, aphrodisiac. See salix nigra. (42)

Salicylas, sodii; Salicylas, lithii: Sodium and lithium salts of salicylic acid, from reaction with sodium or lithium carbonate. (8)

Salicylate of strontium: See strontii salicylas. (32)

Fig. 3-225 Saccharum or sugar cane.

Salicylate; Salicylic acid; Salicylicum, acidum: Salicylic acid can be obtained from a variety of plants and oils, but was also produced synthetically in later years from the reaction of carbolic acid (phenol) with carbon dioxide, neutralized with hydrochloric acid. Salicin and salicylic acid are antiseptics with greater activity than carbolic acid itself, but the salts (sodium salicylate, etc.) do not have this activity. The salts are used orally to treat fever and for their anti-inflammatory effects. They also depress the heart in large doses. (8)

Salicylici compositus, acidi, pulvis: Salicylic acid and boric acid in French chalk, a dusting powder for hyperhydrosis, especially of the feet. (42)

Salicylici dilubiles: See acidi salicylici, stili. (31)

Salicylici, acidi, elixir: Salicylic acid elixir of same with potassium citrate, glycerin, and aromatic elixir. (46)

Salicylici, acidi, glyceritum: Glycerite of salicylate, used topically and also systemically as an alternative method to administer salicylate for anti-inflammatory effect. (34)

Salicylici, acidi, glycerogelatinum: Salicylic acid glycerogelatin, of thirty-five percent glycerin and ten percent salicylic acid in glycerinated gelatin vehicle. Used as an antiseptic and keratoplastic (i.e., for remodeling skin). Similar materials are still in use for removal of warts, etc. (31)

Salicylici, acidi, gossypium: Absorbent cotton soaked in salicylic acid dissolved in alcohol and dried. (42)

Salicylici, acidi, stili: Salicylic acid pencil, stilus acid, salicylici dilubiles. These pencils (see medicamentorum, stili) contain ten percent salicylic acid with tragacanth, starch, dextrin, sugar and distilled water. (31) Use as per unguent, below.

Salicylici, acidi, unguentum: Ointment of salicylic acid in paraffin. Topical salicylate is used today for wart and corn removal, and is an effective keratolytic. (34)

Salicylicum [compositum], collodium: Compound salicylic collodion, corn collodion. Salicylic acid, extract of cannabis (in the compound or compositum form), and flexible collodion. Similar preparations are still used for the removal of corns, calluses, and warts. (31)

Salicylicum compositum (elasticum), emplastrum; Salicyl. Co. Emp.: Corn plaster of salicylic acid in rubber or other adherent dressing, of which a strong (forte) form was also available in the BP. One formulation contained salicylic acid, extract of Indian Hemp, India rubber (masticated), wool fat, copaiba, thymol, and oil of wintergreen, softened with naphtha.

Salicyl-sulphonic acid: Reagent for precipitation of protein in urine, a diagnostic test. (40)

Saligallol: See pyrogallol disalicylate. (40)

Salina, mixtura diaphoretica: See mistura diaphoretica. (39)

Salina, mixtura: Potio riveri, river potion, effervescent mixture of potassium citrate. (3)

Salina, solutio: Normal saline solution, 0.95 percent salt in water, for irrigation. (42)

Salina (anodyna), mistura: Saline mixture, a mixture of ammonium acetate, potassium nitrate, and spirit of nitrous ether in water, diaphoretic and diuretic. The anodyne mixture included two percent tincture of opium. (42)

Salina laxans, mistura: A mixture of magnesium sulfate, potassium citrate, and tincture of hyoscyamus in chloroform water, aperient and diuretic. (42)

Salinaphthol: See naphthol salicylate. (40)

Saline: Salt or a solution of salt. (39)

Saline, normal: Normal saline has the approximate salt content of body fluids (plasma), 0.95 percent by weight, or about 150 meq/L. (42)

Saline julap: See mistura diaphoretica. (39)

Saline solution. B.C.G.: Tuberculin injection, diagnostic test material for intradermal injection. BCG is Bacillus Calmette-Guérin, attenuated strain of tubercle bacillus. (40)

Saline wash: See lotio refrigerans. (34)

Salinus aromaticus, spiritus: Aromatic spirits of ammonia, see ammoniae aromaticus, spiritus. (39)

Salipyrazolon; Salipyrine; Salipyrinum: Salipyrine is a trade name for the salicylate salt of antipyrine, useful as an antipyretic and anti-inflammatory, especially for dysmenorrhea. (8,40)

Salis (fumans), spiritus; Salis marini Glauberi, spiritus: Hydrochloric acid. (3,40)

Salis carolini factitii effervescens, pulvis: See Carolinum factitum effervescens. (42)

Salix; Salix nigra; Salix alba: Tree of genus *Salix*, a willow, including the black and white willow (*S. nigra* and *alba*, respectively) or crack willow (*S. fragilis*, figure 3-226) of Europe. Bark used. Source of salicylic acid (aspirin, acetylsalicylic acid, was derived from willow bark), anti-inflammatory. Also used for various urogenital disorders. (1,32) Genitive form is salicis.

Salmiac {*German*}: Ammonium chloride. (3)

Salocoll: Phenocoll salicylate, analgesic, see phenocol. (40)

Salol; Salolum: Salol, or the pseudo-Latin salolum, is the condensation product of phenol and salicylic acid by dehydration with phosphorus pentachloride. This is an intestinal antiseptic by virtue of decay back to phenol (carbolic acid) and salicylic acid, and also has anti-inflammatory and antipyretic actions similar to salicylate and to aspirin. (8)

Salol etherial solution; Salol varnish; Salolis aetherea, solutio: A solution of salol and shellac in ether and alcohol, pill coating resistant to gastric acid, for delivery of drugs to the intestinal tract, i.e., enteric coated. (42)

Salolis compositus, liquor; Salol, compound solution of; Salol mouth wash: A solution of salol, thymol, spirit of anise, oil of peppermint, elixir of gluside (saccharin), and alcohol, typically added at the rate of a few drops per several ounces of water and used as a mouthwash. (42)

Salomonis, opiata: See opiata Salomonis. (1)

Salop: Variant of salep. (39)

Salophen: Aceto-para-amidophenol salicylate. This was administered orally and in the alkaline environment of the intestine, would break down to salicylate and acetyl-para-amido-phenol. According to White's *Materia Medica*, the latter is "harmless." In fact, this is para-acetylamino-phenol, or acetaminophen, and is an effective analgesic. Salophen was employed as a treatment for rheumatism and as an intestinal antiseptic, and was noted to be "quite efficient." (8)

Salix fragilis

Fig. 3-226 Salix fragilis, or crack willow.

Salsepareille {*French*}: See sarsaparilla. (1)

Salt, bay: Sea salt. (40)

Salt, digestive: See sal, pepsinae. (42)

Salt, spirit of: Strong, impure hydrochloric acid, muriatic acid. (40)

Salt, volatile: See ammonii carbonas. (40)

Salt cake: Crude acid sodium sulfate, by-product in industry. (3)

Salt mixture: See potassii citras, liquor. (39)

Salt of many virtues: See polychrestum (multiple entries). Usually potassium sulfate. (39)

Salt of Mars: Ferrous sulfate. (3)

Salt of Saturn: Lead acetate. (3)

Salt of steel: Ferrum vitriolatum, iron sulfate. (39)

Salt of tartar: Pure potassium carbonate. (3)

Salt of tin: Tin chloride. (3)

Saltpeter; Saltpetre: See potassii nitras. (8)

Saltpetre (or saltpeter) Chili; —, Chilean: Sodium nitrate. (40)

Saltpetre paper: Nitre paper; see potassii nitratis, charta. (40)

Salts (not further specified): Usually Epsom salts, magnesium sulfate. (3)

Salts, bitter; Salts of England: Epsom salts. (3,40)

Salt(s), tasteless: Sodium phosphate. (40)

Salufer: Trade name for sodii silicofluoridum, sodium silicofluoride, a disinfectant in dilute solution. (42)

Salutis, elixir: Compound tincture of senna. (3)

Salvarsan: See arsenobenzol. (40)

Salvia: Sage, leaves of *Salvia officinalis*, used chiefly as a condiment and flavoring, but said to be useful in reducing sweating in hectic fevers and as an infusion (sage water) for treatment of sore throat. Figure 3-227. (8)

Salviae, conserva: Conserve of sage leaves. (35)

Salzburg vitriol: Copper sulfate (see cupri sulphas). (3)

Sambuci, aqua: Water of sambucus. No additional information was located on the water. Sambucus itself is said to be an ineffectual remedy for dropsy, and the water was presumably used for the same purpose. (38)

Sambuci, vinum: Wine of elder, or hydragogue tincture, of elder bark, parsley root, and sherry wine. Good for dropsy, ascites, and exanthematous (rash causing) disorders such as scarlatina. (34)

Sambuci flores; —folia: Elder flowers and leaves, respectively, see sambucis. (42)

Sambuci viride, unguentum: Green elder ointment, of fresh leaves, lard, and prepared suet, emollient and for bruises and sprains. (42)

Sambuci(num), unguentum; Sabucini, U.: Ointment of bark, flowers, and berries of the elder in lard. For gastrointestinal disorders, and said to be antiscorbutic. (35,42)

Sambucinum, oleum: Liniment made by boiling elder flowers in olive oil and discarding insoluble matter. (1)

Sambucis ebulus: See ebulus. (39)

Sambucus (niger): Common elder, *Sambucus niger* of which flowers, fruit, leaves, and bark were used. The flowers were used to flavor medicines and as a mild stimulant and diuretic. While the flowers contain an essential oil similar to other essential oils (see caryophyllus), the flowers were used directly in many cases. Figure 3-228. (1,8)

Sambucus ebulis: Dwarf elder, figure 3-229. Diuretic. Sambucus, unspecified, is usually common elder, above.

Sanctum lignum: See guaiaci, lignum. (1)

Sand acid: Hydrofluorosilicic acid, see salufer. (3)

Sandalum; Sandalwood (red): See santalum. (1,8)

Sandalwood oil, mixture: See santali, oleum, mistura. (42)

Sandarac solution; Sandaracae, solutio: Pill varnish, of sandarach gum in absolute alcohol. (42)

Sandaraca; Sandarach (gum): 1. Sandaracha Graecorum, Greek Sandarach, realgar, arsenic disulfide (not used in this sense after seventeenth century). 2. Sandarach, gum resin obtained from trees of genus *Tetraclinis*. (1,39) Gum juniper. (40)

Sanders (red)(wood): See santalum. (39,40)

Sandiver: See glass gall. (3)

Sandyx: Red lead oxide, see plumbum oxidum. (3)

Sang de salamandre {*French*}: Salamander's blood, a red residue of crude nitric acid left after the distillation of niter. Alchemical, in accordance with the legend that this creature was immune to fire. (39)

Sanguinaria; Sanguinariae rhizoma; —fluidum, extractum; —liquidum, extractum; —, syrupus; —, tinctura; —, acetum.: Bloodroot, the rhizome of *Sanguinaria canadensis*, or the fluid extract, syrup, tincture or simple vinegar thereof. The root has a deep reddish-brown color. Used as an emetic, expectorant, emmenogogue, and for many other purposes. (8,39,42,46)

Sanguinariae acetata composita, tinctura: Emetic tincture, compound acetated tincture of bloodroot, of same with skunk-cabbage root, vinegar, and alcohol. An expectorant and for cutaneous diseases. (34)

Sanguinariae composita, mistura: Compound mixture of bloodroot, cough drops. Syrup of ipecac, syrup of squill, tincture of bloodroot, syrup of balsam of tolu, and camphorated tincture of opium, in equal parts. For cough. (34)

Fig. 3-227 Salvia.

Fig. 3-228 Sambucis (niger) or common elder.

Fig. 3-229 Sambucis ebulis or dwarf elder.

Sanguinariae composita, tinctura: Compound tincture of bloodroot with lobelia and skunk cabbage. An expectorant and for cutaneous diseases. (34)

Sanguis {*Latin*}: Blood. On rare occasions, used by mouth for therapy. (1)

Sanguis draconis: Dragon's blood, highly flammable resinous exudate formed on fruit of climbing palms of the genus *Daemonorops* (formerly *Draco*). Forms a blood red solution in alcohol. Astringent and tonic, later replaced by Brazil wood and gum kino. (1,39)

Sanguisuga {Italian}: Leech. (40)

Sanicula: Sanicle, *Sanicula europea*. Leaves used. Primarily an astringent. (1,39)

Sano et esperto, loch {*Italian*}: See sanum et expertum, lohoch. (1)

Sanocrysin: See sodium aurothiosulphate. (40)

Santal, oil of; Santali, oleum; Santali albi, fluidextractum: Sandalwood oil, distilled from the wood of *Santalum album*, figure 3-230, of southern India, or the fluid-extract prepared from sandalwood. It shared all of the actions of other major volatile oils, of which clove (caryophyllus) oil is an example, but was particularly used for urinary disorders. (8)

Santali, olei, mistura: A mixture of oil of sandalwood with gum acacia and cinnamon water, for gonorrhea and urinary catarrh. (42)

Santali composita (cum morphina), mistura: A mixture of oils of sandalwood, cassia, and pigments in alcohol, to which morphine hydrochloride could be added. (42)

Santali compositus, liquor: A solution of oil of sandalwood, spirit of cinnamon, tinctures of buchu and cubeb, and alcohol. Stimulating disinfectant of mucous membranes and urinary tract (following ingestion) and thus used for gonorrhea. (42)

Santalum (citrinum): Tree or shrub of genus *Santalum*, sandalwood, especially white sandalwood, *Santalum album*. Heartwood, lignum santali, used as a restorative tonic. Figure 3-230. (1,39)

Santalum rubrum: Red saunders, the heartwood of *Pilocarpus (Pterocarpus) santalus*, is finely ground and used to color and flavor various preparations, but has limited therapeutic value. Occasionally a tonic, corroborant, or antivenereal. Figure 3-231. (8,39)

Santonica; Santonicum; Santonini; trochisci; —, tabellae; Santonine: Santonica, or wormseed, is the unexpanded flower heads of *Artemesia pauciflora (*or *santonica)*, of Turkey and the Middle East. The active principal is said to be santonin (santoninium). The troche contained santonin, sugar, tragacanth, and stronger orange-flower water. The tablet (NF) is flavored with vanilla and cocoa and the US Dispensatory warns they are easily mistaken for candy and that no more than a few should be given out at once, as three tablets will kill a child. Santonin is a highly effective anthelmintic against roundworm, but not against the tapeworm. It is toxic, with nervous system side effects, including convulsions and loss of consciousness reported. Figure 3-232. (1, 8, 29, 31)

Santonin; Santoninum: Bitter principal prepared from santonica, primarily anthelmintic. (42)

Santonini composita, trochisci: Compound troches of santonin, resin of jalap, gum arabic, chocolate, sugar, water, and gum arabic. A vermifuge. (34)

Santonini compositae, tabellae: Compound tablets of santonin (santonica), of santonin and calomel (to help purge worms), flavored with cocoa and (in USP) vanilla. (31,42)

Sanum et expertum, lohoch: A "sound and expert lozenge." Antitussive, antiasthmatic medication made from hyssop, fenugreek, maidenhair, fennel, iris, cinnamon, licorice, raisins, dried figs, sweet almonds, etc. (1)

Sapa: Sticky, honey-like residue left when raisins or dried grapes are heated. (39)

Sapan (wood): Heartwood of *Caesalpina sappan*, tree of India, used in place of logwood (haematoxylon) in that location and the eastern British colonies. (42)

Sapientiae, sal: Salt of wisdom, see sal alembroth. (39)

Sapium: Yerba de la flecha, *Sapium salicifolium*, a powerful emetic, cathartic, and diuretic. (32)

Sapo: Soap, white soap, Castille soap, hard soap (sapo durus). Soap in general refers to the reaction products of fats and alkali. In pharmaceutical use, if not otherwise indicated, refers to sodium oleate, the soap formed from the reaction of olive oil (largely containing oleic acid) and caustic soda (sodium hydroxide). Soap was commonly used to bind together pills and prepare plasters. (1,8) Soft soap was a potassium salt, see sapo mollis.

Fig. 3-230 Santalum citrinum or S. album, sandalwood.

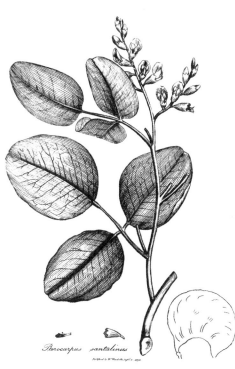

Fig. 3-231 Santalum rubrum of red saunders.

Fig. 3-232 Santonica or wormseed.

Sapo, linimentum: Soap liniment, of soap, camphor, rosemary oil, and alcohol. (39)

Sapo aetheris, liquor; Sap: aether, liq: This is ethereal soap, a liquid solution of soap or fatty acids (oleic acid) in various mixtures of ether (diethyl, methyl-ethyl). Multiple variants were found, including commercial products such as Johnson's Ethereal Soap, evidently used as a surgical disinfectant. (38)

Sapo animalis: Curd or animal soap, soap made from animal fat and sodium hydroxide. A base for plasters, liniments, pills, and suppositories. (8)

Sapo durus: Hard or Castile soap, see sapo above. (42)

Sapo hispanicus (alba)(mot.)(viridis): Spanish soap, white, mottled, or green respectively. This is said to be prepared from olive oil. The mottled variety has some residual water content and is compressed from soap curd, giving a mottled appearance.

Sapo kali: Potash soap. See sapo mollis. (42)

Sapo kalinus (, German): Soft soap (see sapo molis) made with linseed oil. (40)

Sapo medicatus: Medical soap, or white Castile soap. Despite the term, this generally did not contain any other medication or ingredient. (3)

Sapo mollis: Soft, or green soap is prepared from olive oil (occasionally from other oils) reacted with potash, or potassium hydroxide unless otherwise noted. This is in distinction to ordinary (hard) soap, which is produced with caustic soda, or sodium hydroxide. (8)

Sapo niger: Black soap, of lye with oil from whale, fish, or seal. (39)

Sapo tartareus: Soap of tartar, unctuous mass prepared by heating a mixture of saltpeter and tartar with oil of turpentine. (1)

Sapo venetian: Venetian soap, same as sapo alba. (39)

Sapo viridis: See sapo mollis. (8)

Sapocresol: See cresol saponatus, liquor. (40)

Saponaceous pills: Pills of opium or rhubarb made with soap. (39)

Saponaceum, balsamum: See opodeldoc. (3)

Saponaria: Root and leaves of soapwort, soaproot, bouncing bet, fuller's herb, bruisewort, *Saponaria officinalis*. A tonic, diuretic, and alterative. Herb and root used. Figure 3-233. (1,33,39)

Saponatis: An irregularly used genitive form of sapo (soap), see saponis.

Saponatis, spiritus: Spirits of soap, typically of 175 grams castile soap per liter of alcohol and water. Used for cleansing and as a liniment for skin conditions. (34)

Saponato-camphoratum, linimentum: Camphorated soap liniment, solid opodeldoc, containing freshly prepared sodium stearate made by combining sodium carbonate and stearic acid, perfumed with camphor, oils of thyme and rosemary, and ammonia water. "It is a useless survival of a former fad." (31)

Saponato-camphoratum, tinctura; Sap. Camp., Tr.; Sapo Camph., Tr.: Tincture of camphorated soap. This is the same as the liniment, immediately above.

Saponin: See quillain. (42)

Saponis, emplastrum: Soap plaster, of soap and lead plaster, mixed with water and evaporated to the desired consistency. A common base for the addition of active substances to form a plaster. (8,31)

Saponis, enema: Enema of soft soap and water, for bowel evacuation. (42)

Saponis, glyceritum: Glycerite of soap, which forms a mass which will melt when applied to the skin. A base for emollients. (34)

Saponis, linimentum: See saponis viridis, tinctura. (34)

Saponis, linimentum: Soap liniment, of soap, camphor, oil of rosemary, and alcohol. Could be used as such, or as a base for active constituents. Also referred to as opodeldoc. (8)

Saponis (viridis)(camphoratis), tinctura: See saponis mollis linimentum. Although referred to as a tincture, and containing some alcohol, with or without camphor, this is really a soap-based liniment. Also known as spiritus nervinis camphoratis, liquid opodeldoc, or camphorated tincture of soap. (8,34)

Saponis aetherea, solutio: Ether soap, of oleic acid, potassium hydroxide, alcohol, lavender oil, and methylated ether. A pre-surgical scrub. (42)

Saponis composita, pilula: See opii, pilulae. (34)

Saponis et opii, tinctura: See opii, linimentum. (40)

Saponis fuscum, emplastrum; Sap. Fuscum, Emp.: Plaster of brown soap, of wax, soap, vinegar, and lead oxide. (33)

Saponis fuscum: Brown soap, in the BP.

Saponis kalini, spiritus: Spirit of potash soap, of same with lavender in alcohol. (42)

Saponis mollis, linimentum: Liniment of soft (green) soap, of soft soap, oil of lavender flowers, alcohol, and water. (8)

Saponis pulv.: Powdered soap.

Sappan, decoctum: Decoction of sappan, official in India, use as per decoction of haematoxylon. (42)

Sapphire water: Same as aqua aeruginis ammoniatae, a green solution of ammoniated copper. (39)

Sarcocolla: Gum resin of Eastern origin, probably an inferior grade of gum tragacanth. (1)

Sarracenia: Pitcher plant, sidesaddle plant, fly trap, water cup, *Sarracenia purpurea*. A stimulant and laxative. (32)

Sarsa; Sarsae: Generally an abbreviated form of sarsaparilla, from the common name sarsa parilla (as opposed to yellow parilla). (8)

Sarsae compositum, decoctum: Decoction of sarsaparilla, sassafras root, guaiac wood, dried licorice root, mezerion bark, and water. Said to be chiefly used as a vehicle for potassium iodide to treat syphilis. (42)

Sarsae compositus concentratus, (liquor)(decoctum): A solution made from sarsaparilla, sassafras root, guaiac wood, licorice root, and mezereon bark in alcohol and water. This is said to be eight-fold the concentration of the standard decoction and used as a base to administer iodine. (42)

Sarsae liquidum, extractum: Liquid extract of sarsaparilla, BPC, in alcohol with ten percent glycerin. (42)

Sarsae radix: Sarsa root, i.e., sarsaparilla. (42)

Sarsae, decoctum: Simple infusion of sarsaparilla in water. (44)

Saponaria Officinalis.

Fig. 3-233 Saponaria or soapwort.

Sarsaparilla; Sarsaparillae fluidum, extractum: The root of various species of the genus *Similax* (*S. medica, S. papyracea*, etc.), of the tropical Americas. A fluid extract was prepared by maceration in alcohol and water. White's *Materia Medica* of 1894 notes that "it is not known to have any physiological action. It is never given alone, therefore we are ignorant of its therapeutic effects. Probably it has none." Nonetheless, it seems to have acquired some public esteem as a general tonic and stimulant. Figure 3-234. (1,8)

Sarsaparilla, compound decoction of: See sarsae compositus concentratus, decoctum. (42)

Sarsaparilla, decoction: See sarsae, decoctum. (42)

Sarsaparilla, Indian: See hemidesmus. (8)

Sarsaparilla, (Jamaica(n))(Mexican)(Central American)(Equador(i) an): Sarsaparilla of various geographical origins, variously *Similax ornata, medica*, or *officinalis*. Used interchangeably. (7)

Sarsaparillae (compositus), syrupus; Sarsap. Co., Syr.: Syrup or, usually, the compound syrup of sarsaparilla, or syrupus sudorificus, of the fluid extracts of sarsaparilla, glycyrrhiza, and senna, oils of sassafras, anise, and gaultheria, sugar, and water, strained to remove foreign matter. (8)

Sarsaparillae compositum, decoctum: Compound decoction of sarsaparilla, of sarsaparilla, sassafras, guaiacum wood, glycyrrhiza, and mezereum, by boiling in water, maceration ,and straining. (8)

Sarsaparillae fluidum compositum, extractum: Compound fluid extract of sarsaparilla, of sarsaparilla, glycyrrhiza, sassafras, and mezereum, by maceration and percolation with glycerin, water, and alcohol. (8,31)

Sarsarparilla; Sarsar.: Orthographic variant of sarsaparilla.

Sassa gum: Poorly described gum of Asian origin. Unofficial. (44)

Sassafras; Sassafras, oleum: The bark of the root of Sassafras variifolium, of the western and southern United States, from which an oil can be distilled. Sassafras is a mild stimulant and the mucilage is considered a useful vehicle. It does not appear to be of impressive therapeutic value. Figure 3-235. (8)

Sassafras (radix): Inner bark of the root of the tree *Sassafras officinale*. Aperient, tonic, blood purifier, diuretic, diaphoretic, antirhumatic, and antivenereal. (1,39)

Sassafras, spiritus; Sassafras olei, tinctura: Spirit of sassafras, of the oil in alcohol. (34)

Sassafras composita, lotio: Lotion of sassafras and rosewater, used especially for eye conditions. (34)

Sassafras et opii, mistura: Mixture of sassafras and opium, mistura opii alkalina, or Godfrey's cordial, of oil of sassafras, tincture of opium, alcohol, potassium carbonate, molasses, and water. A carminative. (34)

Sassafras medulla; Sassafras, medullae, mucilago: The medulla (core) of sassafras root, which forms a pleasant and useful mucilage when boiled in water and strained. (8,34)

Sassy bark: See erythrophloeum. (8) See casca bark. (40)

Satin spar: Gypsum. (3)

Saturatio: Solution of sodium citrate. (3)

Satureja; Satureia: Summer savory, *Satureia hortensis*. Herb used as an aromatic. (1,33,39)

Saturn; Saturni; Saturnus: Lead, this planet being associated with the metal. (3)

Saturn, extract of; Saturni, extractum: Lead acetate, see also Goulard's extract of Saturn. (39)

Saturni, acetum: Solution of lead subacetate. (3)

Saturni, aqua: See plumbi subacetatis dilutus, liquor. (40)

Saturni, saccharum; Saturni, sal; —, salis: Salt of Saturn, i.e., sugar of lead, lead acetate. (1,39)

Saturni, unguentum; Saturninum, unguentum: Ointment of lead acetate. See plumbi acetatis, unguentum. (1)

Saturnina, aqua: Lead water. (3) Likely the acetate or subacetate, Saturni aqua, above.

Saturnine anodyne pills: Lead analgesic pills of cerussa (lead acetate) with ipecac and opium. (39)

Saturnine ointment: Simple ointment with lead acetate, a refrigerant plaster. (39)

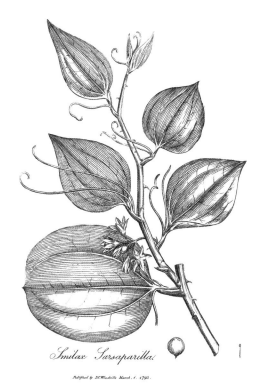

Smilax Sarsaparilla.

Fig. 3-234 Sarsaparilla.

Laurus Sassafras

Fig. 3-235 Sassafras.

Satyrion; Satyrium: Term denoting certain plants of the genus *Orchis*, especially *Orchis mori*, the green-winged orchid and *O. mascul(a) (us)*, figure 3-236. Tuberous root used. The base of an orchid resembles the testicle, from which the name orchid derives, and hence was used to enhance male sexual performance. (1,35,39)

Sauce-alone: See alliaria. (39)

Saucy bark: See erythrophloeum. (8)

Sauerin: Lactic acid bacillus, dried, as a digestive aid. (40)

Saunders: See sanders, see santalum (multiple entries). (39)

Savin(e); Savina {*Italian*}: Savin, see sabina. (1,8)

Savine cerate: See sabinae, unguentum. (34)

Savory, summer: See satureia. (39)

Saw palmetto: See sabal. (31)

Sawyer's (Sir James) asthma powder: See stramonii compositus, pulvis. (42)

Saxafrage, burnet: See pimpinella. (39)

Saxifraga: Meadow saxifrage, *Saxifraga granulata*. Plant used. (Do not confuse with sassafras). Figure 3-237. (1)

Saxin: Saccharin. (3)

Scabiem, unguentum contra: Anti-scabies ointment of sulfur, white lead, calcined lead, litharge, frankincense, etc. (1)

Scabiosa: Field scabious, *Scabiosa arvensis*. Leaves used. (1)

Scabiosum, unguentum: See scabiem, unguentum contra. (1)

Scammonii, confectio: Confection of scammony resin, ginger, oil of caraway, oil of cloves, simple syrup, and clarified honey. A cathartic. (42)

Scammonii, electuarium: Electuary of scammony, of same, with clove, ginger, caraway, and rosewater. A "warm, brisk cathartic." (39)

Scammonii, lac; —, mistura: Scammony mixture, lac scammonii, or emulsio purgans cum scammonia. An emulsion of powdered scammony in whole milk. A pleasant-tasting purgative for adults and children. (34)

Scammonii, resina: Dried resin from an alcoholic tincture of scammony. Use as per the herb. (34)

Scammonii compositus, pulvis: According to Estes this was made in London with scammony, jalap, and ginger but in Edinburgh of scammony and cream of tartar. The BPC specifies scammony resin, jalap powder, and ginger powder. Cathartic. (39,42)

Scammonii cum hydrargyro, pulvis: Powder of calomel and scammony, purgative. (42)

Scammonin: Active components of scammony. (40)

Scammony (juice), Scammonium; Scamoniae radix; Scammonii, resina; —, extractum: Scammony is the resinous exudate of the living root of *Convolvulus scammonia*, sometimes referred to as Scammonium de Aleppo as it was commonly obtained in the Levant. The resin was prepared by extracting with alcohol and precipitating the insoluble resin by addition of water, followed by washing and evaporation to dryness. An alcoholic extract could also be prepared. Scammony is a powerful purgative, or hydrogogue cathartic, i.e., one causing a severe watery evacuation of the bowels. It was used to treat intestinal worms and in adults or children to treat obstinate constipation. Figure 3-238. (1,8,42)

Scammony milk: See scammonii, lac. (40)

Scammony, Mexican: See jalap (7)

Scamonii compositae, pilulae: Compound pills of scammony resin with jalap resin, soap, and strong tincture of ginger. A drastic purgative. (34)

Scarabeus: Dor-beetle, scarab beetle. (1)

Scariola: See endivia. (1)

Scecachul; Scecacul: See secacul. (1)

Schaenanthum; Schénanthe {*French*}: See schoenanthum. (1)

Scheele's acid: Dilute hydrocyanic acid, four percent. (40)

Scheele's green: Copper arsenite. (40)

Schick test: Skin test reagent for diphtheria. (40)

Schilla: See scilla. (1)

Schindler's jelly: Protargol, see argein. (40)

Schlippe's salt: Sodium sulphantimoniate. (40) This is a red-brown photographic toner.

Schoenanthi, herba; Schoenanthum: Grass of genus *Andropogon*, e.g.— camel's hay, *Andropogon schoenanthus*, native to North Africa. (1)

Orchis mascula

Published by D.ʳ Woodville June 1. 1791.

Fig. 3-236 Satyrion or orchis mascula, an orchid.

Saxifraga granulata

Published by D.ʳ Woodville May 1. 1794.

Fig. 3-237 Saxifraga or meadow saxifrage.

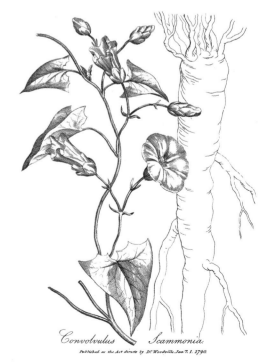

Convolvulus Scammonia

Published as the Act directs by D.ʳ Woodville Jan 7. 1. 1790.

Fig. 3-238 Scamony.

Schulze's solution: Chloro-zinc iodine, a stain used in tissue microscopy. (40)

Schweinfurth's green: Copper arsenite. (3)

Schällibaum's solution: A tissue mounting solution for microscopy. (24)

Scientiae, sal: Sal alembroth. (3)

Scilla: Dried bulb of squill, *Urginea* (or *Scilla*) *maritima*, native to the shores of the Mediterranean, Figure 3-239. Scilla is the source of scillin and a variety of other toxins. It acts upon the heart in a manner similar to digitalis, but due to the presence of other active ingredients (scillin, etc.) is more prone to causing numbness and vomiting. It is also said to be useful as an expectorant in chronic bronchitis. Due to irritancy and other side effects, squill was often used in combination with digitalis and other remedies. White's *Materia Medica* suggests a pill consisting of squill, digitalis, and the mercurial diuretic, calomel, for use in heart failure. (1,8)

Scillae composita, mistura: A mixture of syrup of squill, oxymel of squill, and spirit of nitrous ether in water, use as per scillae, mistura. (42)

Scillae, acetum; Scillae fluidum extractum; —liquidum, extractum; —, oxymel; —, syrupus; —, tinctura: The vinegar, fluid extract, oxymel, syrup, or tincture of squill. (8,42)

Scillae, linctus: Syrup of the oxymel of squill with gum tragacanth, glycerin, emulsion of chloroform, and simple syrup, for cough, especially in children. (42)

Scillae, mel; —, oxymel: Oxymel of squill, see scilliticum, oxymel. (40)

Scillae, mistura: A mixture of syrup of squill, diluted hydrobromic acid, and spirits of chloroform in water, sipped slowly for cough. (42)

Scillae, pilule; Scillaticae, pilule: A pill of squill, gum ammoniac, licorice, and cardamom minus, in simple syrup. Diuretic, diaphoretic, and sialogogue, especially used before the introduction of digitalis. (39)

Scillae compositae, pilulae: Compound squill pills, of powdered squill, ginger, and sal ammoniac with hard soap and syrup. (42)

Scillae compositae, tablettae: Tablet of squill, ginger powder, ammoniac, hard soap, refined sugar, and alcohol to bind. (42)

Scillae compositus, syrupus; Scillae Co., Syr.: Compound syrup of squill or hive syrup, of squill, senega, antimony, and potassium tartrate (antimonii et potassii tartras), sugar, calcium phosphate, and water. For cough. (8,34)

Scillae et ipecacuanhae, mistura: A mixture of vinegars of squill and ipecac with potassium citrate and ammonium acetate in anise water, a diaphoretic and expectorant. (42)

Scillae et opii, mistura: Mixture of squill (scilla) and opium in cinammon water. For cough. (40)

Scilliticum, oxymel: Oxymel of squills, i.e., an oxymel made with vinegar extract of squill. (1)

Sciroppo {*Italian*}**:** Syrup, see syrupus. (1)

Sclavo's serum: Anti-anthrax serum, used for local and systemic treatment of anthrax. (40)

Scolopendrium: Hart's tongue, *Scolopendrium vulgare* or *Asplenium scolopendrium*. Fronds used, deobstruent and "visceral tonic." Figure 3-240. (1,39)

Scoparii, decoctum: Decoction of broom, of dried tops in water, diuretic for dropsy. (42)

Scoparii, infusum: An infusion of broom. The BPC also specified a concentrate with alcohol and chloroform water for storage and reconstitution. (42)

Scoparii, succus: Fresh juice of broom tops (three parts), to which is added alcohol (one part) as a preservative. (34)

Scoparin; Scoparinum: Poorly characterized extract of scoparius, believed to be a diuretic, used in place of the whole herb or for hypodermic injection. (42)

Scoparius; Scoparii cacumina; Scoparii, fluidextractum: Broom, the tops of *Cytisus scoparius*, or the fluid extract thereof. It was prescribed as a diuretic and was also emetic in large doses. (8, 31,39)

Scordium: Water-Germander, *Teucrium scordium*. Herb used as deobstrent, diuretic, and diaphoretic. Figure 3-241. (1,39)

Scorpio: Scorpion. (1)

Scorpions, oil of: Oil in which scorpions have been digested. (40)

Scorza {*Italian*}**:** Bark, peel, rind, crust (in reference to bread). (1)

Scorzonera: Viper's grass, black salsify, *Scorzonera hispanica*. Herb used. (1)

Scot(t)'s pills: See grana angelica and also Anderson's Scots pills. 39)

Scotch paragoric: See opii ammoniata, tinctura. (42)

Scotch soda: Crude sodium carbonate. (3)

Scott's dressing: See hydrargyri compositum, unguentum. (40)

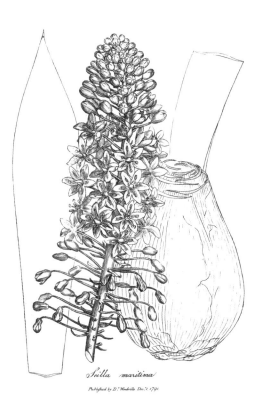

Fig. 3-239 Scilla or squill.

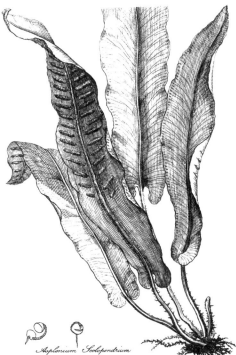

Fig. 3-240 Scolopendrium or hart's tongue.

Fig. 3-241 Scordium.

Scott's liniment: See hydrargyri linimentum. (40)

Scrofula plant; Scrophularia: Carpenter's square, scrofula plant, figwort, heal-all, *Scrophularia nodosa.* A stimulant, tonic, diuretic, etc., particularly used for scrophula, a tuberculous infection of the lymph nodes of the neck. (32)

Scrofula weed: See goodyera. (33)

Scrophulariae, unguentum: Figwort ointment, of the leaves in lard and tallow, for piles and skin disorders. (34)

Scudder's alterative: See corydalis composita, tinctura. (34)

Scullcap: See scutellaria. (8)

Scurvy grass, spirit of: See armoraciae compositus, spiritus. (40)

Scurvygrass; Sea —; Scot's —: See cochlearia, brassica marina, or cochlearia marina, respectively. (39)

Scutellaria; Scutellariae fluidum, extractum: Blue skullcap, the herb *Scutellaria lateriflora,* or fluid extract of same. A mild sedative said to have little therapeutic effect. Used as a remedy for rabies (ineffective). Figure 3-242. (8,39)

Scylla: See scilla. (1)

Scytodephicum, acidum; Scytodepsicum, acidum: Tannic acid. (3,40)

Scytodepsicum, unguentum: Soft (moist) lead tannate. (3)

Sea holly: See eryngium. (39)

Sea lavender: See statice limonium. (39)

Sea onion; Sea-onion: Squill, see scilla. (3)

Sea-colewort: See brassica marina. (39)

Sebesten; Sebestina: Sebesten, a plum-like fruit of the tree *Cordia myxa.* It produces a mucilagenous material used to soothe sore throats and alleviate cough. (1,39)

Sebum (castrati); Sevum: Suet, tallow. The weak form (castrati) was from a castrated ram. (3)

Secacul; Seccacul arabum: Name applied to eastern plant, identity unknown. (1)

Secale: Rye. (1)

Secale cornutum: Literally (from the Latin) horned rye, also referred to as spurned rye. This is rye contaminated with the fungus *Clavaceps pupurea,* source of ergot. The growth of the fungus makes the grain appear to be pointed or horned. See ergota. (39)

Secalis cornuti, tinctura: See ergotae, tinctura. (40)

Secretin; Secretinum; Secretini, liquor: A solution of duodenal secretions, a digestive aid. (40)

Sedaspirin: Acetyl-bromo-salicylic acid, an anti-inflammatory and sedative, see bromide. (40)

Sedativa, aqua: See ammoniacalis camphorata, lotio. (40)

Sedative de raspail, eau: See ammoniacalis camphorata, lotio. (31)

Sedative salt: See sedatum, sal. (40)

Sedative solution of opium: See opii sedativus, liquor. (42)

Sedative water: See ammoniacalis camphorata, lotio. (31)

Sedativus hombergi, sal: Homberg's sedative salt, boracic acid, i.e., boric acid. See Homberg's narcotic salt of vitriol. (3)

Sedatum, sal; Sedativus: Sedating salt, of salt and vitriol volatilized with borax, i.e., boric acid. (39,40)

Sedlicensis, sal; Seidlitz salt: Salt from the spring at Seidlitz, in Bohemia. Essentially Epsom salts, magnesium sulfate. (3,39)

Sedum (acre): House-leek (*Sempervium tectorum*) or Wall-pepper (*Sedum acre*). Emetic, cathartic, diuretic. Figure 3-243. (1,39)

Seidlitz('s) powder: See effervescens compositus, pulvis. (8)

Seidlitz('s) water: See magnesii citratis, liquor. (40)

Seignette, sal polychrestum de: See polychrestum…. (1)

Seignette salt: Rochelle salt, see potassii et sodii tartras. (3)

Sel {*French*}**:** Salt. (1)

Sel anglais: Smelling salt, see ammoniae aromaticus, spiritus. (40) May also refer to English salt, i.e., Epsom salts.

Sel de sagesse; Sel de science: See alembroth, sal. (40)

Sel d'Angleterre: English, i.e., Epsom salts. (40)

Selenite: Gypsum. (3)

Self-heal: See prunella. (39)

Selinum: Root of marsh parsley or marsh smallage, *Selinum palustre.* According to King's, this "is emmenagogue, diuretic, and antispasmodic, but abandoned as an internal remedy on account of its caustic and dangerously poisonous properties." (33)

Sem. (et Flor.) A~M, M~Z, or other letter variants.: Drawer or cabinet pull for alphabetical filing of various seeds (and flowers).

Semen; Seme {*Italian*}**:** Seed. (1)

Semen _____: Seed. See _____, semen if not listed immediately below. (8)

Semen ambrette: Seeds of musk mallow, see abelmoschus. (40)

Mad-dog Skull-cap.   Scutellaria lateriflora.

Fig. 3-242 Scutellaria or blue skullcap.

Sedum acre

Fig. 3-243 Sedum acre.

Semen contra: Barbary wormseed. Herb of the genus *Artemesia*, same as or related to santonica. (3)

Semen cynae: Santonica, Levant worm-seed. (3)

Semen sanctum: Seeds of santonica. (40)

Semen sanitum: Seed of *Artemisia santonica*. (3)

Semencina: Levant wormseed (santonica). (3)

Semina strychni: Nux vomica. (3)

Sempervivum: See sedum. (1) *Supervivum tectorium* is the common house leak, juice applied to bites, stings, and monor skin injuries; unofficial in US (44)

Semplice {*Italian*}**:** Simple, not a mixture. (1)

Sena: See senna, etc.

Seneca (snakeroot): Variant of senega. (7)

Senecio (aureas); Seneci[i][onis], fluidextractum; —, oleoresina: The dried plant *Senecio aureus*, or the fluid extract or dried oleoresin, used as an emmenagogue. (The genitive of senicio is irregularly either senecionis or senecii.) (3,31,34)

Senecio vulgaris: Common groundsel, probably the same as or similar to senecio (aureus), above, as it is described for the same indications. Unofficial. (44)

Senega; Senegae radix; Seneka; Seneca: Root of *Polygala senega*, the active component of which is referred to as senigin or saponin. Seneca is a common orthographic variant, also called seneca Snakeroot. It is a respiratory irritant and expectorant and also acts upon the heart, like digitalis. Used as an expectorant, as a cardiac medication, and as a snuff to induce sneezing. It is said to be useful in chronic bronchial conditions, but as it is an irritatant to the respiratory tract, it is not recommended for acute or inflammatory conditions. Figure 3-244. (8)

Senega oil; Seneka oil; Seneca oil: Crude petroleum. (3) No oil is derived from the botanical source of the same name.

Senegae, decoctum; —, infusum (concentratum): A water decoction or infusion of senega, similar to the fluid extract. (40) The BPC also specified a concentrated infusion with alcohol, ammonia, oil of wintergreen, and chloroform water for storage and reconstitution. (42)

Senegae alcoholicum, extractum: Dry alcoholic extract of senega powder, USP. (44)

Senegae fluidum, extractum; —liquidum, extractum; —, syrupus; —, tinctura; —concentratus, liquor: The fluid extract, syrup or tincture of senega. An expectorant. (8) The BPC specifies a concentrated liquor form for reconstitution as needed.

Seneka: Variant of senega. (39)

Senna (Alexandrina)(Alex.)(Indica)(Ind.)(Tinn.): Senna was a popular laxative and remains in use today. Senna itself consists of the leaves of *Cassia acutifolia* or *C. senna* (Alexandria senna) or *C. augustafolia* (Indian or Tinnivelly senna). The leaf was not used directly, but rather in the preparation of numerous laxative formulations, many of which contain multiple laxative agents. The latter is not entirely irrational, as senna stimulates the motion of the bowels and will cause cramping, or "gripe," which is prevented by laxatives having other modes of action. It is said to induce purgation by the intravenous route, and consumption by the mother is noted to produce laxative properties in breast milk. Figure 3-245. (8)

Senna, American: Wild senna, see cassia (fistula). (39)

Senna, sweet essence of: See sennae, elixir. (42)

Sennae, compositum, infusum: Compound infusion of senna, or black draught, consisting of senna, manna, magnesium sulphate, and fennel in water. (8)

Sennae, confectio: Confection of senna, benedicta laxativa, with senna, oil of coriander, fig, tamarind, cassia fistula, prune, sugar, and water. (8,39) See lenitiva, electuarium.

Sennae, infusum: An infusion of senna and sliced ginger in boiling water. Purgative. The BPC also specified a concentrate with tincture of ginger, alcohol, and chloroform water for storage and reconstitution. (42)

Sennae, syrupus: Syrup of senna, of Alexandria senna, oil of coriander, sugar, alcohol, and water. (8)

Sennae aromaticus, syrupus: Aromatic syrup of senna, made from fluid extract of senna (sennae fluidum, extractum), jalap, rhubarb (rhus), cinnamon, clove (caryophyllum), nutmeg (myristicum), oil of lemon (citrus, oleum), sugar, and diluted alcohol. A compound laxative. (31)

Polygala Senega

Fig. 3-244 Senega or seneca snakeroot.

Cassia Senna

Fig. 3-245 Senna.

Sennae composita, mistura: Compound mixture of senna described by King's as the British equivalent to the compound infusion (below) known as black draught. Of magnesium sulphate, infusion of senna, fluidextract of licorice, tincture of senna, and tincture of cardamom. Use as per the infusion. (34)

Sennae (composita), tinctura: Elixir salutis, tincture of senna, technically a compound tincture, although not always labeled as such, with senna, raisins, caraway fruit, coriander fruit, and spirits. A similarly named preparation consisted of senna, jalap, fennel or coriander seed, raisins, and brandy or alcohol. (34)

Sennae compositus, syrupus: Compound syrup of senna, of fluid extracts of senna, rhubarb, and frangula with oil of gaultheria (wintergreen), alcohol, and syrup. (46)

Sennae dulcis, liquor; Sennae, elixir: Elixir of senna, of root (extracted in process), refined sugar, chloroform, oil of coriander, tincture of capsicum, alcohol, and water. Laxative, especially for use in children. (42)

Sennae et sulphuris, confectio: Confection of senna, sublimed sulphur, acid potassium tartrate, tragacanth powder, simple syrup, tincture of orange, and glycerin. A mild laxative to help with hemorrhoids, or for use in children. (42)

Sennae fluidum deodoratum, extractum: Deodorized fluid extract of senna, prepared from solid senna deodorized by extraction with alcohol. (46)

Sennae fluidum, extractum; —(leguminorum) liquidum, extractum; —concentratum, liquor: A simple fluid extract of senna (pods or beans, leguminae) in alcohol and water, used mainly to produce other formulations. The BPC specifies a concentrate liquor for reconstitution as needed. (8,42)

Sennae folia: Senna leaf.

Sennae fructus; Senna legumes: Senna pods or beans, laxative. (42)

Sennae leguminosum liquidum, extractum: A mild laxative for use in children, from senna pods (leguminae). (42)

Sennae simplex, infusium: Simple senna infusion, of senna and ginger. (39)

Sennae tartarisatum, infusium: Tartarated infusion of senna, of same with coriander and cream of tartar. A cathartic, said to be a more palatable form of senna. (39)

Sennerti, sal: Potassium acetate. (3)

Sentinelle, powder of: Magnesia alba, magnesium oxide. (39)

Sepia: Cuttlefish or cuttle-fish bone. (1)

Septfoil: See tormentilla. (39)

Sericose: Cellulose acetate. (3)

Sericum: Cocoon of silkworm. (1)

Seriparus, liquor: Liquid rennet, usually in solution of alcohol or sherry. (3,42)

Serpentina: See serpentaria. (39)

Serpent(in)aria; Serpent(in)ariae rhizoma; Serpent(in)aria Virgini(an)a: Serpentary, Virginian Snake-root, *Aristolochia serpentaria*. Rhizome and root used for a wide variety of purposes from tonic to enema. Figure 3-246. (1,39)

Serpent(in)ariae composita, tinctura: Compound tincture of serpentaria, of same with ipecac, saffron, camphor, and gin or other diluted alcohol. A powerful sudorific, also called sudorific tincture. (34)

Serpent(in)ariae fluidum, extractum; —concentratum, liquor; —, infusum (concentratum); —, tinctura: The fluid extract, concentrated liquor, infusion, or alcoholic tincture of serpentinaria. Alternately, derived from Texas snakeroot, *Aristolochia reticulata*. It is a typical bitter and is employed as such (see columba). (7,8) The BPC specified a concentrated liquor and also specified a concentrated infusion with alcohol and chloroform water for storage and reconstitution. (42)

Serpyllum: Wild thyme, mother of thyme, *Thymus serpyllum*. Herb used. Figure 3-247. (1)

Serum _____ (BPC); Sera {plural}: A number of sera were specified in the BPC, derived from the blood of immunized animals, including **antidiphthericum** (diphtheria antitoxin); **antipestis** (plague, *Yersinia* (now *Pasteurella*) *pestis*); **antistreptococcum** (for streptococcal infection including erysipelas); **antitetanicum** (tetanus antitoxin); **antithyroideum** (to treat graves disease, of questionable value); and **antiveninosum** (snake or other venom). Those directed against toxins (diphtheritic, tetanus, snake) remain of some clinical importance, those directed at bacterial infections (streptococcal) have been supplanted by antibiotics. (42)

Serum (lactis): Whey (milk). (3)

Sesami, oleum; Sesame oil; Sesamum, oil of: Oil expressed from sesame seed, the seed of *Sesamum indicum*, of Asia. Used for preparing hair oil or as a flavoring. (8)

Fig. 3-246 Serpentinaria.

Fig. 3-247 Serpyllum.

Sesamum (orientale); Sesami folium; Sesamino {*Italian*}: Sesame, *Sesamum indicum* or *Sesamum orientale*. Seeds or occasionally leaves (folium) used. Mucilagenous laxative. (1,39)

Seseli: Plant of genus *Seseli*, hartwort. Leaves and seeds used. (1)

Sesquisulphuret of antimony: See antimonium nigrum purificatum. (40)

Seton: This is a thread or string designed to be passed subcutaneously through a wound or infection to drain pus. (39)

Seven-barks: See hydrangea. (7)

Sevum: Fat. See suet. (8)

Sevum benzoinatum: Benzoinated suet, prepared by digesting suet with three percent powdered benzoin. (31)

Sevum ceti: Fat of a whale, i.e., spermaceti. (39)

Sevum ovillum: Sheep's fat. See suet. (8)

Sevum phosphoratum: Phosphorated suet, of same with carbon disulfide and phosphorus. (42)

Sevum praeparatum: Prepared suet, heated and strained fat from the internal organs (omentum) of sheep. (42)

Sevum salicylatum: Salicylated suet, of prepared suet with salicylic and benzoic acid, for skin disorders. (42)

Seyderhelm's solution: A solution of trypan blue and congo red dye used to stain urinary sediment in urinalysis. (24)

Seydschutzense, sal: Magnesium sulfate. (3)

Shaving cream, aseptic: See paraffini, emulsio. (42)

Sheele's solution; Sheele's Prussic acid: See hydrocyanidum, acidum. This is a four to five percent solution of hydrocyanic acid. (8)

Shell-lac; Shellac: Resin of the shell of the lac beatle, see lacca.

Shepard's purse: See bursa pastoris. (39)

Sherbet: See kali, lemon. (40)

Shikimol: Safrol. (3)

Shoemaker's black: Ferrous sulfate, used as a pigment. (40)

Shohl's solution: Solution of citric acid and sodium citrate, used to treat renal tubular acidosis. (24)

Siberian Snow Rose: See rhododendron. (39)

Siccativus: Siccative, drying. (1)

Sicc[a][us][um]: Dry, dried. (1)

Sideros: Iron. (3)

Sidonal (, new): See quinic anhydride. (40)

Sidonal: Piperazidine quinate, a quinate salt used in treatment of gout, see urol. (40)

Sienna (, terra di): A pigmented earth or bole, do not confuse with senna. Sienna is tan, burnt sienna reddish-brown. Unofficial. (44)

Sigillum salomonis; —Solomonis: Solomon's Seal, *Polygonatum officinale*. Root used. Decoction used for piles and for skin rash caused by contact with certain plants. Figure 3-248. (1)

Signette's salt: Rochelle salt, see potassii et sodii tartras. (3)

Silene virginica: Catchfly or wild pink, of eastern US, anthelmintic. Unofficial. (44)

Silent spirit: Spirit of wine, see vinum, spiritus. (40)

Siler montanum: Denotes certain umbelliferae, mountain laserwort (*Laserpitium siler*) and lovage (*Levesticum officinale*). (1)

Silesian earth: A form of bolus, earth or clay from Silesia (currently on the Czech-Polish border), brownish and not acid-reactive. (39)

Silex (, pulverized): Quartz, or silica, finely pulverized. Pulverized quartz was mainly mixed with volatile oils to finely divide them and enhance incorporation into aqueous preparations. It was removed by filtration. (3)

Silicate of soda: Soluble glass, water-glass, soluble sodium silicate, uricosuric for gout and rheumatism. Unofficial. (44)

Siliqua dulcis: St. John's bread, or carob, *Ceratonia siliqua*, formerly *Siliqua dulcis*. (3) This material, still used for chocolate-like flavoring properties, appears to have been used as a mucilage, laxative, nutritive, and excipient.

Silphium: The root of cup plant, Indian cup plant, or ragged cup, *Silphium perfoliatum*, a tonic, diaphoretic, and alterative, said to be of use for enlarged spleen. (33) Estes (39) indicates that in ancient usage this may have referred to *Ferula tingitana* or *Thapsia garganica*, and that the American genus of weeds known as silphium was not used medicinally, but *King's American Dispensatory* (33) suggests that the latter conclusion is incorrect.

Silver: See argentum (metallic), argenti (compounds). (8)

Silver albuminate: Silver vitellin, a complex of metallic silver and egg albumin, used as a topical disinfectant in solution.

Silver nitrate, mitigated: See argentii nitras mitigatus. (42)

Silver nucleinate: A complex of silver with "nuclein," i.e., DNA. Antimicrobial, specifically a topical for gonorrhea. (40)

Silver proteinate: See argein. (40)

Silver vitellin: See silver albuminate. (40)

Silvestris, prunus: See prunus sylvestris. (1)

Silvius: See sylvius. (1)

Simarouba; Simaruba; Simarubae cortex: Bark of mountain damson, *Simarouba* (or *Quassia*) *amara*, *Quassia simarouba* or *S. officinalis*, a bitter tonic, astringent, and emetic introduced from Guyana ca. 1713. Figure 3-249. (1,39)

Fig. 3-248 Sigillum salomonis or Solomon's seal.

Fig. 3-249 Simarouba or mountain damson.

Similax china: See China root.

Simpitum: See symphytum. (1)

Simple elixir: See elixir aromaticum (8) and simplex, elixir. (42)

Simple plaster: See cerae compositum, emplastrum. (39)

Simple syrup: A concentrated solution of sugar in water. See syrupus. (8)

Simplex, elixir: This is the common base elixir used in formulations of the BPC. Composed of tincture of orange 7.5 parts, syrup 40 parts, and distilled water 100 parts. It was added to mixtures (usually alcohol containing) for flavor and sweetening. (42)

Simplex, emplastrum: Simple plaster, see cerae compositum, emplastrum. (39)

Simplex, unguentum: Simple unguent, of white beeswax, benzoinated lard, and almond oil. Emollient and common base for other ointments. (42)

Simplex: Simple, not composite. (1)

Sinapi; Sinapis; Sinapis alba (semina); Sinapis nigra: Mustard, white mustard, the seed of *Brassica alba* or black mustard the seed of *B. nigra* or *B. sinapoides*, figure 3-250, also called *Sinapis brassica*. Both yield a similar oil. Used as an irritant, counterirritant, and rubifacient. Induces a sense of warmth followed by localized loss of sensation, and stimulates the heart. Internally it is a gastrointestinal stimulant in low dosage and an irritant and emetic if given in sufficiently large amounts. Often used as a poultice with ground flax-seed. A poultice, mustard paper, plaster, or even fresh mustard leaves could be placed upon the affected body part to reduce pain of neuralgia, gastric conditions, pleurisy, etc. Common colds and other febrile conditions, especially in children, were treated with mustard plasters or baths to vasodilate the skin and, presumably, reduce fever (by increasing heat loss). A mustard bath is said to bring on menses, and it was recommended as a stimulant antidote to narcotic drug overdose. (1,8)

Sinapis, cataplasma: Poultice of crushed linseed with powdered mustard and water. Used as a counterirritant in deep inflammation such as pleurisy and bronchitis. (42)

Sinapis, charta: Mustard paper, prepared by percolating black mustard with benzine, drying, mixing the resulting extract with India rubber using benzine and carbon disulphide as solvents, and painting upon heavy paper. It was dipped in warm water prior to application. (8, 42)

Sinapis, linimentum: Mustard liniment, of the oil of mustard, camphor, and castor oil in alcohol, powerful counterirritant for severe pain of chest conditions. (42)

Sinapis, oleum (volatile): Mustard oil, from maceration of black mustard with water, and subsequent distillation. (8)

Sinapis, semen; Sinapis Sem.: Mustard seed.

Sinapis, spiritus: Spirit of mustard, two percent of volatile oil of mustard (sinapis, oleum) in alcohol, used as a counterirritant. (31)

Sinapis, unguentum: Mustard ointment, ointment of oil of mustard, of same (sinapis oleum) in a base of lard and white wax. (31)

Sinapis compositum, linimentum: Compound liniment of mustard, of mustard oil, fluid extract of mezareum, camphor, castor oil, and alcohol. (8)

Sinapis nigrae (semina): Black mustard seed, of *Brassica nigra* or *B. sinapoides*, similar to white mustard. (42)

Sinapism: A plaster of mustard, see sinapis. (39)

Sine quibus esse nolo, pilulae: "The pills I would not wish to be without," Purgative pills of Socotra aloe, scammony, larch agaric, senna leaves, myrobalans, dodder, petals of red roses, mastic, etc. (1)

Sine: Without (Latin). (1)

Sipeira: See bebeeru bark. (40)

Siroem: See sapa. (39)

Sirupus; Sirop {*French*}; **Siropo** {Italian}; **Siroppo** {Italian}: Syrup, see syrupus. (1)

Sisarum: Skirret, *Sium sisarum*. Root used. (1)

Sistomensine: Corpus luetum extract, hormonal. (40)

Sisymbrium: Hedge mustard, *Sisymbrium officinale*, said to be expectorant and perhaps diuretic, particularly of use in kidney stones. (33)

Sium: Water parsnip, *Sium latifolium* or *S. nodiflorum*, a diuretic, emmenagogue, and lithontriptic. Figure 3-251. (39)

606 (, compound): See arsenobenzol. (40)

Skullcap: See scutellaria. (8)

Skunk cabbage: See arum americanum. (39)

Fig. 3-250 Sinapis brassica or nigra.

Fig. 3-251 Sium or water parsnip.

Slate, Irish: See lapis hibernicus. (40)

Slippery elm: See ulmus. (8)

Sloe: See prunus sylvestris. (39)

Small beer: Weak beer, a tonic. (39)

Smallage: See apium. (39)

Smalt: Impure oxide of cobalt, a blue pigment. (44)

Smaragdus: Emerald (gem). (1)

Smartweed: See persicaria. (39)

Smelling salts: Usually ammoniae aromaticus, spiritus, but also simply ammonium carbonate. (40)

Smellon's eye salve: Proprietary copper-based eye ointment, see aeruginis, unguentum. (39)

Smilax china; —sarsaparilla: See china or sarsaparilla, respectively. (39)

Smoking salts: Impure hydrochloric acid. (40)

Snakeroot, seneca; —, senega: See senega. (7)

Snakeroot; —, Virginia; —, black; —, Texas: Snakeroot can refer to the Virginia snakeroot (see serpentinaria) or the black snakeroot, also called black cohosh (see cimicifuga), (8)

Snakeweed: See bistorta. (39)

Snakewood: Wood or roots of *Strychnos colubrina*, a narcotic and bitter tonic, related to nux vomica. (39)

Sneezewort: See ptarmica. (39)

Snig oil: Oil of almonds (amygdale, oleum), used as ear drops. (40)

Snuff: Powdered tobacco (see nicotiana) used as an errhine. (39)

Snuff: See insufflatio or _____, insufflatio. (42)

Snuff, white: Menthol and cocaine snuff. (40)

Soamin: Sodium aminarsonate, antimicrobial. (40)

Soap: See sapo, multiple related entries. (8)

Soap, green: See sapo mollis. (8)

Soap, Marseilles: An olive oil soap, see sapo. (40)

Soap, potash: Soft soap, made with potash, see sapo mollis. (40)

Soap, Venice: Olive oil soap. (40)

Soap bark: See quillaja. (8)

Soap plaster (, white): See saponis, emplastrum. (31,40)

Soapstone: French chalk, see creta gallae. (40)

Soapwort: See saponaria. (39)

Socaloin: Aloin from Socotrine aloes. (40)

Socot(o)rina, aloe: See aloe Socotrina. (1,39)

Sod oil (, degras): Crude wool fat. (3)

Soda: Soda, caustic soda, sodium hydroxide, NaOH, sodium hydrate. Corrosive, of very limited therapeutic use. Sometimes may refer to sodium carbonate or bicarbonate. (8)

Soda, liquor: Aqueous solution of soda, i.e., sodium hydroxide. (8)

Soda, lotion, compound: See sodii composita, lotio. (34)

Soda, muriate of: Sodium chloride, i.e., common salt. (40)

Soda, sal: Crystallized washing soda, sodium carbonate. (3)

Soda, sesquicarbonate of: Sodium bicarbonate. (40)

Soda, sub-borate of: See borax. (40)

Soda, subcarbonate of: Sodium carbonate. (40)

Soda, tartarized; Soda tartar(is)ata: See cream or tartar. (39) See potassae et sodae tartras. (44)

Soda ash: See sodii carbonas. (39)

Soda crystals: Sodium carbonate. (40)

Soda effervescens, aqua: Soda water, i.e., carbonated water, or seltzer. (40)

Soda mint (tablets): See sodae et menthae, liquor and sodae et menthae, mistura. For the tablets, see sodii bicarbonatis, compositae. (31,42)

Soda phosphorata: See sodii phosphas. (39)

Soda vitriolata; Soda, vitriolated: Sodium sulfate, a cathartic, see sodii sulphas. (39)

Sodae, liquor: See sodii hydroxidi, liquor. (42)

Sodae, silicas: See silicate of soda. (44)

Sodae, super-carbonatis aqua: A solution of barilla (crude sodium carbonate and bicarbonate) saturated with carbon dioxide, primarily a lithontriptic. (39)

Sodae, super-carbonatis: Potassium bicarbonate. (39)

Sodae _____: *Sodae* is the genitive form of *soda*, properly sodium hydroxide or carbonate, not elemental sodium, but this variant is common for sodium compounds. See also: sodii _____.

Sodae chlor(in)atae, liquor; ——, lotio: Solution of chlorinated soda, Labarraque's solution, a variable composition consisting of sodium carbonate and chlorinated lime in water. (8,42)

Sodae chlorinatae, cataplasma: Poultice of chlorinated soda, i.e., bleach solution, with linseed and water. Used as a disinfectant for sloughing ulcers. (42)

Sodae composita, mistura: A mixture of gentian root, ginger root, and powdered ginger extracted with sodium bicarbonate in peppermint water, a stomachic. (42)

Sodae et menthae [, liquor][, mistura]: Solution (mixture) of soda and mint, soda mint. Contains sodium bicarbonate, aromatic spirit of ammonia and spearmint or peppermint water (see menthae viridis or piperitae, aqua). Used as an antacid and carminative. (31)

Sodae et potassae tartras: See potassae et sodae tartras. (44)

Sodae potassio-tartras: See potassae et sodae tartras. (44)

Sodae sesquicarbonas: Sodium bicarbonate. (40)

Sodae tartaratae effervescens, pulvis: See effervescens compositus, pulvis. (34)

Sodas chloratae, liquor: Solution of chlorinated soda, i.e., bleach (sodium hypochlorite). (40)

Sodas potassio-tartras: Tartarated soda, see cream of tartar. (40)

Sodas sub-boras: See borax. (40)

Sodas subcarbonas: Sodium carbonate. (40)

Sodic: Irregular chemical name for the sodium ion, Na^+. For compounds see sodii. (29)

Sodii _____: Sodium salts are sometimes named as *Sodae _____*, the genitive form of *soda*, properly sodium hydroxide or carbonate, not elemental sodium. See listings under sodae _____ if not found below.

Sodii acetas: Sodium acetate, by action of acetic acid on sodium carbonate. Rarely used diuretic, mainly for preparation of other materials. (8)

Sodii anilarsonas: Anilarsonate of sodium, an organic arsenical antimicrobial for trypanosomiasis and syphilis, and used topically for skin disorders. (42)

Sodii arsenas Sodium arsenate, Na_2HAsO_4. Like other arsenicals, used for trypanosomiasis, syphilis, and skin disorders. (8,42)

Sodii arsenatis (Pearson), liquor: Solution of sodium arsenate (see sodii arsenas); Pearson's solution is one-tenth the strength of the liquor. (8)

Sodii arsenis; —arsenias: Sodium arsenite. (40,44)

Sodii benzoas; Sodium benzoate: Sodium salt of benzoic acid, see benzoicum, acidum. Expectorant and urinary disinfectant. (8,42)

Sodii bicarbonas saccharatis: Mixture of sugar and sodium bicarbonate, used (with the other component being saccharated tartaric acid) as a pre-mixture for effervescent preparations in the NF. (46)

Sodii bicarbonas: Sodium bicarbonate, $NaHCO_3$. Used, as today, primarily as an antacid and digestive aid. (8)

Sodii bicarbonatis, troschisci; —, tabellae: Troches of sodium bicarbonate with sugar, nutmeg, and tragacanth, for gastric disorders. The tablets (NF) contain ¼ gram of sodium bicarbonate and are flavored with oil of peppermint. (8,31,42)

Sodii biphosphas: See sodii diphosphas. (42)

Sodii bisulphis: Sodium bisulfite, mainly non-medicinal (to neutralize bleach in fabric processing), but a mild antiseptic and used orally for gastric fermentation. (42)

Sodii boras: Borax, the naturally occurring mineral, $Na_2B_4O_7$. Primarily a disinfectant, sometimes used as a bladder irrigant and in diluted forms as a mouthwash. (8)

Sodii boratis compositus, liquor: Compound solution of sodium borate, Dobell's solution, of sodium borate and sodium bicarbonate with 0.3% phenol in glycerin and water. "Widely used as a cleansing wash in inflammations of the nose and pharynx." (31)

S

Sodii boratis, glyceritum: Glycerite of sodium borate, a topical for various inflammations of the skin and mucous membranes. (34)

Sodii boratis, mel: Honey of sodium borate, a simple mixture of these items used as an alkaline (hence antacid) demulcent. (38)

Sodii boro-benzoas: Mixture of sodium borate and benzoate (NF). (46)

Sodii bromidi, elixir: Elixir of sodium bromide. See bromine. (31)

Sodii bromidum (effervescens): Sodium bromide, NaBr. From addition of bromine to a solution of soda (soda ash, NaOH). Primarily used as a sedative, see bromide. The BPC has an effervescent formulation. (8)

Sodii cacodylas: Sodium cacodylate, interchangeable with (see) cacodylic acid. (42)

Sodii carbolatum; Sodii carbolatis, liquor: Sodium carbolate (sodium salt of carbolic acid), or a solution of same with sodium hydroxide, glycerin of cochineal, and water. An antiseptic mouthwash following dilution in water. (42)

Sodii carbonas (, exsiccatus) (, venalis): Sodium carbonate, Na_2CO_3. Used primarily to prepare other materials. May be dehydrated with mild heat (exsiccatus), and may be crude or purified and prepared for commercial use (venalis). (8)

Sodii chloras: Sodium chlorate, $NaClO_3$. For stomatitis, pharyngitis, etc. in gargles, pastilles, and lozenges. (8,42)

Sodii chloridum: Sodium chloride, salt, common or table salt, sal communis. Solutions had many uses as a tonic, enema, antiseptic, stimulant, styptic, catharic, emetic, etc., depending upon concentration and dose. (8,39)

Sodii cinnamas: Sodium cinnamate, an antiseptic, like benzoate. (42)

Sodii cinnamatis, glycerinum: Sodium cinnamate in glycerin, for hypodermic injection in cancer and tuberculosis, ineffectual. (42)

Sodii citras: Sodium citrate. (42)

Sodii citratis, liquor; —, mistura: Solution (mixture) of sodium citrate, potio rivierii, of citric acid and sodium bicarbonate in distilled water, it should be freshly prepared. "The amount of sodium citrate formed…is so small that the solution has scarcely any effect beyond that of a mildly saline drink…it would require upwards of an ounce to exercise any therapeutic effect." (31)

Sodii citro-tartras effervescens: Effervescent formulation of sodium bicarbonate (51 parts), tartaric acid (27 parts), citric acid (18 parts), and refined sugar (15 parts). This is the general formulation of an effervescent powder, which is dissolved in water immediately before use. (42)

Sodii composita, lotio: Compound soda lotion, of zinc sulphate and persulfate of iron. For eye conditions. (34)

Sodii diphosphas: Sodium diphosphate, the monosodium salt of phosphoric acid. For urinary acidification. (42)

Sodii et ammonii phosphas: Combined sodium and ammonium phosphates. (40)

Sodii ethylas; Sodii ethylatis, liquor: Sodium ethylate, the sodium salt of ethyl alcohol, by reaction of same with metallic sodium. The liquor was nineteen percent strength in alcohol. This is a corrosive material used to remove nevi and other skin lesions. It had to be made fresh when needed. (8)

Sodii floridum: Sodium fluoride, highly toxic, small amounts used to increase bone density in rickets. (42)

Sodii formas: Sodium formate, formate being used as a general tonic, often in mixed forms. (42)

Sodii glycerophosphas: Sodium glycerophosphate is used with other glycerophosphates to treat wasting diseases and as a tonic. (42)

Sodii hippuras: Sodium hippurate, for gout. (42)

Sodii hydroxidi, liquor: A solution of approximately five percent sodium hydroxide in water, for making other materials. (42)

Sodii hydroxidum: Sodium hydroxide, caustic soda. (42)

Sodii hypobromitis, liquor: A solution of sodium hydroxide and bromine in water. Analytical reagent for determining urea content of urine via release of nitrogen. (42)

Sodii hypophosphis: Sodium hypophosphite, from sodium carbonate plus calcium hypophosphite. (8)

Sodii hypophosphitis, elixir: Elixir of sodium hypophosphite in aromatic elixir. (46)

Sodii hypophosphitis, syrupus: Syrup of sodium hypophosphite in simple syrup. (42)

Sodii hyposulphis: See sodii thiosulphas. (8)

Sodii iodas: Sodium iodate, a powerful antiseptic and used orally for asthma and hypodermically for rheumatism. (42)

Sodii iodidum: Sodium iodide, NaI, from iodine and sodium hydroxide, dried and heated with carbon to convert the resulting sodium iodate ($NaIO_3$) to iodide. For syphilis. (8)

Sodii lactas: Sodium lactate, mainly for production of other lactate compounds, medicinal value unclear. (42)

Sodii metharsenis: An organic arsenical used as per cacodylic acid. (42)

Sodii naphtholas: Sodium naphtholate, sodium salt of naphthol, a more potent disinfectant than carbolic acid (phenol), used at 1:200 or more dilution in water for lotions and dressings. (42)

Sodii nitras: Sodium nitrate, $NaNO_3$. Noted to be rarely used, the potassium salt being preferred. (8,42)

Sodii nitris: Sodium nitrite, $NaNO_2$. Formed by heating sodium nitrate (sodii nitras) with lead. Used to prepare spirit of nitrous ether (see (a)etheris nitrosi, spiritus). Like other nitrites, it is a vasodilator and used for angina, asthma, and hypertension. (8,42)

Sodii oleatis, liquor: This was the crude sodium oleate, i.e., white Castile soap, in water. Used to produce other oleate solutions. (46)

Sodii peroxidum: Sodium peroxide, Na_2O_2. Used externally in paraffin paste or medicated soaps for acne. (42)

Sodii phosphas: Sodium phosphate, Na_2HPO_4. The BPC also specifies an effervescent form with sodium bicarbonate and citric and tartaric acids. Mainly cathartic, or as a phosphate supplement in rickets, etc. (8,42)

Sodii phosphatis compositus, liquor: Compound solution of sodium, of sodium phosphate, citric acid, glycerin, and water. Used as a laxative. (31)

Sodii pyrophosphas (effervescens): Sodium pyrophosphate, $Na_2P_2O_7$. Used to produce other materials. (8) The effervescvent form was used to clean dentures, etc.

Sodii salicylas; Sodium salicylate: Sodium salt of salicylic acid, see salicylate. The BPC also specifies an effervescent form with sodium bicarbonate, citric and tartaric acids, and refined sugar. (8,42)

Sodii salicylatis compositum, elixir: Compound elixir of sodium salicylate, new (ca. 1926) elixir of sodium salicylate and potassium iodide with gelsemium and cimicifuga. An antirheumatic and anti-inflammatory. (31)

Sodii salicylatis, elixir: Elixir of sodium salicylate in aromatic elixir base. "It is intended for an antirheumatic but is not a very happy combination." (31,46)

Sodii santoninatis, trochisci: Troche of sodium santoninate (see santonin), sugar, gum tragacanth, and orange flower water. (46)

Sodii silicofluoridum: Sodium fluorosilicate, rarely used medicinally as a disinfectant in dilute solutions. (42)

Sodii sulphas: Sodium sulfate, $NaSO_4$. A saline laxative. The BPC also specifies an effervescent form with sodium bicarbonate and citric and tartaric acids. (8,42)

Sodii sulphis: Sodium sulfite, Na_2SO_3. Antiseptic, topical anti-parasitic, and for "gastric fermentation." (8)

Sodii sulpho(-)ricinas: Oil formed by action of sulphuric acid on castor (*Ricinus communis*) oil, a brown to red oil used as a solvent or carrier for other materials such as iodoform. (40)

Sodii sulphocarbolatum: Sodium sulphocarbolate, sodium para-phenolsulphonate, $(HO-C_6H_4-SO_4^-, Na^+)$. An antiseptic, topical and surface disinfectant, and deodorant. Derived from carbolic acid (phenol) it was used in much the same manner. (8)

Sodii taurocholas: Sodium taurocholate is a constituent of bile, used for deficient production of same and as a cholegogue. (42)

Sodii thiosulphas: Sodium thiosulfate or hyposulfite $Na_2S_2O_3$, a topical for ringworm and parasitic diseases, highly toxic systemically. Commonly carried as a photographic chemical, "hypo," for fixing images. (42)

Sodii uras: Sodium urate, non-medicinal. (42)

Sodii valerianas: See valeriana. (8)

Sodio-citro-ferric pyrophosphate (, soluble): See ferri pyrophosphas (solubilis). (40)

Sodium: Sodium, see sodae and sodii for compounds. (8)

Sodium acid phosphate: See sodii diphosphas. (42)

Sodium acid sulphite; Sodium bisulphis: See sodium bisulphis, sodium bisulfite, $NaHSO_3$. (8,42)

Sodium cinnamate: See storax, the sodium salt of cinnamic acid, a component of storax, a disinfectant compound.

Sodium dihydrogen phosphate: See sodii diphosphas. (42)

Sodium dimethyl-arsenate: Sodium cacodylate, see cacodylic acid. (40)

Sodium ethylate: See sodii ethylas.

Sodium hydrate; Sodium hydroxide: Sodium hydroxide, caustic soda. See soda. (8,42)

Sodium hypochlorite: Bleach. A Latin form ("hypochloras") seems to be non-existent, or at least quite rare. Often incorrectly named as a chlorate.

Sodium hyposulphis; —hyposulphite: See sodii thiosulphas. (42)

Sodium metarsenite: See sodii arsenis. (40)

Sodium naphthol(ate): Sodium salt of naphthol, a disinfectant. (40)

Sodium nitroprusside: An intravenous vasodilator used for hypertension.

Sodium orthosulfate: See sodii sulphas. (8)

Sodium phenolsulphonate: Sodium carbolate, sodium salt of carbolic acid (phenol), disinfectant. (40)

Sodium sesquicarbonate: See sodii bicarbonas. (8)

Sodium sulphocarbolate: See sodii sulphocarbolatum. (8)

Sodium sulphoricinate: See sodii sulphoricinas. (40)

Sodium thiosulphas; —thiosulphate: See sodii thiosulphas. (8,42)

Sol: Sun, associated with gold. (3)

Sol. (abr.): A solution in English language, more likely "solutiva" in Latin inscriptions, especially if in combination with another indicator of the dose form, i.e., s. sol. rosarum is *syrupus solutiva rosarum*, purging syrup of rose. (35)

Solanum: In herbal usage, horse nettle, *Solanum carolinensis*, a minor sedative and anti-epileptic. (32)

Solanum (nigrum); Solani, fluidextractum: Black nightshade, *Solanum nigrum*, or a fluid extract therefrom. Leaves used. An anticholinergic, see belladonna. Figure 3-252. (1)

Solanum dulcamara; Solanum lignosum: See dulcamara. (1)

Solanum lethalis: Lethal solanum, i.e., belladonna. (39)

Solanum tuberosum: Potato, *Solanum tuberosum*, usually in reference to the starch therefrom, used as per starch (see amylum), but also a homeopathic.

Solar oil: Kerosene. (3)

Solatrum: See solanum. (1)

Soldanella: See brassica marina. (39)

Solfo {*Italian*}: Sulfur. (1)

Solidago: Sweet golden rod, fragrant-leaved golden rod, sweet-scented golden rod, blue mountain tea, *Solidago odora*. Diuretic and contains an oil used as a carminative. (32)

Solimato {*Italian*}: Sublimate of mercury, mercuric chloride, see hydrargyri chloridum corrosivum. (1)

Solomonis, opiata: See opiata Solomonis. (1)

Solomon's cordial balm of Gilead: Proprietary panacea of unknown composition, used to treat onanism. (39)

Solomon's seal; Solomonis, sigillum: See sigillum Solomonis. (1)

Soluble glass: Sodium silicate. Dried solutions form a glass-like amorphous substance. (3)

Soluble tartar: Sal tartaris, cream of tartar, i.e., sodium potassium tartrate. (39)

Solurol: Thyminic acid. (40)

Solution; _____, solution: See salutio, also see liquor or _____, liquor if not found under solution. For an eponymous solution, i.e., Fowler's solution, etc., see eponym.

Solutiva; Solutive; Solutivum; Solutivus; Solutif {*French*}: "Tending to dissolve or loosen," i.e., a purgative or aperient. For example see rosarum, syrupus solutiva. (1,35)

Solvella; Solvellae {plural}: Soluble tablets, for dissolution in water prior to use, usually for external or topical applications. (42)

Solvellae _____ (BPC); Solvella {singular}: The BPC (42) specifies a number of prepared soluble tablets for topical use following dissolution in water. They generally consist of compressed pure material in a specific size, without other formulation ingredients. Some had a standard and stronger (fortes) and/or weaker (mitis) form or a small form (parvae). These include:

- **Acidi borici**—of boric acid.
- **Acidi carbolici (fortes)**—of carbolic acid.
- **Aluminis**—of alum.
- **Betacainae (fortis)**—of betacaine.
- **Betacainae et sodii chloridi**—of betacaine and salt.
- **Boracis compositae**—of borax, sodium chloride, carbolic acid, and sodium bicarbonate.
- **Boracis et cocainae compositae**—of borax, cocaine hydrochloride, sodium chloride, boric acid, benzoic acid, thymol, and menthol.
- **Boro-salinae**—of borax and saline.
- **Cocainae (fortes)**—of cocaine.
- **Hydrargyri et potassii iodidi (fortes)**—of mercury and potassium iodides.
- **Hydrargyri perchloridi (fortes)(mitis)(parvae)**—of mercuric chloride with sodium chloride and crystal violet.
- **Potassii permanganatis**—of potassium permanganate.
- **Sodii chloridi**—of salt.
- **Zinci sulphatis (fortes)**—of zinc sulfate, fuchsine, and oil of lavender.
- **Zinci sulphatis et aluminis**—of zinc sulfate and alum.
- **Zinci sulphocarbolas (fortes)**—of zinc sulphocarbolate.

Solvellae antisepticae: A prepared soluble tablet dissolved in a glass of warm water and used as a gargle. These contained benzoic acid, boric acid, carbolic acid, sodium bicarbonate, gum acacia, carmine (red coloring), gluside (saccharin), thymol, oils of peppermint and wintergreen, and distilled water. (42)

Solanum nigrum

Fig. 3-252 Solanum nigrum or black nightshade.

Solvens, mixtura: Solution of ammonium chloride with liquorice. (3)

Solvens simplex, mistura: See ammonii chloridi, mistura. (34)

Solvens stibiata, mixtura: Solution of ammonium chloride with liquorice and tartar emetic. Expectorant. (3,34)

Solvin: Petroleum solvent. (3)

Sonchus; Sonco {*Italian*}**:** Common sow-thistle, *Sonchus oleraceus* and related plants of same genus. Herb used. (1)

Soot: Carbon, or soot, usually of wood. Unofficial, but used in various forms—topically, as a decoction, or as an unguent for an almost endless list of conditions. (44)

Sophoria tinctoria: See baptesia. (39)

Sorbus: Tree of genus *Pyrus* (formerly genus *Sorbus*), especially the service tree, *Pyrus domestica*. Fruit used. Source of sorbic acid, commonly used as a preservative. (1)

Sore-throat salt: Sal prunellae. (3)

Sorghum saccharatum: Chinese sugar cane, a source of sugar. (44) This is synonymous with *Sorghum bicolor*, modern sorghum.

Sorrel: May refer to either acetosa or lujula. (39)

Sorrel, acid of: Oxalic acid. (39)

Sorrel, salt of: Potassium oxalate. (40)

Soufre (, fleurs de) {*French*}**:** Sulfur or flowers of (i.e., sublimated) sulfur. (1)

Sour whey: Semi-refined lactic acid. (39)

Southernwood: See arbotanum. (39)

Sowbread: See arthanita. (39)

Soya; Soja: Soybean, *Glycine max*, used as a flour substitute in diabetes to reduce carbohydrate intake. (8)

Soymida: Powdered bark of the rohan tree, *Soymida febrifuga*, or sometimes of mahogany (*Sweitenia mahagoni*, see same and figure 3-257). An apparently unsuccessful substitute for cinchona, as it shared the tonic and astringent properties and had a similar appearance, but was presumably lacking in the critical element, quinine. (39)

Sozoiodolic acid: Diiodopara-phenolsulphonic acid, an antiseptic. (3)

Sozolic acid: Orthophenolsulphonic acid, antiseptic. (3)

Sp.: Spirit(s), spiritus. May on occasion mean species in the apothecary sense, see species.

Spadium stearite: Zinc oxide. (3)

Spagyrica, conserva: Polypharmaceutical preparation for treatment of quartan fevers or jaundice. (1)

Spahlinger's vaccine: Tuberculin injection, for prevention of tuberculosis. (40)

Spanish fly; Spanish flies, ointment of: See cantharis and cantharidis, unguentum, respectively. (34)

Spanish pepper: See capsicum. (40)

Spanish white: 1. Bismuth subnitrate or calcium carbonate. (3) 2. Prepared chalk (same as calcium carbonate) per Hughes. (40)

Sparadrap(um): An adhesive plaster. (3)

Sparagio {*Italian*}**:** Asparagus. (1)

Spartein(a); Sparteinae sulphas; Sparteine sulphate: Sparteine is an alkaloid derived from *Scoparius* species. It is quite toxic, but had infrequent therapeutic uses similar to those of digoxin (see digitalis). (8,42)

Spartium junceum: Spanish broom, diuretic and tonic. Unofficial. (44)

Spasmine; Spasmodin: See benzyl benzoate. (40)

Spathum fluoricum: Fluorspar, source of elemental fluorine. (3)

Spearmint: See mentha viridis. (8)

Species (_____): This general term refers to mixtures of ground and/or powdered plant material used to make various other preparations or formulations as noted under specific forms below. (1)

Species ad infusum pectorale: See species pectorales. (31)

Species aromatica(e); Species, aromatic: See pulvis aromaticus. A mixture of aromatic herbs used to make aromatic baths as well as aromatic pillows and plasters. In essence, this is a *potpouri*. Typically of cubeb, clove, thyme (wild and sweet), lavender, and peppermint. (39)

Species diambrae sine odoratis: See species aromaticae, although the name suggests this was without (sine) odor. (40)

Species e scordio sine opio: See cretae compositus, pulvis. This is the variant without (sine) opium. (40)

Species emollientes: Emollient species, made from equal parts of althea leaves; mallow leaves (malvae folia), melilot, matricaria, and linseed oil (lini, oleum). An emollient, used for making a poultice by adding hot water. (31)

Species hamburgensis: Most likely the herbal material used to prepare (see) Hamburg tea, a laxative.

Species laxativae; Species laxantes: Laxative species, St. Germain tea, containing cut senna, elder flowers (sambucus), bruised fennel (foeniculum), bruised anise, and potassium bitartrate. (31)

Species pectorales: Pectoral species, species ad infusum pectorale, or breast tea, containing peeled althea, coltsfoot leaves (tussilago), peeled Russian glycyrrhiza, anise, mullein flowers (verbascum), and orris root (iris). Used as a pectoral. (31)

Specificum antihecticum Poterii: See antihecticum Poterii. (1)

Specificum purgans: Specific purgative, potassium sulphate. (39)

Speediman's pills: Proprietary cathartic of aloe, myrrh, rhei (rhubarb), and chaemaemelum (chamomile), early 1800s. (39)

Speedwell: See beccabunga. (39)

Spelter; Speltrum: Zinc. (3)

Sperma mercurii: Mercury acetate. (3)

Spermaceti; Sperm. Oil: Spermaceti, i.e., whale oil. See ceratum. (8)

Spermin: See Brown-Sequard's fluid. (40)

Sphagnol: Tar product from peat. (40)

Spica indica: See nardus indica. (1)

Spica: Spiked lavender, *Lavandula latifolia*. Flowers and flowering tops used. (1)

Spicae, oleum: Oil of spike lavender. (1)

Spice plaster: See emplastrum aromaticum. (46)

Spider web: See tela araneae.

Spigelia; Spigeliae fluidum, extractum: Pinkroot, the rhizome and roots of *Spigelia marilandica*, of North America. The fluid extract was a powerful anthelmintic, but carried the risk of narcotic side effects. Figure 3-253. (8)

Spigeliae compositus, pulvis: King's entozoic powder, compound powder of spigelia, of same with swamp milkweed, pinkroot, bitter root, mandrake, and balmony. A vermifuge. Very bitter, thus given in molasses. (34)

Spigelia marilandica
Published by D.r Woodville Sep.t 1, 1794.

Fig. 3-253 Spigelia or pinkroot.

Spigiliae et sennae, fluidum extractum; Spigiliae et Sen., Fl. Extr.: The fluid extract of spigilia and senna, flavored with oils of anise and caraway. A laxative. (34)

Spignel: See meum. (39)

Spignet: See aralia. (7)

Spike: Lavender oil, see lavandula. (40)

Spike, factitious, oil of: Mixture of lavender and turpentine oil, colored with alkanet. (40)

Spikenard (American): See nardus or aralia, respectively. (7,39)

Spikenard (oil); Spica nardi; Spiga nardo {*Italian*}**:** See nardus (, oleum). (1)

Spina alba: Hawthorn, whitethorn, see oxycantha. (1)

Spina cervina (baccae): Buckthorn (berries), see rhamnus. (1,3,7)

Spinae cervinae, syrupus: See rhamni catharticae, syrupus. (31)

Spindle tree: See euonymus. (8)

Spiraea (tomentosa) (trifoliata): Root of the hardhack, steeple bush, or Indian Physic, *Spiraea tomentosa*, astringent, emetic, and tonic. (39)

Spirit: An alcoholic solution.

Spirit, pyro-acetic: Acetone. (3)

Spirit of (a)ether (, compound): See (a)etheris compositus, spiritus.

Spirit of ants: See acidi formici, spiritus. (31)

Spirit of formic acid: See formici acidi, spiritus. (31)

Spirit of nitre: Crude nitric acid. (3)

Spirit of salt: Crude muriatic (hydrochloric) acid. (3)

Spirit of turpentine: Oil of turpentine (see terebinthina). (3)

Spiritus: Liquor obtained by distillation of an aromatic drug, or a mixture of such drugs, with alcohol or wine. (1)

Spiritus _____: Spirits (alcoholic solution) of, see _____, spiritus if not listed immediately below. (8)

Spiritus aromaticus (acetatus): Aromatic spirits, an alcoholic extraction of rosemary and thyme. Vinegar (acetatus) was sometimes added. A "prophylactic fumigant." (39) In the NF, compound spirit of orange in deodorized alcohol. (46)

Spiritus formicarum: See formici acidi, spiritus. (31)

Spiritus muriaticus: See ethyl chloride. (40)

Spiritus vini gallici, mistura: See vini Gallici…. (34)

Spiss[a][us][um]: Hard or dried (Latin). (8)

Spissatus, succus: Dried juice, usually of (see) sambucis. (39)

Spleen mixture; Splenetica, mistura: Mixture of iron sulfate, quinine sulfate, nitric acid, potassium nitrate, and water. (46)

Spodium; Spodio {*Italian*}**:** Crude bone charcoal or ivory black. The term refers, in ancient chemistry or alchemy, to any compound obtained via calcination. In general, this would be an oxide. From the Greek for "ashes." (1,3,39)

Spodium graecorum: Zinc oxide. (1)

Spondium: Burnt ivory, a tonic and antacid, probably the same as spodium. (39)

Spondylium: See heracleum. (39)

Sponge; Spongea (communis)(optima); Spongia: Sponge, sometimes labeled as common (communis) or finest (optima). A sundry and surgical supply.

Sponge, bleached: See spongia decolorata. (46)

Sponge tent; Spongia compressa: Compressed sponge, or sponge tent, of sponge with water and mucilage of acacia. The sponge was saturated, wrapped in twine or otherwise compressed, and allowed to dry. It would expand on becoming moist, and was used to dilate orifices or strictures. It is suggested that it be stored wrapped in twine or otherwise carefully protected from dampness. (46)

Spongia decolorata: Bleached sponge prepared by immersion in potassium permanganate, sodium hyposulfite, hydrochloric acid, and water—a powerful oxidizing and bleaching combination. Sponges of this type tended to harden and it is noted that they could be dipped in dilute glycerin prior to final drying to keep them flexible. (46)

Spruce gum: Spruce gum or resin. See pix burgundia.

Spruce oil: Oil of spruce, i.e., turpentine. See teribinthena.

Spt.; SPT.; SPt.; etc.: Spirit.

Spurge: See euphorbia. (39)

Spurge flax: See daphne gnidium. (40)

Spurge laurel; Spurge olive: See mezereum. (40)

Spurred rye: See ergot. (40)

Squaw root: Blue Cohosh, see caulophyllum. (8)

Squibb's mixture: See diarrhea mixture. (34)

Squibb's podophyllum pills: See podophylli belladonnae et capsici, pilulae. (34)

Squibb's rhubarb mixture: See rhei composita, mistura. (34)

Squill(s) (Indian); Squilla: See Scilla. (1,8,39,40)

Squill(s), oxymel of: See scilliticum, oxymel. (39)

Squinantho; Squinante {*Italian*}**:** See schoenanthum. (1)

Squire's grand elixir: Proprietary opium compound. (39)

Squirting cucumber: See cucumis agrestes. (39)

SSKI: Saturated solution of potassium iodide, see potassii iodidi.

St. Germain('s) tea: See species laxativae. (31)

St. Ignatius' beans: Seeds of *Strychnos ignatii*, closely related to (strychnos) nux vomica, and having similar properties. (39)

St. John Long's liniment: See terebinthinae aceticum, linimentum. (31)

St. John, oil of: Oil of elder, see sambucus. (40)

St. John's wort: See hypericum. (39)

St. John's wort, oil of: Red oil from hypericum in olive oil. (40)

St. Lucy's water: See Luce, eau de. (39)

St. Yves, balsamum: Ointment of red precipitate, see hydrargyri oxidum rubrum, unguentum. (3)

Staechados; Staechas: See stoechas. (1)

Stafford spring water: Water from Stafford Springs, Connecticut. (39)

Stanni amalgama: Amalgam of tin, a powdered mixture of tin in mercury, anthelmintic. (39)

Stanni chloridum: Tin chloride, an analytical reagent. (42)

Stannum; Stanni, pulvis: Tin (metal), usually powdered. Primarily anthelmintic and antihysteric. (1,39)

Stannum cinereum (glaciale): Bismuth. (3)

Stannum (cinereum) Indicum: "Indian tin," which is zinc. (3,40)

Staphisagria; Staphysagria; Staphysagriae semina: Stavesacre, the seed of *Delphinium staphisagria*, of the Mediterranean. Used as a topical treatment for parasites of the skin in the form of various ointments. Figure 3-254. (1,8,32,42)

Delphinium Staphisagria

Fig. 3-254 Staphisagria or stavesacre.

Staphisagriae, lotio: Nursery hair lotion, a lotion of powdered stavesacre seed, acetic acid, alcohol, oils of geranium, lavender, and lemon, glycerin, and distilled water. For head lice, especially in children. (42)

Staphisagriae, tinctura: Tincture of stavesacre. (34)

Staphisagriae, unguentum: Ointment of stavesacre, of the seeds in beeswax and benzoinated lard. For itching and as a pediculocide. (34,42)

Star anise: See illicium and anise. (8)

Starch, iodized: See amylum, iodatum. (42)

Star grass: See aletris. (7)

Starch: See amylum. (8)

Starch gum: See dextrin, the gummy carbohydrate of starch. (40)

Starch paste: Mucilage of starch. (40)

Starkei, pilulae; Starkey's pill: Pills originated by English physician George Starkey, seventeenth century, of opium extract, black and white hellebore, licorice, etc. Used to treat mental illness and as a sedative. (1)

Starkey's soap: A trituration of equal parts of potassium carbonate and Venice turpentine. (40)

Starwort: See aletris (rhizome). (40)

Statice (limonium): Root of sea lavender, marsh rosemary, *Limonium nashii*. Astringent, antiseptic, and expectorant by internal and topical routes. (39)

Stavesacre: See staphisagria. (8)

Stearicum, acidum; Stearic acid: A fatty acid (18 carbons) derived from various fats. Stearic acid is included in glycerin suppositories and various unofficial zinc and copper stearates are used to treat skin conditions. (8)

Stearophanic acid: Stearic acid. (3)

Steatite: Talc. (3)

Stechas; Stechadis; Stecade {*Italian*}**; Stecados** {*Italian*}**:** See stoechas. (1)

Steel drops; **—tincture:** Tincture of ferric chloride. (3) See ferri perchloridi, tinctura. (40)

Steel mixture: See ferri composita, mistura. (3)

Steel wine: See ferri citratis, vinum. (40)

Steer's (celebrated) (chemical) opodeldoc: Steer's version of opodeldoc, marketed as a panacea by Dr. Steer, London, ca. 1780. (39)

Stegnoticus, pulvis: Thickening powder, see aetheops vegetabilis. (39)

Stephen's (Mrs.) cure for stone: A cure for kidney and bladder stones after Johanna Stephens, English, 1700s. Of burnt egg shells, whole snails, soap, honey, bardana, chamomile, daucus sylvestris, fennel, and parsley. (39)

Sterculia; Sterculiae fluidum, extractum: Fluid extract of seed from *Sterculia acuminata*, of Africa, the cola or (see) kola nut. (46)

Stercus diaboli: See asafetida. (40)

Sternutatory powder; Sternutatorius, pulvis: Sternutatory powder, an errhine, i.e., snuff. See asari compositus, pulvis. (1)

Stibiated tartar: Tartarated antimony, see antimonium tartrate. (40)

Stibiatum, unguentum: See antimonii tartarati, unguentum. (40)

Stibio-kali tartaricum: Tartar emetic. (3)

Stibium; Stibiatum: Antimony, for compounds see antimonii. (3)

Stibnite: Antimony ore. (40)

Stibum sulfur nigra; Stib. Sulf. Nig.: This is the black sulfide of antimony, variously referred to as antimony sulphurette, antimony black, black sulfide, etc., Sb_2S_3. Naturally occurring.

Sticade; Stichas: See stoechas. (1)

Sticks, bitter: See chirata. (3)

Sticta: Lungwort, *Sticta pulmonaria*, for asthma and lung conditions. (32)

Stigmata maidis: Corn silk, see zea. Maidis is the Latin genitive form of mays (modern maize is *Zea mays*). (32)

Stili dilubiles: See medicamentorum, stili. (31)

Stillatic[a][um][us]: Distilled, equivalent to distillata. (1)

Stillingia; Stillingiae fluidum, extractum; —, syrupus; —, tinctura: The root of queen's delight, queen's root, *Stillingia sylvatica*, of the southern United States, or the fluid extract or tincture thereof. Stillingia is described as an emetic and cathartic in large doses and an "alterative" in smaller doses, being particularly useful in syphilis, cutaneous diseases and hepatic disorders. The syrup (NF) is of the fluid extract, sugar, and water. (8,31)

Stillingiae composita, trochisci: Compound troches of stillingia oil with oil of prickly ash berries, oil of sassafras, sugar, and gum tragacanth. For "rheumatic, syphilitic, scrofulous, bronchial, and laryngeal affections." (34)

Stillingiae compositum, elixir: Compound fluid extract of same, with aromatic elixir. (46)

Stillingiae compositum, fluidextractum; —fluidum, extractum: Compound fluid extract of stillingia containing stillingia, corydalis, iris, sambucus, chimaphila, coriander, and xanthoxylum berries. "It is a relic of therapeutic superstition." (31)

Stillingiae compositum, linimentum: A liniment of the oils of stillingia, lobelia, and cajaput, in alcohol and glycerine. Useful for a variety of respiratory and systemic inflammatory conditions. (34)

Stillingiae compositus, syrupus: Compound syrup of queen's root, with turkey corn, blue flag, elder flowers, pipsissewa leaves, coriander, prickly ash berry, sugar, and water. A powerful alterative for various chronic diseases including scrofula and syphilis. (34)

Stilus acid: See acidi salicylici, stili. (31)

Stinking orach: See atriplex (foetida). (39)

Stipes: Stalk, stem. (1)

Stipites dulcamarae: See dulcamara. (3)

Stipticae, pilulae: See stypticae, pilulae. (1)

Stirax: See storax. (1)

Stockholm tar: See petroleum, Stockholm.

Stoechadis, syrupus; Stoechados, syrupus de; —, s.d.: Syrup of French lavender. See lavandulae, syrupus. (35,40)

Stoechas; Stoechade; —, oleum: French lavender, cassidony, *Lavandula stoechus*. Flowers or flowering tops used. Oleum is lavender oil, see lavandulae, oleum. (1)

Stokes' expectorant: See pectoralis, mistura. (3)

Stokes' liniment: See terebinthinae aceticum, linimentum. (31)

Stomach drops; Stomachic drops, bitter; Stomachic tincture: See amara, tinctura. (31)

Stomachale, ceratum; Stomachicum, ceratum; Stomatico, cerotto {*Italian*}**:** Cerate (ointment) used in the treatment of gastric disorders. (1)

Stomachic elixir; Stoughton's elixir: See gentianae compositum, elixir. (3)

Stomachic(a), tinctura; Stomachic tincture: Compound tincture of cardamom. See cardamomi composita, tinctura. (3,40)

Stomachicos, tinctura ad: "Tincture for the stomach," same as vinum amarum. (39)

Stomachicum, elixir: See Stoughton's bitters. (39)

Stomachus: Dried stomach, generally porcine. Source of "anti-anemia factor" (later called intrinsic factor) used orally to facilitate B-12 absorption in treatment of pernicious anemia. (7) Supplanted by injectable vitamin B-12.

Stomatik tincture: See Stoughton's bitters. (39)

Stone root: See collinsonia. (40)

Stone-crop: See sedum acre. (39)

Storax; Styrax (praeparatus); Storace {*Italian*}**:** Storax, gum resin obtained in classical times from the inner bark of the tree *Styrax officinalis*, and later times from *Liquidambar orientalis*, of Asia Minor. Used in olive oil to treat skin parasites (scabies, lice, etc.). For additional usage, see balsam of Peru. Figure 3-255. (1,8)

Storax calamita: Solid storax. "Generally sawdust or residue of chinchona preparation mixed with liquid storax." (3)

Stoughton's bitters, elixir; —, tincture; Stoughton's elixir magnum: After Richard Stoughton, Southwark, ca. 1700, as a panacea for stomach ailments, and later becoming the official tinctura gentianae compositum. (39)

Stovaine: Amylocaine hydrochloride, local anesthetic. (40)

Stramonii, semen; Stramo. s.: Seeds of stramonium. (8)

Stramonii, unguentum: Ointment of stramonium, from the extract with alcohol, and benzoinated lard (and lanolin in the BPC). A topical anodyne for ulcers, burns, tumors, scalds, piles, etc. (8,34,42)

Stramonii alcoholicum, extractum: Dry alcoholic extract of stramonium (leaf), USP. (44)

Stramonii compositus, pulvis: Sir James Sawyer's asthma powder, of stramonium leaf, lobelia powder, anise fruit powder (flavor), tea leaf powder, oil of eucalyptus, and potassium nitrate. See discussion of similar formulation, lobelia compositus, pulvis. (42)

Stramonii compositum, unguentum: Compound ointment of stramonium, with bittersweet, stramonium leaves, cicuta leaves, deadly nightshade (belladonna), yellow-dock, lard, and Venice turpentine. For topical treatment of various tumors. As no effective treatment for tumors was available, many eroded through the skin and required topical management, at least of tumor size and odor, even if cure was impossible. (34)

Stramonii (foliorum) extractum: Extract of stramonium leaf, USP. See also stramonii (seminis), extractum, below. (44)

Stramonii folia: Stramonium leaves, i.e., those of *Datura stramonium*. The leaves were used in the form of a cigarette in the treatment of asthma, usually in combination with lobelia (tree tobacco, a source of nicotine), cannabis (marijuana), nitre, and eucalyptus. While the use of smoking to treat asthma now seems counterintuitive, the various agents do act as bronchodilators and modern asthma therapy still focuses on delivery of inhalational medications to limit systemic side effects. (8)

Stramonii (seminis)(exsiccatum), extractum; —fluidum, extractum; —liquidum, extractum; —, tinctura: Solid (dried, exsiccatum) extract, fluid extract, or alcoholic tincture of stramonium seed, respectively. (8,42) The BP specifies a dried aqueous extract of seed, while the USP specifies the dried extract of leaf, stramonii foliorum, extractum, above. (44)

Stramonium; Stramonii folia; —semina; Stramonio {*Italian*}**:** Stramonium is the seed (semina) of the plant *Datura stramonium*, commonly known as jimson weed, thorn apple, or loco weed, and source of atropine, scopolamine, and hyoscyamine. As such, it shares pharmacologic actions with belladonna. It was used for the same purposes, but most particularly for asthma. Leaves (folia) also sometimes used. Figure 3-256. (1,8,42)

Strasbourg turpentine: See terebinthena, argentoratensis. (39)

Strawberry: See fraga. (39)

Strengthening plaster: Plaster of red lead in yellow resin (pine tar) with wax and olive oil, to enhance muscular strength. (39)

Strike: Ammonia water. (3)

Stroh's pine syrup; Strohi compositus, syrupus pini: See pini albae compositus, syrupus. (31)

Strong purging pill: See colocynthidis et hyoscyami, pilulae. (40)

Strontia: Strontium oxide. (40)

Strontia muriate; Strontia nitrate: Strontium chloride and nitrate, respectively.

Strontii bromidum: Strontium bromide, $SrBr_2$. From reaction of hydrobromic acid (see hydrobromicum dilutum, acidum) with strontium carbonate. Primarily used as a sedative and for control of epilepsy. See bromide. (8)

Strontii cinnamas: Strontium cinnamate, use as per the sodium salt. (42)

Strontii iodidum: Strontium iodide, by reaction of hydriodic acid (see acidum hydriodici) and strontium carbonate. (8)

Strontii lactas; Stron. lact.: Strontium lactate, from the carbonate by reaction with lactic acid. Strontium lactate was said to be useful for gastric and certain renal disorders. (8)

Strontii salicylas; Strontium salicylate: Strontium salt of salicylic acid, used as an anti-inflammatory. (32)

Strophanthi, extractum: Extract of strophanthus seed in ether and alcohol, dried and diluted to proper concentration in milk sugar. (42)

Fig. 3-255 Storax or styrax.

Fig. 3-256 Stramonium, jimson or loco weed.

Strophanthi, tinctura: The alcoholic tincture derived from strophanthus. (8)

Strophanthin(um); Strophanthidin: The active principal of strophanthus. (8)

Strophanthus; Strophanthi semina; Strophanthi, tincture: Seed of *Strophanthus hispidis*, of African origin, or the alcoholic tincture. Source of strophanthin (strophanthidin). Strophanthus acts upon the heart in a manner similar to digitalis. (8,42)

Strychni, semen: Seeds of nux vomica. (40)

Strychni, tinctura: See nucis vomicae, tinctura. (40)

Strychnina; Strychnine: Strychnine, the primary alkaloid derived from nux vomica. If not otherwise specified, it is generally the hydrochloride salt. (8)

Strychninae, liquor; Strychninae hydrochlor[atis][idi], liquor: A solution of strychnine hydrochloride in water, for oral or hypodermic use. Specified as a solution of strychnine in hydrochloric acid or, alternately, a solution of strychnine hydrochloride salt, with identical results. (42,44)

Strychninae, unguentum: Ointment of strychnine in oleic acid. (34)

Strychninae acetatis, liquor: A solution of strychnine acetate, dilute acetic acid, alcohol water, and compound tincture of cardamom. (46)

Strychninae acida, mistura; Strych. acid. mist.: An acid mixture of strychnine hydrochloride in dilute nitro-hydrochloric acid with glycerin and compound infusion of gentian. (8) Strychnine, like other alkaloids, is soluble in acid solutions. An acid mixture with acetic acid was apparently standard in the BP (42) but other sources describe many variants in sulfuric, tannic, or other acids. A stimulant tonic and aperient.

Strychninae formas; —hydrochloras; —nitras; —sulphas: Various salts of strychnine, all with activity of the parent compound. (42)

Strychninae sulphas: Strychnine sulphate, by action of sulfuric acid on strychnine. See nux vomica. (8)

Strychninae valerianatis, elixir: Strychnine valerianate in mixture of acetic acid, tincture of vanilla, compound tincture of cudbear, and aromatic elixir. (46)

Strychnos colubrina: See snakewood. (39)

Strychnos ignatii: See St. Ignatius' beans. (39)

Strychnos nux vomica: Strychnine or the plant from which it is derived. See nux vomica. (8,39)

Stupa: Stupa, or tow, refers to broken fibers of jute, flax, or other fibrous plants. In medicine, this was saturated with medicinal materials and used to pack wounds as one would with gauze or lint. The BPC (42) notes the following stupae:

- **Carbolisata composita:** Of tar and carbolic acid.
- **Carbolisata:** Of jute fiber with carbolic acid dissolved in methylated ether (which would evaporate leaving the dry material).
- **Styptica:** Of resin and tar dissolved in benzol (which evaporated).

Stygia, aqua: Mythical water from the river Stygia of Greek mythology, allegedly highly corrosive as per aqua regia. (39)

Stypteria: Alum. (3)

Styptica, aqua: Styptic water, a solution of copper sulfate, see cupri vitriolati composita, aqua. (39)

Stypticae, pilulae: Pills to control hemorrhage. (1)

Stypticin: Proprietary form of (see) cotarinae hydrochloridum. (42)

Stypticus loofii, liquor: Solution of ferric chloride. (3)

Styptirenal: See adrenaline. This product was used as a vasoconstrictor for topical use to control bleeding. (40)

Styrace, pillulae e; Styrace p.e.: Storax (styrax) pills, see storax. Of styrax calamita, opium, and licorice. (35,39)

Styracol: See guaiacoli(s) cinnamas. (42)

Styrax (praeparata): See storax. (42)

Styrax benzoin: See benzoin. (39)

Styrax calamita: Styrax (see storax) packed in reeds for shipment. (1, 8)

Styrone: Cinnamyl alcohol. (3)

Sub-boras, sodae: Same as borax. (39)

Sublimate of sulphur: See sulphur sublimatum. (8)

Sublimato {*Italian*}: Sublimate of mercury, see hydrargyri chloridum corrosivum. (1)

Succaro {*Italian*}: Sugar, see zaccharo. (1)

Succata: Citron. (3)

Succedaneum: Substitute, a drug used in place of another. (1)

Succini (rectificatum), oleum; Succin. rect., oleum: Oil of amber was obtained by destructive distillation of amber. The rectified oil was purified by redistillation. (29)

Succini, sal: Succinic acid. (3)

Succini compositum, linimentum: Liniment of oil of amber, of oils of stillingea, amber, and lobelia in olive oil, for a variety of unrelated conditions such as asthma, epilepsy, rheumatism, etc. (34)

Succinic acid; Succinicum, acidum: Succinic acid may be derived from tartaric acid or amber, but is little used in medicine. (42)

Succinum, sal: Salt of amber, succinic acid, cathartic, diuretic, and antihysteric. (39)

Succinum: Amber, fossil resin. (1,3)

Succolata {*Italian*}: Chocolate. (3)

Succory: Chicory. See chicorea.

Succus; Succo {*Italian*}; Sugo {*Italian*}: Juice, or in some cases sugar. Some juices were plain (ex. lemon juice), but many also contained added alcohol, typically one part alcohol to three parts juice, as a preservative (ex. belladonnae, succus). (1,34)

Succus _____: Juice. See _____, succus if not listed immediately below.

Succus apertivus primum, unguentum e.; Succ. ap. [u][v]. e.: Ointment of aperient juice, of smallage, endive, mint, wormwood, parsley, valerian, oils of wormwood and mint, and wax. (35)

Sucrol: Para-phenitol-carbamide, artificial sweetener, ca. 1892. (3)

Sucrosum: Sucrose, simple sugar, used in simple syrup and as a general sweetener. (7)

Sudorific tincture: Serpentariae composita, tinctura. (34)

Suet (, mutton): Internal abdominal fat of the sheep. Used as a base material, especially in combination with waxes to prepare various cerates. (8)

Suffitus: Fumigation. See, for example, sulphur. (3)

Sugar: See saccharum. (8)

Sugar acid: Oxalic acid. (3)

Sugar ally: Black sugar, licorice (root) juice, see glycyrrhizae, succus. (40)

Sugar color: Caramel. (3)

Sugar sand: Crude milk sugar. (3)

Suint: Oesipus, impure wool fat, an antiseptic. (3)

Sulfarsenol: See salvarsan. (40)

Sulfazol; Sulfazolum: Sulfathiazol, a sulfa antibiotic.

Sulfonal; Sulfonali, tablettae: Sulfonal (see sulphonal) or tablet of sulfonal in glucose, starch, and (see) theobromatis, emulsio. A sedative. (42)

Sulfosot(e): See potassium creosote sulphonate. (40)

Sulfur; Sulphur: Elemental sulfur. Traditional and British spelling is sulphur, modern American spelling sulfur. For related entries, see sulphur. Official forms of elemental sulfur in the USP are the sublimate, the precipitate, and the ointment as detailed below. It was used topically, primarily to treat scabies or other skin parasites, and is also a laxative. Sulfur may also be burned, often in the form of sulfur candles, to produce sulfur dioxide (SO_2) to disinfect sick rooms. (1,8)

Sulfuric acid; Sulphuric acid: See sulphuricum, acidum. (8)

Sulfuric ether; Sulphuric ether: See ether. (8) This name refers to the use of sulfuric acid to dehydrate alcohols, forcing condensation to the ether, which itself contains no sulfur.

Sulpharsenobenzene: See salvarsan. (40)

Sulpharsphenamine: An arsenical antimicrobial, for syphilis. (40)

Sulphas americanus australis: "South American sulfate," i.e., quinine sulphate. (3)

Sulphatum, injectio: Injection of sulfates, zinc, copper, and ferrous sulfates plus alum, 0.25 percent each, in water. Astringent injection for gonorrhea or leucorrhea. (42)

Sulphhydric acid: Hydrogen sulphide, sulphuretted hydrogen, hydrosulphuric acid. (3)

Sulphocarbolic acid: A sulfate ester of carbolic acid (phenol), disinfectant. (40)

Sulphomethylmethanum; Sulphomethylmethane: See methylsufonal. (42,40)

Sulphonal; Sulphonalum; Sulphomethane; Sulphonmethane; Sulphonmenthanum: Sulfonal was a hypnotic related to chloral and chloral hydrate. Formula: $(CH_3)_2C(SO_2\text{-}C_2H_5)_2$. (8,42)

Sulpho-salicylic acid: See salicyl-sulphonic acid. (40)

Sulphur, balsam of; Sulphur balsam(um) (crassum): See sulphurated oil. (39,40)

Sulphur, black: Crude native sulphur. See sulphur nigrum. (40)

Sulphur, flowers of: Sulfur. Elemental sulfur takes many forms, this is sublimated, recondensed sulfur, which is yellow, light, and fluffy. (39)

Sulphur, vegetabile; —, vegetable: See lycopodium. (40)

Sulphur antimoniatum fuscum: Precipitated sulphur of antimony. (3)

Sulphur aurantium antimonii: Golden sulphur of antimony, see antimonium, sulphuratum. (39)

Sulphur auratum: Golden sulphur, antimony sulphide. (3)

Sulphur caballium: Black native sulfur. (40)

Sulphur depuratum: Sulfur purified by sublimation.

Sulphur griseum: Black native sulfur. (40)

Sulphur lotum (sublimatum): Washed sulphur, sulphur sublimatum washed with ammonia water, used to produce other materials. (8)

Sulphur nigrum: Impure native sulfur. (3)

Sulphur praecipitatium: Precipitated sulfur, lac sulphuratum, milk of sulphur. Produced from the sublimate by dissolution in lime water, followed by acidification, producing a fine precipitate. (8)

Sulphur stibiatum rubrum; —rubeum: Kermes mineral, antimony sulphide and oxide. (3)

Sulphur sublimatum: Sublimate of sulfur, flowers of sulphur. Purified from crude sulfur by sublimation. (8)

Sulphur vivum: Crude native sulfur. (40)

Sulphur(,) roll: Roll sulfur is amorphous sulfur heated and formed into rolls typically about ½ to 1 inch in diameter and 2–3 inches long, in contrast to sublimed or flowers of sulfur.

Sulphurated antimony: A crude antimony and potassium sulfide. (40)

Sulphurated oil; Sulphuratum, oleum: Sulphurated oil, of sulfur boiled in olive oil, a pectoral used orally, and also applied to running sores. (39)

Sulphurated potash ointment: A formulation of sulphurated potash (potassa sulphurata), hard paraffin, and soft paraffin, for scabies and chronic skin conditions. (8)

Sulphuret(icum) _____: Sulphurets were crude mixtures of a material, generally a metal, with sulfur, subjected to heat in order to form a mass of variable homogeneity, and reacted with sulfur to an unpredictable degree. Note that sulphuretum is also used irregularly, usually for a sulphate, but at times for a sulphuret. In general, refer to the primary metal, i.e., _____, sulphureticum. While some definitions reference a salt or composition, it is best not to overly focus on the specific chemistry, which was poorly defined at the time and probably highly variable depending upon reactants and conditions. (39)

Sulphureticum antimonii: Golden sulphur of antimony, see antimonium, sulphuratum. (39)

Sulphuretum hydrargyrus [niger] [ruber]: See hydrargyrus sulfuratus niger or ruber respectively. (39)

Sulphuretum potassae: Potassium sulphate, kali sulphuratum, see potassii sulphas. (39)

Sulphuric acid, fuming; —, Nordhausen: Concentrated sulfuric acid saturated with sulfur trioxide (SO_3) to form a mixture of sulfuric acid itself, the gas, and the condensation product, (pyrosulfuric acid) $H_2S_2O_7$. As the name implies, a corrosive and unpleasant material.

Sulphurica acida, mistura: See Haller's elixir. (34)

Sulphurici, acidi unguentum: Ointment of sulphuric acid in lard, a topical for rheumatism and neuralgia as well as for ringworm, itch, and other skin disorders. (34)

Sulphurico-aethereus, spiritus: Spirit of ether, Hoffmann's drops. (3)

Sulphuricum (dilutum), acidum; Ac. Sulphuric. (D.): Sulfuric acid, H_2SO_4. The concentrate is approximately ninety-seven percent sulfuric acid, the dilute form, approximately ten percent by dilution with water. (8)

Sulphuricum alcoholisatum, acidum: A solution of sulphuric acid in alcohol. (40) See vitriol, elixir. (40)

Sulphuricum aromaticum, acidum; Acid. Sulph. Ar.: Aromatic sulphuric acid, approximately twenty percent acid, diluted with oil of cinnamon, tincture of ginger, and alcohol. (8)

Sulphuris, balsamum: See balsamum sulphuris. (1)

Sulphuris, confectio: Confection of sublimed sulfur in orange syrup with the acid tartrate of potassa. (44)

Sulphuris, lotio: Lotion of precipitated sulfur, glycerin, alcohol, rose water, and lime water. For acne and other skin disorders. (42)

Sulphuris, trochisci: Sulphur lozenges, of sulphur, potassium tartrate, sugar, gum tragacanth, and tincture of orange peel. (34) Used as a "mild laxative in rheumatism, gout, chronic skin diseases, etc." (42)

Sulphuris, unguentum: Washed sulphur (sulphur lotum) in benzoinated lard. Sulfur ointments are effective against scabies and other parasites of the skin. (8,34)

Sulphuris alkalinum, unguentum: Alkaline sulphur ointment, made of sublimed sulphur (sulphur sublimatum), potassium carbonate, water, and benzoinated lard (sevum benzoinatum). (31)

Sulphuris camphoratum, unguentum: Camphorated sulfur ointment, of precipitated sulfur, carbolic acid, resorcin, camphor powder, solution of coal tar, benzoinated lard, and soft paraffin. (42)

Sulphuris chloridum: Sulfur chloride. (40)

Sulphuris compositum, unguentum: Compound sulphur ointment, Wilkinson's ointment, Hebra's itch ointment, of precipitated calcium carbonate, sublimed sulphur (sulphur sublimatum), and oil of cade, in a base of soft soap and lard. (31)

Sulphuris et potassii bitartratis, tabellae: Tablets of sulphur and potassium bitartrate, of washed sulphur and potassium bitartrate (potassii bitartras), flavored with oil of orange (aurantii cortex, oleum). (31)

Sulphuris et resorcin, unguentum: Ointment of precipitated sulfur and resorcinol in soft paraffin, for acne and chronic skin disease. (42)

Sulphuris flores: Flowers of sulfur, i.e., sublimed sulfur. (1)

Sulphuris hypochloratis, unguentum: Sublimed sulfur, sulfur chloride, and essential oil of almonds in lard, for acne or psoriasis. (42)

Sulphuris iodid(i)(um) (, unguentum): Sulfur iodide, SI, from direct heating (fusion) of washed sulphur (sulphur lotum) and iodine. A scabicide. The ointment consisted of the compound in paraffin or (in BPC) glycerin and benzoinated lard. Used topically for acne rosacea, ringworm, and parasitic infections of skin. (8,34,42)

Sulphuris lac: Precipitated sulfur. (1)

Sulphurosum, acidum: Sulfurous acid, H_2SO_3, from dissolution of sulfur dioxide (SO_2) in water. The latter is generated by heating sulfuric acid with charcoal, with oxidation of the carbon and release of SO_2. Sulfurous acid is a powerful reducing agent and is used as a general disinfectant. SO_2 gas was also used as an agent to disinfect sick-rooms. (8)

Sulphurous acid: See sulphurosum, acidum. (8)

Sulphydrate: Irregular chemical name for hydrosufide, HS, i.e., "ammonic sulphydrate" is ammonium hydrogen sulphide, NH_4SH. (29)

Sumach; Sumac: Sumach (sumac), *Rhus coriaria* and related species of genus *Rhus*. Berries used. A stomachic. See Rhus glabra. (1,8)

Sumbul (radix); Sumbul, tinctura; —, extractum: Musk root, or sumbul, the root of *Ferula sumbul*, of central and northeast Asia, or the alcoholic tincture or extract (NF) thereof. It is used as per other volatile oils (see caryophyllus), mainly internally as a carminative to treat flatulence, but was also used in a manner similar to valerian to treat various neurotic and mental conditions. (8)

Summitates: Literally (*Latin*) "tops." Young shoots of a plant or shrub, as in summitates sabinae, shoots of savin. (1)

Sun mixture: See diarrhea mixture. (34)

Supradin; Suprarenalin; Suprarenin: See adrenaline. (40)

Suprarenales, extractum; Suprarenalum, extractum: Extract of sheep or ox adrenals in water and glycerin. Said to have topical vasoconstrictive effects in nose and throat and for hemorrhoids, or given internally (but not active by this route). (42)

Suprarenales, tablettae: Tablet of dried adrenal gland in sugar with (see) theobromatis, emulsio. (42)

Suprarenalis, unguentum: Ointment of adrenal gland extract in paraffin and lanolin, vasoconstrictor for hemorrhoids. (42)

Suprarenalis compositus, pulvis: Suprarenal snuff, of dry powdered adrenal gland, boric acid, camphor, menthol, oil of eucalyptus, and lycopodium. To constrict nasal membranes or for asthma or other spasmodic conditions. (42)

Suprarenals; Suprarenales glandulae; Suprarenalum: Desiccated suprarenal, i.e., adrenal, gland from bovine, ovine, or porcine source. Used primarily for content of epinephrine, to treat shock, as a topical hemostatic, and as a cardiac stimulant. It was believed (correctly) to lack oral activity. (7,42)

Suprarenalum siccum; Suprarenal powder: Dried suprarenal (adrenal) gland, taken internally, as a snuff, or as a suppository. (42)

Sureau {*French*}: Elder, see sambucus. (1)

Surfeit water: See ammoniae acetatae, liquor. (40)

Surrenine: Adrenaline. (40)

Swaim's panacea: After William Swaim, Philadelphia, ca. 1820, of sarsaparilla, gaultheria, and corrosive sublimate, with other ingredients later added. Allegedly for purification of blood, scrofula, syphilis, rheumatism, and (fascinatingly) mercury poisoning. (39)

Swallow oil: Infused oil of elder flowers. (3)

Swallow wort: See vincetoxicum. (39)

Swallows, oil of: See hirudinum, oleum. (39)

Swamp milkweed: See asclepias (incarnata). (32)

Sweet almond: See amygdala dulcis. (8)

Sweet birch: See betulae. (8)

Sweet clover: See melilotus. (32)

Sweet flag, oil of: Oil from rhizome of (see) acorus. (40)

Sweet flag: See calamus. (8)

Sweet oil: Olive oil. (3)

Sweet spirits of nitre: See (a)etheris nitrosi, spiritus. Used as a stimulant, stomachic, and carminative, it causes dilation of the blood vessels, is a diuretic, and is diaphoretic. (8)

Sweet's red powder: A powder of mandrake and bloodroot, for various chronic diseases. (34)

Swietenia: Mahagony tree, figure 3-257, bark used as an unsuccessful substitute for cinchona, see soymida. (39)

Swine's seam; —same: Prepared lard, adeps praeparata. (40)

Sydenham's laudanum: Wine of opium, see opii, vinum and opii crocata, tinctura. After Thomas Sydenham, London, seventeenth century. (8,31,39)

Sydenham's plaster: Poultice of bread crumbs, crocus, and rose oil. After Thomas Sydenham, London, seventeenth century. (39)

Sylvestris, malum: See malum sylvestris. (1)

Sylvius, (carminative) spirit of: A variant of spirits of ammonia, after Franciscus du Bois, Latinized to Sylvius, professor of medicine, University of Leyden, 1614-1672. (1,39)

Sympathetic ointment: See unguentum armarium. (39)

Symphiti, syrupus; Symphito, syrupus de {*Italian*}: Syrup of comfrey. (35)

Symphyti compositum, vinum: Compound wine of comfrey, of comfrey root, Solomon's seal, helonias root, chamomile flowers, calumba root, gentian root, cardamom seed, and sassafras bark in sherry wine. A tonic for "diseases peculiar to females." (34)

Symphytum: Common comfry, *Symphytum officinale*. Figure 3-258. (1)

Symplocarpus; Symplocarpi, tinctura: Skunk cabbage (dracontium), or the tincture of the root. For asthma, pertussis, hysteria, and "other irritable or excitable conditions of the nervous system." (34)

Synapi: See sinapi. (1)

Syo; SYo; etc.; {*Italian*}: See entry for syrupus and syrupo.

Fig. 3-257 Swietenia or mahagony.

Fig. 3-258 Symphytum or common comfrey.

Syrup et Rubus: Syrup with blackberries, see rubi, syrupus. (31)

Syrup of triple phosphates; Syrup of three phosphates: See ferri, quininae et strychninae phosphatum, syrupus. (34)

Syrup of wild cherry: See pruni virginianae, syrupus. (40)

Syrup, cuisinier: See sarsaparillae compositus, syrupus. (3)

Syrupus; Syropo {*Italian*}**:** Syrup, simple syrup, consisting of sugar diluted roughly in a ratio of 850 grams of sugar per 1,000 cc of water, and strained. (8)

Syrupus aromaticus: Aromatic syrup, of tincture of orange and cinnamon water in simple syrup. Flavoring agent. (42)

Syrupus corrigens: See eryodictyium aromaticus, syrupus. (34)

Syrupus corticis…: "Syrup of bark (or peel, rind) of…." (1)

Syrupus de quinque radicibus; S. 5. rad.; (S.) (de) quin. rad., etc.: Syrup of five roots. Found on European containers and said to contain smallage, parsley, fennel, broom, and asparagus roots. (35)

Syrupus e spinae cervinae; Syr. e spin. cerv.: Syrup of buckthorn; see rhamni catharticae, syrupus. (40)

Syrupus Eastonii: See ferri, quininae et strychninae phosphatum, syrupus. (34)

Syrupus fuscus: Brown syrup, treacle, i.e., molasses. (40)

Syrupus mineralis: Liquid paraffin, mineral oil. (40)

Syrupus pectoralis: Literally, syrup for the chest, i.e., cough syrup. Many variants existed, often flavored with licorice and often containing opium in one form or another to suppress cough. (36)

Syrupus sudorificus: Sweating syrup, see sarsaparillae compositus, syrupus. (34)

Sys. specific: See os sepiae. (30)

Syzygium: See jambul. (32)

T.: Tabellae (tablets); theriaca, triaca {*Italian*} (see theriaca); tinctura (tincture); trochisci (troches). (1)

T.R.: Tuberculin reagent, new tuberculin, skin test reagent for tuberculosis. (40)

Tab.; Tablet: Tablet, lozenge. Plural (rarely seen except as a heading in formularies organized by dosage form) is tablettae. See also tabella (plural tabellae) below, as this is a distinct form unique to the BPC. (1)

Tabaci, enema: Enema of leaf tobacco in boiling water, cooled and strained. To induce "muscular relaxation," but nicotine is highly toxic and "now rarely used on account of the danger of collapse." (42)

Tabaci, oleum: Distilled residue of tobacco, noted to be similar to residue in smoking pipes, used rarely as a topical ointment in lard or simple ointment base for tumors, buboes, ulcers, and other growths, but with some risk of nicotine toxicity. (44)

Tabaci, unguentum: Ointment of tobacco extract in yellow wax and lard. For various skin conditions, but capable of causing systemic nicotine intoxication if not used with care. (34)

Tabaci, vinum: Wine (sherry) in which tobacco has been macerated, a diuretic said to be "seldom used." (44)

Tabacum; Tabaci folia: Tobacco, leaf of *Nicotiana tabacum,* source of the alkaloid nicotine. While consumed in the form of smoking or chewing tobacco and snuff, nicotine is among the most powerful and deadly toxins known. Therapeutic use in Europe began shortly after discovery of the new world, and included use as a diuretic, errhine (snuff), cathartic, and as a topical insecticide and anthelmintic. The pesticidal activity of nicotine is well known, and it continues to be used as such. Figure 3-259. (8,39,42)

Tabellae (BPC); Tabella (*singular*)**:** The BPC (42) specified a variety of chocolate tablets, or tabellae (distinct from tablets in general, which are tablettae) consisting of chocolate (see pasta, sub-entry for theobroma) and the specified active ingredient, often in multiple doses, i.e., tabellae cocainae could be produced with 2, 3, 6, or 8 mg per 100 tablet batch. These could be chewed (in fact, for erythol, must be chewed) as opposed to swallowed whole. These included:

- **Apomorphinae** (apomorphine hydrochloride)
- **Caffeinae** (caffeine citrate).
- **Cocainae** (cocaine hydrochloride).
- **Erthrol** (erythritol tetranitrate).
- **Mentholis** (menthol).
- **Trinitrini** (nitroglycerin).

Tabloids: Trademark compressed tablets (various contents), Burroughs Wellcome & Co., London. (3)

Tacamahaca, gummi: Tacamahac, resin of tree *Bursera tomentosa.* (1) Estes indicates this is Carolina poplar, *Populus balsamifera* or other American species such as *Faraga octandra.* Supposedly used by Native Americans to treat limb pain and superficial swellings or tumors, used as a diuretic and antiscorbutic.

Tachiol: Silver fluoride. (3)

Tagetes: See calendula. (39)

Tailed pepper: Cubeb. (3)

Talbor's powder: Powdered cinchona bark. (40)

Talci salicylicus, pulvis: Salicylated powder of talcum, of talcum powder and salicylic acid, as a dusting powder for irritated or broken down skin surfaces. (34)

Talcum; Talci, pulvis: Talcum powder, i.e., powdered mineral talc, a magnesium silicate, $Mg_3Si_4O_{10}(OH)_2$. This is of ancient origin, the name coming from Arabic.

Talcum purificatum; Talc, purified: Purified talc, of same, boiled extensively in a weak solution of hydrochloric acid and recovered by filtration. It is extremely fine. Used for dusting powder, or as an aid to filtration to help remove very fine particulates. (42)

Fig. 3-259 Tabacum or tobacco.

Tamarac: See pinus larix. (34)

Tamarac, compound tincture of: See laricis composita, tinctura. (34)

Tamarind; Tamarindus: Preserved pulp of the tamarind, fruit of *Tamarindus indica*, used as a mild laxative. Figure 3-260. (1,8)

Tamarindorum cum senna, infusum: Infusion of tamarinds (an example of the plural genitive, "orum") with senna, by extraction of a mixture of same with cream of tartar, coriander, and crude (brown) sugar. (39)

Tame poison: See vincetoxicum. (39)

Tanaceti, oleum: Oil of tansy. This is quite toxic and rarely used internally except as an abortifacient, often with fatal results to both mother and infant. (34)

Tanacetum; Tenaceti vulgare: Leaves and tops of Tansy, *Tanacetum vulgare*. It is described as an aromatic bitter, irritant, and narcotic, as well as an abortifacient, but is dangerous in large doses and evidently was associated with fatalities. It appears to have been little used. Figure 3-261. (1,8)

Tannacetin: See tannin, diacetyl. (40)

Tannalbin; Tannin albumin: Tannin albumin, or tanninated albumin, astringent for oral use in diarrhea, etc. (40)

Tannici, acidi, glycerinum; Tannic acid, glycerite; —, gargarisma; Tannici acidi, glyceritum: Glycerite of tannic acid, a twenty percent mixture of tannic acid in glycerine, used as an astringent paint for the throat or diluted and used as a gargle or throat spray. The gargarisma (gargle) was a ten percent solution of the glycerite in water. (42)

Tannici acidi, suppositoria: Suppository of tannic acid in cocoa butter, an astringent for hemorrhoids. (42)

Tannici acidi, trochisci; —, unguentum: Troches of tannic acid composed of sugar, tannic acid, gum tragacanth, and strong orange flower water or unguent consisting of tannic acid and benzoinated lard. Used for astringent properties. (8)

Tannici acidi, unguentum: Ointment of twenty percent tannic acid in benzoinated lard. An astringent and antiseptic for skin ulcers, piles, and various skin diseases. (34)

Tannicum, acidum; Tannic acid: Tannic acid, also called gallotanic or digallic acid, is derived from nutgall (see galla), an excrescence of the oak tree caused by insect damage. This is exposed to a damp atmosphere for twenty-four hours, triturated with ether to form a paste, and the ether squeezed from the material. This is repeated several times, after which the collected ether is allowed to evaporate away, leaving tannic acid. Tannic acid is the prototypical astringent, and is considered to be a highly important and useful drug due to the ability of tannic acid and similar organic acids to coagulate protein and albumen, acting as a topical astringent to constrict blood vessels, coagulate protein, and clot the blood. It is said to have mild antiseptic activity and to be only mildly irritating, making it doubly useful for open wounds. It was used topically to treat ulcers, sores, moist eruptions of the skin, tonsillitis, pharyngitis, nasal catarrh, otorrhea, gastric catarrh, diarrhea, leucorrhea, gonorrhea, rectal ulcers, rectal fissures, and rectal prolapse. It was applied as a haemostatic to small wounds, ulcers, the gums, the pharynx, or the nose, and given internally for bleeding of the stomach, intestines, rectum, and bladder. (8)

Tannigen: See tannin, diacetyl. (40)

Tannin: See tannicum, acidum. (8)

Tannin, diacetyl: Acetylated tannin, acetic acid ester of tannic acid, used as per tannicum, acidum. Astringent, for diarrhea. (40)

Tannocol; Tanno-gelatin: Tanno-gelatin, a tanninated gelatin, astringent for oral use in diarrhea, etc. (40)

Tannoform: A reaction product of formalin (formaldehyde) and tannic acid, used as a topical dusting powder to dehydrate skin and mucous membranes, particularly as a nasal astringent for rhinological procedures. Also as a foot powder.

Tannopin: Naphthamine tannate, use as per tannicum, acidum. (40)

Tansy: See tanacetum. (8)

Tapioca: Starch (fecula) of *Janipha manihot*, now *Manihot esculentum*, the manihot plant. (44)

Tapsus: See verbascum. (1)

Tar: See pix liquida. (8)

Fig. 3-260 Tamarind.

Fig. 3-261 Tanacetum.

Tar, Barbados; Tar, green: A mineral pitch tar. (40)

Tar, light, oil of: Rectified (distilled) oil of tar. (40)

Tar, oil of: Creosote, or reddish fluid distilled from tar. (40)

Tar, spirit of: Rectified (distilled) oil of tar (pitch, see pix). (40)

Tar and iodine paint: See pigmentum picis cum iodo. (42)

Tar mixture: See olei picis, mistura. (34)

Tar ointment, compound: See picis compositum, unguentum. (31)

Tar plasma: See picis liquidae, plasma. (34)

Tar tea: Tar water, essentially picis liquidae, aqua. (40)

Tar water (, Berkeley's): A panacea, after George Berkeley, Bishop of Cloyne, simply the supernatant water standing over pix liquida; diuretic, diaphoretic, cathartic, and emetic. (39)

Taraxaci, decoctum: Decoction of dandelion root, a vehicle for bitters. (42)

Taraxaci, extractum (liquor); —fluidum, extractum; —liquidum, extractum: The extract or fluid extract of dandelion root, or taraxacum. It is a typical bitter and is employed as such (see columba for use). (8,40)

Taraxaci, liquor: See taraxaci, succus or may also be taraxicum, extractum (liquor). (40)

Taraxaci, mellago: See taraxicum, extractum (liquor). (40)

Taraxaci, succus: Fresh juice of dandelion leaves (three parts), to which is added alcohol (one part) as a preservative. (34)

Taraxaci compositae, pilulae: Compound pills of dandelion, of bloodroot, podophyllum resin, extract of dandelion, and spearmint. As a laxative, nauseant, diuretic, and for disorders of the liver or kidney. (34)

Taraxaci compositum, elixir; Taraxac. co. elix., etc.: Compound elixir of taraxacum, made from fluid extracts of taraxacum, wild cherry and glycyrrhiza, with the tinctures of sweet orange peel and cinnamon, compound tincture of cardamom and aromatic elixir. Used as a vehicle to cover the taste of bitter substances. (31)

Taraxacum; Taraxaci radix; Tarassico {*Italian*}: The root (radix) or leaves of *Taraxacum officinale*, the common dandelion, of European origin but widespread in North America. It is a typical bitter and is employed as such (see columba for use). Figure 3-262. (8,42)

Tartar: Tartar or argol is a precipitate forming in wine casks during fermentation, and is the source of tartaric acid. (3)

Tartar, acid vitriolated: Potassium bisulphate, see potasii bisulphas. (40)

Fig. 3-262 Taraxacum or dandelion.

Tartar, cream of: See potassii bitartras. (8) Cream of tartar was obtained from the bottom of wine casks and is variably said to be the potassium or combined sodium and potassium salt of tartaric acid. Composition was probably quite variable as to sodium vs. potassium or other counter-ions. Used to raise baked goods and as a hydragogue cathartic, diuretic, and deobstruent. (39)

Tartar, neutral: See potassae, super-tartras. (40)

Tartar, oil of: Deliquesced (allowed to take up water from the air until semi-liquid) potassium carbonate. (40)

Tartar, regenerated; —regeneratum: Potassium acetate. (39)

Tartar, salt of: Potassium carbonate. This appears inconsistent with the Latin term (Sal Tartari), but references consistently document that the English term referred to the carbonate. Recall, however, that the carbonate can be made by calcination of the tartrate, so they are are at least logically related and may not have been distinguished historically. (40)

Tartar emetic ointment: See antimonii tartarati, unguentum. (34)

Tartar emetic: See antimonii et potassii tartras. (8)

Tartar per deliquium, oleum: Concentrated solution of potassium carbonate. (3)

Tartarated antimony: See antimonii et potassii tartras. (8)

Tartareae Quercetanus, pillulae; Tartar. qverc., p.: Tartar pills of Quercetanus (see Quercetanus), of aloe, gum ammoniac, vinegar of squill, tartar of vitriol, and extract of rhubarb. Purgative and for many internal disorders. (35)

Tartari, sal: Potassium tartarate (in a few references, carbonate). Diuretic and cathartic. (39) See discussion above regarding tartar, salt of.

Tartari essentiale, sal: Tartaric acid. (3)

Tartari per delinquum: Crude potassium carbonate by heating of potasium tartrate.

Tartaric acid; Tartaricum, acidum: Tartaric acid, from potassium acid tartrate (potassii tartras) and calcium carbonate, followed by treatment with sulfuric acid. (8)

Tartaricum saccharatum, acidum: Tartaric acid in sugar, a pre-mixed ingredient for effervescent formulations in the NF, in combination with sacharated sodium bicarbonate. (46)

Tartarified soda: Cream of tartar. See potassii bitartras. (8)

Tartarine: Potassium bisulfate. (40)

Tartaris antimoniae: Antimony tartrate, see tartarum emeticum. (39)

Tartarum regeneratum: Potassium acetate. (39)

Tartarum vitriolatum: Vitriolated tartar, crude potassium sulfate by reaction of tartar with sulfuric acid. (1)

Tartarus: Crude potassium bitartrate (argol), later various potassium salts. (1,3)

Tartarus albus: See tartar, cream of. (40)

Tartarus boraxatus: Sodium borotartrate. (40) Potassium and sodium borotartrate. (3)

Tartarus depuratus: Potassium tartrate. (40)

Tartarus emeticum; Tartarum stibiatus; Tartarus emeticus; Tartar emetic: Tartar emetic, potassium antimonyl tartrate. A powerful emetic. (1,40)

Tartarus natronatus: Rochelle salt, see potassii et sodii tartras. (3)

Tartarus ruber: Tartar, crude red tartar as would be derived from a red wine cask. (40)

Tartarus stibiatum: Antimony tartrate, see tartarum emeticum. (39)

Tartarus tartarisatus: Potassium tartrate. (3)

Tartarus vitriolat[um][us]: Potassium sulfate. (1,3)

Tartras potassae et ferri: See iron tartrate. (40)

Tartris potassae (et sodae): See tartari, sal. (39)

Tasteless ague drops: Similar to arsenici, solutio mineralis. (39)

Tasteless tincture of iron: See ferri citro-chloridi, tinctura. (31)

Taurus: Bull. (1)

Taxus: 1. Yew tree, genus *Taxus*, source of modern antineoplastic agent, taxol. 2. Badger (the animal). (1)

Tea: See thea. (39)

Tea, oil of: Oil obtained from seeds of tea plant and related *Camellia* species. (40)

Teel oil: See sesami, oleum. (8)

Tela araneae: Spider web. This description from Ellingwood (1919) is worthy of quotation at length: "The *spider's web* has long been used as an astringent. The freshly spun web free from dust, is macerated in alcohol, and a tincture is prepared, or the *specific tela*, of which from one to ten drops may be given as a dose. The web has been applied directly to fresh wounds to check hemorrhage, but because of the fact that it can seldom be found free from dust, it is not commonly used. Given in intermittent fevers, it is said to produce a positive antiperiodic effect. It is also given in periodical headaches or neuralgias, for this purpose." (32)

Tela gaulteri: Gaultier's web, a form of sparadrapum, a self-adhesive suppurating plaster applied on a backing of linen. (39)

Templinum, oleum: Oil of pine cones and small branches of *Pinus pumilio*. (3)

Tennant's salt: See chlorinated lime. (40)

Tenuior, spiritus: Attenuated spirits, i.e., diluted alcohol, forty-nine percent. (8)

Tenuior: Weakened (*Latin adj.*), altered to reduce strength, most commonly by dilution.

Tephrosa virginiana: Turkey pea or goat's rue, vermifuge, tonic, and laxative. Unofficial. (44)

Terebene; Terebenum: A fraction containing mainly terebene, $C_{10}H_{16}$, distilled from turpentine treated with concentrated sulfuric acid. Used much like turpentine (terebenthina), but particularly by inhalation as an expectorant, as it is readily inhaled if warmed slightly by mixture with hot water. Also given orally for the same purpose. (8)

Terebentha: Orthographic variant of terebintha. (39)

Terebintha: A common variant of terebinthina, with some major references having a preference for this term over the longer form.

Terebinthina; Terebinthinae, oleum: Turpentine, an oleoresin obtained from *Pinus palustris* and other species of pine tree. Turpentine consists mainly of 10-carbon unsaturated hydrocarbons, members of the terpene family. The latter is made up of various combinations of 5-carbon base units, which also constitute many of the other essential oils (clove, lavender, geranium, etc.).The generic term "turpentine" in modern usage generally refers to oil of turpentine (oleum terebinthina), which is distilled from the resin and which is then used to create various formulations. Topically turpentine is a rubifacient, counterirritant, and may serve as an antiseptic or disinfectant. Internally turpentine is a stimulant and carminative, causes purging in large doses, and is an effective anthelmintic. It is readily absorbed, stimulates the heart, and is said to constrict the blood vessels and thus be hemostatic. Inhaled, it is an irritant and expectorant, stimulating cough, and has the same effects after oral administration. It is a sedative and in excessive dose, causes significant nervous system depression. Turpentine is particularly hard on the urinary tract, however, causing flank pain, blood and protein in the urine, and irritation of the urinary tract. Urine after administration is said to smell of violets. It is not uncommon for turpentine to carry a geographical designation, i.e., English, French, etc., and to be derived from predominant local pine species. The "Canadian" form (terebinthina Canadensis) uniquely tended to harden. With age and exposure to oxygen, turpentine oxidizes and forms a gummy resin. The latter, containing oxygen, is said to be a particularly good antidote for phosphorus. (8)

Terebinth(in)a argentoratensis: A form of turpentine, botanical source not known. (39) The region referred to geographically appears to be that surrounding what is now Strasbourg.

Terebinth(in)a canadensis: Canadian turpentine, or Canada balsam, is a liquid oleoresin from *Abies balsamea*, or *Pinus abies*, a Canadian conifer. It was employed for its property of drying to a hard resinous material or varnish and as a component in a few remedies, but not much used directly for therapeutics. See also terebinthina for information regarding other forms of turpentine. Figure 3-263. (8)

Terebinth(in)a venata (oleum)(ol.): Venice turpentine, larch turpentine, i.e., oleoresin of larch tree. Figure 3-264. (1)

Terebinthi(n)a cocta: Turpentine, hard or solid. (3)

Fig. 3-263 Terebinthina canadensis.

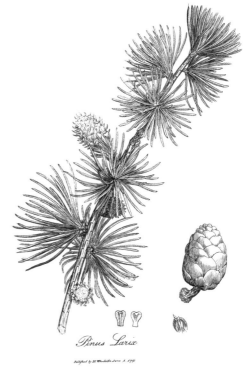

Fig. 3-264 Terebinthina venata.

Terebinthina cypria: See terebinthina pistacina. (40)

Terebinthina lagigna: See terebintina venata. (40)

Terebinthina pistacina: Turpentine from Mediterranian turpentine tree, *Pistacia terebinthus*. Figure 3-265. (40)

Terebinthina venata factitia: A mixture of resin, linseed oil, and oil of turpentine produced to mimic the characteristics of Venice turpentine. Mainly for arts, but occasionally used as a diuretic. (42)

Terebinthina vulgaris: Crude turpentine, mainly for plasters and ointments. (39)

Terebinthinae, confectio: Confection of oil of turpentine and powdered licorice root in clarified honey. Diuretic and antispasmodic, at higher doses purgative and anthelmintic. (42)

Terebinthinae, enema: Enema of turpentine and mucilage of starch, for bowel evacuation. (42)

Terebinthinae, linimentum (BPC): Liniment of soft soap, camphor, and turpentine with water. General counterirritant. (42)

Terebinthinae, linimentum: Liniment of turpentine, of resin cerate (wax) and oil of turpentine. (8)

Terebinthinae, olei fortior, emulsio: Stronger emulsion of turpentine, of same with powdered acacia and water, to be shaken before use (unstable emulsion). (46)

Terebinthinae, olei, emulsio: Oil of turpentine, acacia, egg yolk, aromatic elixir, and cinnamon water. (46)

Terebinthinae, olei, emulsum: Emulsion of turpentine (rectified), expressed oil of almond, syrup, powdered acacia, and water. Antiseptic, anthelmintic, and diuretic. (45)

Terebinthinae, spiritus; Terebinth. sp.: Spirits of turpentine, i.e., turpentine. See terebinthina.

Terebinthinae, unguentum: Ointment of turpentine, of same plus resin and yellow wax in lard. For skin conditions and burns. (34)

Terebinthinae aceticum, linimentum (BPC): Liniment of oil of turpentine and acetic acid in liniment of camphor. General counterirritant. (42)

Terebinthinae aceticum, linimentum: Acetic turpentine liniment, linimentum album, Stokes' liniment, St. John Long's liniment. This liniment contains forty percent oil of turpentine, fresh egg, oil of lemon, acetic acid and rose water. A powerful counterirritant. (31)

Terebinthinae rectificatum, oleum: Rectified oil of turpentine, distilled from a mixture of one part turpentine and six parts lime water. (8)

Teriacum; Teriaca; Tériaque {*French*}**:** See theriaca. (1)

Pistacia Terebinthus

Published by Dr Woodville July 1 1792.

Fig. 3-265 Terebinthina pistacina.

Terpene; Terpene hydrate; Terpin hydrate; Terpini hydras: Rectified oil of turpentine, alcohol, and nitric acid are allowed to react for several days, oxidizing the terebene to terpin hydrate [$C_{10}H_{18}$-$(OH)_2$], i.e., addition of two molecules of water. This crystallizes spontaneously. Used as an antiseptic, antituberculin, and general expectorant as well as in the treatment of cystitis, gonorrhea, and chronic kidney disease. Terpin hydrate is still used as an expectorant. (8,40)

Terpentine: See terebinthina. (8)

Terpentine, Canadian: See terebinthina canadensis. (8)

Terpilenol; Terpineol: A monoterpene alcohol common to pine oil, cajuput, oil, and other sources. Primarily used in perfumery. (3,40)

Terpini hydratis et codeinae, elixir: Elixir of terpin hydrate and codeine, containing terpin hydrate and codeine in alcohol elixir base. A sedative, analgesic, and antitussive. "It is a much misused mixture." (31)

Terpini hydratis et creosoti compositum, elixir: Compound elixir of terpin hydrate and creosote, of terpin hydrate, creosote and the glycerophosphates of calcium and sodium. "These proportions are so small that a fluidounce of the elixir would contain scarcely a therapeutic dose. It contains twenty percent alcohol. The official dose is given as one fluidrachm (4 cc), which is ridiculous." (31)

Terpini hydratis, elixir: Elixir of terpin hydrate, containing terpin hydrate, tincture of sweet orange peel (aurantii dulcis, tinctura cortex), spirit of bitter almond (amygdalae amarae, spiritus), alcohol, glycerin, and syrup. A sedative and expectorant. (31)

Terpinol: A mixture of various terpenes from distillation of terpin hydrate, used in perfumery. (42)

Terra alba: "White earth," variously barium sulfate, clays (kaolin), and other heavy, white minerals. (3,40)

Terra blanche: See whiting, crude calcium carbonate. (3)

Terra cariosa: Rottenstone, abrasive, carried as a sundry item. (40)

Terra damnata: Damned earth, see caput mortuum. (39)

Terra dulcis vitrioli: Sweet earth of vitriol, washed ferrum vitriolatum (ferrous sulfate) used as an astringent. (39)

Terra foliata mineralis: Impure sodium carbonate. (3)

Terra foliata tartari: Potassium acetate. (3)

Terra foliata: Sulfur. (3)

Terra fullonica; —fullorum: Fuller's earth (not eponymous), an absorbent soil used in the processing, or "fulling" of wool. (3)

Terra japonica: See catechu. (1,3) Multiple authoritative sources suggest that this is properly pale catechu, *Terra Japonica,* see gambier. (40)

Terra lemnia: See lemnian earth. (39)

Terra ponderosa salita: Barium chloride. (40)

Terra ponderosa: Natural barium sulfate. (3)

Terra rosas: Rose pink soil of Italian origin, see bolus. (40)

Terra semnia; Terra sigillata (alba)(rubra): "Signed earth," white and red bole (clay) respectively, i.e., a soil or clay from a particular location, and bearing a seal or signature indicating the source. See bolus. (1,3,39)

Terra silesiana: See Silesian earth. (39)

Tersulphuret of antimony: See antimonii sulphuret(ic)um praecipitatum. (40)

Testa: Oyster shells, *Ostrea edula*, source of calcium carbonate, and the oxide when calcined. (40)

Testaceous cerata pulvis: A mixture of wax and crushed oyster shell. (39)

Tetraform: Carbon tetrachloride. (40)

Tetraiodopyrrol: An organified iodine disinfectant, used as per iodoform. (40)

Tetranitrin: See erythritol tetranitrate. A vasodilator, for angina. (40)

Tetrapharmacum, unguentum: "Ointment of four drugs," salve of pine resin, tar, wax, and olive oil. Used as a vulnerary. (1)

Tetronal: A synthetic sedative hypnotic related to sulphonal. See ethylsulfonal. (8,42)

Teucrium: Variously chamaedrys, marum syriacum, or scordium. (39)

Teufelsdreck: See asafetida. (40)

Thalapsus bursa pastoris: Sheppard's purse, fresh herb bruised and applied for rheumatism. Unofficial. (44)

Thalictrum: Common meadow rue, *Thalictrum flavum.* Herb and root used. (1)

Thalline sulphate; Thalinae sulphas: A complex synthetic chemical, quite toxic (causing hemolysis), but used by injection for gonorrhea and as an antipyretic. (8,34)

Thapsia: Root of the deadly carrot, *Thapsia garganica.* A vesicant and counterirritant. See also, silphium. (1,32,39)

Thapsus barbatus: See verbascum. (39)

Thea (pecco): Tea, (orange) peco tea, from the common tea plant, genus *Thea.* Diluent, diuretic, and stimulant beverage whose effects are well known. Original source of the bronchodilator, theophylline, and also contains related caffeine and theobromine. Figure 3-266. (39)

Thebaic[a]: Opium, any opium preparation. (39)

Thebaic electuary: See electuarium opiatum. (39)

Thebaic pill: Any opium pill. Often of opium, licorice, and soap. See pacifick pill, same with added pimento. (39)

Thebaica(e), tinctura: Tincture of thebaic, i.e., a tincture of opium, specifically prepared by soaking 2 oz. opium in 2 pints of spirits, then straining and boiling down to a concentration of 3½ grains opium per drachm. May be flavored with aromatic spices. See opii, tinctura. (3,39,40)

Thebaicum: Adjective, containing opium. In reference to Thebes, believed to be the origin of thebiac or opium. (3)

Thebaicum, extractum: An extract of opium. (40)

Thebaicum, infusum: A water solution of opium, often with added catechu. It is weak, as the active principals are poorly water soluble. (39)

Thebaicum, pulvis: Powdered opium, generally with niter. (39)

Thebaicum, unguentum: See opiatum, linimentum. (39)

Thebaine: An alkaloid derived from opium, and used for the same purposes. (8)

Thebaira, tinctura: Alternate name for tincture of opium, see opii, tinctura. (34)

Theelin: Ovarian hormone extract. (40)

Theine: See caffeine. (8)

Themisalum: Sodium acetate salt of theobromine, used as a diuretic, stimulant, and cardiac tonic.

Fig. 3-266 Thea or tea plant.

Theobroma; Theobromatis semina: Seeds of the cocoa tree, see cocoa. Note this is *Theobroma cocoa,* not the coca tree, *Erythroxylon coca,* source of cocaine. (39)

Theobromae, oleum; Theobromatis, oleum; Theobroma, oil of: See cocoa butter. (8,44)

Theobromatis aethereus, liquor: A solution of oil of theobroma in ether, added to an equal volume of alcohol it was used as a pill excipient to allow for hardened pills when the ether and alcohol evaporated. (42)

Theobromatis, emulsio: Emulsion of theobroma, of the oil of theobroma (cocoa butter), hard soap, tragacanth, benzoic acid, and water. This is a base used for incorporation of powdered materials to form pills. (42)

Theobromatis, pulvis: Cocoa. (42)

Theobromina; Theobromine: The primary stimulant in chocolate, closely related to caffeine.

Theobromine salicylate; Theobromine sodio-salicylate; Theobrominae sodio salicylas: Used as a diuretic, theobromine being closely related to caffeine. (8)

Theobromsal; Theobromsalum: Calcium salicylate salt of theobromine, used as a diuretic, stimulant, and cardiac tonic.

Theocin; Theophylline: Alkaloid derived from tea (see thea), bronchodilator still in use for asthma. Closely related to caffeine, it is the major stimulant in tea and is also diuretic. (40)

Theosalicin: Sodium salicylate salt of theobromine, used as a diuretic, stimulant, and cardiac tonic.

Therebinthina: Orthographic variant, see terebinthina. (1)

Theriaca; Thériaque {*French*}: 1. In nineteenth century, a synonym for treacle (molasses), the uncrystalized residue of refined sugar, used as a flavoring, mainly in England. (1,3,8) 2. Theriac. A polypharmaceutical preparation, usually an electuary or plaster, supposedly introduced by Nicander of Colophon, second century CE, Greek poet and priest of Apollo. This was a universal antidote to poisons, particularly the bites of serpents, but came to be gradually regarded as a universal remedy or panacea. Many types and variants existed, with Theriac of Andromachus (seventy-three ingredients, including the flesh of vipers) being perhaps the most famous. There were five sovereign remedies in ancient times, of which one was Theriac, the others being confectio alkermes, confectio hyacintho, Mithridatum, and Orvietanum. Principal types of theriac were theriaca Andromachi (of Andromachus), theriaca Caelestis (celestial theriac), theriaca Democratis (of Democratis), theriaca Edinensis (per the Edinburgh Pharmacopoeia), theriaca Germanorum, Theriaca Londinensis (per the London Pharmacopoeia), theriaca Venata (of Venice), and theriaca diatessaron. The latter product was a "discount" variety intended as a universal remedy for the poor, and contained only myrrh, bay-laurel berries, gentian root, and root of round birthwort.

Theriacale, acetum: Aromatic vinegar. (3) See acetum aromaticum.

Theriaca veneta; Ther. ven.: Venice treacle, see theriacum andromachus. (35) In later use, molassas as discussed above.

Theriacum andromachus, axungia (or emplastrum or E.): Ointment or plaster of theriac of Andromachus.

Theriacum diachylon (, emplastum or E.) (, axungia or A.); Thericum diatchylon (, emplastum); Thericum diat. (, E.): Diachylon theriac was a plaster of lead oxide and olive oil. See diachylon, emplastrum.

Theriacum edinensis: Edinburgh theriac, per Estes, introduced as a simplified formula in the 1722 *Edinburgh Formulary,* of angelica, camphor, contrayerva, costus, crocus, guaiac, lauryl, myrrh, opium, ruta, scordium, serpentine, and valerian with addition of aromatic powder (pulvis aromaticus), honey, and wine. Estes also notes that castoreum was added in 1744 and then the entire formulation replaced in 1774 by electuarium opiatum (opiatum, electuarium). (39)

Theriacum londonensis: London theriac, i.e., London treacle, of a large number of herbal ingredients in honey. (35) Per Estes (39), similar to Theriac edinensis, above.

Theriacum, emplastrum; Theriac. E.: Emplastrum of theriac. See theriacum.

Thermarum (carolinarum), sal: Carlsbad salt, derived from hot baths of the same name. (3)

Thielemann's mixture; Thielemanni, mistura: See diarrhea mixture. (34)

Thiocol: See potassium guaiacol sulphonate. (40)

Thioform: See bismuth dithiosalicylate, basic. (40)

Thiol: Artificial ammonium ichthosulphonate. See icthamol. (40) Thiol is also a general name for organic compounds containing the sulfur analog of an alcohol, an -SH group.

Thiolin: Salts of thiosulphonic acid, salt of thiolinic acid, sulphonated and sulphurated linseed oil. (3) Ammonium ichthosulphonate. See icthamol. (40)

Thiolinic acid: Sulphurated and sulphonated linseed oil. (3)

Thiosinamina; Thiosinamine: Thiosinamine is a synthetic compound derived from mustard oil, injected to remove or reduce scar tissue or strictures (i.e., urethral strictures, uterine adhesions) but evidently of questionable value. (42) Allyl thiocarbamide. A photographic chemical. (40)

Thiosinamine-sodium salicylate: A febrifuge. (40)

Thiostab: Injection of sodium thiosulphate. (40)

Thlaspi: Name applied to cruciferous plants such as Mithridate mustard (*Thlaspi arvense*) and treacle mustard (*Erysimum cheirantoides*). Seed used. (1)

Thomas' balsam: Balsam of tolu. (3)

Thompson's antibilious pills: See aloes et mastiches, pilulae (approx.). (40)

Thompson's fluid: A solution of borax (sodii boras), glycerin, and water, used as a disinfectant bladder irrigation fluid. (8)

Thompson's panacea: Proprietary antivenereal containing mercury, sulphur, and antimony, ca. 1705. (39)

Thompson's solution of phosphorus: See phosphori, liquor. (31)

Thomsonian number six: See capsici et myrrhae, tinctura. (31)

Thorium; Thorii nitras: Thorium salts, especially the nitrate, have been recommended in malignancy, and "emanations" from thorium were inhaled in phthisis, without any proven utility. Thorium is radioactive and produces a number of gaseous isotopic decay products. One suspects this was the basis of the use in malignancy. The main use of the nitrate is to produce incandescent mantles for gas lamps or lanterns, consisting of cotton mesh soaked in thorium nitrate, dried, and ashed after tying the mantle on the gas outlet. (42)

Thorn apple: See stramonium. (39)

Thorough-root; —wort: See eupatorium. (8)

Three oils: Cajuput, eucalyptus, and olive oils. (40)

Thridace; Thridax: Juice of lactuca, used as a sedative. See lactucarium. (39)

Throat balls: See nitrum, tabulatum. (40)

Thromboplastin: Hemostatic protein, originally prepared from ox brains. (40)

Thuja; Thujae, fluidextractum: Thuja or fluid extract of thuja, *Thuja occidentalis*, a North American conifer, the fluid extract prepared using alcohol as the menstruum. Note that, although the active component of absinthe is referred to as thujone, the plant source is unrelated (see absinthe). (3,31)

Thus (, gum); Thuris (genitive): Frankincense, see olibani, gummi. (1)

Thus (masculum)(faemininum)(corticosum): Various forms of olibanum, i.e., frankincense. (39)

Thus Americana: See frankincense. (8)

Thus, gum.: See frankincense, common. (40)

Thyme, oil of; Thymi (rub.)(ruber), oleum; Thymus (botanical): A volatile oil distilled from (red) thyme, *Thymus vulgaris*, of southern France. The chief use is said to be for the isolation of thymol, but thyme oil shared all of the actions of other major volatile oils, of which clove oil is an example (see caryophyllus). It was particularly used for urinary disorders. Figure 3-267. (8) For the thymic glandular extract see below and thymus.

Thyme camphor: See thymol. (40)

Thymeae, glandulae: Dried thymus gland, action (if any) unclear, but recommended in rickets, hemophilia, and exophthalmic goiter. (42)

Thymelaea: Spurge-flax, *Daphne gnidium*. (1)

Thymi, syrupus: Syrup of thyme, of the fluid extract (thymi, fluidextractum) and simple syrup. (31)

Thymi compositus, syrupus: Compound syrup of thyme. Each fluidrachm of this contains about two grains of ammonium bromide in syrup of thyme (thymi, syrupus). (31)

Thymic acid: See thymol. (40)

Thyminic acid: Solurol, a treatment for gout, said to dissolve uric acid (the crystals of which cause gout). (40)

Thymol: A phenol or stearoptin closely related to camphor, obtained from *Thymus vulgaris*. It is a powerful antiseptic and is non-irritating, making it particularly useful as a wound dressing. A dilute preparation in glycerin is said to be useful for sore throat. Usage otherwise is essentially as per camphor. (8)

Thymol compositum, glycerinum: Glycerite of sodium bicarbonate, sodium biborate, sodium benzoate, sodium salicylate, menthol, thymol, eucalyptol, oil of pine, and oil of wintergreen in glycerin and water, colored with carmine solution. An antiseptic nasopharyngeal wash. (42)

Thymol iodide; Thymolis iodidum; Thymolol: An iodine derivative of thymol, used as per iodoform and other topical iodine compounds as a disinfectant. (3)

Thymolis compositus, liquor: A solution of boric acids, benzoic acid, thymol, eucalyptol, oils of peppermint, gaultheria, and thyme, and alcohol in water. Diluted with water and used as a mouthwash, gargle, or nasal wash, wound wash, or taken internally for flatulence and diarrhea. (42)

Thymus; Thymi liquidum, extractum: Calf thymus or extract of same in the BPC. Said to be used in exophthalmic goiter (Grave's disease) and to improve nutrition in children, especially for rickets. Presumably inactive as this would have no biological basis in current knowledge. (42)

Thymus; Thymi, fluidextractum: Garden thyme, *Thymus vulgaris*, or the fluidextract therefrom. Herb used. (1,31)

Thymus vulgaris.

Published by DT Woodville Oct 1, 1791.

Fig. 3-267 Thymus (botanical) or thyme.

Thymus (botanical use): See thyme.

Thymus siccus: Dried thymus, see thymeae, glandulae. (42)

Thyriaca: See theraica. (1)

Thyroidei, liquor: A solution of fresh thyroid gland (usually sheep), preserved with phenol. As a thyroid hormone replacement. (42)

Thyroidei, tablettae: Tablet of dried thyroid gland in sugar with (see) theobromatis, emulsio. (42)

Thyroidei liquidum, extractum: Liquid extract of thyroid gland of sheep in the BPC, a thyroid supplement. (42)

Thyroidium; Thyrroideae, glandulae; Thyroideum siccum; Thyroid powder: Desiccated thyroid, from bovine, ovine, or porcine source. This remains in infrequent use for the treatment of thyroid insufficiency and is entirely effective, if somewhat unpredictable in potency. It has largely been replaced by synthetic thyroid hormone preparations of consistent potency. (7,42)

Tic plaster: See belladonnae, emplastrum. Tic plasters were cut to approximately one inch size to cover the tic and make it withdraw. (40)

Tiger lily: See lilium tigrinum. (32)

Tiglii, collodium: Collodion with croton oil, counterirritant. (45,46)

Tiglii, oleum: See croton oil. (8)

Tiglii (compositum), linimentum: Liniment (NF) of croton oil with oil of cajuput and alcohol, or the compound liniment with croton oil and oil of sassafras, in turpentine and olive oil. Counterirritant. (46)

Til oil: See sesami, oleum. (40)

Tilia; Tiglio {*Italian*}**; Tilleul** {*French*}**:** Tree of genus *Tilia*, esp. the Lime-tree (not citrus) or Linden-tree, *Tilia europaea*. (1)

Tilia(e), aqua: Lime flower water, from "lime tree," not the citrus tree but a form of Linden. (40)

Tiliae, conserva de floribus: Conserve of the flowers of lime tree, not the citrus tree but a form of Linden. (35)

Tilly drops: See Dutch drops. (39)

Tincal: Native borax. (3)

Tinct.; Tinctura: Tincture. (1)

Tinctoria: Latin for dye. While not the same as tincture, many materials can serve both purposes and the words have a common origin. (39)

Tinctura _____; Tincture___: Tincture of, see _____, tinctura if not listed immediately below. (8)

Tinctura, amara: Bitter tincture, a stomachic or bitter, often same as vinum amarum. (39)

Tinctura aromatica: Aromatic tincture, of cinnamon, cardamom, piper longum, and angelica. Used as a tonic. (39) In the NF, of alcohol, water, cardamom, cloves, galangal root, ginger, and cinnamon. (46)

Tinctura sacra: See aloes, vinum. (39)

Tincturae aethereae, ____: In the NF, a tincture of specified potency made from any desired drug by extraction or dissolution in ether. (46)

Tincture, antacrid: Guaiac mixture with corrosive sublimate. (3)

Tincture, antiperiodic: A type of Swedish bitters with quinine. (3)

Tincture, Indian: Spirit of nitrous ether (etheris nitrosi, spiritus) and compound tincture of rhubarb (rhei composita, tinctura), in simple syrup. (40)

Tinker's Weed: See triosteum. (39)

Tinospora; Tinosporae, infusum; —concentratus, liquor; —tinctura: A bitter of India (BPC), dried stems of gulancha, *Tinospora cordifolia*. Used as an infusion or liquor and as a simple alcoholic tincture. (42)

Tiraica: See theriaca. (1)

Tobacco water: An infusion of tobacco. (40)

Tobacco: See tabacum. (8)

Todaflex; Toad flax: See linaria. (33)

Toddalia; Toddaliae, infusum; —, concentratus liquor: A bitter of India (BPC), dried root bark of *Toddalia aculeata*, used as an infusion. (42)

Toison's solution: A diluent used for counting blood cells. (24)

Tokayense, vinum; —, vin; Tokay wine: A wine from the portion of Transylvania, now Hungary, known as the Tokay, Tokaj, or Tokaji region.

Tolu, balsamum; —, balsam of; —, syrup of: Tolu balsam, obtained from the trunk of *Myroxylon toluiferum*. (1)

Toluene; Toluenum; Toluol: Toluene, i.e., methyl-benzene, a solvent. (42)

Toluifera balsamum: See balsam of Peru. (39)

Tolutana, tinctura; Tolutanum; Tolutanus, syrupus: This is the alcoholic tincture or syrup prepared from balsam of tolu. Used almost exclusively as an expectorant. (8)

Tolutana solubilis, tinctura; Tolu. Tr.: Soluble tincture of tolu, of balsam of tolu, magnesium carbonate, glycerin, water, and alcohol. Expectorant. (34)

Tolutanus, liquor: A solution of balsam of tolu in alcohol and water, stock solution for syrupus tolutanus. (42)

Tonco: See tonka. (42)

Tonga; Tonga bark; Tongae, fluidextractum: Bark of *Raphidorphora vitiensis*, of Fiji, from which a non-standard fluid extract is prepared. It is said to be highly effective in neuralgia, but very expensive. (8, 31)

Tongae et salicylatum, elixir: Elixir of tonga and salicylates, "an imitation of a widely advertised proprietary nostrum," containing tonga, cimicifuga, sodium salicylate, pilocarpine nitrate, and colchicine. The US Dispensatory of 1926 notes that "[i]t is intended for cases of chronic rheumatism and is the type of 'shot gun' that was more popular a generation ago." (31)

Tonic cups: Cups made of (see) Quassia wood. (40)

Tonka (seed)(bean); Tonco semina: Tonka seeds or beans are derived from *Dipteryx odorata* of Guyana, or *D. oppositifolia* of Brazil, large seeds containing two oily cotyledons from which coumarin, or tonka camphor, was derived. Replaced later with synthetic coumarin. Although having some anticoagulant activity (related to coumadin), mainly for perfumery. (42)

Tonquin (beans): See tonka. (42)

Tonquinol: Trinitroisobutyltoluol, substitute for musk. (3)

Toothache jelly: Phenol and collodion, equal parts. Analgesic and disinfectant. (40)

Toothache seeds: Henbane seeds, see hyoscyamus. (40)

Toothache tree: See aralia (spinosa). (39)

Tooth-powder (, oxidizing): See dentifricium (31)

Torcularia: Tournequets, non pharmacological. (39)

Tormentilla: Tormentil, septifoil, *Potentilla tormentilla*. Rhizome used as astringent. Figure 3-268. (1,39)

Toughened caustic: See argentii nitras fusas. (42)

Tous-les-mois {*French*}**:** See canna starch, i.e., arrowroot starch. (3,40)

Fig. 3-268 Tormentilla.

Tow (, styptic): See stupa. (42)

Toxicodendron; Toxicodendri, tinctura: See Rhus toxicodendron, poison oak. Although the plant was typically labeled Rhus or Rhus toxicodendron, the tincture and other preparations were not infrequently labeled toxicodendri. (34)

Tr.: Tincture.

Tragacanth (, gum); Tragacantha (, gumma): A gummy exudate of *Astragalis gummifera* (or *tragacantha*) and related species, of Asia, often referred to as "gum tragacanth." Figure 3-269. (1, 8)

Tragacanthae, mucilago; —, glyceritum: Mucilage of tragacanth, of gum tragacanth, glycerin, and water, heated and strained. Used as a binder or thickening agent or used alone as a demulcent. The glycerite (NF) was of magnesium carbonate, pitch, water, alcohol, and glycerin and was used as an excipient for making pills. (8,31)

Tragacanthae compositus, pulvis: One part each of tragacanth, gum acacia, and starch, with three parts sugar. A pill making excipient, especially good for ferrous carbonate or other heavy powders. (34)

Tragacanthum, glycerinum: Tragacanth powder 20 parts in 60 glycerin and 20 water (adjusted to desired consistency), used primarily as a pill mass. (42)

Tragea granorum actes: Elder seed troches, of same (see ebulus) with rye flower. (39)

Tragea mercurialis: Mercury troche, a panacea, mercury (metallic) and gum tragacanth. (39)

Tragea: Troche or lozenge. (39)

Tranquille, baume: Panacea after Tranquille, a Capuchin monk, seventeenth century, of many ingredients including opium, tobacco, stramonium, absinth, lavender and ruta. (39)

Tranquille, sel {*French*}**:** Sedating salt, see sal sedatum. (39)

Traumatic balsam: See benzoini composita, tinctura. (40)

Traumaticin: See gutta percha, liquor. (42)

Traumaticum, balsamum: Compound decoction of aloes (aloes compositum, decoctum), also applied to compound tincture of benzoin (benzoi, tinctura). (3) See also Turlington's balsam. (39)

Treacle: Originally theriac, in later English prescriptions, uncrystalized residue of refined sugar (molasses), used as a flavoring. (3,8)

Treacle, Venice: See theriaca Andromachi.

Tree of heaven: See ailanthus. (32)

Trementina {*Italian*}**:** Turpentine, see terebenthina. (1)

Tri-iodomethane: See iodoform. (40)

Triaca {*Italian*}**:** See theriac. (1)

Triapharmacum, unguentum: "Ointment of three ingredients," litharge, olive oil, and vinegar. Used to treat skin disorders. (1)

Tribromomethane: See bromoform. (8)

Tribus, mixtura de: "Three part mixture," of theriac, vitriol, and cream of tartar, with added camphor. (39)

Tribus, pilulae de: "Pill of three," a purgative of Socotrine aloe, agaric, and rhubarb. (1)

Tribus, syrupus de: "Syrup of three," a purgative syrup of senna leaves, agaric, and rhubarb. (1)

Tricalcic phosphate: Calcium phosphate, see calcii phosphas. (40)

Trichlor-butylidene glycol: Butyl-chloral hydrate, a sedative-hypnotic. (40)

Trichlor-ethylidene glycol: See chloral hydrate. (40)

Trichloroacetic acid; Trichloroaceticum, acidum: A highly corrosive acid formed by action of nitric acid on chloral hydrate, used mainly for destruction of skin lesions, but dilute solutions are topical disinfectants and may be applied to wounds, inflamed mucous membranes, or to eruptive skin lesions. (42)

Trichloromethane: Modern proper chemical name for chloroform, although the older term remains in preferred use. (40)

Trichomanes: See polytrichum. (1)

Trifera magna {*Italian*}**:** See tryphera magna. (1)

Trifera persica: See tryphera persica. (1)

Trifolii, fluidextractum: Fluid extract of trifolium. "It is without therapeutic virtue." (31)

Trifolii compositum, fluidextractum: Compound fluid extract of trifolium, of 21.5 percent each trifolium, glycyrrhiza, and berberis, with half that quantity of cascara amarga, lappa, phytolacca, stillingia, and also xanthoxylum. "What is to be hoped from such a conglomeration of useless remedies is a conundrum." (31)

Trifolii compositus, syrupus: Compound syrup of trifolium, of compound fluid extract of trifolium and methyl salicylate flavored with oils of sassafras and anise. (31)

Trifolium fibrinum; Trifolium paludosum; Trifolium palustre: Buckbean, bogbean, march trefoil, water trefoil, *Menyanthes trifoliata*. Leaves used. Figure 3-270. (1,3)

Trifolium praetense: Clover. (1)

Fig. 3-269 Tragacanth, source of gum tragacanth.

Fig. 3-270 Trifolium.

Trigemin(e): Butyl-amidopyrine, an analgesic. The form without the final "e" appears to be correct, but the improper form often is observed. (40)

Trigonella: See fenugraecum. (39)

Trilactine: Lactic acid forming bacillus, desiccated. Digestive aid. (40)

Trillii, fluidextractum; —fluidum, extractum: Fluid extract of trillium. (31,46)

Trillium: Trillium, beth root, *Trillium erectum*, dried rhizome and root used. It is an emetic and uterine stimulant also used in bladder disorders. (7)

Trimethylamine; Trimethylamina; Trimethylaminae hydrochloridum: A compound from various plants and from herring brine, occasionally used as the hydrochloride salt in medicinal applications for gout and rheumatism. (42)

Trimethylglycocoll: See betaine. (40)

Trimethylxanthine: Caffeine. (40)

Trinitrin: Nitroglycerin, see glonoin. (42)

Trinitrin: See glonoini, spiritus. (8)

Trinitrini, liquor: A solution of nitroglycerin in the BPC, one percent in alcohol. See glonoini, liquor. (40,42)

Trinitrophenic acid: See picric acid. (40)

Trional: A synthetic sedative hypnotic related to sulphonal. (8)

Trional: Methylsulphonal, a sedative-hypnotic. (40)

Triosteum: Root of the fever root, fever wort, or tinker's weed, *Triosteum perfoliatum*, cathartic, diuretic, and emetic. (39)

Trioxyacetophenone: See gallacetophenone. (40)

Trioxymethylene: See paraformaldehyde. (40)

Trip: Iron subcarbonate. (3) Ferric oxide. (40)

Tripharmacum, unguentum: See triapharmacum, unguentum. (1)

Triphera: See tryphera. (1)

Triple phosphate, syrup of: See ferri, quininae, et strichninae phosphatum, syrupus. (34)

Triplex pills; Triplex, pilula; Triplices, pilulae: Triple pills, of purified aloes, mercury pill mass (see hydrargyri, massa) and resin of podophyllum, a purgative. (34, 46)

Tripoli; Tripolitana, terra: A common sundry, abrasive, jeweler's rouge. (44)

Triticum; Tritici fluidum, extractum; Tritici liquidum, extractum: Couch grass, the root of *Agropyrum repens*, a creeping grass, or the fluid extract thereof. It is a mild sedative and a diuretic with some anti-inflammatory activity in the urinary tract. (8) See also tritcum (wheat) below.

Tritici, amylum; —, amyl.: Wheat starch.

Tritici, decoctum: See tritici fluidum, extractum. (40) In BPC, may also be agropyri, decoctum. (42)

Tritici, farin(a)(um): Farina (Latin) means a flour or seed meal, Farina tritici (flour of wheat) is wheat flour. Farini is grammatically incorrect, but frequently observed. (1,8)

Triticum (aestivum)(hybernum): Wheat, or flour from same. (1,39) See also triticum, Couch Grass, below.

Trituratio _____: Trituration, see _____, trituratio. (8)

Trium phosphatum, pilulae: Pill of three phosphates. See ferri phosphatis cum quinina et strychnina, pilulae. (42)

Trium valerianatum, pilulae: Pill of three valerianates, see ferri valerianatis, pilulae. (42)

Troche, pectoral; Trochisci pectoralis: See lozenge, pectoral and also bechici, troschisci. (39)

Trochi mischi; —, misci: Mixed or assorted troches (drawer or cabinet pull).

Trochisci _____: Troches (lozenges) of, see _____, trochisci. (8)

Trochisci _____ (BPC): The BPC (42) specified numerous troches based on five general formulae in addition to other specific troches listed separately. If you do not locate a troche here, see listing under primary ingredient. The bases are as follows. **Fruit:** of refined sugar, gum acacia, mucilage of gum acacia, and black currant paste, boiled. **Rose:** of refined sugar, gum acacia, mucilage of gum acacia, and rose water, admixed cold. **Simple:** of refined sugar, gum acacia, and mucilage of gum acacia. **Tolu:** of refined sugar, gum acacia, mucilage of gum acacia, tincture of balsam or tolu, and water. **Compressed:** These were produced like tablets, but intended to be sucked, and were bound with (see) theobroma, emulsio, which contains gum acacia. Lozenges (troschisi) include:

- **Ammonii chloridi (et glycyrrhizae)**—ammonium chloride (and licorice extract), fruit base, for pharyngeal catarrh.
- **Antacidi**—calcium and magnesium carbonate, salt, simple base, for indigestion.
- **Benzoici, acidi**—boric acid, fruit base, local antiseptic.
- **Bismuthi compositi**—bismuth oxycarbonate, magnesium and calcium carbonate, rose base, for pyroisis, gastric catarrh, and as an antacid.
- **Boracis**—borax, simple base, for aphthous ulcers.
- **Carbolici, acidi**—phenol, tolu base, antiseptic.
- **Catechu**—catechu, simple base, throat astringent.
- **Catechu compressi**—catechu troches, compressed type, for inflamed or ulcerated throat.
- **Cubebae**—cubebs, fruit base, mucous membrane stimulant and for cough.
- **Eucalypti gummi**—eucalyptus gum, fruit base, astringent for sore throat or cough.
- **Ferri redacti**—reduced iron, simple base, iron supplement.
- **Glycyrrhizae**—extract of licorice, oil of anise, simple base, for cough.
- **Guaiaci resinae**—guaiac resin, fruit base, for chronic tonsillitis or pharyngitis.
- **Ipecacuanhae**—ipecac root, fruit base, expectorant.
- **Kino**—Kino, fruit base, astringent.
- **Krameriae (et cocainae)**—extract of krameria, fruit base, astringent. Cocaine may be added as local anesthetic.
- **Krameriae compressi**—extract of krameria, black currant paste, compressed base, astringent.
- **Mentholis compositi**—of potassium chlorate, menthol, and betacaine, fruit base, for catarrh and ulcerations of the oral cavity.
- **Morphinae (et ipecacuanhae)**—morphine hydrochloride, tolu base, for cough. Ipecac added for expectorant activity.
- **Morphinae et ipecacuanhae compressi**—compressed form of above for same purposes.
- **Opii**—extract of opium, tolu base, for cough.
- **Potassii chloratis (compressi)**—potassium chlorate, rose base or compressed form, disinfectant for inflammatory conditions of oropharynx.
- **Sodii bicarbonas**—sodium bicarbonate, rose base, antacid.
- **Santonini**—santonin, simple base, to expel worms.

Trochisci albi Rhasis: See albi Rhases, trochisci. (1)

Trochisci medicat.: Medicated troches, a drawer or cabinet pull for assorted troches.

Trochiscus: Lozenge, plural trochisci. (1)

Trooper's ointment: See hydrargyri, unguentum. (42)

Trotter oil: See neatsfoot oil. (40)

Trout-lily: See erythronium. (39)

Trypaflavine: See acriflavine. (40)

Tryphera magna: Electuary of opium, cinnamon, galangal rhizome, zedoary rhizome, henbane seeds, etc. Used to treat gastric pain or insomnia. (1)

Tryphera persica: Electuary of senna leaves, larch agaric, rhubarb, thyme dodder, hops, etc. Used as a mild purgative, antidepressant, and in treatment of jaundice. (1)

Trypsin(um): Trypsin is a proteolytic digestive enzyme from hog pancreas, used as a digestive aid. (42)

Tuberculin [old][new]; Tuberculinum (novum): Skin test reagent for tuberculosis, similar to that still in use. New and old forms varied as to culture conditions and necessary dose to get a dermal response. (42)

Tucia {*Italian*}**:** See tutia. (1)

Tulip tree: See liriodendron. (39)

Tully's powder: See morphinae compositus, pulvis. Developed by Dr. Wm. Tully, New Haven, Connecticut. (34)

Tumenol: Artificial ammonium ichthosulphonate. See ichthymol. (40)

Tumenolsulphonic acid: Distillate of mineral oil treated with sulfuric acid. (3)

Tunicae, flores: Clove-scented pink, clove-gillyflower, *Dianthus caryophyllus*. (1)

Turbith: See turpethum. (1)

Turionis pini; Turio pini {*Italian*}**:** Pine cones. (1,3)

Turkey-red oil: See sodii sulphoricinas. (40)

Turks, wine of: See laudanum. (39)

Turlington's balsam (of life): After Robert Turlington, ca. 1744, a patent remedy initially mainly for urinary tract disorders, but later a panacea. It remained on the market in one form or another well into the twentieth century. Estes notes one later formula contained benzoin, styrax, calamita, balsam of tolu, balsam of Peru, aloe, myrrh, and angelica. (39) See balsamum traumaticum and benzoini composita, tinctura. (45)

Turmeric: Usually same as cucuma, but in the US can be *Sanguinaria canadensis*. (39)

Turnbull's blue: See ferri ferricyanidum. (40)

Turner(i)a; Turner(i)a, elixir; Turnerae, elixir; —, fluidum, extractum; —, fluidextractum: See damiana and, for preparations, damianae. (40,46)

Turner's cerate: See calaminae, unguentum. (31)

Fig. 3-271 Tussilago or colt's foot.

Turner's fluid extract: See damiana, fluidextractum. (31) This appears to be an erroneous use of an eponym and should properly be fluid extract of turner(i)a.

Turnsol(e): Litmus. (3,40)

Turpa: Oil of turpentine. (3)

Turpentine: See terebinthina.

Turpentine, American: Oil of turpentine, see terebinthina. (40)

Turpentine, Bordeaux: Turpentine from *Pinus maritima*. (40)

Turpentine, Canada: See terebinthina Canadensis. (40)

Turpentine, chian: Turpentine from Mediterranian turpentine tree, *Pistacia terebinthus*. See terebinthina. (40)

Turpentine, larch: Venice turpentine, see terebenthina venata. (40)

Turpentine drops: See Dutch drops. (40)

Turpeth; Turpethum: Turpeth, root of the plant *Ipomoea turpethum*. A purgative similar to jalap, native to India and Ceylon, and official in India and eastern British colonies. (1,42)

Turpeth mineral; Turpethum mineralis: See hydrargyri subsulphas flavus. (8) See hydrargyri oxysulphatis. (40)

Tusche: India ink. (3)

Tussilaginis farfarae, syrupus: Syrup from dried colt's foot flowers, sugar, and water. For cough. (42)

Tussilago (flores)(folia): Colt's foot, *Tussilago farfaria*. Leaves (folia) and flowers (flores) used, primarily a demulcent and expectorant. Figure 3-271. (1,39,42)

Tussim, pilulae ad: "Pills for cough," antitussive pills of licorice, opium, frankincense, myrrh, and saffron. (1)

Tutenag; Tutia; Tutty (powder): Tutty, impure zinc carbonate or oxide. (1,3,40)

Tutia pro oculis, unguentum de: Eye ointment containing zinc oxide and other ingredients. (1)

Tutiae unguentum: Ointment of tutty, i.e., zinc oxide. This ancient remedy is, with little modification, still readily available as a sunscreen and general emolient. (35)

Tutty: Impure zinc oxide. Estes suggests, reasonably, that this is a corruption of tuttiae. (3,39)

Tuzia {*Italian*}**:** See tutia. (1)

2, II, etc. "Of two," duabus(*f*) or duobus(*m*), i.e., *syrupus de duobus radicibus*, syrup of two roots, might be inscribed as *Sy. 2 Rad.* The Latin numbers beyond three are indeclinable, i.e., do not take a possessive form, but may be accompanied by "de" (of) in some uses. Digits are at times used for Greek prefixes (given parenthetically below), usually specifying a number of ingredients as in *unguentum dodecapharmacum* (ointment of twelve drugs).

2, II	duabus (*f*)/duobus(*m*)
3, III	tribus (tri)
4, IV	quattuor (tetra)
5, V	quinque (penta)
6, VI	sexies (hepta)
7, VII	septem (septa)
8, VIII	octo (octa)
9, IX	novem (nona)
10, X	decem (deca)
11, XI	undecem (undeca)
12, XII	duodecim (dodeca)

Tylcalsin; Tyllithin; Tylnatrin: Calcium, sodium and lithium acetylsalicylate salts, aspirin derivatives, analgesic, antipyretic, and anti-inflammatory. (40)

Tylmarin: Aceto-coumaric acid, see coumarin. (40)

Tylophora; Tylophorae, folia: Tylophora leaf, from *Tylophora asthmatica*, of India and surrounding areas, used as expectorant and emetic in place of ipecac in India and eastern British colonies. (42)

U

U.: A common orthographic substitution for the letter "V." At beginning of inscription: vinum (wine); unguentum (unguent). At end of inscription: usta, ustum (calcined, ashed). (1)

Ulmaria: Meadow-sweet, queen of the meadows, *Filipendula ulmaria*. Leaves used. (1)

Ulmi, decoctum: Decoction of elm bark, bitter and astringent. (42)

Ulmi, trochisci: Troches of elm, of elm flavored with methylsalicylate (wintergreen oil). Used as a demulcent. (31)

Ulmi (fulvae), mucilago: Mucilage of slippery elm bark, by boiling roughly 6 parts elm bark in 100 parts of water and straining. Used as a thickening agent and binder. Used alone as a demulcent. (8,42)

Ulmus (fulvae); Ulmi (fulvae) cortex: Slippery elm bark, the inner bark (cortex) of *Ulmus fulva*, of North America, or related species such as the English common elm, *U. campestris (*or *U. vulgaris)*. Used to produce a mucilage, see ulmi, mucilago. A topical astringent for skin conditions, demulcent, and diuretic. Figure 3-272. (1,8,39)

Ulmus rubra: Inner bark of the slippery elm, *Ulmus rubra*, preparations used as an emollient, expectorant, or antidiarrheal, and as a demulcent wound dressing. (39)

Ultramarin[e][um]: A pigment derived from a mineral of the same name by repeated grinding. More generally, a deep blue pigment. This has no clear pharmaceutical indication and most likely is a paint, pigment, or dye, but noted in a number of apothecary bottle collections.

Umber: An earth pigment, tan; burnt umber is dark reddish-brown. (44)

Ulmus campestris

Fig. 3-272 Ulmus or elm (English).

Umbilicus veneris: Pennywort, navelwort, *Cotyledon umbilicus*. Herb used. (1)

Uncaria: See catechu. (39)

Unction (not further specified): Usually a mild mercurial ointment. (3)

Ung.; Ungt.: Unguent.

Unguent(a)(um) pro oculi; Unguentum (BPC) for ocular use: The BPC (42) specified numerous eye ointments of soft paraffin, the added materials being finely powdered. Many are noted as "dilutum" despite the absence of a specified stronger formulation to distinguish them from other ointments of the same materials, which would be too strong for ocular use. These include unguentum pro oculi:

- **Acidi borici dilutum**—boric acid.
- **Atropinae (cum cocaina) dilutum**—atropine with or without cocaine.
- **Cocainae dilutum**—cocaine.
- **Flavum (cum atropina)**—yellow mercuric oxide, with or without atropine.
- **Hydrargyri ammoniati dilutum**—ammoniated mercury.
- **Iodoformi cum atropina**—iodoform and atropine.
- **Iodoformi praecipitati**—precipitated iodoform.

Unguent, cosmetic: An unguent of arum maculatum. (39)

Unguentum; unguento {*Italian*}**:** Unguent, ointment, liniment. (1)

Unguentum _____: Unguent, see _____, unguentum if not listed immediately below.

Unguentum ad vesicatorum: Ointment to blister, of hog's lard plus blistering agent (cantharidin, mylabridis, etc.), to produce blisters, not treat them. (35)

Unguentum alkalinum camphoratum: Camphorated alkaline ointment, of potassium bicarbonate and camphor in lard. (34)

Unguentum alkalinum: Alkaline ointment, of sodium carbonate and tincture of opium in lard, for skin disorders. (34)

Unguentum ammoniacale: Ammoniacal ointment, Gondret's pomade, of stronger solution of ammonia, almond oil, and lard. A vesicant and rubifacient. (34)

Unguentum antipsoricum: Ointment for skin disorders such as psoriasis, made from sulphur, pork fat, and oil of either lemon or lavender for scent. (39)

Unguentum armarium: The sympathetic unguent of Paracelsus, which sounds more akin to witchcraft than pharmacy. According to Estes, it is made in the autumn from a mixture of bear and pig fat with multiple ingredients including burnt worms, dried boar's brain, sandalwood, powdered mummy, bloodstone, and moss (collected under moonlight) from the skull of a dead individual (ideally not hung, but not buried). As if this is not sufficiently strange to the modern reader, this was intended (perhaps mercifully) to be applied to the weapon which had inflicted the injury, not to the patient. (39)

Unguentum aureum: Golden ointment, of yellow wax, oil, turpentine, pine rosen, colophony, frankincense, mastich, and saffron. (35)

Unguentum des(s)iccativium rubrum; Ung. Desicca. Rub.: Desiccating (drying) ointment, of oil of roses, wax, bole (clay), calamine, litharge, ceruse, and camphor. (35)

Unguentum glycerini: Ointment of (or with) glycerin, of which there are many variants.

Unguentum irritans: See cantharidis, unguentum. (34)

Unguentum matris: Mother's ointment, see fuscum, unguentum. (31)

Unguentum neopolitanicum: See hydrargyri, unguentum. (34)

Unguentum oculare; U. oculare; Unguentum opthalmicum; — ophthalmos: Eye ointment. (35)

Unguentum pectorale: Ointment for disorders of the chest. There are many variants, generally of a pleasant aromatic nature, to be rubbed on the chest as a counterirritant and for volatile components, like camphor or eucalyptus, to be inhaled. (35)

Unguentum simplex: Simple ointment, of olive oil and wax. Same as linimentum simplex. (39)

Unguentum stibiatum; —stibio-kali tartarici: See antimonii tartarati, unguentum. (34)

Unguentum suppurativum: Suppurating ointment, same as basilicon, unguentum. (39)

Unguentum tussivum: Cough liniment, see ammoniae, linimentum. (39)

Ungula caballina: Coltsfoot, see tussilago. (1)

Ungula: Hoof. (1)

Unicorn root: See aletris. (7)

Unique, pill: See pill unique. (39)

Universal antidote: A supposed antidote given orally to absorb poisons, consisting of activated charcoal, magnesium carbonate, and tannic acid. (See also theriac and confectio universalis.) (24)

Universale, balsamum: Universal ointment, composed of lead subacetate, yellow wax, and rape-seed oil. (3) Ointment of lead acetate, white wax, and olive oil. (1)

Unna's paste: See zinci, gelatinum. (40)

Upas antiar; —tieute: Arrowhead poisons from trees native to Java. Later study of arrowhead poisons would lead to the discovery of neuromuscular blockers, like curare, used in surgery. (44)

Uranii acetas; Uranii nitras: Uranium acetate or nitrate, rarely used in medicine, but induces renal dysfunction with loss of sugar in the urine, hence tried in diabetes. Highly toxic. (42)

Urao, unguentum: An unguent of native hydrous sodium carbonate. (3)

Urari: See curare. (8)

Urea; Urea quinate: An oral medication for dissolution of urate kidney and bladder stones. (40)

Urethane; Urethanum: Urethane, ethyl carbamate, at one time a very popular sedative-hypnotic as it produced few side effects. (8)

Urginea; Urginia: Urginea, Indian squill, *Urginea indica*, has similar activity to scilla. It is used in place of squill and is official in the BPC for India and eastern British colonies. Urginia is an incorrect but common variant. (39,42)

Urgineae, acetum: Similar to scillae, acetum. (42)

Urgineae, oxymel; —, syrupus; —, tinctura: Oxymel or syrup of urginea, of bruised urginea in acetic acid, distilled water, and clarified honey. The tincture was a simple alcoholic extract. Use as per similar formulations listed for scillae. (42)

Urgineae compositae, pilulae: Urginea was used in place of squill in India and the British eastern colonies, see scillae compositae, pilulae. (42)

Uric acid; Uricum, acidum: Uric acid is excreted by animals and obtained from guano or other excrement. It is relatively inert and does not appear to have been used regularly in therapeutics. (42)

Urinalis, herba: See linaria. (39)

Urine, sal: Sodium phosphate. (3)

Urisol; Uritone: See hexamethyleneamine. (40)

Urol; Urosin: Urea or lithium quinate, respectively. Quinate inhibits the excretion of urate in urine and was used as a preventative for renal stones. (40) Urosin is now a trade name for several medications including allopurinol, used to treat gout.

Uropherin: See lithium theobromine salicylate. (40)

Uropurgol: See formamol. (40)

Urotropine: See hexamethyleneamine. (32)

Ursus: Bear (Latin). (1)

Urtica; Urticae fluidum, extractum: Plant of genus *Urtica*, the nettles, or fluid extract of same. Leaves and seeds used as astringent and for gastrointestinal hemorrhage. Figure 3-273. (32,46)

Urtica dioica

Fig. 3-273 Urtica or nettle.

Urucu: Anatta, arnatto, dye obtained from the roucou tree, *Bixa orcellana*. (1)

Usta; Ustus; Ustum: Calcined, ashed, or burnt, or simply heated and dehydrated (dried) as in alumen ustum. (1)

Ustilago: Corn ergot, *Ustilago maidis*, a fungus affecting corn, similar in all respects to (and perhaps identical to) ergot, which afflicts rye. Used for vasoconstrictive and uterine contractile properties, as is ergot today. (32)

Uterine elixir; Uterinum, elixir: Uterine elixir, see sabinae composita, tinctura. (39)

Uterine tincture; Uterinum, tinctura: Tincture of myrrh, crocus, castor, camphor, hartshorn, and wine. For uterine disorders, i.e., antihysteric and emmenagogue. (39)

Uva; Uvae: Grape(s), raisin(s). Uvae is plural. (1,8)

Uva passa; Uvae passae (plural): "Dried berry," i.e., raisin or raisins.

Uva ursi (folia); Uvae ursi, extractum; Uvae ursi fluidum extractum; —, infusum (concentratum); —, decoctum: Bearberry (Uva ursi translates "grape of the bear"), or leaves (folia) of same, *Arbutis Uva ursi*, or the dry or fluid extract or infusion (decoction). Uva ursi is a disinfectant and astringent, particularly of the urinary tract, and was used to treat pyelitis, cystitis, gonorrhea, etc. Figure 3-274. (8,44) The BPC also specified a concentrated infusion with alcohol and chloroform water for storage and reconstitution. (42)

Uvae passae minores: Currant berries. (40)

Uvaleral: See bromural.

Fig. 3-274 Uva ursi or bearberry.

V

V.: Common orthographic substitution for the letter "U." At beginning of inscription: vinum (wine); vngvento {*Italian*}, vngventum (unguent). In the middle or at the end of inscription: veneris, veneta (of Venus); viride, verde {*Italian*} (green); verum (true); vino (wine); violatum (of violets); vstum (ustum, burnt or calcined). (1)

V.S.: Abbreviation for venisection, i.e., bleeding, not a medication. (39)

Vaccinium: See myrtillus. (1)

Vaccinum: Many vaccines were listed in BPC (42) and other sources, not always effective. These included **vaccinum: antibubonicum** (plague); **antityphosum** (typhoid); **antistaphlococcicum** (staph); and **vacciniae** (vaccinia, the original material used in smallpox vaccination).

Val. amm. elix.; Valer. amm., el'x: See ammonii valeratis, elixir.

Valerene: See amylene. (3)

Valerian; Valeriana; Valerianae rhizoma; Valerianae, fluidextractum; —, liquidum, extractum; infusum (concentratum); —, pulvis; —, tinctura: The rhizome and roots of *Valeriana officinalis* or *sylvestris*, Figure 3-275, or fluid extract, infusion, powder, or tincture therefrom. Valerian and its oil were used in a manner similar to that of clove oil (caryophyllus). In addition, valerian was used for a variety of nervous and mental disorders and for neuralgia, although the benefit was questionable. Valerian was prepared often as a "valerianic acid" salt, although the purity and identity of valerianic acid is questionable and the salts not necessarily purified chemically. These include ammonium, ferric, sodium, and zinc valerianate. (1,8,31,34, 42) According to Hughes (40), this is the European usage, and American valerian was (see) *Cypripedium hirsutum*. The BPC (42) specified a concentrated infusion with alcohol and chloroform water for storage and reconstitution.

Valeriana officinalis

Fig. 3-275 Valeriana or vlerian.

Valeriana indica; Valerianae indicae rhizoma: Indian valerian, from *Valeriana wallichii*, of India, used in place of valerian in India and eastern British colonies. (42)

Valerianae, elixir: Elixir of valerian, of the liquid extract with adjuvant elixir, BPC, as an antispasmodic and stimulant in hysteria and nervous disorders. (42)

Valerianae, tinctura: Simple tincture of powdered valerian root in alcohol, used as per the ammoniated tincture, below. (42)

Valerianae alcoholicum, extractum: Dry alcoholic extract of powdered valerian, USP. (44)

Valerianae ammoniata, tinctura; —composita, tinctura: Ammoniated tincture of valerian, of valerian extracted into aromatic spirit of ammonia. For heartburn and for hysterical or nervous attacks. (34)

Valerianae compositae, pilulae: Compound pills of valerian, of extracts of skullcap, chamomile, boneset, quinine sulfate, capsicum, and oil of valerian. A tonic and nervine. (34)

Valerianae indicae ammoniata, tinctura: A tincture of Indian valerian, oils of nutmeg and lemon, solution of ammonia, and alcohol, specified in BPC as official in India and eastern British colonies. (42)

Valerianic ether; Valerianate, ethyl: The ethyl ester derivatives of valerian alkaloids, used as per valerian. (40)

Valerianicum, acidum: Isovaleric acid. (40)

Validol: Menthol valerianate, menthol in menthyl ester of valerian (latter is a liquid). (40)

Vallet's pills; —mass; Valetti, pilula: See ferri carbonatis, massa. Tincture of ferric chloride (ferri chloridi) with diluted acetic acid, solution of ammonium acetate (ammonii acetas), aromatic elixir, glycerin, and water. (8)

Valsol: See parogen. (40)

Van Swieten, liqueur de: Mercuric chloride (van Sweiten's antivenereal, below) one percent in an approximately eight percent solution of alcohol, for venereal diseases. (40)

Van Swietens' antivenereal: Corrosive sublimate, see hydrargyri chloridum corrosivum. (39)

Van Swieten's bark: Cinchona preparation after Dr. Gerhard van Swieten, Vienna, ca. 1750. (39)

Vanilla; Vanill(in)ae, tinctura: Fruit of *Vanilla planifolia*, of Central America. Tincture of vanilla is prepared with sugar, vanilla, and alcohol, or the flavoring principal, vanillin, can be produced synthetically. Used for flavoring purposes only. (8,46)

Vanillae, essentia: Essence of vanilla bean, i.e., the distilled essential oil, often diluted with alcohol.

Vanillae, fructus: Vanilla "fruit," i.e., the vanilla bean.

Vanillin; Vanillic aldehyde: Vanillin, flavoring component of vanilla. (40,42)

Vanillini compositum, elixir: Compound elixir of vanillin, a new (ca. 1926) elixir used as a vehicle, and containing compound spirit of vanillin colored with tincture of caramel. (31)

Vanillini compositus, spiritus: Compound spirit of vanillin, containing vanillin, oil of orange (aurantii cortex, oleum), oil of cardamom, and oil of cinnamon in alcohol. Used as a flavoring agent. (31)

Vanilloes: Vanilla bean pods. (40)

Vapor; Vapores: A dosage form administered by inhalation, usually by addition to boiling water, similar to the use of volatile medicaments in a vaporizer today, ex.– eucalyptus compositus, vapor. Modifiers of vapor take the Latin masculine form. Not official in the USP, but several existed in the BP, including chlorine, pine oil, iodine, hydrocyanic acid, etc. (34)

Vaporole: Trademark capsules containing material for inhalation, Burroughs, Welcome Co., London. (3)

Varium: Ovarian extract, hormonal (estrogen). (40)

Vasoconstrictine: See adrenaline. (40)

Vasogen; Vasoliment: See parogen. (40)

Vasotonin: See adrenaline. (40)

Veal marrow: Red bone marrow from calves, nutritive and for anemia. (40)

Vegetabile, sal: Potassium tartrate. (3)

Vegetable acid, potus: Usually an infusion of lixivia (crude potassium carbonate), sometimes cream of tartar, dissolved with flour and water. For relief of thirst and for "weak stomach." The name is odd, as this is clearly alkaline. (39)

Vegetable alkali, fixed: See alkali, vegetable. See also, lixivia. (39)

Vegetable black: A fine lamp-black, i.e., vegetable derived carbon. (40)

Vegetable calomel: Resin of podophyllum, a powerful cathartic. (40)

Vegetable gum: Dextrin. (3)

Vegetable mercury: See manaca. (3)

Vegetable salt: Potassium tartrate, see potassii tartras. (40)

Vegetable sulphur: See lycopodium. (3,8)

Vegeto-mineral water: See Goulard's extract of Saturn. (39)

Velpeau's mixture: See diarrhea mixture. (34)

Venalis: From the Latin, meaning for sale, i.e., of marketable condition, usually in relationship to a slave. In apothcary use it refers to a chemical or product of commercial quality. Thus, cupri sulphas (copper sulfate) may be crude as naturally found, while cupi sulphas venalis has been purified by recrystallization for commercial sale or use.

Venene: Snake venom. (40)

Veneris, spiritus: Acetic acid. (3)

Venetian red: Red bole, a red clay. (40)

Venice turpentine: See terebenthina venata. (40)

Ventriculin: Desiccated hog stomach, digestive aid. (40)

Venus fly trap: See melilotus. (32)

Venus, crystals of: Copper acetate. (3)

Venus: Planet associated with or equal to copper. (3)

Ver[a][us][um]: True or genuine, Latin.

Veratri albi, unguentum: Ointment of *Veratrum album*, white hellebore, composed of the root plus lemon oil, in lard. For itch. (34)

Veratri viridis fluidum, extractum; Veratri (viridis), tinctura: The fluid extract and alcoholic tincture of veratrum viride. (8,42)

Veratria; Veratrine (, crystalline); Verine: A mixture of alkaloids obtained from the seed of cevadilla, *Asagraea officinalis* (not related to veratrum viride). It is a powerful dermal irritant and modest topical anesthetic used to treat neuralgia. Given internally it causes severe slowing of the heart, muscular tetany and paralysis and is rarely used in that manner. The official US preparations are, accordingly, topical. (8)

Veratrinae, ole(in)atum: Veratrine in oleic acid with olive oil, as a topical for pain or neuralgia. (42)

Veratri(n)ae, unguentum: Veratrine ointment, of veratrine, expressed oil of almond (amygdalae expressum, oleum) and benzoinated lard (sevum benzoinatum). (31,44)

Veratroidine: One of several active principals in veratrum viride. (8)

Veratrum, American: Veratrum viride. (40)

Veratrum album; Veratri albi rhizoma: Rhizome of white hellebore, *Veratrum album*. Used for dropsy and as an external parasiticide. The powdered root is used as an insecticide to prevent moth infestations of clothing. Figure 3-276. The variant, viratrum, is not uncommon. (39,42)

Veratrum viride: The roots of *Viratrum viride*, or American (Green) Hellebore. This is a complex remedy consisting of jervine and many other active components. Primarily a cardiac depressant and emetic, it was apparently not extensively used due to high toxicity, including loss of cardiac function and seizures. White's *Materia Medica* notes that "aconite and antimony are much safer" which, considering the toxicity of these materials, does not speak highly for veratrum viride. (8)

Verbascum; Verbasci foliorum, fluidextractum; Verbasci fluidum, extractum: Plant of genus *Verbascum* (mullein) or the fluid extract therefrom. Petals and leaves used. An emollient for lung or intestinal disorders and used topically for skin disorders. Figure 3-277. (1,31,39,46)

Verbena, factitious, oil of; Verbena, Indian, oil of: Oil of (see) lemon grass. (40)

Fig. 3-276 Veratrum album or white hellebore.

Fig. 3-277 Verbascum or mullein.

Verbena; Verbenae fluidum, extractum: Vervain, *Verbena officinalis*, or fluid extract of same. Herb used. Figure 3-278. (1)

Verde {*Italian*}**:** Green. (1)

Verderame {*Italian*}**:** Verdigris. (1)

Verdigris, spirit of: Acetic acid, see same. (40)

Verdigris: "Green substance," see copper acetate. (39)

Vermes, unguentum contra; Vermifugum, unguentum: Ointment with anthelmintic action made of wormseed, rue, oil of wormwood, wax, etc. (1)

Vermifuge oil: See oleorum composita, mistura. (34)

Vermifugus: Vermifuge, i.e., eliminates intestinal worms. (1)

Vermillion; Vermillion: Red mercuric sulphide. See hydrargyrus sulphuratus ruber. (3,40)

Vermis: Worm, generally in reference to an intestinal parasite. (1)

Veronal (sodium): Barbitone or the sodium salt, see barbitone. (32,40)

Veronica: See beccabunga. (1)

Verum; Verus; Vera: True, genuine (Latin). (1)

Verum, balsamum: See gileadense, balsamum. (3)

Vervain: See verbena, American usage said to be *Verbena hastata*, British usage, *V. officinalis*. (40)

Vesaloine; Vesalvine: See hexaminium. (40)

Vesicatorium, emplastrum: See epispasticum, emplastrum. (1)

Vessicativium, tinctura: Blister tincture, usually cantharidis, tinctura. (39)

Veterinaria alba, lotio; Veterinary white lotion: See alba veterinaria, lotio. (31)

Vetiver, oil of: An aromatic oil said to be sedative, from *Vetiveria zizanoides*. (40)

Viburni compositae, pilulae: Compound pills of highbush cranberry, of same with blue cohosh, unicorn root, and partridgeberry. For menstrual disorders and habitual miscarriage, or to reduce uterine cramping in pregnancy. (34)

Viburni opuli composita, tinctura; Viburn. Opul. Co., Tr.: Compound tincture of viburnum, of same plus dioscorea and scutellaria in glycerin, alcohol, and water, flavored with cinnamon and cloves (caryophyllus). Alternately, of the fluid extracts of viburnum opulus, trillium and aletris with compound elixir of taraxicum. (31,38)

Viburni opuli compositum, elixir: Compound elixir of viburnum opulus, of viburnum opulus, aletris and trillium, with compound elixir of taraxacum. "It is probably destitute of therapeutic virtues." (31)

Viburni prunifolii compositum, elixir: Compound elixir of viburnum prunifolium, of the liquid extract, with dry extract of hydrastis, oils of coriander and caraway, and glycerin. Use same as the fluid extract, below. (42)

Viburni prunifolii, elixir: Elixir of *Viburnum prunifolium*, elixir of black haw, made from fluid extract of *Viburnum prunifolium*, compound tincture of cardamom and aromatic elixir. Use as per the fluid extract, above. (31,42)

Viburnum (prunifolii); Viburni prunifolii (fluidum)(liquidum), extractum; ———liquidum, extractum: The bark of *Viburnum prunifolium*, or Black Haw, of North America, or the solid or fluid extract thereof. Used as an antispasmodic, diuretic, and tonic, and especially to treat nervous diseases of pregnancy and to prevent miscarriage. It is recommended for spasmodic dysmenorrhea, treatment of after pains (of birth), and in metrorrhagia. (8,31,42)

Viburnum opulus; Veburni opuli fluidum, extractum: Cramp bark, High Bush Cranberry, the bark of *Viburnum opulus*, or the fluid extract. Use is as per viburnum prunifolia, below. (8)

Vichy salt: Sodium bicarbonate. (40)

Vichy water: Water from the mineral spa at Vichy, France.

Vichyanum factitium (effervescens), sal; Vichyani factitii effervescens (cum lithio), salis, pulvis: Artificial Vichy salt, of sodium bicarbonate, potassium carbonate, magnesium sulphate and sodium chloride, optionally with lithium (presumably carbonate) to produce a water similar to Vichy water in its main constituents. The effervescent form is made so in the usual manner, with sodium bicarbonate, tartaric acid, and citric acid. (31)

Vicia faba: See faba. (39)

Vienna mixture: A three-to-one mixture of ether and chloroform. General inhalational anesthetic. (40)

Vienna paste: See potassa cum calce. A mixture of the latter, usually with caustic potash (i.e., potassium hydroxide), used as a caustic to destroy skin growths, tumors, etc. (8) In the BPC, pasta potassae et calcis. (42)

Verbena officinalis

Published by Dr Woodville Feb.ʳ. 1. 1794.

Fig. 3-278 Verbena or vervain.

Asclepias Vincetoxicum.

Published by Dr Woodville. April. 1. 1794.

Fig. 3-279 Vincetoxicum.

Vienna powder: Potassa with lime (the mineral), potassium, and calcium carbonates. (3)

Vigo(nium), emplastrum (de): Poultice for treatment of wounds, devised by Giovanni da Vigo, 1460–1525, surgeon to Pope Julius II. A mercurial plaster, consisting of earthworms, frogs, viper flesh or human fat, wine, camel's hay, lavender, chamomile, white lead, and mercury with additional ingredients. Also used for venereal disease. (39)

Villate's solution: See adstringens et escharotica, mistura. (34)

Vin.: Vinum, wine. (29)

Vinaigre des quatre voleurs: Vinegar of the four thieves, per Estes, this was used by thieves to protect themselves from the plague while robbing the dead in France, ca. 1628, and revealed to medicine when the thieves were taken into custody. Originally a vinegar with ruta, rosemary, peppermint, and absinth. It became more complex over time, eventually becoming the official acetum aromaticum. (39)

Vincent's mixture: A solution of sodium hypochlorite (bleach) and boric acid, used as a wound dressing. (24)

Vincetoxicum: German contrayerva, swallowwort, *Vincetoxicum officinale* or *V. asclepiade* (also called *Asclepias vincetoxicum*); a diaphoretic, emmenagogue and alexipharmic (i.e., *vince + toxicum*, victor over toxins). Rhizome used. Figure 3-279. (1,39)

Vinegar, Marseilles: See acetum, prophylacticum. (40)

Vinegar, prophylactic: See acetum prophylacticum.

Vinegar, toilet: See acetum odoratum. (42)

Vinegar (, white): Ordinary vinegar, diluted acetic acid. (40)

Vinegar, white wine: Vinegar prepared from white wine. (40)

Vinegar, wine: Vinegar prepared from wine (red or white). (40)

Vinegar acid: Acetic acid. (3)

Vinegar naphtha: Ethyl acetate. (3)

Vinegar salts: Calcium acetate. (3)

Vini (Calif., etc.), spiritus: Wine, sometimes designated as to source (California, etc.) or type of grape.

Vini, oleum: Oil of wine. This is essentially sulfuric or vitriolic ether (diethyl ether) made from distillation of a mixture of wine and concentrated sulfuric acid (vitriol) over potassium. (39)

Vini gallici, spiritus, mistura: Brandy with cinnamon water, egg yolks, refined sugar, and oil of cinnamon (latter omitted in the BP), a nutritive and stimulant useful for low-grade fevers and general debility In the NF, lithium citrate could be added. (34,46)

Vini gallici, spiritus: Brandy, thirty-nine to forty-seven percent alcohol. (8)

Vinosus rectificatus [purissimus], spiritus: A form of rectified spirits, by distillation of wine to achieve roughly ninety-five percent alcohol content. (39)

Vinum (Muscatel, etc.): Various types of wine designated by location or type, California, Muscatel, etc.

Vinum ____: Wine, a wine solution, see _____, vinum if not listed below. (8)

Vinum adustum: Alcohol, sometimes brandy. (3)

Vinum album (fortius); Vinum rubrum: White and red wine, respectively, with ten to fourteen percent alcohol content. Fortified (fortius) white wine, enhanced with distilled spirits, appeared in the early USP and was later removed. (8)

Vinum amarum: Bitter wine, generally a mixture of herb bitters in wine, typically gentian, orange rind, and coriander. (39)

Vinum antimonii; Vin. Antimon.: Wine of antimony, see antimonii, vinum.

Vinum aromaticum: Aromatic wine, of stronger white wine (vinum album fortior) with lavender, oreganum, peppermint, rosemary, sage, and wormwood. A vulnerary, but over time became mainly a flavoring or excipient in other preparations. (34)

Vinum benedictum: See vinum antimonii. (39)

Vinum carnis ((et) ferri)(et cinchonae): Wine of iron, extract of beef in sherry, with iron (the citro-chloride) or with iron and quinine sulphate. A general nutritive, restorative, and tonic. (34)

Vinum carnis et bynes: Wine with beef concentrate and malt, nutritive. (40)

Vinum chalybeatum: See ferri citratis, vinum. (40)

Vinum crematum; Vinum destillatum: Brandy. (1,3)

Vinum martis: See ferri citratis, vinum. (40)

Vinum portens; Vinum portense: Port wine, a wine fortified with distilled spirits.

Vinum stibiatum: Wine of antimony, see antimonii, vinum.

Vinum xericum; Vin. xeric.: Sherry. (29)

Viola: Plant of genus *Viola*, a violet. Petals, leaves, seeds used. Gentle cathartic used for children, emollient, expectorant, and nephritic. Figure 3-280. (1,39) See also Jacea, *V. tricolor.*

Violaceum, mel: Honey of violets, decoction of violets in honey. (1)

Violae, pulvis: Violet powder, of orris root and oils of bergamot and neroli in starch, a fine dusting powder for use on infants. Named, evidently, for its scent as it does not actually contain violets. (42)

Violae, syrupus: Syrup of violet petals in sugar and water, coloring agent and demulcent. (42)

Violarum, tabellae de succo: Tablets of violet juice, a mild cathartic electuary. (39)

Violarum; Violatum; Violato {*Italian***}:** Made from violets. (1)

Violet root: Orris root, see iris. (40)

Violi: Variant, see listings for violae.

Viosterol: Irradiated ergosterol, i.e., vitamin D. (40)

Vipera: Viper. The flesh of a venomous snake, per Estes, the flesh of Great Britain's only venomous species, *Pelias berus*. Said to be a restorative and to treat chronic skin conditions. (1,39)

Vipera, trochisci de: Viper troches, for prevention of the plague and an antidote to poisons, as with theriac. A paste made of boiled snake meat, salt, dill seed, and white bread, kneaded into oil of nutmeg or opobalsam, and cut into lozenges. (35)

Viperae, oleum; Vipers, oil of: Oil derived from the flesh of venomous snakes.

Viperina: Viper's bugloss, *Echium vulgare*. Root used. (1)

Viratrinae, oleatum; Viratrinae unguentum: This is a variant of (see) veratrinae. Oleate and ointment of veratrine, respectively. The former was approximately two percent in oleic acid, the latter in a mixture of a small amount of olive oil with benzoinated lard. A powerful local stimulant for neuralgia, paralysis, and amaurosis (blindness). (8,34)

Viratrum album: Variant of (see) veratrum. White hellebore, *Veratrum album*, a violent and fairly toxic emetic. (39) This variant remains present in botanicals to date.

Virdigris, Viride aeris: Verdigris (which is a contraction, i.e., "green substance"), crude copper acetate. (3,39)

Fig. 3-280 Viola or violet.

Virga aurea: Golden rod, *Solidago virgaurea*. Herb used. See solidago. (1)

Virgin oil: Virgin olive oil, which separates first from the olives, without pressing. (40)

Virginia Snakeroot: See serpentinaria. (8)

Virgins' milk: A mixture of tincture of benzoin and rose water. (3)

Virgin's bower: See flamula. (39)

Viride aeris: See aerugo. (1)

Viride; Veridis; Veridum: Green. (1)

Viride, balsamum: Green balsam, a lotion of verdigris, oil of linseed, and oil of turpentine. Used for treatment of ulcers. (1)

Viride, oleum: Liniment made by heating bay-laurel, rue, chamomile, marjoram, and wormwood with olive oil, followed by straining to remove insoluble matter. (1) Alternatively, oil of elder, see sambucis. (40)

Viridem, balsam: Green balsam, balsam with verdigris (copper acetate). (39)

Virol: A proprietary bone marrow preparation. (40)

Viscerale, elixir: Compound tincture of orange peel and gentian. A nonstandard item, sources suggest this is much like vinum aurantii. (3)

Viscum (album); Viscus: Mistletoe (*Viscum album*) or yellow mistletoe (*Loranthus europaeus*). Twigs and leaves used. Antispasmodic, general antidote, and plant worn to prevent witchcraft. Figure 3-281. (1,39)

Viscum quercum: Oak mistletoe, probably now *Phoradendron leucarpum*. (1)

Vitae, aqua: "Water of life," i.e., brandy or whisky. (1,3)

Vitae, lignum: See guaiaca, lignum. (1)

Vitae, sal: Sal alembroth. (3)

Vitae hoffmanni, balsamum: Alcoholic solution of various balsamic oils. (3) See oleo-balsamica, mistura. (46)

Vitelli, glyceritum: Glycerite of egg yolk, or glyconin, is a mixture of egg yolk, forty-five percent and glycerin, fifty-five percent. Used as an emulsifying agent. (31)

Vitellin: See silver albuminate. (40)

Vitellus; Vitellum ovi (recens): Egg yolk, generally of the chicken, stored or fresh (recens). An emollient and nutritive. (1,8)

Vitis (vinifera): Vine (grape), *Vitus vinifera*. Leaves used. Astringent, anti-inflammatory, and diuretic. Figure 3-282. (1,39)

Vitriol: May refer to sulfuric acid itself, or to one of a variety of reaction products of metals with sulfuric acid, i.e., sulfates, such as green vitriol (ferrous sulfate). (8)

Vitriol, aromatic: See vitrioli aromaticum, acidum. (39)

Vitriol, blue: Copper sulfate, see cupri sulphas. (39)

Vitriol, elixir of; Vitrioli acidum, elixir: See vitrioli aromaticum, acidum. (39)

Vitriol, green: Crude ferrous sulfate (ferri sulphas). (3)

Vitriol, Roman: Copper sulfate. (40)

Vitriol, salt of: Zinc sulfate. (40)

Vitriol, spirits of; Vitrioli, spiritus: Diluted sulfuric acid. (3)

Vitriol, sweet, spirit of: See vitrioli dulcis, spiritus. (40)

Vitriol, Vigani's volatile elixir of: A formulation of fuming sulfuric acid in ether. (39)

Vitriol, white: Zinc sulfate. (39)

Vitriol of heavy earth: "Heavy earth" is the source of barium ("bary," from the Greek for heavy). Thus, barium sulfate. (39)

Vitriolated magnesia: Magnesium sulphate, see magnesii sulphas. (40)

Vitriolated tartar: See kali sulphricum, a crude preparation of potassium sulfate. (39)

Vitriolatum calcinatum: The calcined vitriol (sulfate) of iron. See ferrum vitriolicum, exsiccatum. (39)

Vitriolatum sulphuratum lixivia: Equivalent to kali sulphuratum. (39)

Vitrioli aromaticum, acidum: Aromatic vitriol, of vitriol (sulfuric acid) in wine, with cinnamon and ginger. Tonic, astringent, and stomachic. (39)

Vitrioli dulcis, spiritus: Hoffmann's anodyne, see (a)ether, sulphuric. (3)

Vitrioli mynsichti, elixir: Aromatic sulphuric acid, see Mynsicht. (3)

Vitrioli narcoticum, sal: Boracic acid, i.e., boric acid. (3)

Vitrioli, oleum: Oil of vitriol, sulfuric acid. Same as vitriol itself, not a true oil. (1)

Vitrioli, sal: Zinc sulfate. (3)

Vitriolicum dilutum, acidum: Sulfuric acid, diluted with seven parts water. (39)

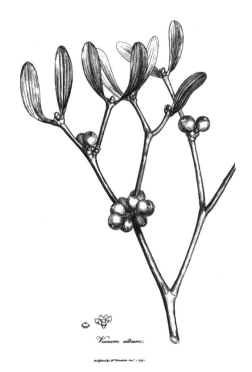

Fig. 3-281 Viscum album.

Fig. 3-282 Vitis vinifera or grape vine

Vitriolicum, linimentum; Vitriolicum, unguentum: Sulphuric liniment or unguent, with one part vitriolicum dilutum in eight of olive oil. Rubifacient. (39)

Vitriolum, oleum: See vitrioli, oleum. (1)

Vitriolum album: White vitriol, zinc sulfate. (1)

Vitriolum caeruleum; Vitriolum cupri; —Romanum: Blue vitriol, copper sulfate (see cupri sulphas). (1,3)

Vitriolum martis: Ferrous sulfate, after Mars, god of war and symbol or iron. (40)

Vitriolum viride: Green vitriol, ferrous sulfate. (1)

Vitulus: Calf (bovine, not anatomical). (1)

Vivicantes imperialis, tabellae: Royal tablets of long life, a heart stimulant, similar to kermes, confectio. (39)

Vlemincks' solution; —lotion: A solution of sulfurated lime. See calcis sulphurata, liquor. (24,31)

Vol: See ammonii carbonas. (40)

Volatile, sal: Ammonium carbonate. (3)

Volatile alkali: Ammonia. See ammoniae, spiritus. (39)

Volatile drops: 1. Spirits of ammonia. 2. Ammonia praeparata or smelling salts. 3. A variety of other volatile medications including cajeput, camphor, sal ammoniac, sal tartari or tartaric acid, or "volatile alkali" (same as ammonia spirits). (39)

Volatile liniment: See ammoniae, linimentum.

Volatile liquid, sal: Ammonia water. (3)

Volatile oil of betulae: See betulae. (8)

Volatile ointment: See ammoniae, linimentum.

Volatile oleosum, sal: Salt of volatile oil, see ammoniae aromaticus, spiritus. (39)

Volatilis fetidus, spiritus: See ammonias fetidus, spiritus. (40)

Volatilis oleosus, spiritus: Spirit of volatile oils, see ammoniatis aromaticus, spiritus. (40)

Vomiting salt; Vomitorium vitrioli, sal: Zinc sulfate. (3)

Vulpes; Volpe {*Italian*}**:** Fox. (1)

Vulpinum, oleum; —, ol.: Oil of fox, i.e., a mixture of fox fat (obtained by boiling a whole fox with white wine, water, salt, and various herbs) and oil, used primarily for joint discomfort, gout, and back or kidney pains. This would appear to be a recipe for fox soup, save for the fact that the soup is discarded and the fat retained. (35)

Vultur: Vulture (Latin). (1)

Vuzin: Iso-octylhydrocupreine, a local anesthetic. (40)

V

W

Wade's balsam; —drops: A liniment similar to tincture of benzoin. See benzoini, tinctura. (39)

Wafer cachets: Thin starch wafers between which material was enclosed and the edges sealed to form a cachet or lozenge.

Wahoo (bark): See euonymus. (7,8)

Wake robin: See arum (maculatum). (39)

Wallwort: See urtica. (39)

Walnut: See juglans. (39)

Warburg's pills: See pilulae antiperiodicae.

Warburg's tincture (without aloe): See Antiperiodica (sine aloe), tinctura. (31)

Ward's drops: After Joshua Ward, London, eighteenth century, of antimonii vitrificatum in Malaga wine. (39)

Ward's dropsy purging powder: A hydragogue and cathartic of jalap, cream of tartar, and iris florentina, the later replaced by Armenian bole at a later date. See Ward's drops. (39)

Ward's essence for headache: Eventually standardized as an official formulation, see camphorae compositum, linimentum. See Ward's drops. (39)

Ward's liquid sweat: A tincture of opium with crocus, cinnamon and sal tartari, a diaphoretic. See Ward's drops. (39)

Ward's paste: A remedy for hemorrhoids, later the official formula, piper nigrum, confectio. See Ward's drops. (39)

Ward's pills: Pills of antimonium vitrificatum and sanguis draconis. See Ward's drops. (39)

Warming plaster: See cantharidis, emplastrum. See also: emplastrum calefaciens. (8,40)

Warner's gout cordial: A mild cathartic formulation of senna and rhubarb. (39)

Warren's styptic: See adstringens, lotio. (34)

Warwick, powder of Earl of: A cathartic and panacea, after Robert Dudley, Earl of Warwick, seventeenth century. Of scammony, antimony tartrate, and cream of tartar. (39)

Wash, _____ Wash: A lotion, see _____, lotio. (31)

Washed sulphur: See sulphur lotum. (8)

Water, plague: See aqua odorifera.

Water avens: See geum; see benadicta, herba. (44)

Water caltrop: Water chestnut, *Trapa natans*, used in poultices as a demulcent. (39)

Water dock; —hemlock; —lily; —pepper: Respectively, see lapathum, cicuta, nymphaea (alba), and persicaria. (39)

Water glass: See silicate of soda. (40,44)

Water of saturn: See plumbi subacetatis dilutus, liquor. (40)

Water-pepper: See polygonum. (34)

Water: Unspecified—see aqua. With a proper or location name, a specific therapeutic water, usually listed by eponym, of which many were available: Carlsbad, Marienbad, Tarasp, Villacabras, Rubinat, Condal, Aesculap, Hunyadi, Janos, or Franz Joseph waters. (8)

Watercress: See nasturtium aquaticum. (39)

Waterglass: Sodium or potassium silicate. See silicate of soda. (3)

Watermelon: See cucurbita. For seed, see pepo. (32)

Wax: See cera. (8)

Wax, aseptic: See cera aseptica. (42)

Wax, Japan: Wax from Japanese wax tree, *Rhus succedaneum*. (40)

Wax, oil of: Oil from beeswax. (40)

Wax solution, (a)etherial: See cerae aetherea, solutio. (42)

Weapon salve: See unguentum armarium. (39)

Web, spider: See tela araneae. (32)

Wedel's oil: Oil of almonds with oil of bergammot and camphor. (40)

Wertheim's ointment: Ointment of ammoniated mercury, bismuth, and glycerin, for chloasma (a discoloration of the skin in pregnancy). (24)

Wet ash: Commercial grade potassium carbonate (potasii carbonas). (40)

Wheat, oil of: Oil from bruised wheat (triticum) grains. (40)

White, permanent: Artificial barium carbonate or sulphate. (3)

White acid: Mixture of hydrofluoric acid and ammonium bifluoride, for etching glass. (3)

White arsenic: Arsenic trioxide, see acidum arsenosum. (8)

White cinnamon: Canella. (3)

White flake; —lead: Lead carbonate. (3)

White lac: Shellac bleached with chlorine, see lacca. (40)

White liniment: See album, linimentum. (42)

White liquor: "Southern Negro term for alcohol." (3)

White lotion: See lotio alba. (24)

White mixture: See mistura alba. (42)

White nix: Crude zinc oxide. (3)

White pearl: Bismuth subnitrate or chloride. (3)

White precipitate (, insoluble): See hydrargyrum ammoniatum. (See also précipité blanc, which has a different meaning.) (8,39,40)

White precipitate ointment: See hydrargyri ammoniati, unguentum. (42)

White rose, essence: Essence of white rose, i.e., the distilled essential oil, often diluted with some alcohol. See Rosa (alba).

White wash: See plumbi subacetatis dilutus, liquor. (40)

White wood: See liriodendron (tulipifera). (39)

Whitehead's varnish: See pigmentum iodoformi compositum. (42)

Whitfield's ointment: Ointment of benzoic and salicylic acids. (24)

Whiting: A prepared chalk, a pigment (Paris white), but also a fine abrasive, commonly used to clean leaded windows after soldering. (44) In some sources, calcium carbonate.

Whitworth's red bottle: After John Taylor, Whitworth (Lancashire), late eighteenth century, of camphor, oreganum, and buglossum. (39) Hughes describes composition as eight parts alcohol, four compound tincture of lavender, and one oil of oregano. (40)

Whortleberry: See uva ursi. (39)

Wickersheimer's fluid: An arsenic containing solution used in the preservation of anatomical specimens. (24)

Wild cherry: See prunus virginiana. (8)

Wild cucumber: See cucumus (agrestis). (39)

Wild potato; —rhubarb: See mechoacanna. (39)

Wilkinson's ointment: See sulphuris compositum, unguentum. (31)

Willow: See salix and, for preparations, salicis. (42)

Wind root: See aesclepias. (39)

Wine, oil of: See ethereum, oleum. (40)

Wine bitters: See hydrastis compositum, vinum. (34)

Wine of antimony: See antimonii, vinum. (8)

Wine of iron (citrate): See ferri citratis, vinum. (31)

Wine of the Turks: Same as laudanum. (39)

Winkler's electuary: A compound remedy for tuberculosis. (39)

Winter cherries: See alkekengi. (39)

Winterberry: See prinos (verticillatus). (39)

Wintergreen (, oil of): See gaultherium. (8) The term was also used for chimaphila (pipsissewa) in the US as well as the unrelated mountain laurel, *Kalmia latifolia* and in British use for the round-leaf wintergreen, *Pyrola rotundifolia*. (39,40)

Winter's bark; Winteranus [cortex]: Winter's bark, the bark of *Drimys winteri*, after John Winter, vice admiral under Sir Frances Drake, ca. 1577, a cathartic and antiscorbutic. Figure 3-283. See coto. (39,40):

Wisdom, salt of: See alembroth, sal. (40)

Witch hazel foam; Witch hazel snow: See pasta hamamelidis. (42)

Witchhazel: See hamamelis. Generally refers to the astringent fluid extract. (8)

Witherite: Barium carbonate. (40)

Wolf's bane; Wolfsbane: See aconitum. (39,40)

Wood, bitter: See quassia. (3)

Wood ash: See lixivia. (39)

Wood ether: Methylic ether, i.e., dimethyl-ether, from condensation of wood alcohol. (40)

Wood lice: See millepeda. (39)

Wood naphtha: Crude methyl alcohol. (40)

Wood oil: See gurjun oil. (40)

Wood soot, oil of: Oil from soot of burnt wood, similar to tar oil. (40)

Wood Sorrel: See oxalis acetosella. (40)

Wood spirit: Methyl alcohol. (40)

Wood tar: See pix liquida. (8)

Wood wool: Finely divided pine wood treated with corrosive sublimate (mercuric chloride). It is antiseptic and very absorbent and was used in sanitary towels for menstruation or post-partum bleeding, for uterine discharges, or in "infant napkins," i.e., diapers. (8)

Woods, decoction of: See guaici compositum, decoctum. (39)

Wool fat: See lanolin. (8)

Wool, _____: In the BPC, one of several preparations of cotton (not wool) soaked in various materials and dried, including:
- **Biniodide of mercury**—see hydrargyri iodidi, gossypium.
- **Blue**—see sal alembroth, gossypium.
- **Boric (acid)**—see acidi borici, gossypium.
- **Capsicum**—see capsici, gossypium.
- **Carbolized**—see carbolisatum, gossypium.
- **Ferric chloride**—see ferri perchloridi, gossypium.
- **Hamamelis**—see hamamelis, gossypium.
- **Iodine**—see iodisatum, gossypium.
- **Iodised**—see iodisatum, gossypium.
- **Iodoform**—see iodoformi, gossypium.
- **Menthol**—see mentholis, gossypium.
- **Mercuric chloride**—see hydrargyri perchloridi, gossypium.
- **Mercuric iodide**—see hydrargyri iodidi, gossypium.
- **Perchlorate of iron**—see ferri perchloridi, gossypium.
- **Perchloride of mercury**—see hydrargyri perchloridi, gossypium.
- **Red iodide of mercury**—see hydrargyri iodidi, gossypium.
- **Sal alembroth**—see sal alembroth, gossypium.
- **Salicylic (acid)**—see acidi salicylici, gossypium.
- **Styptic**—see sal alembroth, gossypium.
- **Sublimate**—see hydrargyri perchloridi, gossypium.

Wool, philosophers': Zinc oxide, see zinci oxidum. (40)

Woorara; Wourari; Wourali: See curare. (8)

Worm Grass: See spigelia. (40)

Worm mixture; Wormseed mixture: See chenopodii composita, mistura. (34)

Wormseed, American; Wormseed, levant: American wormseed, see chenopodium. Levant (European) wormseed, see Santonica. (8) Unexpanded flower-heads of *Artemisia maritima*. (40)

Wormseed, oil of: Oil from chenopodium. (40)

Wormwood salts; Wormwood, salt of: An impure potassium carbonate (see potassii carbonas). (40)

Wormwood: See absinthum. (39)

Wort: Old English "wort" or "wyrt" for an herb, most often a woody plant or shrub, but used widely for almost any botanical, often based upon function, i.e., "liverwort" was believed good for the liver. (39)

Wound balsam: See benzoini composita, tinctura. (40)

Wound stone: See lapis divinus. (40)

Wound water: See arquebuscade. (40)

Wrightia antidysenterica: A tree of East India, *Nerium antidysentericum*, for diarrhea, dysentery, and febrile illness. Unofficial. (44)

Wurrus: See kamala. (40)

Fig. 3-283 Winteranus or winter's bark.

X

X-ray bismuth: Bismuth carbonate, an insoluble bismuth salt used as a contrast material in radiographic procedures, as with a barium enema. (40)

Xametrin: See hexaminium. (40)

Xanol: See caffeinae sodio-salicylas. (40)

Xanthium: Cocklebur, clotbur, *Xanthium spinosum*, a diuretic and sialogogue. (32)

Xanthorhiza apiifolia; —tinctoria: Stem and root of the yllowroot, *Xanthorhiza simplicissima*, green dye and bitter tonic. (39)

Xanthorrhoea resin(s): Yellow or red resinous exudates of various plants, similar to storax or balsam of tolu. Unofficial. (44)

Xanthoxyli, fructus: Fruit of xanthoxylum. (7)

Xanthoxyli compositus, pulvis: Compound powder of xanthoxylum, of oleoresin of prickly ash bark, berberine hydrochloride, quinine sulphate, and sugar of milk. A stimulating alterative for many chronic debilitating conditions. (34)

Xanthoxylum; Xanthoxylon; Xanthoxyli fluidum, extractum; —, oleoresina; —, tinctura: The bark of prickly ash, *Xanthoxylum americanum*, of North America or perhaps of the southern prickly ash, *X. clava-herculis*, from which a fluid extract was prepared by percolation with alcohol, which could in turn be dried to the oleoresin. A tincture was prepared directly from the berries. Use was essentially as per guaiac, particularly for chronic rheumatism, hepatic conditions, and, when chewed, as an anodyne for toothache. The tincture was said to be effective for cholera. (7,8,34)

Xaxa: Acetylsalicylic acid, i.e, aspirin. (40)

Xaxaquin: Quinine acetylsalicylate, a quinine salt used as an antirheumatic and anti-inflammatory, i.e., an aspirin substitute. (40)

Xeroform: Bismuth tribromphenate, a disinfectant. (40)

Xylene; Xylol: The volatile solvent dimethylbenzene. (40)

Xylobalsamum: Fragrant wood of the tree *Commiphora opobalsamum* and related trees. (1)

Xymine: See pancreatin. (8)

Xyrus: Orthographic variant, see iris (various entries). (39)

Y

Yam root, wild: See dioscorea. (7)

Yaw root: See stillingia. (40)

Yeast poultice: A poultice of yeast, of which many variants exist. Often with wheat, linseed (flax) meal, and milk or water, much like a bread starter. The idea was, in fact, to precipitate fermentation, as indicated by the Latin name for such poultices, cataplasma fermenti. Thus, waxy or fatty components of other typical poultices are absent. (40)

Yeast: Yeast, brewers yeast, *Saccharomyces cerevisiae* (formerly *Cerevisiae fermenti*). Yeast was used as a poultice for sloughing sores and ulcers on occasion. (8)

Yellow arsenic: Yellow arsenic sulphide. (3)

Yellow bark: Bark of cinchona calisaya. (40)

Yellow basilicon: Resin ointment, see basilicon. (40)

Yellow dock: See rumex. (8)

Yellow lotion: See flava, lotio. (31)

Yellow ointment: A mercurial ointment of hydrargyum, spirit of niter, and pork fat. (39)

Yellow parilla: See menispermium. (8)

Yellow precipitate: Yellow mercuric oxide. (3)

Yellow prussiate of potash: Potassium ferrocyanide. (40)

Yellow Puccoon: See hydrastis. (8)

Yellow root; —sandalwood; —thistle; —wood; —wax: Respectively see xanthorhiza, santalum, argemone (mexicana), xanthoxylum, and cera flava. (39)

Yellow thistle: See argemone. (39)

Yellow wash: See flava, lotio. (31)

Yellow wood: See fustic. (40)

Yera picra: See hiera picra. (1)

Yerba mate: See ilex (Paraguariensis).

Yerba sania; Yerba santa: See eriodictyon. (8)

Yerba santa, aromatic elixir; —, syrupus, etc.: See eriodictyi aromaticum, elixir, syrupus, etc.

Yohimbe; Yohimbine: The yohimbe or yohimbeye tree, *Corynanthe yohimbe*, is the source of yohimbine, a local anaesthetic and stimulant. Used for "sexual neurasthenia" and still popular as an aid to enhance male sexual function. (32)

Yohimbine; Yohimbenine: Various active principals of yohimbe.

Yolk (egg): See vitellus. (8)

Yolk of eggs, oil of: Oil from hard-boiled egg yolks. (40)

Yrino, olio: See irino, oleo. (1)

Yssopus: See hyssopus. (1)

Yva arthritica: See chamaepitys. (1)

Y

Z

Z.Z.: Anciently myrrh, in more modern use, "zinziber," i.e., ginger, see zingiber. (3)

Zafferano {*Italian*}: Saffron, see crocus. (1)

Zanaloin: Aloin derived from Zanzibar aloes, a small, spiny variant not clearly botanically distinct from aloe vera. (40)

Zanthoxylum: Orthographic variant, see xanthoxylum. (39)

Zea (mays); Zeae Stigmata; Zeae, fluidextractum; —fluidum, extractum: The silk of corn, *Zea mays*. Corn silk was boiled in water to produce a tea and was a mild diuretic. Said to be helpful in dropsy, and perhaps having some of the beneficial cardiac effects of strophanthus. A very mild cardiac stimulant, and used in acute and chronic cystitis. (7,8,31,40,46)

Zedoaria; Zedoariae, tinctura: Zedoary, rhizome of zingiberaceous plant (ginger family), *Curcuma zedoaria*, probably same as *Zedoaria* or *Kaempferia rotunda*, or the tincture therefrom. Figure 3-284. (1,34)

Zedoaria Semina; Zedoariae, semen: An alternate name for santonica. (40)

Zedoariae amara, tinctura: Bitter tincture of zedoary, with aloes, rhubarb, gentian, white agaric, saffron, glycerin, alcohol, and water. (46)

Zeller's ointment: Ammoniated mercury ointment, for example see hydrargyrum ammoniatum, unguentum. (40)

Zenker's solution: A tissue fixative of mercury bichloride (corrosive sublimate), potassium dichromate, acetic acid, and water. (24)

Zenzero {*Italian*}: Ginger, see zingiber. (1)

Zibethum: See civet. (1,44)

Ziels' solution: A tissue stain for microscopy. (24)

Zinc, subcarbonate of: Zinc carbonate. (40)

Zinc dust; Zinc powder: Powdered metallic zinc. (40)

Zinc phenolsulphonate: Used orally as an intestinal disinfectant. (40)

Zinc sulphocarbolate; Zinci sulphocarbolas: Zinc sulphocarbolate, an antiseptic formed by reacting sulfuric acid with carbolic acid (phenol) followed by addition of zinc oxide. $Zn(SO_4-C_6H_5)_2$. Useful for topical treatment of indolent ulcers. Not used internally. (8)

Zinc white: Zinc oxide or carbonate. (3,40)

Zinci, flores: Flowers of zinc, zincum ustum, see zinci oxidum. (39)

Zinci, gelatinum: A mixture of zinc oxide in melted gelatin with water and glycerin. Stored cold, but melted for application to the skin. (40)

Zinci, oleatum: Ointment of zinc oxide and oleic acid. For skin conditions. (8)

Zinci acetas; Zinci acetatis, solutio: Zinc acetate, from action of acetic acid on zinc. The solution was used as a topical for gonorrhea. (8,39)

Zinci bromidum: Zinc bromide, $ZnBr_2$. From direct action of hydrobromic acid (hydrobromicum dilutum, acidum) on metallic zinc. Primarily used as a sedative and for control of epilepsy. See bromine. (8)

Zinci butyrum: Butter of zinc, i.e., zinc chloride. See zinci chloridum. (39)

Zinci carbonas praecipitatus: Probably a mixture of zinc carbonate and oxides formed by boiling zinc sulphate with sodium carbonate. (8)

Zinci carbonatis, ceratum: Cerate of zinc carbonate in "lard ointment," i.e., ceratum album. (44)

Zinci carbosulphocarbolas: Zinc sulphocarbolate, astringent and antiseptic used as other sulfocarbolates for gonorrhea or leucorrhea. (42)

Zinci chloratis: Zinc chlorate.

Zinci chloridi et cocainae, guttae: Eyedrops (BPC) consisting of 0.5 percent zinc chloride and 0.25 percent cocaine, powerfully astringent, disinfectant, and anesthetic. (42)

Zinci chloridi, lotio: A 0.25 percent solution of zinc chloride in water, astringent and antiseptic, topical for skin and eye and topical injection for gonorrhea or leucorrhea. (42)

Zinci chloridum; Zinci chloridi, liquor: Zinc chloride, $ZnCl_2$, from action of hydrochloric acid on metallic zinc. Highly corrosive, it is used directly or as a stick or pencil with plaster of Paris, or as a paste with flour or starch to destroy warts or other growths. A twenty percent solution (liquor), Burnett's fluid, is used as an antiseptic on surfaces and objects (not for topical or internal use). (8,42)

Zinci composita, lotio: Compound lotion of zinc, of zinc sulphate and alum in water. An eyewash and for ulcers, fungal growths or tumors on mucous membranes, or topically for gangrene. (34)

Fig. 3-284 Zedoaria or Zedoary.

Zinci [durum][molle], glycerogelatinum: Firm (durum) or soft (molle) zinc glycerogelatin. This preparation contains 25 (durum) or 35 (molle) percent glycerin, and 10 percent zinc oxide in glycerinated gelatin vehicle. Used as a local sedative and protective. (31)

Zinci et alumini compositus, liquor: Solution of zinc and aluminum sulfates, naphthol, oil of thyme, and water. (46) See also the zinci et ferri preparation immediately below.

Zinci et ferri compositus, liquor: Deodorant solution, a solution of zinc, iron (ferrous) and copper sulfates, naphthol, oil of thyme, diluted hypophosphorus acid, and water. A deodorant for sick room use. It is noted that the zinc and aluminum solution above was preferred when iron stains were to be avoided. (46)

Zinci iodidum: Zinc iodide, ZnI_2, by reaction of iodine directly with zinc. For syphilis. (8)

Zinci oleatis compositus, pulvis: Compound zinc oleate powder, of same with boric acid, oil of rose, and starch. A pleasant dusting powder. (42)

Zinci oleatum, unguentum: Zinc sulfate and hard soap (which together form the oleate) in water, mixed with soft paraffin, similar to other zinc protective ointments. (42)

Zinci (oxidi), unguentum: Zinc oxide ointment, of zinc oxide in benzoinated lard. (8,42)

Zinci oxidi compositus, unguentum: Compound ointment of zinc oxide, of same in olive oil, spermacetti, and white wax, with benzoic acid, morphine sulphate, and oil of roses. Used for various eye conditions and skin conditions, including wounds and ulcers. (34)

Zinci oxidi et [acidi borici][acidi salicylici][amyli], pulvis: Ordinary dusting powders, of zinc oxide powder with, respectively, boric acid, salicylic acid, or starch. (42)

Zinci oxidi et belladonnae, pilulae: Zinc oxide and alcoholic extract of belladonna in milk sugar and syrup. (42)

Zinci oxidi, emplastrum: Zinc oxide plaster. In the BPC this is emplastrum adhaesivum elasticum with added zinc oxide. (42)

Zinci oxidi, plasma: Plasma of zinc oxide in glycerin and starch. For burns, chaps, irritations, and various skin infections. (34)

Zinci oxidum (venale): Zinc oxide, flowers of zinc, or burnt zinc (zinci ustum), ZnO, from heating of the carbonate to eliminate carbon dioxide. It may be crude or purified for commercial use (venale). It was used topically as a suspension or in dry form to treat irritation or injury. This relatively inert material is still used in ointments to treat skin conditions and protect from the sun. (8)

Zinci phosphidum: Zinc phosphide, from reaction of phosphorus vapor with elemental zinc. (8) Zinc phosphide, ZnP, reacts with water to produce the deadly fumigant gas, phosphine (PH_3) and remains in use as a fumigating agent.

Zinci stearatis, unguentum: Ointment of zinc stearate, of same in an equal weight of white petrolatum. (31)

Zinci sulphanilas: Zinc sulphanilamide, antibiotic. (40)

Zinci sulphas; Zinc, sulphuric: Zinc sulfate, from sulfuric acid acting on metallic zinc. An emetic and astringent. (8)

Zinci sulphatis, lotio: A 0.5 percent solution of zinc sulfate in water, astringent and antiseptic, topical for skin and eye and topical injection for gonorrhea or leucorrhea. (42)

Zinci sulphatis, unguentum: Ointment of zinc sulphate in butter. For various skin eruptions, fungal growths, fistulas, hemorrhoids, corneal ulcerations, etc. (34)

Zinci sulphitis, carbasus: Antiseptic gauze treated with solution of zinc sulfate, sodium sulfite, and water, then dried. (42)

Zinci sulphocarbolatis, lotio: A 0.5 percent solution of zinc sulphocarbolate in water, astringent and antiseptic, topical for skin and eye and topical injection for gonorrhea or leucorrhea. (42)

Zinci ustum: See zinci oxidum. (39)

Zinci valeratis, elixir; Zinci valerianatis, elixir; Zinci valerian., elix.: Elixir of zinc valerate (valerianate), the NF version of which consisted of zinc valerate, ammonium citrate, alcohol, spirit of bitter almond, compound tincture of cudbear, water, and aromatic elixir. For nervous conditions. (38)

Zinci valerianas: See valerian. (8)

Zinci valerianatis compositae, pilulae: Compound pill of zinc valerianate with crushed compound asafoetida pill, milk sugar (lactose), and water. (42)

Zinci valerianatis compositae, tablettae: Compound tablet of zinc valerianate, with asafetida, galbanum, myrrh, refined sugar, and ethereal solution of theobroma. (42)

Zincum: Zinc (metallic). Zinc compounds are variously corrosive to astringent and are used as topical agents. Soluble zinc salts (i.e., not the oxide) are also effective emetics although the chloride is too corrosive for such use. (8)

Zincum praecipitatum: Zinc precipitated out of zinc sulfate (zincum vitriolatum) with spirits of ammonia, used as an antispasmodic. (39)

Zincum vitriolatum: Vitriol of zinc, from the reaction of zinc and sulfuric acid, i.e., zinc sulfate, see zincum sulphas. (39)

Zingiber (Jam.) (race), Zinziber: Ginger, the rhizome of *Zingiber officinalis*, or *Amomum zingiber*, of Indian origin, from which an oleoresin can be extracted using alcohol, followed by evaporation. Sometimes referred to as Jamaican (Jam.) or Race Ginger. Use is as per clove oil (caryophyllus). Figure 3-285. (1,8)

Zingiberi (Jam.), essentia: Essence of ginger, i.e., the distilled essential oil, often diluted with some alcohol.

Zingiberis, liquor: Solution of fluid extract of ginger with pumice (to suspend) and water, filtered after agitation to remove pumice. (46)

Zingiberis (Jam.)(race), oleoresina; —fluidum, extractum; —tinctura; —, syrupus; —, trochisci: The oleoresin extracted from (Jamaican)(race) ginger root, the fluid extract, the tincture, the syrup made with fluid extract, or ginger troches composed of the tincture and syrup plus tragacanth and sugar. (8)

Zingiberis compositae, tablettae: Compound tablets of ginger, of the oleoresin of ginger, sodium bicarbonate, ammonium carbonate, gluside (saccharin), gum acacia, oil of peppermint, and (see) theobromatis, emulsio. (42)

Zingiberis (R. or Rad.) conditum: Condiment or sweetmeat of ginger (root). (36)

Fig. 3-285 Zingiber or ginger.

Zingiberis fortior, tinctura: Strong tincture or essence of ginger, an extract of ten ounces of powdered ginger root in one pint of rectified spirits. (34)

Zittmann's pills: See calomelanos et colocynthidis et hyoscyami, pilulae. (42)

Zittman's decoction; —mixture: A decoction of sarsaparilla and cinnabar, as an escarotic and antisyphilitic, ca. 1750. (39,40)

Zizyphus (spina-Christi) (vulgaris): See jujuba. (1,39,44)

Zolfo {*Italian*}**:** Sulfur. (1)

Zootic acid: Prussic acid. (3)

Zooticum: A hydrocyanate. (3)

Zuccaro {*Italian*}**; Zucchero** {*Italian*}**:** Sugar. (1)

Zuccaro buglossato {*Italian*}**:** Candied confection of bugloss, see buglossum. (1)

Zuccaro rosato {*Italian*}**:** Sweetmeat of sugar and petals or oil of red roses. (1)

Zuccaro violato {*Italian*}**:** Candied confection of violets. (1)

Zwelfer: Johann Zwelfer, 1618-1668. Apothecary and physician in Germany, Italy, and Austria, and author of multiple works including revision of the Augsburg Pharmacopoeia. Name often seen in eponymous formulations. (1)

Zylonite: Celluloid, used to make various devices. (3)

Zymin: Dried yeast. The catalyic proteins were first discovered in yeast, and hence called "en-zymes." (40)

NOTES ON LATIN

A complete description of Latin grammar and syntax is beyond the scope of this text, but is also, fortunately, unnecessary. The vast majority of Latin nouns appearing on labels will be in either the nominative case or in the genitive (possessive) case. For example, "*Glycyrrhiza*" (nominative, "licorice") will often appear as "*Glycyrrizae*" (genitive, "of licorice") as in "*Radix Glycyrrizae*," or root of licorice. Other cases, far less likely to be encountered, are the accusative (object of a verb or of certain pronouns, or the ablative, which follows *cum* (with) or *sine* (without). Latin adjectives are relatively simple, being declined, with few exceptions, to match the noun modified. Verbs appearing on labels are largely in the form of participles modifying a noun—either past (ex.—boiled) or present (ex.—boiling), and those appearing in prescriptions are generally in the imperative (command) form, as in *Rx* itself, abbreviating the imperative *Recipe* ("Taketh thou"), or occasionally the subjunctive.

Further details are left to those who choose to learn Latin as an applied language—an endeavor hardly necessary to enjoy the collecting of apothecary paraphernalia. While a discussion of Latin in general can be found in any modern Latin primer, this is of little help in regards to specific pharmaceutical terms, many of which arose late in history, and are in fact pseudo-Latinate terms. A relatively complete discussion of pharmaceutical Latin can be found in DeLorme's *A Manual of Pharmacy for Physicians* (11), and a comprehensive discussion—indeed an entire book—in Howe and Beard's *Latin for Pharmacists* (12).

NOUNS

There are four declensions of Latin nouns, with the bulk of pharmaceuticals being of the first declension. Each declension has an associated gender, and is declined in a unique manner. Nouns of a particular declension are generally identifiable by their ending letter or letters, but numerous exceptions exist, a few of which will be mentioned below. The declensions of nouns are as follows:

First Declension

All first declension nouns are feminine. Example: Herba (herb)

	Singular	Plural
Nominative	herba	herbae
Genitive	herbae	herbarum
Accusative	herbam	herbas
Ablative	herba	herbis

The word *aloe* is of Greek origin and is first declension, but is irregularly declined, i.e., *aloes* (gen), *aloen* (acc), and *aloe* (abl).

Although most terms ending in "-*a*" are 1st declension, *Aspidosperma*, *Physostigma*, and *Theobroma* are third declension (genitive = ...*atis*). The common term *folia* is a plural (leaves) of the second declension neuter *folium* (leaf), not a first declension singular.

Second Declension

Some second declension nouns end in –*us* and may be masculine or feminine, example: *syrupus* (syrup)

	Singular	Plural
Nominative	syrupus	syrupi
Genitive	syrupi	syruporum
Accusative	syrupum	syrupos
Ablative	syrupo	syrupis

The remaining second declension nouns end in -um and are neuter, example: *extractum* (extract):

	Singular	Plural
Nominative	extractum	extracta
Genitive	extracti	extractorum
Accusative	extractum	extracta
Ablative	extracto	extractis

In words ending in "ium" such as Kalium (potassium) the singular genitive may be formed as Kali, rather than Kalii.

Third Declension

Medical terms in this declension have various endings, some of which are determined by the nature of the term, i.e., those ending in –*as* (masculine) are all negatively charged ions such as *bicarbonates* (bicarbonate), with the genitive form –*atis*, giving most simple salts a form similar to that of sodium bicarbonate, *sodium bicarbonatis* or "sodium of bicarbonate." Example: *boras* (borate):

	Singular	Plural
Nominative	boras	borates
Genitive	boratis	boratum
Accusative	boratem	borates
Ablative	borate	boratibus

Exception: *Asclepias* is feminine and forms the genitive *Asclepiadis*. Those third declension nouns ending in –*is* will decline as follows:

	Singular	Plural
Nominative	hypophosph**is**	hypophosph**ites**
Genitive	hypophosph**itis**	hypophosph**itum**
Accusativ	hypophosph**item**	hypophosph**ites**
Ablative	hypophosph**ite**	hypophosph**itibus**

This declension also contains a large number of nouns with irregular declension, some of which are common terms and worthy of note. *Anthemis, Berberis, Cantharis, Colocynthis, Hammamelis,* and *Iris* form the singular genitive *–idis,* i.e., *iridis,* etc. *Cannabis, Digitalis, Hydrastis, Panis,* and *Sinapis* remain unchanged in the genitive.

A limited number of terms ending in *–o,* such as *lotio* (lotion) are irregularly declined in the singular as per *lotionis* (gen), *loteonem* (acc) and *lotione* (abl). *Carbo, confectio, pepo, sapo,* and *triturato* are similarly declined.

Many other exceptions occur (11) and will be noted when important in the glossary, most notably being the formation of the singular genitive of the following: *alcohol (alcoholis), elixir (elixiris), flos (floris)* (flower), *lac (lactis)* (milk), *pars (partes)* (part) and *semen (seminis)*(seed).

Fourth Declension

The forth declension contains a small number of terms ending in *–us,* as in *spiritus* (spirit):

	Singular	Plural
Nominative	spirit**us**	spirit**us**
Genitive	spirit**us**	spirit**uum**
Accusative	spirit**um**	spirit**us**
Ablative	spirit**u**	spirit**ibus**

Indeclinable Nouns

A limited number of nouns are considered indeclinable, i.e., *Azederach, buchu, catechu, condurango, curare, cusso, diachylon, eryodictyon, jaborandi, kino, matico, quebracho, sago,* and *sassafras.* The form of these nouns, primarily plant species, will not change with use.

ADJECTIVES

Proper treatment of the adjectives is complex, as there are many irregular forms. The adjective must match the associated noun in number (singular or plural), case (nominative, etc.), and gender. The vast majority take the following forms as per the adjective *alba* (white):

	Masculine	Feminine	Neuter
Nom:	: alb**us**	: alb**a**	: alb**um**
Gen:	: alb**i**	: alb**ae**	: alb**i**

Other common adjectives similar to *Canadensis* (Canadian) scarcely change:

	Masculine	Feminine	Neuter
Nom:	Canadens**is**	Canadens**is**	Canadens**e**
Gen:	Canadens**is**:	Canadens**is**	Canadens**is**

Exceptions outside of these classes are, however, numerous. One should also be aware of the superlative, generally formed by the addition of *–issim-,* i.e., *grandus* (great) becomes *grandissimus* (greatest).

VERBS

There are four conjugations of verbs in Latin, and the imperative is simply the root form of a particular verb, i.e.,

Typical Example

Conj.	Vowel	(infinitive)	Meaning	Imperative	Meaning
1.	: ā	*siccare*	to dry	*sicca*	: dry
2.	: ē	*miscere*	to mix	*misce*	: mix
3.	: ĕ	*recipere*	to take	*recipe*	: take
4.	: ī	*finire*	to end	*fini*	: end

The verb to make, *facere,* has an irregular imperative, *fac.*

The imperative (order or command) form is generally preferred to the use of the active subjunctive. Formation of the various imperative forms for the four declensions of verbs is given below for the 3rd person active singular (ex—let it stand) or plural (ex—let them stand) and passive singular (ex—let it be shaken) and plural (ex—let them be shaken).

Active Voice

	3rd Singular	3rd Plural
1.	: -et	: -ent
2.	: -eat	: -eant
3.	: -at	: -ant
4.	: -iat	: -iant

Passive Voice

	3rd Singular	3rd Plural
1.	: -etur	-entur
2.	: -eatur	-eantur
3.	: -atur	-antur
4.	: -iatur	-iantur

The present participle (in English usually produced by adding "-ing," i.e., boiling) regularly ends in *–ns,* i.e., *bulliens* (boiling). The past participle (in English usually produced by adding "-ed," i.e., boiled) ends in *–tus* or *–sus* (masculine form) and is declined to match the modified noun (*-ta* or *-sa* for feminine, *-tum* or *–sum* for neuter). Thus the past participle for liquefied could be *liquifactus* (m), *liquifacta* (f) or *liquifactum* (n), contingent upon the gender of the associated noun.

The gerund (in English, "to be" plus the ending "-ed," i.e., "to be boiled",) regularly ends in *–ntus* and is similarly declined to match the gender of the modified noun.

There are a limited number of quite commonly occurring participles and gerunds worthy of mention here:

demulcens (demulcing)	*fervens* (hot, literally–heating)
fumens (fuming)	*roborans* (strengthening)
calefaciens (warming)	*calcinatus* (calcined, i.e., dried by heating)
carbolisatus (carbolized)	*compressus* (compressed)
expressus (expressed)	*contusus* (bruised)
liquifactus (liquefied)	*exsiccatus* (dried)
rectificatus (rectified)	*pulveratus* (powdered)
dividendus (divided)	*formandus* (to be formed)
servandus (to be preserved)	*utandus* (to be used)

PREPOSITIONS AND CONJUNCTIONS

Prepositions in Latin are relatively simple, but do require use of the appropriate case in the object, as noted below:

Preposition	Meaning	Case (of object)
ana	of each	genitive
ad	to	accusative
in	into	accusative
infra	below	accusative
supra	above	accusative
ante	before	accusative
post	after	accusative
cum	with	ablative
pro	for	ablative
sine	without	ablative
secundum	according to	accusative

The only commonly occurring conjunctions are *et* ("and") and *vel* ("or"). Certain subordinate clauses may be joined using *ut* ("as" or "in order that"), as in *divide ut dictum* ("divide as directed").

APPENDIX 2

LATIN ABBREVIATIONS
COMMONLY USED IN PRESCRIPTIONS

The following abbreviations are commonly used in the writing of prescriptions or medical orders for care in modern times, reflecting the widespread use of pre-manufactured remedies. A much more comprehensive list of terms was used to provide compounding orders, i.e., detailed instructions to the apothecary regarding the preparation of a prescription from individual ingredients (see Appendix-3). The prescription is itself generally begun with the abbreviation Rx or symbol, ℞, for the Latin *Recipe,* an imperative form meaning "take" or "taketh thou" which is also the source of the modern English word, recipe.

Abbreviation	Latin	English Equivalent
a.c.	*ante cibum*	before food (meals)
a.h.	*alternis horis*	alternate hours
(q) a.m.	*ante meridian*	(each) morning
ad.lib.	*ad libitum*	freely as wanted
aq.	*aqua*	water
b.i.d.	*bis in die*	twice a day
cap.	*capula*	capsule
c̄	*cum*	with
div.	*divide*	divide
eq.pts.	*equalis partis*	equal parts
gtt.	*gutta*	a drop
h.	*hora*	hour
no.	*numero*	number
O.	*octarius*	pint
o.d.	*oculus dexter*	right eye
o.s	*oculus sinister*	left eye
o.u.	*oculus uterque*	each eye /both eyes
p.r.n.	*pro re nata*	as occasion requires (as needed)
(q) p.m.	*post meridien*	(each) afternoon
p.o.	*per os*	by mouth / orally
q.s.	*quantum sufficiat*	a sufficient quantity (i.e., to make up to a final volume)
q4h	*quaque 4 hora*	every 4 hours
q6h	*quaque 6 hora*	every 6 hours
q1d or qd	*quaque 1 die*	every day
q1w	*(pseudo latin)*	every week
q.i.d.	*quater in die*	four times a day
s.i.d.	*semel in die*	once a day
Sig., S.	*signa*	write on the label
stat.	*statim*	immediately
tab.	*tabella*	a tablet
t.i.d.	*ter in die*	three times a day

APPENDIX 3

MAGISTRAL PHARMACY

LATIN TERMS USED IN COMPOUNDING INSTRUCTIONS

Historically, a complete prescription contained a full set of instructions to the apothecary for producing a therapeutic material from raw ingredients. The practice of specifying such instructions was referred to as Magistral Pharmacy (see Remington's Pharmacy (3) for a complete discussion). A magister, or master (origin of the modern term magistrate), i.e., a competent person such as a physician, would specify the preparation of such a remedy at the time of need. The remedy itself also came to be called a "magestral," in distinction to those remedies specified in official documents (pharmacopoeias or formularies) and known as "officials" or "official remedies."

The 1926 edition of Remington's states that Magistral Pharmacy is "unquestionably the most important division of true pharmaceutical practice." Today, almost all therapeutics are commercially produced in advance of prescription and the majority of physicians would be hard pressed to write a complete prescription in their native tongue, let alone in the traditional Latin. Lest one think the art is completely lost, however, the competent pharmacist of today remains capable of producing a wide variety of pills, liquids, suppositories, ointments, and other medications on demand if necessary, so long as the proper equipment remains at hand.

Each complete prescription consists of the following parts:

Superscription— the symbol Rx for the Latin *Recipe*, or Take.

Inscription—the specific ingredients and quantities, including:
   Basis—the primary ingredient.
   Adjuvant—an ingredient intended to assist the primary ingredient.
   Corrective—an ingredient to modify or alter primary action.
   Vehicle—a diluent or other carrier for the therapeutic components

Subscription—detailed instructions for compounding the ingredients listed and preparing them to produce a certain volume of completed product, specified number of pills or suppositories, etc.

Signa—the sign, i.e., label or instructions to accompany the medication.

This should look entirely familiar to the modern cook when compared to the modern "recipe" in any cookbook: A list of ingredients and quantities (2 eggs, 3 cups flour, etc.), details for the compounding (mix together liquid ingredients, fold in flour, etc.), and instructions for use (bake at 350 degrees for 60 minutes and serve hot, with ice cream if desired).

A complete list of terms used in magistral pharmacy is impractical, as it could encompass almost any instruction one might wish to give—in Latin of course. The following is a set of terms traditionally and recurrently used for these purposes. Symbols for units of measure are included here for convenience. For a more complete explanation of these symbols and units, see Weights and Measures in the Background Matter.

Latin Phrase:	Abbreviation(s):	Meaning and/or Explanation
Accuratissime	Accuratis.	Most carefully, accurately
Ad	—	To, up to
Ad libitum	Ad. Lib.	At pleasure, as desired, i.e., not limited.
Ad partes dolentes	Ad. Part. Dolent.	To the affected part
Ad tertiam vicem	—	For three times
Adde (addantur, addendum, addendo)	Add	Add, let them be added, to be added, by adding
Admove, admoveatur, admoveantur	Admov.	Apply, let it be applied, let them be applied.
Adversum	Adv.	Against
Agita	Agit.	Shake or stir
Albus	Alb.	White
Alcoholizatus	—	Alcoholized, finely powered (by dissolving in alcohol and allowing to evaporate, leaving a fine powder)
Aliquot	—	Some, a few (in modern use, a portion or sample)
Alter	—	The other
Alternis horis	—	Every other hour
Alvo adstricta	Alv. adst.	The bowels being confined. (constipation)
Amplus	—	Large
Ana	A, āā	Of each
Ante cibum	a.c.	Before meals
Aqua aerata	Aq. aerat.	Carbonated water
..... astricta	Aq. astr.	Frozen water (ice)
..... bulliens	Aq. bull.	Boiling water
..... communis	Aq. Comm..	Common water
..... fervens	Aq. ferv.	Hot water
..... fluviatus	Aq. fluv.	River water
..... fontalis, fontis, Fontana	Aq. font.	Spring water
..... marina	Aq. mar.	Sea water
..... nivalis	Aq. niv.	Snow water (i.e., from melted snow)
..... pluvialis, pluviatus	Aq. pluv.	Rain water
Aut	—	Or
Baccillum	—	Bougie
Balneum arenae	B.A.	Sand bath (heated sand, for warming)
..... maiae, maris	B.M.	Sea water bath (for warming)
..... vaporosum, vaporis	B.V.	Vapor bath (steam, for warming)
Barbadensis	B.B, B.B.S.	(of or from) Barbadoes
Bene	—	Well (i.e.– mix well)
Bibe	Bib.	Drink
Biduum	—	Two days
Bis	—	Twice
Bis in die(s)	Bis in d., bid	Twice a day
Bolus	Bol.	A large pill
Bonus	—	Good
Brevis	—	Short
Bulliat, bulliant	Bull.	Let boil
Calcifactus	—	Warm
Capiat	Cap.	Let him/her take
Capsulae amylaceae	—	Starch capsules, i.e., cachets (for oral dosage)

Latin Phrase:	Abbreviation(s):	Meaning and/or Explanation
Carbasis	Carbas.	Lint, linen
Caute	—	Cautiously, with care
Charta	Chart.	Paper
Charta cerata	Chart. cerat.	Waxed paper
Chartula	—	Small paper
Cibus	—	Food
Cito dispensetur	Cito disp.	Dispense quickly
Cochlear(e), cochleatim	Coch., cochleat.	Teaspoon
..... amplum	Coch. amp.	Tablespoon (3 teaspoons)
..... magnum	Coch. mag.	Large spoonful (about ½ oz, or 15 cc)
..... medium, modicum	Coch. med.	A dessert spoon full, about two fluidrachms
..... parvum	Coch. parv.	A teaspoon (one fluidrachm)
Cola	Col.	Strain
Colatus, colentur, coletur	Colat.	Strained, let them be strained, let it be strained
Collunarium	—	A nosewash
Collutorium	Collut.	A mouthwash
Collyrium	Collyr., coll.	An eyewash
Coloretur	—	Let it be colored
Commisce	—	Mix together
Compositus	Comp.	Compounded
Confection	Conf.	Confection (a candy-like dosage form)
Confricamentum	—	A linament
Congius	Cong.	A gallon
Conserva	Cons.	Conserve or keep (usually for later use)
Consperge	Consperg.	Dust or sprinkle
Continuandur remedia	Cont. rem.	Let the medication be continued
Contra	—	Against
Contuses	—	Bruised
Cor, cordis	—	The heart
Cortex	Cort.	The bark
Cortula	—	A measure
Cujus, cujuslibet	Cuj.	Of which, of any
Cum	C.	With
Da, detur	D., det.	Let it be given
De	—	Of, from
De die in diem	De.d.in.d.	From day to day
Deaurentur pilulae	—	Let the pills be gilded
Debita spissitudo	Deb. spiss.	Of the proper consistency
Decanta	—	Poor off
Decem, decimus	—	Ten, the tenth
Deglutiatur	Deglu.	Let it be swallowed
Dein	—	Thereupon
Dentur tales doses no iv	D.t.d.no. iv	Let 4 (or other inserted number) of doses be given
Denturc in duplo	—	Let twice as much be given
Dexter, dextra	—	Right (masculine and feminine forms)
Diebus alternis	Dieb.alt.	Every other day
Diebus tertiis	Dieb tert.	Every third (or other inserted number) of days
Digere	—	Digest

Latin Phrase:	Abbreviation(s):	Meaning and/or Explanation
Dilue, dilutus	Dil.	Dilute, diluted
Dimidius	Dim.	One half
Directione propria	D.P., direc. Prop.	With a proper direction (i.e., instruction)
Dividatur in partes aequalies	D. in p. aeq.	Divide into equal parts
Dividendus, -a, -um	—	To be divided
Donec	—	Until
Eadem (feminine)	—	The same
Ejusdem	Ejusd.	Of the same
Electuarium	Elect.	An electuary (a candy-like dosage form)
Emulgens	—	An emulsifying agent
Enema (pl. enemata)	En.	An enema or clyster (or plural thereof)
Epistomium	Epistom.	A stopper of cork
Et	—	And
Etiam	—	Also, besides
Ex, E	E.	From, one of
Ex modo prescripto	E.m.p.	In the manner prescribed
Extende	Ext.	Spread
Fac, Fiat, Fiant	F., Ft.	Make, let it be made, let them make
Fac pilulas duodecem	F.p. xii	Make 12 (or other specified number) pills
Farina	—	Flour
Febris	—	Fever
Fervens	Ferv.	Boiling
Fiant chartulae xii	Ft. Chart. xii	Let 12 (or specified number) powders be made (literally, 12 papers, used to wrap powdered doses)
….. pilulae	—	Let 12 (or specified number) pills be made
….. pulveres	—	Let 12 (or specified number) powders be made
….. suppositoria	—	Let 12 (or specified number) suppositories be made
Fiat cataplasma	Ft. cataplasm.	Let a poultice be made
….. ceratum	Ft. cerat.	Let a cerate (wax) be made
….. colyrium	Ft. collyr.	Let an eye wash be made
….. confectio	Ft. confect.	Let a confection be made
….. electuarium	Ft. elect.	Let an electuary be made
….. emplastrum 4x6	Ft. emp. 4x6	Let a plaster be made, 4 x 6 inches (or as specified)
….. emplast. epispasticum	Ft.emp.epispast.	Let a blister be made (by rubbing)
….. emplast. vesicatorium	Ft.emp.vesicat.	Let a blister be made (by rubbing)
….. emulso	Ft. emuls.	Let an emulsion be made
….. enema	Ft. enema	Let an enema (rectal) be made
….. gargarisma	Ft. garg.	Let a gargle be made
….. haustis	Ft. haust.	Let a draught be made
….. infusum	Ft. infuse.	Let an infusion be made (i.e., by soaking matter in liquid, not an intravenous form)
….. injection	Ft. inject.	Let an injection (urethral) be made
Fiat lege artis	F.L.A.	Let it be made by the rules of the art
….. linimentum	Ft. linim.	Let a liniment be made
….. massa	Ft. massa	Let a mass be made
….. massa et divide in pillulas xii	Ft. mas. div. in. pil. xii	Let 12 pills be made (make a mass and divide in 12 pills)
….. massa in pilulas xii dividenda	(same)	(same)

Latin Phrase:	Abbreviation(s):	Meaning and/or Explanation
..... massa in trochiscos xl dividenda	Ft. mas. in troch. xl div	Let 40 troches be made (make a mass and divide into 40 troches)
..... mistura	Ft. mist.	Let a mixture be made
..... pulvis	Ft. pulv.	Let a powder be made
Fiat pulvis et divide in chartulas xii	Ft. pulv. et div. in char. xii	Let 12 powders be made (let a powder be made and divided among 12 papers, i.e. 12 wrappers)
Fiat secundum artis regulas	F.S.A.R.	Let it be made according to the rules of the art
Fiat solution	Ft. solut.	Let a solution be made
..... suppositorium	Ft. suppose.	Let a suppository be made
..... trochisci xxiv	Ft. troch. xxiv	Let 24 (or specified number) troches be made
..... unguentum	Ft. ung.	Let an ointment be made
Filtra	—	Filter (imperative, i.e., thou shalt filter)
Fistula armata	—	Syringe fitted for use ("armed")
Flavus	Flav.	Yellow
Folium	Fol.	A leaf
Fuerit	—	Shall have been
Gargarisma	Garg.	A gargle
Gradatim	—	By degrees, gradually, slowly
Grana sex pondere	—	Six (or specified number) of grains by weight
Granum, grana	—	Grain, grains (unit of weight)
Gratus	—	Pleasant
Grossus	—	Large or coarse
Gutta (pl. guttae)	Gtt.	Drop or drops
Guttatim	Guttat.	By drops
Haustus	Haust.	A draught
Herba	—	An herb
Hic, haec, hoc	—	This
Hirudo	—	A leech
Hora	H.	Hour
..... decubitus	H.D.	At the hour of reclining, i.e., at bedtime
..... somni	H.S., hor.som.	At the hour of sleep
..... unis spatio	Hor. un. spat.	At the expiration of the hour
..... intermedius	Hor. Interm.	In the intermediate hours, between other events
Idem	—	The same
Identidem	—	Repeatedly
Inde	—	Therefrom
In dies	In d.	From day to day, i.e., daily
Ingerendo capsulas	—	Put in capsules
In impetus effervescentae	—	At the height of effervescence
Injection	—	An injection
Injiciatur enema	—	Let an enema or clyster be given
In lagena bene obturata	—	In a well-stoppered bottle
Inter	—	In between
Involve gelatina	—	Coat with gelatin
Ita	—	In such a manner
Jam	—	Now
Lac	—	Milk
Lamella	—	Leaf or scale

Latin Phrase:	Abbreviation(s):	Meaning and/or Explanation
Laridum	—	Lard
Leniter terendo	—	By rubbing gently
Leviter	—	Lightly
Magnus	Mag.	Large
Massa, massa pilularis	—	Pill mass (i.e., the body of material prepared to be pressed into pills or tablets)
Mica pannus	Mic. Pan.	Crumbs of bread
Minimum	M. or Min.	Minim (unit of volume)
Minutum	—	Minute
Misce	M.	Mix (imperative form)
Mitte, mittatur, mittantur	—	Send, let it be sent, let them be sent
Mitte talis	—	Send of such, or send this
Modicus	—	Middle sized
Modo praescriptio	Mod. praesc.	In the manner prescribed
More dictum	More dict.	In the manner dictated
More solito	More sol.	In the usual manner
Mortarium	—	Mortar
Necnon	—	Also
Ne tradas sine numo	Ne. tr. s. num.	Do not deliver unless paid
Nisi	—	Unless
Non	—	Not
Non repetatur	Non. rep.	Do not repeat
Nox, noctis	—	Night
Numerus	No.	Number
Nunc	—	Now
Obduce	—	Cover, conceal, or coat
Octarius	O.	A pint (i.e., the eight part of a gallon)
Octavus	—	Eighth
Octo	—	Eight
Oculus	—	Eye
Oleum olivae optimum	O.O.O.	Best olive oil
Omni hora, omni bihorio, omni	Omn. hor., Omn. bihor, etc.	Every one, two, or more (as specified) hours; quadrante horae
Omne nocte	—	Every night
Omni mane	—	Every morning
Ovum	—	Egg
Panis	—	Bread
Pars (pl. parties)	—	Part, parts
Partes aequalis	P. ae.	Equal parts
Partitis vicibus	Part. vic.	In divided doses
Parvulus	—	An infant
Pastillus, pastillum	—	A little ball (pastille, an oral lozenge)
Pectus	—	The breast, chest
Pediluvium	—	A footbath
Per	—	Through, by, i.e.– *per os* means by mouth
Perinde	—	In the same manner as before
Pes (pl. pedes)	—	Foot, feet
Phiala prius agitate	P.P.A.	The bottle having first been agitated
Pilula	—	A pill

Latin Phrase:	Abbreviation(s):	Meaning and/or Explanation
Pilus	—	Hair
Pinguis	—	Fat, grease
Placebo	—	To please (lit. I please, an inactive dose form)
Poculum, pocillum	Pocul., pocill.	A small cup
Pondere	P.	By weight
Pondis medicinale	—	Medicinal (apothcary's) weight
Pone aurem	—	Behind the ear
Post cibo, post cibum	P.c.	After meals
Potus	—	Drink
Prandium	Prand.	Dinner (i.e., post-prandial = after meals)
Primo mane	—	Very early (first) in the morning
Primus	—	The first
Pro	—	For
Pro ratione aetatis	—	According to the age of the patient
Pro re nata	P.r.n.	As the thing is needed, as necessary
Proximo	—	Nearest
Prius	—	Before, former
Pulpa	—	Pulp
Pulvis, pulverizatus	Pulv.	Powdered, pulverized
Pyxis	—	Pill box
Quam libit	—	As much as desired
Quantum libit	q.l.	As much as desired
..... placet	q.p.	As much as desired
..... vis	q.v.	As much as desired
..... volueris	q.v	As much as desired
..... sufficiat, ... satis	q.s.	Sufficient quantity (usually to make up to specified volume)
Quaque	Q.Q.	Each or every (q.q.h. = every hour) (see also quoque)
Quarter	—	Four times
Quartus	—	Fourth (i.e., a fourth part, one quarter)
Quatuor	—	Four
Qui libet	—	Whatever you please
Quibus	—	From which
Quninque	—	Five
Quintus	—	The fifth
Quoque	Q.Q.	Also (see also—quaque)
Quorum	Quor.	Of which
Quotidie	—	Daily
Quoties	—	As often as
Ratio	—	Proportion
Recens	—	Fresh
Recepe	Rx	Take
Redactus (or ridigatur) in pulverum	Red. in pulv., redig. in pulv.	Reduce to a powder
Renovetur semel	—	Renew once only
Repetatur, repetantur	—	Let it be repeated, let them be repeated
Res (pl. rei)	—	Thing or things
Residuus	—	Remaining
Respondere	—	Answer, to answer

Latin Phrase:	Abbreviation(s):	Meaning and/or Explanation
Ruber	—	Red or ruddy
Saccellatio	—	A dry poultice
Saepis	—	Often, frequently
Saltem	—	At least
Scatula	Scat.	A box
Scilicet	—	Namely
Secundum artem	S.A.	According to (the) art (of apothecary)
….. naturam	S.N.	According to nature
Secundus	—	Second
Semel	—	Once
Semidrachma	Semidr.	Half a drachm
Semihora	Semih.	Half an hour
Semis	Ss.	A half
Septem	—	Seven
Septimana	—	A week (i.e., seven days)
Sescuncia	—	An ounce and one half
Sesqihora	—	An hour and a half
Sex	—	Six
Sextus	—	Sixth
Si	—	If
Sic, Sic?	—	So, is it so?
Siccus	—	Dry, dried
Signa	Sig. S.	Mark it (so), i.e., label the prescription as follows
Signetur nomine proprio	—	Let it be written with a proper name (generic, not a trade name)
Simul	—	Together, at the same time
Sine	s	Without
Si opus sit	Si op. sit	If necessary
Sit	—	Let it be
Solitus	—	Accustomed, ordinary
Solus	—	Alone
Solve	—	Dissolve (imperative form)
Solvo, solvere, solutus	—	To dissolve, dissolved
Somnus	—	Sleep
Sparadrapus	—	A spread plaster
Spiritus vini rectificatus	S.V.R.	Rectified (i.e., distilled) spirit of wine, i.e., alcohol
Spiritus vini tenuis	—	Proof spirit (in US Pharmacopoeia, 50% alcohol, or 100 Proof)
Spiritus vinosus	—	Ardent (distilled) spirit of unspecified strength
Spissus	—	Dense, hard
Statim	Stat.	Immediately
Stet, Stent	St.	Let it stand, let them stand
Stillatim	—	By drops or small quantities
Stilus	—	Pencil, stick, or crayon
Stratum super stratum	S.S.S.	Layer upon layer
Subinde	—	Frequently
Subtilis	—	Fine, smooth, nice
Succus	—	Juice or sap
Sumat talem	—	Let the patient take one like this

Latin Phrase:	Abbreviation(s):	Meaning and/or Explanation
Sume, sumat, sumatur, sumendus	Sum.	Take (imperative form), let him take, let it be taken, let them be taken, to be taken
Superbibendo haustem	—	Drinking afterwards this draught
Supra	—	Above
Tabella	Tab., Tabel.	A lozenge (diminutive form of tabula, a table)
Talis	—	Such, like this
Tandem	—	At last, finally
Tantum	—	So much, so many
Tegmen or tegument	—	A cover
Tempus, temporis	—	Time (or temple)
Tenuis	—	Fine, thin
Ter	—	Three times
Ter (in) die	t.i.d., t.d.	Three times a day
Tere	Ter.	Rub (imperative form)
Tertius	—	Third (i.e., one-third)
Tres	—	Three
Triduum	—	Three days
Tritura	Trit.	Triturate (see pharmaceutical processes)
Tussis		A cough
Ubi		Where, wherever, whenever
Uncia		An ounce
Unctulus		Besmeared, anointed
Unguilla		An ointment box
Ustes		Burned
Ut dictum	Ut. Dict.	As directed
Utendum	Utend.	To be used
Uto, uti	—	To be used
Vas vitrium	—	A glass vessel
Vehiculum	—	A vehicle (a solvent, ointment base, etc.)
Vel	—	Or
Venosus	—	Poisonous
Verus	—	True, genuine
Vesper, vesperis	Vesp.	Evening
Vitello ovi solutus	—	Dissolved in an egg yolk
Vitellus	—	Yolk (i.e., egg yolk)
Vitreum, vitrum	—	Glass (the material, not a drinking glass)

ALCHEMICAL AND ASTROLOGICAL SYMBOLS

Alchemical symbols continue to appear as decorative motifs on apothecary containers despite the fact that their role in chemical notation has been completely displaced by modern nomenclature based upon the periodic table. The astrological symbols, a subset of the vast family of alchemical symbols, were associated not just with heavenly bodies, but with chemical substances (the seven known metals and others) and with specific laboratory processes as well. They are included here with notations regarding their astrological and chemical significance. This collection is certainly far from complete, and as alchemical usage shifted significantly over time and place, there are many conflicts in meaning among available sources.

Astrological Signs

The astrological signs and associated alchemical processes are shown below. The meaning of the processes conforms to modern usage unless otherwise noted, although the alchemical understanding often varied from our own, i.e., dissolution or digestion involved not just the dissolving of a substance in solution in intact form (as we understand today), but the actual separation of the various intrinsic properties of the material so that one might alter those properties (by some method such as projection) to achieve a desired transformation of matter.

♈	Aries	Calcination (i.e., drying with heat)
♉	Taurus	Congelation
♊	Gemini	Fixation (to capture or preserve in a certain state)
♋	Cancer	Dissolution
♌	Leo	Digestion (similar to dissolution)
♍	Virgo	Distillation
♎	Libra	Sublimation (distillation out of the solid phase)
♏	Scorpio	Separation
♐	Sagittarius	Ceration (i.e., wax formation)
♑	Capricorn	Fermentation
♒	Aquarius	Multiplication (to increase the volume of, usually by alloying)
♓	Pisces	Projection (transfer of properties, i.e., gold properties onto lead)

Assignment of the Metals and "Planets"

The reader may wish to note, and will see in the tables below, the traditional planetary assignments of the metals dating back at least to ancient Persia (16). These were also used as decorations for apothecary wares. These are (18): Saturn (lead), Venus (tin), Jupiter (copper), Mercury (Mercury/quicksilver), Mars (Iron), Moon (silver), and Sun (gold). The latter two are not now recognized as planets, but were considered as such in pre-Copernican astronomy.

Other Alchemical Symbols

Alchemy as an art spanned the ancient world both geographically—from Egypt to China, and temporally—from perhaps 300 BCE until displaced by the rise of modern chemistry in the seventeenth century. The underlying alchemical concepts of matter and the chemical processes applied display a remarkable degree of homogeneity across time and place, and the stated goal of exoteric (transmutation of metals) and esoteric (prolongation of life) alchemy remain relatively constant across the ages. Thus, one might expect that the application of alchemical symbols would demonstrate a similar degree of consistency…and one would be badly mistaken.

Alchemical secrets were closely guarded. In part, this was a matter of "trade secrecy," as the successful transmutation or the ability to offer eternal life would have obvious commercial value. Alchemy was, however, not well looked upon by the church for religious reasons—one was meddling in eternal life and the creation of matter. Further, the manufacture of gold would have undermined existing wealth and power. Although many of the educated and powerful regarded the alchemists as charlatans, the alchemists did in fact possess considerable skills in metallurgy. Transmutation aside, these skills allowed them to debase currency or engage in counterfeiting by creating gold alloys having the appearance of undiluted gold or by plating base metals with gold. To make matters worse, these same skills could be used to detect debased currencies and to thereby uncover the fraudulent acts of others. Alchemy, in other words, represented a considerable threat to many individuals and institutions across time, and was consequently the subject of innumerable bans and restrictions.

Alchemical symbols were thus originated for the very purpose of obscuring the interpretation of alchemical texts. The application of these symbols across time and place is highly inconsistent, often idiosyncratic to the level of a particular alchemist and their disciples, with multiple symbols applied to a given term and with multiple meanings applied to the same symbol. Layered upon this is the generally inconsistent use of chemical, botanical, and mineralogical names, and the reasons for our confusion at this time are evident.

If this were not enough cause for confusion relative to the assignment of modern chemical terms, it is also important to recall that the modern concept of chemical elements was not yet extant. "Elements" consisted of earth, air, fire, water and the "fifth element"—quintessence, or vital essence. Matter consisted of various combinations or ratios of these elements, and the properties of a material could be extracted and/or transferred to other materials. The latter is the basis of the belief in transmutation of the elements and the ability to "multiply" or "expand" gold, as well as the source of such concepts as the Arabic "el-kahul," a distilled essence—our modern alcohol. Having no concept of fixed elements and few skills in what is now called qualitative or quantitative chemical analysis beyond the confirmation of gold (as a result of its stability to heat and degradation), materials were identified simply by physical characteristics such as weightiness (density), color, and behavior under various conditions. Thus, materials of different chemical composition (in the modern sense) were frequently confused—orpiment was usually red sulfide or arsenic, but could be a red lead oxide, or even mercuric sulfide (cinnabar), and perhaps even hematite—all red minerals of similar density

In an attempt to provide information on at least the more common chemical symbols, I have drawn from two sets of published figures. The first table (page 310) is derived from Partington's multi-volume history of chemistry (13). This figure provides Latin definitions for the numbered symbols, and similarly numbered English definitions are provided on page 311. A number of the symbols are compound and many are combined with a Latin ending to form an imperative (-are, –ere) or other verb form, as these symbols were commonly used for word roots in alchemical texts. The English meaning of the root symbol is provided.

The second table (pages 312 to 320) is derived from *Medicinisch-Chymisch—und Alchemistisches Oraculum*, published in Ulm, ca. 1755 (14). This table lists multiple symbols in use for particular terms. The alchemical symbols are original, but the original mixed Latin and German text has been replaced with Latin terms alone and English definitions have been provided. Cross references to other items within the table are present in the original text.

Mineral or chemical assignments are provided where any degree of consistency appeared among the reference materials. However, the reader should take these assignments "*cum grana salis*" (with a grain of salt)—even those that are generally correct are likely to be incorrect in at least some uses across the vast scope and time of alchemy.

Ref. No.	Symbol meaning
1	∿tio, ⊙tio solutio
2	re praecipitare
3	io fusio
4	re vaporare
5	re digerere
6	tio digestio
7	re coquere
8	re incinerare
9	re pulverisare
10	re fundere
11	re calcinare
12	destillare
13	re sublimare
14	aa, aaa ana
15	āāā, ááá amalgama
16	arena
17	minera
18	MB balneum maris
19	VB vaporis balneum
20	retorta
21	recipiens
22	cucurbita
23	alembicus
24	crucibulum
25	SSS stratum super stratum
26	pulver
27	libra
28	drachma
29	uncia
30	scrupulus
31	dies nox
32	hora
33	mensis
34	corpora volatilia
35	corpora fixa
36	sublimatum, spiritus
37	caput mortuum
38	ignis
39	aer
40	aqua
41	terra
42	sales
43	sal communis
44	salia
45	sal neutrum, salsum, enixum
46	borax
47	alcalia
48	sal ammoniacus
49	tartarus
50	acida, acetum
51	acetum destillatum
52	crystalli
53	silex
54	alumen
55	nitrum
56	sulphur
57	phosphorus
58	phlogiston
59	oleum
60	tinctura
61	sapo
62	urina
63	vitrum
64	regulus
65	aurum, sol
66	argentum
67	cuprum, aes
68	ferrum
69	chalybs
70	stannum
71	plumbum
72	mercurius
73	mercurius sublimatus corrosivus
74	mercurius praecipitatus
75	antimonium
76	orichalcum
77	magnesium (manganese)
78	zincum
79	bismuthum
80	arsenicum
81	regulus niccoli
82	regulus cobalti
83	platinum
84	uranium
85	auripigmentum
86	cinnabaris
87	cancer (crab)
88	c.c. cornu cervi
89	calx (lime)
90	calx viva
91	aqua calcis
92	magnes
93	magnesia, terra muriatica
94	sal amarus
95	argilla
96	terra ponderosa
97	sal alcalinus
98	sal alc. purus (causticus)
99	potassinum
100	natrum
101	sal neutralis
102	sal metallicus
103	alcalia fixa
104	alcalia volatile
105	sal tartari
106	vitriolum
107	vitriolum cupri
108	vitriolum ferri
109	vitriolum zinci
110	viride aeris, aerugo
111	cinis, cineres clavellati
112	acidum carbonicum
113	acidum vitriolicum
114	acidum nitricum
115	spiritus vitrioli
116	spiritus nitri
117	spiritus vini
118	spiritus tartari
119	spiritus urinae
120	aqua fortis
121	aqua regis
122	sal sedativum
123	acidum boracicum
124	acidum tartarosum
125	acidum phosphoricum
126	acidum urinae, phosphori
127	acidum salis
128	acidum arsenici
129	acidum fluoricum
130	acidum oxalicum
131	acidum benzoicum
132	acidum formicarum
133	acidum prussicum
134	acidum succinicum
135	acidum minerale
136	acidum vegetabile
137	acidum animale
138	oleum vitrioli
139	oleum empyreumaticum
140	tartar tartarisatus
141	oleum essentiale
142	aether
143	saccharum
144	resina
145	gummi

Table of alchemical symbols from *Partington*.

See following table for English translation of numbered items.

Notes: "Vitriol" is a crude sulfuric acid. "Sugar" could be any sweet tasting compound as in "sugar of lead" (lead acetate). A spirit (essence) can be any distilled vapor of volatile substance. "Ether" in ancient use refers to a pervasive medium as in the ether theory of light transmission, only later becoming associated with a class of volatile organic molecules.

1	dissolve	49	tartar	98	pure alkaline salt, possibly KOH (18)
2	precipitate	50	acid	99	potassium
3	melt	51	distilled vinegar	100	sodium
4	vapor (vaporize)	52	crystal	101	neutral salts (18)
5	digest	53	silica SiO_2	102	metallic salt
6	digest	54	alum	103	fixed alkali
7	boil down or cook	55	nitre (potassium nitrate)	104	volatile alkali
8	burn	56	sulfur	105	potassium carbonate (18)
9	powder, pulverize	57	phosphorus	106	vitriol (a sulfate)
10	pour	58	phlogiston	107	copper sulfate
11	calcine/dry	59	oil	108	iron sulfate
12	distill	60	tincture	109	zinc sulfate
13	sublimate	61	soap	110	green copper
14	of each	62	urine	111	potassium carbonate (18)
15	amalgam	63	glass	112	carbonic acid
16	sand	64	pure form, i.e., of metal (18)	113	vitriolic (crude sulfuric) acid
17	mineral, a compound of metal	65	gold (sun)	114	nitric acid
18	water bath/double boiler	66	silver (moon)	115	distilled vitriol
19	steam bath	67	copper	116	distilled nitric acid
20	retort (for distillation)	68	iron	117	wine spirits / alcohol
21	receiver (for distillation)	69	iron (18)	118	spirit of tartar (18)
22	a globular type of flask	70	tin	119	distilled urine
23	alembic (distilling flask)	71	lead	120	concentrated nitric acid
24	crucible	72	mercury	121	nitric + Hydrochloric acid
25	supernatant	73	corrosive sublimate	122	sedative salt (borates) (18)
26	powder	74	mercuric oxide (18)	123	boric acid
27	pound (Troy weight)	75	antimony	124	tartaric acid
28	drachms	76	golden metal, bronze/brass (18)	125	phosphoric acid
29	ounce	77	manganese	126	same, from urine
30	scruple	78	zinc	127	hydrochloric acid (18)
31	day / night	79	bismuth	128	arsenic acid
32	hour	80	arsenic	129	hydrofluoric acid (18)
33	month	81	pure nickel	130	oxalic acid
34	vapor phase (distillation)	82	pure cobalt	131	benzoic acid
35	residual phase (distillation)	83	platinum	132	formic acid
36	sublimated spirit	84	uranium	133	Prussic acid
37	residue of dry distillation (18)	85	golden metal, bronze/brass (18)	134	succinic acid
38	fire (i.e., essential element)	86	cinnabar (mercuric sulfide)	135	mineral (derived) acid
39	air (i.e., essential element)	87	cancer / crab (zodiac)	136	vegetable (derived) acid
40	water (i.e., essential element)	88	impure ammon. carbonate (18)	137	animal (derived) acid
41	earth (i.e., essential element)	89	lime	138	oil of vitriol, sulfuric acid
42	salt	90	quicklime	139	oil with burnt taste/smell (18)
43	common salt (NaCl)	91	lime water	140	potassium tartrate (18)
44	salt (19)	92	magnesia (see #93)	141	essential oil
45	neutral salt or KSO_4 (18)	93	magnesium sulfate/carbonate (18)	142	ether (a pervasive medium)
46	borax (sodium borate)	94	magnesium sulfate (18)	143	sugar, as sweet compound
47	alkali	95	clay	144	resin
48	sal ammoniac (NH_4Cl)	96	barium sulfate (18)	145	gum
		97	alkaline salt (18)		

Abstrahere- to abstract or draw off	(symbol)
Acetum, Vinum mortuum- vinegar from dregs of wine	(symbol)
Acetum cydoniorum- vinegar from dregs of wine	(symbol)
Acetum destillatum- distilled vinegar	(symbols)
Acetum ter destillatum- triple distilled vinegar	(symbol)
Acetum vini rubri- red wine vinegar	(symbol)
Acies f. chalybs, Ferrum- steel	(no symbol)
Ad pondus omnium- add amount equal to weight of existing ingredients	ad p.o
Adde- add (imperative verb)	add.
Aer- gas	(symbols)
Aerugo, f. aes destillatum- verdigris, basic copper acetate	(symbols)
Aes, cuprum, venus- copper	(symbols)
Aes destillatum, flores viridis aeris, aeris crystalli, aerugo- flowers of green copper	(symbols)
Aes ustum, crocus veneris- Cupric oxide	(symbols)
Aes viride- green copper (oxide)	(symbols)
Aestas- Summer	(symbols)
Ahenum- pot to boil water over a flame, a cauldron	(symbols)
Albumen- albumen (egg white)	(symbols)
Alcali, alkali sal, f. cineres clavellati, sal alcali- fixed or alkaline salt, potassium carbonate	(symbols)
Alcohol vini, Spiratus vini rectificatissimus- rectified (distilled) wine spirits	(symbols)
Alembicus- Alembic (a distillation vessel)	(symbols)
Alumen- alum	(symbols)
Alumen calcinatum or ustum- alum, calcined (dried)	(symbols)
Alumen catinum- potash, mainly potassium carbonate	(symbols)
Alumen plueum or plumosum- feather alum, fine crystals. of alum, later use, fibrous minerals like asbestos	(symbols)
Alumen saccharinum or zaccarinum- alum sugar, a preparation of alum, protein, and rose water, which formed crystals	(symbols)
Alumen ustum- burnt alum	(symbols)
Amalgama- amalgam	(symbols)
Ammoniacum, Sal ammoniacum- sal ammoniac	(symbols)
Ana.- each (Latin)	ā, āā, āā, āā, āā, āā
Animalia- animal	(symbol)
Antimonii flores- flowers of antimony	(symbols)
Antimonii hepar- antimony trisulfide	(symbol)
Antimonii regulus- antimony metal	(symbols)

Alchemical Signs from *Medicinisch-Chymisch- und Alchemistisches Oraculum*-1.

Alchemical Signs

Antimonii vitrum- antimony sulfate	(symbols)
Antimonium- antimony	(symbols)
Antimonium spagyriae praeparatum- prepared metallic antimony	(symbols)
Aphronitrum- saltpeter	(no symbol)
Aqua- water	(symbols)
Aqua fontana- spring water	*Font*
Aqua fortis simplex, aqua gehennae, stygia- nitric acid	(symbols)
Aqua pluvialis- rain water	(symbols)
Aqua regis- aqua regia, nitro-hydrochloric acid, which will dissolve gold	(symbols)
Aqua vitae- alcohol	(symbols)
Arena- sand	(symbols)
Argentum, Luna- silver, equated with the moon	(symbols)
Argentum foliatum- silver leaf	(symbols)
Argentum musicum- mosaic silver, artificial silver pigment.	(symbols)
Argentum pictorium- pictorial or artist's artificial silver	(symbols)
Argentum vivum, Mercurius vivus, Hydrargyrum- quicksilver, i.e.- mercury	(symbols)
Armenia bolus- Armenian clay	(symbols)
Arsenicum album- white arsenic (oxide)	(symbols)
Arsenicum citinum, Flavum luteum- arsenic citrate	(symbols)
Arsenicum rubrum, Sandaracha graecorum- red arsenic or realgar, arsenic disulfide	(symbols)
Arsenicum sublamatum- arsenic sublimate (flowers of arsenic)	(symbols)
Atramentum vitriolum- ferrous sulfate	(symbols)

Alchemical Signs from *Medicinisch-Chymisch- und Alchemistisches Oraculum-2.*

Atramentum album, Vitrolum album- ferrous sulfate		**Bezoardicum minerale**- antimony "butter" (trichloride)	
		Bezoardicum saturninum- lead chloride	
Aurichalcum, Cuprum citrinum- orichalcum- various gold-colored alloys, usually zinc, copper, and tin		**Bezoardicum solare**- gold chloride	
		Bezoardicum venerium- mixture of copper with corrosive sublimate and ammonia	
Auripigmentum, Resigallum- orpiment or realgar, golden arsenic disulfide		**Bismuthum marcasita**- marcasite, yellow-red mineral of bismuth	
		Bolus alba or aremen(i)a- aluminum silicate	
		Bolus communis- aluminum silicate	
Aurum, Sol- gold, equated to the sun		**Borax, Borrax**- borax, sodium borate	
Aurum foliatum- gold leaf		**Cadmia factitia or fornacum**- see next item, fake or furnace cadmia	(no symbol)
Aurum musicum- mosaic gold, i.e.- an imitation gold used in mosaic work, etc. tin sulfide or other compound		**Cadmia fossilis or pativa, Lapis calaminaris**- cadmia- flue deposits of zinc smelting, variable composition, later source of cadmium	
Aurum pictorium- a false gold alloy		**Calcinare**- calcine (imperative verb)	
Aurum potabile- colloidal or drinkable gold		**Calcinatio argenti**- calcined silver	
Autumnus- autumn		**Calcinatio auri**- calcined gold	
Balneum- bath, water bath for heating		**Calx**- calx, metal oxide formed by heating in presence of air	
Balneum arenae- sand bath, for heating			
Balneum mariae or maris- bain Marie, a water bath or double boiler		**Calx ouorum**- probably calcined gold, "ourum" being a variant of aurum	
Balneum roris or vaporis- steam bath (i.e.- for heating)		**Calx solis**- cold calx, or calcined gold	
Benzoe flores- flowers of (sublimated) benzoin	(no symbol)	**Calx viva**- quicklime (calcium oxide)	
Bezoar occidentalis or orientalis- gallstones of oxen			
Bezoardicum joviale- antimony "butter" (trichloride)			
Bezoardicum lunare- silver chloride		**Camphora**- camphor	
Bezoardicum martialis- iron chloride		**Cancer, Astacus, Gammarus**- cancer or crab (zodiac)	

Alchemical Signs from *Medicinisch-Chymisch- und Alchemistisches Oraculum-3*.

Capella- small dish or plate often used as a heated sand bath	*(alchemical symbols)*
Caput mortuum- residue following dry distillation, sometimes ferric oxide	*(alchemical symbols)*
Catinus tigillum- "beam-bowl," bowl with facility to suspend an object to be heated within	*(alchemical symbols)*
Caementare, Stratificare- Layer or cementate, process of reacting solids by layering upon one another	*(alchemical symbols)*
Cera citrina- citrus wax	*(alchemical symbols)*
Cerussa, Plumbago, Plumbum album- white lead oxide	*(alchemical symbols)*
Chalybs, Ferrum- iron	*(alchemical symbols)*
Cineres clavellati, Alkali sal- potassium carbonate, ash of clavella, a wedge of wood	*(alchemical symbols)*
Cines, Cineres- incinerate or reduce to ash by heating	*(alchemical symbols)*
Cinnabaris- cinnabar, the ore of mercury, i.e.- mercuric sulfide	*(alchemical symbols)*
Coagulatio- coagulate	*(alchemical symbols)*
Colbaltum- cobalt	*(alchemical symbols)*
Colaturae- strainer or filter	Col. Colat.
Completus- complete (adjective)	C...... compl.
Compositio- mix (imperative verb)	*(alchemical symbols)*
Cornu cervi- impure ammonium carbonate, see cururbita	C C
Cornu cervi ustum- calcined ammonium carbonate	ccV, X, *(symbol)*
Cornuta- horned, a salt, often a carbonate as immediately above	*(alchemical symbols)*
Creta- chalk, gypsum (calcium sulfate)	*(alchemical symbols)*
Crocus, Crocus aromaticus- a yellow to red oxide of a metal	*(alchemical symbols)*
Crocus martis- iron oxide (19)	*(alchemical symbols)*
Crocus metallorum- impure antimony oxide and sulfide mixture	*(alchemical symbols)*
Crocus veneris- cupric oxide	*(alchemical symbols)*
Crucibulum- crucible	*(alchemical symbols)*
Crystallus- crystal or crystalline	*(alchemical symbols)*
Cucurbita- a gourd-shaped flask often of copper or later glass. See also cornu cervi	CC
Cucurbita caeca cuprum or venus- a copper cucurbit (flask)	*(alchemical symbol)*
Cum vino- with wine	C.V.
Da. et Signa- give and sign (prescription)	D.S.
Destillare, Destillatio- distill (verb)	*(alchemical symbols)*
Dies- day	*(alchemical symbols)*
Dies et nox- day and night	*(alchemical symbols)*
Digerere, digestio- digest	*(alchemical symbols)*
Drachma, Holca- drachm	*(alchemical symbols)*
Drachma semis- half-drachm	*(alchemical symbol)*
Ebullitio- effervesce by fermenting, allow to bubble	*(alchemical symbol)*
Elementa, Principia corporum- elements or principles (properties) of a body	*(alchemical symbols)*
Essentia- essence	*(alchemical symbol)*
Excipulum, Receptaculum- receptacle for distillates	(no symbol)

Alchemical Signs from *Medicinisch-Chymisch- und Alchemistisches Oraculum*-4.

Extractio sicca- make a dry extract (imperative verb)	(symbol)
Farina- flour, in reference to wheat or to other fine powders	(symbol)
Farina laterum- brick flour, a finely ground baked clay or ceramic material	(symbols)
Faex, Faex vini or aceti- dregs of wine of vinegar	(symbols)
Fel vitri, Sal vitri- glass salt, i.e.- alkaline sodium or potas-sium sulfate used to make glass	(symbols)
Ferrugo, Ferri vitium or situs- rust (iron oxide)	(symbols)
Ferrum- iron, associated with mars	(symbols)
Filtratio, Philtratio- filter (verb)	(symbols)
Filtrum, Philtrum- filter (noun)	(symbol)
Fimus equinus- horse dung	(symbols)
Fixus, Fixum- fixed (adjective)	(symbol)
Figere, Fixatio- fix (verb), to capture or make permanent	(symbols)
Flores, Flores antimonii- flowers of antimony	Fl.
Flores benzoe- flowers of benzoin	(symbol)
Flores martis- flowers of iron oxide	(no symbol)
Flores vitrioli- flowers of vitriol- i.e.- ferrous sulfate	(symbol)
Flores viridis aeris- flowers of green copper oxide	(symbols)
Fluere- to flow / flowing	(symbols)
Fornax, Furnus- furnace	(symbols)
Fuligo- soot (Latin), includes condensed metallic vapors such as cadmia	(symbols)
Fumus- fume or smoke (noun)	(symbols)
Furnus- see fornax above	(no symbol)
Fusio- fuse or melt (verb)	(symbol)
Gummi- gum	(symbols)
Gummi arabicum- gum arabic	(symbol)
Gradatio- measure (verb)	(symbols)
Gradus ignus- stepwise or gradual heating	(symbol)
Granatus- a red jewel	(symbol)
Granum- grain (unit of weight)	gr.
Gutta, Guttae- drop (noun)	(symbols)
Hematites- hematite (iron ore)	(no symbol)
Herba- herb	(symbols)
Hermetice sigillatum- hermetic (air tight) seal	H. S.
Hora- hour	(symbols)
Hiems, Hydrargyrum- mercury, see argentum vivum	(symbols)
Ignis- fire (noun)	(symbols)
Ignis circulatorius- Gentle heating in a closed vessel, recirculating distillation, or vessel for same	(symbols)
Ignis fortis- strong fire	(symbols)
Ignis lentis- slow (low) fire	(symbols)
Ignis reverberius- reverberatory fire or furnace	(symbol)
Ignis rotae- "round fire," intense fire around crucible, etc.	(symbol)
Imbibere- drink (imperative verb)	(symbol)
Incompletus- incomplete, unfinished	(symbols)
Jupiter, Stannum- tin, equated with Jupiter	(symbols)
Lege artis- "by the laws of (the) art"	(symbols)
Lamina- layer (noun)	(symbols)
Lana illota, Erion- probably unwashed (illota) lanolin or wool	(symbol)
Lapides- stones (singular is lapis)	(symbols)
Lapis amenius or armenus, Malachites- Armenian stone, malachite	(symbol)
Lapis bezoar occidentalis or orientalis- see bezoar	(no symbol)
Lapis calaminarius- calamine (zinc carbonate)	E
Lapis calcarius- chalk or a similar white mineral	(symbol)
Lapis hematites- hematite (iron ore)	(symbols)
Lapis lazuli- a blue stone, term still in modern use	(symbols)

Alchemical Signs from *Medicinisch-Chymisch- und Alchemistisches Oraculum*-5.

Lapis magnes- magnetic iron, lodestone)	*(symbols)*
Lapis fabulosus, Osteocolla- fabled or legendary stone, probably limestone, also called osteocolla	*(symbol)*
Lapis silex- in Latin, lava or flint, a siliceous mineral	*(symbol)*
Later- brick or tile	*(symbols)*
Lateres cribrati- seive (literally perforated tile, Latin)	*(symbols)*
Libra- Lb, pound (Troy weight)	*(symbols)*
Libra civilis, Pondus civile- civil pound, or 500 grams	c. p.
Libra medicinalis- medicinal pound, about 358 grams	m. p.
Libra pencilis- a pendant-beam scale or balance	*(symbol)*
Lignum- wood	*(symbols)*
Limatura chalybis martis- iron filings	*(symbols)*
Lixivium- alkaline solution, sodium or potassium hydroxide or carbonate (poorly distinguished)	*(symbols)*
Luna- moon, see argentum	(no symbol)
Lutatio- lute (verb), to seal or "lute" a flask or joint	*(symbols)*
Lutum- a mud, clay, etc. used in luting (see above)	*(symbols)*
Lutum philosophorum or sapientiae- philosophers mud, to coat and protect equipment from fire or heat	*(symbols)*
Magnes- magnet, see lapis magnes	(no symbol)
Manipulus, Mannes- a handful	M. man.
Magnesia- magnesium carbonate	*(symbols)*
Marcasita- pyrite-like mineral, see bismuth	*(symbols)*
Marcasita aurea- golden marcasite, see zinc	*(symbols)*
Mars, Ferrum- iron, associated with the planet mars	*(symbols)*
Massa- mass, generally a pill mass	*(symbols)*
Massa pilularum- pill mass	*(symbol)*
Materia- material	ãa, maa
Materia prima- quintessence, essential or vital essence	*(symbols)*
Mel- honey	*(symbols)*
Mensis- month	*(symbols)*
Mercurius vivus, Hydrargyrum, Argentum vivum- mercury	*(symbol)*
Mercurius praecipitatus albus- white precipitate of mercury	*(symbols)*
Mercurius praecipitatus ruber- red precipitate of mercury	*(symbols)*
Mercurius saturni precipitatis, Minium- cinnabar or red lead oxide, which may be difficult to distinguish	*(symbols)*
Mercurius sublimatus- mercuric sublimate (corrosive sublimate of mercury, HgCl2)	*(symbols)*
Minium- see murcurius saturni praecipitatus above	(no symbol)
Misce- mix (imperative verb)	M.
Mixtura simplex Ludovici- Simple mixture of Ludovici	M. S L
Numero- number	Nr. N°
Nitrum commune- common niter, potassium nitrate	*(symbols)*
Nox- night	*(symbols)*
Nux moschata, Nycthemeron- nutmeg	NM
Obulus, scrupulus semis- half scruple (unit of weight)	*(symbol)*
Oleum- oil	*(symbol)*
Oleum commune, olivarium or gremiale- olive oil	*(symbols)*
Oleum saturni- oil of lead, i.e.- lead sulfide	*(symbols)*
Oleum sulphuris- sulfuric acid	*(symbols)*
Oleum Talci, Talchi- talc	*(symbols)*
Oleum tartari senerti- potassium carbonate	*(symbols)*

Alchemical Signs from *Medicinisch-Chymisch- und Alchemistisches Oraculum*-6.

Oleum vitrioli- sulfuric acid	(symbol)
Ovum- egg	(symbol)
Pars cum parte- alloy, equal parts gold and silver	(symbol)
Per deliquium- deliquescent material (liquefies by drawing moisture from air)	p d.
Phlegma, Aqua insipida- an aqueous distillation fraction	(symbol)
Picis, Ichthys- fish	(symbol)
Plumbago, Plumbum album- see cerussa	(no symbol)
Plumbum, Saturnus- lead, associate with planet Saturn	(symbols)
Praecipitatio, Praecipitatus- precipitate (verb and noun)	(symbol)
Preparatio, Praeparatus- prepare	(symbol)
Pugillus- a unit of volume	(symbol)
Pugillus semis- half pugillus	(symbol)
Pulvis- powder (noun)	(symbols)
Pulverifare- powder or pulverize (verb)	(symbols)
Purificatio- purify	(symbols)
Putrificatio- putrify or ferment	(symbols)
Quantum placet- a pleasing quantity, add the amount desired	q. pl.
Quantum satis- sufficient quantity	q. s.
Quantum uis- right or correct quantity (uis- "just" or "fair")	q. v.
Quinta essentia- quintessence	(symbol)
Radix, Radices- root (plant) plural is irregular- radices	Rad.
Rasura, Raspatum- probably scrapings or shavings	Ras. P. rasur. rasp
Realgar, fumus, exhalatio & concretio- realgar, arsenic sulfide, or fumes from same	(symbols)
Receptaculum, Recipiens, Excipulum- receiver for distillate, a receiving flask	(symbols)
Receptum, Formula, Medica, Recepta- recipe or prescription	Recept.
Recipe- make (imperative verb), Rx appears on every modern prescription	(symbols)
Reductio- reduce, boil down, decrease in mass or volume	(symbols)
Regulus- a pure form, generally in reference to a metal	(symbols)
Regulus antimonii medicinalis- pure medicinal antimony	(symbol)
Renovatio metalourum- reconstituted metal via condensation or reaction	(symbol)
Resina- resin	(symbol)
Retorta, Cornuta, Matracium- a retort or distilling vessel	(symbols)
Reverberatio- heat in a reverberatory furnace	(symbols)
Reverberatorium, Reverberium- reverberatory furnace, used in metallurgy	(symbols)
Rhabarbarum, Resigallum- synonyms realgar or orpiment	Rhab.
Saccharum- sugar or sweet tasting compound (lead acetate is sugar of lead)	Σ
Sal- salt (any)	(symbol)
Sal alcali- alkaline salt, i.e.- potash, mainly consisting of potassium or sodium carbonate or the hydroxides, poorly distinguished historically	(symbols)
Sal ammoniacum, Ammoniacum- ammonium chloride	(symbols)
Sal commune- common salt, table salt	(symbols)
Sal colcotharum, vitriolatum vomitivum- colcothar, an impure iron oxide, latter term can be any emetic.	(symbol)
Sal essentiale vini- essential salt of wine, potassium acetate, see terra foliata tartarti	(no symbol)

Sal gemmae- impure potassium carbonate from wood ash	(symbols)
Sal marinum- sea salt	(symbols)
Sal petrae, aphronitrum, flos parietis, faex nitri, nitrum graecorum, nitrum stolidum- saltpeter, potassium nitrate	(symbols)
Sal tartari fixum- fixed salt of tartar, potassium carbonate from heating the tartrate	(symbols)
Sal essentiale, Terra foliata tartari, Sal vini essentiale- potassium acetate	(symbols)
Sal volatile- various ammonium salts, carbonate, etc.	(symbols)
Sal urinae- salt of urine various salts, mainly ammonia and phosphate compounds	(symbols)
Sapo- soap	(symbols)
Saturnus, Plumbum- Saturn, planet associated with lead	(symbols)
Scriptulus, Scripuius- unclear, possibly same as scrupulus	(no symbol)
Scrupulus- scruple (unit of weight)	(symbols)
Secundum artem- according to the art	(symbols)
Semen, Semina- seed	(symbols)
Semis, semina- half	(symbols)
Semiuncia, Semuncia, Uncia semis- half ounce	(symbols)
Sextarius- one sixth congius (gallon), about 570 ml	(symbols)
Siccare- dry (imperative verb)	(symbols)
Siccum- dry (adjective)	(symbols)
Signa, signetur, simplex & compositum- a sign or indication, simple & composite (probably two merged entries)	(symbols)
Sine vino- without wine	(symbols)
Sine stipitibus- possibly "without attendants" or coverings (Latin- retine/bodyguard), i.e.- isolated in pure form	(symbols)
Soda- sodium or potassium carbonate	(symbols)
Sol, Aurum- sun, associated with the metal gold	(symbols)
Solutio, Solvere- dissolve	(symbols)
Species- species, a mixture of dried herbs	(symbols)
Spiritus- spirit	(symbols)
Spiritus vini, Spiritus vini rectificatus- wine spirits	(symbols)
Stratum super stratum- layer above the layer, i.e.-supernatant	(symbols)
Sublimatio, Sublimare- Sublimate (verb)	(symbols)
Succinum album, Leucelectrum- amber	(symbols)
Succus- juice or sap	(symbols)
Sulphur- sulfur	(symbols)
Sulphur nigrum- black sulfur	(symbols)
Sulphur philosophorum- philosopher's sulfur or stone	(symbols)
Sulphur stillatitium- distilled (sublimated) sulfur	(symbols)
Sulphur tartari, Tinctura sulphuris- tincture of sulfur, liver of sulphur in alcoholic solution	(symbols)
Sulphur vivum- elemental sulfur	(symbols)
Talca, Talcum- talc	(symbols)
Tartarus- tartar, potassium hydrogen tartrate	(symbols)

Alchemical Signs from *Medicinisch-Chymisch- und Alchemistisches Oraculum*-8.

Tartarus emeticus- tartar emetic, potassium antimony tartrate	
Tauri priapus- bull's penis, an aphrodisiac	
Terebinthini- terabinth, turpentine	
Terra- earth or soil, a clay	
Terra foliata tartari- regenerated potassium acetate from distillation of tartar salt and vinegar	
Terra lemnia- soil of Lemnos (Greek island), a red earth	
Terra sigillata alba- white "signed" or "sealed" earth	
Tigillium- a type of crucible	
Tinctura- tincture	
Terbithum, Turpethum minerale- mercuric sulfate	
Tutia alexandrina- zinc oxide, calamine	
Tutia officinarum, Cadmia factita, Cadmia fornatum- zinc oxide, calamine	
Uncia- ounce	
Uncia semis- half ounce	
Urina lotium- urine for washing, urine, esp. of infants for bleaching or fixing dyes.	
Vaporis balneum- see balneum vaporis	(no symbol)
Venus cuprum- copper, associated with planet Venus	
Ver.- spring (veris) most likely, possibly truth (verum)	
Vesica destillatoria- distillation vessel	
Vinum- wine	
Vinum adustum, Spiritus frumenti, Venum- fermented spirits, may be distilled	
Vinum album- white wine	
Vinum alkalisatum, circulatum, or correctum- bitter wine with orange peel or other bitter ingredients	(no symbol)
Vinum emeticum- emetic wine with antimony salts	
Vinum Hippocraticum- hippocras, a spiced wine	
Vinum medicatum- medicated wine	
Vinum mortuum- "dead" wine, i.e.- vinegar	
Vinum rubrum- red wine	
Viride aeris, Viride graecum or hispanicum- green copper, the oxide, verdigris	
Vitellus, Luteum, Luteum ovi- egg white	
Vitriolum- vitriol, a reaction product with oil of vitriol (sulfuric acid), a sulfate, typically ferrous sulfate	
Vitriolum album- white vitriol, zinc sulfate	
Vitriolum Romanus- Roman vitriol, or green atrament, may refer to ink or a native mineral	
Vitrum- glass	
Vitrum antimonii- see antimonii vitrum	(no symbol)
Volatile- vaporize or volitilize (verb) or volatile (adjective)	
Zincum, Zinctum, Zinck, Zink- zinc, see marcasita aurea	(no symbol)
Zingiber, Zinziber- ginger	

Alchemical Signs from *Medicinisch-Chymisch- und Alchemistisches Oraculum*-9.

APPENDIX 5

MANUFACTURERS OF AMERICAN APOTHECARY GLASS

The following is derived from Griffenhagen and Bogard (5), which contains a great deal more information on the individual firms than is presented here, and represents, no doubt, a considerable effort on their part. I have omitted this detailed information except for that necessary to understand the operation names, locations, and approximate dates of operation for the various manufactories. Hyphenated entries without a second date indicate unknown date or in some cases, as indicated in the notes, a merger or other event without termination of activity. Non-hyphenated dates are singular occurrences of presumably short-lived companies. Manufacturing dates are generally only approximate, and listings are primarily for firms still in existence in 1800, as earlier history is difficult to reconstruct. Similar information is available in online sources (10).

Firm Name	Location	Dates	Notes
Henry Allen	New York City	1871–1880	
American Flint Glass Works	Boston	1843–1858	
American Glass Works	Richmond, VA	1908–1935	
Anchor-Hocking Glass Co.	—	—	See Carr-Lowry Glass Co.
Armstrong Cork	Pittsburgh	1860–1998	Purchased **Hart Glass** and **Whitall, Tatum** (1939)
Atlas Glass			See **Hazel-Atlas Glass Co.**
Atterbury & Co.	Pittsburgh	1859–1899	Est. as **White House Glass Works**
Baker Brothers & Co.	Baltimore	1853–1904	Est. as **Baltimore Glass Works** 1790
Bay State Glass Co.			See **Neidlinger Brothers**
Boston Crown Glass Co.	Boston	1793–1943	Acq'd by Am. Flint Glass, 1943
Boston Flint Glass Works	Boston	1849–1867	
Brockway Glass Co.	Brockway, PA	1907–1970	Made plastics after approx 1970
Brooklyn Green Glass Co.			See **Hagarty Bros.**
Burgin and Pearsall	Philadelphia	1833–	Took over **Millville Glass Works** (1806), mfg. of apothecary wares, Acq'd by **Scattergood,**
		&	
		1844–1910:	**Booth & Co.** in 1836 and became **Whitall, Tatum**. Started another firm in 1844, became **Philadelphia Glass Works** (by 1848), **Burgin and Sons** (1853).
Carr—Lowrey Glass Co.	Baltimore	1889–1990+	Acq'd by **Anchor Hocking** (1944) and **Swindell Bros** (1959), operated as Carr Lowrey.
Coventry Glass Works	Coventry, CT	1813–1848	
Dawes Manufacturing	Pittsburgh	1868–1900	
Dean, Foster & Co.	Boston	1875–1990+	
Diamond Glass Co.	Royersford, PA	1899–1931	
Dyottville Glass Co.	Philadelphia	1824–1838	Dyott was a famous Patent Medicine purveyor who took over **Philadelphia and Kensington Glass Vial and Bottle Factories** in 1824, re-named 1833.
East River Flint Glass Works	Pittsburgh	1877–1880	
Excelsior Flint Glass Works	Pittsburgh	1856–1871	Name change to **Leach, Schneider & Pelatier** some time before 1871.

Firm Name	Location	Dates	Notes
Fay and Schueler	St. Louis	1892–?	Purchased by **T.C. Wheaton Co.**, 1928.
A.M. Foster & Co.	Chicago	1885–1929	Merged to **Foster-Forbes** 1929
Foster-Forbes Company	Chicago	1929–	Purchased **Standard Glass** (Marion, OH, 1932) and **Kerr Glass** (1984), Continued operations as **Ball-Foster** beyond 1995.
Fox, Fultz & Webster	Boston	1876–1900	
Franklin Glass Factory	Franklin, MA	1812–1816	
Hagerty Brothers & Co.	New York City	1850–1954	Operated as **B.B.&J. Hagerty** & **Hagerty & Burrows** at various times.
J.T.&A. Hamilton & Co.	Pittsburgh	1863–1943	Operated as **W.H. Hamilton** by 1897
Harmony Works	Glassboro, NJ	1813–1835	Purchased by **Whitney Bros**. 1835, **Owens Bottle** 1918.
Hazel-Atlas Glass Co.	Wheeling, WV, Washington, PA	1902–1964	Merger of Hazel and Atlas firms, Merged with **Kearns-Gorsuch Bottle Co** 1920, Purchased by **Brockway Glass Co**. 1964.
Hygeia Glass Co.	Lancaster, PA	1927	Relocated to Buffalo, discontinued apothecary goods.
Illinois Glass Company	Alton, IL	1873–1929	Merged with **Owens Bottle Co**, 1929
Iron City Glass Co.	Pittsburgh	1864–1876	Begun as **Pastorium, Schultz & Co.,** Iron City from 1873
Jersey Glass Co.	Jersey City, NJ	1824–1860	
Kentucky Glass Works	Louisville, KY	1849–1873	Name change to **Louisville Glass Works**, 1856
Kerr Glass Manufacturing Co.	Altona, KS	1903-	Moved to Sand Springs, OK 1912 and began making pharmaceutical bottles, Part of National Can's **Foster-Forbes** division after 1984.
King & Sons Co.	Pittsburgh	1872–1890	
Kimble Glass Co.	Vineland, NJ	1946	Moved to Toledo, OH by 1959, subsidiary of **Owens-Illinois**
Lancaster Glass Works	Lancaster, NY	1849–1890	
Libbey Glass Company	Toledo, OH	1874–1888	Founded—WM Libbey, New England Glass Co. 1974 and relocated to Toledo. Held the Toledo Glass Company where Michael J. Owens invented the bottle machine, Libbey continues to operate as a division of Owens-Illinois
Manheim Glass Works	Lancaster, PA	1965–1774	One of multiple works founded by Wm. Stiegel
Maryland Glass Works	Baltimore	1849–1982	Later operated as **Maryland Glass Corp.**
Marion Flint Glass Co.	Marion, IN	1890–1917	Founded 1831, advertising vials by 1890
Maysville Glass Mfg. Co.	Maysville, KY	1813–1816	
Wm. McCully & Co.	Pittsburgh	1837–1892	
Mount Pleasant Glasshouse	Mt. Pleasant, NY	1845–	
Muncie Glass Co.	Muncie, IN	1895–1910	
Neidlinger Brothers	Cambridge, MA	1853–1899	Agent of **Bay State Glass Company**
New England Glass Company	E. Cambridge, MA	1818–1883	See **Libbey Glass** for history after 1883
New Jersey Glass Manufact.		1798–1816	**Olive Glass Works** after 1810, part of **Dyottville Glass** after 1816.
Obear-Nestor Glass Co.	E. St. Louis, IL	1900–1961	Successor to **Allison-Obear** 1891, apothecary goods from about 1900
Ottawa Bottle & Flint Gl. Co.	Ottawa, IL	1891–1899	
Owens Bottle Machine Co.	Toledo, OH	1903	Merger with **Illinois Glass** 1929 to form **Owens-Illinois**. Held **Owens Eastern Bottle Co.**

Firm Name	Location	Dates	Notes
Owens-Illinois	Multiple	1929	See Owens Bottle and Libby for additional history.
Patapsco Glass Co.	Baltimore	1895	
Pennsylvania Glass Prod. Co.	Pittsburgh	1933	
Philadelphia & Kensington			See **Dyottville Glass Works**
Philadelphia Glass Works	Philadelphia	1771–1848+	Closed in 1777 and re-opened later, still producing at least until 1848
Phoenix Glass Works			See **Whitall, Tatum**.
Pittsburgh Glass Works	Pittsburgh	1797–1887	Spotty production of apothecary goods including shop furniture and a number of well known patent medicine bottles.
Providence Flint Glass Co.	Providence, RI	1831–1835	
Jeremiah Quinlan	New York City	1868	
F.E. Reed Glass Co.	Masssilon, OH	1903–1947	Relocated to Rochester, NY, by 1912
Andrew Ross	New York City	1859–1871	
Saltsburg Bottle Works Co.	Pittsburgh	1890–1899	
Scattergood, Booth & Co.		1836	**Scattergood, Haverstick** (1844) and **Scattergood & Whitall** (1844, operating Phoenix Glass Works), see **Whitall, Tatum**.
Sheldon Foster Glass Co.			See **Dean, Foster Glass Co.**
Albert G. Smalley & Co.	Boston	1866–1899	Factories in Clayton NJ, Pittsburgh
South Boston Glass Co.	Boston	1824–1843	Acq'd, **American Flint Glass**, 1843
Standard Flint Glass Works	Philadelphia	1890–1900	Esp. homeopathic vials
Swindell Brothers	Baltimore	1872–1959	Part of **Carr-Lowrey** after 1948
Tibby Brothers Glass Works	Pittsburgh	1866–1930	
Union Glass Works	Wheeling, WV	1850	
Walton Druggist Glass Works	New York City	1862–1889	Patented recess label jar in 1862
Warren Glass Works	New York City	1877	Associated with **Walton**, above
West Phila. Flint Glass Works	Philadelphia	1877	
Whitall, Tatum	Millville, NJ	1857–	Window glass mfg.; became **Whitall Bros.** in 1848 and **Whitall, Tatum** in 1857. Premier producer of apothecary shop furniture, by 1894
T.C. Wheaton Co.	Millville, NJ	1888–	Later **Wheaton Glass** and **Wheaton industries**, provided apothecary glass until well after 1970.
White Glass Co.	Zanesville, OH	1815–1851	
White House Glass Works			See **Atterbury & Co.**
Whitney Glass Works	Glassboro, NJ	1775–	Became part of **Owens Bottle** in 1918
Witte's Glass Factory	White Mills, PA	1876–1890	
Wistar's Glass House	Salem County, NH	1739–1776	

APPENDIX 6

MANUFACTURERS' MARKINGS —AMERICAN APOTHECARY GLASS

This appendix is based upon Griffinhagen and Bogard (5), which in turn acknowledges as source material Toulouse's *Bottle Makers and Their Marks* (T. Nelson Publishers, New York, 1971) and a computer disk by William J Hunt, now available for download on-line (9).

The marks listed were employed either by the bottle manufacturer (listed) or by particular patent medicine manufactures, listed with the indication "used by." Dates are approximate.

Symbol	Manufacturer or User	Dates
A	Used by Warner's Safe Cure	1890s
A (in circle)	American Glass Works	1909-1936
	American Cork Co.	1938-1969
A & Co.	Agnew and Co., Pittsburgh	1876-1892
A.& D.H. Co.	Pittsburgh Glass Works of A. & D.H. Chambers	1860-1886
Abbott & Co.	C.W. Abbott and Co., Baltimore	1890s
A B Co	American Bottle Co. Chicago	1905-1915
A.D.S.	Used by American Drug Syndicate	1905-1926
A G M	Used by W.H. Comstock	1880-1900
A.G.S.	Albert C. Smalley	1877-1907
A.G.W.	American Glass Works	1927-1930
A.M.F. & Co.	A.M. Foster and Company	1895-1911
A.P. Ordway	A.P. Ordway & Co.	1890s
Atlas	Hazel-Atlas Glass Co.	1896-1964
A.W.C.	T.C. Wheaton Co.	1959-1960
B	Used by E. L. Soule & Co, NYC, Feldt & Co, Peoria IL, Hygienic Supply, Cincinnati	1860-1880
B (in circle)	Brockway Glass Co.	1930s
Baltimore	Charles A. Voegler Co.	1870s
B&B	Bauer and Black	1900s
B&R	Standard Works, NY	1890s
Banner	Obear-Nestor Glass Co.	1899-1920
B.B. & Co.	Baker Brothers	Patent 1889
Blue Ribbon	Standard Glass Co.	Trademark 1908
C	Used by Cheeseborough Mfg. Co.	1920s
C & Co.	Cunningham and Co. Pittsburgh	1879-1907
	Colgate and Co.	1900s
C & I	Cunningham & Ihmson	1865-1879

Symbol	Manufacturer or User	Dates
C I & Sons	C. Ihmson & Sons, Pittsburgh	1867-1885
C.L.G. Co.	Carr-Lowrey Glass Co.	1889-1920
(Diamond, ◇)	Diamond Glass Co.	1924-1940
D.F. & Co.	Dean Foster 7 Co.	1888-1900
D.F. & D.	Dean, Foster & Dawley	1888-1900
D&O Co.	Used by Dodge & Olcott	1860-1870
Duffield	Used by Duffield, Parke & Co. (later Parke-Davis)	1866-1875
E.L. & Co.	Used by Eli Lilly & Co.	1880-1890
E.R.S. & S.	Used by E.R. Squibb & Sons	1860-1895
F (in keystone)	Flaccus Glass Co.	1900-1920
F & S	Fay and Scueler Co.	Patented 1894
F E R G Co.	F.E. Reed Glass Co., used by Guggenhein Mfg.	1912-1920
F C & Co.	Used by French, Cave & Co., Philadelphia	1890s
F.G. Mfg. Co.	Used by Jones & Primley, Elkhart, IN	1890s
FGW	Fairmount Glass Works, used by Lash's Bitters	1898-1930
F.S. & Co.	Used by Frederick Stearns	1855-1875
G & D	Used by Wengert & Co., York, PA	1880s
G.B. W.L.	Used for Clement's Tonic	1920s
G.W.C. Co.	Used by G.W. Carnrick Co.	1900
H (in star)	W.H. Hamilton & Co	1863-1884
H (in triangle)	J.T. & A. Hamilton	1884-1935
Hazel	Hazel Glass Co.	1886-1902
HB	Hagerty Brothers	1880s
H.B. Co.	Hagerty Brothers	1880-1920
H. M. & P.	Used by Hornick & Porterfield	1908
H. T. Co.	Used by Henry Thayer	1850-1900

Symbol	Manufacturer or User	Dates
I (in circle)	Owens Illinois	1932-1943
I (in diamond)	Owens Illinois	After 1943
I.C.C.O.	Used by Dr. B.L. Bull, Racine, WI on Vegetable Bitters	1890s
I.C. Co.	Used by Home Bitters Co., St. Louis	1873-1881
I. G. Co.	Ihmsen Glass Co., Pittsburgh	1870-1895
	Illinois Glass Co.	1900-1916
I P & L R	Used on Iron Tonic Bitters	1892
IPGC	Illinois Pacific Glass Co.	1902-1930
IPG Co.	Illinois Pacific Glass Co.	1902-1930
I.S. P.	Used by J. H. Salisbury, Hinsdale, NY	1870s
J.F.L.	Used by M.M. Fenner, Fredonia, NY	1872-1900
J Quinlan	Jeremiah Quinlan glass works	1868-1875
JT & AH	J.T. & A. Hamilton	1884-1920
J.W. & B.	Used by John Wyeth & brother	1860-1920
J. Walker/V.B.	Used on Joseph Walker's Vinegar Bitters	1870-1900
K (in hexagon)	Kimble Glass Co.	1917-1947
K & O. Co.	Used by Kress & Owen Co., New York City	1910-1920
Kerr	Kerr Glass Co.	1912-1960
K P	Used by S. Kutnow, New York City	1920s
K.Y.G.W. Co.	Kentucky Glass Works	1849-1855
L&W	Used by Lorenz & Wrightman	1862-1871
L. Bros.	Used by Lloyd Brothers	1885-1920
L. Co.	Used by Lycosine Co., Philadelphia	1900s
L.F.	Used by L.F. Atwood, Atwood's Jaundice Bitters	1876-1901
L.F. & Co.	Used by L. Fundler Co., Milwaukee	1890s
L.G.	Used by E. Fougera & Co.	1920s
LGC	Used by McConnon & Co., Winona, MN	1880s
L.G. Co.	Louisville Glass Works	1880s
L.G.W.	Louisville Glass Works, used by Reed Drug	1870-1900
M	Maryland Glass Co.	1907-1916
M (in triangle)	Used by Murray & Lanman Florida Water	1890s
M & C	Used by McLean Medicine Co., McLeans Volcanic Oil	1900-1920
M B Co.	Muncie Glass Co.	1895-1910
M B W	Millville Bottle Works	1903-1930
Mc C	William McCully & Co.	1850-1885
Mc C & Co	William McCully Co.	1850-1885
M.G. Co.	Millgrove Glass Co	1898-1911
Minneapolis	Lavoris Chemical Co.	1920s
M.P. & Co.	Used by Morrison, Plummer & Co., Chicago	1880-1900

Symbol	Manufacturer or User	Dates
N (in circle)	Obear-Nestor Glass Co.	1895-1915
O (in square)	Owned Bottle Co.	1911-1929
Paris	Dean, Foster & Co.	1888-1900
Patd Feb 6 66	George Stoeckel, used on Mischler's Herb Bitters	Patented 1866
Patent 1867	Walton & Co, Phila., Used on National Bitters	1867-1880
Pat March 10 68	Used by Rumford Chemical Works	1870s
Pat Jan 22 78	Used by W.R. Holmes, Macon, GA	1878
Pat. June 17 88	Used by Log Cabin Remedy, Rochester, NY	1887
Pat June 17 88	Swindell Brothers	1888
Pat. May 27 90	Used by Houts Mfg. CO, St. Louis	1890
Pat. June 2 96	Used by Dr. Van Dyke	1896
Pat. Nov 23 97	Used by George Benz & Sons	1897
Pat May 16 99	Used by John Wyeth & Brother	1899
P C G W	Pacific Coast Glass Works	1902-1924
P.D. & Co.	Parke Davis & Co.	1875-1920
PR	Used by S.B. Hartman & Co., for Peruna	1900s
R	Used by Van Schaack Stevenson & Reid, Chicago	1880-1890
R & C / N.Y.	Used by Reed & Carnrick	1880-1900
R.C.& A	Reed Carnrick & Andrus	1860-1875
R.C.S.	Used by H.K Mulford	1890s
Rex	Obear-Nester Glass Co, used by Fannie Briggs Carr	1896-1920
S (in circle)	Swindell Bros.	1920-1959
S & D	Used by Sharp and Dohme	1860-1920
S. B.	Swindell Bros.	Patent 1888
S.B. & Co.	Used by L.G. Jung, New Orleans (Swindell Bros. Glass?)	1890s
S.B.C.C.	Used by Smith Brothers, Fresno, CA	1900s
S.B. & G. Co.	Streator Bottle and Glass Co.	1881-1905
S.B.H. & Co.	Used by Samuel B. Hartmann & Co., for Peruna	1900s
S.B.W. Co.	Used by C.P. Herrick, Tilton, NH	--
Sheldon	Sheldon Foster Glass Co.	1888
S K & F	Used by Smith Klein & French	1890-1920
S. McKee & Co.	S. McKee's Co., Pittsburgh, used on Hostetter's Bitters	1860s
Stoeckel's Grad	George Stoekel for Hartman & Co., Mishler's Herb bitters	Patented 1866
S.W.C.W.Co.	Used by Schroeder Pharmacy, Baltimore	1890s
TCW	T.C. Wheaton & Co.	1888-1900
T.C.W. Co.	T.C. Wheaton & Co.	1900-1920
Tilden	Used by Tilden & Co.	1873-1876
T O R	Used by T. Pieters & Co.	1920s

Symbol	Manufacturer or User	Dates
T.W. & Co.	Thomas Wightman & Co.	1880-1895
Usona	Obear-Nester Glass Co.	1902-1920
U.C.	Used by Mineral Wasteer CO, Manitou, CO	1900
U D Co.	United Drug Company	1910-1930
Victor	Obear-Nester Glass Co.	1902-1920
W	A.C. Meyer & Co., Baltimore	1880s
W (in circle)	T.C. Wheaton & Co.	1946-1971
W / II	T.C. Wheaton & Co for Bishops Citrate of Magnesia	1900s
W.F. & Sons	William Frank & Sons	1866-1876
W.H.H.	W. H. Hamilton Co.	After 1880
W.H. Ware	Used by W.H. Ware for Fish Bitters	Patented 1866
Whiteman	Warren Glass Works	1879
WI / WT	Whitall, Tatum	1924-1938
W.I.M. Co.	Used by West India Mfg. Co.	1880-1910
W. McC & Co.	William McCully & Co. by Ball Lyons and others	1860-1880

Symbol	Manufacturer or User	Dates
	Wm. McCully, used by Thompson's Philadelphia	1866-1891
Wm F. & Co.	William Frank & Co., Pittsburgh	1890s
W. N. Walton	William N. Walton & Co.	Patented 1862
W P G Co	Used by W. J. Parker & Co., Baltimore	1900s
W.R.W. & Co.	Used by William R. Warner	1870-1920
WR Warner & Co	Used by William R. Warner	Patented 1875
W S M Co.	Used by Wm. S. Merrell	1880-1920
WT (in triangle)	Whitall, Tatum	1935-1938
W.T. & Co.	Whitall, Tatum, used by multiple vendors (see (9))	1868-1903
W.T.& Co./USA	Whitall, Tatum, used by multiple vendors (see (9))	1890-1903
W.T. Co.	Whitall, Tatum, for Hiram Pond, California	1903-1924
Wyeth	Used by John Wyeth & Brother	1880–1910

APPENDIX 7

BOTANICAL PARTS AND TERMS

Botany was an essential part of medicine until nearly modern times. The latter part of the nineteenth century saw the isolation and identification of pharmacologically active substances, "active principals," from plants. As plants are highly variable, therapeutics could be much improved by the use of purified dosage forms. Even then, the largely botanical science of naming drugs, or pharmacognosy, remained essential. With the rise of synthetic chemistry in the late nineteenth and early twentieth centuries, driven largely at the outset by the pursuit of dyes, the source of drug materials shifted from meadow to laboratory, and even those drugs derived from plants became standardized products and were increasingly provided by large pharmaceutical manufacturers in standardized dosage forms. Thus, pharmacognosy has receded in the minds of physicians and in apothecary practice over the past century and has become relegated to the arcane.

Despite this, it should be recognized that we continue to derive many of our drugs from botanical and other natural sources, or begin with natural sources as feedstock for further chemical alteration. Examples of such modern, botanically derived agents include digoxin and digitoxin (congestive heart failure), the opiates (codeine, morphine, etc., used for pain), caffeine (for infantile apnea, migraine and a generic stimulant), theophylline (asthma), vinca alkaloids (cancer), psyllium (laxative), atropine, scopolamine, cocaine, the canabinoids, and ergot alkaloids (migraine) to name a few. In other instances, we no longer use the botanical source for practical and economic reasons, but the active principal remains in use. Perhaps the best example is aspirin (acetylsalicylic acid), a derivative of salicylic acid. The latter was originally derived from the willow, genus *Salix*, a remedy for fever and inflammatory conditions whose first use precedes recorded history.

Greater attention has lately been paid to plants as possible sources of drugs; largely driven by the realization that extinction, particularly in the rainforest, may forever deprive humanity of this potentially valuable resource. Such discovery will not likely bring back the art and science of pharmacognosy, vestiges of which remain largely in the form of generic chemical names whose origin goes largly unrecognized by the modern physician, i.e., Taxol from the yew (genus *Taxus*) or Vincristine from the periwinkle (genus *Vinca*).

Finally, one should recognize that many pharmaceuticals arise within the animal kingdom. While no further space is devoted to the naming of animal parts, the source of these wonder-drugs should not be forgotten. In ancient times animal-derived materia medica consisted largely of mythical remedies having little or no therapeutic value— everything from goat bezoar to bull penis. These were generally intended to confer upon the user some characteristic of the animal or organ from which the matter derived. Recall, however, that the estrogenic preparation Premarin in fact was originally derived from Pregnant Mare's Urine, and that the first useful paralytic agent, curare, originated with a frog. While largely replaced by agents derived synthetically or through the use of recombinant DNA technology, virtually all of the hormonal substances were originally derived from animal sources: insulin, the steroid hormones (estrogens, androgens, progestins, corticosteroids, etc.), growth hormone and other pituitary hormones, thyroid hormone, etc. Considering this list, one cannot help but realize that the ancients, in fact, were on the right track. They lacked, however, proper understanding of the function of many organs, technology to preserve and isolate the active principals from those organs, and the ability to effectively administer these principals, as most are active only by injection.

BOTANICAL PARTS

The following is but a small subset of botanical terms selected for occurrence in pharmaceutical descriptions, not in common use (i.e., "thorn"), and not referring to the microscopic scale.

anther—the part of the stamen, usually on top, which bears the pollen, commonly consisting of two of four thecae, which contain the pollen.

aril—an extra, often colored, coat or covering on a seed.

blade—expanded part of a leaf, petal etc.

branch—division of a stem or axis of a plant, a shoot or secondary stem growing from the main stem.

branchlet—a minor form of a branch; a small branch or the terminal or ultimate subdivision of a branch.

bud—tightly packed unexpanded initial stages of a new organ, i.e., stem, flower, and root.

bulb—short, modified, underground stem surrounded by fleshy modified leaves that contain stored food.

calyx— outmost series of leaves in a flower, a collective term for all sepals of a flower.

carpel—female organ of a flower, consisting of a modified leaf and containing the ovules, normally with a style with a stigma at the top. Several can be fused to form a (compound) ovary.

corm—short, thick, solid food-storing underground stem, sometimes bearing papery scale leaves.

corolla—a collective term for all the petals of a flower.

corona—a crown-like structure on some corollas i.e., "trumpets" of the daffodils.

cortex—region of a stem or root surrounding the vascular cylinder.

cotyledon—a food-storage organ in seeds. Monocot seeds have one cotyledon (ex. grasses); dicot seeds have two (ex. broadleaf plants, as in a pea or bean).

crown—the upper part of a tree (branches and leaves); the part of a plant, usually at ground level, where the stem and roots merge; the persistent base of a perennial herb.

cuticle—the waxy surface that reduces water loss from a leaf.

dioecious—having male and female flowers on separate plants. For fruit and seed production to take place, there needs to be a male and female plant present.

filament—the usually thin to thread-like short or elongated stalk of the stamen, which carries the anther at the upper end.

herb—a vascular plant which is not woody.

inflorescence—a plant branch that carries the flower(s)

integument— the coating of an ovule that becomes the skin of a seed.

latex—milky exudate, drying rubber-like.

leaves—a usually green, flattened, lateral structure attached to a stem.

locule—the hollow chamber of an ovary formed by the union of several carpels.

monoecious— having separate male and female flowers but on the same plant.

ovary—the female parts of a flower, made up by one or several free or united carpels.

ovule—the embryonic seed which only develops after fertilization.

pedicel—the stalk of a single flower. Opposite—peduncle.

peduncle—the main axis or stalk of a whole inflorescence.

perianth—the protective envelope of a flower.

petiole—stalk of a leaf.

pistil—the female reproductive organ of flowers.

radicle—first embryonic root of a seedling.

rhizoid—filamentous root-like structure.

rhizome—modified underground stem, usually growing horizontally

root—underground extension stem that tends to grow downwards, not bearing leaves and absorbing minerals and water.

saprophyte—a plant that feeds on dead or decayed matter. Saprophytes do not have chorophyll (ex. fungi).

sepals—the individual part of the calyx, i.e., leaves of the outer floral envelope.

shrub—a woody perennial without a dominant trunk, and generally less than 5 m high.

stamen—(pl. stamens or stamina) the male organ within a flower, usually consisting of a filament and anther.

stigma—the topmost receptive region of the style, often divided into stigma lobes, which captures and nourishes pollen grains.

stiple—the stalk-like structure carrying a gynoecium or carpel, or its tapered base.

tree—a woody perennial, mostly more than 5 m high.

trunk—the main stem of a tree; usually covered with bark.

tuber(s)—rounded underground fleshy stem or stem segment with several buds.

vein(s)—a visible vascular bundle, especially of the leaf.

BOTANICAL DESCRIPTORS

The following terms occur commonly in proper Latin plant names. They may appear in a variety of guises, particularly with various endings, but the meanings of the root remain reasonably constant. (Adapted from (25) and other botanical references)

acaula—stemless

acma—anvil-shaped

aestive—of summer

alatus—having wings

alba—white

alternifolia—leaves arranged alternately

amabilis—lovely, beautiful

angustifolia—narrow-leaved

arena—sand

argenta—silvery

arvensis—of fields, generally cultivated

aspera—rough

augusta—august, noble

aurea—yellow, orange or golden

auriculara—having lobes, like the human ear

autumnale—of the autumn

bacillarus—staff or rod-like

barbinerva—with veins

belladonna—beautiful lady

biennis—biennial

blanda—bland or pleasant

bombycina—silky or furry

bracteata—with bracts

caerulea—blue, literally sky-colored

campanulata—bell-shaped

campeste—of the fields, generally cultivated fields

canadense—of Canada

candidissimum—"most white"

candida—pure or white

capitata—head, i.e., having a densly flowering head

carnea—meat-like, flesh colored, or pink

caudata—having a tail

cepa—clustered

chinensis—of China

chryso—golden

chrysogonum—green-and-gold

ciliata—with hairs

cinerea—ash-like, gray

citrioda—citrus like, generally in reference to odor

coccinea—scarlet

compacta—small or compact

cordatus, cordifolia—heart-like or with heart shaped leaves (foliae)

cornuta—literally "horned," i.e., posessing spikes or thorns

crassifolia—fleshy or thick leaved

crenulate—finely scalloped (leaf edges)

crispula—wavy (leaf edges)

cristata—crested or crowned

cultriformis—knife-shaped

cyparissa—cyprus-like

dealbata—whitened

deltoides—triangular

dentate, denticulate—toothed, finely toothed (leaf edges)

dioica—male and female flowers on separate plants

divaricata—sprawling, spreading

echinate—having stiff prickly hairs

ensata—sword-shaped

erecta—upright, vertical

ericoides—heath-like

erythro—red

excortica—peeling (bark)

fatuosa—proud, i.e., grandiose, spectacular, a show-off

fenestra—window-like, usually leaf vein pattern, sometimes holes

filiform, filamentosa—thread- or filament-like, or posessing same

fimbriate—fringed

floribunda, florida—flowering abundantly

flora—flowers, thus grandiflora means large flowers.

foetidus—fetid, foul-smelling

folia, folium, folius—leaves, thus longifolia means long-leaves

fragrans—fragrant

frutescens, fruticans, or fruticosus—shrubby, bush-like

fulgens, fulgida—shiny

fulva—tawny or beige colored

furcate—forked, i.e., bifurcate means split in two, etc.

galeobdola—like a nettle

glaber, *glabra*, *glabrous*—smooth (hairless)

glaucous—having whitish waxy coating that is easily removed

globose—round or spherical, globe-like

glutinosa—sticky

gracilis—graceful, slender, delicate, or fragile

grandi—large

graveola—heavy, i.e., heavily scented, intense smelling

guttata—spotted, from Latin meaning "drops"

hirta, *hirsutus*—hirsute, covered with hairs

hispida—brush-like, bristly

hygrometrica—measuring moisture, responds to moisture by flowering, etc.

ignea—in flames, glowing, brightly colored

imbricate—overlapping (usually leaves)

inaperta—closed, without an aperture

incana—hoary or gray

indicus—from India, applied to plants throughout Asia

infundibular—funnel shaped (usually flowers)

japonicus—of Japan

koreanus—of Korea

labiate—lip-like (usually flowers)

lact—milky

laevigatus—smooth

lanata—wooly

lanceolate—lance-like, pointed (usually leaves)

latifolia—wide-leaved

leuco—white

ligneous—woody

lobata—lobed

leucens, *lucidus*—bright, shining, or clear

lutea—yellow

macrophylla—large leaves

maculatus—spotted

majalis—of (flowering during) May

margaritacea—pear-like

melanocarpa—black fruited

meleagra—spotted

meridionalis—flowering at mid-day

micro—very small

mollis—velvety

montana—of the mountains

moschata—musk like, musk scented

mutabilis—mutating or changing (flower color)

nana, *nanus*—dwarf

napella—like a small turnip

nemerosa—of the woods

niger, *nigra, etc.*—black, or a very dark green

nipponicus—of Japan

nitida—shiny

niveus, *nivalis, etc.*—snow or snow-like

nucifera—nut-bearing

nudiflora—flowering naked, when leaves are shed

nuta—nodding or bobbing

odora, *odorata*—fragrant

officinalis—official, i.e., listed in a formulary or pharmacopeoea

pallida—pale

palmata—shaped like a hand (usually in reference to leaves)

palustris—of the swamp, marsh, or bog

paniculata—bearing flowers in panicles

pannosa—felt-like

parvi—small

patens, *patulus*—spreading

pavia—flesh-colored

pectinata—comb-like

perennis—perennial

petraea—growing on rocks

picta—painted

pinguifolia—having fat leaves

pisifera—bearing pea-like seeds

pluvia—of rain, i.e., flowers following rain

polychroma—many colored

praecox—early (blooming)

pratense—of the meadows

procumba—supine, prostrate, i.e., grows lying down

pulchra—pretty

pumila—small or dwarfed

pungens—sharp-pointed or pungent

purpurens—purple

quercifolia—shaped like oak leaves

radicans—with rooting stems, producing aerial roots

recurvata—curved downwards, bent backwards

reptans—creeping or low, like a reptile

resupinate—upside down (usually in reference to flowers)

reticulata—webbed, net-like

riverens—growing by streams

robustus—strong, robust

rosea, *rosacea*—rose-colored

rostrata—hooked or beaked

rotunda—rounded

rubra—red

rugosa—wrinkled

rupestris—growing on rocks

salicifolius—having leaves, like willow

sanguinea, *sanguis*—blood red

sarmentosa—producing runners

sativus—cultivated, i.e., not wild

saxatilis—growing on rocks

scandens—climbing

scopulorum—of rocks or cliffs

sempervirens—always green, evergreen

setosa—densely hairy

sororia—sisterly, resembling others in genus

speciosa—showy

spectabilis—showy, spectacular

spicata—spiked

spinosa—spiny

squamata—scaly

stagnalis—of still water

stolonifera—spreading by stolons (shoots)

strictus—erect or upright

suaveolens—sweetly scented

sylvestri—of the woods

tardiflora—late flowering

tectora—growing on roofs

tenui—means "slender or thin"

tinctoria—used for dye

tomemtosa—hairy

tuberosa—having tubers or rhizomatous roots

umbellata—flowers appear in umbrels (clusters)

uvaria—like a bunch of grapes

velutinus—velvety

venusta—charming

vernalis—of spring

verruculosa—warty

verticillata—whorled

villosus—covered in soft hair

virens, *viridens, etc.*—green

virgatus—twig or wand-like

viscosus—sticky

vulgaris—common

xanth—yellow

GUIDE TO SOURCES

The following are the bibliographic sources referenced by number and found in parentheses in the Compendium:

1) Drey, REA. *Apothecary Jars*. Faber & Faber, London/Boston, 1978. This beautiful and classic reference focusing on European apothecary material, contains an extensive glossary.

2) Stewart, FE. *Quiz-Compends No. 11, Pharmacy*. P. Blakiston Son & Co., Philadelphia, 1886. This is a pocket compendium obviously intended as a study review guide and thus densely packed with information. It is stated to be based on Remington's Textbook of Pharmacy.

3) Cook, E.F., and C.H. LaWall (eds). *Remington's Practice of Pharmacy, 7th ed*. J.B. Lippincott and Co., Philadelphia/London, 1926. *Remington's* is the standard US textbook of Pharmacy. Prior (1889, 1894, 1905, 1907, and 1917) as well as later editions exist.

4) Baldwin, J.K. *A Collector's Guide to Patent and Proprietary Medicine Bottles of the Nineteenth Century*. Thomas Nelson, Inc., Nashville, 1973. This classic collectors reference is devoted to patent medicines, but contains a great deal of background information on American glass, techniques, dating, and manufacturers. It has become an uncommon find, but is not expensive if located.

5) Griffenhagen, G,, and M. Bogard. *History of Drug Containers and their Labels*. American Institute of the History of Pharmacy, 1999.

6) Munsey, C, *Collecting Bottles*. Hawthorne Books, Inc. New York, 1970. A classic general reference for collectors with a generous section on patent medicine bottles and a well-illustrated section on dating North American bottles using characteristic markings. Illustrated with a myriad of black and white photographs.

7) Mansfield, W. *Materia Medica, Toxicology and Pharmacognosy*. C.V. Mosby and Company, St. Louis, 1937.

8) White, W.H., and R.W. Wilcox. *Materia Medica. Pharmacy, Pharmacology, and Therapeutics*. P. Blakiston, Son & Co., 1012 Walnut Street (i.e., Philadelphia), 1896.

9) Hunt, W.J. (compiler), 1995, *Embossed Medicine Bottle Labels: An Electronic Finding Aid for the Identification of Archeological Specimens*. National Park Service, Midwest Archeological Center, Lincoln, Nebraska. Revised August, 1997.

10) *Some Common Bottle Marks and Their Manufacturers*. On line at: www.angelfire.com/tn/traderz/marks.html (accessed 12/28/2005).

11) DeLorme, M.F. *A Manual of Pharmacy for Physicians*, 3rd ed. P. Blakiston's Sons & Co., Philadelphia, 1913.

12) Howe, G., and J.G. Beard. *Latin for Pharmacists*. P. Blakiston's Sons & Co., Philadelphia, 1916.

13) Partington, J.R. *A History of Chemistry, Volume II*. St. Martin's Press (Macmillan and Company, Ltd.), New York, 1961.

14) *Medicinisch-Chymisch—und Alchemistisches Oraculum*, Ulm, 1755 available online at http://levity.com/alchemy/.

15) *The Alchemy Website*. (accessed 1/16/2006).

16) Taylor, F.S. *The alchemists*. Collier Books, New York, 1962

17) Stillman, J.M. *The Story of Alchemy and Early Chemistry*. Dover Publications, Inc. New York, 1960.

18) Eklund, J. *The Incompleat Chymist: Being an Essay on the Eighteenth-Century Chemist in His Laboratory, with a Dictionary of Obsolete Chemical Terms of the Period*. Smithsonian Studies in History and Technology, Number 33, Smithsonian Institute Press, Washington, DC, 1975. Available online at: http://dbhs.wvusd.k12.ca.us/webdocs/Chem-History/Obsolete-Chem-TermsTOC.html.

19) Giunta, C. *Glossary of Archaic Chemical Terms*. Online resource at: http://web.lemoyne.edu/~giunta/archema.html.

20) de Morveau, Louis Bernard Guyton, Antoine Lavoisier, Claude-Louis Bertholet, and Antoine deFourcroy. *A Dictionary of the New Chymical Nomenclature from Method of Chymical Nomenclature (Paris, 1787); translated by James St. John (London, 1788), available online at: http://web.lemoyne.edu/~giunta/nomenclature.html .

21) *Eilodon's Lexicon*. Online reference (German) at: http://www.hermetik.ch/eidolon/lexikon/lexikon_symb_index.htm.

22) Hughes, I. Pharmaceutical Latin Abbreviations. Herbal Data New Zealand, available online at: http://www.herbdatanz.com/pharmaceutical_latin_abbreviations.htm.

23) *A Lexicon of Alchemy by Martin Rulandus the Elder*, Translated by Arthur E. Waite. John M. Watkins, London, 1893 / 1964. Available online at RexResearch: http://www.rexresearch.com/rulandus/rulxa.htm.

24) *Dorland's Illustrated Medical Dictionary, 26th ed.*, W.B. Saunders Co., Philadelphia, 1981.

25) *Glossary of Botanical Terms*, Gee Farms, Stockbridge, Michigan. http://www.geefarms.com/botanical_terms.htm.

26) Gilman, A.G., T.W. Rall, A.S. Nies, and P. Taylor (eds). *The Pharmcological Basis of Therapeutics, 8th ed*. Pergammon Press, New York, NY, 1990.

27) Watson, R. *Bitters Bottles*. Thomas Nelson & Sons, New York, 1965. Primary collector's reference on bitters bottles produced in North America. Excellent line drawings.

28) Ketchum, W.C., A *Treasury of American Bottles*. Rutlidge Books, New York, 1975.

29) *Catalog, Whitall, Tatum & Co, 1880*. The American Historical Catalog Collection, Pyne Press, Princeton, NJ, 1971. Contains addendum with historical information and engravings dating to much later than 1880.

30) *The British Pharmaceutical Codex*, 1911, available online via Henrietta's Herbal Home Page at: http://www.henriettesherbal.com/eclectic/bpc1911/index.html.

31) Wood et al., *United States Dispensatory*, 1926, 21st edition.

32) Ellingwood, F. *American Materia Medica, Therapeutics and Pharmacognosy*, 1919, available online at http://www.henriettesherbal.com/eclectic/ellingwood/index.html (accessed December 1, 2007).

33) Felter, H.W., and J.U. Lloyd. *King's American Dispensatory*, 1898. The Ohio Valley Co., Cincinnati, OH. Available online at Henretta's Herbal Homepage, Scanned version copyright © 1999-2007 Henriette Kress. http://www.henriettesherbal.com/eclectic/kings/index.html.

34) Felter, Harvey Wickes, and John Uri Lloyd. *King's American Dispensatory*, 1905. The Ohio Valley Co., Cincinnati, OH. available online at Google Books.

35) Hudson, B. (ed). *English Delftware Drug Jars: The Collection of the Museum of the Royal Pharmaceutical Society of Great Britain*. Pharmaceutical Press, London, 2006.

36) Beasley, H. *Medical Formulary Comprising Standard and Approved Formulae for the Preparations and Compounds Employed in Medical Practice*. Lindsay and Blakiston, Philadelphia, 1856.

37) Garrod, A.B. *The Essentials of Materia Medica and Therapeutics*, 1885. Longmans, Green and Company, London.

38) Hewlett, A.W., et al. *Epitome of the Pharmacopeia of the United States and the National Formulary, with Comments*. The American Medical Association, Chicago, 1916 (as available from Google Books).

39) Estes, J.W. *Dictionary of Protopharmacology—Therapeutic Practices 1700-1850*. Science History Publications, Watson Publishing International, Canton, MA. 1990.

40) Hughes, I. *Dictionary of Synonyms And Trade Names in Common Use—The Pharmaceutical Pocket Book*. 1913.

41) Wood, H.C., J.P. Remington, and S.P. Sadtler. *The Dispensatory of the United States of America. 16th ed. J.B. Lippincot Company, Philadelphia, 1892.*

42) *British Pharmaceutical Codex. An Imperial Dispensatory for the Use of Medical Practitioners and Pharmacists*. Pharmaceutical Society (of Great Britain), London, 1907.

43) Darling, E.R. *Inorganic Chemical Synonyms*. D. van Nostrand and Co., New York, New York, 1922.

44) Wood, G.V., and F. Bache. *The Dispensatory of the United States of America*. 16th ed. J.B. Lippincot Company, Philadelphia, 1868.

45) Hallberg, C.S.N., and J.H. Salisbury. *Physician's Manual of the Pharmacopeia and the National Formulary*, American Medical Association, Chicago, Illinois, 1909.

46) *The National Formulary of Unofficial Preparations*. American Pharmaceutical Association, 1896.

CREDITS FOR IMAGES AND FIGURES

Permission obtained from currrent copyright holders and acknowledgment for use of public domain materials not in the author's personal collection is specifically indicated below. If permission is not specified, the material has been determined by the author to reside in the public domain.

Frontmatter

Opposite Copyright (page 5):
Advertisement for Remington's Practice of Pharmacy From: Stewart FE. Quiz-Compends No.11, Pharmacy. P. Blakiston Son & Co., Philadelphia, PA, 1886.

Opposite Dedication (page 6):
T.W. Dyott Glass Works, Philadelphia Advertisement in *Whitley's Philadelphia Advertiser Directory* for 1820 (author's personal collection, electronically restored) from: Young, James Harvey, *The Toadstool Millionaires*, copyright 1961 Princeton University Press, 1989 renewed PUP. Reprinted with permission of Princeton University Press.

Engraving of "Flint-Glass Factories," Whitall Tatum, 1891. Obtained from Whitall, Tatum and Co. Catalog, 1880, Pyne Press, Princeton, NJ, 1971. With permission of the original copyright holder, Armstrong Industries.

Chapter 2

2-1: Apothecary Wares, from Munsey C, *Collecting Bottles*. Hawthorne Books, Inc. New York, 1970. With permission of the author (current copyright holder)

2-1: Apothecary Wares, from Munsey C, *Collecting Bottles*. Hawthorne Books, Inc. New York, 1970. With permission of the author (current copyright holder)

2-3: Assorted poison bottles, stoppers, and corkscrew with warning bell. Corkscrew from Griffenhagen G and Bogard M. *History of Drug Containers and Their Labels*. American Institute of the History of Pharmacy, Madison, Wisconsin, 1999, with permission. Remaining images compiled from Munsey C, *Collecting Bottles*. Hawthorne Books, Inc. New York, 1970. With permission of the author (current copyright holder)

2-4: Cook EF, LaWall CH (eds). *Remington's Practice of Pharmacy, 7th ed*. J.B. Lippincott and Co., Philadelphia/London, 1926. With permission, Wolters Kluwer Health for Lippincott, Williams & Wilkins

2-5: A puzzle card advertising Brown's Bitters from Watson, R. *Bitters Bottles*. Thomas Nelson & Sons, New York, 1965

2-6: Embossed dispensing wares from Munsey C, *Collecting Bottles*. Hawthorne Books, Inc. New York, 1970. With permission of the author (current copyright holder)

2-7: Sample embossing plate images from *Catalog, Whitall, Tatum & Co, 1880*. The American Historical Catalog Collection, Pyne Press, Princeton, NJ, 1971.

2-8: Des Moines Drug Co., Catalog, 1906-07. Published by Des Moines Drug Company, 110 SW. Fourth St., Des Moines, Iowa. Illustration courtesy of O.J. Cloughly Library, St. Louis College of Pharmacy.

2-9: From Ketchum, WC, A *Treasury of American Bottles*. Rutledge Books, New York, 1975.

2-10: Figure by author based upon orthographic variations observed on containers or images thereof, particularly as documented in Drey, 1978 (1).

2-11: Cook EF, LaWall CH (eds). *Remington's Practice of Pharmacy, 7th ed*. J.B. Lippincott and Co., Philadelphia/London, 1926. With permission, Wolters Kluwer Health for Lippincott, Williams & Wilkins.

2-12: Cook EF, LaWall CH (eds). *Remington's Practice of Pharmacy, 7th ed*. J.B. Lippincott and Co., Philadelphia/London, 1926. With permission, Wolters Kluwer Health for Lippincott, Williams & Wilkins.

2-13: Cook EF, LaWall CH (eds). *Remington's Practice of Pharmacy, 7th ed*. J.B. Lippincott and Co., Philadelphia/London, 1926. With permission, Wolters Kluwer Health for Lippincott, Williams & Wilkins.

2-14: Cook EF, LaWall CH (eds). *Remington's Practice of Pharmacy, 7th ed*. J.B. Lippincott and Co., Philadelphia/London, 1926. With permission, Wolters Kluwer Health for Lippincott, Williams & Wilkins.

Chapter 3

3-1: Woodville, William. *Medical Botany*. Volumes 1-4 (1790, 1792, 1793, and Supplemental Volume 1794). Published by James Phillips, George Yard, London, Plate 119. Courtesy Missouri Botanical Garden (with permission). Text and images available online at www.botanicus.org.

3-2: Woodville. Plate 120. Courtesy Missouri Botanical Garden.

3-3: Woodville. Plate 67. Courtesy Missouri Botanical Garden.

3-4: Woodville. Plate 69. Courtesy Missouri Botanical Garden.

3-5: Woodville. Plate 6. Courtesy Missouri Botanical Garden.

3-6: Woodville. Plate 173. Courtesy Missouri Botanical Garden.

3-7: Mathews, F. Schuyler. *Fieldbook of American Wildflowers*. G.P. Puntam's Sons, New York, 1905. Plate, page 151. Author's personal collection.

3-8: Woodville. Plate 222. Courtesy Missouri Botanical Garden.

3-9: Woodville. Plate 258. Courtesy Missouri Botanical Garden.

3-10: Woodville. Plate 224. Courtesy Missouri Botanical Garden.

3-11: Woodville. Plate 245. Courtesy Missouri Botanical Garden.

3-12: Woodville. Plate 168. Courtesy Missouri Botanical Garden.

3-13: Woodville. Plate 202. Courtesy Missouri Botanical Garden.

3-14: Woodville. Plate 53. Courtesy Missouri Botanical Garden.

3-15: Woodville. Plate 83. Courtesy Missouri Botanical Garden.

3-16: Woodville. Plate 239. Courtesy Missouri Botanical Garden.
3-17: Woodville. Plate 92. Courtesy Missouri Botanical Garden.
3-18: Woodville. Plate 214. Courtesy Missouri Botanical Garden.
3-19: Woodville. Plate148. Courtesy Missouri Botanical Garden.
3-20: Woodville. Plate159. Courtesy Missouri Botanical Garden.
3-21: Woodville. Plate50. Courtesy Missouri Botanical Garden.
3-22: Woodville. Plate 180. Courtesy Missouri Botanical Garden.
3-23: Woodville. Plate 103. Courtesy Missouri Botanical Garden.
3-24: Woodville. Plate 107. Courtesy Missouri Botanical Garden.
3-25: Woodville. Plate 150. Courtesy Missouri Botanical Garden.
3-26: Woodville. Plate 4. Courtesy Missouri Botanical Garden.
3-27: Woodville. Plate 121. Courtesy Missouri Botanical Garden.
3-28: Woodville. Plate 25. Courtesy Missouri Botanical Garden.
3-29: Woodville. Plate 8. Courtesy Missouri Botanical Garden.
3-30: Mathews. Plate, page 99. Author's personal Collection.
3-31: Woodville. Plate 86. Courtesy Missouri Botanical Garden.
3-32: Woodville. Plate 145. Courtesy Missouri Botanical Garden.
3-33: Woodville. Plate 183. Courtesy Missouri Botanical Garden.
3-34: Woodville. Plate 193. Courtesy Missouri Botanical Garden.
3-35: Woodville. Plate 7. Courtesy Missouri Botanical Garden.
3-36: Woodville. Plate 1. Courtesy Missouri Botanical Garden.
3-37: Woodville. Plate 259. Courtesy Missouri Botanical Garden.
3-38: Woodville. Plate 72. Courtesy Missouri Botanical Garden.
3-39: Woodville. Plate 234. Courtesy Missouri Botanical Garden.
3-40: Woodville. Plate 241. Courtesy Missouri Botanical Garden.
3-41: Woodville. Plate 34. Courtesy Missouri Botanical Garden.
3-42: Woodville. Plate 217. Courtesy Missouri Botanical Garden.
3-43: Woodville. Plate 189. Courtesy Missouri Botanical Garden.
3-44: Woodville. Plate 230. Courtesy Missouri Botanical Garden.
3-45: Woodville. Plate 229. Courtesy Missouri Botanical Garden.
3-46: Woodville. Plate 155. Courtesy Missouri Botanical Garden.
3-47: Woodville. Plate 117. Courtesy Missouri Botanical Garden.
3-48: Woodville. Plate 228. Courtesy Missouri Botanical Garden.
3-49: Woodville. Plate 144. Courtesy Missouri Botanical Garden.
3-50: Woodville. Plate 30. Courtesy Missouri Botanical Garden.
3-51: Woodville. Plate 131. Courtesy Missouri Botanical Garden.
3-52: Woodville. Plate 42. Courtesy Missouri Botanical Garden.
3-53: Woodville. Plate 161. Courtesy Missouri Botanical Garden.
3-54: Woodville. Plate 45. Courtesy Missouri Botanical Garden.
3-55: Woodville. Plate 80. Courtesy Missouri Botanical Garden.
3-56: Woodville. Plate 135. Courtesy Missouri Botanical Garden.
3-57: Woodville. Plate 211. Courtesy Missouri Botanical Garden.
3-58: Woodville. Plate 163. Courtesy Missouri Botanical Garden.
3-59: Woodville. Plate 66. Courtesy Missouri Botanical Garden.
3-60: Mathews. Plate, page 153. Author's personal Collection.
3-61: Woodville. Plate 157. Courtesy Missouri Botanical Garden.
3-62: Woodville. Plate 243. Courtesy Missouri Botanical Garden.
3-63: Woodville. Plate 263. Courtesy Missouri Botanical Garden.
3-64: Woodville. Plate 248. Courtesy Missouri Botanical Garden.
3-65: Mathews. Plate, page 321. Author's personal Collection.
3-66: Woodville. Plate 236. Courtesy Missouri Botanical Garden.
3-67: Woodville. Plate 268. Courtesy Missouri Botanical Garden.
3-68: Woodville. Plate 200. Courtesy Missouri Botanical Garden.
3-69: Woodville. Plate 201. Courtesy Missouri Botanical Garden.
3-70: Woodville. Plate 27. Courtesy Missouri Botanical Garden.
3-71: Woodville. Plate 82. Courtesy Missouri Botanical Garden.
3-72: Mathews. Plate, page 129. Author's personal Collection.
3-73: Woodville. Plate 29. Courtesy Missouri Botanical Garden.
3-74: Woodville. Plate 177. Courtesy Missouri Botanical Garden.
3-75: Mathews. Plate, page 391. Author's personal Collection.
3-76: Woodville. Plate 175. Courtesy Missouri Botanical Garden.
3-77: Woodville. Plate 22. Courtesy Missouri Botanical Garden.
3-78: Woodville. Plate 51. Courtesy Missouri Botanical Garden.
3-79: Mathews. Plate, page 35. Author's personal Collection.
3-80: Woodville. Plate 137. Courtesy Missouri Botanical Garden.
3-81: Mathews. Plate, page 149. Author's personal Collection.

3-82: Woodville. Plate 181. Courtesy Missouri Botanical Garden.
3-83: Woodville. Plate 261. Courtesy Missouri Botanical Garden.
3-84: Mathews. Plate, page 163. Author's personal Collection.
3-85: Woodville. Plate 176. Courtesy Missouri Botanical Garden.
3-86: Woodville. Plate 43. Courtesy Missouri Botanical Garden.
3-87: Woodville. Plate 191. Courtesy Missouri Botanical Garden.
3-88: Woodville. Plate 132. Courtesy Missouri Botanical Garden.
3-89: Woodville. Plate 79. Courtesy Missouri Botanical Garden.
3-90: Woodville. Plate 199. Courtesy Missouri Botanical Garden.
3-91: Woodville. Plate 216. Courtesy Missouri Botanical Garden.
3-92: Mathews. Plate, page 95. Author's personal Collection.
3-93: Woodville. Plate 116. Courtesy Missouri Botanical Garden.
3-94: Woodville. Plate 242. Courtesy Missouri Botanical Garden.
3-95: Woodville. Plate 24. Courtesy Missouri Botanical Garden.
3-96: Woodville. Plate 172. Courtesy Missouri Botanical Garden.
3-97: Woodville. Plate 33. Courtesy Missouri Botanical Garden.
3-98: Mathews. Composite figure derived from plates, page 499 and 501. Author's personal Collection.
3-99: Woodville. Plate 102. Courtesy Missouri Botanical Garden.
3-100: Woodville. Plate 244. Courtesy Missouri Botanical Garden.
3-101: Woodville. Plate 220. Courtesy Missouri Botanical Garden.
3-102: Woodville. Plate 130. Courtesy Missouri Botanical Garden.
3-103: Woodville. Plate 49. Courtesy Missouri Botanical Garden.
3-104: Woodville. Plate 160. Courtesy Missouri Botanical Garden.
3-105: Woodville. Plate 158. Courtesy Missouri Botanical Garden.
3-106: Woodville. Plate 36. Courtesy Missouri Botanical Garden.
3-107: Woodville. Plate 88. Courtesy Missouri Botanical Garden.
3-108: Woodville. Plate 12. Courtesy Missouri Botanical Garden.
3-109: Woodville. Plate 269. Courtesy Missouri Botanical Garden.
3-110: Woodville. Plate 89. Courtesy Missouri Botanical Garden.
3-111: Woodville. Plate 156. Courtesy Missouri Botanical Garden.
3-112: Woodville. Plate 112. Courtesy Missouri Botanical Garden.
3-113: Mathews. Plate, page 231. Author's personal Collection.
3-114: Woodville. Plate 192. Courtesy Missouri Botanical Garden.
3-115: Mathews. Plate, page 303. Author's personal Collection.
3-116: Woodville. Plate 167. Courtesy Missouri Botanical Garden.
3-117: Mathews. Plate, page 79. Author's personal Collection.
3-118: Woodville. Plate 58. Courtesy Missouri Botanical Garden.
3-119: Woodville. Plate 47. Courtesy Missouri Botanical Garden.
3-120: Woodville. Plate 16. Courtesy Missouri Botanical Garden.
3-121: Woodville. Plate 17. Courtesy Missouri Botanical Garden.
3-122: Woodville. Plate 28. Courtesy Missouri Botanical Garden.
3-123: Woodville. Plate 19. Courtesy Missouri Botanical Garden.
3-124: Woodville. Plate 18. Courtesy Missouri Botanical Garden.
3-125: Woodville. Plate 128. Courtesy Missouri Botanical Garden.
3-126: Woodville. Plate 52. Courtesy Missouri Botanical Garden.
3-127: Woodville. Plate 10. Courtesy Missouri Botanical Garden.
3-128: Woodville. Plate 65. Courtesy Missouri Botanical Garden.
3-129: Woodville. Plate 35. Courtesy Missouri Botanical Garden.
3-130: Woodville. Plate 255. Courtesy Missouri Botanical Garden.
3-131: Woodville. Plate 108. Courtesy Missouri Botanical Garden.
3-132: Woodville. Plate 203. Courtesy Missouri Botanical Garden.
3-133: Woodville. Plate 39. Courtesy Missouri Botanical Garden.
3-134: Woodville. Plate 40. Courtesy Missouri Botanical Garden.
3-135: Mathews. Plate, page 63. Author's personal Collection.
3-136: Woodville. Plate 252. Courtesy Missouri Botanical Garden.
3-137: Woodville. Plate 21. Courtesy Missouri Botanical Garden.
3-138: Woodville. Plate 127. Courtesy Missouri Botanical Garden.
3-139: Woodville. Plate 95. Courtesy Missouri Botanical Garden.
3-140: Woodville. Plate 250. Courtesy Missouri Botanical Garden.
3-141: Woodville. Plate 178. Courtesy Missouri Botanical Garden.
3-142: Woodville. Plate 15. Courtesy Missouri Botanical Garden.
3-143: Woodville. Plate 240 (original plate misnumbered 230). Courtesy Missouri Botanical Garden.
3-144: Woodville. Plate 32. Courtesy Missouri Botanical Garden.
3-145: Woodville. Plate 55. Courtesy Missouri Botanical Garden.

3-146: Woodville. Plate 152. Courtesy Missouri Botanical Garden.
3-147: Mathews. Plate, page 409. Author's personal collection.
3-148: Woodville. Plate 190. Courtesy Missouri Botanical Garden.
3-149: Woodville. Plate 273. Courtesy Missouri Botanical Garden.
3-150: Woodville. Plate 205. Courtesy Missouri Botanical Garden.
3-151: Woodville. Plate 101. Courtesy Missouri Botanical Garden.
3-152: Woodville. Plate 184. Courtesy Missouri Botanical Garden.
3-153: Woodville. Plate 221. Courtesy Missouri Botanical Garden.
3-154: Woodville. Plate 111. Courtesy Missouri Botanical Garden.
3-155: Woodville. Plate 213. Courtesy Missouri Botanical Garden.
3-156: Woodville. Plate 63. Courtesy Missouri Botanical Garden.
3-157: Mathews. Plate, page 235. Author's personal collection.
3-158: Mathews. Plate, page 287. Author's personal collection.
3-159: Woodville. Plate 54. Courtesy Missouri Botanical Garden.
3-160: Woodville. Plate 225. Courtesy Missouri Botanical Garden.
3-161: Woodville. Plate 97. Courtesy Missouri Botanical Garden.
3-162: Woodville. Plate 56. Courtesy Missouri Botanical Garden.
3-163: Woodville. Plate 249. Courtesy Missouri Botanical Garden.
3-164: Mathews. Plate, page 45. Author's personal Collection.
3-165: Mathews. Plate, page 215 (left side of figure). Author's personal collection.
3-166: Mathews. Plate, page 215 (right side of figure). Author's personal collection.
3-167: Woodville. Plate 147. Courtesy Missouri Botanical Garden.
3-168: Woodville. Plate 169. Courtesy Missouri Botanical Garden.
3-169: Woodville. Plate 170. Courtesy Missouri Botanical Garden.
3-170: Woodville. Plate 23. Courtesy Missouri Botanical Garden.
3-171: Woodville. Plate 64. Courtesy Missouri Botanical Garden.
3-172: Woodville. Plate 129. Courtesy Missouri Botanical Garden.
3-173: Woodville. Plate 134. Courtesy Missouri Botanical Garden.
3-174: Woodville. Plate 48. Courtesy Missouri Botanical Garden.
3-175: Woodville. Plate 223. Courtesy Missouri Botanical Garden.
3-176: Woodville. Plate 267. Courtesy Missouri Botanical Garden.
3-177: Woodville. Plate 266. Courtesy Missouri Botanical Garden.
3-178: Woodville. Plate 136. Courtesy Missouri Botanical Garden.
3-179: Woodville. Plate 113. Courtesy Missouri Botanical Garden.
3-180: Woodville. Plate 164. Courtesy Missouri Botanical Garden.
3-181: Woodville. Plate 165. Courtesy Missouri Botanical Garden.
3-182: Woodville. Plate 20. Courtesy Missouri Botanical Garden.
3-183: Woodville. Plate 247. Courtesy Missouri Botanical Garden.
3-184: Woodville. Plate 99. Courtesy Missouri Botanical Garden.
3-185: Woodville. Plate 185. Courtesy Missouri Botanical Garden.
3-186: Woodville. Plate 186. Courtesy Missouri Botanical Garden.
3-187: Woodville. Plate 142. Courtesy Missouri Botanical Garden.
3-188: Mathews. Plate, page 309. Author's personal Collection.
3-189: Woodville. Plate 59. Courtesy Missouri Botanical Garden.
3-190: Woodville. Plate 73. Courtesy Missouri Botanical Garden.
3-191: Woodville. Plate 26. Courtesy Missouri Botanical Garden.
3-192: Woodville. Plate 179. Courtesy Missouri Botanical Garden.
3-193: Woodville. Plate 209. Courtesy Missouri Botanical Garden.
3-194: Woodville. Plate 207. Courtesy Missouri Botanical Garden.
3-195: Woodville. Plate 187. Courtesy Missouri Botanical Garden.
3-196: Woodville. Plate 188. Courtesy Missouri Botanical Garden.
3-197: Woodville. Plate 14. Courtesy Missouri Botanical Garden.
3-198: Mathews. Plate, page 155. Author's personal collection.
3-199: Woodville. Plate 271. Courtesy Missouri Botanical Garden.
3-200: Woodville. Plate 204. Courtesy Missouri Botanical Garden.
3-201: Woodville. Plate 85. Courtesy Missouri Botanical Garden.
3-202: Woodville. Plate 84. Courtesy Missouri Botanical Garden.
3-203: Woodville. Plate 171. Courtesy Missouri Botanical Garden.
3-204: Woodville. Plate 212. Courtesy Missouri Botanical Garden.
3-205: Woodville. Plate 104. Courtesy Missouri Botanical Garden.
3-206: Woodville. Plate 77. Courtesy Missouri Botanical Garden.
3-207: Woodville. Plate 126. Courtesy Missouri Botanical Garden.
3-208: Woodville. Plate 246. Courtesy Missouri Botanical Garden.
3-209: Woodville. Plate 114. Courtesy Missouri Botanical Garden.

3-210: Woodville. Plate 46. Courtesy Missouri Botanical Garden.
3-211: Woodville. Plate 149. Courtesy Missouri Botanical Garden.
3-212: Woodville. Plate 74. Courtesy Missouri Botanical Garden.
3-213: Woodville. Plate 75. Courtesy Missouri Botanical Garden.
3-214: Woodville. Plate 61. Courtesy Missouri Botanical Garden.
3-215: Woodville. Plate 141. Courtesy Missouri Botanical Garden.
3-216: Woodville. Plate 140. Courtesy Missouri Botanical Garden.
3-217: Woodville. Plate 139. Courtesy Missouri Botanical Garden.
3-218: Woodville. Plate 87. Courtesy Missouri Botanical Garden.
3-219: Woodville. Plate 138. Courtesy Missouri Botanical Garden.
3-220: Woodville. Plate 68. Courtesy Missouri Botanical Garden.
3-221: Mathews. Plate, page 103. Author's personal Collection.
3-222: Woodville. Plate 237. Courtesy Missouri Botanical Garden.
3-223: Woodville. Plate 37. Courtesy Missouri Botanical Garden.
3-224: Woodville. Plate 94. Courtesy Missouri Botanical Garden.
3-225: Woodville. Plate 196. Courtesy Missouri Botanical Garden.
3-226: Woodville. Plate 198. Courtesy Missouri Botanical Garden.
3-227: Woodville. Plate 38. Courtesy Missouri Botanical Garden.
3-228: Woodville. Plate 78. Courtesy Missouri Botanical Garden.
3-229: Woodville. Plate 260. Courtesy Missouri Botanical Garden.
3-230: Woodville. Plate 264. Courtesy Missouri Botanical Garden.
3-231: Woodville. Plate 254. Courtesy Missouri Botanical Garden.
3-232: Woodville. Plate 123. Courtesy Missouri Botanical Garden.
3-233: Woodville. Plate 251. Courtesy Missouri Botanical Garden.
3-234: Woodville. Plate 194. Courtesy Missouri Botanical Garden.
3-235: Woodville. Plate 31. Courtesy Missouri Botanical Garden.
3-236: Woodville. Plate 90. Courtesy Missouri Botanical Garden.
3-237: Woodville. Plate 232. Courtesy Missouri Botanical Garden.
3-238: Woodville. Plate 5. Courtesy Missouri Botanical Garden.
3-239: Woodville. Plate 118. Courtesy Missouri Botanical Garden.
3-240: Woodville. Plate 272. Courtesy Missouri Botanical Garden.
3-241: Woodville. Plate 57. Courtesy Missouri Botanical Garden.
3-242: Mathews. Plate, page 402. Author's personal Collection.
3-243: Woodville. Plate 231. Courtesy Missouri Botanical Garden.
3-244: Woodville. Plate 93. Courtesy Missouri Botanical Garden.
3-245: Woodville. Plate 162. Courtesy Missouri Botanical Garden.
3-246: Woodville. Plate 106. Courtesy Missouri Botanical Garden.
3-247: Woodville. Plate 110. Courtesy Missouri Botanical Garden.
3-248: Woodville. Plate 44. Courtesy Missouri Botanical Garden.
3-249: Woodville. Plate 76. Courtesy Missouri Botanical Garden.
3-250: Mathews. Plate, page 173. Author's personal Collection.
3-251: Woodville. Plate 182. Courtesy Missouri Botanical Garden.
3-252: Woodville. Plate 226. Courtesy Missouri Botanical Garden.
3-253: Woodville. Plate 105. Courtesy Missouri Botanical Garden.
3-254: Woodville. Plate 154. Courtesy Missouri Botanical Garden.
3-255: Woodville. Plate 71. Courtesy Missouri Botanical Garden.
3-256: Woodville. Plate 124. Courtesy Missouri Botanical Garden.
3-257: Woodville. Plate 235. Courtesy Missouri Botanical Garden.
3-258: Woodville. Plate 215. Courtesy Missouri Botanical Garden.
3-259: Woodville. Plate 60. Courtesy Missouri Botanical Garden.
3-260: Woodville. Plate 166. Courtesy Missouri Botanical Garden.
3-261: Woodville. Plate 115. Courtesy Missouri Botanical Garden.
3-262: Woodville. Plate 3. Courtesy Missouri Botanical Garden.
3-263: Woodville. Plate 208. Courtesy Missouri Botanical Garden.
3-264: Woodville. Plate 210. Courtesy Missouri Botanical Garden.
3-265: Woodville. Plate 153. Courtesy Missouri Botanical Garden.
3-266: Woodville. Plate 256. Courtesy Missouri Botanical Garden.
3-267: Woodville. Plate 109. Courtesy Missouri Botanical Garden.
3-268: Woodville. Plate 9. Courtesy Missouri Botanical Garden.
3-269: Woodville. Plate 98. Courtesy Missouri Botanical Garden.
3-270: Woodville. Plate 2. Courtesy Missouri Botanical Garden.
3-271: Woodville. Plate 13. Courtesy Missouri Botanical Garden.
3-272: Woodville. Plate 197. Courtesy Missouri Botanical Garden.
3-273: Woodville. Plate 146. Courtesy Missouri Botanical Garden.
3-274: Woodville. Plate 70. Courtesy Missouri Botanical Garden.
3-275: Woodville. Plate 96. Courtesy Missouri Botanical Garden.

3-276: Woodville. Plate 100. Courtesy Missouri Botanical Garden.
3-277: Woodville. Plate 125. Courtesy Missouri Botanical Garden.
3-278: Woodville. Plate 218. Courtesy Missouri Botanical Garden.
3-279: Woodville. Plate 227. Courtesy Missouri Botanical Garden.
3-280: Woodville. Plate 81. Courtesy Missouri Botanical Garden.
3-281: Woodville. Plate 270. Courtesy Missouri Botanical Garden.
3-282: Woodville. Plate 195. Courtesy Missouri Botanical Garden.
3-283: Woodville. Plate 257. Courtesy Missouri Botanical Garden.
3-284: Woodville. Plate 133. Courtesy Missouri Botanical Garden.
3-285: Woodville. Plate 11. Courtesy Missouri Botanical Garden.

Appendix-4

p. 310 Table of alchemical symbols from Partington, J.R. *A History of Chemistry, Volume II*. St. Martin's Press (Macmillan and Company, Ltd.), New York, 1961.

p. 312 Alchemical Signs from *Medicinisch-Chymisch—und Alchemistisches Oraculum*, Ulm, 1775. Available online at: http://www.alchemywebsite.com/index.html (accessed Dec. 21, 2013), courtsey of website author.

p. 313 Ibid.
p. 314 Ibid.
p. 315 Ibid.
p. 316 Ibid.
p. 317 Ibid.
p. 318 Ibid.
p. 319 Ibid.
p. 320 Ibid.

Endplate

From: *Catalog, Whitall, Tatum & Co, 1880*. The American Historical Catalog Collection, Pyne Press, Princeton, NJ, 1971.

Frontispiece from Whitall, Tatum and Co. Catalog, 1880, American Historical Catalog Collection, Pyne Press, Princeton NJ, 1971.